Learned and lucid, this multiauthor survey of Western th
and the world from the Greeks and Hebrews to the exo......,
vagaries of our own time will be a boon to serious students. It is a major
achievement.

—*J. I. Packer, professor of theology, Regent College*

Revolutions in Worldview is a magnificent intellectual and spiritual tour
de force—indeed, a feat of strength and virtuosity. This work is everything
that a primer to worldview thinking should entail. From the early Greeks
to present-day postmodernists, these authors explore what the human race
has done to illustrate Solomon's admonition "to search and seek out wisdom and the 'reason of things.' " (Eccl. 7:25). Solomon concluded: "As for
that which is far off and exceedingly deep, who can find it out?" This is the
lament of modern and postmodern man after 2,500 years of probing the
"exceedingly deep" of theology (Is there a God?), philosophy (What is reality?), ethics (What is good and evil?), biology (What is life?), physics (What
is dark energy?), and so forth. I cannot recommend this book too highly.

—*Dr. David Noebel, founder and president of Summit Ministries and
author of* Understanding the Times *worldview curriculum*

Having taught history of philosophy and Christian thought at the graduate
level for many years, I am delighted to welcome *Revolutions in Worldview*.
Andy Hoffecker, who has long been a recognized leader and expert in this
field, has brought together an impressive faculty to present a worldviewish
survey of the history of Western thought—a kind of contemporary course
in moral philosophy for the undergraduate, or an introduction to this important material for the graduate student who escaped college or university without adequate exposure to this vital subject matter. This volume
joins Colin Brown and Jacques Barzun in providing the student a window
into how outlook has informed life in key stages of the development of
the Western mind. Written from a standpoint that emphasizes the majesty
and lordship of God, and his sovereignty in his redemptive purposes, these
chapters provide us with knowledge and perspective crucial for an integrated understanding of history and philosophy, and for current cultural
analysis and engagement.

—*Ligon Duncan, senior minister, First Presbyterian Church, Jackson, MS*

Revolutions in Worldview is about ten major worldview revolutions, and several sub-revolutions, in Western culture and civilization. Like its predecessor, *Building a Christian World View*, the authors of this well-written volume recognize the immense intellectual and practical importance of the concept of worldview itself and its inescapable human significance. This book's historical orientation sheds light on the past up to our own day. Its grounding in Scripture and the Reformed tradition gives it authority and perspective. Its wealth of theological and philosophical insight is sure to make readers better lovers of God and wisdom. I hope, as the editor does, that it will be used as a formidable text in capstone courses for undergraduates regardless of discipline. I also believe it will help cast a new vision for graduate and seminary education.

—*David K. Naugle, professor of philosophy, Dallas Baptist University and author of* Worldview: The History of a Concept *(Eerdmans, 2002)*

A dreadful irony of our times is that much of the world is looking to the West for constructive models of cultural patterns, while many in the West are cynically refusing their own heritage. When I travel to China, or the African continent, I am regularly asked what ingredients from Western history can bring inspiration to their local problems and opportunities. Far from perfect, and perhaps not entirely unique, yet the West gave the world so much: health care, human rights, freedom of conscience, the separation of church and state, technology, humane labor laws, and flourishing arts. This book challenges the cynics and encourages advocates by explaining how it all came about, and by setting forth conditions whereby the West may continue to stay alive.

—*William Edgar, professor of apologetics, Westminster Theological Seminary, Philadelphia*

At a time when knowledge of the history of ideas, either by neglect or design, seems to have fallen out of favor, *Revolutions in Worldview* is a welcome antidote. Sweeping in its scope, without being simplistic, *Revolutions* shows how the ideas of today, together with their consequences, have not come to us ex nihilo. The impetus to bring together the disparate elements and institutions that make up a culture is embedded in human nature. In this volume, that impetus is laid out clearly as each historical era builds on the other. Providing historical perspective as well as critical analysis, these essays give the reader both a telescopic and a microscopic view on present-day Western culture.

—*K. Scott Oliphint, professor of apologetics and systematic theology, Westminster Theological Seminary, Philadelphia*

W. Andrew Hoffecker's *Revolutions in Worldview* offers insightful accounts of the intellectual, political, and social movements and forces that have shaped Christian worldviews through the course of Western history. All by themselves, the chapters "Christianity from the Early Fathers to Charlemagne," "Medieval Theology and the Roots of Modernity," and "The Renaissance" justify the price of the book! The book as a whole demonstrates two important reasons for Christians today to take worldview analysis seriously. First, the various essays show that the task of bringing our own thinking and affections into conformity with Scripture is both perpetual and complicated. The spirit of the world in every age is more diverse and more subtly attractive than we like to admit. Second, the essays show that worldview analysis can serve many different valuable ends, from making us appreciate the faithfulness of Christians in the past, to displaying the ways that Christian worldviews can respectfully differ, to inspiring us to resist the encroachment of a worldly mindset. For readers ready to enrich their pursuit of a biblical worldview with a historical perspective, this book will be a valuable and challenging resource.

—*William Davis, professor of philosophy, Covenant College*

If ideas have consequences, *Revolutions in Worldview* shows definitively that ideas also have contexts. For those interested in defending, maintaining and promoting a Christian worldview, this book gives ample material for considering the complications and importance of the work of cultivating Christian minds.

—*D. G. Hart, PhD, director of partnered projects,*
Intercollegiate Studies Institute

Professor Hoffecker's *Revolutions in Worldview* is an incisive collection of essays by leading Reformed scholars who examine the historical, philosophical, and cultural roots of Western civilization—and those ideas and movements that continue to challenge the credibility and vitality of Christian faith. I warmly recommend it for use as a text in all Christian colleges and seminaries.

—*John Jefferson Davis, professor of systematic theology and Christian*
ethics, Gordon-Conwell Theological Seminary

Much is said, but little understood, about worldview, yet the recognition of its importance is gaining adherents daily. You cannot afford to be uninformed about worldview and its shaping influence on all of life. If you must choose one volume to orient you to this critical subject, you can do no better than *Revolutions in Worldview*, edited by Andrew Hoffecker, one of the foremost experts on this subject.

—*Luder Whitlock, The Trinity Forum*

Students of intellectual history have become accustomed to a vocabulary that highlights the struggle for the meaning of Western civilization. Terms such as *metanarrative, paradigm shift, weltanschauung, worldview, presuppositions,* and *hermeneutics* are weighty yet commonplace words that reflect the evolution and revolution in the history of ideas. But what is not so common is a succinct and historically logical presentation of this flow of ideas, simultaneously developed by a cadre of profoundly competent and deeply committed Christian scholars. If you seek to better understand the flow of Western thought, then *Revolutions in Wordlview* will sharpen your vision into the essence of the ideas that have created the way we view our world.

—*Dr. Peter A. Lillback, president, Westminster Theological Seminary*

Revolutions in Worldview

Understanding the Flow of Western Thought

Edited by W. Andrew Hoffecker

P U B L I S H I N G
P.O. BOX 817 • PHILLIPSBURG • NEW JERSEY 08865-0817

Page design by P&R Publishing and Bits & Bytes, Inc.
Typesetting by Bits & Bytes, Inc.
Edited by John J. Hughes

Printed in the United States of America

Library of Congress Cataloging-in-Publication Data

Revolutions in worldview : understanding the flow of western thought / W. Andrew Hoffecker, editor.

    p. cm.

Includes bibliographical references and indexes.
ISBN 978-0-87552-573-0 (pbk.)
1. Philosophy--History. 2. Christianity--Philosophy. I. Hoffecker, W. Andrew, 1941-

B72.R48 2007
190--dc22

2007004796

Dedicated to my three sons:

Drew, Scott, and Timothy

"My son, do not forget my teaching,
but let your heart keep my commandments,
for length of days and years of life and peace they will add to you."
Proverbs 3:1–3

For additional helpful material and resources about worldview,
we invite you to visit
www.prpbooks.com/RIW.

Contents

Abbreviations

BL/BRBK	*The Blue and the Brown Books*
ESV	English Standard Version
JBQ	*Jewish Bible Quarterly*
JSNT	*Journal for the Study of the New Testament*
NIV	New International Version
NT	New Testament
OT	Old Testament
PL	*Patrologia Latina*
PG	*Philosophical Grammar*
PI	*Philosophical Investigations*
RTR	*Reformed Theological Review*
ST	*Summa Theologiae*
T	*Tractatus Logico-Philosophicus*
WTJ	*Westminster Theological Journal*

Preface

W. Andrew Hoffecker

Of the writing of books on worldview—as a philosophical category and as specific belief systems—there is no end! For example, over the last twenty years a myriad of texts have probed the cacophony of worldviews that characterize modernity and postmodernity, and yet, ironically, the first full-scale treatment of *worldview* as a philosophical category appeared only recently in David Naugle's analysis *Worldview: The History of a Concept* (Grand Rapids: Eerdmans, 2002). Other publications exploring related topics with titles such as *The Soul of the American University* and *The Outrageous Idea of Christian Scholarship* remind us of the remarkable influence of worldviews on academics. They highlight the failure of evangelicals to tackle the challenge of identifying and confronting underlying principles that shape scholarly pursuits.

Evangelicals' interest in understanding how worldviews influence life has not been limited to the rarefied air of the academy. Various types of publications, along with church conferences, leadership seminars, and summer institutes, testify to sustained evangelical interest in worldview-related issues. The appearance of Mark Noll's *The Scandal of the Evangelical Mind*, toward the end of the twentieth century (1994), highlighted the irony that characterized American evangelicalism at that time. Despite cultural leadership at the earliest stages of American intellectual life, Noll contended, evangelicals sowed seeds in the nineteenth century that bore anti-intellectual fruit in the twentieth century. Thus, evangelicals abandoned their heritage of making substantial contributions to the American mind. About the time Noll's book appeared, evangelicals began to awaken to the challenge of articulating a distinctively Christian worldview—a hope-filled trend that Noll documented. The prevalence of texts about Christian worldview issues justifies this hope.

I awakened from my own "dogmatic slumbers" to worldview concerns in the mid-1960s during my last year at seminary—a heady time for theological graduate studies. I had thoroughly devoured my coursework—historical, biblical, theological, and practical. Equipped with the tools of an evangelical seminary education, I eagerly looked forward to ministry, though I had no idea what form my service would take. This changed radically when Arthur Holmes (*Contours of a World View*) and another guest lecturer challenged our graduating class with a bold proposition. Our theological education, they contended, was severely impoverished if it consisted only of the traditional disciplines of a seminary curriculum. They argued that the cultural crisis of the 1960s demanded that every responsible Christian, not just ministers and ministerial candidates, articulate a vibrant, compelling, Christian worldview to challenge the contemporary unbelief that threatened to engulf American life. Similarly, during the closing years of that turbulent decade, Francis Schaeffer inspired the rising generation of evangelicals by preaching that "people act as they think," further solidifying my growing conviction that the academy needed Christians who were self-consciously committed to thinking and acting in terms of their worldview. Therefore, I enrolled in a PhD program, not only to be equipped to teach "religion" courses but to do so with a firm conviction that the Christian worldview should influence all the disciplines of higher education.

Evangelicals preoccupied with worldview concerns occasionally are criticized for overintellectualizing Christianity. Defenders of "worldview thinking" deny the validity of such charges. Everyone has a worldview, and one's worldview, they argue, influences every aspect of a person's thought and life. One's worldview gives coherence to how one thinks and lives, provides moral parameters, and directly motivates behavior.

Thus, "worldview thinking" is not merely an academic issue and concern. Worldview issues and influences pervade every area of human existence, from individual reflection to all forms of social and cultural activity—family and marriage, labor and management, economic transactions, scientific investigation, technological development, political and judicial practices, arts and entertainment, and leisure and recreational activities. Worldviews determine the cultural activities in which individuals and people groups immerse themselves.

Before beginning our survey of revolutions in Western worldviews, we need to understand what constitutes a worldview and how this term has been used in the history of ideas. David Naugle's *Worldview: The History of a Concept*, mentioned above, offers the first extensive analysis of the concept and its role in intellectual history.[1] The term *worldview* is modern in origin, stemming from one of the most dramatic philosophical shifts in

---

1. David Naugle, *Worldview: The History of a Concept* (Grand Rapids: Eerdmans, 2002), 55–67.

Western thought: the Enlightenment. In his *Critique of Judgment* (1790), Immanuel Kant, who thought of his own epistemology as a "Copernican revolution," coined the term *weltanschauung*. Kant was referring simply to one's empirical perception of the world—one's "worldview." Later, *worldview* was expanded to include not only one's sensory apprehension of the natural order, but also the categorization of moral experience. Thus, early on, *worldview* encompassed how one experienced the phenomenal and moral aspects of reality.

In the nineteenth century, there was an explosion in the use of the term *worldview* among philosophers in their discussions of the existence of the cosmos and the meaning of reality. As its use proliferated, *worldview* as a comprehensive way of understanding human existence transcended strictly philosophical inquiry. Worldview vocabulary captured the attention of thinkers outside the field of philosophy, until scholars throughout the academic disciplines—language, music, art, theology, history, and the physical sciences—adopted the term. For many, *worldview* became a help maid to philosophy.[2]

Widespread use of *worldview* in other academic fields testifies to its significance in the abstract world of ideas, and to its implications for every form of human activity. One's worldview, or world-and-life view, consists of one's most basic beliefs and framework of understanding. Basic beliefs can be expressed by several terms—*ideas, assumptions, convictions, presuppositions*, and *premises*. Directly or indirectly, basic beliefs influence every dimension of human life: they guide thought, stimulate imagination, influence intuition, direct moral choices, and determine the value and priority given to each of these faculties. Collectively, basic beliefs function as the grid or matrix by which we comprehend reality and attempt to live consistently within that framework.

All humans are committed to their basic beliefs; otherwise, these beliefs would not be *basic*. Our commitments to our basic beliefs are *core* commitments—we cling to them; they are nonnegotiable; we express them in every facet of our lives. Basic beliefs and core commitments are the fundamental aspects of a worldview, since, by definition, they determine how we understand the world and what aspects of that understanding are nonnegotiable. Thus, having and living out a worldview are inescapable aspects of being human. To be human is to have a worldview. So although we might associate *worldview* with complex philosophical systems—from Platonism to Cartesianism to postmodernist proposals—*worldview* also is fundamental to what it means to be human.

Basic beliefs are religious in nature because they are *basic* beliefs; core commitments are religious in nature because they are *core* commitments. Religion is fundamentally a matter of *basic* beliefs and *core* com-

---

2. Naugle notes that in the early nineteenth century, a German dissertation included in its bibliography about two thousand entries with "weltanschauung" in the title.

mitments—a worldview. Thus all worldviews are religious, and all people are religious. All thinking and doing arise from or are motivated by our core commitments, our basic beliefs—what the Bible terms "the heart" and describes as the center of our being.

Since everyone has a worldview, Christian truth addresses people not just theologically and doctrinally but in other ways as well. One's worldview encompasses not only what one believes about God but also everything about which one can think or do. A worldview influences how one comprehends everything from the exterior vastness of the cosmos to the most interior reflection of our hearts. It does so in several ways, at different levels, and in every conceivable subject matter and vocational calling.

Though worldview as a category is modern in origin, "worldview thinking" describes a universal feature of human experience. Evangelicals understand that the concept of worldview has immense implications for Christianity. If everyone possesses a worldview—a comprehensive, unifying perspective in terms of which we interpret the cosmos and live our lives—then it is in terms of our worldview that Christians should live in the world to God's glory, defend the faith to unbelievers, and live out the implications of God's revealed will. The Christian worldview is rooted in the Bible: the transcendent, triune God, who sovereignly created and redeemed heaven and earth, provides the ultimate context for understanding all reality.

The previous two-volume work, *Building a Christian World View*, was an introductory, college-level discussion of the history of Western worldviews from the ancients to contemporary thought. The present volume attempts a similar survey but is directed toward upper-level undergraduates and graduate students. As a historian of the old Princeton theology (which arguably represents traditional Reformed thinking at the peak of its influence in American life), I see the present volume as analogous to the "exiting course" on moral philosophy that most nineteenth-century American colleges required. Princeton and other American colleges framed this course using Scottish Common Sense philosophy to rebut the skepticism of David Hume, which had undermined the foundations of Christian orthodoxy. The lectures ranged widely over epistemology, natural theology, and social and political relations, thus providing students a Christian framework for all that they had learned. Many college presidents taught these capstone courses to round out their graduates' education, no matter what vocation they would pursue. Although I hope such a vision is not quixotic, I am convinced that Christian undergraduates need assistance in clarifying their own worldviews as they seek to serve Christ in various vocations.

The present volume follows the basic schema of *Building* by dividing the study of worldviews into ten discrete historical eras, but it differs from the earlier work in several ways. We do not separate our discussion into subtopics, such as theology, anthropology, and epistemology, but treat the worldviews as wholes. We also delineate the historical eras differently.

To probe the medieval era in more detail, we divide the vast Middle Ages into two sections, showing the variety of perspectives from Augustine to Charlemagne in one chapter and the High Middle Ages in another. We also add a separate chapter on the Renaissance to enable readers to compare and contrast its thinkers with those of the Middle Ages, which preceded, and those of the Reformation, which was contemporaneous with it and which extended past it. We also divide modernity into two segments: the Enlightenment, which in the name of modernity departed radically from the philosophy and religion of the past, and the nineteenth century, which furthered that rupture. Finally, we devote a separate chapter to the twentieth century, giving special emphasis to the emergence of postmodernity, which broke from modernity by denying the very idea of philosophy and thus of worldview. Each of these changes enables us to engage in more detailed study of the worldviews and movements they have precipitated.

The thesis of this book is that Western thought has experienced a series of changes so profound they should be called *revolutions*. Chronicling these revolutions should enable Christians living in the twenty-first century to understand the flow of Western thought—how key ideas persisted over time; how unique perspectives such as the nature of the deity, the question of human nature, and that of the cosmos got their original impetus and developed to their present state; how ideas spawned debates that remain with us; and how shifts from theism to secularism have intensified.

Although the contributors to this work teach in various academic milieus—most are seminary professors, while others teach at the undergraduate and graduate levels—they affirm what traditionally has been called a "Reformed perspective." Thus, we identify at the outset of this project the worldview within which we practice our scholarship: the Reformed worldview. The Reformed worldview, examined more fully in chapter 8, views all reality in terms of the majesty and lordship of God and his redemptive purposes. Reformed thinkers believe that all of life and thinking should be shaped or reformed according to the Word of God.

Our goal in this book is to present honestly and forthrightly the worldviews that characterize the periods assigned. The early chapters on ancient Greece and the Old and New Testaments establish a basic sense of antithesis between biblical revelation and other systems of speculative thought. In virtually every chapter besides those probing the Old and New Testaments, more than one perspective comes to light. Our assumption as scholars from the Reformed tradition is that despite obvious differences between and within the Old and New Testaments, we can affirm confidently that the Bible is the Word of God and speaks with a unified voice. The Bible serves as the qualitative touchstone for implicit and explicit criticism found in the remaining chapters.

Acknowledgments

W. Andrew Hoffecker

The vast majority of books are not the product of a single mind. Those who pursue writing as a vocation readily acknowledge a variety of individuals who contributed to what they have written. How much more does an editor of a joint project such as *Revolutions in Worldview* owe to those whose efforts combined to give birth to this book.

I acknowledge first the colleagues who wrote the chapters. Their teaching and writing had already established them as respected scholars in their various disciplines. Thus, they were an easy choice as I projected the book's scope. They waited patiently as several years marched by from the time they first signed on with this endeavor. May your teaching ministry prosper and your next manuscript be accepted!

I thank Reformed Theological Seminary for the sabbatical that enabled me to bring to completion another book on worldview. I extend my appreciation to those who sat through courses and weekend seminars on worldview during the past three decades, first at Grove City College, then at RTS. Your questions and contributions to discussion enhanced my thinking about worldview issues.

Thanks also to Allan Fisher, former director of publications for P&R Publishing, who expressed enthusiasm for the project and guided me through initial hurdles; to Bryce Craig, president of P&R, and Marvin Padgett, P&R's present editorial director, who offered words of advice and encouragement; and to Eric Anest, P&R's associate director of editorial, who brought the manuscript to its completion.

I offer special words of thanks to John J. Hughes, president of Bits & Bytes, Inc., who shepherded the other authors and me in a timely manner. His suggestions for improving the book as a whole, as well as the individual chapters, have made the text more attractive and reflect his commitment to excellence in Christian publishing.

Finally, I thank my wife, Pam. In our forty-four years of marriage, she has always been my most faithful encourager and critic. She combines those two qualities not only in the most loving manner possible but also at times when they are most needed.

1

Greeks Bearing Gifts

John M. Frame

The ancient Greeks were not the first civilization in the West, but they made such immense contributions to art, architecture, science, politics, warfare, education, poetry, history, and philosophy that many discussions of these subjects, even today, begin with them. Until the twentieth century, when Eastern religion and philosophy began to make a major impact, Western thought had two roots: Greek and biblical. Some thinkers tried to synthesize these traditions in various ways; others saw an antithesis and sought to be consistent with one or the other.

Although I greatly admire the creative brilliance of the Greek thinkers, I believe it is a serious mistake to adopt their worldviews or to try to synthesize their thinking with the worldview of the Bible. The Greeks and the biblical writers did explore many common themes: God and gods, the nature of reality, the origin of the world, human nature, wisdom, knowledge, ethics, politics, and even salvation. We can still learn much from the Greek discussions of these topics. But the ancient wariness about "Greeks bearing gifts" should be applied to the study of Greek worldviews.[1] The chief benefit in studying Greek thought is to understand better the philosophical and cultural consequences of rejecting biblical theism.

The word *rejecting* may seem harsh. Did the Greeks have access to Scripture? And if not, how could they have rejected it? The early Christian writer Justin Martyr thought that Plato got the idea for his Demiurge (a godlike figure in the dialogue *Timaeus*) from the writings of Moses. Justin's hypothesis is historically unlikely, and it is a symptom of Justin's overesti-

> *The ancient wariness about "Greeks bearing gifts" should be applied to the study of Greek world-views. The chief benefit in studying Greek thought is to understand better the philosophical and cultural consequences of rejecting biblical theism.*

---

1. The phrase "beware of Greeks bearing gifts" paraphrases a text from Virgil's *Aeneid* and other sources. The allusion is to the Trojan horse. The Greeks sent the Trojans a huge wooden horse as a supposed gift. After it was brought into the city of Troy, Greek soldiers emerged from the wooden structure, wreaking havoc.

mation of the coherence between Platonism and the Bible. But whatever we may say about the commerce in ideas between Greece and the Near East, the Bible does tell us that the Greeks, like all people, had the resources for formulating a theistic worldview. According to Romans 1:18–23,

> For the wrath of God is revealed from heaven against all ungodliness and unrighteousness of men, who by their unrighteousness suppress the truth. For what can be known about God is plain to them, because God has shown it to them. For his invisible attributes, namely, his eternal power and divine nature, have been clearly perceived, ever since the creation of the world, in the things that have been made. So they are without excuse. For although they knew God, they did not honor him as God or give thanks to him, but they became futile in their thinking, and their foolish hearts were darkened. Claiming to be wise, they became fools, and exchanged the glory of the immortal God for images resembling mortal man and birds and animals and reptiles.

Because of God's self-revelation in creation, Paul states, all people, Greeks included, know the biblical God, but the human race has rejected this knowledge and has come to worship images of created things.

When Paul visited Athens, he found it "full of idols" (Acts 17:16). He preached there to an audience that included Epicurean and Stoic philosophers, and concluded by demanding their repentance for the sin of idolatry. Although Epicureans and Stoics had little use for traditional Greek gods, Paul evidently believed that Stoic materialistic pantheism and Epicurean atomism were no better than the worship of Zeus and Apollo. The world is not governed by impersonal fate (Stoicism) or impersonal (occasionally random) movements of atoms (Epicurus) but by a personal God who "has fixed a day on which he will judge the world in righteousness by a man whom he has appointed; and of this he has given assurance to all by raising him from the dead" (Acts 17:31). When Paul said this, some mocked, some withheld judgment, and a few believed.

The biblical God tolerates no rivals. It is wrong to worship Baal, Moloch, Dagon, Marduk, Zeus, Apollo, or Aphrodite. It also is wrong to regard the natural order as absolute, as an uncreated, self-sufficient reality. For both the "religious"[2] and the "secular" alternatives deny God the worship due him alone. In this sense, both the materialistic Stoics and Epicureans and the spiritualistic Plato are idolaters.

> *None of the Greeks believed the world was created and directed by a personal, supreme, absolute being. The idea of a **personal** absolute being is virtually unique to the Bible.*

Greek Worldviews: One and Many

We sometimes speak of "Greek philosophy" or even "Greek thought" as if it represented a single worldview. However, even at first glance, there

---

2.   I put "religious" in quotes, for in a larger sense all worldviews are religious, even those called "secular." A person's religious faith is his "ultimate concern" (Paul Tillich), the passion or allegiance that governs his life, whether or not he expresses that faith in ceremonial rites.

seem to be vast disagreements among Greek thinkers. Besides the disagreement between materialists and spiritualists, we note that Homer and Hesiod believed in the traditional gods; Heraclitus, Xenophanes, and Epicurus had little use for them. Parmenides believed that nothing changes, Heraclitus that everything changes—well, almost everything. Plato despised sense experience; Heraclitus, the Stoics, and Epicurus affirmed it. Protagoras denied, and Plato affirmed, the possibility of objective knowledge. Parmenides and Plotinus believed that reality is a perfect oneness; Democritus and Epicurus believed that the world was irreducibly plural. Epicurus advised people to avoid politics; the Stoics encouraged such involvement. The tragedians and Stoics were fatalists; the Epicureans were not.

But Greek thinkers had much in common. First of all, none believed in the God of the Bible, despite the revelation of God to them mentioned earlier. None of the Greek philosophers even considered the theistic worldview, as far as we can tell from their writings. Since the theistic hypothesis was excluded from the outset, Greek thinkers had the common task of explaining the world without reference to the biblical God, that is, of explaining the world by means of the world.

Unbelief in the biblical God also meant that the human mind had to do its work without help from a higher mind. Although Anaxagoras taught that the world was directed by *nous* (mind), according to Plato's *Apology* Socrates expressed his disappointment that Anaxagoras didn't make much use of this idea. Nor did Heraclitus, who taught that the world was ordered by *logos* (word or reason). And although Aristotle also believed in a higher mind—the Unmoved Mover, a being whose entire activity consists in thinking about his own thoughts—this god did not reveal his thoughts to Aristotle but instead is a hypothesis of Aristotle's own reason and thus an idol.

To consider the issue more broadly: none of the Greeks believed the world was created and directed by a personal, supreme, absolute being. The idea of a *personal* absolute being is virtually unique to the Bible.[3] Hinduism, like Aristotle's and Plato's philosophies, teaches the existence of an absolute being, but that being (like those of the philosophers) is impersonal. The Homeric gods (as those of the Canaanites and other polytheists) are personal, but they are not absolute. Only the biblical God is both absolute and personal.[4]

> *Both the materialistic Stoics and Epicureans and the spiritualistic Plato are idolaters. . . . Since the theistic hypothesis was excluded from the outset, the Greek thinkers had the common task of explaining the world without reference to the biblical God, that is, of explaining the world by means of the world.*

3. I say "virtually" to interject a note of caution. I have not studied all the religions and philosophies of the world in order to prove the negative proposition that no other worldview includes a personal absolute. But I do believe this generalization is true. Scripture itself teaches that idolatry is universal among fallen people. God's revelation and grace, revealed only through the gospel of Christ, are the necessary antidote.

4. The god of Islam is absolute and often is presented as personal. But, (1) this emphasis ultimately comes from the Bible, from Mohammed's respect for the "peoples of the book," and (2) Muslim theology compromises absolute-personality theism when it takes divine predestination in a fatalistic sense and when it presents its god as a super-transcendent being about whom nothing may truthfully be said in human language.

The Greek Way of Worship

In Greek religion, the philosophical and religious absolute was fate. Although sometimes this is symbolized by the three women ("fates") who together weave and terminate the fabric of human life,[5] to the Greeks, fate was impersonal. The tragic heroes of Aeschylus and Sophocles are propelled by fate to transgress the proper boundaries of human life, whereupon they are destroyed, again by fate. The dictates of fate may agree with those of morality in some measure, but not necessarily. Fate is an impersonal force like gravity or electricity, and even the gods are subject to it.

Dooyeweerd says that the older, pre-Homeric Greek religion

> deified the ever-flowing stream of organic life, which issues from mother earth and cannot be bound to any individual form. In consequence, the deities of this religion are amorphous. It is from this shapeless stream of ever-flowing organic life that the generations of perishable beings originate periodically, whose existence, limited by a corporeal form, is subjected to the horrible fate of death, designated by the Greek terms *anangke* or *heimarmene tuche*. This existence in a limiting form was considered an injustice since it is obliged to sustain itself at the cost of other beings so that the life of one is the death of another. Therefore all fixation of life in an individual figure is avenged by the merciless fate of death in the order of time.[6]

He later describes the "central motive" of this religion as "that of the shapeless stream of life eternally flowing throughout the process of birth and decline of all that exists in a corporeal form."[7]

For the tragedians, however, fate governs not only birth and death but the rest of life as well. A fate that governs birth and death must govern all the events leading to birth and death. How, then, can we reconcile such a comprehensive fatalism with the amorphousness of the stream of life? One of these, it seems, will have to yield to the other; maintaining both leads to an unstable worldview. Neither fate nor the "shapeless stream" gives any meaning to the historical process. Things happen just because they happen (the shapeless stream) or because they were made to happen (fate); there is no rational or moral purpose. We often contrast fatalistic worldviews with worldviews based on chance, but in the end these coincide: both leave history meaningless and human beings helpless. Both types of worldview present a world that is not governed by purpose, goodness, or love.

Homer

Gradually, the old nature-religion gave way to the religion of the Olympian gods. The transformation was not too great, for the gods were basically personifications of the various forces of nature: Poseidon of the sea, Hades of the underworld, Apollo of the sun, Hephaestus of fire, Demeter of the earth, and so on. Then the gods became patrons of human activi-

---

5.   Clotho spun the thread, Lachesis measured it, and Atropos cut it.
6.   Herman Dooyeweerd, *In the Twilight of Western Thought* (Nutley, NJ: Presbyterian and Reformed, 1960), 39.
7.   Ibid.

ties: Hera of marriage, Ares of war, Athena of education, Artemis of the hunt, Aphrodite of love, Hermes of commerce, and so forth.[8] Zeus was the most powerful but not all-powerful. He had a father and mother, the Titans Cronos and Rhea. He gained knowledge by consulting the fates and suffered irrational fits of jealousy and rage.

Dooyeweerd describes this "younger Olympian religion" as "the religion of form, measure and harmony."[9] The Olympians lived far above the "shapeless stream of life." So worship of these gods became the official religion of the Greek city-states who, of course, preferred order to chaos. Apollo especially became the embodiment of orderliness. But "in their private life the Greeks continued to hold to the old earthly gods of life and death."[10]

Dionysus, god of wine and revelry, was one of the Olympian gods, but not one honored much by Homer or by the politicians. His worship was an intentional violation of form, order, and structure—a religion of drunken revelry and sexual orgy. So Dionysus, for all his Olympian transcendence, came to be seen as the patron of the old religion, the religion of shapelessness and chaos.

By providing some meaning to history, some reason why things happen as they do, the Olympian religion improved somewhat on the older one. Now, not only impersonal fate, or the chaotic life stream, but rational thought, the thinking of the gods, became part of the process. Ultimately, however, history remained in the hands of irrational fate, which was superior to the gods, and of the stream of life, over which the gods had little control.

Thus the old religion and the Olympian religion have pessimistic implications for human life. Human beings are essentially pawns, of fate, of chaos, or of the Olympians. Unlike the God of the Bible, none of these elements of Greek religion has a moral character, nor is any of these beings "a very present help in trouble" (Ps. 46:1).

Philosophy, the New Religion

A new movement began around 600 BC, when some thinkers tried to understand the world without the help of religion. They were called philosophers—lovers of wisdom. There had been wisdom teachers earlier in the ancient world, in Egypt, Babylon, and elsewhere, and the wisdom literature in Scripture (Proverbs, Song of Solomon, Ecclesiastes) is similar to extrabiblical wisdom literature in many ways. But, unlike it, the biblical wisdom

> *We often contrast fatalistic worldviews with worldviews based on chance, but in the end these coincide: both leave history meaningless and human beings helpless. Both types of worldview present a world that is not governed by purpose, goodness, or love.*

> *A new movement began around 600 BC, when some thinkers tried to understand the world without the help of religion. They were called philosophers—lovers of wisdom.*

---

8. One is reminded of how the later church appointed dead saints as patrons of human endeavors.

9. *Twilight*, 40.

10. Ibid.

teachers declare that "the fear of the LORD is the beginning of wisdom" (Ps. 111:10; Prov. 9:10, 15:33; compare Eccl. 12:13).

What distinguishes Greek philosophers from Greek religions and other ancient wisdom teachers is their insistence on the supremacy of human reason, what I shall call rational autonomy. Wisdom teachers in other cultures treasured the traditions of fathers and mothers, the teachers of past generations (as in Prov. 1:8–9; 2:1–22; 3:1–2; etc.) They saw themselves as collectors and guardians of such traditions, occasionally adding something and passing on the collection to their sons and daughters. The philosophers, however, wanted to accept nothing on the basis of tradition. Although Parmenides and Plato occasionally resorted to myth, they considered mythological explanations second best and, in the end, rationally inadequate. Reason must be autonomous, self-authenticating,[11] and subject to no standards other than its own.

Although the philosophers disagreed on much, they all agreed that the good life was the life of reason.[12] To them reason, not the fear of the Lord, was the beginning of wisdom; reason itself became something of a god—though they did not describe it as such—an object of ultimate allegiance, and the ultimate standard of truth and falsity, of right and wrong.

The philosophers' attitudes toward the traditional Greek religion ranged from ridicule (Xenophanes) to genial acceptance (Epicurus, who affirmed belief in the gods but denied that they caused anything to happen on earth). Socrates, considered the most admirable model of the philosophic temperament, was executed for his failure to believe in the gods of Athens, as well as for corrupting the youth by teaching them also to disbelieve. So Greek philosophy was indeed a "revolution in worldview." It represented a radical break from what had gone before.

A Survey of Greek Philosophy

Now we will survey Greek philosophers in more detail and in roughly chronological order. In our discussion, the following themes will apply to almost all of the individual philosophers: (1) the supreme authority of human reason, (2) the consequent attempt to make rational claims about the nature of *all* reality, (3) the consequent claim that all reality is basically one, but (4) the continuing problem of dualism: the antagonism between impersonal fate and the shapeless stream of life. And (5) the shapeless stream challenges the power of reason to grasp reality. The philosophers

> *What distinguishes Greek philosophers from Greek religions and other ancient wisdom teachers is their insistence on the supremacy of human reason, what I shall call rational autonomy.*

---

11.   I.e., validated only by itself.

12.   The sophists of the fifth century (Protagoras, Gorgias, Thrasymachus) and the skeptics of the later Academy (Pyrrho, Timon, Arcesilaus) denied the possibility of knowing objective truth. But (paradoxically) they offered rational arguments for this conclusion. They never considered abandoning reason. For Plotinus, ultimate knowledge is mystical, not rational. But the path to mystical experience is rational. For him (also paradoxically) it is reason that teaches us how to transcend reason.

try to deal with this problem in various ways, without compromising their fundamental allegiance to autonomous reason. But (6) the philosophers' inability to maintain the rationality of their enterprise indicates the failure of their attempt to understand the world autonomously. For in the end, we must conclude that they have set themselves an impossible task: imposing autonomous reason on an essentially irrational world. (7) These difficulties invalidate much of what they say about the soul, ethics, and society.

The Milesians

Only fragments remain from the teachings and writings of the first group of Greek philosophers, named for their city, Miletus, in Asia Minor. Most of what we know about them comes from other writers, particularly Aristotle, who were not entirely sympathetic. Still, it is less important for us to know what these philosophers actually said or meant than to know how they were understood by later thinkers; for it was by these later interpretations that the Milesians influenced the history of philosophy.[13]

Thales (ca. 620–546 BC) taught that "all is water" and that "all things are full of gods." Anaximenes (d. 528 BC) believed that "all is air." Anaximander (610–546) taught that "all is indefinite" (*apeiron*, boundless). To understand this, it helps to remember that, generally speaking, the Greeks thought the universe consisted of four elements: earth, air, fire, and water. So the Milesians were seeking to discover which of these, if any, was the fundamental one, the element of the elements, the basic constitution of the universe.

The Greek philosophers sought answers to three questions that continue to interest scientists and philosophers: (1) What is the fundamental nature of reality? (2) Where did everything come from? (3) How did the universe get to be as it is?

For Thales, (1) the fundamental nature of the universe is water. That is the essence of everything, what everything really is, despite appearances to the contrary. (2) Everything came from water and will return to water. (3) The world developed out of water by various natural processes. Perhaps by saying that "all things are full of gods" he meant to indicate that these natural processes were governed by thought or mind in some way.

Anaximenes thought similarly about air, doubtless provoking arguments about whether water or air was the most plentiful element, the element most able to account for other phenomena, and so forth. For him, the diversity of reality results from the condensation and rarefaction of air. Later, Heraclitus would make the case for fire. To my knowledge, nobody

But the philosophers' inability to maintain the rationality of their enterprise indicates the failure of their attempt to understand the world autonomously. For in the end, we must conclude that they have set themselves an impossible task: imposing autonomous reason on an essentially irrational world.

---

13. This also is true with regard to other thinkers discussed in this essay. For the most part, I shall be assuming traditional interpretations of these thinkers, even though I know that many of these are controversial among specialists. I cannot enter here into detailed interpretative controversies, and I believe the traditional interpretations reveal the nature of the impact these philosophers have had on later history.

hypothesized the primacy of earth, perhaps because earth seemed to be less changeable than the other three elements. Anaximander believed that none of the four elements could explain the variety of the world, so he said the essence of things was a substance without a definite nature (in that sense "unbounded") that takes on limitations to create the visible world.

Commentators sometimes describe the Greek philosophers as children looking at the world in wonder. This picture, however, is far from that of the apostle Paul, who, in Romans 1:18–23, says that those without the biblical God are suppressing the truth in unrighteousness. It is hard not to sympathize with Thales and his colleagues as they forge ahead to look at the world in a new way. We cannot hold against them the fact that modern science has transcended their perspectives. But if we consider seriously what they are doing, we may evaluate their work differently.

Thales' statement that all is water does not arise from what we would call scientific research. Doubtless, Thales' observations influenced his view: the vast amount of water in the world, the need for water to sustain life, and so forth. But the "all" goes far beyond any possible observations. It is the language of a man sitting in an armchair, dogmatically asserting what the whole universe must be like. The "all" statements of these thinkers represent human reason vastly exceeding its limits. This is rationalism, an awe over the power of reason that turns it into a god.

On the other hand, water (and air, and even more obviously the "boundless") represents the "shapeless stream" of the old religion. Water moves in waves and currents; it cannot be leashed or controlled. There is a randomness about it that calls into question the power of reason to give an account of it. Thales' statement about everything being "full of gods" may be an attempt to give a rational direction to the random flow. But that raises further questions: are the gods, too, made of water? If not, then his hypothesis fails to explain "all." If they are water, then they, like Zeus and Apollo, are victims of the flowing stream, not controllers of it. And we cannot ignore the fact that on Thales' basis the human mind, too, is water. My thoughts are essentially waves and wavelets, occurrences that just happen to take place in the movements of my inner sea. So why should we think that one wave is more true than another, more valid, more illuminating, more profound? Mechanistic natural processes can account for waves, but they cannot account for the truth or falsity of human thoughts.

So, Thales is an extreme rationalist, but his worldview calls his reason in question. He is a rationalist *and* an irrationalist. He calls to mind Cornelius Van Til's philosophical reading of Genesis 3: Our mother Eve was faced with two claims. God told her she would die from eating the fruit. Satan told her she would not die but would become like God. Eve should have disregarded Satan's claim at the outset. Instead, she asserted her own right to make the final judgment (rationalism). Satan's claim presupposed God did not exist as the ultimate determiner of truth and meaning, and

[In Thales' statement, "All is water,"] the "all" goes far beyond any possible observations. It is the language of a man sitting in an armchair, dogmatically asserting what the whole universe must be like.

that therefore there was no absolute truth (irrationalism). Van Til says that every unbeliever is caught in this tension between rationalism and irrationalism. Some emphasize the former, others the latter. But when they get uneasy with one, they leap to the other.[14] I shall mention this pattern with other Greek philosophers. I mention it, not just as a fact of possible interest, but to show that the main inadequacies of Greek philosophy, in the end, are not to be blamed on primitive science, incomplete observations, or remediable logical mistakes, but on religious rebellion. Although these thinkers all absolutize human intellect, their nontheistic worldviews call human intellect itself into question.

The Milesians' epistemological failure is linked to a metaphysical failure. For the "all" of the Milesians excludes the biblical relation between Creator and creature. If all is water, then God, if he exists, also is water, and we are water. There is no fundamental difference between him and us. God and the world are one stuff. There is no creation. God has no intrinsic sovereignty over the world. The Milesians' scheme, therefore, rules out the biblical God. And if the biblical God is the only possible ground of meaning or truth in the world, the Milesians also rule out meaning and truth.

Although these thinkers all absolutize human intellect, their nontheistic worldviews call human intellect itself into question.

Heraclitus (525–475)

Heraclitus lived in Ephesus (not far from Miletus) and thought the most fundamental element was fire, the most dynamic and changeable of the four. But he was less concerned with identifying the fundamental substance than with describing the pervasiveness of change, with the ways in which fire changes into other things and others into still others. He is quoted frequently as saying, "You cannot step in the same river twice," meaning that when you step in the second time, you are stepping into different waters. Since the waters are different, it is a different river. Actually, what he said was this:

"On those stepping into rivers staying the same, other and other waters flow."[15]

The river stays the same, but the waters constantly change. Evidently, his view was that the elements of things are indeed constantly changing, but such change makes it possible for sameness to occur at other levels of reality.[16]

Thales

14. Van Til's discussion can be found in his *A Christian Theory of Knowledge* (Nutley, NJ: Presbyterian and Reformed, 1969), 41–71. For his application to Plato, see Van Til, *A Survey of Christian Epistemology* (Den Dulk Christian Foundation, 1969), 14–55. Cf. my *Cornelius Van Til: An Analysis of His Thought* (Phillipsburg, NJ: P&R Publishing, 1995), 231–38 passim.

15. Hermann Diels and Walther Kranz, *Die Fragmente der Vorsokratiker* (Zurich: Weidmann, 1985), DK22B12. Translated by Daniel W. Graham in "Heraclitus," in *The Internet Encyclopedia of Philosophy*, http://www.utm.edu/research/iep/h/heraclit.htm.

16. See Graham, ibid.

So, the world is constantly changing, but somehow these changes occur in regular patterns. If absolutely everything was in constant change, rational thought would be impossible; rational thought requires stability—objects that remain themselves long enough to be examined. Horses must remain horses, houses houses, people people, rivers rivers.

Heraclitus called the source of such stability the *logos*—probably the first philosophically significant use of this term. Logos has a variety of meanings: word, reason, rational account. Heraclitus believed that change was governed by a principle that kept change within rational bounds.

We can understand Heraclitus's philosophy as common sense. When we look at the world, nothing seems perfectly at rest; everything moves and changes, even if ever so slightly. Yet there is enough stability that we can talk about rivers, horses, houses, people, and many other things. The question is whether Heraclitus sheds any light on this change and stability. To say there is a logos is to say that the stability in the world must have a source. But what is that source? Is logos really an explanation of anything, or is it just a label for an unknown? Heraclitus's writings are paradoxical, multi-layered, full of symbols. They are fascinating, but in the end it isn't clear (to me, at least) what he is trying to tell us.

The logos is another assertion of Greek rationalism. Heraclitus tells us that reason must be our guide, even if we don't see how it can be a reliable one. By arguing that rationality must exist, not only in our minds but as an aspect of the universe, Heraclitus invokes reason by an act of faith. On the other hand, the changing flux amounts to irrationalism; Heraclitus virtually concedes that reason cannot deal with reality unless reality somehow is constant. But at the elemental levels, reality is anything but constant. Yet, rationalistically, he tries to develop a rational analysis of the elemental change.

Like the Milesians, Heraclitus rejects biblical theism and therefore the One who originates and sustains change. He is left with a world that is *somehow* changing and a rational constancy that is *somehow* there. The God who alone can give meaning to constancy and change is not a part of Heraclitus's philosophy.

Parmenides (510–ca. 430)

Parmenides lived in Elea in southern Italy, and agreed with Heraclitus that reasoning requires something changeless. So, turning 180 degrees from Heraclitus, he denied the existence of change altogether. He wrote a poem describing an encounter with a goddess, who reveals to him that "Being is." The goddess, however, does not deliver this revelation on her own authority; she appeals to reason as a properly philosophical goddess should do.[17]

> *Heraclitus called the source of such stability the logos—probably the first philosophically significant use of this term.*

17. Parmenides usually is considered a follower of the religious teacher Xenophanes (570–475), who rejected the Olympian gods in favor of a kind of pantheistic monism. Par-

"Being is" means that nothing can change from what it "is" to what it "is not." Red cannot change to green, for then red would be changing into non-red, or non-green would be changing into green. And how can that be? Where does the green come from, if the previous state is non-green? Therefore, change cannot be real; it must be an illusion.

Indeed, the very idea of "nonbeing" must be rejected. There is no change from nonbeing to being, for there is no such thing as nonbeing. Nonbeing simply is not, nor are non-red, non-green, and all other negative expressions.[18]

What *is* the real world, then? Parmenides tries to describe what a world without nonbeing, and thus without change, would be like. It would be ungenerated, homogeneous, solid, symmetrical, spherical. If it is not homogeneous, for example, it must be a combination of one element and what it is not, for example, water and non-water. But that cannot be. The same holds true for the other characteristics Parmenides ascribes to reality.

Parmenides

Parmenides' worldview, which he calls the "way of truth," is so removed from common sense that it provides no help for living in the world of our experience. In fact, it requires a drastic *rejection* of our experience. Parmenides' poem also includes, however, an elaborate cosmology that the goddess calls the "way of belief." This cosmology includes change and is very different from the "way of truth." Most likely, Parmenides regards the "way of belief" as an error to be rejected. But he may also have intended for us to use the "way of belief" as a practical guide, as a way to think about the world that our senses presents to us.

Parmenides may well be the most consistent rationalist in the history of philosophy. He said there is no difference between "what is" and "what can be thought." Therefore, having determined what can be thought by human reason, he believed he had discovered the true nature of the world. To serve reason he was willing to deny (almost entirely) the testimony of sense experience, thereby positing a world vastly different from anything we have seen or heard. But what happens to reason in this unchanging world? Human reason is temporal, or seems to be. We think one thought after another. Our minds experience change, even in our most intellectual activities. How can we think at all if we cannot advance from less adequate to more adequate ideas? So, Parmenides' rationalism actually invalidates reason, leading to irrationalism.

> Parmenides' world-view, which he calls the "way of truth," is so removed from common sense that it provides no help for living in the world of our experience. In fact, it requires a drastic rejection of our experience.

menides' "Being" is roughly equivalent to Xenophanes' god.

18.   Critics of Parmenides have pointed out there is a difference between existential (e.g., "horses are" = "horses exist") and the predicative ("horses are mammals") senses of the verb "to be." Parmenides evidently confuses these. Obviously, it is contradictory to say that "Being is not," for in that phrase *Being* refers to existence. It is not obviously contradictory to say "the horse is not green," for "is" in that sentence is used predicatively, rather than existentially.

Perhaps Parmenides knew this and provided the "way of belief" as an alternative philosophy, one that would account for the structure of our sense experience.[19] If so, we can detect rationalism in Parmenides' "way of truth" and irrationalism in his "way of belief." On this understanding, Parmenides would have anticipated Plato's distinction between the world of Forms, which really Is, and the world of our sense experience, which is less knowable and less real.

Again, we must ask how Parmenides' thought might have been different had he started with the existence of the biblical God and listened to his revelation.

The Atomists

Parmenides is classified as a "monist," someone who believes that the universe is basically one. Indeed, Parmenides systematically excluded all diversity from the world in his attempt to exclude "nonbeing." In the "way of truth" there cannot be different things, one that is red (for instance) and one that is not.

Other philosophers have been pluralists, maintaining that the universe is fundamentally many, rather than one. In ancient Greece, those who held this position most consistently were the atomists, Empedocles (major work ca. 450), Anaxagoras (500–428), Leucippus (fifth century), Democritus (460–360), and Epicurus (341–270).[20]

Empedocles thought that the world was originally something like Parmenidean Being: one, homogeneous, and so forth. But the opposing forces of love and strife start things in motion, separating out the four elements and combining them in different ways. The four elements are "roots" of all reality, in effect the atoms, the basic stuff of which everything is made.

According to Anaxagoras, there were an indefinite number of elements. Fire could not produce earth, he thought, unless some earth already was present in fire. Nor can a person's bread become muscle and hair unless there are little bits of muscle and hair already in the bread. Anaxagoras also taught the existence of *nous* or mind, a principle that maintains the rationality of change, and is similar to Heraclitus's logos and Empedocles' love and strife. In Plato's *Apology*, Socrates complained that he had hoped to find in Anaxagoras some account of how mind directed the world but was disappointed to find only mechanistic explanations of nature.

Empedocles and Anaxagoras are called "qualitative atomists," which means they believed the world is composed of elements with different qualities—four (Empedocles) or indefinitely many (Anaxagoras). Some-

> *Parmenides is classified as a "monist," someone who believes that the universe is basically one. Indeed, Parmenides systematically excluded all diversity from the world in his attempt to exclude "nonbeing."*

---

19. Plato also introduced myths (e.g., *Republic* and *Timaeus*) to deal with subjects his philosophy was unable to treat adequately. We might compare here the "custom" of David Hume, the "practical reason" of Immanuel Kant, and the "mystical" of Wittgenstein.

20. The atomists were pluralists only in a sense. They were monists in that like Thales they believed there was only one kind of thing in the world—atoms.

what like Parmenidean Being, the elements are unchanging, but reality as a whole changes as these elements combine in different ways.

Leucippus, Democritus, and Epicurus were "quantitative atomists." Their atoms, or elements, had the same qualities, except for size and shape (Democritus) or weight (Epicurus). These atoms moved through space and collided with one another to form objects. On this view, reality consists entirely of atoms and empty space.

Since Epicurus's atoms had the quality of weight, they tended to fall in one direction, a sort of cosmic "down." Normally they fell in lines parallel to one another. How, then, did they ever collide to form objects? Epicurus posited that occasionally an atom would "swerve" from the vertical path. The swerve is entirely uncaused, and accounts for the formation of objects. It also accounts for human free choice. Human beings are able to act apart from causal determination because the atoms of their bodies sometimes swerve inexplicably.

Epicurus is probably the first philosopher to identify human freedom with causal indeterminacy and to make this indeterminacy the basis of moral responsibility. This view of freedom is sometimes called libertarianism or incompatibilism.[21] A number of theologians have argued for such an understanding of free will, including Pelagius, Molina, Arminius, and the recent open theists.[22] But how does the random swerve of atoms in my body make my acts morally responsible? If I walk down the street and some atoms in my head swerve and collide, making me rob a bank, why am I to blame? I didn't make them swerve; indeed, the swerve had no cause at all. It seems more plausible to say the swerve *happened* to me and therefore I am *not* responsible for its consequences. It is like a chemical imbalance in my brain that makes me do strange things. In reality, this is an odd kind of *determinism*, rather than freedom. Should we not say, then, that such a swerve precisely *removes* our responsibility?

The question of responsibility leads us to think of ethics. Writing after the time of Plato and Aristotle, Epicurus was eager to apply his atomism to moral questions. One wonders, indeed, what kind of ethics can emerge from such a thoroughgoing materialism?

Essentially, Epicurus's ethic is that we should avoid pain and seek pleasure, which he defines as the absence of pain. Unlike the Cyrenaics and some later Epicureans, Epicurus distinguished short-term from long-term pleasures and taught that on the whole a quiet, peaceful, contemplative life is the most pleasurable. This view of ethics is called hedonism, from the Greek word meaning pleasure. There are several problems with it:

> *Epicurus is probably the first philosopher to identify human freedom with causal indeterminacy and to make this indeterminacy the basis of moral responsibility.*

---

21. It is called incompatibilism because it is incompatible with determinism. Other views of freedom are compatible with determinism. For example, the view called "compatibilism" is the view that freedom is simply doing what you want to do.

22. I have criticized libertarianism extensively in my *No Other God: a Response to Open Theism* (Phillipsburg, NJ: P&R Publishing, 2001) and in *Doctrine of God* (Phillipsburg, NJ: P&R Publishing, 2002).

(1) In the normal sense of *pleasure*, there are many things that human beings value more. One example is sacrificing one's life to save the life of another. Epicurus offers no good reason to pursue pleasure rather than some other value. (2) If we define *pleasure* so broadly that it includes all other values, even self-sacrifice, then it loses its meaning by failing to distinguish pleasurable from non-pleasurable activities. (3) Even if it is true that in some sense people value pleasure above all else, it is a logical jump to say that we *ought* to value pleasure above all else. But the *ought* is what ethics is all about. I doubt that anyone can derive an ethical ought from a materialistic philosophy.[23] Matter in motion simply cannot tell us what we ought to do.

Atomism, then, tries to explain everything in terms of matter, motion, and chance. If Thales was unable to account for human thought by means of water, how can the atomists expect to account for it by means of nondescript bits of matter in motion? The atomists are rationalistic in trying to use reason to reduce all reality to its smallest components. But, having done that, they have left us little if any reason to trust our minds. So rationalism and irrationalism again combine. The problem becomes even more difficult when we try to account for human responsibility and moral obligation on a materialistic basis.

The religious roots of this way of thinking become especially clear in Epicurus's writings: he is most explicit in wanting to exclude the supernatural from any role in the world. But without a personal God, how can one account for the validity of thinking and the authority of moral principles?

Pythagoras (572–500)

We know little of the specific views held by Pythagoras, but he influenced a school of thought that in turn influenced other philosophers. Plato visited the Pythagorean religious community in southern Italy and reworked many of its ideas in his own writings. The Pythagoreans followed a religion known as Orphism, which taught that the human soul was a divine being imprisoned in the body. According to this view, the soul undergoes repeated reincarnations until it is sufficiently purified to return to the divine realm. Our souls are divine because they are rational; so salvation comes through knowledge. Thus, the Pythagoreans followed the common Greek emphasis on the autonomy of the intellect. They also divided human beings into three classes: lovers of wisdom, lovers of honor, and lovers of gain, which may be the source for Plato's similar threefold distinction in the *Republic*. And they developed an elaborate cosmology, similar to that of Anaximander and of Parmenides' "way of belief."

However, we remember Pythagoras chiefly for his work in mathematics, including the Pythagorean Theorem that is found in every high school

> *Even if it is true that in some sense people value pleasure above all else, it is a logical jump to say that we ought to value pleasure above all else. But the ought is what ethics is all about. I doubt that anyone can derive an ethical ought from a materialistic philosophy. Matter in motion simply cannot tell us what we ought to do.*

---

23. The question of whether one can derive obligations from facts about material objects came up again in the modern period. David Hume denied that one could deduce "is" from "ought," and G. E. Moore labeled the attempt to do that the "naturalistic fallacy."

geometry book. This theorem tells us that in a right triangle the square of the hypotenuse is equal to the sum of the squares of the other two sides. In a right triangle whose sides measure 3, 4, and 5 inches, the squares of the shorter sides would be 9 and 16, totaling 25, the square of the longest side. Pythagoras and/or his disciples also most likely discovered that harmonious combinations of musical notes arise from different vibrations related by simple fractions. If A on the scale is 440 vibrations, the next higher octave is 880, and so on.

These data may have suggested to the Pythagoreans that everything in the universe can be described in terms of the application of a mathematical formula. Hence the slogan "all is number," reflecting the "all" formulae of the Milesians. Since everything is the outworking of a mathematical formula, mathematics is the ultimate reality. This was the Pythagorean version of the common Greek theme that reason is the nature of reality as well as the nature of thought.

The Pythagoreans, however, did not ask, so far as we can tell, where the formulae came from. The existence of such formulae would seem to be a remarkable fact. Indeed, it should have suggested a personal creator, for the natural home of numbers and formulae is in the mind of a person. For the Pythagoreans, numbers "just are." They exist as brute facts. For the Pythagoreans, like the other Greeks, were unwilling to acknowledge a rational person higher than themselves. The greatest mind is the mind of the human mathematician.

But the cost of this rationalism is the loss of cogency. If mathematical formulae just are, why should we trust them? Is it perhaps an accident that mathematical formulae neatly apply to right triangles and some musical intervals? And by what process do abstract numbers get converted into concrete things? Like other Greek philosophies, the Pythagoreans' rationality terminates in irrationality.

Pythagoras

> *But the cost of this rationalism is the loss of cogency. If mathematical formulae just are, why should we trust them? . . . Like other Greek philosophies, the Pythagoreans' rationality terminates in irrationality.*

The Sophists

The Sophists were traveling educators in fifth- and fourth-century Greece who went from one city to another teaching young men the skills needed for success in public life: rhetoric, grammar, history, science, art, and the virtues of character that lead to public admiration. These teachers had many clients, for the traditional aristocracy was losing ground to the mercantile class, creating opportunities for upwardly mobile sons of wealthy families. Also, there was much political upheaval, raising philosophical questions about the ground and legitimacy of political rule.[24]

Thus philosophy took a new turn. No longer were philosophers mainly concerned with the structure of the natural world. Now human nature and the problems of human society became prominent.

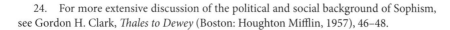

24. For more extensive discussion of the political and social background of Sophism, see Gordon H. Clark, *Thales to Dewey* (Boston: Houghton Mifflin, 1957), 46–48.

If one's main concern is getting along with various political factions, then relativism will have a strong appeal, as we know from contemporary politics. If there is no absolute or objective truth, no truth that everyone must acknowledge, then one's convictions are free to move here and there, with every wave of political opinion. So it is not surprising that the Sophists were relativists.

We learn about them mainly through the dialogues of Plato, an unsympathetic witness, to be sure, but most likely a fair one. The sophist Protagoras, for example, advocated acceptance of traditional ways of thinking, not because they were true, but because we need to use them to gain power and acceptance. Gorgias denied the existence of objective truth and so wanted to substitute rhetoric for philosophy. Thrasymachus taught that "justice is the interest of the stronger," so that laws are (and should be) means by which the strong keep the masses subordinate. Callicles held, on the contrary, that laws are the means used by the masses to check the power of the strong.[25] Critias, later described as the cruelest of the thirty tyrants, said that a ruler must control his subjects by encouraging fear of nonexistent gods.

Socrates, as Plato presents him in the same dialogues, replies that indifference or hostility to objective truth is unacceptable. For one thing, the Sophists themselves are making assertions of fact. If there is no objective truth, then the Sophists' positions are not objectively true, and there is no reason for anyone to listen to them. This argument has been a standard answer to relativism ever since, and we still hear it used over against, for example, contemporary postmodernism.

Furthermore, Socrates argues, justice cannot merely be the interest of the stronger. For the interest of the stronger is not what makes it *just*, as opposed to unjust. There must be some other quality that *defines* justice, that serves as a criterion to evaluate the conduct of rulers.

Thus Socrates refutes the irrationalism of the Sophists, or rather shows that such irrationalism is self-refuting. But the Sophists were also rationalists in the typical Greek way. Protagoras said that "man is the measure of all things." This statement expresses the Sophists' irrationalism: reality is what any man thinks it is. But it also is rationalistic, for it makes human reason the ultimate criterion of truth and falsity, right and wrong. One asks, how could Protagoras *know* this, especially given his overall relativism? He asserts rational autonomy arbitrarily. That is, he asserts rationalism irrationalistically, as he asserts irrationalism rationalistically—by the measure of his own mind.

> *If one's main concern is getting along with various political factions, then relativism will have a strong appeal . . . . If there is no absolute or objective truth, no truth that everyone must acknowledge, then one's convictions are free to move here and there, with every wave of political opinion.*

25. The distinction between Thrasymachus and Callicles reminds us of the differing attitudes of Marx and Nietzsche to Christianity. Marx considered Christianity an "opiate" by which the strong kept the poor in their place. Nietzsche considered it a "slave religion" by which lesser people inhibited those with ability and power. That such opposite conclusions can be derived from the same (relativistic) premises indicates some problem with the premises themselves.

No other course was open to the Sophists, for they were skeptical about the traditional gods and would not consider the God of biblical theism.

Socrates (470–399)

But Socrates did more than refute the Sophists. He is a figure of such towering importance that all of the other thinkers discussed to this point traditionally bear the label "pre-Socratic." He is a major saint in the religion of philosophy, a martyr. He was executed in 399 by the Athenian state for disbelief in the official gods[26] and for corrupting the youth by teaching them also to disbelieve.

Socrates is revered, not so much for his ideas (which are hard to disentangle from those of his student Plato, our major source of information about him), as for his way of life, his style of argument, his passion for truth. Having rejected the relativism of the Sophists, he insisted on getting to the roots of philosophical questions, exploring first here, then there. And he insisted on living in accord with his philosophy. He refused opportunities to escape death, wanting to show himself loyal to the government of Athens.

The Oracle at Delphi, he says, told him he was the wisest of men because he alone was aware of his own ignorance. So he sought out people he thought might be able to answer important questions, and he interrogated them rigorously. He regularly exposed flaws in the reasoning of the experts. Then he sought to define terms: what is justice, really? What is virtue? Characters in the dialogue would bring up examples of these qualities, but Socrates wanted to know more than examples. What is common to the examples of justice that makes them just? Usually, his interrogation yielded nothing definitive. But his use of dialogue (the technical term is *dialectic*) as a way of finding truth has inspired philosophers and other educators for centuries. Hence all disciplines have adopted his slogan, "The unexamined life is not worth living."

For Socrates, however, the use of dialogue was subordinate, as a source of truth, to something inward, to the human soul itself. He claimed that within him was a *daimon*, a divinity, and he believed that everyone could find the truth by looking within. So another Socratic slogan is, "Know yourself."

Dialectic and introspection together, then, constitute the Socratic epistemology. The emphasis on dialectic renews the Greek rationalistic tradition. The emphasis on introspection, however, locates truth in individual subjectivity.[27] This subjectivism is uncomfortably like that of the Sophists. If we are not to dismiss it as irrationalistic, we need to know how human subjectivity is related to the objective world, and to the Author of truth.

> "Socrates is revered, not so much for his ideas . . . as for his way of life, his style of argument, his passion for truth. Having rejected the relativism of the Sophists, he insisted on getting to the roots of philosophical questions, exploring first here, then there.

---

26. Though Plato says that one of his last acts was to ask someone to deliver a cock to Asclepius, the god of healing.

27. So Socrates has been compared to Søren Kierkegaard.

Plato (427–347)

Plato was the greatest student of Socrates and one of the greatest philosophers of all time. The greatest philosophers (among whom I include Aristotle, Aquinas, Kant, and Hegel) tend to be those who bring together many ideas that at first seem disparate. As an example: Parmenides said that Being is fundamentally changeless; Heraclitus that the elements of reality are in constant change. Plato's genius is to see truth in both of these accounts and to bring them together in a broader systematic understanding. Similarly, Plato provides distinct roles for reason and sense experience, soul and body, concepts and matter, objects and subjects, and, of course, rationalism and irrationalism.

Plato's epistemology begins with the observation that we can learn very little from our sense organs. So far, he agrees with the Sophists. Our eyes and ears easily deceive us. But the remarkable thing is that we have the rational ability to correct these deceptions and thus to find truth. It is by our reason also that we form concepts of things. We have never, for example, seen a perfect square. But somehow we know what a perfect square would be like, for we know the mathematical formula that generates one. Since we don't learn the concept of squareness by sense experience, we must learn it from reason. Similarly concepts of treeness, horseness, humanity, justice, virtue, goodness, and so forth. We don't see these, but somehow we know them.

These concepts Plato calls *Forms* or *Ideas*. Since we cannot find these Forms on earth, he says, they must exist in another realm, a world of Forms, as opposed to the world of sense. But what are Forms, exactly? In reading Plato we sometimes find ourselves thinking of the form of treeness as a perfect, gigantic tree somewhere, which serves as a model for all trees on earth. But that can't be right. Given the many different kinds of trees, how could one tree serve as a perfect model for all of them? And even if there were a gigantic tree somewhere, how could there be a gigantic justice, or virtue, or goodness? Furthermore, Plato says that the Forms are not objects of sensation (as a gigantic tree would be). Rather they are known through intelligence alone, through reason. Perhaps Plato is following the Pythagoreans here, conceiving the Forms as quasi-mathematical formulae, recipes that can be used to construct trees, horses, virtue, and justice as the Pythagorean Theorem can be used to construct a triangle. I say "quasi," because Plato in the *Republic* said that "mathematicals are a class of entities *between* the sensibles and the Forms."[28] Nevertheless, he does believe that Forms are real things and are the models of which things on earth are copies.

The Forms, then, are perfect, immaterial, changeless, invisible, intangible objects. Though abstract, they are more real than the objects of our sense experience, for only a perfect triangle, for example, is a real triangle.

> *Plato's epistemology begins with the observation that we can learn very little from our sense organs. . . . Our eyes and ears easily deceive us. But the remarkable thing is that we have the rational ability to correct these deceptions and thus to find truth. It is by our reason also that we form concepts of things.*

28. Diogenes Allen, *Philosophy for Understanding Theology* (Atlanta: John Knox Press, 1985), 20. Allen's further comments on this issue are helpful.

And the Forms are also more knowable than things on earth. We may be uncertain as to whether a particular judge is just, but we cannot be uncertain as to the justice of the Form Justice. As such, the Forms serve as models, exemplars, indeed criteria for earthly things. It is the Forms that enable us to know the earthly things that imitate them. We can know that someone is virtuous only by comparing him with the norm of Ideal Virtue.

The Forms exist in a hierarchy, the highest being the Form of the Good. For we learn what triangles, trees, human beings, and justice are when we learn what each is "good for." Everything is good for something, so everything that exists participates in the Form of the Good to some extent. The world of Forms, therefore, contains not only formulae for making objects but also norms defining the *purposes* of objects.

In *Euthyphro*, Socrates argues that piety cannot be defined as what the gods desire. For why should they desire it? They must desire it because it is good. So piety is a form of goodness, and goodness must exist independently of what gods or men may think or say about it. So it must be a Form. We should note, however, that if courage, virtue, goodness, and so forth are abstract forms, then they have no specific content. To know what is good, for Plato, is to know the Form of Goodness. But Goodness is what all individual examples of goodness have in common. How, then, does it help us to know specifically what is good and what is bad?

Any time we try to define Goodness in terms of specific qualities (justice, prudence, temperance, etc.), we have descended to something less than the Form of Goodness. The Form of Goodness serves as a norm for human goodness, because it is utterly general and abstract. Any principle that is more specific is less normative, less authoritative. Such is the consequence of trying to understand goodness as an abstract Form rather than, as in biblical theism, the will of a personal absolute.[29]

The world of sense experience is modeled on the world of Forms. Plato's *Timaeus* is a sort of creation account in which the Demiurge, a godlike figure, forms matter into patterns reflecting the Forms, placing his sculpture into a "receptacle" (presumably, empty space). The Demiurge is very different from the God of the Bible, for he is subordinate to the Forms and limited by the nature of the matter. The matter resists formation, so the material objects cannot be perfect, as the Forms are. So the Demiurge must be satisfied with a defective product. It is not clear whether Plato intended this story to be taken literally. He sometimes resorted to myth when he could not come up with a properly philosophical account of something. But it is significant that he saw the need for some means to connect the

Plato

"And the Forms are also more knowable than things on earth. We may be uncertain as to whether a particular judge is just, but we cannot be uncertain as to the justice of the Form Justice. As such, the Forms serve as models, exemplars, indeed criteria for earthly things.

29.   And if anyone asks the relation of goodness to the God of the Bible, the answer is as follows: (1) Goodness is not something above him, that he must submit to; (2) nor is it something below him, that he could alter at will; but (3) it is his own nature: his actions and attributes, given to human beings for imitation. "You therefore must be perfect, as your heavenly Father is perfect" (Matt. 5:48).

Forms with the sensible world. And it is significant that he made that connection personal rather than impersonal.

But how do we know the Forms, located as we are in this defective, changing world? Here Plato reflects the subjectivism of the Sophists and Socrates: we look within. We find within ourselves recollections of the Forms. Recollections? Then at one time we must have had experience of the Forms. When? Not in this life, where our experiences are limited to imperfect and changing things, but in another life before this one. So Plato embraces the Pythagorean-Orphic doctrine of reincarnation. We lived once in a world in which the Forms were directly accessible to us. Then we "fell" from that existence into the sense-world, into bodies. Our knowledge of the Forms remains in memory, but sometimes it has to be coaxed out of us by Socratic questioning. One famous example is in Plato's *Meno*, where Socrates asks questions of an uneducated slave boy, leading him to display knowledge of geometry nobody expected him to have.

The world of sense is not strictly knowable. Plato compares it to the shadows cast by a fire in a cave. Prisoners chained in the cave all their lives can see the shadows, but they mistake them for the Truth, so in fact they know virtually nothing. Their notions are "conjecture," not "knowledge." We can move beyond conjecture to "belief" by distinguishing between images (such as shadows and pictures) and actual objects. Thus we come to know the visible world. But we do not "understand" the visible world until we see the things of the world as instances of general concepts. Thus we move from conjecture, to belief, to understanding. Pure knowledge is still a fourth stage: intuitive vision of the Forms. The first two stages Plato calls "opinion," the last two "knowledge." The first two come through sense experience, the last two through reason. Our sense experience is illumined by the sun; our knowledge of the intelligible world is illumined by the Form of the Good.

In *Phaedrus*, Plato considers knowledge from another perspective: knowledge is motivated by love. In beautiful objects,[30] we see an echo of true beauty, and we are moved by passion to seek the Form of Beauty itself. Here is another example of the Greek focus on inwardness. People have sometimes said that the search for knowledge must be disinterested, without passion. Although Plato advocated the dominance of intellect over the appetites, he saw a positive use of the passions, even in philosophy.

Since we once lived apart from the body in the world of the Forms, it must be the case that the human soul can exist separately from the body. In *Phaedo*, as Socrates prepares for death, he bases his hope for immortality on this epistemological argument. Plato divides the soul into three parts.

> *Plato embraces the Pythagorean-Orphic doctrine of reincarnation. We lived once in a world in which the Forms were directly accessible to us. Then we "fell" from that existence into the sense-world, into bodies. Our knowledge of the Forms remains in memory, but sometimes it has to be coaxed out of us by Socratic questioning.*

---

30. His example is the beauty of a boy, as a pederastic love interest. As many Greek thinkers, Plato favored homosexual relationships between men and boys, another indication of how far the Greeks were from the biblical revelation. Paul's argument in Romans 1 presents homosexuality as a particularly vivid example of the depths to which people fall when they reject God's revelation.

The lowest is the appetitive, which seeks physical necessities and pleasures. Next higher is the spirited, which includes anger, ambition, desire for social honor, and so forth. The highest is the rational, which seeks knowledge for its own sake.[31] We can see how, with a bit of emendation, these divisions correspond to the later common distinction between emotions, will, and intellect, respectively. They correspond even more closely to Freud's distinction between id (appetitive), ego (spirited), and superego (rational). In *Phaedrus*, Plato sees the spirited part as a driver with two horses, white (the rational) and black (the appetitive). The spirited is swayed, sometimes by the appetitive, sometimes by the rational. The more it subordinates its appetites to its intellect, the better off it will be.

And if virtue is knowledge, then knowledge of what? Knowledge of the Good? But good is more difficult to define than virtue is.

But Plato's major interest, like that of Socrates, was to tell us how to live. His metaphysics and epistemology are all a prelude to his ethics and political theory. But it is in these areas that he is most disappointing. Socrates discusses at length the nature of justice and courage but comes to no firm conclusion. He does conclude that the definition of virtue is knowledge. One never does wrong except out of ignorance. If one knows what is right, he will necessarily do it. But most of Plato's readers through the centuries (including his pupil Aristotle) have dismissed this statement as naïve, and Christians have found it superficial in comparison with the Bible's view of human depravity.

And if virtue is knowledge, then knowledge of what? Knowledge of the Good? But *good* is more difficult to define than virtue is. Like all Forms, it is abstract. So how can it settle concrete ethical disputes, such as whether abortion is right or wrong? For Plato, to live right is to know the Good. But to say that is to leave all specific ethical questions unanswered.

Plato did come to some specific recommendations in the area of politics. But these recommendations have been almost universally rejected. In the *Republic*, he divides the body politic into groups corresponding to the divisions of the soul. In his ideal state, the peasants are governed by the appetitive soul, the military by the spirited, and the rulers by the rational. So the rulers of the state must be philosophers, those who understand the Forms. Such a state will be totalitarian, claiming authority over all areas of life. The upper classes will share their women communally, and children will be raised by the rulers. Art will be severely restricted, because it is a kind of shadow of which one can have only conjecture, the lowest form of opinion. Images detract from knowledge of Beauty itself (the Form) and they can incite to anarchy. Donald Palmer says that Plato's *Republic* "can be viewed as a plea that philosophy take over the role which art had hitherto played in Greek culture."[32]

---

31. In *Phaedo*, the soul is only the higher part, but in *Phaedrus*, the soul includes all three parts, even prior to its bodily existence.

32. Palmer, *Looking at Philosophy* (Mountain View, CA: Mayfield Publishing Co., 1988), 73.

*We may applaud
Plato's rejection of
relativism, but his
absolutism is what
makes him a totali-
tarian. He thinks the
philosophers have
Knowledge, so they
must rule everything.*

Most all modern readers look at these ideas with distaste. Where did Plato get them? It would not be credible for him to claim that he got them by contemplating the Good. Rather, the whole business sounds like special pleading. Plato the philosopher thinks that philosophers should rule. He is rather like a Sophist here, claiming to be the expert in the means of governance. But he certainly has not shown that philosophers in general have any of the special qualities needed to govern. And the Sophists denied what Plato claims: access to absolute truth. We may applaud Plato's rejection of relativism, but his absolutism is what makes him a totalitarian. He thinks the philosophers have Knowledge, so they must rule everything.

Plato engages in special pleading because he has no nonarbitrary way of determining what is right and wrong. But as we've seen, once one identifies Goodness as an abstract form, one cannot derive from it any specific content. So Plato's ideas about ethics and politics lack any firm basis or credibility.

The best thing that can be said of Plato is that he knew and considered seriously the criticisms that could be made against his system. He treats a number of these in the *Parmenides*, without actually answering them. In this dialogue, Parmenides asks the young Socrates whether there are Ideas (Forms) of such things as mud, hair, and filth. He might also have asked whether there are Ideas of evil, of imperfection, of negation. But how can there be a Form of imperfection, if the Forms, by definition, are of perfection? But if there is no form of imperfection, then the Forms fail to account for all the qualities of the material world.

Another objection (called the "third man") goes like this: if the similarity between men requires us to invoke the Form man to account for it, then what of the similarity between men and the Form man? Does that require another Form (a "third man")? And does the similarity between the first Form and the second Form require a third, *ad infinitum*?

The first objection shows that the Forms are inadequate to account for experience. The second objection shows that on Plato's basis, the Forms themselves require explanation and that they are inadequate to provide that explanation themselves.

Plato also explores other objections to his theory that I cannot take the time to describe here. The main problem is that the Forms cannot do their job. The Forms are supposed to be models for everything in the sensible world. In fact, they are not, for perfect Forms cannot model imperfection; changeless Forms cannot model change. So the imperfection and change of the experienced world has no rational explanation. Plato tries to explain them by the story of the Demiurge in *Timaeus*. But that, after all, is myth. Plato gives us no reason to believe in a Demiurge, and in any case the Demiurge does not account for the existence of matter or the receptacle. So the changing world of matter and space is for Plato, as for Parmenides, ultimately irrational. Parmenides had the courage to say that the changing world is therefore unreal. Plato does not go quite this far; rather, he ascribes a greater *degree* of reality to the Forms than to the sense-world. But we must question Plato's assumption that there are degrees of reality. What does it mean to say that one thing is "more real" than another?

The picture should be clear by now. Though Plato is far more sophisticated than the pre-Socratics, his position, like theirs, incorporates rationalism and irrationalism. He is rationalistic about the Forms and irrationalistic about the sense-world. For him, reason is totally competent to understand the Forms but not competent to make sense of the changing world of experience. Yet he tries to analyze the changing world by means of changeless forms—an irrational world by a rationalistic principle. Eventually, in *Parmenides*, he has the integrity to admit that his fundamental questions remain unanswered.

With Plato as with the pre-Socratics, the tension between rationalism and irrationalism has a religious root. If Plato had known the God of Scripture, he would have known in what fundamental ways our reason is competent, yet limited. And he would have understood that the world of change is knowable, but not exhaustively, because God made it that way. He also would have been able to consult God's revelation for ethical guidance, rather than teaching his students to rely on the abstract form of the Good, which has nothing specific to say to them.

> *[Plato] is rationalistic about the Forms and irrationalistic about the sense-world. For him, reason is totally competent to understand the Forms but not competent to make sense of the changing world of experience.*

Aristotle (384–322)

Aristotle, Plato's student, was certainly Plato's equal in terms of brilliance, comprehensiveness, and influence on later thought. Someone has said that no pupil has had a greater teacher and no teacher a greater student.

Aristotle demythologizes Plato. He continues to distinguish between form and matter, but for him form is not found in a separate world (hence, I am no longer capitalizing the term). Rather, form is an element of things in the world we perceive.

The main category[33] of Aristotle's philosophy is the substance. A substance is an individual thing: a rock, a tree, a table, an animal, a person. With one exception that we shall examine later, all substances contain both form and matter. In general, the matter is what something is made of: the ingredients of bread, the clay of the statue. The form is the "whatness" of a thing, the qualities that make the thing what it is: bread, tree, statue, person. The matter is the "thisness." The matter is what distinguishes one piece of bread from another, one brick from another, one person from another. Socrates and Plato share the same form, the form "man," but not the same matter. So "man" or "manness" includes both Socrates and Plato, but "this man" points to one or the other.

---

33. For Aristotle, "categories" are the general types of subjects and predicates, the things we talk about and the things we can say about those subjects. He gives different lists of categories in different places in his writings, and the lists include such things as substance, quality, place, relation, time, posture, state, action, and passion.

Form and matter are usually relative. In a brick, clay is matter and the form is its brickness, the qualities that make it a brick rather than something else. But when the brick is used to build a house, the brick itself can be considered matter and the house itself (or rather its houseness) is the form. So the brick is form in one relationship, matter in another.

Yet it seems that there must be some kind of absolute matter or "prime matter." The house is made of bricks; the bricks are made of clay; the clay is made of various other things. Each of these can be described as a form, because each is a substance, bearing various qualities. But this sequence cannot go to infinity. Let's say that we reach the smallest possible particle, perhaps one of Democritus's atoms. What is *that* made of? Presumably a kind of matter that has no qualities, but is only a bearer of qualities. But something without qualities is not a substance. It is nothing. Thus the matter that underlies all reality, the stuff of which all reality is made, is indistinguishable from nonbeing. Aristotle avoids saying that, but the consequence is hard to avoid.

Aristotle insisted that such prime matter is not actually found in nature. In the natural world, there are only substances, and matter exists only in conjunction with form. But the problem reoccurs in every substance. For in every case we must ask, what is the form the form of? What is the stuff that the forms are attached to? And the answer must be, ultimately, nothing.

That is the main problem in Aristotle's philosophy. But we must continue to follow his thinking. For Aristotle, the combination of form and matter in individual things injects an element of purposiveness or teleology into everything. Form is what each thing is, but it also is the purpose of the thing: for Aristotle, the nature and purpose of a thing are the same. So the form of bread defines it as food, a statue as art. Recall that for Plato, too, purpose and essence were closely related: everything partook of Goodness and therefore was good for something. So form is not just what things are, it also is what they should be, what they strive to be. Form is a normative category as well as a descriptive one.

> *Thus the matter that underlies all reality, the stuff of which all reality is made, is indistinguishable from nonbeing. Aristotle avoids saying that, but the consequence is hard to avoid.*

So an acorn bears the form of an oak. The acorn is not now an oak, but it has the *potentiality* to be one, and in the normal course of events it will become an *actual* oak. So potentiality and actuality are important aspects of reality for Aristotle. The form directs the matter to realize its potential. As potentiality becomes actuality, the object becomes fully formed: it becomes what it inherently is. So Aristotle says that in potentiality matter is prominent, but in actuality form is prominent.

For Aristotle, the distinction between potentiality and actuality is a general explanation (or perhaps description) of change. Change, which bewildered previous philosophers, is for Aristotle simply the movement from potentiality to actuality. When my car moves from Atlanta to Orlando, it changes from being potentially in Orlando to being actually there.

Aristotle also uses the form/matter distinction to describe human nature. For him, the soul is the form of the body. This is a radical departure from Plato, for whom the soul was quite independent of the body, though at present confined to the body. This idea would suggest that for Aristotle soul and body are inseparable and that the soul vanishes when the body dies. Certainly, Aristotle doesn't affirm personal immortality as Plato does. But some interpreters think that his epistemology, like that of Plato's *Phaedo*, contains an argument that leads from epistemology to personal immortality.

So we should look at Aristotle's epistemology. For Aristotle, there are two givens that we must start with in order to know anything. The first is the "first principles," principles of logic, as well as general propositions such as "the whole is greater than any part." These first principles cannot be proven; they are known intuitively. The second given is the substance, presented by sense experience. For Aristotle, both these starting points are important. He criticizes the "definition mongers," who try to derive everything from first principles without paying attention to the facts of experience. And he criticizes those who look at facts only as "no better than plants."

Aristotle

Now for Aristotle the intellect has two aspects, passive and active. The passive intellect receives data from the senses. The active intellect examines, analyzes, tries to understand that data by abstracting the forms from the material things given in the data. In Plato's terms, the active intellect tries to bring conjecture to the levels of belief and understanding. For Aristotle as for Plato, true knowledge is knowledge of form, not matter. True knowledge is an understanding of what things are.

There has been much interpretive controversy over the nature of the active intellect in Aristotle's thought. The most common understanding is that each human being has his own active intellect. But in *De Anima*, Aristotle speaks of the active intellect (as he would not speak of the individual soul) as something separable from the body. So some have thought that for Aristotle there was only one active intellect, common to mankind: either a cosmic principle of intelligence, as in Heraclitus, Anaxagoras, and Plotinus, or a kind of god.[34] Perhaps Aristotle did not try to reconcile the apparent contradiction between *De Anima* and his general view of the soul.[35] But an Aristotelian who wants to make a case for personal immortality would have to begin here.

> *The passive intellect receives data from the senses. The active intellect examines, analyzes, tries to understand that data by abstracting the forms from the material things given in the data.*

Aristotle believed that the process of movement from potentiality to actuality must begin somewhere. Each motion is caused by another. But

34.   For a helpful discussion of these interpretations, see Ronald Nash, *Life's Ultimate Questions* (Grand Rapids: Zondervan, 1999), 111–12.

35.   For epistemological reasons also, it is regrettable that Aristotle did not clarify the relation between the active intellect and the soul. If the active intellect is a cosmic principle of intelligence, how does it enter into relation with the individual person? How does the cosmic intellect illumine my mind? And if each individual has his own active intellect, how can that intellect be separable from the body while the soul is not separable?

the chain of causes cannot go back to infinity. So at some point there must be an unmoved mover who starts the process going. Like the other Greek philosophers, Aristotle did not believe the world had a beginning. So his unmoved mover is not like the biblical God, who creates the world at the first moment of time. Rather, for Aristotle, every state of affairs at each moment is explained ultimately by a Prime Mover.[36]

The Prime Mover[37] is pure form, the one exception to the rule that every substance contains both form and matter. If there were a material component in his nature, then he would have some unrealized potentiality, and that would move him toward actuality. Then he would not be unmoved. Similarly, he must not, in Aristotle's view, be influenced in any way by the world; else he will be the moved, not the mover. So this being must not know the world (since to know is to be influenced in some way by the object of knowledge), or love the world, or act in the world.

How, then, does he cause motion? Aristotle's answer is that he is supremely attractive and thus influences things in the world to turn toward him. Interpreters of Aristotle have compared the Prime Mover to a goal to which runners run or to a magnet attracting iron to itself. This writer thinks of a rock concert, in which frenzied fans throw themselves at the performer's feet, while the performer himself remains (apparently) in a daze.

Aristotle distinguished four kinds of causation: formal, final, efficient, and material. These are "causes" in a broad sense, four ways of answering the question "why is something as it is?" They involve four meanings of the word "because." Let us see how the four causes answer the question "Why is Bill thinking?" The formal cause tells what something is: Bill thinks because he is a man. The final cause tells the purpose, the reason something happened: Bill thinks because he wants to complete his philosophy paper. The efficient cause tells what made something happen: Bill thinks because his brain generates thoughts. The material cause tells what something is made of: Bill thinks because his brain is composed of materials that generate thinking. Now on Aristotle's account, the Prime Mover causes motion as the final cause, rather than the efficient. But that leaves open the question as to what is the efficient cause of motion in the world.

What does the Prime Mover do, if he does not efficiently cause things to happen, and if he does not know or love the world? Aristotle's answer is that he thinks. One wonders why Aristotle suddenly starts using personal

> *Interpreters of Aristotle have compared the Prime Mover to a goal to which runners run or to a magnet attracting iron to itself. This writer thinks of a rock concert, in which frenzied fans throw themselves at the performer's feet, while the performer himself remains (apparently) in a daze.*

36.   It helps to consider that causal sequences are either sequential (as one domino toppling the next, and so on) or simultaneous (as the gears of a watch moving one another along). Aristotle's view of a chain of causes is more like the watch than like the dominos. So it is not necessarily a *temporal* sequence and does not require a first mover at the beginning of time. Rather, each event requires a Prime Mover at the very time it is taking place.

37.   Although Aristotle speaks of one Prime Mover as explaining all motion in the universe, he also maintains that every circular motion in the heavens requires an unmoved mover to get it started. Since he believes that the universe consists of a number of concentric spheres revolving around the earth, he postulates that there is an unmoved mover for each. So Aristotle is a philosophical polytheist.

language here, when his argument so far proves at most an impersonal principle. But what does this "god" think about, if not the world? Aristotle replies, he thinks of himself. But what facts about himself does he contemplate? Aristotle replies, his thoughts. The Prime Mover is "thought thinking thought." If the Prime Mover were to think of something about himself other than his thoughts, then his thoughts would be moved by that something else. For his thoughts to be entirely unmoved, they can be caused only by themselves.

What shall we make of this? First, the Prime Mover is a quasi-philosopher. As Plato believed that philosophers should be kings, Aristotle believes that God is a philosopher. Furthermore, Aristotle's deity reduces to tautology. He cannot know the world, lest he be relative to it. His thought cannot be of anything other than itself, lest it be relative to something else. It can not be about any quality he has except his thinking, lest his thinking be moved by something else. So in the end his thought is a thought of a thought of a thought, or, to put it differently, a thought of nothing in particular.

> *First, the Prime Mover is a quasi-philosopher. As Plato believed that philosophers should be kings, Aristotle believes that God is a philosopher.*

Plato thought he had found the ultimate philosophical principle in the Form of the Good; but the Form of the Good turns out to be abstract and empty. Though bearing rational authority, it tells us nothing specific. So with Aristotle's Prime Mover: it is so abstract that its mind is virtually nothing.

We can see that Aristotle's Prime Mover is vastly different from the biblical God. The biblical God is not only the final cause of the world, but the efficient cause as well. He is not only the logical beginning of the universe, but its temporal beginning as well. And he knows and loves the world, without endangering his own absolute nature. This is possible because the world itself is what it is because he created it according to his eternal thought. His mind contains real content, which he freely reveals to human beings.

We should also consider Aristotle's ethics. For Aristotle, each being should act in accordance with its form, that is, its nature and purpose. He defines human beings as rational animals, so for him, as with all the Greek philosophers, the good life is the life of reason.

Reason tells us that the goal of human life is happiness. Happiness is not pleasure, at least not in the narrow sense of Epicureanism. Happiness is general well-being. Pleasure is at most a means to the end of happiness. In general, Aristotle sees the good life as contemplative, philosophical (again, Aristotle exalts his particular vocation to a universal principle).

Aristotle, like Plato, distinguishes three aspects of the soul, the vegetative, the sensitive (perhaps roughly equivalent to Plato's "spirited"), and the rational. We share the first with plants, the second with animals; the third is unique to human beings. He also distinguishes moral from intellectual virtues. Moral virtues pertain to the will, intellectual to reason.

We learn the moral virtues, courage, temperance, and justice, from imitating others who exemplify these qualities. Such imitation leads us in time to form good habits, and those habits form a good character. The intellectual virtue is prudence, and that comes from teaching. Aristotle distinguishes philosophic wisdom (disinterested, contemplative) from practical wisdom (wisdom to make decisions leading to happiness). One who has wisdom, he thinks, will seek moderation in all things. It is often possible to determine our specific duties by calculating the mean between two extremes. For example, a buffoon makes a joke out of everything; a boor takes everything too seriously. But wit is the "golden mean" between these extremes. Aristotle didn't offer any precise formula for defining the extremes or locating the mean. Doubtless, he knew that with a bit of cleverness any act could be justified as being between two extremes (e.g., robbing one bank as the mean between robbing many and robbing none). And he did see that sometimes a right decision might be on one extreme, such as the very decision to do right rather than wrong. But he assumed that the wise man would be able to furnish a proper context for these judgments.

The State is the whole of which individuals and families are parts. Thus its interests take precedence over theirs. Yet the ruler ought to seek the happiness of his subjects. Aristotle was nothing if not balanced! Yet his impulse, like Plato's, is toward statism and totalitarianism, an impulse that may have influenced his most famous pupil, Alexander the Great.

There is a question as to how we can begin to acquire moral virtues. Aristotle teaches that we need to have virtuous dispositions to perform virtuous acts; but we need to perform moral acts in order to form the habits that produce virtuous dispositions. Aristotle is aware of this circularity and counsels readers to begin the process by doing things that "resemble" virtuous acts. But how one gets from resemblance to actuality is a mystery.

The Christian revelation has an answer: God's grace creates moral dispositions in sinners and enables them to follow those dispositions. And it also answers another major problem in Aristotle's ethics. For Aristotle assumes that we can learn our moral obligations simply by observing our own natures and what makes us happy. This is the root of the "natural law" tradition in ethics. But as David Hume pointed out, one cannot derive moral obligations from natural facts. One can't infer what we *ought* to do from statements of what is the case; we cannot derive "ought" from "is." The fact that we are rational does not prove that we ought to live according to reason; the fact that we seek happiness does not imply that we ought to seek it. Scripture points to God's revelation as the source of our knowledge of ethical obligation. For God is both fact and value. To know him is to know at the same time the ultimate source of reality and the ultimate source of ethical obligation.

To summarize, the fundamental contrast in Aristotle's philosophy, as in Plato's, is that between form and matter. But form at the highest level (as

> *We learn the moral virtues, courage, temperance, and justice, from imitating others who exemplify these qualities. Such imitation leads us in time to form good habits, and those habits form a good character. The intellectual virtue is prudence, and that comes from teaching.*

illustrated in the Prime Mover) is entirely contentless and abstract: a kind of "being in general." And matter in its purest form is nonbeing. We see again the contrast between the Olympian order and the "shapeless stream" of the old religion. But in Aristotle the order is empty. He cannot really account for motion on its basis or for ethical obligation. And the shapeless stream, in Aristotle, is more shapeless than ever. The lack of an absolute-personal God leaves Aristotle's system in incoherence.

Stoicism

The Epicurean and Stoic schools arose during the Hellenistic period, the time when Greek culture spread throughout Western and Near Eastern civilization. Alexander the Great (356–323), whose tutor was Aristotle, conquered most of the known world—doubtless his means of seeking happiness.[38] His empire broke up quickly after his early death, was divided among his lieutenants, and eventually passed to the Romans. Although Greek culture attained a kind of supremacy during this time, its most creative period was past. Yet philosophical schools continued the discussions begun by their predecessors.

I discussed Epicurus with the atomists at an earlier point, so I shall here focus on the Stoics, a school founded by Zeno of Cyprus (334–262). The Stoics were materialists, teaching that only physical objects were real. But they acknowledged many differences within the broad category "matter." The soul was made of very fine matter, rocks and dirt out of coarser matter. Even virtues are material, but they can exist in the same place as other matter, so virtues can be in the soul. Gordon Clark suggests that the Stoics' "matter" is more like a field of force than like a hard stuff.[39] Or, perhaps, for the Stoics to say that something is material is simply to say that it really is, that it has being. Perhaps for them (whether or not they were aware of it), the proposition "reality is material" was tautological.

For the Stoics, knowledge begins in self-authenticating sensations. General skepticism about sense experience defeats itself, for it can be based only on the experiences it presumes to doubt.

The world is a single reality, governed by its own world soul. This pantheistic "god" rules all by natural law. As Plato's Republic was ruled by a philosopher king, so the world of the Stoics is ruled by a divine philosopher king.

Everything happens by law, so the Stoics took a fatalistic attitude toward life. Aristotle, like present-day open theists, had said that propositions about the future were neither true nor false, because the future was not an object of knowledge. The Stoics held, on the contrary, that if I say

> *For the Stoics, knowledge begins in self-authenticating sensations. General skepticism about sense experience defeats itself, for it can be based only on the experiences it presumes to doubt.*

Zeno

---

38. One wonders, however, how such conquest could be justified under the doctrine of the golden mean.

39. Clark, *Thales*, 158–60.

"the sun will rise tomorrow" and it does, that proposition was already true when I uttered it. Therefore, the rising of the sun *had* to happen.

So the Stoics sought to act in accord with nature. They sought to be resigned to their fate. Their ethic was one of learning to want what one gets, rather than of getting what one wants. But they did not advocate passivity. Contrary to Epicurus, they sought involvement in public life (the emperor Marcus Aurelius was a Stoic). They taught, as did all Greek thinkers, that one should live according to reason, which also is according to nature and according to the universal structure of society. They considered human society to be a universal brotherhood.

Stoicism is one major source, after Aristotle, of natural law thinking in ethics. Again, I ask David Hume's question: how does one reason from the facts of nature to conclusions about ethical obligation? The lack of a true theistic position made the answer to this question, for the Stoics as for Aristotle, impossible.

Even though the Stoics tried to overcome the form/matter dichotomy by making the whole world material, there remains a secondary dichotomy between the world soul and the beings within it. The Stoics failed to answer how the world soul accounts for individual facts, or how it gives moral direction to finite creatures.

Plotinus (AD 205–70)

The school of thought begun at Plato's Academy continued for many centuries, but it endured some radical philosophical shifts. In the third century BC, a number of its members were skeptics: Pyrrho (d. 275), Timon (d. 230), and Arcesilaus (315–241). This was odd, because Plato himself had expended considerable energy disputing skepticism. But his dialogues rarely ended with cogent definitions of philosophical terms, and the *Parmenides*, as we have seen, leaves the theory of Forms itself hanging in uncertainty. So perhaps the skeptical turn of the Academy was not entirely a surprise.

The period of "Middle Platonism" (100 BC–AD 270), was a time of world-weariness. Politics and economics gave people little reason to treasure the affairs of this life but desire to escape from it. The mystery religions and Gnosticism[40] offered people various means of transcending the

> *Stoicism is one major source, after Aristotle, of natural law thinking in ethics. Again, I ask David Hume's question: how does one reason from the facts of nature to conclusions about ethical obligation? The lack of a true theistic position made the answer to this question, for the Stoics as for Aristotle, impossible.*

40.   Gnosticism is similar to Plotinus's Neoplatonism in many ways. In Gnosticism, too, there is a scale of being. At the top there is a nameless being, connected to the material world by semi-divine intermediaries. The "fall" occurs when the least of these beings mistakenly creates a material world. We are trapped in that world and must be reabsorbed into the nameless Supreme Being by various intellectual and moral disciplines taught by the Gnostic teachers. However, Plotinus opposed the Gnostics. I'm inclined to regard that as a family quarrel. We can see that Gnosticism and Neoplatonism represent a common way of thinking, a common worldview (with variations of course) that was in the air during the early centuries of the Christian era. The idea that God and man are on a continuum and we can become God by various means is still in the air today. See Peter R. Jones's comparison between Gnosticism and the "new spiritualities" in *The Gnostic Empire Strikes Back* (Phillipsburg, NJ: P&R Publishing, 1992) and *Spirit Wars* (Escondido: Main Entry, 1997).

space-time world and being absorbed into divinity. The Platonic school also turned in a religious direction, emphasizing Plato's teaching that the soul belonged to a world other than this one and needed to return to that world through the exercise of mind. Into this tradition came Plotinus, the founder of the movement known as "Neoplatonism."

Plotinus opposes the materialism of the Epicureans and Stoics by using various arguments: Materialism cannot explain thought. Materialism cannot identify the subject of knowledge, the one who knows, the one who uses the senses to gain knowledge. As Plato said, the most real beings are immaterial, including the human soul.

Plotinus describes a chain of being with a supreme being ("the One") at the top of the scale, and descending levels in order: mind (*nous*), soul (*psyche*), and the material world. He conceives of this ladder as a downward path and an upward path.

To examine the downward path, we shall start at the top of the scale, with the highest being, the One. The One cannot be described in human words. Even the term "one" is not literally applicable. But Plotinus thinks that the idea of oneness, unity, captures much of what he wants to say about this being. The One has no qualities, no properties (else there would be a division between subject and predicate). The only way to know the One is through being mystically united to him in a trance that itself cannot be described.

Yet, Plotinus does say a great deal about the One: that it exists, that it does not have the qualities of beings in the material world, that it is immaterial, that it is possible for souls to enter a mystical relation with it. He particularly emphasizes that the One communicates its excellence to lower beings. This communication is an emanation, like light coming from a fire. The One does not freely choose to emanate; rather, it cannot help but do so.[41] To emanate is its nature. The emanations produce the lower beings. In the end, all reality is an emanation of the One. So in one sense all reality is divine in character. Plotinus is fundamentally a monist.

The first product of the emanation, and the second level of reality, is *nous*, or Mind. Plotinus represents it as the result of the One's thought. It corresponds to Plato's world of Forms and, perhaps, to Aristotle's active intellect. Here, some multiplicity enters in: the distinction between subject and object, the many things of which there are Ideas.

The third level is that of Soul (*psyche*). Mind generates objects of its thought and thus produces Soul or life. Plotinus's Soul is like Plato's Demiurge, Heraclitus's *logos*. It governs the world from within the world. Plotinus describes three aspects of Soul: (1) The world Soul (compare the Stoic world Soul), which explains motion and change; (2) the middle Soul,

Plotinus

> *Materialism cannot explain thought. Materialism cannot identify the subject of knowledge, the one who knows, the one who uses the senses to gain knowledge. As Plato said, the most real beings are immaterial, including the human soul.*

---

41. This is in contrast with the God of the Bible. In Scripture, (1) God is not constrained to create. He creates the world freely and voluntarily. (2) The product of creation, the world, is not divine in character, not in any sense a part of God.

31

which gives life to particular souls; and (3) the lower Soul, which gives rise to bodies. Human souls are immortal.

The fourth level is the material world. We are souls, contained in material bodies. This condition is the result of a "fall," which results because our souls have accepted the guidance of sensation and become entangled with the material.[42] Union with the body in itself is not evil, unless we linger too long in this condition. But we should seek to rise from it as soon as possible by knowledge and virtue. At the bottom level of the material world is prime matter (compare Aristotle's teaching on this). Prime matter is really nothing, or empty space (compare Plato's "receptacle"). As rays of light disappear into the darkness, prime matter represents the farthest extent of the emanation of the One.

We can ascend on the ladder of being as we first descended, being absorbed into Soul, then Mind, then the One. The method of ascent is gaining knowledge, which also is growth in virtue.

Plotinus probably noticed that Plato's Forms did not account for all reality. So he advocated a broader principle, higher than the Forms, that would account for all of reality, including mud, hair, filth, evil, negativity, and imperfection. So the One can be understood as the result of a rationalistic impulse. Plotinus commends Parmenides' statement that "to be and to be thought are the same."

Significantly, however, it turns out that the One cannot be described at all. It has no qualities. It is not tall or short, because it is the principle of tallness and shortness. It is not good or evil, because it is the principle of good and evil, and therefore beyond good and evil. It is not even literally one, for it is the principle underlying both unity and plurality. So the One explains everything and nothing. The explanation of everything turns out to be the greatest unexplained mystery of all.

Ultimate knowledge, therefore, comes not from reasoning but from mysticism, from ineffable union with the One. Thus Plotinus's extreme rationalism devolves into irrationalism. As Plato's Good was empty and Aristotle's Prime Mover a self-referential tautology (thought of thought of thought), so Plotinus's One communicates to us no knowledge at all.

> So the One explains everything and nothing. The explanation of everything turns out to be the greatest unexplained mystery of all.

Conclusion

Recall the general themes I listed under the introduction to "A Survey of Greek Philosophy." We have seen now many specific examples of the "form-matter motive" (Dooyeweerd's phrase[43]) that unites the various

---

42. It is not clear in Plotinus whether or not this fall is the result of a free choice. Given that the whole movement from the One to the material world is a necessary emanation, it would seem that the fall, too, was necessary. But when speaking of the fall and redemption of the human soul, Plotinus refers to choices we make.

43. Dooyeweerd, *Twilight*.

strains of Greek thought. Though very different in many ways, these philosophies all seek to understand reality without the guidance of an absolute person. Therefore they affirm the autonomy of their own reason. Yet they note as they must that their reason is fallible, not omnicompetent. There are areas of reality that defy rational analysis (change to Parmenides, the world of sense to Plato, prime matter for Aristotle, etc.). The Greek response to these mysteries is to say that part of the world is essentially unknowable, essentially irrational. We can't know it, because it can't be known.[44] It is the chaos of the "shapeless stream." It is illusion (Parmenides), nonbeing, or nothingness. But the shapeless stream is found everywhere, as Aristotle's matter underlies all substances. So if matter is irrational, the whole universe is irrational. Thus the irrationalism of the Greeks undermines their rationalism; and when they (as Parmenides) force their way to a consistent rationalism, they end up denying the entire world of experience.

Their project was to impose autonomous reason upon an irrational world.[45] That project was bold, even revolutionary, as we have seen; but it could not hope to succeed.

The only ultimate alternative is the absolute-personality theism of Scripture. God has created a knowable world and has given human beings the power to know it. But they can never hope to know it exhaustively as he does. So there are mysteries—not because there is an irrational element in the world, not because there is an element of nonbeing that somehow exists in order to frustrate philosophers—but because God has hidden from us some of his rational understanding of his creation.

Combining the Christian perspective with the Greek is not advisable. We can learn today from the questions the Greeks asked, from their failures, from the insights they express in matters of detail. But we should rigorously avoid the notion of rational autonomy and the form-matter scheme as a comprehensive worldview.[46] Unfortunately, during the medieval period and beyond, Christian theologians relied extensively on Neoplatonism and (beginning with Aquinas) Aristotelianism. Aquinas, for example, distinguished between natural reason (which operates apart from revelation) and faith (which supplements our reason with revelation). Then he referred over and over again to Aristotle as "the Philosopher" who guides us in matters of natural reason. The problems generated by this combination of Christian and pagan thought will occupy our studies of the medieval period.

> *[The project of Greek philosophy] was to impose autonomous reason upon an irrational world. That project was bold, even revolutionary, as we have seen; but it could not hope to succeed.*

44. We recall the slogan, "What my net can't catch isn't fish." See Cornelius Van Til's pamphlet "Why I Believe in God" (Philadelphia: Orthodox Presbyterian Church, n.d.).

45. As Van Til often says, imposing abstract forms on abstract particulars, stringing beads without holes.

46. It is sometimes useful to distinguish form and matter on a micro-level. It is not wrong to distinguish what things are made of (matter) from what they are (form). It is wrong to try to bring all reality under this schema. For to do that would either leave God out of our worldview or would make him a form (as Aristotle), matter, or both.

For Further Reading

Allen, Diogenes. *Philosophy for Understanding Theology*. Atlanta: John Knox Press, 1985. An introductory text that goes into considerable depth. Insightful.

Bahnsen, Greg. "Socrates or Christ: The Reformation of Christian Apologetics," in Gary North, ed., *Foundations of Christian Scholarship*. Vallecito, CA: Ross House, 1976), 190–239. Interesting thoughts about Greek epistemology evaluated from a Christian perspective.

Bakewell, Charles M. *Source Book in Ancient Philosophy*. New York: Charles Scribner's Sons, 1939.

Burnet, John. *Early Greek Philosophy*. London: A. and C. Black, 1952.

———. *Greek Philosophy, Part 1. Thales to Plato*. London: Macmillan, 1914.

Clark, Gordon H. *Thales to Dewey*. Boston: Houghton Mifflin, 1957. A history of philosophy to around 1920. Clark enters into the arguments of the philosophers in considerable depth. He is himself a Christian philosopher, and the book contains a subtle Christian apologetic.

Copleston, Frederick C. *A History of Philosophy*, vol. 1. Garden City, NY: Doubleday, 1962. Copleston was a Roman Catholic priest. Very rich analysis.

Dooyeweerd, Herman. *In the Twilight of Western Thought*. Nutley, NJ: Craig Press, 1968. An introduction to this great Dutch thinker, whose thought can be studied in more depth in his four-volume *A New Critique of Theoretical Thought*. Philadelphia: Presbyterian and Reformed, 1955. I am critical of Dooyeweerd's view of Scripture and of the relationship of philosophy to theology, so I don't recommend chapters 5–7 of this volume. But the earlier chapters provide great insight into Greek philosophy and non-Christian thought generally.

Edwards, Paul, ed. *The Encyclopedia of Philosophy,* eight volumes in four. New York: Macmillan, 1967. Contains valuable articles on many philosophers and philosophical topics.

Frame, John M. *Apologetics to the Glory of God*. Phillipsburg, NJ: P&R Publishing, 1994. Develops my argument that ethics and knowledge presuppose absolute-personality theism.

Hoitenga, Dewey J. *Faith and Reason From Plato to Plantinga*. Albany, NY: State University of New York Press, 1991. A Christian philosopher who presents some insights into Plato's epistemology and makes comparisons with Scripture, Augustine, Calvin, and Alvin Plantinga.

Jones, Peter R. *The Gnostic Empire Strikes Back*. Phillipsburg, NJ: P&R Publishing, 1992.

———. *Spirit Wars*. Escondido: Main Entry, 1997. These books make the important comparison between the worldview of Gnosticism/Neoplatonism and that of contemporary New Age thought.

Jordan, James B. "Van Til and the Greeks," photocopied, available from Biblical Horizons, PO Box 1096, Niceville, FL 32588.

Jowett, B., tr. *The Dialogues of Plato*. Chicago: Encyclopedia Britannica, 1952.

Kirk, G. S., and Raven, J. E. *The Presocratic Philosophers: A Critical History with a Selection of Texts.* Cambridge: Cambridge University Press, 1963.

Nash, Ronald H. *The Gospel and the Greeks: Did the New Testament Borrow from Pagan Thought?* Richardson, TX: Probe Ministries, 1992.

———. *Life's Ultimate Questions: an Introduction to Philosophy.* Grand Rapids: Zondervan, 1999. A Christian analysis of some historical figures (Greek philosophy, Augustine, and Aquinas) with discussion of some philosophical topics, such as logic, epistemology, and God.

Oates, Whitney, ed. *The Stoic and Epicurean Philosophers.* New York: Random House, 1940. All their extant writings.

Palmer, Donald. *Looking at Philosophy.* Mountain View, CA: Mayfield Publishing Co., 1988. Not a distinctively Christian treatment but a competent analysis told with conciseness and wit. Illustrated with cartoons. This is the most readable of the histories of philosophy.

Ross, W. D., ed. *The Works of Aristotle.* Chicago: Encyclopedia Britannica, 1952.

Van Til, Cornelius. *Christian Theistic Ethics.* No place of publication listed: Den Dulk Foundation, 1971. Includes Van Til's positive presentation of Christian ethics and his negative criticisms of Greek and other ethicists. This and other Van Til works can be found on the CD-ROM *The Works of Cornelius Van Til* (published by Labels Army Co., available through the Logos Library System).

———. *A Christian Theory of Knowledge.* No place of publication listed: Presbyterian and Reformed, 1969. Deals with a number of historical figures and also presents Van Til's Christian epistemology.

———. *A Survey of Christian Epistemology.* No place of publication listed: Den Dulk Foundation, 1969. This is Van Til's analysis of the history of epistemology. At times difficult to follow, but in my judgment no one has done more to develop a consistently biblical analysis and critique.

For Further Discussion

1. Why does Frame advise against combining the Greek world view with the Christian? Evaluate his position.

2. What propositions, if any, did the Greek philosophers hold in common? In what ways did they differ from one another?

3. Distinguish the "shapeless stream," "fate," and "order," in the older and younger Greek religions. Do these same concepts appear in the Greek philosophical tradition? Where and how?

4. Following Cornelius Van Til, Frame alleges that each Greek philosopher combined rationalism and irrationalism. Define these isms, show how they apply to each philosopher, and explain why these

categories are so regularly present. Or, rebut the whole idea.

5. Describe some of the Greek philosophers' views of ethics. Do any of them succeed in showing us what we ought to do? Why or why not?

6. Distinguish form and matter as these categories are used by Plato and Aristotle. What is the purpose of this distinction? Does the distinction accomplish its purpose? Explain.

7. Does Aristotle prove the existence of the God of the Bible? Why or why not?

8. Give an example of determinism and an example of indeterminism among the Greek philosophers. How is each position argued? Is either position cogent? Present your own view, and an argument for it.

9. Frame says, "The only ultimate alternative (to the Greek philosophies) is the absolute-personality theism of Scripture." Explain and evaluate.

10. Should Christians try to synthesize Greek thought with the biblical message? If so, describe how the two would fit together. If not, why not?

2

The Hebrew World-and-Life View

John D. Currid

You ask, what was the philosophy of the Hebrews? The answer will be a very short one—they had none. . . . In short, we find in them only an ignorant and barbarous people, who have long united the most sordid avarice with the most detestable superstition and the most invincible hatred for every people by whom they are tolerated and enriched. Still, we ought not to burn them.

Voltaire, Dictionnaire philosophique *(1764)*

Today the modern skepticism of Voltaire finds its greatest advocacy in a cadre of scholars often called biblical minimalists.[1] To them, the history of Israel before the Exile is principally fabrication; it is really nothing more than a Judaic *Iliad*, King Arthur legend, or even *Winnie-the-Pooh*. One of the primary advocates, T. L. Thompson, puts it this way: "We have seen that the biblical chronologies are not grounded on historical memory, but are rather based on a very late theological schema that presupposes a very unhistorical world-view. Those efforts to use the biblical narratives for a reconstruction of the history of the Near East, in a manner comparable to the use of the archives of Mari and similar finds, can justly be dismissed as fundamentalist."[2] Although sometimes painted as extremism, this position has most recently gained a host of scholarly followers.

A great danger of minimalist thinking is that it not only attempts to undercut the veracity of the biblical accounts but also calls into question

> *A great danger of minimalist thinking is that it not only attempts to undercut the veracity of the biblical accounts but also calls into question any succeeding history or thought based on the reliability of the Bible.*

---

1. Three important works of this position are P. Davies, *In Search of "Ancient Israel"* (Sheffield: JSOT Press, 1992); K. Whitelam, *The Invention of Ancient Israel: The Silencing of Palestinian History* (New York: Routledge, 1996); and T. L. Thompson, *The Mythic Past: Biblical Archaeology and the Myth of Israel* (New York: Basic, 1999).

2. T. L. Thompson, *The Historicity of the Patriarchal Narratives: The Quest for the Historical Abraham* (Berlin: de Gruyter, 1974), 315.

any succeeding history or thought based on the reliability of the Bible. It is true that for at least two thousand years the Hebrew world-and-life view has had a tremendous impact on world thinking and, especially, on the beliefs of the Western mind. But what if, as Dever asks, "ancient Israel was 'invented' by Jews living much later, and the biblical literature is therefore nothing but pious propaganda? . . . there was no ancient Israel. There was no actual historical experience of any real people in a real time and place from whom we could hope to learn anything historically true, much less anything morally or ethically enduring. The story of Israel in the Hebrew Bible would have to be considered a monstrous literary hoax, one that has cruelly deceived countless millions of people."[3]

The biblical minimalism, however, rests on faulty assumptions that manifest more the speculative worldview of modernity and postmodernity than any clear evidence from the biblical texts themselves. Secure and sound historical connections between the Bible and other ancient Near Eastern documents make it nearly impossible to defend their approach. That the biblical authors set incidents such as the invasions by Sennacherib (2 Kings 18:13; 19:16, 20; 2 Chron. 32:1–22) and Nebuchadnezzar (2 Kings 24:1–10; 1 Chron. 6:15) in their proper chronological framework and setting is confirmed by contemporary ancient Near Eastern texts—the Prism of Sennacherib for the former campaign and the Lachish Letters for the latter. Moreover, excavations at Lachish and Jerusalem furnish positive evidence of the historical accuracy of the biblical account of those events. If the books of Kings and Chronicles were free literary creations by late and disparate authors, how could they have placed so many events in their "right time and pew"?[4]

Denouncement and denigration of the Hebrew people, their history, and their view of life did not originate with twenty-first century biblical minimalists. Throughout history, at least as early as Marcion in the second century AD, the Jews have been considered a primitive or even a barbaric people whose worldview has not contributed to the realm of ideas and progress. Adolf von Harnack remarks about Marcion's view of the Hebrews in the following manner: "The God of the Old Testament is pictured, approximately as Marcion had done, as a limited, petty, and contradictory national deity who also does immoral things; the Mosaic legislation is a wholly unsatisfactory, particularly limited and offensive work, a distortion of the *lex naturae*, very little different from the pagan religions. The nation of Israel, of bad character from the outset, runs aground of this law."[5]

> *Biblical minimalism
> . . . rests on faulty
> assumptions that
> manifest more the
> speculative world-
> view of modernity
> and postmodernity
> than any clear evi-
> dence from the bibli-
> cal texts themselves.*

---

3. W. Dever, *Who Were the Israelites and Where Did They Come From?* (Grand Rapids: Eerdmans, 2003), ix.

4. This section is taken from J. Currid, *Ancient Egypt and the Old Testament* (Grand Rapids: Baker, 1997), 173.

5. A. von Harnack, *Marcion: The Gospel of the Alien God* (Durham, NC: The Labyrinth Press, 1990; 1924 original), 136.

Much of the so-called higher criticism of the last two hundred years has been presuppositionally based on the idea that the Hebrews borrowed many, if not most, of their ideas from surrounding cultures. They were not very original. Friedrich Delitzsch's strident book *Babel und Bibel* (1903) is the apex of this perspective.[6] Delitzsch, for example, "drew sharp attention to the Babylonian ingredient in Genesis, and went on to conclude that the Bible was guilty of crass plagiarism."[7] His distaste for any originality in Hebrew thought manifests itself when he emphatically states, "How utterly alike everything is in Babylon and the Bible!"[8] The influence that Delitzsch and others of his ilk have had on modern biblical scholarship should not be underestimated.

Adolf von Harnack

We contend, on the other hand, that such views severely underestimate the originality of thought of the Hebrews and their influence on centuries of succeeding generations. And, clearly, Hebrew thought is not a mere mouthpiece of other ancient Near Eastern cultures. Even the notorious higher critic H. Gunkel recognized that fact: "How incomparably superior the Hebrew legend is to the Babylonian! . . . and this also we may say, that the Babylonian legend strongly impresses us by its barbaric character, whereas the Hebrew legend is far nearer and more human to us." Although we sharply disagree with Gunkel's characterization of Hebrew writing as legend, we affirm his statement of the unique Hebrew conception of the universe and its workings. The impact of the Hebrew world-and-life view, in addition, has exercised a powerful influence on world thinking and, in particular, the beliefs of the Western world. It largely shaped cultural structure and moral direction in Western life. We contend that the primary features of the Old Testament worldview treated in this chapter—its view of God, who creates, speaks and acts in history; its view of human nature, both its dignity in the *imago Dei* as well as its moral failure in the space/time fall; its covenantal conception of law and redemption, and their corresponding implications for individual and public morality—provided intellectual and moral underpinnings for Western culture before they were challenged by the worldviews of modernity and postmodernity. What influence has there been from the philosophy of Babylon?

Revelation

The belief that God has revealed himself and given his word to his people forms the foundation of the Hebrew perspective and alerts us to the utter centrality of theological concerns to their worldview. Whatever else may be said of the Hebrews, theological matters inform their fundamental beliefs

The belief that God has revealed himself and given his word to his people forms the foundation of the Hebrew perspective and alerts us to the utter centrality of theological concerns to their worldview.

6. F. Delitzsch, *Babel and Bible* (Chicago: Open Court, 1903).
7. E. A. Speiser, *Genesis* (Garden City, NY: Doubleday, 1964), lv–lvi.
8. F. Delitzsch, *Babel and Bible* (New York: Putnam, 1903), 175.

more than any other concern. Theology was never peripheral to any discussion; sooner or later it manifested itself regardless of what topic was probed.

In contrast with those other ancient religions and philosophies, the Old Testament writings propose the revolutionary idea that a transcendent-personal God reveals truth not through myth and magical practices but through the creation itself, actual historical events which are interpreted by means of language and words disclosed by God to prophets and other messengers. Hebrew life and culture gains its central core of beliefs, as well as the vast diversity of its practices, from God's self-revelation. Revelation may be defined as "the view that God communicates to mankind the literal truth about his nature and purposes."[9] The Hebrews believed that God's revelation appears in both nonverbal and verbal form. Psalm 19 provides a striking example of how the wonders of creation manifest both the glory and wisdom of God. The heavens and the pattern of day and night reveal God's wisdom and power in concrete form. Although neither speech nor words occur, metaphorically their "voice" permeates the earth, "even to the end of the world."

Events in Israel's history and the history of its neighbors, the rise and fall of kingdoms, also reveal God's purposes (Ps. 78; Amos 1, 2). The very fact God speaks and human beings develop language as a cultural tool illustrates the belief that people can legitimately formulate fundamental metaphysical questions (Job 11:7; Ps. 13:1–2) that in turn yield authoritative, though not exhaustive, answers (Deut. 29:29; Job 38–40). The cultural mandate in Genesis 1:26–28 presupposes that God and the cosmos are knowable and that human life consists of living morally responsible lives. The moral component of revelation is evident in God's commandments (Ex. 20). But the list of diverse acts condemned in Amos 1–2 implies that knowledge of good and evil does not rest exclusively on contents of biblical law but is accessible even to people who do not have access to covenantal law. Truth about God, mankind, and the entire order of creation is accessible and can be expressed in words that people can understand.

וְהָאָ֗רֶץ הָיְתָ֥ה
תֹ֙הוּ֙ וָבֹ֔הוּ וְחֹ֖שֶׁךְ
עַל־פְּנֵ֣י תְה֑וֹם
וְר֣וּחַ אֱלֹהִ֔ים
מְרַחֶ֖פֶת עַל־פְּנֵ֥י
הַמָּֽיִם׃

*The Hebrew text of
Genesis 1:2*

Many moderns dismiss this thought by saying that the written word, specifically the events recorded in the Old Testament, is mere man-made myth. But the Hebrews themselves clearly understood that "Thus says Yahweh" is exactly that, the very word of God. The term *myth* does not occur in Old Testament literature. Myth is more compatible with Israel's polytheistic neighbors' religions that God repeatedly commanded Israel to avoid. Even when mythological language appears in the text (e.g., Job 7:12; Ps. 74:13), it is ridiculed or contrasted with the truth of revelation.[10]

---

9. C. F. H. Henry, *God, Revelation and Authority*, vol. 1 (Waco, Texas: Word, 1976), 44.

10. Cf. Michael A. Grisanti, "Mayim" in VanGemeren, ed., *Dictionary of Old Testament Theology and Exegesis*, vol. 2 (Grand Rapids: Zondervan, 1997), G. Ernest Wright, *God Who Acts* (London: SCM Press, 1952), "Myth Become Fact" in C. S. Lewis, *God in the Dock* (Grand Rapids: Eerdmans, 1970), "Revelation and Myth" in Carl F. H. Henry, *God, Revelation and Authority* (Waco: Word Books, 1976).

When Hebrew prophets invoked the expression "Thus says Yahweh," which occurs hundreds of times, they employ a common Near Eastern formula to preface the commands of a deity. The Egyptians "would have been well aware of that idiom because many of their own texts, such as the *Book of the Dead*, introduce the directives of the gods with the words: 'Thus says . . .' It is an introductory formula that signifies that the words following derive directly from the deity, and are not to be altered or changed in any manner. The role of the prophet is to communicate the word without modification."[11] Similarly, in the book of Amos, no less than sixty times, the prophet proclaims that he is declaring what God revealed to him. The prophet truly labored under the conviction that the words he uttered were the very words of God.[12]

Oftentimes, the personality of the prophet seems to disappear, and the speaker becomes God himself. For instance, Amos 1:3 reads: "Thus says the LORD, 'For three transgressions of Damascus and for four I will not revoke its punishment.' " God directly speaks in the first person singular, yet it is the prophet who pronounces the word to the people.

Numerous sections of the Pentateuch begin with the remark: "Yahweh said to Moses." In the book of Leviticus alone, the expression appears at least forty times. The Holiness Code concludes with the words: "These are the statutes and ordinances and laws which the LORD established between Himself and the sons of Israel through Moses at Mount Sinai" (Lev. 26:46). And the entire book ends with the statement, "These are the commandments which the LORD commanded Moses for the sons of Israel at Mount Sinai" (27:34).

At times, God did not use a human mediator but spoke his word directly to the people. The giving of the Ten Commandments is one such incident (Ex. 20:1–17). The people so feared God's presence and his direct revelation that they pleaded with Moses that God would no longer speak to them but that Moses should intercede on their behalf (Ex. 20:18–19). At other times, God even wrote down his revelation by his own hand (Ex. 24:12; 31:18; Deut. 4:13; 5:22).

Three New Testament passages confirm the nature of the Old Testament as revelation from God. Second Timothy 3:16a sums up the implication of the Jewish writings by affirming their full authority and inspiration as "Scripture": "All Scripture is inspired by God." As a person fully versed in the Hebrew worldview, Paul draws upon his extensive rabbinic background

> *The Old Testament writings propose the revolutionary idea that a transcendent-personal God reveals truth not through myth and magical practices but through the creation itself, actual historical events which are interpreted by means of language and words disclosed by God to prophets and other messengers.*

> *At times, God did not use a human mediator but spoke his word directly to the people. The giving of the Ten Commandments is one such incident (Ex. 20:1–17).*

---

11. J. Currid, *Exodus I* (Darlington, England: Evangelical Press, 2000), 114.

12. Ironically, the human fall into sin and disobedience of the Lord's commands (see below) brings drastic epistemological consequences. Error and false prophecy emerge. Prophets may claim to speak "the word of the Lord," yet they propagate lies and visions of their own imagination that lead God's people into further error, rather than the pursuit of truth. Knowing and possessing the truth in the Hebrew worldview is never merely a matter of intellectual cognition but depends on adherence to ethical norms (Jer. 23:16–22; 5:20–21; Ezek. 13:6–8).

to affirm the Old Testament as "inspired." He uses the word *theopneustos*, a term literally meaning "God-breathed": the Old Testament Scriptures were "expired" by God, breathed out through the writers by divine exhalation in a way that did not override the writer's personality or choice of words. The Hebrew Scriptures owe their origin and substance to God alone.[13]

The apostle Peter, also a product of the fully developed Old Testament worldview, affirms the divine character of prophetic utterances: "But know this first of all, that no prophecy of Scripture is a matter of one's own interpretation, for no prophecy was ever made by an act of human will, but men moved by the Holy Spirit spoke from God" (2 Peter 1:20–21). What Peter means by this statement has frequently been called into question, the confusion stemming from a misunderstanding of his use of "interpretation." To the modern reader, "interpretation" implies an explanation of some problem or issue. The Greek word *epilusis* is poorly translated as "interpretation." It literally means "release." Thus Peter claims that Old Testament prophecy is released from the prophet himself. The origin and substance of prophecy does not arise from the human will but from God speaking through man.

Verse 21 confirms that conclusion by indicating that the Old Testament prophets spoke from God merely by being "moved by the Holy Spirit." Peter reflects the relationship between the Holy Spirit and the prophet by the word *phero*, often applied in maritime contexts to denote a ship born along by the wind (cf. Acts 27:15, 17). The metaphor is clear: as a ship is moved by the wind, so is a prophet (like sails) filled with the Holy Spirit and carried in the direction God wills.[14] Thus the apostle Peter also declares the prophecies of the Old Testament are expired from God through prophets, who are the means or instruments of his word.[15]

Finally, in the Sermon on the Mount, Jesus confirms the Hebrew view of revelation when he describes the extent of inspiration. Matthew 5:17–18 is a worldview argument on behalf of his teaching ministry: "Do not think that I came to abolish the Law or the Prophets; I did not come to abolish but to fulfill. For truly I say to you, until heaven and earth pass away, not the smallest letter or stroke shall pass away from the Law, until all is accomplished." The King James Version translates part of the last verse as not "one jot or one tittle" shall pass away of the Old Testament until Christ accomplishes all his work. The Greek word for "jot" refers to the Hebrew letter *yod* that is the tiniest letter in the Hebrew alphabet. The word "tittle" is used of the Hebrew serif marking, a small stroke that distinguishes one conso-

> *Paul . . . uses the word **theopneustos**, a term literally meaning "God-breathed": the Old Testament Scriptures were "expired" by God, breathed out through the writers by divine exhalation in a way that did not override the writer's personality or choice of words.*

---

13. A common contention is that the writers of the Scriptures are inspired. While that idea is true, Scripture uses the term "inspiration" primarily as a description of the writings themselves. See A. M. Stibbs, "The Witness of Scripture to Its Inspiration," in *Revelation and the Bible*, ed. C. F. H. Henry (Grand Rapids: Baker, 1959), 107–18.

14. M. Green, *The Second Epistle of Peter and the Epistle of Jude* (London: Tyndale, 1970), 91.

15. This does not presuppose the view of mechanical dictation, since the person and personality of each writer of the Bible is clearly in evidence in the writings.

nant from another. Thus Jesus articulates a fully developed Old Testament worldview of revelation: the Scriptures are true, inspired, and authoritative even to the smallest strokes and letters of the text.[16] Jesus frames his argument in a context where beliefs about revelation already carried full authority and takes them to another level. They support his teaching in the following verses (5:19–48) where he proposed a radical understanding of the laws concerning murder, adultery, "an eye for an eye," and loving one's enemy. Taken together, therefore, Paul's, Peter's and Jesus' teaching on the inspiration and authority of the Old Testament Scripture provides a further development of the biblical worldview on revelation.

Theology

Revelation is primarily God's self-disclosure of who he is. Thus, first and foremost it is theological. The term *theology*—a combination of two Greek words: *theos* (god) and *logos* (word)—in the biblical worldview is not a word about God or man's thoughts about God—what some people call *religion*—but properly speaking is God's word to man about himself. In this section, we will briefly consider what revelation says about God—his being and character—that provides the foundation of the Old Testament worldview.

Monotheism

The most fundamental theological belief of the Hebrew faith is monotheism as summarized in Deuteronomy 6:4: "Hear, O Israel! The LORD is our

> *Revelation is primarily God's self-disclosure of who he is. Thus, first and foremost it is theological. The term theology . . . in the biblical worldview is not a word about God or man's thoughts about God—what some people call religion—but properly speaking is God's word to man about himself.*

---

16.   Theologians call this verbal (to the word) and plenary (full) inspiration. For the Christian, the critical aspect of the nature of the Old Testament revelation is how Jesus understood and used it. To him, it is the very word of God and, therefore, bears divine authority in all respects. This can be demonstrated in various ways. First, Jesus does not hesitate to base his entire argument on a single passage from the Old Testament (cf. Matt. 21:16; 21:42; 22:43–44; 26:64; 27:46; Luke 20:17; 20:42–43; 22:69; 23:46). He also relies heavily, and sometimes solely, on the authority of the Old Testament as verification of his own person. In Matt. 27:35–46, Jesus answers the taunts of his enemies at the cross, a modification of Ps. 22:8, by quoting Ps. 22:1, "My God, my God why have you forsaken me?" Jesus cites the same messianic psalm that the Jews had just mockingly quoted, to underscore his claim that he is indeed the hoped-for Messiah. Similarly, authors of the New Testament also consider the Old Testament completely authoritative for the church. They often concentrate their message on a single Old Testament passage when testifying to the truth of the gospel. For example, Paul's gospel witness at Antioch recorded in Acts 13 is based on two quotes from the book of Psalms. One points to Christ's person as Son of God and the other to his resurrection. Peter similarly proclaims the doctrine of Christ's resurrection by quoting Ps. 16:8–11 in Acts 2:22–28. The Old Testament carries utmost authority for the church's doctrine and theology; it is so important that it is quoted by every author of the New Testament, and often it is referred to extensively. Church tradition has been almost unanimous in regard to the authority of the Old Testament. It is seen as the very word of the Holy One of Israel. It is not mankind's word stemming from his own imagination and creativity but God's word "breathed out" to the human writers of Scripture. Because they are divine oracles, and not man-made literature, it then follows that they are completely trustworthy, dependable, and authoritative.

God, the LORD is one!" This verse, called the *shema* by Jews, has a unique scribal calligraphy: the last letters of the first word and the last word of the verse are enlarged beyond the normal script. This scribal activity draws attention to the fact that the two letters together spell a Hebrew word. They form the word *'ad,* which means "witness or testimony." The point being made is that Deuteronomy 6:4 forms the most weighty theological doctrine of Judaism. This belief lasted well into New Testament times and beyond. Commenting on first-century Jewish teaching, Hurtado says, "devout Jews proclaimed their faith in monotheistic professions which emphasize the universal sovereignty and uniqueness of the one God of Israel."[17]

The Hebrews were not the first and only monotheists in antiquity. In reality, the first humans were monotheists (Gen. 2–3). Not until after the fall of mankind into sin does polytheism appear. Perhaps the best-known monotheist of ancient times was the Egyptian Pharaoh Akhenaton (Amenophis IV, reigned ca. 1350–1334 BC). Some historians have argued that Akhenaton's belief was not a true monotheism but rather a form of henotheism (worshiping one god without denying the existence of other gods).[18] But that is untrue. Akhenaton had, in Redford's words, "an uncompromising monotheism that denied other gods."[19] Aldred adds that Akhenaton's was a "worship of an omnipotent and singular divinity."[20]

Akhenaton worshiped the sun-god Aton alone, and he suppressed the worship of other gods in his kingdom. He attempted to sweep away the old cults by eliminating their priesthoods. Later in his reign he suppressed the use of the plural form "gods" in earlier texts. He imposed a revolution from above, one that he forced on the people of Egypt. In addition, during Akhenaton's rule the sun-god's name was enclosed in double-bordered cartouches, and the god was given names and titles like pharaoh. No other gods had ever received such treatment.

Because of Akhenaton's monotheism, some have argued that he was the true mentor of Moses and the instigator of Jewish monotheism. None other than Sigmund Freud believed it: "I venture now to draw the following conclusion: if Moses was an Egyptian and if he transmitted to the Jews his own religion, then it was that of Ikhnaton, the Aton religion."[21] The claim is hollow and spurious, however. There is no evidence that any Hebrew was ever influenced by this unique Egyptian concentration on one god. In fact, Akhenaton's "heresy" had no lasting effect even on his own people. Almost immediately after his death and in subsequent generations, he was branded a rebel and heretic.

Akhenaton

---

17. L. Hurtado, "First-Century Jewish Monotheism," *JSNT* 71 (1998): 26.

18. A synonymous term is *monolatry.* See H. Cohn, "From Monolatry to Monotheism," *JBQ* 26 (1998): 124–26.

19. D. B. Redford, *Egypt, Canaan, and Israel in Ancient Times* (Princeton, NJ: Princeton University Press, 1992), 381.

20. C. Aldred, *Akhenaten, King of Egypt* (London: Thames and Hudson, 1988), 240.

21. S. Freud, *Moses and Monotheism* (New York: Random House, 1939), 27.

Although the Hebrews and Akhenaton were both monotheists, Israel's monotheism differed radically from the Egyptian. In Egypt, the Aton was a god personified in the sun; to the Hebrews, Yahweh was a spirit, not part of or personified in nature. Yet, Yahweh is a personal God who enters into covenant with his people; he is holy and commands his people to behave in a moral way. The Aton is quite impersonal and mechanistic and has little relationship to the Egyptians, except perhaps to Pharaoh. Aton appears in art forms, usually as a disc with multiple arms. Yahweh, on the other hand, is never to be portrayed in physical form. Moses told the people just before they crossed into the Promised Land to "watch yourselves carefully, since you did not see any form on the day the LORD spoke to you at Horeb from the midst of the fire, lest you act corruptly and make a graven image for yourselves in the form of any figure" (Deut. 4:15–16).

The radical differences between Egyptian and Hebraic monotheism illustrate how elements within a worldview correlate with one another or stand in tension with each other. The monotheism of Akhenaton, for example, never truly integrated into the Egyptian worldview, which continued to be dominated by polytheism. Because Akhenaton imposed it from his position as ruler, belief in one god stood in marked contrast with the remaining features of Egyptian belief, for example, their view of the cosmos. In fact, monotheism actually contradicted other beliefs, never received widespread acceptance, and quickly disappeared. On the other hand, because theological concerns dominated, Hebraic monotheism not only penetrated but harmonized with every other aspect of the Hebrews' worldview—their cosmology, their view of human nature and of humans' capacity to relate to a personal God, and the highest ethical standards commanded for human behavior. Hebrew beliefs and customs reflect the fact that its monotheism of a personal God who transcends creation, yet works immanently within it, exercised a powerful influence on every institution in Hebrew life. For this reason, monotheism "worked" within the biblical worldview and did not "work" within the Egyptian.

The highest assertion of Old Testament monotheism contends that Yahweh is not just the greatest of the gods but the only God, utterly incomparable to all rival claimants (Isa. 40–48). Whereas polytheistic deities personified powers within the cosmos and were associated with idols crafted out of natural materials and were tied to repetitive events in the cycle of nature, Israel's Yahweh created all that exists and reigned supremely by determining the courses of history and nature (Ps. 104; 115:3–8; Isa. 9–17; Jer. 10:1–10). Numerous passages claim that people become like what they worship, that individuals and nations take on the characteristics of their gods (2 Kings 17:15; Ps. 115:8; Isa. 44:9–20; Jer. 2:5). On the other hand, Yahweh's people are to manifest his unique righteousness and holiness (Ex. 19:5–6; Lev. 19; 1 Chron. 16:29).[22] To argue that Israel's monotheism com-

> *The radical differences between Egyptian and Hebraic monotheism illustrate how elements within a worldview correlate with one another or stand in tension with each other.*

> *The highest assertion of Old Testament monotheism contends that Yahweh is not just the greatest of the gods but the only God, utterly incomparable to all rival claimants (Isa. 40–48). . . . Israel's Yahweh created all that exists and reigned supremely by determining the courses of history and nature.*

---

22. Cf. below on *imitatio Dei*.

"

The name of a person in the Old Testament often reflects either the character of the person or an important event in which the person has been involved. . . . Israel also had many names for God, attesting to the multitude of attributes that set Yahweh apart as unique within the Hebrew worldview.

pares with or developed from another monotheism ignores the radical differences between the two.

Names of God

The name of a person in the Old Testament often reflects either the character of the person or an important event in which the person has been involved. For example, the name "Abraham" literally means "the father of many," which is significant because he became the father of the entire nation of Israel. "Abel" means "fleeting," and indeed how that reflects the brevity of his life. "Isaac" means "laughter," a reference to both Abraham and Sarah who laughed at the supposed pregnancy of Sarah. Sometimes names can be prophetic, as, for instance, Isaiah's son is named "Maher-shalal-hash-baz," which means "swift is the booty, speedy is the prey"—a reference to the advancing Assyrian army (Isa. 8:1–4).

The same principle applies to the names of God in the Old Testament. While consistently adhering to its monotheism, Israel also had many names for God, attesting to the multitude of attributes that set Yahweh apart as unique within the Hebrew worldview. Each of his names expresses a different aspect of his character and separates him from the vast pantheons of deities held by Israel's neighbors. Israel's contemporaries posited a vast diversity of gods, each of which accounted for a specific power that worked within nature or upon human existence. In contrast, Israel held to one sovereign deity who revealed himself with characteristics manifested in his many names. We will consider only a few of these names in order to illustrate the application of the principle.

Yahweh. In Exodus 3:13–15, God identifies himself by the name *YHWH*, often referred to in modern literature as the tetragrammaton (literally the "four letters"). The original pronunciation of the name has been lost because traditional Judaism refused to pronounce it. It was considered too holy and sacred to say out loud. An indication of how the Hebrews' understanding of God shaped their worldview becomes evident in how they treated the divine name. Whenever a Jew saw the consonants *YHWH* written, he would replace it in speech with the term *Adonai* (see below). Although the pronunciation has been lost, many argue that it should be pronounced as "Yahweh." It is the personal name for God in the Old Testament, and his most frequent designation, occurring at least five thousand times. It also is often found in compound with other names. For example, the name Joab means "Yahweh is father"; Isaiah means "the salvation of Yahweh."

Yahweh is the awesome, personal, serious covenantal name for God in the Old Testament. Often it is simply called "the name" (Lev. 24:11–16). It is derived from the simple Hebrew verb "to be." God's name means, "Being, I am who I am." The name signifies, first of all, that God is self-existent and self-sufficient. That is, "he determines his own experience and he is independent of anything else for his being. He is autonomous of creation. Secondly, it means that he is immutable or unchanging. He is not in the process of becoming something else. God is the same yesterday, today and for ever. Finally, it implies the eternity of his being. He has always been and he will always be."[23]

El. This name for God derives from a term that means "strong, powerful." It is used to present the idea of God's might. Thus, it establishes a solid connection between God's nature and the activities he performs. Often, when God is pictured as performing mighty deeds and acts in the Bible, this name is given to him, as in the creation account in Genesis 1, in which a derivative of *El* is used exclusively of God's wondrous creative acts. There are some variations or derivatives of the name *El* in the Old Testament, and they are commonly used.

El Shaddai. Often translated in English Bibles as "God Almighty," it appears forty-eight times in the Old Testament. The first occurrence is Genesis 17:1. The meaning of the term *Shaddai* has caused much debate. It may derive from the word "breast," and, thus, may signify the "blessings of the breast," that is, grace. So the full name may denote a mighty God who also is a God who blesses his people. The name seems to be used in that manner in Genesis 17:1–2 and 28:3. *El Shaddai* is principally used by the patriarchs (Gen. 28:3; 43:14; 48:3).

El Elyon. This title is first used in Genesis 14:18–22, where it is translated as "God Most High." *Elyon* derives from the verb "to go up, to exalt." It is used to designate God as the most elevated being in all reality. He is God over all (Ps. 57:2; 78:56).

Elohim. This derivative, the most commonly used in the Old Testament, is employed throughout Genesis 1. It is a masculine *plural* form of the word that means "strength, might." When used of the God of the Hebrews it takes singular agreement; when it designates other gods, it takes plural agreement (as in Ex. 20:3). The plurality of God's name probably reflects the Hebrew practice of the honorific plural or plural of majesty (*pluralis majestatis*) in which a singular object is so characterized by a quality that a plural is used for the object. Others have attempted to argue for the Trinity based on the plurality of this name. Higher critical scholars view the plurality as a vestige or remnant of polytheism; that is, the Hebrews originally worshiped many gods but through a process of syncretism the many evolved into one. The fact that *Elohim* is combined with *Yahweh* (e.g., Gen. 2:4–3:23) may indicate that God is the sovereign, universal creator and also Israel's personal deity.[24]

> "Yahweh is the awesome, personal, serious covenantal name for God in the Old Testament.... God's name means, "Being, I am who I am." The name signifies ... that God is self-existent and self-sufficient.... He is autonomous of creation ... the same yesterday, today and for ever.... He has always been and he will always be.

---

23. Currid, *Exodus I*, 91.
24. Testifying to the importance of the names of God is the Hebrew practice of implementing various names of God into names of people.

Special Names for God

Throughout the Old Testament, God also is given particular names that include an attribute of his character and being. These are expressions that help us to understand who he is and how he works in creation. We will consider three of these titles.

Lord of Hosts. In Hebrew this title is *Yahweh Tsebaoth.* It is first found in 1 Samuel 1:3, which mentions a man named Elkanah who had the habit of going yearly to sacrifice to "the Lord of Hosts." The term "hosts" carries military overtones, and it can simply be translated as "armies, forces." For example, when the Hebrews leave Egypt in martial array, they are called "the hosts of Yahweh" (Ex. 14:41). The title indicates that God has a host of armies at his right hand to implement his will. He is attended by an army of angels (see Isa. 6:2–3), and even the stars are the "host of heaven" and do his bidding. For further references, see Psalm 24:10; Isaiah 1:9, 24.

Yahweh will provide. In Genesis 22, God calls on Abraham to offer his son Isaac as a burnt offering. At the moment of sacrifice, however, God shows Abraham a ram that is to be offered in the place of Isaac. Afterward, the patriarch consecrates the site by giving it a name, "Yahweh will provide" (Hebrew *Yahweh yireh*). This name is based on verse 8, where Isaac asks about the missing sacrifice. Abraham responds: "God will provide for Himself the lamb for the burnt offering."

This story underscores the reality that God does indeed provide for his people, and he does so abundantly. He did not require Abraham to sacrifice his son, for God one day would send his own son as a sacrifice! It also should be noted that the verb "to provide" is the same as the verb "to see" in Hebrew. This highlights the fact that this whole scene of the sacrifice of Isaac has been anticipated by God and unfolds according to his will and purpose. God is totally in control of the situation.

The Angel of Yahweh. In the episode of the burning bush in Exodus 3, the text says that "the angel of the LORD appeared to him in a blazing fire from the midst of a bush" (v. 2). Who is this? The angel is identified with God in the passage and speaks as if he is God (3:4). That identification appears elsewhere in Judges 13:17–22. Some commentators argue that the Angel of the LORD is the second person of the Trinity, a pre-incarnate Christ. As John Calvin remarks, "But let us enquire who this Angel was? . . . The ancient teachers of the church have rightly understood [it to be] the Eternal Son of God in respect to his office as Mediator."[25]

25. Currid, *Exodus I*, 81.

The number of names and the manner in which the Hebrews used the names of God clearly indicate the centrality of theology to their worldview.

Cosmogony

Creation constitutes a unique feature of the biblical worldview, and along with the existence of God comprises the very first worldview issues that a person confronts in reading the Bible. Creation as a primary component of Israelite thought pervades the Old Testament. The Psalms extol God and his creation as the basis for worship (e.g., Ps. 8, 19, 50, 95–97, 104, 145–47); the prophets support their condemnation of human wickedness on the moral demands implicit in creation (Isa. 40–44; Jer. 5); and the wisdom literature presupposes creation in its view of reflective thinking and pedagogy (Job 28:12–28; 37:1–13; 38; Prov. 8:22–36; 9:1–6).

Earth from Apollo 17

Creation provides the context out of which the rest of the biblical narrative, with all of its many dimensions, develops. It not only set the Hebrew worldview over against its ancient counterparts but also supplied Western thought with its distinctive account of origins well into the modern period.[26] Whereas Israel's contemporaries incorporated elaborate myths to depict the origin of the cosmos with the result that the gods merely personified the forces of nature,[27] Genesis presents creation in the context of its radical monotheism. Mesopotamian polytheism portrayed the world as a function of the origins of both gods and the world out of primordial matter. In Israel's account, however, Yahweh stands as the exclusive creator and sovereign ruler of the cosmos and is sharply distinguished from creation, which though thoroughly "good," is nevertheless not divine (Gen. 1:4–31).

> *Creation provides the context out of which the rest of the biblical narrative, with all of its many dimensions, develops. It not only set the Hebrew worldview over against its ancient counterparts but also supplied Western thought with its distinctive account of origins well into the modern period.*

26.   One advantage the biblical worldview held over naturalistic perspectives until the nineteenth century was its depiction of beginnings—not only of the cosmos but also human history and the covenant people of God. Genesis 1–3 gave the Judeo-Christian tradition a unique advantage over other naturalistic perspectives, which lacked an account of origins. Alternative perspectives, whether originating in primitive nature myths or in civilized, rationalistic settings such as Greece, portrayed the cosmos as the result of an infinite regress or as an artifact, fashioned out of some pre-existent matter. Charles Darwin's *On the Origin of the Species* (1859) filled the gap in the naturalistic worldview by proposing an alternative "creation story" that in the words of one of Darwin's advocates made it possible for him to be "an intellectually fulfilled atheist."

27.   "The language of the Genesis account of creation can be described as a demythologization of ancient creation accounts. Mythical terminology is still found in the references to creation in the Psalter (Ps. 74:12–17; 18:10–12 [11–13]) and Job (3:8; 26:12). However, in Genesis the mythical elements have been excised radically; instead we find an explicit polemic against the creation myth. Polytheism is removed, and with the theogony and the theomachy that are so vital in the Mesopotamian mythology." A. H. Konkel, "bohu" in Van-Gemeren, ed., *Dictionary of Old Testament Theology and Exegesis*, vol. 1 (Grand Rapids: Zondervan, 1997).

49

The Creator

The Bible's opening words, "In the beginning God . . ." (Gen. 1:1), make God the true subject of the creation account. The fundamental belief in one creator God (Job 38; Ps. 24:1–2; 104) is an almost unknown tenet in the rest of the ancient Near East. Mesopotamians, for example, clearly believed in a multiplicity of gods who had creative powers and performed creative acts.[28]

In the Old Testament, the manner of God's creative activity is called the *logos doctrine*. God created the universe by the mere power of his speech: "Then God said, 'Let there be light'; and there was light" (Gen. 1:3). The entire biblical record of creation in Genesis 1 highlights God's creative effort through the word (vv. 8–11, 14, 20, 22, 24, 26). Other Old Testament texts, such as Psalm 33:6, support the Hebrews' belief in God's creation by mere verbal fiat.

The Hebrew creation account implies a creation divinely fashioned *ex nihilo*—out of nothing.[29] This presentation serves to emphasize that God is all-powerful, incomparable, and sovereign. He owes nothing to the agency of another. In addition, creation did not occur as the result of a contest or a struggle between gods, as it did in the Mesopotamian myths. In the *Enuma Elish* myth, creation was a mere consequence of a war aimed at determining who would be the main god.

The Hebrew creation account also is unique because it is not *theogonic*.[30] Other societies of the ancient Near East taught that the gods came into being either by self-creation or through creation by other gods. Theogony played an important and vital role in ancient Near Eastern cosmological myths.[31] The myths' purpose was to establish the hierarchy of the gods in the pantheon. Never in Hebrew thought is God merely the consequence of some other god's creative efforts. Instead, Israel's God alone creates and superintends the boundaries of natural forces (Job 38) and providentially cares for creatures he has placed in nature (Ps. 104), even as he cares for the people whom he formed by his covenant call (Isa. 42:5–9). God's uniqueness as creator leads prophets to ridicule vain attempts to worship

> *The Hebrew creation account implies a creation divinely fashioned **ex nihilo**—out of nothing. This presentation serves to emphasize that God is all-powerful, incomparable, and sovereign. He owes nothing to the agency of another.*

28. A. Heidel, *The Babylonian Genesis* (Chicago: University of Chicago Press, 1951), 96–97.

29. The New Testament explicitly affirms creation *ex nihilo* in Heb. 11:1–3.

30. A "theogony" is an account of the creation of the gods by other gods.

31. In his chapter "The Temple in the Moonlight: The Primeval Religious Experience," Thomas Cahill portrays the Sumerian prehistoric worldview with its polytheistic origin of the gods and endless cycles of nature. He then contrasts it with "The Journey in the Dark: The Unaccountable Innovation"—the worldview revolution of Genesis's Abrahamic narrative with its personal, transcendent deity who interacts "face-to-face" with people. In enumerating *The Gifts of the Jews: How a Tribe of Desert Nomads Changed the Way Everyone Thinks and Feels* (New York: Random House, 1998), Cahill focuses on history, the Jews' concern to underscore the concreteness and specificity of historical events as foundational to their worldview. Cahill's work is the second of his own "revolution" series, "The Hinges of History," which explores turning points in history.

idols made of woods and metals, which God alone created (Isa. 40:18–20; Jer. 10).

The Creation

Though God himself has no beginning, the universe does. The Old Testament begins with the phrase "In the beginning . . ." In Hebrew, the phrase is one word, often used to describe the first phase or step in an event. Creation simply took place at the beginning of time. Although such a teaching is unique when compared with Greek or Roman thought, it is not unique in the ancient Near East, for the Egyptians as well believed that the event of creation had a real beginning.

The Hebrews believed that God's creative work at the beginning was comprehensive. However, they had no single word to describe the universe. When they wanted to express the concept of all reality, they used the expression "the heavens and the earth," which is a merism, that is, two opposites that are all-inclusive (cf. Gen. 14:19). Thus, in Genesis 1:1, when the writer proclaims that God created the heavens and the earth, he was saying that God had fashioned the entire universe.

Genesis 1:2 presents the earth in the process of formation. First, we read that it was created in a state of *tohu wabohu*, that is, "formlessness and emptiness." These two terms appear together two other times in the Old Testament (Isa. 34:11 and Jer. 4:23). In both cases, the prophets report visions of what the earth would look like after God's judgment. It will return to a wild and dark state as it was in the beginning.

Genesis describes creation in a six-day structure. The first three days picture God as ordering and organizing the creation. The motif of separation dominates these three days: God is portrayed as dividing the light from the darkness (vv. 1:4, 18), the waters above from the waters below (vv. 6–7), and earth from sky (v. 9). Thus, in the first three days, God is taking the *tohu* ("formlessness") and giving it form and order.

The next three days (including part of day three) present God as filling creation. He commands the earth to sprout forth vegetation, the luminaries to be set in the sky, and, finally, the creation of animals and mankind. Thus God is taking the *bohu* ("emptiness") of Genesis 1:2 and filling it with creatures and things.

The structure of the creation account in six days has stirred great debate among evangelical scholars that has resulted in four different positions. Each view attempts in its own way to articulate the centrality of creation in the biblical worldview.

The Framework Interpretation. Adherents of this view emphasize the pervasive influence of creation as a theme running from the creation account in Genesis to the new creation in Revelation. This position states that the

> "The Hebrews believed that God's creative work at the beginning was comprehensive. However, they had no single word to describe the universe. When they wanted to express the concept of all reality, they used the expression "the heavens and the earth.""

days of Genesis 1 are not to be understood as sequential.[32] Instead, they are a figurative description of actual events, and the days are structured in a strophic or poetic framework that manifests a topical structure depicted below.

KINGDOMS (DOMAINS)	KINGS (RULERS)
Day 1. Light vv. 3–5	Day 4. Light Bearers vv. 14–19
Day 2. Sea, Sky vv. 6–8	Day 5. Fish, Birds vv. 20–23
Day 3. Land vv. 9–13	Day 6. Land animals vv. 24–31
Day 7. Sabbath	

The six days of creation are thus structured as two sets of three days in parallel. The first triad (days 1–3) describes the creation of three kingdoms, and the second triad (days 4–6) pictures the creation of the three rulers of those kingdoms. The author draws a portrait of creation by presenting individual pictures of what happened at creation. The "days" do not constitute a chronology as one frame ends and another begins. These events truly happened in history but not in the apparent sequence that a literal reading of Genesis 1 would portray.

Those who hold to the framework view argue that for one to accept a chronological or sequential account of creation, one must presuppose extraordinary providential care. Thus, light and darkness exist before the text records the creation of the luminaries that divide the night and day. God creates vegetation prior to the sun upon which it fully depends. Certain natural laws must be discounted if one holds to a sequential account of creation. Framework advocates deny that such discrepancies are problematic. In an important study, Kline says that the "presupposition of Gen. 2:5 is clearly that the divine providence was operating during the creation period through processes which any reader would recognize as normal in the natural world today."[33] Thus Genesis 2:5 describes a time "when the earth was without vegetation, an environmental state that flies in the face of the six-day sequence recorded in Genesis 1. This demonstrates that God used normal providential procedure in creation—and if that be the case, Genesis 1 must be understood in light of ordinary providence. It is therefore a figurative account."[34]

Day Age View (Concordist Position). This interpretation developed as scientific evidence mounted that supported a very old cosmos. Concordists formulated their position to reaffirm the credibility of creation as central to

> *The six days of creation are thus structured as two sets of three days in parallel. The first triad (days 1–3) describes the creation of three kingdoms, and the second triad (days 4–6) pictures the creation of the three rulers of those kingdoms.*

---

32. For examples of this view, see M. G. Kline, "Because It Had Not Rained," *WTJ* 20 (1958): 146–57; M. Futato, "Because It Had Not Rained: A Study of Gen 2:5–7 with Implications for Gen 2:4–25 and Gen 1:1–2:3," *WTJ* 60 (1998): 1–21.

33. Kline, "Because It Had Not Rained," 150.

34. J. Currid, *Genesis I* (Darlington, England: EP, 2003), 36.

the biblical worldview. The day age view affirms the sequence of creation in Genesis 1. However, each "day" (Hebrew *yom*) equals an indeterminable length of time; that is, each day could last aeons. In support of this position is the fact that the Hebrew term for "day" is sometimes used, even in the creation account itself, of an extended period (see Gen. 2:1–3; Ps. 90:4). Day 7, the Sabbath day, appears to extend over thousands of years. Why would not the other six as well?

This theory eliminates the problem of harmonizing geological evidence with the Scriptures. Yet, the Concordist still confronts the problem of chronology or sequence. Even with the elongation of the days, there is the question of an unnatural creation.[35]

Anthropomorphic Days. C. J. Collins has recently presented a somewhat different view on the issue. He says, "the seven 'days' of the creation week are an anthropomorphism to describe God's activity. If we wish to specify their relationship to time as we know it, perhaps we may view them as successive periods of undefined length (with perhaps some overlap). This idea has the advantage of arising from the Biblical narrative itself and it does not involve supposed (and questionable) 'figurative' meanings for the word 'day,' but instead takes this usage as part of a well-known class of anthropomorphisms."[36] In other words, the days of creation in Genesis 1 are God's days, not the days of nature (i.e., 24-hour periods). Thus, earthly time is not a main issue of the Hebrew creation account.

Collins's view appears similar to the Concordist's position when he says the creation is "successive periods of undefined length." Collins also inherits the same problems of the Concordist—the question of chronology. If one holds to the historicity of the sequence of Genesis 1, then it must have been an unnatural creation that took place (e.g., light before the sun).

24-hour Solar Day View. This position, often called "the literal view," maintains that each day mentioned in Genesis 1 is a literal twenty-four hour period. And each day of creation sequentially follows the one before it. So during the first "day," God created the light; on the second "day," the firmament; and so forth until the completion of creation at the end of six days. It is nothing less than a historical account of creation.

The following points may be made in support of the literal position. First, in biblical Hebrew there is a grammatical device called a "vav-consecutive-plus-imperfect." Its purpose is to present events in a historical sequence. This device appears throughout the Old Testament narratives

Moonrise, British Columbia. "God made the two great lights ... the lesser light to rule the night—and the stars." Gen. 1:16

"This theory eliminates the problem of harmonizing geological evidence with the Scriptures. Yet, the Concordist still confronts the problem of chronology or sequence. Even with the elongation of the days, there is the question of an unnatural creation.

---

35. A primary advocate of the day age view is D. Kidner, *Genesis* (London: InterVarsity, 1967), 55–56.

36. C. J. Collins, "How Old is the Earth? Anthropomorphic Days in Genesis 1:1–2:3," *Presbyterion* 20/2 (1994): 120–21.

but rarely in poetry. For example, it appears at least twenty times in Joshua 2. In Genesis 1, it appears fifty-one times. If the text was not meant to be taken chronologically, why did the biblical writer employ this device so freely? Second, there is little or no figurative language in Genesis 1: no symbols, tropes, or metaphors. The dearth of figurative language in a chapter that some consider figurative is quite striking. Third, it is worth noting that the days of Genesis 1 are numbered, and numbers imply sequence. In other words, counting is sequential and chronological by its very nature. As Kidner comments, "the march of days is too majestic a progress to carry no implication of ordered sequence; it also seems over-subtle to adopt a view of the passage which discounts one of the primary impressions it makes on the ordinary reader."[37]

The major problem with the literal interpretation is it presupposes extraordinary providential care. That is, natural processes must be discounted in the creation of the universe. The literalist would respond to the criticism by saying that God was not bound by natural law when he created the universe. He may create in any way he pleases. In fact, the very event of creation *ex nihilo* is an unnatural act.

At this point, non-literalists argue from Genesis 2:5. In an important study of that verse, Kline argues: the "presupposition of Gen. 2:5 is clearly that the divine providence was operating during the creation period through processes which any reader would recognize as normal in the natural world today."[38] His point is simple yet profound. Genesis 2:5 "describes a time when the earth was without vegetation, an environmental state that flies in the face of the six-day sequence recorded in Genesis 1. Thus, Genesis 2:5 demonstrates that God used normal providential procedure in creation—and if that be the case, Genesis 1 must be understood in light of ordinary providence. It is therefore a figurative account."[39]

The literalist responds by saying that Kline misreads Genesis 2:5. The first part of the verse says, "every shrub of the field was not yet in the earth," and that would seem to confirm Kline's interpretation. However, the second half of the verse declares that "every plant of the field had not yet sprouted." The Hebrew verb "to sprout" is used in the Bible only of the process of growth, and not of bringing into existence (see Gen. 41:6, 23; Ex. 10:5; Ps. 104:14). It appears then that the plants exist in the earth, but they have not yet blossomed because there has been no rain and no man to cultivate them. How then are they kept alive? By the extraordinary providence of God!

Each of the four positions has advantages and disadvantages. Each viewpoint upholds creation as a nonnegotiable element of the biblical

> "Kidner comments, "the march of days is too majestic a progress to carry no implication of ordered sequence; it also seems over-subtle to adopt a view of the passage which discounts one of the primary impressions it makes on the ordinary reader.""

---

37. Kidner, *Genesis*, 54–55. Other supportive data may be seen in a recent article that I wrote as introductory for a Genesis commentary, Currid, *Genesis I*, 34–43.

38. Kline, "Because It Had Not Rained," 150.

39. Currid, *Genesis I*, 36.

worldview. Christians may advocate any of the positions and still hold to the authority of Scripture. But regardless of which view one holds, creation inherently demands the role of extraordinary providence. Whether it be creation *ex nihilo* or the sequence of the days or the length of the days, creation implies the supernatural power of God as its underlying presupposition.

Creation of Mankind

The final object that God fashions is mankind, and that is why humanity often is called the "crown of creation." In addition, humans differ from all other parts of creation because they are made *imago Dei* ("in the image of God"). On the sixth day of creation, the biblical author reports God saying, " 'Let Us make man in Our image, according to Our likeness; and let them rule over the fish of the sea and over the birds of the sky and over the cattle and over all the earth, and over every creeping thing that creeps on the earth.' And God created man in His own image, in the image of God He created him; male and female He created them" (Gen. 1:26–27). Sometimes called "the cultural mandate," this passage not only affirms in the highest possible terms the inherent value and dignity of mankind but assigns mankind a role in cultural formation appropriate to that status. Other elements in Genesis 1 and 2—marriage and family (1:28), the Sabbath (2:1–2), the task of tilling and keeping the garden (2:15), and the prohibition against eating the fruit of the Tree of Knowledge of Good and Evil (2:16–17)—reinforce the unique status and function of humans as created in the image of God.

The creation narrative portrays what it means for man to be created *imago Dei* in three ways. First, the initial three days of creation, Genesis 1:1–10, picture God bringing about an ordered world. The first man is to reflect God in such activity by subduing and ruling over creation. He does this by cultivating the garden (2:15) and, especially, by naming the animals. Previously, God demonstrated his authority over the elements of creation by naming them. For example, when God created the light on day 1, he gave a name to it. Verse 5 literally says: "And God called to the light 'day,' and to the darkness he called 'night.' " By analogy, man subdues and rules the animal kingdom through the medium of the word by naming the different creatures. Both acts involve creative intelligence, something that no other creature possesses.

In the second three days of creation, God fills the heavens with a starry host and the earth with animate life. Adam, as well, is to fill the earth with his progeny (1:28). This role is accomplished by humanity as plural, male and female, as they populate the earth with their image-bearers (cf.

> *The final object that God fashions is mankind, and that is why humanity often is called the "crown of creation." In addition, humans differ from all other parts of creation because they are made imago Dei ("in the image of God").*

5:1–3). They also fulfill their cultural role as gardeners by producing a harvest of produce (2:15).[40]

Finally, on the seventh day of creation, God rests from his subduing and filling activity. It is implied here that Adam would work six days and rest on the seventh day (see Ex. 20:8–11).

Thus as one created in the *imago Dei*, Adam was created to act according to the *imitatio Dei* ("imitation of God"). Thus, mankind fulfills the cultural mandate of Genesis 1:26–27 by copying God's character and activity. No matter the activity—thought, word, or deed—people are to impersonate and behave like God.

The Hebrew term for "image" in Genesis 1:26–27, *tselem*, occurs sixteen times in the Old Testament. Most of its occurrences depict idols as representatives of gods (see 2 Kings 11:18). It also portrays a king setting up a statue of himself in a land he has conquered (see Dan. 3:1ff.) to demonstrate his sovereignty over the land and its inhabitants. Thus, *tselem* describes a god or a king, and specifically rulership or sovereignty that pertains to deity or kingship. For the creation of mankind in Genesis 1, it indicates humanity's dominion over God's creation and that men and women are likenesses or representations of God's image. The dignity and value of human life appear in its protection by sanctions against murder (Gen. 9:6; Ex. 20:13) and in its relative importance in comparison with creation, its other inhabitants, and God himself (Ps. 8). But above all, the biblical worldview elevates human worth; after the fall, God engages in the massive enterprise of restoration and salvation (Ps. 16; 51:10–17; 103:1–5).

> For the creation of mankind in Genesis 1, it [**tselem**, "image"] indicates humanity's dominion over God's creation and that men and women are likenesses or representations of God's image.

The Fall

From the exalted view of mankind as bearers of God's image, Genesis 3 proceeds to narrate the fall into a state of sinfulness. Man fails to exercise dominion over the creation and refuses to wield the authority God had given to him. He fails by not keeping the Word of God. In Genesis 2:16–17, God had given mankind a commandment that people were bound to keep: "And the LORD God commanded the man, saying, 'From any tree of the garden you may eat freely; but from the tree of the knowledge of good and evil you shall not eat, for in the day that you eat from it you shall surely die.'" God gives our first parents the freedom to eat from every tree of the garden, save one. If, however, they eat from that one tree, then they will die.

In Genesis 3:1–6, the serpent approaches the woman to see whether she has understood God's command. In the discussion, she reveals her ignorance of God's word. First, she exaggerates the prohibition. God never

40. Thus the first cultural activity is *agriculture* (Latin *ager*, "field," and *colere*, "to till or cultivate"), which was supplemented later with other cultural activities—animal husbandry, music, and forging of metals (Gen. 4:21, 22).

commanded that they not touch the fruit (3:3). Second, she omits the name of the tree, that is, the Tree of Knowledge of Good and Evil. Third, she adds to the commandment by giving the location of the tree "in the middle of the garden." Fourth, the woman minimizes the penalty by saying "lest you die," when in fact God had said "you shall surely die" (there is a double verb in Hebrew not present in the woman's statement). And, finally, she minimizes her privileges by proclaiming that "we may eat" of the fruit of the trees; God had said that they "may eat freely" from the trees (again a double verb appears for emphasis).

This ignorance of God's word is as much Adam's fault as Eve's. When the commandment had been given in Genesis 2:16–17, Eve had not yet been created. Apparently it was up to Adam to teach and train the woman in the word of God, and in this regard he failed.

The serpent capitalizes on the woman's ignorance of God's word by proclaiming the first lie. He says: "you will surely not die!" (3:4; note that the serpent uses the double verb when the woman does not). This is the lie from the beginning that Jesus refers to in John 8:44. The core of the lie is the serpent's discrediting of the character of God, as if the Lord had been holding humanity back from its potential.

Once the prohibition has been reasoned away, the practical and aesthetic appeal draws Eve to the tree. She sees that the tree is "desirable"—the Hebrew term used in the Ten Commandments of coveting (Ex. 20:17). The woman has an uncontrolled craving for the fruit. Thus, the deception of mankind occurs as a consequence of two things: (1) mankind's ignorance of the word of God and (2) the tree's overwhelming appeal to the physical senses.

The results of the fall of mankind into sin are many and immediately become apparent. Humanity itself was greatly affected in all its aspects:[41] (1) Because of their sin, the man and woman were *alienated from God*. After the sin, they "hid themselves from the presence of the LORD God among the trees of the garden" (3:8). The remainder of the Old Testament reinforces this alienation. The first four of the Ten Commandments presuppose the alienation from God, caused by sin, by commanding worship of God alone, forbidding images of God for worship, forbidding the misuse of God's name, and commanding the keeping of the Sabbath (Ex. 20:1–11). Mankind continues to manifest the image of God by increasing in numbers and creating cultural institutions, but we do so in distorted ways (Gen. 4). Old Testament writers portray man as sinful and in need of redemption. Evil is not simply incidental to the human condition, that is, occurring in discrete acts of wickedness, but is rather deeply seated in human nature.

Adam and Eve
(detail),
Titian (Tiziano Vecelli)

This ignorance of God's word is as much Adam's fault as Eve's. When the commandment had been given in Genesis 2:16–17, Eve had not yet been created. Apparently it was up to Adam to teach and train the woman in the word of God, and in this regard he failed.

41.   Cf. Albert M. Wolters, *Creation Regained* (Grand Rapids: Eerdmans, 1985) for an excellent worldview analysis of creation in terms of structure and direction. As it came from the hand of God, creation was ordered and good; but sin corrupted every aspect, thus necessitating a program of redemption to restore what sin distorted.

Biblical writers describe human evil as rooted in the heart (Ps. 32; 51; Jer. 17:9–10). The Old Testament inveighs against evil, whether manifest in intention, thought, or overt behavior (Gen. 6:5; 8:21; Ps. 14:1–3; 139). The Old Testament writers condemn sin not only in individual terms but also in corporate and social terms.[42] Throughout Old Testament history, Israel and Judah flagrantly disobey God's commands (1 Kings—2 Chronicles), and prophets condemn their rebellion, which frequently exceeds even the wickedness of pagan practices (2 Chron. 36:15–16; Amos 1, 2). Despite alienation from God, mankind still accomplishes much good through the ordinary institutions of family, labor, and government. But human sin requires repentance and restoration (Deut. 30:1–3; 2 Chron. 7:14; Jer. 3:22).[43]

(2) Adam and Eve also were *alienated from each other*. Prior to their sin, they had been naked before one another, a symbol of complete openness and intimacy. Now they covered themselves because they were ashamed. Whereas previously human nature was characterized by innocence, now it manifests itself in guilt. As in the case of the first four commandments of the Mosaic law, commandments five through ten presuppose the alienation between humans by forbidding the sins of dishonoring parents, murder, adultery, stealing, false witness and covetousness (Ex. 20:12–17). The commandments are not justified; they are merely asserted. Although only ten in number, whatever else people may correctly affirm as immoral or sinful behavior can be deduced from them. For centuries these mandates singularly framed the moral foundation for civilized culture. Old Testament law in all its forms presupposes human sinfulness, and these commands become the moral norms to restrain evil and to encourage behavior that glorifies God and benefits others. Although the word "conscience" does not appear in the Old Testament, gestures of guilt and sorrow for sin indicate that the Hebrews believed that people knew what God required of them (2 Sam. 24:10; Job 27:6; Ps. 51:1–9).

(3) They were *alienated from the Garden of Eden*. In Genesis 3:24, God drove them out of the garden so that they would not continue to enjoy its pleasures, and he placed cherubim and a flaming sword to guard the entrance. Expulsion from the garden and God's presence continues as a leitmotif in the Hebraic worldview, thus creating the context for the longing to be reconciled with God.

> *Although the word "conscience" does not appear in the Old Testament, gestures of guilt and sorrow for sin indicate that the Hebrews believed that people knew what God required of them (2 Sam. 24:10; Job 27:6; Ps. 51:1–9).*

---

42. The Old Testament manifests a delicate balance between individual and collective perspectives in assessing human behavior. In many instances individual responsibility provides the primary context for assigning moral blame. Ezek. 18:1–9 and Jer. 31:29 state the individualist principle, and numerous examples from patriarchal sins (viz., Abraham's and Isaac's lies about their marriages) to those of the kings of Israel and Judah (viz., David's adultery) illustrate individual culpability for specific sinful acts. Yet in notable instances, collective responsibility determines the assigning of moral guilt. Ex. 20:5 and 34:6–7 affirm corporate guilt and responsibility. And the judgment of Israel for Achan's sin, the tribal spies' unbelief, and economic evil (see, e.g., the book of Amos) illustrate instances where writers pronounced collective guilt.

43. See discussion below on covenant.

(4) They were *alienated from eternal life*. God had told them that they would die if they ate of the fruit of the tree. Throughout the remainder of the Old Testament, the ultimate result of human sin is death (Jer. 21:8; Ezek. 18:4). Within the biblical worldview, the overwhelming question becomes that of Job, "If a man dies, will he live again?" (Job 14:14). The *imago Dei* was twisted by sin and under the judgment of death. Thus the Old and New Testaments represent Adam in a period of probation, serving as the covenant representative of all mankind. As the first and the head of God's covenant people, what would happen to Adam while on probation would happen to all people to be born. Because Adam sinned, all people eventually die; we all share in the curses on Adam. All the descendants of Adam thus bear his fallen nature. This is clear from Genesis 5:3 when it says that Adam "became the father of a son in his own likeness, according to his image, and named him Seth." The reversal of the two terms "likeness" and "image" from Genesis 1:26 underscores the twisted nature that has now been inherited.

The fall, however, not only dramatically altered human nature, but also resulted in great consequences for the entire creation. In Genesis 3:17–18, Yahweh cursed the very ground because of mankind's sin: "Cursed is the ground because of you; in toil you shall eat of it all the days of your life. Both thorns and thistles it shall grow for you; and you shall eat the plants of the field." The earth will now resist efforts to cultivate it, and human attempts to fulfill the creation mandate meet with frustration.[44] Thus, after the fall, the cosmos itself falls prey to vanity and futility. The Deuteronomic covenant reinforced the consequences of moral disobedience by enumerating cosmic evils as punishments (Deut. 28),[45] a theme that the eighth-century prophets repeated (Amos 4:6–10; 5:11; Mic. 6:15). The New Testament reinforces the cosmic consequences of sin; Paul pronounces the world subject to "corruption" (Rom. 8:21). The universe is in a process of decay and deterioration, and it appears to be running down.

> *The fall, however, not only dramatically altered human nature, but also resulted in great consequences for the entire creation. . . . The New Testament reinforces the cosmic consequences of sin; Paul pronounces the world subject to "corruption" (Rom. 8:21). The universe is in a process of decay and deterioration, and it appears to be running down.*

Redemptive Anticipation in the Old Testament

Immediately after the fall, God spoke to the serpent and pronounced the first prophecy of the Bible. In Genesis 3:15, God, the first prophet, proclaimed:

> And I will put enmity
> Between you and the woman,
> And between your seed and her seed;

44. Note that labor is not a curse resulting from the fall. In the biblical worldview, God institutes labor before the fall as a means by which we fulfill God's call (vocation) and glorify God. Through work, mankind imitates God's work in creating; as a result of the curse after the fall, labor becomes more difficult (cf. Rom. 8:18–22).

45. Perhaps the most graphic being "The heavens over your head shall be bronze, and the earth under you shall be iron. The Lord will make the rain of your land powder. From heaven dust shall come down on you until you are destroyed" (Deut. 28:23–24).

He shall bruise you on the head,
And you shall bruise him on the heel.

The passage begins with the statement, "And I will put enmity . . ." The Hebrew term for "enmity" signifies hostile intent that escalates to the degree of murder (see Ezek. 25:15; 35:5). God as the speaker establishes a new order of animosity.

The first conflict will be between "you" (i.e., the serpent) and "the woman" (i.e., Eve). This has already begun to happen at the start of Genesis 3, in the dialogue between the serpent and the woman that helped to bring about the fall. The second stage of the conflict is between "your seed" and "her seed." The Hebrew word for "seed" is commonly used of posterity or lineage. Thus, the ones who proceed from the serpent and the ones who proceed from the woman will be at odds. It is crucial to understand that these words refer not to a physical lineage but to a spiritual descent. There is no evidence that the serpent (or the devil) could produce physical heirs. This is a spiritual descent where one can be of the devil by will, heart, and intent. In John 8:44, Jesus says to the Pharisees, "You are of your father the devil."

This conflict between the two seeds finds immediate fulfillment in the murder of Abel by his brother Cain. Cain was "of the evil one" (1 John 3:12) and Abel was "righteous" (Heb. 11:4). This theme of conflict continues through the Scriptures to the very end of time, as related in the book of Revelation (see Rev. 12:13–17).

This ages-long conflict will reach its climax in a confrontation between two individuals, that is, "you" (i.e., the serpent) and "he." In this last clause, the "he" is mentioned before the "you." It demonstrates the primacy and preeminence of the "he." This is the great battle, and the "he" will be victorious.[46] That is clear from the locations of the battle wounds: the blow to the serpent is to the head—a mortal wound. The "he" will be struck on the heel—not a fatal blow.

Genesis 3:15 is messianic. Immediately after the fall, in the curse on the serpent, God provides a prophecy that he will send a redeemer to crush the enemy. No one has ever lived in a time in which this promise did not exist. The identity of the said descendant is clear: Jesus Christ is the "he" of Genesis 3:15. The New Testament genealogies, such as Luke 3, pointedly trace Jesus' ancestry back to Adam and Eve—Jesus is in the direct lineage of the woman. Luke further confirms Jesus as fulfilling the prophecy in Genesis by following the genealogy with the Spirit's leading Jesus into battle

> This ages-long conflict will reach its climax in a confrontation between two individuals, that is, "you" (i.e., the serpent) and "he." In this last clause, the "he" is mentioned before the "you." It demonstrates the primacy and preeminence of the "he." This is the great battle, and the "he" will be victorious.

---

46. Interpreters commonly argue that "he" refers to the "seed" of the earlier part of the verse. See, for instance, C. Westermann, *Genesis* (Neukirchen-Vluyn: Newkirchener Verlag des Erziehungsvereins, 1966), 355. Recent studies, however, have shown that Genesis 3:15 exhibits the pattern found when "he" refers to an individual and not to humanity in general. See J. Collins, "A Syntactical Note (Genesis 3:15): Is the Woman's Seed Singular or Plural?" *TB* 48 (1997): 139–48.

with Satan in the wilderness. This begins a raging war that finds its climax at the cross where the Messiah lands a mortal blow on the serpent.

Scripture from Genesis 3 to Revelation 22 narrates the unfolding of the prophecy of Genesis 3:15. Redemption is promised in this one verse, and the Bible traces that redemptive theme to its end. Redemption, a payment of a ransom, appears in the Old Testament as both individual and corporate. In the Mosaic legislation, Yahweh provided a means of redemption by which offending individuals and Israel collectively offered animal sacrifices as substitutes—the innocent for the guilty—to make atonement for sin. Atonement was necessary to take away the guilt of sin (Lev. 16). On the level of everyday life, redemption also played a fundamental role politically and economically. Israel's enslavement in Egypt and later deportation into Babylon is portrayed in spiritual terms as a consequence of sin. Thus Israel's deliverance from Egyptian slavery (Ex. 6:6; 15:13) serves as the prototype of corporate redemption in the biblical worldview; and the later release of captives from Babylon reaffirms redemption as God's gracious saving activity (Isa. 40:1–5; 44:21–28). Economically, a person who lost his inheritance or who sold himself into servitude could be redeemed if a close relative paid the appropriate price of redemption (Lev. 25:25–27). The primary image of redemption presented Yahweh as a loving God who redeems life, including the forgiveness of sins, restoration of harmony, and reconciliation between God and his children and within the covenant community (Ps. 111:9; 130:7–8). Additionally, the Old Testament has various other forms of redemptive anticipation but none as important as the prophets.[47]

Cain and Abel, attributed to Vouet and to Pietro Novelli

My Servants the Prophets

The prophets of the Old Testament further anticipated this future redemption by the work of the Messiah. They proclaimed that one day God would redeem his people and restore them to a right relationship with himself. Much of the language of these prophecies centered on a renewal of the covenant between God and his people. For example, the prophet Ezekiel declared: "And I [God] will make a covenant of peace with them; it will be an everlasting covenant with them. And I will place them and multiply them, and will set My sanctuary in their midst forever. My dwelling place also will be with them; and I will be their God, and they will be My people" (Ezek. 37:26–27). The prophet Jeremiah provides another description of mankind's future deliverance:

> "Behold, days are coming," declares the LORD, "when I will make a new covenant with the house of Israel and with the house of Judah, not like the covenant which I made with their fathers in the day I took them by the hand to bring them out of the land of Egypt, My covenant which they broke, although I was a husband to them," declares the LORD. "But this is the covenant which I will make with the

Scripture from Genesis 3 to Revelation 22 narrates the unfolding of the prophecy of Genesis 3:15. Redemption is promised in this one verse, and the Bible traces that redemptive theme to its end. Redemption, a payment of a ransom, appears in the Old Testament as both individual and corporate.

---

47. For a study of each particular form of messianism in the Old Testament, see W. Kaiser, *The Messiah in the Old Testament* (Grand Rapids: Zondervan, 1995).

house of Israel after those days," declares the LORD, "I will put My law within them, and on their heart I will write it; and I will be their God, and they shall be My people." (Jer. 31:31–33)

The Messiah in the Old Testament is pictured as bringing about this redemption or restoration in two principal ways. First, he will come as the conquering king who will destroy the enemies of God and deliver his people (Ps. 2). But he also is portrayed as the Suffering Servant who will bear the pains and sufferings of his people and so deliver them through his own sacrifice (Isa. 53).

In addition to atonement for personal sin, the Old Testament anticipated redemption on a broader scale. A cosmic fall requires a cosmic redeemer. And the Old Testament prophets announce that the entire creation will share in the redemptive work of God. The universe that is now twisted, broken, and subject to futility will one day be restored to harmony. Redemption extended to the very cosmos itself. Prophets foresaw a renewed order in which the cosmic curses were reversed: abundant harvests result in sowers overtaking reapers (Amos 9:13), a new heavens and new earth bring joy instead of weeping and suffering, labor no longer is marked by vanity, and creatures live in peace instead of struggling for survival (Isa. 11:6–9; 65:17–25). D. Martyn Lloyd-Jones comments:

> It is only then that creation will really be free to develop as it was meant to do, as God created it to do. It is only then that it will be entirely delivered from every element of disintegration. We saw that, at the present time, it is "subject to vanity," that there is a kind of futility about it, that there is this element of decay and putrefaction in it. Then, it will be free from everything of that nature. There will be no more strife, no more discord, no more disease.[48]

Eschatological passages such as Isaiah 11:6–9 and 65:17–25 confirm that the Hebrews possessed a full-orbed worldview, one that anticipated redemption not just of mankind but also of the cosmos, which also suffered the effects of the fall. Although these expectations were not realized in Israel's history, they held out hope of future fulfillment, and worldview heirs of Old Testament thought expanded on them in the New Testament and the life of the Christian church.[49]

History

As is clear from our discussion thus far, the Hebrews held to a linear history. They believed there was a beginning to time and creation (cosmogony) and a movement to a consummation (eschatology). And the Hebrews believed that this history unfolded according to the plan of God,

> *The Messiah . . . is pictured as bringing about this redemption or restoration in two principal ways . . . as the conquering king who will destroy the enemies of God and deliver his people . . . [and] as the Suffering Servant who will bear the pains and sufferings of his people and so deliver them through his own sacrifice.*

48. D. Martyn Lloyd-Jones, *Romans: An Exposition of Chapter 8:17–39* (Grand Rapids: Zondervan, 1975), 76.

49. Cf. Wolters, *Creation Regained*.

the Lord of history. Scholars have traditionally distinguished the Hebraic view of history from those of their contemporaries—the Egyptians, Mesopotamians, and Canaanites. Many have understood the latter groups' perception of the universe as locked in an unending cycle of nature, heading nowhere—a repetition of birth, life, death, and rebirth. Thus, many authors believe that linear history is one of the great gifts or treasures that the Hebrews have given to the world.[50]

In reality, the issue is not as simple as supposed. Although the Egyptians, for example, did see the unending cycle working throughout existence, they were not ahistorical or nonhistorical. In fact, they were quite aware of history, and they kept voluminous records and documents that prove it. The Babylonians and Assyrians, as well, were masters of keeping annals and historical documents.[51] It is not as if they were unaware of the movement of history from one era to another.

The contrast between the two conceptions of history focuses on the basis and foundation of history. To the Hebrews, again due to the centrality of theology in their worldview, history is "his-story." Everything in the universe occurs according to the plan of God, the Lord of history. He created the universe, he determines what happens in it, and God moves history toward a final climax. The pagan cultures had no such beliefs. And, therefore, though both espoused forms of linear history, their underlying worldviews conflicted radically. And, as we shall see, the Hebrew conception of linear history has powerfully influenced the way that people have thought throughout the centuries.

Israel's Place in Redemptive History

One of the major events of Old Testament history is God calling a people as his own, creating a nation out of them, and establishing them in the land of promise. The Hebrews were the chosen people: "For you are a holy people to the LORD your God; the LORD your God has chosen you to be a people for His own possession out of all the peoples who are on the face of the earth" (Deut. 7:6). Israelite notions of a chosen people and a Promised Land, correctly understood, reveal a theological focus, rather than an ethnocentric emphasis (as frequently maintained), as we have consistently argued throughout this chapter. Israel's God, not Israel ethnically or geographically, formed the primary belief. True, Israelite sinfulness frequently manifested itself in racial terms and led to anthropocentric pride. But their claims of being chosen and given a land was premised on God's gracious gift, not any inherent superiority. And their status of being

One of the major events of Old Testament history is God calling a people as his own, creating a nation out of them, and establishing them in the land of promise . . . . Israelite notions of a chosen people and a Promised Land, correctly understood, reveal a theological focus, rather than an ethnocentric emphasis.

---

50. For a popular presentation of this view, see T. Cahill, *The Gifts of the Jews: How A Tribe of Desert Nomads Changed the Way Everyone Thinks and Feels* (New York: Anchor, 1999).

51. See J. Pritchard, *Ancient Near Eastern Texts Relating to the Old Testament* (Princeton, ,NJ: Princeton University Press, 1955).

chosen and granted a land implied enormous responsibilities to manifest moral integrity and God-centered qualities in their national life.[52]

The relationship between God and Israel is configured according to a covenant, which may be defined as "a bond in blood sovereignly administered."[53] It is a binding contract between God and man, one that God has initiated and administered. This pact involves promises on God's part and obligations on mankind's part. The extent of the covenant embraces the very extremes of life and death. At the heart of the covenant is the *Immanuel principle*, that is, Yahweh's recurring statement, "I will be their God, and they will be my people" (Jer. 24:7; 30:22; 31:33; 32:38). Covenant served as a primary element that integrated the various aspects of the Hebrew world-and-life view. It served as the archetypal interpretive device not only for the divine-human relationship in general but also for the special relationship between Yahweh and Israel. Covenant even provided the framework for the constancy of day and night in the orderly functioning of the cosmos (Jer. 33:20, 21). Yahweh's claim to be Israel's God relates the two parties together. God binds himself to his people, bestowing blessing in the form of faithfulness, lovingkindness, and covenant love (Deut. 7:6–11; Ps. 103:4; Isa. 63:7; Jer. 9:24; Hos. 2:19). And the people devote themselves wholeheartedly to God, owing absolute obedience to Yahweh and his commandments (Ex. 19:5–6; Deut. 13:4).

Why did God choose a particular people, one so seemingly insignificant, to enter into covenant with? The Old Testament answer is that God chose Israel not for its significance measured by size but merely to demonstrate to the world God's covenant love in fulfilling promises made to patriarchs who preceded (Deut. 7:6–11). The apostle Paul addressed this issue when he said the Jews "were entrusted with the oracles of God" (Rom. 3:2). When Moses gave the law of God to Israel, he said to them, "What great nation is there that has statutes and judgments as righteous as this whole law which I am setting before you today?" (Deut. 4:8). In a sense, Israel was to be prophetic, that is, bringing the word of God to the world.

At Mount Sinai, when God gave the Torah (including the Ten Commandments) to the Israelites, he said to them, "Now then, if you will indeed obey My voice and keep My covenant, then you shall be My own possession among all the peoples, for all the earth is mine; and you shall be to Me a kingdom of priests and a holy nation" (Ex. 19:5–6). The Hebrews were chosen by God to fulfill an exalted spiritual task: they were to be a priestly people. As a nation, they were to be mediators between God and the other nations—a priesthood. They were to be priestly ambassadors of Yahweh!

Additionally, according to their call at Sinai, Israel was to be a "holy nation." The Hebrew term for "holy" literally means "set apart/distinct/

> *The relationship between God and Israel is configured according to a covenant . . . [which] embraces the very extremes of life and death. At the heart of the covenant is the **Immanuel principle**, that is, Yahweh's recurring statement, "I will be their God, and they will be my people."*

---

52. The prevailing theme of Old Testament prophets focused on Israel's repeated refusal to manifest holiness and righteousness in the context of its pagan neighbors. Cf. Alex Motyer, *The Message of Amos* (Downers Grove, IL: InterVarsity Press, 1974).

53. O. P. Robertson, *The Christ of the Covenants* (Phillipsburg, NJ: P&R Publishing, 1981), 4.

unique," an elective term, signifying that Israel had been chosen and set apart by Yahweh into a covenant relationship with him. No other nation or kingdom on earth could make that claim.

Parts of Exodus and the entire book of Deuteronomy contain the primary elements of the covenantal relationship between Yahweh and Israel. Leviticus 19 presents an encapsulated view of the covenant. It presents concrete elements of the Hebrew worldview and defines how "holiness" appears in everyday life. It begins with the affirmation that Hebrew life should manifest holiness—Israelites should be separate, distinct, set apart in their lives—because God is holy (v. 2). The remainder of the chapter commands and forbids specific behavior in keeping with that holiness. Some of the commands deal with what might be identified traditionally as "religious" activity: Sabbath-keeping (vv. 3, 30), rejection of idolatry (v. 4), offering sacrifices in an appropriate manner (vv. 5–8), refraining from misusing God's name (v. 12), and avoiding magical practices such as wizardry and consulting mediums (v. 31). These statutes govern the cultic life of Israel. They set Hebrew worship apart from practices associated with their pagan neighbors and protect the holiness of God. To engage in what God forbids and to refuse to do what God commands breaks the bond of the covenant. On the other hand, faithful obedience continues the personal relationship between God and his covenant people.

Mt. Sinai

The remaining statutes in Leviticus cover the wide diversity of activities that constitute Hebrew culture. Holiness in marriage and family requires honoring parents (v. 3), preventing daughters from becoming prostitutes (v. 29), and paying special homage to the elderly (v. 32). Covenant faithfulness makes demands on farming practice, specifically harvesting. In verses 9 and 10, Hebrews could not strip their fields of grain or vineyards of grapes while gleaning; they must leave portions "for the needy and for the stranger." Restrictions about harvesting in verses 23–25 guaranteed the growth and maturity of fruit trees when they reached the Promised Land. Other stipulations assured the rights of private property by general commands not to steal, oppress, or deal falsely with one's neighbor (vv. 11, 13). Holiness in specific terms requires people to pay wages promptly (v. 13). Not only did holiness provide in some measure for the poor by the gleaning laws, verse 14 protects those weakened by blindness and deafness from acts that would take advantage of people's handicaps, and verses 33 and 34 prohibit mistreatment of strangers and visitors. In judicial matters, those responsible for administering justice must not defer to either the rich or the poor but issue their judgments impartially (v. 15). Laws also covered Hebrew economic life. According to verses 35–37, measurements of length, weight, and quantity and use of proper balances must ensure that people receive what they pay for in the marketplace (vv. 35–36). Interestingly, laws also reached beyond overt actions by probing motivation; Hebrews must not harbor hatred in their hearts or bear grudges. Instead, they are to love

The Hebrew term for "holy" literally means "set apart/distinct/unique," an elective term, signifying that Israel had been chosen and set apart by Yahweh into a covenant relationship with him. No other nation or kingdom on earth could make that claim.

their neighbors as themselves (vv. 17–18). Finally, detailed laws covering such diverse elements as breeding cattle, sowing fields, and cloth used in garments (v. 19), eating meat with blood, the cut of one's hair, and the use of tattoos (vv. 26–28) indicate various ways in which Hebrew life was set apart and distinguished from pagan culture.

Hebraic holiness laws, therefore, penetrated every aspect of life. Holiness did not consist of a separate part of life—private and "religious" in nature—but so pervaded all cultural activity that one must conclude that all of life is religious, not just certain narrowly defined cultic activities. The comprehensive notion of religion distinguishes the Hebrew world-and-life view. Covenantal demands reached into daily labor, legal matters, and economic transactions, thus ensuring that God's sovereignty did not remain an abstraction but made concrete demands over the widest possible horizon. Yahweh's sovereignty extended from his transcendent control of the cosmos to an immanent reign—a moral rule reaching down into everyday affairs that made the Hebrews accountable to God for their actions.[54]

As a kingdom of priests and prophets, the Israelites were called to be a light to the nations (Isa. 42:6). They were to testify to the truths of Yahweh, that he is the Lord of history and of all things. A wonderful example of this witness occurs in Exodus 18 where Moses recounts to his father-in-law Jethro all that "the LORD had done to Pharaoh and to the Egyptians for Israel's sake, all the hardship that had befallen them on the journey, and how the LORD had delivered them" (v. 8). After hearing this message of redemption, Jethro responds by saying, "Blessed be the LORD who delivered you from the hand of the Egyptians and from the hand of Pharaoh, and who delivered the people from under the hand of the Egyptians. Now I know that the LORD is greater than all the gods" (vv. 10–11). This incident perhaps reflects the conversion of Jethro to follow Yahweh.

Central to the witness of Israel was to be the advent of the Messiah. Israel's primary purpose was to pave the way for the coming Redeemer, the final and ultimate Deliverer. This occurs in the Old Testament in two principal ways. (1) *Direct verbal prophecy* is a foretelling of future events, such as the arrival of the Messiah, merely and directly through words. So, for example, Zechariah prophesies that the Messiah will be "humble, and mounted on a donkey, even on a colt, the foal of a donkey" (Zech. 9:9). This predicts the triumphal entry of Christ into Jerusalem (see Matt. 21:1–11). (2) *Typology* may be defined as "a preordained representative relationship which certain persons, events and institutions bear to corresponding per-

> *Hebraic holiness laws, therefore, penetrated every aspect of life. Holiness did not consist of a separate part of life—private and "religious" in nature—but so pervaded all cultural activity that one must conclude that all of life is religious, not just certain narrowly defined cultic activities.*

---

54. Two works by Christopher J. H. Wright explore the cultural and moral aspects of the Hebraic worldview: *An Eye for an Eye: The Place of Old Testament Ethics Today* (Downers Grove, IL: InterVarsity Press, 1983) and *God's People in God's Land: Family, Land and Property in the Old Testament* (Grand Rapids: Eerdmans, 1990). Both probe worldview implications for Old Testament individual and social ethics.

sons, events, and institutions occurring at a later time in salvation history."[55] In other words, New Testament writers often see in certain Old Testament persons, events, and institutions prefigurations of New Covenant truths. Thus Jonah's three-day ordeal inside the fish and his miraculous deliverance foreshadow the death and resurrection of Christ (see Matt. 12:39–41). The event of the exodus from Egypt in which God redeems Israel from bondage by a blood sacrifice prefigures Christ's atoning work for his people (see 1 Cor. 5:7).[56]

The reality is that both "direct verbal prophecy and typology are prophetic, but they convey prophecy by different means. The former foretells future events directly through words, but the latter foretells future events indirectly through history. Thus they differ in form, not substance."[57] Regarding messianic predictions in the Old Testament, both of these methods play a significant role in God's revelation. The messianic message is the heart of the Old Testament.

The reality is that both "direct verbal prophecy and typology are prophetic, but they convey prophecy by different means. The former foretells future events directly through words, but the latter foretells future events indirectly through history."

Conclusion

After this brief analysis of Hebrew thought, we are ready to answer the question that Voltaire raised at the beginning of this chapter. The question was "What was the philosophy of the Hebrews?" Voltaire responded by saying that they had none; we vehemently disagree. Not only did the Hebrews have a well-defined and well-thought-out world-and-life view, but one that has had great impact on subsequent history and, in particular, on the history of the Western world. Although not exhaustive, the effects of Hebrew thinking on the West may be summarized according to the following points:

1. The Hebrew view of God has had a profound impact on theology in the West. In particular, the concept of monotheism, as the Hebrews presented it, has been a foundational one. In addition, the idea that there is a God who speaks and reveals himself to humanity derives directly from the Hebrews.

2. Much of modern anthropology in the West teaches that mankind has been created with dignity and inalienable rights. Again, this belief stems directly from Hebrew thought in which mankind was created in the image of God. That is so unlike the pagan peoples of antiquity, many of whom held that the gods created humanity to do the labor of the gods. Mankind in the Bible was created to be God's royal steward over the creation and to glorify God through stewardship.

---

55. H. A. Virkler, *Hermeneutics: Principles and Processes of Biblical Interpretation* (Grand Rapids: Baker, 1981), 184.

56. Much of this material is taken from J. Currid, "Recognition and Use of Typology in Preaching," *RTR* 53 (1994): 115–29.

57. Currid, *Genesis*, 54.

3. Humanity in the *imago Dei* determines how the Hebrew was to live: he was to act, in all areas of life, by *imitatio Dei*. This principle is summarized in Leviticus 19:1–2: "Then the LORD spoke to Moses, saying, 'Speak to all the congregation of the sons of Israel and say to them, "You shall be holy, for I the LORD your God am holy." ' " For the Hebrews, this principle applied to all areas of existence: the food they ate, the clothes they wore, how they worshiped, and even how they practiced such things as agriculture were to be done *imitatio Dei*.

Indeed, all spheres of life are affected by this principle, areas such as government, economics, family, and the judicial setting. But how do the Hebrews know how to act in these various spheres? The written revelation of the Word of God was given to them: Scripture reveals God's nature and his purposes for his people. For example, in the area of economics, the Hebrews were commanded by God to have "righteous" weights/scales (Deut. 25:15). But how do the Hebrews know what are "righteous" weights? The answer is that God himself is righteous (Ps. 7:11; Dan. 9:14) and his ways are righteous, and these are revealed to his people through his word. Hebrew ethics are thus rooted in the very being and character of God.

The New Testament believer stands on the same principle: the *imitatio Dei*, but now in the person of the Son of God, Jesus Christ. Jesus is the true image of God (2 Cor. 4:4; Col. 1:15–16), and humanity is called to live according to that image. This is done only by one being "in Christ" (Eph. 1:1, 3, 5, 7) and increasingly becoming like him. The theological term for this process is sanctification; that is, the Holy Spirit develops godliness and Christlikeness in a believer. It is a simple fact: Christians are to live in this world in such a way that they reflect the character and person of Jesus Christ.

> *The New Testament believer stands on the same principle: the **imitatio Dei**, but now in the person of the Son of God, Jesus Christ. Jesus is the true image of God (2 Cor. 4:4; Col. 1:15–16), and humanity is called to live according to that image.*

And this principle transforms every area of life, from vocation to vacation. As the apostle Paul says: "Whether, then, you eat or drink or whatever you do, do all to the glory of God" (1 Cor. 10:31). And again he states: "And whatever you do in word or deed, do all in the name of the Lord Jesus, giving thanks through Him to God the Father" (Col. 3:17). All of life, every sphere of existence, is to be redeemed and brought under the lordship of Jesus Christ.

4. The relationship between God and man is intimate and personal. That is never the case in pagan religion of antiquity. The gods in them are removed, and they have as little contact with humanity as possible. The Hebrews were tied to their God by covenant, a use of covenant unknown elsewhere in the ancient Near East. In the modern day, the individual's close relationship to the Creator is accentuated almost to the unfortunate degree of invalidating the communal aspect of the relationship.

5. The type of linear history that the Hebrews first taught is the form in which history has been understood in the West. It is not, as Henry Ford was once purported to say, "one damn thing after another." History is not

a matter of mere chance. Rather, it has a beginning, it is moving toward an end, and it is being driven and guided by the hand of God.

6. English common law was clearly founded on the biblical laws given to the Hebrews. For example, if a person owns an animal with a history of violence, and if that animal harms someone, the act is considered a felony. The owner is guilty of criminal negligence. This law reflects the laws of the ox found in Exodus 21:29–36.

7. Messianism, that is, the expectation and anticipation of a coming savior and king who would deliver his people, has always been a central hope of many in the West. This hope of a glorious future ushered in by the Messiah is a primary Old Testament message, and it is found in no other culture of the ancient Near East.

As is clear from this discussion, the Hebrew world-and-life view is distinct from pagan religions and cultures that surrounded the Hebrews. And it was Hebrew thought that had such a profound impact on later centuries of history. I ask again, what influence has there been from the philosophy of Babylon?

English common law was clearly founded on the biblical laws given to the Hebrews. For example, if a person owns an animal with a history of violence, and if that animal harms someone, the act is considered a felony. The owner is guilty of criminal negligence. This law reflects the laws of the ox found in Exodus 21:29–36.

For Further Reading

Alexander, T. D. *From Paradise to the Promised Land*. Grand Rapids: Baker, 2002.

Baker, D. W., and B. Arnold, eds. *The Face of Old Testament Studies: A Survey of Contemporary Approaches*. Grand Rapids: Baker, 1999.

Block, D., and A. Millard. *The Gods of the Nations*. Grand Rapids: Baker, 2001.

Currid, J. *Ancient Egypt and the Old Testament*. Grand Rapids: Baker, 1997.

Hess, R., and D. T. Tsumura, eds. *"I Studied Inscriptions Before the Flood": Ancient Near Eastern, Literary, and Linguistic Approaches to Genesis 1–11*. Winona Lake, IN: Eisenbrauns, 1994.

Kaiser, W. C. *A History of Israel: From the Bronze Age through the Jewish Wars*. Nashville: Broadman and Holman, 1998.

———. *The Messiah in the Old Testament*. Grand Rapids: Zondervan, 1995.

Kitchen, K. A. *On the Reliability of the Old Testament*. Grand Rapids: Eerdmans, 2003.

Long, V. P., D. W. Baker, and G. J. Wenham, eds. *Windows Into Old Testament History: Evidence, Argument, and the Crisis of Biblical Israel*. Grand Rapids: Eerdmans, 2002.

Millard, A., J. Hoffmeier, and D. W. Baker, eds. *Faith, Tradition, and History: Old Testament Historiography in Its Near Eastern Context*. Winona Lake, IN: Eisenbrauns, 1994.

For Further Discussion

1. Why would anyone conclude that the Old Testament is guilty of "crass plagiarism" in its relationship to ancient Near Eastern literature? How would you respond to that claim?

2. How would you demonstrate to a non-Christian that the Old Testament is truly God's word, that is, it is his revelation of himself and his plan to humanity?

3. How do the names for God in the Old Testament help us to understand his character?

4. Define what you think is the purpose(s) of the Hebrew creation account?

5. How are we to put into effect the cultural mandate today?

6. According to the Old Testament, what is the means of redemption? How is one saved from sin?

7. How do you define history?

8. How has the Hebrew world-and-life view affected beliefs and thoughts in the Western world?

┌─────┐
│ 3 │
└─────┘

New Testament Worldview

Vern Sheridan Poythress

What worldview does the New Testament present? The documents of the New Testament derive from a number of different human authors, who write with a variety of circumstances in view. They show diversities in theme and emphasis such as we might expect. However, they also show harmony at a deep level, not only because they all come from the first century church but also because they share a common divine authorship. God the Father caused the documents to be written as his own Word. For this purpose, he raised up men whom he providentially shaped (cf. Acts 1:17–26; Gal. 1:15). They were commissioned with the authority of Jesus Christ (Mark 3:14–15; Acts 1:8), and like the Old Testament prophets, in their teaching and writing "they were carried along by the Holy Spirit" (2 Peter 1:21).

The common origin from the Holy Spirit implies a commonality of thought in the product. We can examine the worldview implied by one document by itself, but we also can examine them all together.

> *The common origin from the Holy Spirit implies a commonality of thought in the product. We can examine the worldview implied by one document by itself, but we also can examine them all together.*

Authority

What motivates people to pay attention to these documents? For us[1] who are Christians, discipleship to Christ motivates us. At the heart of the New Testament stands the gospel, the message of salvation through Jesus Christ. Salvation comes through faith in Jesus Christ. It is the gift of God. However, it is accompanied by discipleship. Being a disciple or "slave" of

---

1. I shall regularly use the first person plural ("we," "us") as the New Testament letters often do, to indicate how we who are followers of Christ ought to receive the New Testament's instruction.

Christ (Rom. 1:1 ESV marginal note; 1 Cor. 7:22) involves acknowledging his comprehensive lordship.

Acknowledging Christ as Lord implies believing his instruction and obeying his commands. Confession of lordship becomes meaningless if we choose what we will believe and what we will obey. If *we* choose, we are, in the end, only obeying our own will. By contrast, discipleship implies having a clear word from the Lord, a word other than what we invent for ourselves.

Christ endorses the authority of the Old Testament (e.g., Matt. 5:17–20; Luke 24:25–27, 44–49; John 10:35). Receiving the Old Testament as the Word of God is therefore one aspect of discipleship, and it has implications for a worldview. The New Testament endorses the Old Testament and its worldview, on which it builds. The Old Testament in turn contains a concept of covenantal words of God centrally deposited (Deut. 31:9–13), to which later words by divine messengers may be added (Deut. 18:15–22). In the New Testament, Jesus' commission to the apostles, giving them his authority, anticipates the formation of the New Testament canon.

To that canon we now turn as disciples of Christ, if we are to hear a word from him that we must obey. The New Testament thus enjoys an authority on the level of the Old Testament. Both the Old Testament and the New Testament give us the Word of God himself. But, in fact, in one respect the New Testament has a functional priority, since it interprets the earlier words from God and gives us words addressed to our phase in the history of redemption, in contrast with earlier phases that now have passed away. For example, the laws concerning animal sacrifice (Lev. 1–7) still offer instruction to Christians, but the sacrifices themselves have been made obsolete through the accomplishment of Christ's self-sacrifice.

In sum, through the Old Testament and New Testament together, in their historical relation, God speaks to us, meets us, and gives to us reliable instruction.[2] We find not merely interesting ideas but authoritative knowledge of God and his ways. This knowledge furnishes, among other things, the basis for a worldview.

In crucial ways, the worldview offered by the New Testament is not new but builds on that found in the Old Testament. The Old Testament also heavily influenced the great majority of first-century Jews, who regarded the Old Testament as God's Word. We begin by noting some of these important commonalities.

> *Acknowledging Christ as Lord implies believing his instruction and obeying his commands. Confession of lordship becomes meaningless if we choose what we will believe and what we will obey. If we choose, we are, in the end, only obeying our own will.*

---

2. See the excellent discussions in D. A. Carson and John Woodbridge, eds., *Scripture and Truth* (Grand Rapids: Zondervan, 1983); John Woodbridge, *Biblical Authority: A Critique of the Rogers/McKim Proposal* (Grand Rapids: Zondervan, 1982); D. A. Carson and John Woodbridge, eds., *Hermeneutics, Authority, and Canon* (Grand Rapids: Zondervan, 1986); Benjamin B. Warfield, *The Inspiration and Authority of the Bible* (Philadelphia: Presbyterian and Reformed, 1948).

Part I: Aspects of Worldview Shared with the Old Testament and Intertestamental Judaism

God

At the center of this worldview lies one's view of God. There is only one God, who created all things and who governs and sustains them by his power. Both New Testament and Old Testament contrast radically with the polytheism that dominated the surrounding cultures.[3]

In becoming disciples of Christ, both Gentiles and Jews submit to Christ's revelation of the Father as "the only true God" (John 17:3). They also accept Christ's claim to be the only Son and the exclusive revealer of the Father (Matt. 11:25–27). They accept Christ's teaching about the authority of the Old Testament. Therefore, they owe absolute and exclusive obedience to the "jealous" God of the Old Testament.

What are the implications? They refrain from the idolatry of the Roman Empire, offering worship to none except the true God. Recognizing that the entire world has been created, they do not invest created things with spiritual power. They make a clear distinction between the Creator and the creature.

God's speech. The disciple who submits to Christ's word continues a pattern already found in the Old Testament. The Old Testament calls for absolute submission to God as Lord. And the God of the Old and New Testaments is a God who speaks. He transcends the world in his authority and power. Simultaneously, he is immanent in the world, both through deeds of power and through words. In fulfillment of his plan, his words take specific, permanent embodiment in written form in the Scriptures. The biblical religion differs from the surrounding paganism by repudiating competing sources of supernatural knowledge, such as oracles from gods, divination, and soothsaying (Deut. 18:9–18; Acts 16:16–18).[4]

God's sovereignty over creation. God rules over all things and controls all things for his own wise purposes (Job 1:21; Lam. 3:37–38; 42:2; Eph. 1:11). Since Jews in New Testament times recognized God's sovereignty, the New Testament typically contains reminders rather than arguments to support it (Matt. 6:25–34; Luke 12:22–34). However, it becomes an explicit topic when Paul preaches to pagans (Acts 14:15–17; 17:24–29). Created things are distinct from the Creator. They are not to be worshiped (Rom.

Ephesian Artemis

> *The biblical religion differs from the surrounding paganism by repudiating competing sources of supernatural knowledge, such as oracles from gods, divination, and soothsaying (Deut. 18:9–18; Acts 16:16–18).*

3. See the excellent discussion in Donald Guthrie, *New Testament Theology* (Downers Grove, IL: InterVarsity, 1981).

4. John M. Frame, "God and Biblical Language: Transcendence and Immanence," in *God's Inerrant Word*, ed. John Warwick Montgomery (Minneapolis: Bethany Fellowship, 1974), 159–77; John M. Frame, "Scripture Speaks for Itself," in *God's Inerrant Word*, ed. John Warwick Montgomery (Minneapolis: Bethany Fellowship, 1974), 178–200; Guthrie, *New Testament Theology*, 953–82.

1:20–23) but display clearly the nature of God who created and sustains them (Rom. 1:19–20).[5]

Humanity

The New Testament also agrees with the Old Testament in its basic assumptions about humanity. God created human beings in his image (1 Cor. 11:7; James 3:9). They have a status superior to animals, although in being made from "dust from the ground" (Gen. 2:7) and in their reproductive capacity, they share some affinities with animals. Under God's direction, human beings exercise dominion over the animals and the whole of the lower creation (Gen. 1:28–29; 9:1–3). Human beings are morally responsible to God, and this includes individual and corporate social dimensions. The fall of Adam plunged the entire human race into bondage to sin (Rom. 5:12–21).[6]

Redemption

However, sin, death, and curse do not have the final word, because God promises redemption, beginning right after the fall (Gen. 3:15). God's words and deeds of redemption work out progressively in the time of the Old Testament. The promise to Adam and Eve in Genesis 3:15, the call of Abraham, the redemption from Egypt, the raising up of the Davidic kingship, and other acts of God all look forward to a great, climactic redemption that is still to come.[7]

Part II: Transformations in the New Testament

*What the proph-
ets hoped for has
arrived (Luke 4:21;
10:24; 24:25–27,
44–49) as the "down
payment" (Eph. 1:14
ESV marginal note)
or first installment of
what is yet to come
in the new heavens
and the new earth
(Rev. 21:1–22:5).*

The New Testament unfolds the story of the climactic redemption that takes place in the person and work of Christ the Lord. It presupposes not only the truthfulness and reliability of the Old Testament but its sense of direction; that is, it looks forward to what God will do in the future. This "forward longing" of the Old Testament now has come to realization. What the prophets hoped for has arrived (Luke 4:21; 10:24; 24:25–27, 44–49) as the "down payment" (Eph. 1:14 ESV marginal note) or first installment of what is yet to come in the new heavens and the new earth (Rev. 21:1–22:5).

The New Testament differs fundamentally from the Old Testament because it announces that Christ now has come. Because of his coming, our position in time within the total scheme of God's purposes has fundamentally advanced. As Hebrews puts it,

---

5. Guthrie, *New Testament Theology*, 75–115.
6. Ibid., 116–218.
7. See the excellent discussions in Geerhardus Vos, *Biblical Theology: Old and New Testaments* (Grand Rapids: Eerdmans, 1948); Edmund P. Clowney, *The Unfolding Mystery: Discovering Christ in the Old Testament* (Colorado Springs, CO: Navpress, 1988).

> Long ago, at many times and in many ways, God spoke to our fathers by the prophets, but in these last days he has spoken to us by his Son, whom he appointed the heir of all things, through whom also he created the world. (Heb. 1:1–2)

The coming of Christ has advanced the content of God's revelation, not only because the New Testament adds to revelation ("he has spoken to us by his Son") but also because that revelation is climactic and final. The Son is superior to the prophets (Luke 10:24; 11:31–32; 20:9–18) and reveals God in a way that is final and permanent ("He is the radiance of the glory of God and the exact imprint of his nature, and he upholds the universe by the word of his power," Heb. 1:3).

Advance also takes place in the deeds that accomplish redemption. "He has delivered us from the domain of darkness and transferred us to the kingdom of his beloved Son, in whom we have redemption, the forgiveness of sins" (Col. 1:13–14). Jeremiah 31:31–34 looked forward to a new covenant in which God would write his law on the hearts of his people, but that fundamentally new transformation of the heart did not happen until the Spirit was poured out on the day of Pentecost. Zechariah looked forward to a time when God would "remove the iniquity of this land in a single day" (Zech. 3:9), but the removal happened only when Christ was crucified. Through the life, death, and resurrection of Christ, God accomplished the work of salvation, and it is important to realize that it was *not* accomplished before that. There is a permanent before and after to history, with the crucifixion and resurrection of Christ in the very middle.[8]

Although the Old Testament predicted the coming of Christ and his redemptive work…, the exact manner and the total meaning of his coming remained mysterious…. First-century Jews primarily expected a political deliverer and warrior.

Newness

Although the Old Testament predicted the coming of Christ and his redemptive work (Luke 24:25–27, 44–49), the exact manner and the total meaning of his coming remained mysterious (Eph. 3:1–6; Col. 1:26–28). First-century Jews primarily expected a political deliverer and warrior, who would enable them to throw off the oppression of the Roman government and regain political independence, international prominence, prosperity, peace, and respect. They were surprised, and sometimes offended, by the unconventional form that Jesus' ministry took. Many said that he was a prophet (Matt. 16:14), but it took divine revelation for Peter to see that he was the Messiah, "the Son of the living God" (Matt. 16:16–17).

Thus, the New Testament introduces "surprise" elements. The Old Testament leads up to the New Testament but does not allow us to see beforehand what the New Testament reveals. Consequently, the New Testament leads to a reevaluation and rereading of the Old Testament. Having

---

8. See the excellent discussions in Geerhardus Vos, *The Pauline Eschatology* (Grand Rapids: Eerdmans, 1961); George E. Ladd, *A Theology of the New Testament*, rev. ed. (Grand Rapids: Eerdmans, 1993); Herman Ridderbos, *Paul: An Outline of His Theology* (Grand Rapids: Eerdmans, 1975); Thomas R. Schreiner, *Paul, Apostle of God's Glory in Christ: A Pauline Theology* (Downers Grove, IL: InterVarsity, 2001).

seen and experienced "the end of the story," we look back to the earlier parts of the story with deeper insights into their significance. The change at times may be as radical as what happened to Saul of Tarsus on the Damascus road. He had been a persecutor of the church and of what he interpreted as false messianic claims. Christ turned his world upside down by announcing from heaven: "I am Jesus, whom you are persecuting" (Acts 9:5). Saul had to reread the Old Testament and reevaluate what he thought he knew, on the basis of this spectacular undermining of his beliefs.

We therefore need to look at ways in which the New Testament adds to or transforms the teaching given in the Old Testament.

The Trinity

The New Testament deepens our view of God. The Old Testament indicates that there is only one God (monotheism; cf. Deut. 6:4). It contains adumbrations or foreshadowings of the Trinitarian character of God, but the New Testament and the coming of Christ give further light. They make it clear that there are personal distinctions within the godhead. For a thorough discussion of and backing for Trinitarian doctrine, one may consult the discussions in systematic theologies.[9] We shall content ourselves with a summary of the material in the New Testament.

First, the whole New Testament builds on the Old Testament teaching about God, rather than repudiating or attacking it. Most of the New Testament books were written by Jews, who knew from childhood there is only one God. The New Testament affirms the unity of God when it addresses pagans (1 Cor. 8:6; Acts 14:15–17; 17:22–31; Rom. 1:18–32).

Second, the New Testament affirms the deity of Christ by affirming that he is God (John 1:1; 20:28), that he is eternal (John 1:1), and that he had a mediatorial role in creation (John 1:1–3; 1 Cor. 8:6; Col. 1:16; Heb. 1:2). He also receives the key title "Lord" (*kurios*), which was used in Greek to translate the special, proper name of God, *Yahweh*. In the New Testament, "lord" is used in some contexts without implying deity. However, in Romans 10:13, "Lord" is applied to Jesus in the context of a quotation from Joel 2:32, whose Hebrew texts have the tetragrammaton *Yahweh*, the special personal name of God. In other contexts, the exalted character of the title becomes clear (John 20:28; Phil. 2:10–11). In the book of Revelation, Christ has the same title, "the Alpha and the Omega," that God the Father has (Rev. 1:8; 22:13; cf. 1:17).

These uses are all the more striking because the true God is a jealous God who demands exclusive allegiance and does not share his glory with creatures (Ex. 20:3–5; Isa. 42:8). If Jesus Christ is not God, giving him such

Tetragrammaton
Yahweh

9. See, for example, Louis Berkhof, *Systematic Theology* (Grand Rapids: Eerdmans, 1941), 82–99; John M. Frame, *The Doctrine of God* (Phillipsburg, NJ: P&R Publishing, 2002), 619–742. For an approach oriented to biblical theology, see Guthrie, *New Testament Theology*, 219–407.

honor is blasphemous. Moreover, in the New Testament the deity of Christ seems to be presupposed more often than explicitly taught, confirming that it is a deep, rather than superficial, aspect of the New Testament.

The gospel of John is particularly pointed in its exposition of God's character. It emphatically affirms the deity of Christ in its opening verses (John 1:1–3). Then it clearly distinguishes the Father and the Son, describing their relationship to one another. The Son addresses the Father as a distinct person in John 17. He affirms the indwelling of the Father in the Son and the Son in the Father, which is meaningless if there is no difference or distinction between the two (John 17:21). At the same time, the language of indwelling indicates the mystery of the unity that exists between the two, which is expressed elsewhere when the Son says, "I and the Father are one" (John 10:30). In a rich multitude of ways, John expresses both the unity of the godhead and the distinctions of the persons. He does not "solve" the mysteries that cannot be solved by finite human knowledge, but he affirms and presupposes them.

The gospel of John also clearly implies the deity of the Holy Spirit by indicating that in his coming, Christ himself will be present (John 14:23; 16:16). Against the background of the Old Testament, it is clear that the Spirit is not less than God. What is not so clear is that he is a distinct person. John makes that clear by speaking of the Spirit as "another Helper" (John 14:16). The word "another" makes it clear that he is distinct from the Son. As the one sent from both the Father and the Son (14:26; 16:7), he can be distinguished from both.

The apostle Paul does not use exactly the same phraseology as does John, but one can see that his affirmations are compatible with those in John. Christ has divine prerogatives as Creator (1 Cor. 8:6), has the name of Yahweh (Rom. 10:13), possesses "the whole fullness of deity" (Col. 2:9), and can be distinguished from the Father (1 Cor. 8:6; Phil. 2:11).

The book of Revelation presupposes Trinitarian thinking when it places the Father, the Son, and the Spirit side by side as the source of grace and peace (Rev. 1:4–5). Hebrews affirms the deity of Christ in its opening verses (Heb. 1:1–3).

Matthew 28:18–20 presupposes Trinitarian thinking in the baptismal formula: "in the name of the Father and of the Son and of the Holy Spirit" (28:19). The unity suggested by the singular "name" underlines the unity of God. Against the background of the holiness and jealousy of God in the Old Testament, it is unthinkable that this central formula (28:19) could bring together on the same level the Creator and a mere creature. Thus, the formula presupposes the deity of the Son and the Spirit. The appearance of distinct roles for Father, Son, and Spirit in the earlier incident of the baptism of Christ presupposes a distinction of persons (Matt. 3:16–17). The voice from heaven says: "This is my beloved Son," which indicates that the voice is the voice of the Father.

"The New Testament affirms the deity of Christ by affirming that he is God (John 1:1; 20:28), that he is eternal (John 1:1), and that he had a mediatorial role in creation (John 1:1–3; Col. 1:16; 1 Cor. 8:6; Heb. 1:2).

"The gospel of John is particularly pointed in its exposition of God's character. It emphatically affirms the deity of Christ in its opening verses (John 1:1–3). Then it clearly distinguishes the Father and the Son, describing their relationship to one another.

New Testament scholars often have observed that New Testament language about the godhead *predominantly* focuses on redemption and on practical issues. There are exceptions. John 1:1–2 describes God in himself, independent of the creation of the world.[10] Almost everywhere else, God is described in his relations to the world in general and to human beings in particular. The New Testament devotes the most space to articulating God's activity in redemption, which has come to realization and climax in Jesus Christ. To put it another way, the New Testament primarily focuses on God in his "economic" or functional relations to us, not on God in his "ontological" character, as he exists in and of himself.

In the New Testament, we do not receive a philosophical treatise concerning what has always been the case about the nature of God and the world but a proclamation about what God has done in "the fullness of time" (Gal. 4:4), "in these last days" (Heb. 1:2). In the context of this proclamation, God reconciles us to himself in Christ (2 Cor. 5:18–21), so that we come to know him (2 Cor. 4:6). Hence, we *do* obtain true knowledge of God in the context of the dynamics of redemption, and this overcomes the human resistance to knowing God.

The New Testament's practical, redemptive focus has tempted some people to open the door and speculate about ultimate ontology, beyond the New Testament's functional focus. These people argue that God is more ultimate than what we observe and what has been revealed. Yes, in some sense he is (1 Cor. 13:12; 1 Tim. 6:16). He is incomprehensible, so that we never master him in our knowledge. But he is not *other than* what he has revealed. Precisely in its valuable practical focus, the New Testament vigorously resists any attempt to exceed its revelation by speculatively going beyond its bounds. It resists in two practical ways.

First, the *finality* and *exclusivity* of revelation in Christ assure us that what we have come to know in Christ is indeed the very truth about God (Heb. 1:1–3).

> *In the New Testament, we do not receive a philosophical treatise concerning what has always been the case about the nature of God and the world but a proclamation about what God has done in "the fullness of time" (Gal. 4:4), "in these last days" (Heb. 1:2).*

---

10. John 1:1–2 is still written in human language, and this language, in its detailed texture, is surely not independent of creation, or of the concrete features of the Greek grammar in particular and the surrounding Greek culture in general. But the same might be said for anything that philosophers, mystics, or students of religion care to say about God. If we insist on having language independent of the world, we shall say nothing. By contrast, the New Testament speaks confidently of God, thereby repudiating the idea that God is unknowable and unspeakable. Yes, God is incomprehensible but not unknowable or unspeakable.

In fact, although the New Testament talks about "mystery," the preeminent mystery concerns what was partially concealed and veiled in Old Testament times but has now been revealed and is openly proclaimed (Rom. 16:25–27; Eph. 3:1–12). New Testament teaching is scandalously open and public, in comparison with competing conceptions in Gnosticism, mystery religions, and esotericism. Secret, esoteric knowledge available to a privileged few becomes a source of pride to those who possess it. The New Testament teaching, by contrast, is determined to destroy human pride, in order that God alone would be glorified (1 Cor. 1:18–31).

He is the radiance of the glory of God and the exact imprint of his nature. (Heb. 1:3)

Philip said to him, "Lord, show us the Father, and it is enough for us." [One might equally imagine a person interested in speculation saying, "Give us the final knowledge of God as he is in himself."] Jesus said to him, "Have I been with you so long, and you still do not know me, Philip? Whoever has seen me has seen the Father. How can you say, 'Show us the Father'? Do you not believe that I am in the Father and the Father is in me?" (John 14:8–10)

"I am the way, and the truth, and the life. No one comes to Father except through me." (John 14:6)

"All things have been handed over to me by my Father, and no one knows the Son except the Father, and no one knows the Father except the Son and anyone to whom the Son chooses to reveal him." (Matt. 11:27)

Second, the demands of worship require that we worship God alone and not idols. If the God who has revealed himself in Christ in the pages of the New Testament is other than God as he is in himself, we are worshiping only a substitute for God, and our worship is vain. If we are to worship exclusively the true God, as he calls on us to do, it demands *in practice* the exclusion of any attempt to drive a wedge between God as revealed and God as he is. The speculator who erects the distinction *in practice* already has removed himself from the worship of the New Testament church. He has ceased to come to God through Jesus Christ alone, and in consequence he turns from light back to darkness.

Later creedal Trinitarian formulations should be seen as accurate summaries of the implications of New Testament affirmations. They do not rely exclusively on the vocabulary and phraseology of the New Testament. Naturally, they try to draw out the implications. Therefore, they have been criticized for being too "philosophical" or "theoretical," and are alleged to be a decline from the vitality of the New Testament. But, rightly interpreted, they affirm the same affirmations that the New Testament makes, while not dissolving the mysteries that remain for human knowledge. And, most pointedly, they warn against all attempts to dissolve the mysteries into some kind of rationalized "explanation" that would in the end bring God down to the level of human conceptuality or would speculatively construct a god other than the God who has revealed himself definitively and finally in Christ.

The uniquely focused character of revelation in Christ has led some people to go to another extreme by confining the revelation of God *exclusively* to the incarnate Christ. However, during his life on earth, Christ affirmed the genuineness of the Old Testament Word of God. In addition, John 1:1 indicates that the eternal Son existed as God before he became incarnate. Precisely through the incarnation, we see that God's revelation is broader than the incarnation and that the One who became incarnate was God before he was incarnate.

> The demands of worship require that we worship God alone and not idols. If the God who has revealed himself in Christ in the pages of the New Testament is other than God as he is in himself, we are worshiping only a substitute for God, and our worship is vain.

Creation

The New Testament deepens Old Testament teaching about creation and providence by indicating the role of the Son of God in both. The Son who is the image of God from eternity was the mediator in creating all things (1 Cor. 8:6; Col. 1:15–17; Heb. 1:2; John 1:4). The statement in John 1:4, "In him was life," suggests that his uncreated life lies behind the act of creating life during the six days of creation.

By starting with creation, John is preparing to indicate the mediatorial role that Christ has in *redemption*. Christ is the source of redemptive eternal life for those now subject to death. "Truly, truly, I say to you, whoever hears my word and believes him who sent me has eternal life. He does not come into judgment, but has passed from death to life" (John 5:24). "For as the Father has life in himself, so he has granted the Son also to have life in himself" (John 5:26). John focuses on the functional role of the Son in coming to give redemptive life. For this role, the Father has given life to the Son. But, as usual, with redemption comes the revelation of who God is in his Trinitarian character, and we may infer that God as revealed is consistent with God as he is. The Father and the Son share divine life eternally. By virtue of their mutual indwelling and their personal relationship as Father and Son, it is fitting that the Son serve as mediator both in creation and in re-creation.

The apostle Paul also indicates the close relation between the Son's mediation of creation and his mediation of redemption. Colossians 1:15–17 speaks of creation, and Colossians 1:18–20 speaks of redemptive re-creation. Likewise, the book of Hebrews joins creation with redemptive purification of sins (Heb. 1:2–3).

Providence

The exhibition of God's sovereignty in the work of creation coheres with the continued exhibition of sovereignty in providence. The New Testament continues the Old Testament conviction that God sovereignly governs all events, both blessings (Ps. 65) and disasters (Job 1:21), events in general (Lam. 3:37–38) and events in detail (1 Kings 22:34; Job 2:10; Matt. 6:25–33; 10:29–31).[11] Christians, having been reconciled to God through Christ, have God as Father, and what happens to them transpires in terms of his Fatherly care (Luke 12:22–34). Christians are to seek his kingdom and his righteousness, knowing that the Father will take care of everything else (Matt. 6:33; Luke 12:31).

The events that come to us come not only from the Father but also from the Son, who "upholds the universe by the word of his power" (Heb. 1:3). Christ's governance is to be construed not only as the rule of the second person of the Trinity but also as the rule of the God-man, who has received as a reward for his sufferings exaltation to the right hand of God

> *The Son who is the image of God from eternity was the mediator in creating all things (Col. 1:15–17; 1 Cor. 8:6; Heb. 1:2; John 1:4). The statement in John 1:3, "In him was life," suggests that his uncreated life lies behind the act of creating life during the six days of creation.*

11. Guthrie, *New Testament Theology*, 79–80.

(Phil. 2:9–11; cf. Matt. 28:18–20; Heb. 10:12–14). As the enthroned last Adam, he reigns on behalf of renewed humanity.[12]

Miracle

God has power to bring about extraordinary as well as ordinary events. In the Old Testament, he divided the waters of the Red Sea (Ex. 14–15) and provided manna in the wilderness (Deut. 8:2–3). In the New Testament, he brought about miraculous healings and exorcisms through Jesus and then through the apostles (Luke 9:1–2, 16–17; Acts 19:11–12; etc.). These miracles are preeminently signs of salvation. They are not simply marvels but events symbolizing and signifying that the kingdom of God has come in power. The supreme miracle is the resurrection of Christ from the dead, because it represents not only the culmination of his work but also God's seal of approval and the inauguration of new creation (cf. Rom. 6:9; Rev. 1:18). The proclamation of the gospels centers on the resurrection of Christ, as a central event by which people are called to put faith in Christ (Acts 17:30–31).

Christ "upholds the universe by the word of his power." (Heb. 1:3)

In the modern West, the Bible's testimony to miracles has become a stumbling block to many whose modern worldview makes them think such things are impossible. However, ancient people were not naïve or inferior to us. They knew that such things were extraordinary, rather than ordinary, and that is why they reacted with amazement. The New Testament presupposes that such events were possible, because God is God and does as he pleases (Ps. 115:3).[13] The extraordinariness of miracles fits their function of drawing people's attention to the significance of what God is doing in Christ. It also provides an illustration of the marvel of regeneration, reconciliation to God, and the promise of a cosmic renewal in the new heaven and the new earth (Rev. 21:1–4). If Christ is indeed the incarnate Son of God, and if God is God, it would in fact be extraordinary if no miracles accompanied him.

Humanity

The New Testament presupposes that human beings were created in the image of God, as Genesis indicates (Gen. 1:26–28; 9:6; 1 Cor. 11:7; James 3:9). But it also states that Christ is the image of God (Col. 1:15; cf. Heb. 1:3; Phil. 2:6). Colossians 1:15 places this affirmation at the beginning of an exposition of the role of the Son as mediator of creation (Col. 1:15–17), thereby implying that Christ was the image of God even *before* his participation in creation. At the same time, the language of imaging clearly links itself thematically with the creation of man in Genesis 1. When we put all this together, we conclude that the preincarnate Son is the original

Christ's governance is to be construed not only as the rule of the second person of the Trinity but also as the rule of the God-man, who has received as a reward for his sufferings exaltation to the right hand of God (Phil. 2:9–11; cf. Matt. 28:18–20; Heb. 10:12–14). As the enthroned last Adam, he reigns on behalf of renewed humanity.

---

12.   See Dan G. McCartney, "Ecce Homo: The Coming of the Kingdom as the Restoration of Human Vicegerency," *WTJ* 56/1 (1994): 1–21.

13.   See the excellent discussion in C. John Collins, *The God of Miracles: An Exegetical Examination of God's Action in the World* (Wheaton, IL: Crossway, 2000); see Vern S. Poythress, *Redeeming Science* (Wheaton, IL: Crossway, 2006), 18–20, 177–95.

image, while man is created in the image of God in a derivative sense. A link by analogy exists between the eternal Son and humanity by virtue of the act in which God created human beings.

As we already observed, the New Testament views the renewal accomplished in redemption as re-creation. Redemption naturally focuses on human beings, who are made a "new creation" (2 Cor. 5:17). This re-creation also expresses itself in the language of imaging. Christians are "to put on the new self, created after the likeness of God in true righteousness and holiness" (Eph. 4:24). Similarly, Colossians says, " . . . you have put off the old self with its practices and have put on the new self, which is being renewed in knowledge after the image of its creator" (Col. 3:9–10).

In Colossians 3 the language of "image" or "likeness," linking with the term "created" or "creator," alludes to Genesis 1. Redemptive renewal, however, does not constitute an exact return to the situation of Adam but a conformity to Christ, who is the new man. Immediately following Colossians 3:10, verse 11 says, "Here there is not Greek and Jew, circumcised and uncircumcised, barbarian, Scythian, slave, free; but Christ is all, and in all." The classification into Greek and Jew, circumcised and uncircumcised, barbarian, Scythian, slave, and free concerns features derived from the first or original creation (and of course taking into account the fall). The new creation has its foundation in its union with Christ.

Moreover, the translation of Ephesians 4:24 and Colossians 3:10 in terms of "old self" and "new self" is not altogether accurate. The underlying word in Greek is *anthropos*, "human being" or "man." In the new creation, Christ is the first and archetypal human being. Everyone else receives renewal according to the pattern that he established. First Corinthians 15:45–49 expresses it well in the context of the future resurrection:

> Thus it is written, "The first man Adam became a living being"; the last Adam became a life-giving spirit. But it is not the spiritual that is first but the natural, and then the spiritual. The first man was from the earth, a man of dust; the second man is from heaven. As was the man of dust, so also are those who are of the dust, and as is the man of heaven, so also are those who are of heaven. Just as we have borne the image of the man of dust, we shall also bear the image of the man of heaven.

In Colossians 3 the language of "image" or "likeness," linking with the term "created" or "creator," alludes to Genesis 1. Redemptive renewal, however, does not constitute an exact return to the situation of Adam but a conformity to Christ, who is the new man.

The final verse says: "We shall also bear the image of the man of heaven," that is, the image of Christ in his exaltation, having a resurrection body. The resurrection of our bodies is to take place in the future. But, by being united to Christ now, we already participate in the new order that he inaugurates. Renewal of people within the present life is renewal with the goal of being conformed to the image of Christ.

Second Corinthians 3:18 contains a similar idea, that Christians reflect the pattern of Christ: "And we all, with unveiled face, beholding the glory of the Lord, are being transformed into the same image from one degree of glory to another. For this comes from the Lord who is the Spirit."

The character of humanity itself is thus to be understood in relation to Christ. The first humanity, belonging to the first creation, was created from the dust, in the person of Adam. Adam is the model and representative for all who are descended from him. Christ in his resurrection body is the model and representative for all who are united to him. The restoration of our humanness, which was broken and twisted in the fall, comes not by a return to Eden and Adam's original situation but by an advance toward the goal of being conformed to the image of Christ. New humanity even now comes about as human beings are united to Christ by faith and renewed by his life in the Spirit (2 Cor. 5:17). We are headed toward the consummation of that renewal, which will occur when we are transformed at the time of the future resurrection of the body (1 Cor. 15:35–49).

Human beings, made in the image of God, have a central role within the larger created order. In the renewal and consummation, the same appears to be true, but the center is occupied by Christ, who represents all of the new humanity. Thus in Romans 8 we find that Christ's sonship is the pattern for our becoming adopted sons: "For those whom he foreknew he also predestined to be conformed to the image of his Son, in order that he might be the firstborn among many brothers" (Rom. 8:29). Our status as sons is a present reality, as the testimony of the Holy Spirit indicates:

> For all who are led by the Spirit of God are sons of God. For you did not receive the spirit of slavery to fall back into fear, but you have received the Spirit of adoption as sons, by whom we cry, "Abba! Father!" The Spirit himself bears witness with our spirit that we are children of God, and if children, then heirs—heirs of God and fellow heirs with Christ, provided we suffer with him in order that we may also be glorified with him. (Rom. 8:14–17)

Adoption will be consummated in the future, as another place in Romans 8 indicates: "And not only the creation, but we ourselves, who have the firstfruits of the Spirit, groan inwardly as we wait eagerly for adoption as sons, the redemption of our bodies" (Rom. 8:23). Christ's sonship becomes the pattern for our sonship, and our sonship in turn is linked to the freeing of the rest of creation: "that the creation itself will be set free from its bondage to decay and obtain the freedom of the glory of the children of God" (Rom. 8:21). Indeed, Christ is the one in whom all things are summed up: " . . . a plan for the fullness of time, to unite all things in him [Christ], things in heaven and things on earth" (Eph. 1:10).[14]

Sin

The New Testament accepts and reaffirms the Old Testament view that sin is an offense to God and a violation of his righteousness and holiness. It affirms also that sin is universal (Rom. 3:9–20). However, the coming of Christ results in a deepening of the viewpoint. The coming of Christ

> *The restoration of our humanness, which was broken and twisted in the fall, comes not by a return to Eden and Adam's original situation but by an advance toward the goal of being conformed to the image of Christ.*

---

14. See the excellent discussion in Vos, *The Pauline Eschatology*.

is the coming of the Holy and Righteous One, whose crucifixion shows the exceeding wickedness in human hearts: "But you denied the Holy and Righteous One, and asked for a murderer to be granted to you, and you killed the Author of life, whom God raised from the dead" (Acts 3:14–15).

The coming of the true Light in the person of Christ shows up the darkness for what it is: "And this is the judgment: the light has come into the world, and people loved the darkness rather than the light because their works were evil. For everyone who does wicked things hates the light and does not come to the light, lest his works should be exposed. But whoever does what is true comes to the light, so that it may be clearly seen that his works have been carried out in God" (John 3:19–21).

Jesus' teaching in the Sermon on the Mount and elsewhere indicates that sin does not consist only in outward transgressions of obvious moral standards but in the thoughts and intents of the heart (Matt. 5:2–7:27, and especially 5:20–48). "But what comes out of the mouth proceeds from the heart, and this defiles a person. For out of the heart come evil thoughts, murder, adultery, sexual immorality, theft, false witness, slander. These are what defile a person. But to eat with unwashed hands does not defile anyone" (Matt. 15:18–20; see Matt. 23; Mark 7:1–23).

Jesus' teaching and his miracles increase guilt: "If I had not come and spoken to them, they would not have been guilty of sin, but now they have no excuse for their sin. Whoever hates me hates my Father also. If I had not done among them the works that no one else did, they would not be guilty of sin, but now they have seen and hated both me and my Father" (John 15:22–24). John does not imply that there was literally no sin in Old Testament times. Rather, he heightens the effect by stating a relative contrast (Jesus versus what came before) in absolute terms. The parable of the wicked tenants makes a similar point. It is bad enough that the tenants mistreat the owner's servants. But when they kill the son, they have come to a climax of wickedness (Matt. 21:33–44).

Though sins of all kinds exist, the central sin is sin in reaction to the coming Light: "whoever does not believe is condemned already, because he has not believed in the name of the only Son of God" (John 3:18).

Expulsion from the Garden of Eden, (detail), Masaccio (Tommaso Cassai)

Epistemology

Knowing God and fearing God are the heart of wisdom and the heart of true life, according to the Old Testament (Prov. 1:7). In the New Testament, the revelation of God comes to focus and climax in Jesus Christ (Heb. 1:1–3). The revelation in the Old Testament, though genuine, is but a shadow and preparation for this climax. Hence, the New Testament can make the astounding claim that true knowledge of God is to be found only through Christ (Matt. 11:25–27; John 14:6, 9–11; 8:19; 1 Cor. 1:30; Col. 2:3).

All human beings inescapably know God after a fashion, through his revelation in the things he has made (Acts 14:15–17; 17:24–29; Rom. 1:18–

23). But "by their unrighteousness [they] suppress the truth" (Rom. 1:18). Humans pervert the knowledge of God into idolatry (Rom. 1:21–23). They are in darkness (John 3:19–20). They have given themselves over to the realm of darkness and Satan (Col. 1:13), and Satan holds them captive (cf. 2 Tim. 2:26; 1 John 5:19). Satan has "blinded the minds of unbelievers, to keep them from seeing the light of the gospel of the glory of Christ, who is the image of God" (2 Cor. 4:4).

Man, in his fallen condition, has desperate, insuperable problems in his knowledge. Moreover, his problems are not the result of mere innocence, as if man simply had not yet been exposed to the truth. Rather, human beings already know the truth about God—his eternal power and divine nature (Rom. 1:20)—and they simultaneously reject or suppress it. Man hates God and will do anything not to be subject to him (Ps. 2:1–3). Ours is a sinful, culpable darkness in knowledge.

The Gentiles walk "in the futility of their minds. They are darkened in their understanding, alienated from the life of God because of the ignorance that is in them, due to their hardness of heart" (Eph. 4:17–18). With respect to spiritual things and spiritual knowledge, with respect to God, they are dead:

> And you were dead in the trespasses and sins in which you once walked, following the course of this world, following the prince of the power of the air, the spirit that is now at work in the sons of disobedience—among whom we all once lived in the passions of our flesh, carrying out the desires of the body and the mind, and were by nature children of wrath, like the rest of mankind. (Eph. 2:1–3)

What hope is there then? God must come and act in grace, with resurrection power:

> But God, being rich in mercy, because of the great love with which he loved us, even when we were dead in our trespasses, made us alive together with Christ—by grace you have been saved—and raised us up with him and seated us with him in the heavenly places in Christ Jesus. (Eph. 2:4–6)

Apart from this action in giving new life and renewing the mind, even when the Light comes, it is rejected: "And this is the judgment: the light has come into the world, and people loved the darkness rather than the light because their deeds were evil" (John 3:19).

In sum, man's epistemological powers are sinfully corrupted and can be remedied only through God's own redemption in Christ. The gospel contained in Scripture is the epistemological key to the whole of human existence. Redemptive renewal in the human heart and mind offers the only basis for seeing the world as a whole, as it really is—a world created by God in such a manner that it reveals his glory and his attributes (Rom. 1:20).[15]

Though sins of all kinds exist, the central sin is sin in reaction to the coming Light: "whoever does not believe is condemned already, because he has not believed in the name of the only Son of God" (John 3:18).

Man, in his fallen condition, has desperate, insuperable problems in his knowledge. . . . his problems are not the result of mere innocence . . . . Rather, human beings already know the truth about God— his eternal power and divine nature (Rom. 1:20)—and they simultaneously reject or suppress it.

---

15. See the discussion of this issue in John M. Frame, *The Doctrine of the Knowledge of God* (Phillipsburg, NJ: Presbyterian and Reformed, 1987).

Redemption Accomplished

The predominant emphasis of the New Testament falls not on the pit of sin but on what God has come and done "in these last days" (Heb. 1:2) to accomplish the one remedy, in Jesus Christ. The Old Testament saw God rescue his people and have mercy on them, in the times of the patriarchs, in the exodus, in the wilderness, in the conquest, with the judges, with the monarchy, in the return from exile. But all these deliverances were partial and temporary. By themselves, they did not result in the "circumcision of the heart" that would represent a permanent deliverance from the inward dominion of sin (Deut. 30:6). The prophets looked forward to a final day of glorious and comprehensive deliverance that included the renovation of the heart (Jer. 31:31–34; Ezek. 36:25–27).

The New Testament announcement that the kingdom of God has come means that through the work of Christ, the day of decisive deliverance has at last arrived. Christ's coming means fulfillment of a whole network of Old Testament prophecies that looked forward to God's coming. God would save Israel decisively, and the nations would turn to God as they see his salvation (Isa. 2:2–4; 52:10; 56:7). Early in his ministry, Christ announced that the time has come: "Repent, for the kingdom of heaven is at hand" (Matt 4:17). In the synagogue at Nazareth, after reading from Isaiah 61:1–2, he commented, "Today this Scripture has been fulfilled in your hearing" (Luke 4:18–21).

Most of the Old Testament prophecies announced the fact of God's coming and his future action in salvation, but they did not specify the chronological arrangement in detail. Many Jews in Jesus' day wanted God to act for their benefit, to bring deliverance from Roman rule, and to bring prosperity and peace to the nation. But they wanted it to happen immediately. They did not realize that the decisive events would be spread out over time and would not take the exact form they envisioned.

In reply to popular expectations, the parable of the mustard seed indicates that the kingdom of God can take time in coming (Matt. 13:31–32). It starts in small and unassuming form but in the end is imposing. Interpretations of this and other parables vary. Nevertheless, from the earlier announcement in Matthew 4:17, it seems that Jesus equates the beginning of his ministry with the beginning of the dawning of the kingdom of God. It is the "small" beginning that his contemporaries are in danger of missing or misinterpreting. The big ending must be nothing less than the consummation of God's salvific purposes, just as Daniel 2:34–35, 44–45 depicts the kingdom of God like a stone that grows to fill "the whole earth."

Eschatology

The fulfillment of Old Testament prophecies and the realization of God's final purposes come in stages. Theologians studying the New Testament rightly speak of "inaugurated eschatology." "Eschatology" is used

> *The predominant emphasis of the New Testament falls not on the pit of sin but on what God has come and done "in these last days" (Heb. 1:2) to accomplish the one remedy, in Jesus Christ.... The prophets looked forward to a final day of glorious and comprehensive deliverance that included the renovation of the heart.*

here in a broad sense, not merely to designate the events associated with the creation of the new heaven and the new earth (Matt. 19:28; 24:35; Rev. 21:1), but with events fulfilling Old Testament prophecies of climactic acts of salvation. These climactic acts come to focus in the earthly ministry—the life, the death, and the resurrection—of the Son of God. The new heaven and the new earth of Revelation 21:1 have not yet come as a cosmic reality, but Christ the Redeemer has come. God has come in Christ. And, with his coming and the completion of his work on earth, he has accomplished salvation for the world and has opened a new age of salvation.

Old Testament prophecies describe a coming climax to God's salvific work, usually without clearly separating the work into a fixed number of distinct chronological stages. The whole process is woven together into a single complex description, because in a fundamental way it is *one* process in which the different aspects and different stages have a close relation to and continuity with one another. Some of the Old Testament prophecies focus directly on God: God comes and brings salvation (Isa. 40:10–11; Jer. 31:33–34; Ezek. 36:24–28). Others give a prominent role to a human (messianic) leader (Isa. 11:1–10; 52:13–53:12; Ezek. 37:24–28). Both of these promises find fulfillment in Jesus Christ, who comes as the Messiah who is both God and man (John 1:1–18; see Isa. 9:6–7; Dan. 7:13–14). The different stages of salvation find unity in the person whose action accomplishes salvation.

The New Testament records the first stage, the first coming of Christ. It announces to the whole world the events that have already taken place and their significance. Acts 10:38–43 summarizes apostolic preaching:

> God anointed Jesus of Nazareth with the Holy Spirit and with power. He went about doing good and healing all who were oppressed by the devil, for God was with him. And we are witnesses of all that he did both in the country of the Jews and in Jerusalem. They put him to death by hanging him on a tree, but God raised him on the third day and made him to appear, not to all the people but to us who had been chosen by God as witnesses, who ate and drank with him after he rose from the dead. And he commanded us to preach to the people and to testify that he is the one appointed by God to be judge of the living and the dead. To him all the prophets bear witness that everyone who believes in him receives forgiveness of sins through his name.

The second stage, the second coming of Christ, now becomes the chief focus for future hope. "He is the one appointed by God to be judge of the living and the dead" (Acts 10:42), as Peter shows by pointing to his resurrection. The resurrection is not only a proof of the verity of his teaching and the claims made concerning his life. Logically, it also is part of his vindication, which leads to his ascension and enthronement:

> He humbled himself by becoming obedient to the point of death, even death on a cross. Therefore God has highly exalted him and bestowed on him the name that is above every name, so that at the name of Jesus every knee should bow, in

The new heaven and the new earth of Revelation 21:1 have not yet come as a cosmic reality, but Christ the Redeemer has come. . . . And, with his coming and the completion of his work on earth, he has accomplished salvation for the world and has opened a new age of salvation.

heaven and on earth and under the earth, and every tongue confess that Jesus Christ is Lord, to the glory of God the Father. (Phil. 2:8–11)

In his resurrection and ascension, Jesus was given authority over death, which implies authority to make all things new:

> I died, and behold I am alive forevermore, and I have the keys of Death and Hades. (Rev. 1:18)

Jesus' present authority thus guarantees the complete victory that we will see when "Death and Hades [are] thrown into the lake of fire" (Rev. 20:14). A new Jerusalem comes "down out of heaven from God" (Rev. 21:2), and "the throne of God and of the Lamb" is central in it (Rev. 22:1; see 21:22). The Lamb who was slain has the right to take the scroll from the hand of him who is seated on the throne (Rev. 5:1–10) and to bring about the realization of God's purposes, which issue in the new heaven and the new earth and a renewed humanity (Rev. 5:9–10).[16]

Thus, an inner unity exists between Jesus' victory over death already accomplished and the final abolition of death at the consummation. Jesus' victory, in fact, becomes the pattern for the victory of the saints when they are resurrected:

> As was the man of dust [Adam], so also are those who are of the dust [his descendants], and as is the man of heaven [Christ ascended], so also are those who are of heaven [resurrected saints]. Just as we have borne the image of the man of dust, we shall also bear the image of the man of heaven. (1 Cor. 15:48–49)

The Holy Spirit who empowered the resurrection of Christ (Rom. 1:4) now has been given to those who belong to Christ. He is "the guarantee of our inheritance" (Eph. 1:14; see 2 Cor. 1:22), a down payment on the full possession that we are yet to receive. Even now we have received new life through him that leads us to anticipate future resurrection life:

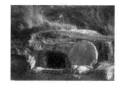

The empty tomb. "He is not here, but has risen." Luke 24:6

> But if Christ is in you, although the body is dead because of sin, the Spirit is life because of righteousness. If the Spirit of him who raised Jesus from the dead dwells in you, he who raised Christ Jesus from the dead will also give life to your mortal bodies through his Spirit who dwells in you. (Rom. 8:10–11)

Already and Yet to Come

Because of the continuity between the present down payment and the future full inheritance, the New Testament uses similar language to describe the present and the future. As we observed earlier, Romans 8 assures us that we already have become sons of God through adoption (Rom. 8:15–17; cf. Gal. 4:5–7), but then a few verses later it places our adoption in the future: "And not only the creation, but we ourselves, who have the firstfruits of the

16. Guthrie, *New Testament Theology*, 790–892.

Spirit, groan inwardly as we wait eagerly for adoption as sons, the redemption of our bodies" (Rom. 8:23).

The gift of the Spirit gives us spiritual life now (Rom. 8:10), and the promise of future resurrection life (Rom. 8:11). John 5 and John 11 also move back and forth between "life" that we have now through Christ and "life" that consists in bodily resurrection (John 5:24–29; 11:23–26). Spiritually, we "have been raised with Christ" already (Col. 3:1), but bodily we *will* be raised in the future, at the second coming (1 Thess. 4:16–17).

In Acts 2:38 and 10:43, Peter announces "forgiveness of sins" as a present reality. And, indeed, Jesus announced it during his earthly life (Luke 5:20; 7:48; cf. 19:9–10). But this present forgiveness also implies a final proof of forgiveness at the time of the last judgment (Rom. 8:30–39).[17]

Aspects of Redemption

The redemption that Christ has achieved runs as broad and deep as the effects of sin. Indeed, it reaches further than the effects of sin, since Christ does not simply return us to Eden in order to start over but brings us forward to the consummation. Redemption touches every aspect of life. Accordingly, a variety of descriptions show its breadth of reach. We were slaves to sin, but now we have become sons of God (Rom. 8). We were alienated from God, but now we have been reconciled (Rom. 5:8–11; 2 Cor. 5:17–21). We were separated from God's people, but now we have become fellow citizens (Eph. 2:11–22; cf. Matt. 21:43). We were under guilt and liable to punishment and condemnation, but now we are free from condemnation. We were guilty, but now we are reckoned as innocent and righteous (Rom. 4). We were captive to Satan, but now Christ has defeated him (Col. 2:15). We were subject to death, but Christ has triumphed over death (Rom. 6:9–11; Heb. 2:14–15; Rev. 1:18). We were poor and blind and captive, but now we have been liberated in the year of jubilee (Luke 4:18–19). We were in darkness, but now we have come to the light (John 1:9–13; 3:18–21; 8:12; 9:39–41; Eph. 5:8–14). We were fools, but now we have become wise (1 Cor. 1:18–31; Eph. 4:17–18). We were unholy, but now we have become holy (Heb. 10:10). We were characterized by hate, but now we love (1 John 3:11–24). We were subject to lies, but now we know the truth (1 John 2:18–27).

Subsequent reflection on redemption sometimes has attempted to polarize the issues, first by emphasizing one aspect of Christ's work, then by denying complementary aspects. One person observes that Christ was victorious over Satan. But does he then infer that there was no need for Christ to be our sin bearer (1 Peter 2:24)? There is the mistake.

The instincts of Christians, as well as the explicit teachings of the New Testament, point us toward affirming the comprehensive character of

> *Thus, an inner unity exists between Jesus' victory over death already accomplished and the final abolition of death at the consummation. Jesus' victory, in fact, becomes the pattern for the victory of the saints when they are resurrected.*

> *The redemption that Christ has achieved runs as broad and deep as the effects of sin. Indeed, it reaches further than the effects of sin, since Christ does not simply return us to Eden in order to start over but brings us forward to the consummation.*

---

17. See the excellent discussions in Richard B. Gaffin Jr., *Resurrection and Redemption: A Study in Paul's Soteriology* (Phillipsburg, NJ: Presbyterian and Reformed, 1987); Ladd, *A Theology of the New Testament.*

Christ's redemption. We magnify and praise Christ, and in doing so honor the Father as well (John 5:23). We see the applicability of Christ's work to every aspect of life. The worldview of the New Testament thus affirms the truth of all the aspects of redemption that it proclaims. It assumes that these aspects are complementary and mutually reinforcing, rather than mutually exclusive alternative explanations.[18]

Union with Christ

The centrality of Christ in accomplishing redemption includes his centrality when people receive the benefits of redemption. What Christ accomplished, he accomplished for others. Those who belong to Christ participate in a whole host of benefits. At the heart of these benefits is the person of Christ himself. Those who belong to Christ are united to him. In the writings of Paul, especially, union with Christ comes to expression in the phrase "in Christ" and its variants: "in the Lord," "in him," "through him," "with him." John talks about dwelling in Christ and Christ in us (e.g., John 14:20–23; 17:22–26). But the idea of participating in Christ is not confined to one fixed set of expressions.

Union with Christ includes many aspects. We may begin with fellowship with the risen Christ in a person-to-person relation. Through the gift of the Holy Spirit, Christ promises to continue, in altered form, the fellowship that he had with the disciples on earth (John 14:18–21). We speak to him in prayer (e.g., 2 Cor. 12:8), and he speaks to us through the Spirit (John 16:13–15; 2 Cor. 12:9).

Union with Christ includes dwelling in Christ and Christ dwelling in us (John 14:20). Living now means "Christ who lives in me" (Gal. 2:20). "For as many of you as were baptized into Christ have put on Christ" (Gal. 3:27).

Union includes the fact that Christ in his work on earth and in heaven represents us, in a manner parallel to Adam's representative function as head of the human race (Rom. 5:12–21; 1 Cor. 15:22, 45–49). Through Christ's vindication and "acquittal" in his resurrection, we are acquitted and justified (Rom. 4:25; 5:18–19). Our sin was taken by him in order that we might receive his righteousness (2 Cor. 5:21; 1 Peter 2:24). Christ is "made our wisdom and our righteousness and sanctification and redemption" (1 Cor. 1:30). Specific events that happened to Christ are ascribed to us as well, typically using the language of "with Christ." For example, "I have been crucified with Christ" (Gal. 2:20). "With Christ you died . . . " (Col. 2:20). "You have been raised with Christ" (Col. 3:1). "[God] raised us up with him and seated us with him in the heavenly places in Christ Jesus" (Eph. 2:6). Since Christ is the Son, we have been made sons: "God sent forth his Son . . . so that we might receive adoption as sons" (Gal. 4:4–5).

The centrality of Christ in accomplishing redemption includes his centrality when people receive the benefits of redemption. What Christ accomplished, he accomplished for others. Those who belong to Christ participate in a whole host of benefits. At the heart of these benefits is the person of Christ himself.

18. Guthrie, *New Testament Theology*, 409–509.

Through Christ, we become heirs to Old Testament promises. "And if you are Christ's, then you are Abraham's offspring, heirs according to promise" (Gal. 3:29). "You yourselves like living stones are being built up as a spiritual house, to be a holy priesthood, to offer spiritual sacrifices acceptable to God through Jesus Christ" (1 Peter 2:5).

> Therefore, brothers, since we have confidence to enter the holy places by the blood of Jesus, by the new and living way that he opened for us through the curtain, that is, through his flesh, and since we have a great priest over the house of God, let us draw near with a true heart in full assurance of faith, with our hearts sprinkled clean from an evil conscience and our bodies washed with pure water. (Heb. 10:19–22)

The Old Testament anticipates a day when Gentiles also will receive blessing from God through Abraham and his offspring (Gen. 12:2–3; 22:18). Certain Gentiles such as Rahab and the Queen of Sheba found blessing even within the bounds of the Old Testament story. But the details remain unclear as to how a multitude of Gentiles will participate in the promised final salvation. Now that Christ has come, it is made clear. Gentiles are saved by being joined to Christ, as are Jews. "This mystery [not revealed before] is that the Gentiles are fellow heirs, members of the same body, and partakers of the promise in Christ Jesus through the gospel" (Eph. 3:6).

> But now in Christ Jesus you who once were far off [Gentiles] have been brought near by the blood of Christ. For he himself is our peace, who has made us both [Gentiles and Jews] one and has broken down in his flesh the dividing wall of hostility. . . . For through him we both have access in one Spirit to the Father. So then you [Gentiles] are no longer strangers and aliens, but you are fellow citizens with the saints and members of the household of God, built on the foundation of the apostles and prophets, Christ Jesus himself being the cornerstone. (Eph. 2:13–14, 18–20)

Union with Christ implies union with the Father and the Spirit (John 14:16–23; Eph. 2:18). This union is unbreakable ("Who shall separate us from the love of Christ?" Rom. 8:35). The Spirit as the "firstfruits" (Rom. 8:23) is the guarantee that the union we now have with Christ will come to consummation (John 6:39–40). On our side, faith is a key aspect in our participation in this union (John 6:40). But faith does not arise unless it is granted as part of the Father's drawing us to himself (John 6:44, 65). Our faith is preceded by the outgoing love of the Father in the Son (John 10:14, 27–29; Eph. 1:4–5). God receives glory, rather than human beings receiving it (1 Cor. 1:28–31; 2:5; 4:7).[19]

Through Christ, we become heirs to Old Testament promises. "And if you are Christ's, then you are Abraham's offspring, heirs according to promise" (Gal. 3:29).

---

19. See the excellent discussions in Ridderbos, *Paul: An Outline of His Theology*; Schreiner, *Paul*.

The Church

Union with Christ means renewal, re-creation, and new existence in both individual and corporate ways. When a person is united to Christ, he also is united to everyone else who is united to Christ. Salvation in Christ means not only salvation for individuals but salvation and renewal *in community*.

Theologians as well as practitioners of Christianity have sometimes polarized the issue by acting as if the individual aspect excluded the corporate, or vice versa. But human beings are both individual and social creatures. Hence, renewal or re-creation works at undoing the effects of sin in both arenas. God's purpose includes a new Jerusalem with the corporate unity of a city, but it also is a place where each individual has unhindered access to God and therefore supreme blessedness (Rev. 22:3–5). The consummation of humanity brings to fulfillment both individual and corporate aspects of human nature. The individual is not crushed into monistic unity in which his personality is dissolved (Luke 22:28–30). Neither is the group in its corporate fellowship and unity dissolved into isolated individuals (Rev. 19:7–8; 21:9). The individual and corporate are in harmony at the end. The individual finds his fulfillment precisely in fellowship with God and, subordinately, in fellowship with those who are filled with his presence and glory. The corporate group finds fulfillment precisely in enhancing the glory of God throughout all its subdivisions, and this implies the affirmation of the significance of every individual.

During the present, the church is headed toward the goal of the consummation, but it has not yet reached it. Already the church is the new humanity in a nutshell, but it has not yet achieved its full stature (Eph. 4:13). In accordance with that goal, the church expresses individual and corporate dimensions in a harmony. The pictures of the church as the body of Christ (1 Cor. 12; Rom. 12) and the temple of the Holy Spirit (1 Cor. 3:10–17; Eph. 2:19–22; 1 Peter 2:5) indicate the principial harmony of the individual and the group. The members of the body serve the body, while the body also serves the health of each member in it. And all serve the glory of Christ.

The life of each individual should not turn inward and serve only self; each one is to serve God and find blessedness in giving himself to God. Because God commands love to neighbor as well as love to God, we subordinately find life and blessing in serving one another. In an analogous way, the life of the community—the church—should not turn primarily inward, but be directed to serving God. The church is denominated *ecclesia*, "assembly," a word used in secular Greek for political assemblies. But, theologically speaking, the primary conceptual background must be located in the assembly of God's people in the Old Testament. There are various assemblies: the assembly at Mount Sinai, in which the people are formed by the Word of God into God's holy people; the assemblies for feasts in the presence of God, celebrating God's goodness and giving thanks for har-

"Salvation in Christ means not only salvation for individuals but salvation and renewal in community."

vests; and the assemblies for fasting and repentance and petition, in which people call on God for deliverance.

The church is the assembly called by God, assembling in the presence of God. It is also the body of Christ, united to him by faith. And it is the fellowship in the Holy Spirit, empowered by the dwelling of the Holy Spirit in both individual (1 Cor. 6:16–19) and group (1 Cor. 3:10–17). All three persons of the Trinity are involved. The church is the beginning of a new humanity that will be consummated in the new heaven and the new earth, but it is not, in the end, man-centered. Humanity itself, by creation and by destiny, finds its meaning not in itself but in relation to God. The church is thus God-centered, in the present as well as in the future.

Though the church is first of all conceived in terms of invisible realities, those realities manifest themselves concretely in human activity. Christians meet together (Acts 2:42–47). They serve one another in concrete acts of love (James 2:14–17). They become a light and a leaven, influencing those around them (Matt. 5:14–16). Outsiders continue to come to faith and are added to the community (Acts 2:37–41; 4:4; 5:14; 6:7; etc.). The community grows both in extent and in maturity (Eph. 4:9–16).

At the same time, within this world the Christian community remains imperfect. Within it arise hypocrites, false teachers, immoral persons, and creators of dissension (Gal. 1:7–9; 5:12, 19–21; 6:12; 1 John 2:18–23; 2 John 7–10; 3 John 9–10). The church must discipline those who continue in sin (Matt. 18:15–20; 1 Cor. 5:1–13). The Christianity of the New Testament is exclusivist about truth; it firmly rejects false teachings within its ranks as well as pagan religions (Acts 14:15–16; 1 Cor. 10:20; Gal. 1:7–9; 1 John 4:1–6; Rev. 13:1–18). It also is exclusivist in membership, in the practice of excluding unrepentant members. At the same time, it welcomes all who repent (Luke 19:10; 2 Cor. 2:7–11).

Students of society sometimes have postulated a tension between innovative, destabilizing forces from unofficial "charismatic" individuals and conservative, stabilizing forces from official, institutionalized leadership. No doubt, within sinful humanity and within a church still beset by sin, such tensions can be real. But the purpose of the church presupposes ultimate harmony between members with different gifts from the Holy Spirit. There is one God, one Lord, one Spirit, as Ephesians reminds us (Eph. 4:4–6). The gifts that he gives include "teachers, . . . helping, administrating," which are typically more stabilizing, and "prophets, . . . miracles," which are more innovating (1 Cor. 12:28). The appointment of elders in every church (Acts 14:23; cf. Phil. 1:1; 1 Thess. 5:12; 1 Tim. 3:1–13; Heb. 13:17; 1 Peter 5:5) does not imply a "quenching of the freedom" of the Spirit but a movement of the Spirit to enhance and support the functioning of the Spirit's own gifts of administrating and ruling, under the transforming power of Christ. Of course the power of rule can be abused (Matt. 20:25–28), but so can an appeal to "freedom" be abused to produce license or anarchy (2 Peter 2:19–22). When the

> The members of the body serve the body, while the body also serves the health of each member in it. And all serve the glory of Christ.

> The church is the assembly called by God, assembling in the presence of God. It is also the body of Christ, united to him by faith. And it is the fellowship in the Holy Spirit, empowered by the dwelling of the Holy Spirit in both individual . . . and group . . . . All three persons of the Trinity are involved.

church as the body of Christ is healthy and growing, the aspects of stability and innovation function harmoniously. We grow based on the stability of a foundation (Eph. 2:20–22; Matt. 16:18).

We can see all this working out in the book of Acts, as well as in the churches to which the New Testament letters are addressed. Acts shows that specific individuals such as Lydia (Acts 16:14–15) and Cornelius (Acts 10) came to Christ. But it also shows that people became part of churches that were dynamic, growing communities (Acts 2:42–47; 4:32–37; 14:23). It also shows the struggles that took place as people adjusted to the new realities of Christians living together (Acts 6:1–7; 15:1–35). Sin continued to threaten to disrupt the new pattern of Christian living (Acts 20:29–31). First-century churches did not perfectly model the doctrine and life that arose from union with Christ, and, like churches later on, sometimes they were racked by heresy and dissension (Galatians; 1 Cor. 1:11–13). Yet, in spite of failings, the church as a whole attracted Jews and Gentiles through the truth that it proclaimed and the life of love that it manifested (Matt. 5:14–16).[20]

Ethics

Where do Christians get direction for their new lives? Once again, the New Testament builds on the Old Testament. The Old Testament affirmed that God is the absolute Lord. He and he alone is the ultimate source for ethical direction. He possesses the right to command his creatures, the goodness and righteousness to assure that his commands are worthy, and the power to reward obedience and punish disobedience. Moreover, man created in the image of God has a sense of right and wrong due to his very nature. Although sin can pervert and confuse the conscience, by suppressing the truth (Rom. 1:18), people never escape responsibility to God (Rom. 1:32; 2:13–15; 1 Tim. 4:2).

> *Salvation in Christ renews our knowledge of God and our fellowship with him, and so also renews our moral power and moral direction. Precisely in the context of ethics and behavior, Paul calls for a continual transformation....*

Salvation in Christ renews our knowledge of God and our fellowship with him, and so also renews our moral power and moral direction. Precisely in the context of ethics and behavior, Paul calls for a continual transformation: "Do not be conformed to this world, but be transformed by the renewal of your mind, that by testing you may discern what is the will of God, what is good and acceptable and perfect" (Rom. 12:2).

Christ is the final revelation of God to human beings (Heb. 1:3). Therefore, he also is the final revelation of God's righteousness and goodness. The moral goal for Christians is to be conformed to his image (2 Cor. 3:18; Eph. 4:13–16, 22–24). This renewal also is closely associated with the Holy Spirit, who comes as the Spirit of Christ (Rom. 8:6–11). Paul's contrast between "the works of the flesh" and "the fruit of the Spirit" fulfills the Old Testament contrast between the way of life and of death, the way of wisdom and of folly (Prov. 6–9).

---

20.   Guthrie, *New Testament Theology*, 701–89; see the excellent discussion in Edmund P. Clowney, *The Church* (Downers Grove, IL: InterVarsity, 1995).

But in what concrete directions does the Spirit work? The New Testament puts love of God and love of the brothers at the center of its exhortations (Gal. 5:14; 1 Cor. 13; Heb. 13:1; 1 John). This love is an outgrowth of the Old Testament commands to love God and love neighbor (Matt. 22:34–40). Genuine love is not in tension with the commandments of God, but leads to fulfilling them (John 14:15; Rom. 13:8–10; Gal. 5:14). Love is deepened by the example of Christ's love (John 13:34–35) and the empowering of the Holy Spirit (John 14:15–26).

Since God remains righteous in both Old and New Testament, the basic principles of Old Testament moral standards continue into the New Testament. Not only the basic principles but every detail finds fulfillment in the kingdom of God that Christ inaugurates (Matt. 5:17–20). But the way of fulfillment involves changes and displacement of what was temporary and shadowy, because it is superseded by the reality of Christ (Mark 7:19; Acts 15:9–10; Col. 2:16–17; Heb. 8–10).

New Testament ethics is also distinctive in its goal. The goal is honoring the name of Christ (Phil. 2:11). We look forward to a new heaven and a new earth in which God and the Lamb are central (Rev. 21:1–22:5). Our short-range tactics, as well as long-range strategy, should derive from our awareness that we are soldiers of Christ involved in spiritual warfare (Eph. 6:10–20; 2 Tim. 2:3–4; Rev. 2–3). The New Testament presents us with this spiritual warfare, involving angels and demons as well as human beings, not merely to enlarge our understanding of the various kinds of beings in the world but so that we might reckon practically with the importance of our allegiance to our Commander and Chief. We are citizens of heaven (Phil. 3:20; Eph. 2:19) and pilgrims and sojourners on earth (Heb. 11:13–16; 12:22–29; Rev. 7:13–14).[21]

> *The New Testament presents us with this spiritual warfare, involving angels and demons as well as human beings, not merely to enlarge our understanding of the various kinds of beings in the world but so that we might reckon practically with the importance of our allegiance to our Commander and Chief.*

Culture

One might naïvely think that Christians' citizenship in heaven implies they should have minimal interaction with things on earth. And, indeed, certain aspects of later monasticism and asceticism have drawn this conclusion. But such a conclusion is unwarranted. The commandment to love one's neighbor, central in both Jesus' teaching and in the New Testament letters, demands involvement with one's fellow human beings, not withdrawal from them. On the other hand, involvement must not lead to entanglement with the evil practices of a surrounding non-Christian world. Jesus' prayer for his disciples formulates it succinctly: "I do not ask that you take them out of the world, but that you keep them from the evil one" (John 17:15). And then: "They are not of the world, just as I am not of the world" (John 17:16). One must use the entire New Testament, and indeed the entire Bible, in thinking through what this implies about our cultural involvement.

---

21. Guthrie, *New Testament Theology*, 893–952.

The driving force of Christian living does not lie either in a positive or a negative attitude toward "culture," as such. The driving motivation should not be things or human institutions, but God. The kingdom of God is primary:

> Therefore do not be anxious, saying "What shall we eat?" or "What shall we drink?" or "What shall we wear?" For the Gentiles seek after all these things, and your heavenly Father knows that you need them all. But seek first *the kingdom of God and his righteousness*, and all these things will be added to you. (Matt. 6:31–33, emphasis added)

We are servants of the King, and everything we do should be animated by and empowered by the desire to serve and honor and please him. The admonition that Paul gives to Timothy in his capacity as a preacher and church leader is, at one level, applicable to all Christians: "No soldier gets entangled in civilian pursuits, since his aim is to please the one who enlisted him" (2 Tim. 2:4). Elsewhere Paul confirms this emphasis on exclusive loyalty as he points to the temporary character of various tasks on earth:

> This is what I mean, brothers: the appointed time has grown very short. From now on, let those who have wives live as though they had none, and those who mourn as though they were not mourning, and those who rejoice as though they were not rejoicing, and those who buy as though they had no goods, and those who deal with the world as though they had no dealings with it. For the present form of this world is passing away. (1 Cor. 7:29–31)

Some interpreters think that Paul spoke as he did because he anticipated a coming time of severe persecution, and that may be the case. But, in view of early Christians' fervent hope for the second coming, the language of "the appointed time" and the statement that "the present form of this world is passing away" seem to go beyond a mere concern for a temporary hardship. Yes, there may be persecution, but the most fundamental way in which the "present form of this world" passes away is when Christ comes. And even if Christ does not come back while we are in the midst of some unfinished business, James points out that we do not know when we will die (James 4:14–15).

The expression "civilian affairs" in 2 Timothy 2:4 (NIV) could be interpreted rigidly to mean that no truly obedient Christian should marry, or engage in business, or rejoice with others' happiness. According to this "withdrawal" interpretation, "civilian affairs" means any dealing with the world. But even in 1 Corinthians 7:29–31, the apostle Paul shows that this is a thorough misunderstanding. Christians are to go on with their marriages, with their rejoicing, with their mourning, with their buying, with their "dealing with the world," but they are to do so "as though they had no dealings with it." Whatever does Paul mean in practical terms?

Careful inspection shows that the very passage that we are looking at in 1 Corinthians 7 agrees with the God-centered emphasis found elsewhere

> "The driving force of Christian living does not lie either in a positive or a negative attitude toward "culture," as such. The driving motivation should not be things or human institutions, but God. The kingdom of God is primary.

in the New Testament. The principles involve using the gift that one has from God (v. 7), leading "the life that the Lord has assigned to him, and to which God has called him" (v. 17), and being fully committed to pleasing the Lord (vv. 32, 34). The driving force is serving the Lord in all things. It is not a question of excluding certain kinds of activity, as if we would say, "You may engage in business, but not marry," or "You may marry, but not serve as a tax collector" (see Luke 3:13). Or, "You may serve as a tax collector but not as a Roman soldier" (see Luke 3:14; Acts 10). Some activities such as thievery are indeed immoral (Eph. 4:28), but that is because God forbids them in his moral law, not because they include some contact with "the world."

Serving the Lord in all things includes reckoning with the Lord's plan for all things, and that plan looks forward to the coming of Christ and the day of judgment. All things are to be summed up in Christ (Eph. 1:10), and God will be "all in all" (1 Cor. 15:28). Unlike pagans, one must *not* continue to act under the illusion that we now live with what is normal or final (2 Peter 3:4–8).

"Serving the Lord in all things includes reckoning with the Lord's plan for all things, and that plan looks forward to the coming of Christ and the day of judgment. All things are to be summed up in Christ (Eph. 1:10), and God will be 'all in all'" (1 Cor. 15:28).

The physical stuff of this world—the plants and animals and rocks and rivers—still belongs to God, by virtue of providence as well as creation: "the earth is the Lord's and the fullness thereof" (1 Cor. 10:26). The New Testament continues the Old Testament affirmation of the goodness of the created order, over against all ascetic denial (see 1 Tim. 4:3–5).

The New Testament also acknowledges the goodness of human institutions, to the degree that these still conform to the moral will of God. Christians serve the Lord by appropriate positive action in marriage, family, and business (Eph. 5:22–6:9; Col. 3:18–4:1; 1 Peter 2:13–3:7). God has ordained governmental authorities for our good (John 19:11; Rom. 13:1–7; 1 Peter 2:13–17).

But we are not to idolize any of these things. Nor, given the New Testament eschatological teaching, are we to imagine that the things and institutions in their present form are permanent. The coming resurrection of the body involves transfiguration, not destruction, of the old (1 Cor. 15:12–57); but it *is* transfiguration, with definite discontinuities with the old (1 Cor. 15:42–49). Far from becoming a motive for passivity and withdrawal, precisely this hope for the future becomes a ground for positive service.

At the end of the famous chapter on the resurrection (1 Corinthians 15), Paul paints this picture of vigorous activity:

> Therefore, my beloved brothers, be steadfast, immovable, always abounding in the work of the Lord, knowing that in the Lord your labor is not in vain. (1 Cor. 15:58)

And in Ephesians, before proceeding to give detailed instructions about marriage (Eph. 5:22–33), family (6:1–4), and business (slaves and masters, 6:5–10), Paul points to the "inheritance in the kingdom of Christ and God" (Eph. 5:5), "the wrath of God [coming] upon the sons of disobedience" (v. 6), and the light that has dawned in association with the resurrection of Christ:

> "Awake, O sleeper, and arise from the dead, and Christ will shine on you." Look carefully then how you walk, not as unwise but as wise, making the best use of the time, because the days are evil. Therefore do not be foolish, but understand what the will of the Lord is. (Eph. 5:14–17)

Precisely in the *concrete circumstances fully involving us in the world*, we serve *the Lord*, not the things or institutions idolatrously.

Conclusion

The New Testament builds on the worldview of the Old Testament, and so one should see it as an advance rather than an overthrow of the Old Testament. But it includes new depths and new revelations, accompanying climactic redemption in Christ. The work that Christ accomplished, and the teaching that he brought, amazed observers, and he spectacularly displayed the wisdom and power and grace of God (2 Cor. 3:7–18; Eph. 3:8–10).

The message of the gospel amazed the Jews, who did not expect that God's promises would come to realization in such a way. And it confounded the thinking of Greeks, who had their own worldly ideas of wisdom (see Acts 17:22–32). In fact, it scandalized both the Jews and the Greeks, as Paul himself says, "For Jews demand signs and Greeks seek wisdom, but we preach Christ crucified, a stumbling block to Jews and folly to Gentiles" (1 Cor. 1:22–23). But by God's power some both from Jews and from Gentiles came to faith: "but to those who are called, both Jews and Greeks, Christ the power of God and the wisdom of God" (1 Cor. 1:24).

The gospel brought a revolution—in life, in power, and in worldview—to all those who received it, both Jews and Gentiles. Even those who were already familiar with the Old Testament, both the faithful Jews and the "God-fearing" Gentiles such as Cornelius, found themselves relearning and rethinking much of what they thought they knew. Those coming straight from paganism experienced an even more profound revolution as they repudiated the gods and superstitions and religious practices of their past in order to embrace the true God whom they had come to know in Christ. "He [God] has delivered us from the domain of darkness and transferred us to the kingdom of his beloved Son, in whom we have redemption, the forgiveness of sins" (Col. 1:13–14).

> "Precisely in the *concrete circumstances fully involving us in the world*, we serve *the Lord*, not the things or institutions idolatrously.

For Further Reading

Frame, John M. *The Doctrine of God*. Phillipsburg, NJ: P&R Publishing, 2002. Further exposition of the biblical teaching on God, including the biblical basis for the doctrine of the Trinity.

———. *The Doctrine of the Knowledge of God.* Phillipsburg, NJ: P&R Publishing, 1987. Biblical epistemology.

Gaffin, Richard B., Jr. *The Centrality of the Resurrection: A Study in Paul's Soteriology.* Grand Rapids: Baker, 1978. Focus on the transition in history through the work of Christ.

Guthrie, Donald. *New Testament Theology.* Downers Grove, IL: InterVarsity, 1981. Exposition of the theology of the New Testament by topics.

Ladd, George E. *A Theology of the New Testament.* Grand Rapids: Eerdmans, 1974. Focus on inaugurated eschatology, already and yet to come.

McCartney, Dan G. "Ecce Homo: The Coming of the Kingdom as the Restoration of Human Vicegerency," *WTJ* 56/1 (1994): 1–21. Focus on Christ's work as the last Adam.

Poythress, Vern S. *Symphonic Theology: The Validity of Multiple Perspectives in Theology.* Grand Rapids: Zondervan, 1987. The harmony in the diversity of writings in the New Testament.

Ridderbos, Herman. *The Coming of the Kingdom.* Philadelphia: Presbyterian and Reformed, 1969. The exposition of Christ's work in the Synoptic Gospels.

———. *Redemptive History and the New Testament Scriptures.* Phillipsburg, NJ: Presbyterian and Reformed, 1988. The authority of the New Testament.

For Further Discussion

1. How can the New Testament introduce new teaching without being in tension with the Old Testament?

2. Why is the Trinitarian character of God an important aspect of New Testament teaching? How is it important for practical Christian living? And how does it protect us against speculations that claim to offer more "ultimate" accounts of God?

3. What is the significance of the fact that Christ is the image of the invisible God (Col. 1:15)?

4. In what sense do unbelievers know God, and in what sense is knowing God the privilege only of believers?

5. In what ways have some people overlooked either the corporate aspect or the individual aspect of the benefits of Christ's redemption?

6. How do order and freedom fit together within the church?

7. What does it look like for Christians to be in the world but to refrain from entanglement with evil? Can you illustrate from one of the challenges in your life?

4

Christianity from the Early Fathers to Charlemagne

Richard C. Gamble

T he first eight centuries of Western civilization after the birth of Christ witnessed a remarkable cultural and intellectual phenomenon. At the end of the first century, Christianity was a miniscule group in the Middle East and Asia Minor, comprising just over 1 percent of the population of the Roman Empire. As Christianity expanded rapidly westward in the second and third centuries, it experienced waves of persecution from Roman authorities. Yet, ironically, Christianity grew from its small beginnings to constitute over 50 percent of the population by 350; and by the reign of Charlemagne, Christianity had permeated Western Europe. The biblical worldview established in Scripture unfolded in the writers and movements covered in this chapter, whose purpose is to trace the emergence and growth of the Christian worldview up to the time of Charlemagne.

> *Christianity grew from its small beginnings to constitute over 50 percent of the population by 350; and by the reign of Charlemagne, Christianity had permeated Western Europe.*

The Apostolic Fathers

One of the best ways to view the thought world of the earliest post–New Testament era is through the lens of that period's extant Christian literature, a body of writing known as the Apostolic Fathers. This term, which first appeared in the seventeenth century, refers to figures and writings that emerged in the aftermath of the apostolic witness. These writings appeared alongside others that eventually comprised the canon of the New Testament. Because the Apostolic Fathers often interpret and apply the emerging Christian worldview, these documents reflect concerns of the church as it confronted impending persecution and heresy. The following representative sampling of the Apostolic Fathers reveals the Christian worldview of the earliest post–New Testament era.

Clement of Rome

Clement was supposedly the third successor of the apostle Peter. Although we know little of his early life, he rose to become a prominent bishop in Rome.[1] Toward the end of Emperor Domitian's reign (81–96), a debate broke out between the leaders of the congregation and some members of the church in Corinth. Clement wrote a letter, *1 Clement*, or the *Epistle to the Corinthians*,[2] to admonish them to submit to the leaders.[3] After the New Testament, this is the earliest known Christian writing.[4]

Dissensions erupted within the church, and some leaders were repudiated. Clement, much like Paul, wrote to settle the differences, and he pleaded for unity, discipline, and love. The epistle insisted that God had prescribed the time, place, and way that worship was to be conducted.[5] When believers follow God's laws, then they do not sin. If they fail to obey, they will be visited by death.[6] Clement also taught that God bestowed on the ordained clergy authority that made an indelible mark on the priest. The document has rightly been dubbed the birthplace of the Roman Catholic notion of the rights of the church.[7]

Icon of the martyrdom of Saint Ignatius

Ignatius of Antioch

Ignatius suffered a martyr's death in Rome during Emperor Trajan's reign (98–117). On the way to his execution, he wrote seven letters.[8] From

1. See Johannes Quasten, *Patrology* (Westminster MD: Newman Press, 1951), 1:42–44.
2. For an English translation, see Alexander Roberts and James Donaldson, trans., *The Ante-Nicene Fathers* (Grand Rapids: Eerdmans, 1950–), 1:1–23.
3. Ernst Shaehelin, *Die Verkündigung des Reiches Gottes in der Kirche Jesu Christi.* Erster Band, *Von der Zeit der Apostel bus zur Auflösung des Römischen Reiches* (Basel, 1951), 85.
4. Bertrand Altaner, Alfred Stuiber, *Patrologie: Leben, Schriften und Lehre der Kirchenväter.* (Freiburg: Herder, 1978), 45. Karl Heussi, *Kompendium der Kirchengeschichte* (Tübingen: Mohr Siebeck, 1991), 26. Quasten, *Patrology,* 1:43.
5. Hans Lietzmann, *Geschichte* (Berlin u. Leipzig: Walter de Gruyter, 1932), 1:203. *The Ante-Nicene Fathers,* 1:16, chap. 40: "He has enjoined offerings to be presented and service to be performed to Him, and that not thoughtlessly or irregularly, but at the appointed times and hours. Where and by whom He desires these things to be done, He himself has fixed by His own supreme will, in order that all things being piously done according to His good pleasure, may be acceptable unto Him."
6. An English text is found in the *Ante-Nicene Fathers,* 1:16, chap. 41. "Those, therefore, who do anything beyond that which is agreeable to His will, are punished with death." He continued: "And what wonder is it if those in Christ who were entrusted with such a duty by God, appointed those ministers before mentioned, when the blessed Moses, also a faithful servant in all his house, noted down in the sacred books all the injunctions which were given him, and when the other prophets also followed him, bearing witness with one consent to the ordinances which he had appointed," 43.
7. Lietzmann, *Geschichte,* 1:204. Shaehelin, *Die Verkündigung,* 1:116. See Heussi, *Kompendium,* 26. J. N. D. Kelly, *Early Christian Doctrines,* 5th ed. (London: Black, 1977), 35.
8. Shaehelin, *Die Verkündigung,* 1:90–93. See Heussi, *Kompendium,* 26.

> *Clement also taught that God bestowed on the ordained clergy authority that made an indelible mark on the priest. The document has rightly been dubbed the birthplace of the Roman Catholic notion of the rights of the church.*

Smyrna, he wrote to churches in Ephesus, Magnesia, and Tralles, exhorting the communities to obedience and thanking them for their faithfulness to him. He also wrote to Rome, imploring Christians not to attempt to intervene on his behalf to hinder his martyrdom. Letters were sent from Troas to the cities of Philadelphia and Smyrna, and to the presbyter Polycarp. Ignatius requested that these churches send delegates to congratulate survivors of the persecution. Ignatius's letters indicate the strength of the ties between churches and a shared consciousness that led them to seek consensus on matters of great concern. They also convey the high value attributed to faithfulness under persecution and to martyrdom's stature as the ultimate witness a Christian could bear in such circumstances.

Polycarp of Smyrna

According to tradition, Polycarp sat at the feet of John the apostle before suffering martyrdom (ca. 155). Polycarp wrote the *Epistle to the Philippians*, a letter of exhortation and defense of the doctrine of the incarnation and Christ's death on the cross. He enjoined prayer for the civil authorities.[9] The graphic description of Polycarp's courage in the face of martyrdom, as well as his refusal to proffer worship to the emperor, lent confidence to the church as persecution spread in the second century and signaled how, from its inception, the good news of the New Testament emboldened followers to die for their faith.

The Epistle of Barnabas

The *Epistle of Barnabas*, which appeared during Emperor Hadrian's reign, is more a theological tract than a letter. The author, definitely not the apostle Barnabas, but probably a gentile convert, wrote from the city of Alexandria with the goal of imparting what he called "perfect knowledge" and faith.[10] The letter consists of a theoretical section and a practical one. The work asserts the preexistence of Christ. It also teaches that baptism confers adoption to sonship and makes believers temples of the Holy Spirit. Of contemporary relevance, the work obligates Christians to protect the lives of infants, even the unborn (19:5).

The author's exegetical method[11] set the tone for interpreting Scripture for centuries. The author thought that the Old Testament is best understood not as straightforward history but rather by the use of "allegory." Under the allegorical method, events in Israelite history derived their importance not from their historicity but from their spiritual or moral meaning. In this

> *The graphic description of Polycarp's courage in the face of martyrdom, as well as his refusal to proffer worship to the emperor, lent confidence to the church as persecution spread in the second century . . . .*

---

9. Heussi, *Kompendium*, 26.

10. Shaehelin, *Verkündigung*, 1:96.

11. Lietzmann, *Geschichte*, 1:229.

way, the Old Testament speaks clearly of that which was to come in the New Testament.[12]

The epistle probes the change of celebration from Saturday to Sunday for Christians. The author underlined the Sabbath[13] command in the Ten Commandments, as well as the covenantal promise that when the Sabbath was embraced in the heart, God's love would be poured out on his people. He also called the Sabbath the "beginning of creation."[14]

In his allegorical elaboration of the completion of creation in six days, the author was convinced that it meant that in six thousand years the Lord would complete the history of the earth. Each creation day stood for one thousand years. Concerning Isaiah 1:13, where God says that he rejects their Sabbaths and new moons, this passage meant that the present Sabbath was not unwelcome: rather, a time will come when God will bring all things to rest, and then he will create another world. The new world will last for eight days, which means the beginning of, perhaps, another world. This period of days will be a time of joy.[15]

Israel's dietary law prohibiting pork also was allegorical. The law actually forbade too much interaction with men who are, in fact, like pigs.[16] Finally, the writer turns his attention to Jesus as presented in the Old Testament. He sees the cross in the outstretched hands of the praying Moses and the snake that Moses lifted up in the wilderness. Additionally, he believes the scapegoat in Leviticus 16:7–10 pictures the coming Christ.[17] Barnabas's allegorizing method gained wide acceptance in the early church, leading many to search for hidden meanings instead of receiving the literal, historical meaning as the basis for their worldview.

The Shepherd of Hermas

This is a book of "revelations," supposedly granted to the Roman Christian Hermas. They were delivered by two heavenly beings: an old woman and a shepherd. The first section of the work contains four visions and a transition section that is followed by the second section, which contains twelve commands and nine parables.[18] Like Barnabas, the *Shepherd* depends heavily on allegory. Hermas views the church as a tower made of stones drawn from water. It exercised strong pastoral influence by saying

> *[The **Shepherd of Hermas** was] a book of "revelations," supposedly granted to the Roman Christian Hermas. They were delivered by two heavenly beings: an old woman and a shepherd.*

---

12. Shaehelin, *Verkündigung*, 1:96. By the word "allegory," the author probably means what we refer to as "typology." For more information on allegory, see Kelly, *Early Christian Doctrines*, 70.

13. Shaehelin, *Verkündigung*, 1:97.

14. The original Greek text can be found in *MSG*, 2:727ff.

15. *The Epistle of Barnabas*, chap. 15, 1–9. See Shaehelin, *Verkündigung*, 1:97–98.

16. Lietzmann, *Geschichte*, 1:231. See *Barnabas*, 10, 1–8.

17. On Moses, see *Barnabas* 12, 1–7. For information on the scapegoat, see *Barnabas* 7, 6–10.

18. The English text can be found in *Ante-Nicene Fathers*, 2:9–55.

that the stones, if damaged, can only be cleansed once. This led people to postpone baptism for fear of sinning after they received it.

The Didache

The full title of this work reads, "The Lord's instruction to the Gentiles through the twelve Apostles." Although not actually written by the apostles, the text provides a brief summary of early doctrine, ethical norms, and church practice.[19] The first part of the text (chaps. 1–10) contains a moral treatise that articulated the way of life and the way of death. Six chapters present the two ways for the newly baptized. They summarize the way of life by using segments from the Ten Commandments and ethical injunctions against abortion, infanticide, and practices that involve magic or omens. The way of life fosters qualities that would prove winsome to outsiders, by enjoining attitudes consistent with the highest standard of ethics—humility, kindness, patience, and receptivity, rather than rebellion in the face of difficult circumstances. By contrast, the way of death includes an extended list of sins that range from obvious external acts of murder and idolatry, to pride, hypocrisy, boasting, refusal to pity the disadvantaged, and oppressing the afflicted. Chapters 7–10 propose liturgical suggestions for Christian baptism, fasting, prayer, and the Lord's Supper. The second part (chaps. 11–15) contains disciplinary regulations and instructions regarding bishops, deacons, and prophets. The last chapter discusses the return of the Lord. Thus, as a whole, the *Didache* is a compilation of material that is not as consistent a unit as we might wish![20] Nevertheless, its worldview assumes a close-knit community that adheres to clearly defined moral absolutes that contrast sharply with the surrounding culture.

Thus, the Apostolic Fathers provide a first glimpse of the new Christian worldview. They demonstrate the second-century concern for church order—in polity, liturgy, and morality. The documents also display a clear self-consciousness that with the emergence of Christianity a radically new perspective had arrived. They unequivocally commend obedience to biblical ethical standards, in contrast to surrounding pagan fashions, and they helped formalize early Christian belief and behavior. Their writings provide the first bridge between biblical revelation and the more fully balanced and developed Christian worldviews that followed.

Portion of the Didache

Heretics

Besides this relatively small collection of literature, the earliest life of the ancient church witnessed the appearance of those whom we call "her-

---

19. The text was not known to the scholarly world until 1883. Since the work is a compilation, it is difficult to determine a precise composition date. Scholars estimate that it was written either in Syria or in Egypt between the years 100 and 150. See K. Heussi, *Kompendium*, 26.

20. Shaehelin, *Verkündigung*, 1:88. Lietzmann, *Geschichte*, 1:213.

etics"—those whose ideas differed sharply from the biblical worldview and the developing tradition of the church. The emergence of radically different views illustrates the antithesis between truth and error that is present in the pages of the Old and New Testaments and throughout history. Two movements—Marcionism and Montanism—deserve special attention, since they posed significant threats to biblical Christianity in the second century.

Marcion

Marcion's father was a bishop from an area near the Black Sea. Apparently, his own father dismissed him for espousing false theological positions. Marcion traveled to the West, visiting Smyrna, where he met the leader Polycarp, then continued to Rome. Conflict seemed to accompany him, and in July of 144 his refusal to retract heretical ideas led the congregation to excommunicate him. His writing, *Antitheses*, depicts an enormous difference between the God of the Old Testament—a cruel, ignorant, and fickle deity—and the New Testament God of love, mercy, and forgiveness. His denial of the unity of biblical revelation spread rapidly throughout the church. In support of his radical dualism, he proposed a canon that consisted of his own work, the gospel of Luke with all passages favorable to the Old Testament expurgated, and a similarly altered Pauline corpus. Thus, the first list of authoritative writings came from a heretic, and this forced the church to propose its own list in response. Marcion died about 160.[21]

Montanus and Montanism

About 156, Montanus, a converted pagan priest, appeared in the small town of Ardabau in Phrygien. He claimed to have received spiritual revelations from God. More importantly, he contended that God the Father, the Son, and especially the Holy Spirit worked in him and spoke through him, and that he had to communicate those revelations to the whole church. Montanus also preached the imminent arrival of the heavenly Jerusalem, preceded by a general distribution and filling of the Holy Spirit, and claimed that God had commissioned him as a forerunner for this great occurrence. To prepare for the arrival of the heavenly Jerusalem, the church was to engage in certain ascetic practices, particularly fasting.[22]

From a worldview perspective, Gnosticism and Montanism posed a profound threat to Christian belief and practice because their extreme views created radical alternatives to scriptural teaching and the emerging doctrine of the church. Self-appointed leaders and new customs at odds with biblical practice challenged orthodox leaders to form standards that would oppose fallacious systems of thought and aberrant religious activities.

From this brief survey of writings, we find Christianity taking root as a worldview. Various forms of literature display a vigorous faith, concern

> *Thus, the Apostolic Fathers provide a first glimpse of the new Christian worldview. They demonstrate the second-century concern for church order—in polity, liturgy, and morality.*

> *More importantly, [Montanus] contended that God the Father, the Son, and especially the Holy Spirit worked in him and spoke through him, and that he had to communicate those revelations to the whole church.*

21. Lietzmann, *Geschichte*, 1:265–81. K. D. Schmidt, *Grundriss der Kirchengeschichte*, 69.
22. Shaehelin, *Verkündigung*, 1:110.

for unity and organization, celebration of the sacraments, and ethical principles demanding a vital Christian life consistent with biblical teaching. But the emergence of false teaching and charismatic groups that contrasted sharply with biblical truth and practice illustrates competing worldviews that necessitated clear standards, or norms, for the young faith.

The Apologists

In the second and third centuries, a group of writers called "apologists" emerged and defended Christianity as it came under attack from pagan sources. While early heresies illustrate internal threats to the integrity of Christianity, opposition arose from various external groups as well. Rome regarded the profession of Christianity a capital crime, and since the time of Emperor Hadrian, believers wrote letters or tracts defending Christianity against the misunderstandings and slanders of the opposition. Additionally, the Roman intelligentsia disparaged the "new" religion and subjected it to virulent ridicule.[23] In response, apologists demonstrated that converting to Christianity did not entail treason against the state nor demand committing intellectual suicide.[24]

The apologists presented Christianity as a "philosophy," in fact as the sole true philosophy, set in competition with Greek religions and worldviews. Some argue that because of this goal, apologists adopted the methods, words, and even the perspectives of Hellenistic philosophical thinking. This approach could be called a "Hellenization" of Christianity.[25] Other apologists viewed philosophy as the archenemy of Christianity, and they portrayed Christian belief and philosophical speculation as polar opposites.

Aristides of Athens

Aristides, formerly a philosopher in Athens, addressed the earliest surviving apology to the Emperor Hadrian (ca. 140). Claiming that he came to this knowledge through contemplation of the world and its existing harmonies, Aristides described the Divine Being using Stoic terminology. According to Aristides, the attributes of the Godhead could be determined only negatively. We can say what God is not. This type of theology is termed a *via negativa*. Aristides also represented Christianity as a philosophy that competed with other philosophies because of its consistency with reason and its answers to the questions that philosophers ask.

> *The apologists presented Christianity as a "philosophy," in fact as the sole true philosophy, set in competition with Greek religions and worldviews.*

---

23. Altaner and Stuiber, *Patrologie*, 60. The Emperor Marcus Aurelius had issued a law in 176 that prohibited new religions—a law clearly directed against Christianity.

24. Heussi, *Kompendium*, 33.

25. Heussi, *Kompenium*, 33–34. He charges that they not only took on the methods of Hellenic thought, but that they also were responsible for "the hellenization of the Christian thought world."

He criticized polytheism by use of *reductio ad absurdum*; he systematically demonstrated that all other religions worship false deities.[26]

Justin Martyr

Born in Palestine to pagan parents, Justin was arguably the most important of the apologists. His worldview thinking included forays in Stoicism, Aristotelianism, Pythagoreanism, Platonism, and several other studies before his conversion to Christianity. Following his conversion in Ephesus, he defended Christianity the rest of his life, wearing a philosopher's cloak.[27]

Justin Martyr

Justin authored a number of works. As did many of the apologists, he addressed his *Apology* (ca. 150–55) to the emperor. The first part boldly pointed out the injustice of a government that punished believers solely because they were Christians, rather than because of proven immoral behavior. He protested against the prefect Urbicus's beheading believers merely for the fact that they were Christians. Since Christian belief had not been shown to be criminal, the empire was in danger of committing a worse injustice than the Athenians when they killed Socrates. Christians are not atheists; they are the intellectual and spiritual heirs of truth wherever it is found. The second part of the apology justified Christianity through a positive presentation of doctrines.

Next, Justin wrote the *Dialogue with Trypho*, a lengthy work consisting of 142 chapters—actually a transcript of a two-day discussion with a learned Jew, perhaps the Rabbi Tarphon, who is mentioned in the Mishna. The introduction includes a narrative of Justin's conversion. The main section presents a Christian understanding of the Old Testament, defends the deity of Christ, and presents Christians as the "New Israel."[28]

Justin placed God at the heart of his worldview, depicting him as without origin and nameless (*Apol.* 2, 6). Unfortunately, his description sounds quite similar to Plato's description of the "Demiurge." Additionally, in Justin's Christology there is a Logos mediator and a clear subordination between the Father and the Logos (*Apol.* 2, 6). Justin refers to Jesus as a "teacher." Justin's "Logos Christology" provided a point of contact between pagan philosophy and Christianity. He considered Christ, the incarnate Reason (Logos) of God, to be superior to all philosophers. Using

> " Justin was arguably the most important of the apologists. ... Following his conversion in Ephesus, he defended Christianity the rest of his life, wearing a philosopher's cloak.

26. His speaking of God in negative terms and his advocacy of the unknowability of God runs counter to the biblical teaching that God has revealed his attributes so that the supreme goal of life itself is to know God. Another figure from this time was Quadratus. All that we know of him comes from Eusebius's *Church History*. He presented an apology to Emperor Hadrian about the year 125 in which he presented Jesus' miracles as proof of his being the savior.

27. Justin founded a school at Rome during the time of Emperor Antonius Pius (138–61). He received his name when Rome beheaded him, ca. 165, with six of his companions.

28. Justin also composed other works, including *Against All Heresies*, written against Marcion; *Discourse Against the Greeks*; *On the Sovereignty of God*; and *On the Soul*.

Stoic terminology, Justin argued that the philosophers have the seed of the Logos (*logos spermaticos*), which is the source of truth for all people. But Christians have more than the seed; they have the Logos himself. Wherever truth appeared prior to Christianity, the Logos mediated it. Platonic philosophy, for example, had only plagiarized Moses! But both Jews and Greeks nevertheless knew the truth. Whoever lived according to reason was a genuine believer, even though he lived among godless people. Only among Christians, however, has the Logos been fully revealed and thus come to fruition.

Justin's doctrine of human nature proved significant for the development of Pelagianism in the fifth century and Arminianism in the seventeenth century. Justin believed humans possess unlimited free will, that we are completely independent. While attempting to protect the idea of human responsibility, Justin presented moral autonomy as the way to resist the Stoic doctrine of fate and determinism. According to Justin, God did not foreordain human events; he only foreknew them. Thus, the idea of free will entered into Christian doctrine by the apologist's marriage of Greek philosophy and Christianity (i.e., the world's independence from the Platonic Forms).

Tatian the Syrian

Tatian came to Rome and became a Christian and student of Justin. He opposed marriage, drinking wine, and eating meat. His works include *The Discourse to the Greeks*, written after 165, which was perhaps not really intended to be an apology for Christianity. Whatever the purpose of the book, Tatian, unlike his mentor, utterly rejected and sharply criticized Greek cults. Four sections juxtapose Christian thinking and pagan thought: cosmology, demonology (astrology and the nature of demons), a critique of Greek society, and the moral value of Christianity.

Athenagoras of Athens

The most eloquent of the Christian apologists,[29] Athenagoras was kinder than Tatian in his attitude toward Greek culture. *The Supplication for the Christians* was written about 177. Athenagoras rebutted the three standard legal charges made against Christians: they are atheists; they practice cannibalism; and they commit incest. His *On the Resurrection of the Dead* attempted to prove the doctrine of the resurrection from the viewpoint of reason. The resurrection of the dead in no way interferes with God's nature. Furthermore, it is consistent with the nature of humanity—God created humans for eternity. Athenagoras also illustrated early Trinitarian belief among apologists. He carefully avoided subordinationism in his teaching,[30] and he affirmed the deity of the Holy Spirit. He was convinced that true wisdom depends on revelation (*Suppl.* 7).

> *Justin believed humans possess unlimited free will, that we are completely independent. While attempting to protect the idea of human responsibility, Justin presented moral autonomy as the way to resist the Stoic doctrine of fate and determinism.*

29. Quasten, *Patrology*, 229.
30. Sadly, subordinationism was common among the other apologists.

Theophilus of Antioch

Theophilus converted from a pagan background. His writings include *Ad Autolycum* (ca. 180), in which he defended Christianity against the objections of his pagan friend Autolycus. His defense of Scripture stands out as the first postbiblical work to develop the doctrine of the inspiration of Scripture, illustrating that Scripture's infallibility and the continuity of the Old and New Testaments were assumed from the earliest times. Theophilus called Paul's writings and the gospels, the "holy word of God" (2:22; 3:13ff.).[31]

Melito of Sardis

Very little is known about Melito of Sardis. We know that he wrote an apology (ca. 170), parts of which appear in Eusebius's *Church History*. Another work, *Homily on the Passion*, discovered only recently, contains the story of the exodus and the Passover, both of which served as types of Christ's redemptive activity. Melito asserted Christ's divinity, his preexistence, his incarnation, and the doctrine of original sin.

Thus the apologists wrote in a difficult time, and they attempted to present Christianity in a manner that would appeal to their persecutors. Their writings clearly indicate the persistence of Christian belief in a hostile environment and a perceived need to defend the faith as something true, substantial, and worthy of intellectual adherence. Although some apologists adopted Greek philosophical categories in order to defend Christianity, others repudiated philosophy.

> "
> *The apologists wrote in a difficult time, and they attempted to present Christianity in a manner that would appeal to their persecutors. . . . Although some apologists adopted Greek philosophical categories in order to defend Christianity, others repudiated philosophy.*

Persecution of the People of God

Christianity was a persecuted religion until the momentous year 313, when the Emperor Constantine acknowledged the faith as legitimate. Persecution formed a unique part of the church's history and profoundly shaped Christian thinking. The history of persecution had worldview significance. Historically speaking, the book of Acts narrates the earliest persecutions of Christianity—first at the hands of Jews,[32] then afterward from Gentiles. Persecution persisted, but not continuously, for over two hundred years.[33]

---

31. Kelly, *Early Christian Doctrines*, 69.

32. During the famous Bar-Cochba wars (132–35), when Judaism suffered severe restrictions, the leader of the insurrection forced all Christians to either join him or be murdered. The rebellion failed, and the Roman government nearly destroyed Judaism. It appears to many scholars that the Talmud, written toward the end of the second century, as well as the Babylonian Talmud (430–521), are inherently anti-Christian as well.

33. Classifying and counting the number of persecutions prove difficult. Some, such as Augustine in the *City of God*, put the number of persecutions at ten. Lactantius cited six; other ancient writers have suggested nine. The exact number is not important to remember. We need to investigate the various background elements that provide a unified structure to

Persecution under the Roman Government

Christianity was an illegal religion from the time of Emperor Trajan (98–117), who first pronounced Christianity a forbidden religion. He prohibited all secret societies, or clubs, thus reviving an earlier statute. Trajan's policy regulated the treatment of Christians for more than a century. Under Trajan, Ignatius of Antioch was torn to shreds by beasts in Rome.

The terror of the Diocletian persecution covered the entire Roman Empire, lasted from 303 to 311–13, and exceeded all previous official outbursts. Edicts grew progressively worse and worse: to destroy church buildings, to burn Bibles, to remove all Christians from public office, and to demand that Christians, on pain of death, sacrifice to the pagan gods. The famous church historian Eusebius witnessed the persecutions in Egypt and narrated how churches were razed, Bibles burned in marketplaces, and pastors hunted, seized, and tortured. Christians frequently faced death at the fangs of wild beasts. It was so terrible and bloody, Eusebius reported, that even the beasts got tired of their frequent attacks on the innocent Christians.

The Meaning or Interpretation of the Persecutions

The story of persecution in the early church elicits various responses, and a proper interpretation is not an easy task. Believers today must wonder whether God would give them strength to endure torture or even bear commonplace insults. They should reflect on what it would be like to worship in secret and to have all property confiscated.

Certain interpretive factors must come into consideration. First, persecutions were intermittent. They did not occur continuously to 313. Still, the possibility of outbreak always existed.[34] Many maintain that this is the case because popular opinion remained uniformly hostile to the church.[35] The reasons for this may be varied, but the main one is that Christianity required a certain way of life. How did this Christian worldview appear to the average Roman citizen?

First, Christians were generally known as what we would call "killjoys" or "stick-in-the-muds." The *Epistle to Diognetus* (ca. 130) reported, "the world hates the Christians, though it receives no wrong from them, because they set themselves against its pleasures." We also have a complaint

"Alexamenos worships his god."
Roman graffiti mocking the crucifixion

all the persecutions of the ancient church. Generally, Christianity existed in urban environments that provided the context for the persecutions.

34.   B. J. Kidd, *A History of the Christian Church to AD 461* (Oxford: Oxford University Press, 1922), 227.

35.   Nero knew there was sufficient popular opinion against Christians to use them as scapegoats as early as AD 64. See F. F. Bruce, *The Growing Day: The Progress of Christianity from the Fall of Jerusalem to the Accession of Constantine* (Grand Rapids: Eerdmans, 1953), 15.

from the *Octavius* of Miniscus Felix (ca. 180): "You abstain from the pleasures of a gentleman"—that is, the theatre and the gladiatorial games.[36]

Texts also blamed Christians for their slight interest in public affairs, for their separateness from the rest of society, and for shirking their social duties. Romans found Christianity so unpopular that Tacitus described Christians as "a class of men loathed for their vices." And Suetonius's *A Life of Nero* called Christianity "a new and baneful superstition."[37] The people found Christians loathsome, and philosophers joined the critique. Philosophers saw Christianity as an intellectual rival; the kingdom over the minds of men was gradually slipping from their grasp.[38]

The problem was further complicated because most of the population did not know much about Christianity, and much of what they "knew" was not true. For example, since only Christians were permitted to partake of the Lord's Supper, false stories, not based on actual observation, circulated about it.

Finally, opponents of Christianity leveled several general charges against the new faith. Many called Christians "atheists," since Christians did not worship a visible god.[39] Atheism, however, carried an additional meaning in Roman culture. "Atheism" implied indifference to a citizen's duties, political or social, as well as disloyalty to the state.[40] Because Christians did not participate in daily cultural activities—many practices entailed an immoral lifestyle—atheism seemed like a legitimate charge. Other accusations focused on the Lord's Supper. Grossly fallacious claims circulated that Christians sacrificed their children, practiced cannibalism, and committed incest (Christians greeted each other with a "holy kiss" and called each other "brothers and sisters"). Christian apologists warded off such attacks by informing their accusers of the true nature of their faith.

Because God controls all events, summarizing the cause of Christian persecution involves acknowledging the sovereign mercy of God in ordaining all things that happen. But, the outstanding observation concerning second-century persecutions in particular is that they were sporadic and prompted by the mob.[41] It was the masses who were moved against a religion that was considered a novelty, that had barbarian origins, that perhaps most importantly, had no national basis, and that was perceived as having a blind, irrational faith. Also of note is the fact that the average Christian appears to have lacked "culture" and "social standing" and, generally speaking, was poor. Christians also lacked "patriotism" (even in modern

> *Romans found Christianity so unpopular that Tacitus described Christians as "a class of men loathed for their vices."*

> *Because Christians did not participate in daily cultural activities—many practices entailed an immoral lifestyle—atheism seemed like a legitimate charge.*

---

36. Kidd, *History*, 228.
37. Bruce, *Growing Day*, 15.
38. L. Duchesne, *Early History of the Christian Church from Its Foundation to the End of the Fifth Century* (London: Murray, 1965), 146.
39. Bruce, *Growing Day*, 15.
40. Kidd, *History*, 233.
41. Kidd, *History*, 233.

America, this is considered a sin) and were perceived as being "gloomingly serious."[42]

Taken together, the apologist movement and the persecution of Christianity benefited the church in at least two ways. The apologists enabled Christians to solidify their views in the context of intellectual opposition. The worldview that emerged out of a rigorous defense of the faith manifested itself as individual believers lived out that faith under duress. Persecution enabled the church to grow through suffering. As Tertullian said so famously, "The blood of the martyrs is the seed of the church." The strength of conviction that led men and women to refuse to sacrifice to the emperor lent believability to the gospel. The Christian faith became something worth dying for. The burgeoning numbers of converts, even in the face of martyrdom, helped facilitate its growth. The rapid rise of Christianity, including its worldview, owed much to the simple faith, patience, and composure that men and women manifested as they lived out their beliefs in the face of persecution and martyrdom.[43]

Early Western and Eastern Writers

In addition to the apostolic fathers and the apologists, the early church produced theologians who further fleshed out the nature of Christian belief. Although apologists defended the faith, a corps of thinkers in both east and west helped to further develop Christian doctrines. Schools of thought in Asia Minor, Alexandria, and North Africa gave rise to distinctive perspectives that provided breadth and depth to the unity of Christian thought.

School of Asia Minor: Irenaeus of Lyons (ca. 130–200)

Irenaeus was born in Smyrna in Asia Minor. He was sent from Gaul (France) to Rome to help mediate the Montanist problem.[44] Irenaeus figured prominently in the development of the Christian worldview in several areas. As an apologist, he leveled a devastating attack against Gnosticism. In his defense of the authority of the Scripture and the teaching of the church, he articulated one of the earliest full-orbed theologies to counter false views of Christian teaching.

Detection and Overthrow of the Pretended but False Gnosis is his main work.[45] The Latin title is usually translated *Against Heresies*. This work attacked the Valentinians, Marcionites, and other Gnostic schools because their doctrines contradict the writings of the apostles. No secret teachings,

> *The rapid rise of Christianity, including its worldview, owed much to the simple faith, patience, and composure that men and women manifested as they lived out their beliefs in the face of persecution and martyrdom.*

---

42. Philip Schaff, *History of the Christian Church* (Grand Rapids: Eerdmans, 1979), 2:103.

43. Cf. Rodney Stark, *The Rise of Christianity: How the Obscure, Marginal Jesus Movement Became the Dominant Religious Force in the Western World in a Few Centuries* (San Francisco: Harper, 1997).

44. Later mythology lists him dying as a martyr, but this cannot be established firmly.

45. We have no copy of the original Greek, but we do possess a Latin translation.

such as the Gnostics claimed, actually derive from Jesus and the apostles. Genuine Christianity appears not in secret myths and the incoherent teachings typical of Gnosticism but in the "rule of truth" that is consistent with the content of the Bible and church tradition. Irenaeus exposed the errors of Gnosticism by showing that his own teaching reflected what his teacher, Polycarp, learned from the apostle John. Over against the Gnostic denigration of the material world, Irenaeus affirmed the biblical God as Creator and Redeemer of both the material and spiritual worlds, and this has important worldview implications.[46]

Against Heresies contains a unique Christology and anthropology. Irenaeus speculated, for example, that Jesus must have lived to be approximately fifty years old! This teaching, which contradicts the content of the Gospels, is a by-product of his theory of recapitulation. He interpreted Ephesians 1:10 as saying that unlike Adam who sinned, Christ brought redemption by recapitulating, or summing up, all the stages of human life in sinless obedience. This recapitulation necessitated Jesus living to an old age—a period longer than the thirty years presented in the Bible. Additionally, some have asserted that Irenaeus is the father of biblical theology because he saw God actively working in this world. In his reaction against Gnosticism, whose god could not get his hands dirty, God, in Irenaeus's thought, not only touches but also acts in the world from Genesis to the consummation.

In rebutting the Gnostics, Irenaeus constantly appealed to tradition. However, it is difficult to determine exactly what he meant by *tradition*. Sometimes, he seemed to appeal to a shorter form of the old Roman creed, which is similar to our Apostles' Creed. At other times, his citations entailed the authority of bishops and presbyters. The bishop teaches true exposition to the presbyter. Especially important for Irenaeus were those bishops who could be traced back to the first century, thus ensuring continuation of apostolic truth.

Thus, Irenaeus cited many sources and emerged as the first theologian of stature in the post-apostolic church. His works display a thorough, constructive wrestling with the rationality and coherence of the gospel message, presenting the themes of creation, fall, and redemption, while opposing beliefs clearly antithetical to the biblical message. Some of his ideas have been discarded, and some of his treatments of Scripture raise more problems than they solve.[47] But, on the whole, he remained faithful to apostolic teaching and defended it aggressively against rival worldviews.

> *Irenaeus cited many sources and emerged as the first theologian of stature in the post-apostolic church. His works display a thorough, constructive wrestling with the rationality and coherence of the gospel message, presenting the themes of creation, fall, and redemption, while rebutting beliefs clearly antithetical to the biblical message.*

---

46. In another, smaller work, *Demonstration of the Apostolic Preaching*, Irenaeus defends the truth of Christianity in simpler terms than in *Against Heresies*. He demonstrates from the Old Testament that Jesus was the Son of David and the Messiah as well. He ends by saying that Christians should live in godliness.

47. An example is his chiliasm or millenarianism. See Kelly, *Early Christian Doctrines*, 469.

North Africa: Tertullian (ca. 160–225)[48]

Quintus Septimius Florens Tertullian was born to pagan parents in the city of Carthage. He became an accomplished lawyer in Rome, was converted sometime around 193–95, and subsequently left Rome to return home, where he pastored a church. At a later date, certainly by the year 207, he joined a group called the Montanists. With his talents and leadership abilities, he became the head of a subgroup named the "Tertullianists," a sect that lasted until the time of Augustine (350). Except for Augustine, Tertullian is considered the most important and original ecclesiastical author in the Latin tongue.[49] His writings express the most comprehensive theological vision in the West prior to Augustine.[50]

Tertullian's literary works fall under various headings. He treats almost every topic that has to do with Christian thinking and behavior. Among Tertullian's apologetic works,[51] the *Apology* (197) is his most important. He directed it to governors of the Roman provinces to demonstrate how Christians were hated because of their refusal to venerate the gods. He demonstrated that Christians were not enemies of the state, and disputed the idea that Christ was a new God. He argued that Christianity is divine revelation. The *Scorpiace* was an antidote, he said, against the scorpion's sting. The stinging scorpions were the Gnostics. The Gnostics thought that it was foolish for Christians to permit martyrdom; Tertullian praised martyrdom. *On the Flesh of Christ* opposed the docetic denial of the reality of Christ's flesh. In *The Resurrection of the Flesh*, Tertullian took on pagans, heretics, and Sadducees. He used reason to conclude that since body and soul were created by God, both need judgment. He cites numerous biblical references to reinforce the importance of the incarnation.

A number of his writings are classified as controversial treatises.[52] The *Prescription of Heretics* was intended to end controversies between "catholic" Christians and heretics. The Latin word *praescriptio*, a technical term in Roman law, describes the defendant's objection to the way the plain-

> *Except for St. Augustine, Tertullian is considered the most important and original ecclesiastical author in the Latin tongue. His writings express the most comprehensive theological vision in the West prior to Augustine.*

---

48. Further information on Tertullian, especially on the Trinity, may be found in B. B. Warfield, *Studies in Tertullian and Augustine* (New York: Oxford University Press, 1930).

49. Quasten, *Patrology*, 2:247.

50. Altaner and Stuiber, *Patrologie*, 148. His Latin is extremely difficult; there have been many scholarly studies concerning his style. Quasten, *Patrology*, 2:247. He used new terms and preferred uncommon forms.

51. Other works include *To the Heathen*, written in 197, which is similar in content to the *Apology*. *To Scapula* was written in 212 and consists of five chapters. Scapula was a Proconsul (211–13) of Africa, and Tertullian wrote regarding the persecution. *Against the Jews* was written to clarify a dispute between two proselytes. Tertullian probably used parts of Justin's *Dialogue with Trypho*. For more information, see Altaner and Stuiber, *Patrologie*, 153; and Staehelin, *Verkündigung*, 1:143.

52. Some of Tertullian's other polemical writings include *Against Marcion*, which gives us the main source of our knowledge of Marcion (written between 207–12), and *Against Hermogenes*. Hermogenes of Carthage was a Gnostic, and this work was written after 200. Tertullian also wrote *Against the Valentinians* and *Against Quintilian*.

tiff presented his legal case. The legal objection had to be written before the case appeared for trial, thus termed a *praescribere*. The problematic issue between Christians and heretics involved the Scriptures. Tertullian contended that heretics cannot even use the Bible. The *praescriptio* against non-Christians using the Bible argued that it was not theirs to use. Some consider this to be his most valuable work.[53]

In other works, Tertullian developed key Christian ideas. *The Testimony of the Soul* (197) contended that the soul knows there is a God and life after death.[54] Tertullian argued that the believer must use God's revelation, not pagan thought, for information about the world. *On Baptism* is the only ante-Nicene work on the nature of the sacraments. In twenty chapters, Tertullian used the images of Israel passing through the Red Sea, the water that came from the rock, and John the baptizer to prefigure Christ.[55] Prior to the Council of Nicea, *Against Praxeas* clearly presented the church's teaching on the doctrine of the Trinity. Praxeas was a "patripassian" who argued that since Father, Son, and Holy Spirit are merely different modes or manifestations of the one divine being in different eras, it was actually the Father who suffered on the cross. To express both the oneness and threeness of the Godhead, Tertullian coined the Latin term *Trinitas*. This work emerged as a very important work for the doctrine of the Trinity.[56]

Tertullian

Tertullian addressed an almost endless number of worldview issues as he took up his pen to address Christian living. He applied the rigorous New Testament ethic to marriage, family, and the pagan culture and Christians' participation in it. Throughout, he prescribed a life of absolute moral obedience. *The Shows* condemned Christian participation in all public games. In *On the Dress of Women*, a pre-Montanist writing, Tertullian warned women not to be dominated by pagan fashion but to show modesty in dress. Condemning ornaments and cosmetics as diabolical in origin, he prohibited wearing objects of gold and silver, pearls, and precious stones. Tertullian forbade his readers to change the work of the Creator by adding dye to the hair and paint to the face. He forbade intermarriage with pagans. *To His Wife* illustrated how Christian marriage differed from pagan marriage. He instructed his wife to remain a widow after his death, explaining there were no good excuses for remarriage. *Exhortation to Chastity* was dedicated to a friend who had recently lost his wife.[57] In *Monogamy*, Tertullian rejected all second marriages. *The Veiling of Virgins* advocated the practice because etiquette at that time required it.[58]

> *Tertullian addressed an almost endless number of worldview issues as he took up his pen to address Christian living. He applied the rigorous New Testament ethic to marriage, family, and the pagan culture and Christians' participation in it.*

53. Altaner and Stuiber, *Patrologie*, 153–54.

54. For the text, see the collection edited by Maurice Wiles and Mark Santer, *Documents in Early Christian Thought* (Cambridge: Cambridge University Press, 1975), 49.

55. Altaner and Stuiber, *Patrologie*, 156.

56. See Wiles and Santer, *Documents*, on Christology, para. 10.

57. See Altaner and Stuiber, *Patrologie*, 156–60.

58. Several treatises address the issue of Christians and the state. *The Crown*, written about Christians in military service, argued that Christians would not wear crowns. In *Con-*

> *Because of two
> remarks, consid-
> erable contro-
> versy exists over
> Tertullian's view of
> philosophy. He said
> that Christian belief
> is true because it
> is absurd, and he
> posed a famous
> question: "What
> does Athens have to
> do with Jerusalem?"*

He also furthered thinking on matters of pious devotion and ecclesiastical discipline. His *Concerning Prayer* (198–200) is the earliest surviving exposition of the Lord's Prayer. *Concerning Repentance* debated ecclesiastical reconciliation. Tertullian believed that reconciliation required public confession by the sinner. *Fasting* attacked Catholics from a rigorous Montanist perspective. *On Modesty* argued that the power of the keys (church discipline) lay not in Rome or with a particular bishop but was "spiritual," that is, tied to apostolic origin. In *Pallium*, he stated that he wore the pallium, an ecclesiastical vestment, instead of the Roman toga.

Because of two remarks, considerable controversy exists over Tertullian's view of philosophy. He said that Christian belief is true because it is absurd, and he posed a famous question: "What does Athens have to do with Jerusalem?" Although he has been accused of an irrational fideism, Tertullian merely opposed the subtleties of Greek speculative thinking with the clear, straightforward, apostolic teaching of the Bible. He favored using philosophical insights if they were compatible with the overall Christian worldview. He believed the being of God and the immortality of the human soul could be known through human reason and reflection on creation. And he believed God's eternity and immensity also could be known in a similar manner.[59]

Tertullian illustrated a full-blown world-and-life view. His contributions to apologetics, philosophy, theology, and ethics became the foundation for those who followed him in the Western church. His contributions in these areas illustrate a comprehensive vision of thought and life. His reflections on philosophy and ethical matters manifested an early form of moral asceticism that supported monasticism and withdrawal from participation in cultural formation.[60]

School of Alexandria: Clement of Alexandria (ca. 150–215)

Titus Flavius Clemens was born about 150, the son of non-Christian parents in Athens, where he received much of his training. When he

cerning *Flight in Persecution*, Tertullian urged Christians not to flee. In *Concerning Idolatry*, he elaborated the same theme as in *De Corona* but added more prohibitions: there were to be no artists and no professors of literature in the church.

59. Altaner and Stuiber, *Patrologie*, 160.

60. Other Western writers followed Tertullian. Hippolytus (ca. 170–236) fought with the bishop of Rome, Callistus, who was lax in his treatment of bigamous bishops and who was theologically questionable. Hippolytus, who had himself elected bishop of Rome, was what has been called in the Roman Catholic Church the first "anti-Pope." Novatian, a leading pastor in Rome in 250, is famous for the schism that bears his name. He said that the church should forever excommunicate those who lapse during times of persecution. In earlier correspondence, Novatian held that when a lapsed believer truly repented, especially one who was on the verge of death, he should be forgiven. Novatian argued that God alone knew what he was going to do with them and the nature of their hearts. Cyprian (d. 258), bishop of Carthage, reflected Tertullian's influence by cautioning against uncomely dress, but he departed from Tertullian's view with a strong treatise: *On the Unity of the Church*. He also held that those who lapsed during persecution should be admitted back into the church after a long time of penance.

became a Christian, he searched the empire for the best tutors. He finally settled in the famous city of Alexandria, where he studied at the feet of Pantanenus[61] and eventually led the school (ca. 200). A few years later, fleeing the persecution of Septimus Severus, he found refuge in Cappadocia, where he died.

Clement read widely, citing more than 360 profane writers, and he had a fair, though not brilliant, knowledge of the Scriptures.[62] Clement's writings include *Warning to the Gentiles*, in which he presented Christ as the true teacher of the new world and presented a critique of the heathen world. *The Teacher* continued by instructing converted heathen how to live as new Christians.[63] *The Carpet* was another, not highly organized presentation, concerning Greek philosophy. Clement believed philosophy borrowed much from the Hebrew Bible.[64] *What Kingdom Will Be Saved?* demonstrated that even the state can be saved. The state was not kept out of the kingdom of heaven. Only unrepentant sinners are excluded from heaven. As a demonstration, he appealed to the legend of John the apostle and the young man.[65]

The *Stromata* or *Miscellanies* was an unsystematic collection of religious and theological thoughts that demonstrated Clement's deep thinking and wide philosophical training.[66]

Clement made contributions toward developing a relationship between Christian faith and philosophy. He implemented a "method" that was important in developing theology. He opposed those whom he derogatorily termed the "orthodoxists," who rejected all philosophical thinking. They were anti-intellectual. Clement believed that philosophy, far from being opposed to Christianity, greatly aided the Christian faith. He did not claim that it could lead someone to faith, but it could make Christianity attractive to outsiders. He also maintained that "faith" is before philosophy. This faith is not necessarily Christian—someone did not have to believe in Christ to have this faith. It is general; that is, it intuits or senses the basic principles of reasoning. It is a faith that knows the methods we have to follow to reason properly.

Plato and Aristotle exemplified this type of faith. In Clement's view, faith and reason originate from God. Thus, both philosophy and Christianity are gifts from God. Philosophy is God's covenant with the Greeks, just as the law was God's covenant with the Jews. The one river of truth has different tributaries. Thus, Christians can use Greek philosophy to understand

> "Clement believed that philosophy, far from being opposed to Christianity, greatly aided the Christian faith. He did not claim that it could lead someone to faith, but it could make Christianity attractive to outsiders.

61. He was apparently a converted Stoic philosopher. See Williston Walker, *A History of the Christian Church* (New York: Scribner, 1985), 72.

62. Shaehelin, *Verkündigung*, 1:169. See Altaner and Stuiber, *Patrologie*, 190–96. See also Schmidt, *Grundriss der Kirchengeschichte*, 101.

63. Altaner and Stuiber, *Patrologie*, 192.

64. Ibid., 193.

65. Ibid., 194. See Shaehelin, *Verkündigung*, 1:170–80.

66. W. Walker, *History*, 73.

Christianity.[67] Philosophy was given to the Greeks to take them to Christ.[68] Clement was not uncritical in his understanding of Greek philosophy—he opposed the Sophists, but he believed we should follow closely the teachings of Plato and Aristotle.[69]

Origen (185–254)[70]

Origen was born into a Christian family about 185. His father suffered martyrdom in 202. To keep her son from following in his father's footsteps, his mother hid his clothes! At the age of eighteen, Origen was put in charge of the largely destroyed catechumen school at Alexandria. He followed an ascetic lifestyle, which apparently resulted in his emasculating himself in misguided obedience to Matthew 19:20.[71]

At first, Origen taught all the preparatory courses, until this became too much of a burden. He found an assistant and then instructed only the advanced students. He attended the lectures of the philosopher Ammonius Saccas, the so-called founder of Neoplatonism.[72]

Origen's writings were vast.[73] He had seven or more stenographers in his lecture room. He worked in textual criticism, creating the *Hexapla* (sixfold Bible), the basis of which was the Hebrew text of the Old Testament; a Hebrew text in Greek letters to aid pronunciation; the Greek translation

> *Origen was born into a Christian family about 185. His father suffered martyrdom in 202. To keep her son from following in his father's footsteps, his mother hid his clothes!*

67. Walker, *History*, 73. "Clement would interpret Christianity as Philo did Judaism, by Philosophy, into scientific dogmatics."

68. Clement, *Stromata* 1:5 "For this was a schoolmaster to bring the Hellenic mind, as the law the Hebrews, to Christ," as cited by Walker, *History*, 73.

69. In response to these ideas, we should remember the truth in Clement's approach, i.e., that Christians should not want to be anti-philosophical. There is no imperative from Reformed theology to say that Plato and Aristotle have nothing true to say to us. We do maintain (as in chapter 1) the essential antithesis between Plato's worldview and that of biblical revelation (chapters 2, 3). Although his system as a whole stands over against that of the Bible, he does say some things that are true. Yet, Clement had an inadequate view of the nature and impact of Adam's fall. He did not acknowledge, as he should have, that because of the noetic effect of sin, pagan philosophers were attempting to avoid God's revelation—which Paul condemns in Romans 1. Clement did not understand the antithesis between the Christian and the non-Christian points of view.

70. See John A. Southwell, *Origen: His Life at Alexandria*, trans. R. Cadiou (London, 1944). William Ralph Inge, *Origen* (London: Cumberlege, 1946). Charles Bigg, *The Christian Platonists of Alexandria* (Oxford, 1913). Walker says: "No man of purer spirit or nobler aims ornaments the history of the ancient church" (*History*, 74).

71. Walker, *History*, 74. Origen was not ordained, which caused problems with his bishop in Alexandria when later he became famous. Origen was then ordained by other bishops—from Jerusalem and Caesarea—which caused even more problems. In the year 231, a synod excommunicated Origen, and he left Alexandria and taught at Caesarea (232–53). Origen was imprisoned and tortured during the Decian persecution and died in 253–54 at age 69.

72. Asserted by Eusebius, *Church History*, 6.19.6, as cited by Walker, *History*, 75. Shaehelin, *Verkündigung*, 1:180. Schmidt, *Grundriss*, 101ff., 106, 161–62. Altaner and Stuiber, *Patrologie*, 197–208.

73. According to Jerome, his titles number two thousand. According to Epiphanius of Salamis, there were six thousand. However, because of his condemnation by the church in the sixth century, we know the titles of a "mere" eight hundred works!

of Aquila; another Greek translation; the *LXX*; and finally another Greek translation. Origen wrote about all of the books of the Bible.

Origen's writings are classified according to their topics. The first grouping includes his apologetic works, the most important of which is *Against Celsus*, written between 246 and 248. Origen responded to Celsus's *The True Word*, an intemperate attack on basic Christian beliefs. Celsus, an able Platonic philosopher, attempted to re-convert Christians using, among other techniques, Jewish arguments against Christianity. He ridiculed Christ as a magician and imposter and argued for the superiority of Greek thinking. Origen's lengthy rebuttal stands as one of the most detailed apologetic pieces in the early church. Despite repeated appeals to allegory, Origen argued for the truth and historical reliability of the gospel's claims, contending these make it superior to Greek philosophical speculation.

Origen

Origen's most important theological work, *First Principles*, is considered to be the first true systematic theology (220–30). Unfortunately, none of the original Greek text has survived. The earliest remaining copy is a Latin translation by the church father Rufinus.[74] Origen's theology is one of the most prominent illustrations of a "synthesis" worldview; he attempted to unite the basic insights of Greek and Christian thought, despite their vast differences. Origen made Christianity "scientific," as that word was understood at the time, by interpreting Christianity through the lens of Greek philosophical thought. To cite but one example, Origen incorporated in his system Plato's belief in the preexistence of souls.[75] This removed the fall from the realm of history into a pre-creation existence. All souls choose in their pre-incarnate state to turn from God. Thus, Origen transformed the biblical view of human sinfulness from a historical space-time fall (which interprets human sin in terms of individual responsibility yet also corporate solidarity with our first parents) to a pre-cosmic myth (in which each person is a sinner solely because the individual made such a choice before history began). Origen also understood the process of redemption primarily in terms of education. Salvation entailed becoming like God through a process of *theosis,* or divinization, which would lead to the restoration (*apokatastasis*) of all moral creatures—a form of universalism.[76]

Origen's theology is one of the most prominent illustrations of a "synthesis" worldview; he attempted to unite the basic insights of Greek and Christian thought, despite their vast differences.

Augustine (354–430)

Few figures in history rival Augustine, bishop of Hippo, for his influence on the Western church, as well as on philosophy, theology, and culture. Augustine's penetrating understanding and development of Christian

---

74.   Walker, *History*, 75. Walker describes the work as "not merely the first great systematic presentation of Christianity, but its thoughts and methods thenceforth controlled Greek dogmatic development."

75.   Cf. Plato's "Myth of Er" in the last chapter of his *Republic*.

76.   Origen's thought on many topics came under sharp criticism in several contexts in early church history. His ideas were condemned at the second Council of Constantinople in 553.

truth, and the breadth of his interests and literary production,[77] surpass all who preceded him and establish him as one of the "Doctors of the Church." Warfield did not exaggerate when he said that Augustine did not merely create "an epoch in the history of the Church, but has determined the course of its history in the West up to the present day."[78] More recently, it has been said that Augustine had a more biblical worldview than any of his predecessors, as well as a more biblical idea of the Bible itself.[79]

Augustine was born in Thagaste, North Africa, to a pagan father and a devout Christian mother, Monica. Augustine was educated to become a philosopher, studying grammar, dialectic, rhetoric, music, geometry, astronomy, and arithmetic. Reading Cicero's *Hortensius* (now lost) was like a "conversion."[80] However, Augustine rebelled against his Christian upbringing, maintaining that Christianity was a religion for old women. In Milan, however, Ambrose's preaching presented Christianity to Augustine in an intellectually acceptable form.[81] Augustine experienced true internal struggles, which are chronicled in the *Confessions*,[82] one of Augustine's most innovative contributions to the history of literature.[83]

Warfield did not exaggerate when he said that Augustine did not merely create "an epoch in the history of the Church, but has determined the course of its history in the West up to the present day."

77. Augustine's literary remains are vast. From my own investigations of the Migne collection, I estimate that his entire corpus contains approximately thirty thousand small-print pages. Even over Augustine's long life that would still have necessitated writing nearly one thousand pages per year! Augustine reckoned that by 427 (three years before his death), he had composed 93 literary works and 232 books. Added to that are his sermons and letters. Most of this massive corpus has been saved.

78. B. B. Warfield, *Studies in Tertullian and Augustine* (Oxford: Oxford University Press, 1930), 306.

79. Cornelius Van Til, *Christian Theory of Knowledge* (Nutley, NJ: Presbyterian and Reformed, 1969), 118. Concerning Augustine and philosophy, Van Til continued: "Though in some measure subject to the principles of Platonism and particularly neo-Platonism, Augustine yet produced from Scripture more clearly than any one before him, such concepts as have enabled his followers to set off the Christian idea of Scripture and of its system of truth clearly against all kinds of non-Christian speculation."

80. R. A. Markus, "Victorinus and Augustine," in *The Cambridge History of Later Greek and early Medieval Philosophy* (Cambridge: Cambridge University Press, 1970), 342. "It had led him to break through the limits of the purely rhetorical conception of his education: he used the work not 'for the sharpening of his tongue,' but followed its 'exhortation to philosophy.' It had given him a new purpose and a new concern, the pursuit of immortal wisdom. . . . Looking back on the experience, Augustine could interpret this turning to philosophy as the beginning of his journey of return to God."

81. Augustine learned much from Ambrose. While not considered a positive benefit today, Ambrose taught Augustine an allegorical or "typical" Old Testament exegetical method. This helped relieve some of Augustine's tensions concerning the Old Testament. While in Milan, Augustine also became acquainted with Neoplatonism. This philosophical grid helped him to comprehend the relationship between God (as spiritual substance) and the presence of evil in the world (evil as a negation).

82. See Books 6–8.

83. In his *Confessions*, Augustine exposed his moral failures from his youthful vagaries and depravity to his prideful search for intellectual recognition. But, even more importantly, the *Confessions* expresses a positive witness to the God who saved him from wickedness, restored his soul, and now served as the foundation for his deepest convictions.

As an epistemological foundation for his worldview, Augustine made a connection between Plotinus's conception of the Nous as fulfilled in John's notion of the Logos.[84] By articulating a theory of illumination that drew upon the Greek theory of ideas and the Bible's teaching about revelation, Augustine demonstrated that Christian thinking demands the respect of both philosophy and theology.

In the first work written after his conversion, *Contra Academicos* (386), Augustine laid the groundwork for his worldview by rebutting the epistemological skepticism of the New Academy. If, as the skeptics contended, no knowledge is possible, then even the most rudimentary truth claims, such as those about our own existence, are questionable. And, more importantly, the search for God is rendered impossible at the outset. As an antidote to agnosticism, Augustine offered his theory of illumination. Adopting the phrase *credo ut intelligam*, "I believe in order that I might understand,"[85] Augustine affirmed that faith precedes reason in the search for truth.[86] In fact, all knowledge rests upon faith in what is indubitable to the human mind. Despite faith's precedence over reason, Augustine did not espouse a mere fideism. Augustine combined the a priori Forms of Platonism, as modified by John's assertion of the transcendent Logos in John 1. Augustine believed that the Logos is "the light that enlightens every man" (John 1:4, 9). As a universal gift to mankind, this intelligible "light" bestows seminal ideas, such as goodness, justice, and beauty, by which the mind makes rational judgments. The light, or categories by which we think, corresponds to the order of the universe God created. Thus, all people are logically endowed, or "lighted," and this makes objective truth accessible. Knowledge, therefore, rests on a priori, God-given ideas that reside in the mind as the precondition to knowledge. These ideas also are subservient to the transcendent Logos (John 1:4, 9) that exists outside the mind. This paradox of an interior "light" and exterior "Light" affirms the individuality of human thought, which enables people to apprehend truth, and also certifies the existence of Truth, which transcends our subjectivity.[87]

> *Adopting the phrase **credo ut intelligam**, "I believe in order that I might understand," Augustine affirmed that faith precedes reason in the search for truth. In fact, all knowledge rests upon faith in what is indubitable to the human mind.*

84. J. G. Davies, *The Early Christian Church* (New York: Holt, Rinehart and Winston, 1965), 224.

85. Later in the Middle Ages, theologians such as Thomas Aquinas would espouse the converse: *intelligo ut credam*: "I understand in order that I might believe." Theologians, philosophers, and apologists have debated the merits of Augustinian and Thomistic epistemologies. Both affirm faith and reason as compatible but disagree on which takes priority in knowing.

86. Augustine took his cue from Isaiah 7:9, which he translated: "Unless you believe you shall not understand."

87. Thus, Augustine's paradox avoids the errors of human autonomy and pantheism. Cf. Van Til, *Christian Theory of Knowledge*, 118–42, for a discussion of the development of Augustine's epistemology from his earlier works to his later writings. Cf. Ronald H. Nash, *The Light of the Mind: St. Augustine's Theory of Knowledge* (Lexington, KY: The University of Kentucky Press, 1969) and "The Christian Rationalism of St. Augustine" in *The Word of God and the Mind of Man: The Crisis of Revealed Truth in Contemporary Theology* (Phillipsburg, NJ: Presbyterian and Reformed Publishing, 1982).

> *Against Man-
> ichaeism's positing
> of two equally ulti-
> mate entities—good
> and evil—Augus-
> tine affirmed the
> sole sovereignty of
> God. Metaphysical
> dualism is logically
> impossible because
> there cannot be two
> equally ultimate,
> but antithetical, first
> principles.*

Augustine addressed all philosophical and theological questions from this epistemological base. He made important contributions in several areas, all of which manifest a fully realized biblical perspective. Augustine's first ten years in North Africa[88] involved a prolonged dispute with Manichaeism, a dualistic religion in which he was formerly an auditor. Manichaeism taught a dualism between two warring worlds—a good one with a perfect deity and an evil one with a wicked adversary to the deity. This worldview most likely reflected Augustine's own inner struggles prior to his conversion.[89]

Augustine's anti-Manichaean writings reject its dualism, fatalism, and intrinsic connection between matter and evil, and substitute the superior biblical truths of creation and evil. Against Manichaeism's positing of two equally ultimate entities—good and evil—Augustine affirmed the sole sovereignty of God. Metaphysical dualism is logically impossible because there cannot be two equally ultimate, but antithetical, first principles. Therefore, God alone is ultimate, the sole source of all being, and he created the cosmos *ex nihilo*. Not only is evil not equally ultimate with God, it has no substantial being and therefore is not to be identified with any "thing" in creation. All of creation, coming from the hand of God, is good, including the body. Evil, therefore, is best considered a privation. Although evil sometimes is a mere absence of good (as blindness is an absence of sight), it frequently is an active privation that wreaks havoc within creation, for example, bodily pain and the ravages of disease. Evil originated ultimately from sin, first in Satan, then in man—a rebellious turning of the will from God as the end or goal of true being. Thus, Augustine firmly posed the Christian answer to the origin and problem of evil not as a metaphysical issue rooted in the cosmos's ontological structure but as a moral issue that stems from disobedience.

For a decade, Augustine was embroiled in controversy with a virulent schismatic sect called the Donatists, which by Augustine's time actually outnumbered the church in North Africa. Claiming to be the visible, pure church of God's elect, the Donatists separated themselves from the church they judged to be lenient in discipline and wrong in its view of the priesthood and its celebration of the sacraments. In response, Augustine elaborated the difference between an invisible church, which consisted of the elect, and the visible church, which was a mixed company. Yet, the community of believers also was the "*Communio sanctorum*"; "the true and full number of the elect" is the invisible church. Augustine believed there were

---

88.   After his conversion and baptism, Augustine arrived in Hippo, North Africa, and set up a small monastic community. He became a presbyter and later was consecrated bishop.

89.   When someone was a Manichaean "elect," he thought that he belonged to the good or pure world—the world of light. For a while, he was entrapped in this dark world. Deliverance from darkness occurred by repudiating the body as something foreign, something to be discarded. This view had previously appealed to his profound spiritual longing, and his emotional character.

some Catholics who were not elect and some outside the church who were. He based this thinking on Jesus' parable of the wheat and the tares. The church's holiness, therefore, depended not on the character of its leaders but solely on God's grace.

Augustine hoped to win the schismatics by persuading them through leaflets, treatises, and debates. When these failed, Augustine concluded that since God had providentially placed the power of the state in Christian hands, the state could end the schism. Whereas previously the church had only the spiritual power of excommunication as a means of discipline, Augustine resorted to a policy that had fateful results for centuries. Citing Jesus' words in Luke 14:23, "Compel them to come in," Augustine urged imperial coercion as the means of ending heresy and restoring unity to the church. State authority could seize property, impose penalties, and bring other pressures to bear on heretics who persisted in false belief. Although the policy eventually ended the schism, it established a precedent that lingered into the Middle Ages and beyond. Augustine intended coercion as a pragmatic method of last resort to bring schismatics and heretics to their senses. Later, church and political leaders baldly adapted coercion as a missionary strategy to "Christianize" the descendants of the Germanic invaders in the fifth century. They forced the "barbarians" to "convert" to Christianity at the point of the sword and to become part of the Holy Roman Empire.[90]

Augustine

On a more positive note, many consider *On the Trinity* to be Augustine's most important writing. He spent twenty years (399–419) composing it.[91] Despite his confidence in reason as God's unique gift,[92] because of three deficiencies, human reflection on the nature of the Trinity cannot begin with reason. First, human reason operates slowly, and even a lifetime would not provide sufficient time to reach correct conclusions concerning God. Second, human reason is darkened by sin and therefore cannot exercise its functions properly. Third, only by contemplation can human reason apprehend God with certitude, and this requires a starting point in either sense experience or the intellect. But, God's nature is not directly accessible to either of these. To resolve the dilemma, the seeker needs to turn to revealed truth. If the seeker fails to do this, then his or her conception of God will be inherently faulty.

In broad strokes, *On the Trinity* presents two main themes. Augustine first defines the content of the Christian faith. Then he presents analogies to

> *Citing Jesus' words in Luke 14:23, "Compel them to come in," Augustine urged imperial coercion as the means of ending heresy and restoring unity to the church. State authority could seize property, impose penalties, and bring other pressures to bear on heretics who persisted in false belief.*

90. For a full discussion of the transformation of Augustine's policy from a means of dealing with heresy to a missionary strategy for converting unbelievers, see David J. Bosch, "The Medieval Roman Catholic Paradigm," *Transforming Mission: Paradigm Shifts in Theology of Mission* (Maryknoll, NY: Orbis Books, 1992).

91. Ambrose (bishop of Milan) had personal contacts with Augustine, yet close connections between his Trinitarian theology and Augustine's are difficult to demonstrate. Ambrose affirmed three persons of the Trinity who are united in one substance and divinity. His doctrine of the Holy Spirit was developed in *De Spiritu Sancto*.

92. Cf. discussion above on Augustine's epistemology.

help his readers understand the nature of the Trinity. Foundational for the content of Christianity was the deity of Jesus Christ. Augustine acknowledged that some scriptural passages pose difficulties concerning Christ's deity, for example, where it appears Christ did not know the future and where he questioned the claim of being "good." To understand such passages, Augustine suggested that the Bible presents Christ not only as the powerful Son of God but also as the humble servant.[93] Thus, although the Son was "sent" from the Father, he was not ontologically subordinate to the Father.[94] From that foundation, Augustine probed the Old Testament theophanies. In contrast to earlier writers, to underline Trinitarian equality, Augustine contended that the theophanies were not exclusively pre-incarnate, earthly appearances of the Son but were appearances of the Father.[95] The incarnation and theophanies were miraculous occurrences Augustine exploited to further his argument for Jesus' deity.[96] From there, he presented arguments for the co-equality of the three persons of the Trinity.[97]

Augustine presented the co-equality of the persons of the Trinity during a time of tremendous contention in the church—from Arius and others. Although he focused on Christ's nature, he did not neglect the Holy Spirit.[98] Augustine argued that the Holy Spirit had the same nature as the Father and the Son. The persons of the Trinity were differentiated not in terms of degrees of being but in terms of the nature of causality. Augustine believed the Father was the "beginning" of the Godhead. The other two persons relate to God the Father in terms of procession and being born. Actually, the Holy Spirit became the "unifying" principle of the Godhead; the Holy Spirit proceeds from both the Father and the Son.[99]

On this point, Augustine's thought concerning the nature of the persons of the Godhead differed sharply from his Greek-speaking colleagues. He was probably not fully aware of the complex discussions going on concerning the nature of "ousia" and "hypostasis." For Augustine, distinctions within the Godhead should not be described in terms of essence or substance but in terms of relations. However, this particular approach had inherent problems and limitations, and fortunately Augustine recog-

> "Augustine presented the co-equality of the persons of the Trinity during a time of tremendous contention in the church—from Arius and others. Although he focused on Christ's nature, he did not neglect the Holy Spirit.

93. *De Trinitate*, Book 1. Augustine's analysis of the incarnate Son did not permit an actual limitation of Christ's knowledge. For example, Christ did in fact know the hour of his return to earth in power.

94. Ibid. In Christ's "sending," all three persons of the Trinity were involved, including the Holy Spirit's coming as a dove.

95. Ibid., Books 2–3.11. Augustine did not deal with questions such as how the Father, who is "spiritual," took visible form.

96. Ibid., Books 3–4.

97. Ibid., Book 4.20.

98. Immediately before his arguments on the equality of the Holy Spirit, Augustine had argued that the Son is an emanation from the Omnipotent and hence was himself omnipotent.

99. *De Trinitate*, Book 4.20.29. This "double procession," that the Holy Spirit proceeds from the Son as well as from the Father (*filioque*), would be debated later and sadly helped to cause separation between the Eastern and Western churches.

nized them. Although the Cappadocian discussion of the Trinity tended toward tritheism, Augustine's presentation could be seen as leaning toward a unitarianism.[100] That is, the term "person" tries to express the ineffable, to describe God's "essence." But God has only one "essence"; that is, he is God. Thus, it could be argued that there is only one "person" (one essence) of the Trinity. Augustine rejected that alternative, but struggled to express his teaching in a coherent and readily comprehensible manner. He knew that to call a human being a "person" implies that the being has a human personality. This drove Augustine to his second main theme.

God created humanity in his image, and Augustine believed this means all three persons of the Trinity are reflected in human beings. However, Augustine acknowledged that all analogies developed to help us understand the Trinity are "reflections," and will prove to be inadequate. Humans never will rise to the knowledge of God as he actually is. Nevertheless, the first analogy between God and humanity is that of love. The human mind knows love within itself, and hence the mind knows God because God is love.[101] More precisely, the human mind must first know itself in order to love itself. Thus, there is the trinity of the mind itself, the love of it, and the knowledge of it.[102] A second analogy of the Trinity was memory, understanding, and will. They are equal to each other and each to all, or else they could not mutually contain each other.[103]

In *On the Trinity*, therefore, Augustine of Hippo drew on a rich heritage in Latin Christianity; his Trinitarian doctrine was especially dependent on Tertullian, Hilary of Poitiers, and Marius Victorinus.[104] It extended the ideas of Christians such as Athanasius and the Cappadocian fathers. But, perhaps even more importantly, his trinitarianism offered a powerful alternative to classical thinking. Instead of the personal but morally flawed and competitive Homeric deities, the Trinity presents the holy tripersonal God who sovereignly rules the cosmos. The Trinity also provides a satisfying basis for personal values—especially love—that the impersonal, abstract Goodness of Plato and Aristotle's Unmoved Mover could not. Augustine's trinitarianism challenged his contemporaries to revise their first principles and to shift civilization from a naturalistic, autonomous foundation to Christian presuppositions based on the triune God.

> *Augustine acknowledged that all analogies developed to help us understand the Trinity are "reflections," and will prove to be inadequate. Humans never will rise to the knowledge of God as he actually is. Nevertheless, the first analogy between God and humanity is that of love.*

---

100.   The Cappadocians used the concept of "ousia" and "hypostasis" as "common" and "particular."

101.   *De Trinitate*, Book 8.10.14.

102.   Ibid., 9.4.4. First, there is equality. The love and the knowledge are equal. Second, there is an identity of essence; the whole mind is involved in knowing and loving itself. Third, they are all in all—one substance and essence. Fourth, there is an indication of the begetting of the Word and the procession of the Spirit. When true knowledge arises in a mind, a word or concept is begotten within us, a concept or word that is equal to the mind.

103.   Ibid., Book 10.11.17–18.

104.   Recent work in Marius Victorinus and Hilary of Poitiers has indicated that Augustine's Trinitarian formulations are perhaps not quite as original as had earlier been thought.

Augustine also forged a view of human nature in his dispute with the British monk Pelagius, a rather popular teacher in Rome.[105] For Pelagius, morality was of highest importance. With this theological presupposition, Pelagius challenged any system that suggested that men and women were mere puppets, wholly determined by the movements of divine grace. Therefore, the keystone of Pelagius's system was the idea of unconditional free will and responsibility. Pelagius did not extricate mankind from the purview of God's sovereignty,[106] though it is true that his followers did.

At the root of Pelagius's thought is his denial that any bias toward evil exists in human nature because of the fall. If there were such a bias toward evil, the will would not be free to choose between good and evil. Likewise, since people have no inclination toward sin, then it is at least hypothetically possible for a human being to obey God's commandments without committing sin.[107] To facilitate further discussion, Pelagius's followers developed and propagated Pelagius's doctrine. Celestius (Coelestius) emphasized (though Pelagius himself would not) the idea that Adam would have died whether or not he sinned, since he was created mortal. Additionally, Julian of Eclanum (in South Italy) asserted man's complete independence from God.

Augustine's response[108] resulted in the most fully developed biblical view of the fall, original sin, and predestination up to that time. As opposed to Pelagius's view of one, uniform state of human nature from Adam throughout history, Augustine posed a threefold state. Prior to the fall, Adam possessed moral freedom to sin or not to sin.[109] But the entrance of sin brought about a profound change—the second stage of human nature. Although the fall did not destroy the image of God in humanity, it radically altered human nature, resulting in a loss of moral freedom—not able not to sin,[110] which reflected the Pauline description of human nature in Romans 7:15–20 and Ephesians 2:1. Adam's disobedience resulted in the human race being subject to original sin—an inherited guilt and stain that left the human will unable to produce any good apart from God's sovereign grace. Because of original sin, only God's predestinating grace, based solely on his inscrutable wisdom, can free people from bondage to sin. The third and final state of human nature is that of the redeemed in heaven

> At the root of Pelagius's thought is his denial that any bias towards evil exists in human nature because of the fall. If there were such a bias toward evil, the will would not be free to choose between good and evil.

105. Pelagius was active between 384 and 400 and probably died before 420. His works: *Exposition of Paul's Letters* and *Letters*.

106. Kelly, *Early Christian Doctrines*, 358.

107. To be fair to Pelagius, he did not envision some state in the believer's walk on earth where he or she has reached and remains in a state of perfection. On the contrary, the state of perfection can be maintained only by continuing strenuous effort.

108. The Pelagian controversy was not the catalyst for Augustine's thoughts concerning grace and free will. Rather, he developed his thought prior to Pelagius.

109. Adam possessed genuine moral freedom in being able not to sin (*posse non peccare*); he also was free to die or not to die (*posse non mori*).

110. To describe the state of original sin, Augustine used the phrase *non posse non peccare*, not able not to sin.

who experience the ultimate state of freedom—they are not able to sin. Augustine's doctrine of the threefold state of human nature profoundly influenced philosophical and theological thinking throughout the history of Western thought. By it, Augustine rebutted not only Pelagianism but also Manichaeism, classical Greek philosophy, and previous, less consistent, forms of Christian thinking, such as Origen's.

Augustine's last major work, the *City of God*, was published in parts from 413 to 426. It was an apologetic work, not in the same sense as the earlier "apologists" who had to fight for their lives, but as a defense of Christianity against the charge that it was faith in Jesus Christ that destroyed the Roman Empire. Augustine's answer was that Rome fell because of its internal corruption—it was not Christian enough—not because it adopted Christianity. The *City of God* also was the first true theology of history (besides the Scriptures!). "Secular" history cannot be separated from "sacred" history; the true story of the development of humanity is the unfolding struggle between faith and unbelief. Augustine reprised many of his earlier themes but also developed ideas that would figure prominently in Western culture. Worth noting is the fact that although Augustine drew a sharp division between the City of God and the City of Man, due to their respective allegiances—one to God, the other to self, the world, or the devil—he did not relinquish hope for transformation of both individuals and culture. Because believers and nonbelievers seek peace in the earthly city, they can have common cause in matters that relate to purely human living.[111]

Thus, in his many writings, Augustine bequeathed to the West a full-orbed worldview that interpreted the Bible and posed a magisterial perspective that anchored the medieval period. He inspired his interpreters to implement this worldview in all dimensions of life: the theology and practice of the church, philosophical speculation in all spheres of thinking, the wielding of political power, and cultural differentiation.

> *Christians are to subject themselves to one another in divinely ordered relationships: wives submitting to husbands, children submitting to parents, slaves submitting to masters, and all submitting to the civil authorities.*

Early Christian Church Life

The Apostolic Age

Christians are to subject themselves to one another in divinely ordered relationships: wives submitting to husbands, children submitting to parents, slaves submitting to masters, and all submitting to the civil authorities. Christians are called to be holy. The church is to stand against pagan society. Moreover, within the church there are to be no social distinctions. However, during the apostolic age the church did not attempt to set aside slavery as a system.[112]

---

111. See *City of God*, Part 5, Book 19, Chapter 17.

112. Although slavery in ancient Rome could be cruel, it differed significantly from slavery in the New World. In the first century, almost 35–40 percent of the inhabitants

Work, or labor, acquired a new meaning within the Christian community. For a Christian, there is a threefold motivation for work: that Christians might not be a burden on others, that Christians might thereby obtain the wherewithal to help the needy, and that Christians might make a good impression on non-Christian workers, thus commending the faith to them. The Greeks saw work as servile activity, and the Romans regarded it as beneath the dignity of a Roman citizen. The church disagreed with the pagan notion that work is unworthy of free men and women,[113] and the church gave a dignity even to the lowest form of work—slavery.

By the second century, there was a continuing emphasis on right conduct. Abortion, for example, was forbidden. In *The Rise of Christianity*, Rodney Stark stresses that Christianity's prohibition of infanticide and abortion stood in stark opposition to prevailing pagan practices and contributed powerfully to the rapid rise of Christianity and the decline of paganism as a worldview.[114] Widely practiced within the Greco-Roman world, both practices were abhorrent to early Christians. Tertullian described an abortion kit and the procedures used to abort fetuses. A series of injunctions, or system of precepts, regarding what was and was not acceptable developed within the church. The Christian life was in the process of being defined in terms of observing a "set of rules." Some of those rules forbade certain jobs—for example, interpreting omens or being an enchanter or an astrologer. At this time, there was no prohibition to enlisting in the armed service. Additionally, Christians still came predominately from the lower classes. Within the church, however, humble origins were no hindrance to advancement. We know of pastors of larger churches, for example, who were former slaves.

There was an emphasis on restraint—a movement against luxury in food and dress. Christians refused to participate in many pagan festivals. We know more about what was forbidden than what was positively suggested as acceptable leisure activities, though one description exists of three friends taking a walk from Rome to the coast in order to paddle in

> *There was an emphasis on restraint—a movement against luxury in food and dress. Christians refused to participate in many pagan festivals.*

---

of Rome and the Italian peninsula were slaves. Roman-era slavery was transracial; there were slaves from all races. Slaves worked at a variety of occupations, including household management, teaching, business, and industry. Many slaves owned property. Because free laborers often lived in poverty, slaves frequently enjoyed far better economic and living conditions than freemen. Because of this, many free laborers sold themselves into slavery to achieve economic advancement. Thus, being set free often could place a person in less advantageous social and economic conditions. Without the connections provided by belonging to a family, an emancipated slave would not have social, legal, or occupational relationships. Perhaps one practical reason the New Testament does not speak out against the first-century institution of slavery is that freeing a slave often did not change his situation much. Although a freeman, he might remain in the same situation in his former master's household—only his legal status would have changed. Interestingly, in the first century, most slaves reasonably expected to be set free by the time they were thirty years old.

 113. Heussi, *Kompendium*, 93.

 114. Rodney Stark, The *Rise of Christianity* (Princeton, NJ: Princeton University Press, 1996), 115–25.

the sea. Christians also were enjoined to spend time in godly conversation and to enjoy nature.

The Third Century

By the third century, attitudes toward Christian activity in culture developed still further. Christianity influenced believers' attitudes toward work, and some rules forbade certain forms of work. It is interesting to read the list of social changes required of Christian converts. The *Apostolic Tradition* said: "If a man is a pimp, he must desist or be rejected. If a man is a sculptor or painter, he must be charged not to make idols; if he does not desist, he must be rejected. If a man is an actor or pantomimist, he must desist or be rejected. A teacher of young children had best desist, but if he has no other occupation, he may be . . . ."[115]

As Christianity dealt with more and more aspects of life, an increasingly complex and detailed set of rules developed. For example, eating meat was acceptable, but it should be boiled and not roasted! The most commonplace aspects of Christianity's worldview were evident in Christians' attitudes of love and mercy. As opposed to their Greco-Roman contemporaries, whose gods despised pity and compassion and who knew nothing of love between the gods and men, let alone an ethic in which people were to demonstrate love for one another, Christians became distinguished for acts of mercy and compassion. In his *Apology*, Tertullian claimed: "It is our care of the helpless, our practice of loving kindness that brands us in the eyes of many of our opponents. 'Only look,' they say, 'look how they love one another!'"[116] Because showing compassion is an obligatory and foundational aspect of Christianity, Christianity gave rise to organized efforts to maximize good works.

Social Life After the Council of Nicaea

We know that Christianity continued to be a religion of the working class, and that there was continued admonition in the church to work hard and to be frugal. Prohibitions against certain forms of labor continued. There was one addition to the list of forbidden occupations, that of being a moneylender. One of the canons of the Council of Nicea required any minister who had lent money at interest to be deprived of office. Many Eastern and Western fathers condemned usury (charging excessive interest) within the church. The issue of usury appeared frequently in subsequent church history.

Ruins of the Temple of Artemis in Ephesus, scene of pagan activities

> *As opposed to their Greco-Roman contemporaries, whose gods despised pity and compassion and who knew nothing of love between the gods and men, let alone an ethic in which people were to demonstrate love for one another, Christians became distinguished for acts of mercy and compassion.*

115. *Ante-Nicene Fathers*, vol. 1.

116. Stark, *Rise*, 87. Stark traces the Christian ethic to the radical New Testament ethic to perform good not only to one's neighbor but even to one's enemies. His comment: "This was revolutionary stuff. Indeed, it was the cultural basis for the revitalization of a Roman world groaning under a host of miseries" (212). Stark developed his account of Christianity's rise not as an attempt to develop a triumphalist apologetic but as a sociological explanation for the rapid rise of Christianity in the first four centuries. Cf. opening comments of this chapter.

Admonitions concerning food continued. Food is meant to nourish the body, not to be a luxury. We find pastoral admonitions for Christians to eat only one meal a day, so that only one hour in twenty-four would be dedicated to satisfying the body. Prayers were always to be said before meals.

Regarding leisure time, Christians still were admonished to avoid going to the theater and to public sporting events, not to gather together for drinking, and not even to enter taverns. They were to rest at home and read the Scriptures. However, in their homes they were to show simple hospitality to fellow Christians and to spend time with them in godly conversation.

Recent studies have detailed how Christianity spread with remarkable rapidity and how its worldview provided a new moral vision for Western culture.[117] Although it has long been recognized that the moral absolutes of the Old and New Testaments brought a radically new and transcendent base for moral norms, not as much attention has focused on the specifics of how this was implemented. We have noted how the apostolic fathers, apologists, and early theologians developed key principles within the Christian tradition. Because significant changes occurred in the moral a priori that demanded concrete changes in everyday behavior, Christian compassion and mercy were manifested in many cultural areas. In addition to matters covered earlier in the chapter, we now notice how care for the sick and the poor were direct results of the Christian worldview, as it developed in the fourth century.

Greco-Roman culture had little humanitarian concern for the disadvantaged, sick, and dying. During plagues, unbelievers tended to desert stricken areas. The practices of exposing infants and thrusting out the sick and dying were commonplace. In contrast to Roman *liberalis*, which entailed giving to others who would later return the favor, Christian *caritas* gave merely to benefit the recipient. Thus, Romans tended not to give to the poor, sick, or disadvantaged. Compassion became a major distinguishing feature of Christian public behavior.[118] Christians established orphanages, took up collections to support such works, and formed *collegia* to distribute aid to orphans and the elderly.[119] Public good works also were encouraged. When possible, food was to be provided for the very poor.

The establishment of hospitals was a direct result of Christian *caritas*. Hospitals existed in Greco-Roman culture but only for soldiers and gladiators. Ordinary citizens could not utilize them for illness or injury. Schmidt refers to the absence of health care as a "colossal void" in the classical era. Fear of contracting disease from those afflicted by plagues resulted in leaving

> *In contrast to Roman liberalis, which entailed giving to others who would later return the favor, Christian caritas gave merely to benefit the recipient. . . . Compassion became a major distinguishing feature of Christian public behavior.*

---

117. Cf. Stark, *Rise*, and Alvin J. Schmidt, *Under the Influence: How Christianity Transformed Civilization* (Grand Rapids: Zondervan, 2001). Earlier studies such as Charles Cochran's *Christianity and Classical Culture: A Study of Thought and Action* (New York: Oxford University Press, 1944) demonstrated how Augustine's Trinitarianism provided an alternative to the norms of classical culture.

118. Schmidt, *Under the Influence*, 125–32.

119. Ibid., 136–37.

the ill without recourse to medical treatment.[120] But, with the legalization of Christianity in 313, Christians were able to implement their moral principles openly. The Council of Nicaea mandated that bishops establish hospital facilities within their dioceses. Hospices provided health care, shelter, and lodging for the poor and for pilgrims. Schmidt notes that the famous bishop Basil of Caesarea in Cappadocia constructed the first hospital in 369 as part of a larger monastic community. Other bishops followed suit in the East and West—in Constantinople, Rome, and North Africa. Schmidt calls these institutions "the world's first voluntary charitable institutions."[121]

Church Structure After Constantine

In general, a profound change occurred in church development after Constantine became emperor,[122] a period sometimes described as the Imperial State Church. Constantine began the process by acknowledging Christianity as a legitimate religion. By 321, churches were legally established; Sunday was to be kept throughout the empire as a holy day; bishops were permitted to adjudicate legal questions; and church buildings were constructed with state funds. The church was now connected to the imperial order. The way "heresy" was dealt with changed; heretics now were treated as "outlaws." There was more imperial change in the Eastern church than in the Western.[123]

The new church structure also affected particular congregations. Local pastors (bishops) officially were put under the new officers, or metropolitans, who may not have been connected to their city at all. Additionally, these regular pastors now were state employees.[124]

The union of state and church under Constantine[125] had positive and negative consequences. There were consequences for church discipline as well. The crisis of Arianism, and later controversies within the empire, solidified discipline regarding those who had lapsed from the faith, resulting in a prescribed way of returning to the church. As the church and state became more closely related, civil penalties became associated with church penalties. For example, the death penalty was decreed against the Priscillianists; heresy was considered the worst crime against society.

In the face of such zeal against theological heresy, the church became more lax against practical errors and morals. Additionally, with the marriage of church and state, the "secularization" of the church began. This secularization, concomitant with the church aligning herself with the mass of hea-

> *In the face of such zeal against theological heresy, the church became more lax against practical errors and morals. Additionally, with the marriage of church and state, the "secularization" of the church began.*

---

120. Schmidt examines the various facilities such as shrines and hospitals and their uses (Ibid., 151–54).

121. Ibid., 157.

122. Heussi, *Kompendium*, 81.

123. Ibid., 81–82.

124. Ibid., 83.

125. Schaff, *History of the Christian Church*, 356ff.

thendom, which had not yet experienced an inward change of heart through redemption, affected church leaders.

Bishops became more concerned with worldly favor than with having the courage to pursue discipline with the rich and powerful members of their communities. An exception to this rule occurred in John Chrysostom, whose example of pursuing even the empress with discipline stands out against the laxity of the age.[126]

Another great exception to this rule was Ambrose of Milan. The year was about 390. The bishop refused communion to the theologically orthodox emperor Theodosius I and even refused to let him come forward to receive it. The reason for the refusal was that the emperor had seven thousand persons executed in Thessalonica after some type of riot had broken out. Eight months after being denied the Lord's Supper, the emperor publicly repented and announced that he would always wait thirty days before inflicting the death penalty so that nothing would be done in the heat of rage and that the penalty could be revoked if necessary.

Apparently, in great contrast to earlier practice and to the Eastern church, which had previously guarded the Lord's Supper, the Western church now permitted everyone who felt worthy to do so to take the Lord's Supper. Additionally, in 390 the Eastern church abandoned its practice of having prescribed penance under the supervision of a deacon or minister.

Monasticism[127]

During persecution, there was no great drive within the church toward monasticism. The church always stood against the ways of the world, and it was relatively easy to do so when the world was actively persecuting you! The situation changed when the church shifted from the hidden catacombs and suddenly found herself enjoying the privileges of being the state religion. With the rise of Christianity as the state religion, there also was a rise in the desire for monastic life.

Thus, from the time of Constantine, a new form of ascetic life called "monasticism" developed. The oldest and most extreme forms were the hermits, or anchorites. These monks fled from the world, supposedly to fight with demons in the wilderness. Monasticism began in Egypt but spread rapidly, particularly from the fourth century onward. First it spread eastward and then westward.[128]

> *During persecution, there was no great drive within the church toward monasticism. The church always stood against the ways of the world, and it was relatively easy to do so when the world was actively persecuting you!*

---

126. Chrysostom said to those who administer communion: "Though a captain, or a governor, nay, even one adorned with the imperial crown approach the table of the Lord unworthily, prevent him; you have greater authority than he . . . Beware lest you excite the Lord to wrath, and give a sword instead of food. In addition, if a new Judas should approach the communion, prevent him. Fear God, not man. If you fear man, he will treat you with scorn; if you fear God, you will appear venerable even to men." See Philip Schaff, *History of the Christian Church* (New York: Charles Scribner's Sons, 1910), § 68.

127. See Richard C. Gamble, "Medieval Monasticism," *Tabletalk* (January, 1995).

128. Heussi, *Kompendium*, 89–90.

By the end of the fourth century, there were thousands of monks. There were more than seven thousand Pachomian monks alone—an amazing development! Until the Reformation, the monasteries were the places where literacy continued for much of Christian life.[129] After the Reformation, monasteries continued in the Roman Catholic and Greek churches.

During its initial development, the monastic movement was motivated by a type of "martyrdom." This was a voluntary martyrdom, a gradual self-destruction—unhappily put, a sort of religious suicide.

Types of monasticism. In the beginning, there were three types of monastic movements. First, there were the ministers who followed ascetic practices but did not separate from regular social life. These types of men were more like half monks. Second, there were those who separated themselves from all work and social interaction. Such people often wore animal skins, ate only bread and salt, and dwelt in caves. Because of the West's harsher climate, this monastic movement did not prosper there. Third, there were those who lived in cloisters. In these monasteries, life was spent in manual labor and religious devotions, and excess food was given to the poor.

Emperor Constantine

The monastic movement was aided by the church father Augustine of Hippo. When he returned to North Africa from his time in Italy, Augustine gathered a group who were willing to give up their belongings, and he prescribed rules for their communal living. This marked the beginning of the Augustinian monks, from whose ranks Martin Luther eventually came.

Certainly, there were some extreme monastic expressions. Whatever judgments one makes of monasticism as a movement, the stories of self-denial are interesting. Although there are many such stories, and many of them are only stories, some are easily verifiable. We know that one monk ate only once a week and slept standing, leaning on a staff. Some monks never ate bread. Some would go nights without sleep and fast for seven days at a time. Additionally, a monk named Symeon spent thirty-six years praying, fasting, and preaching on the top of a pillar that was thirty to forty feet high, and he ate only once a week. These monks tended never to cut their hair or beards or, perhaps, to cut them only at Easter. They would sometimes spend their entire adult lives in one cell, never coming out.

Whatever judgments one makes of monasticism as a movement, the stories of self-denial are interesting. . . . We know that one monk ate only once a week and slept standing, leaning on a staff.

Sometimes, however, monastic life was simply a highly structured existence that "institutionalized" piety. One monastery described their lives as follows. They rose before sunrise, sang hymns praising God, prayed, and read the Scriptures before going to work. They took time to pray again at nine, twelve, and three o'clock. After work, they ate a simple meal of bread,

---

129.   Thomas Cahill, in *How the Irish Saved Civilization: The Untold Story of Ireland's Heroic Role from the Fall of Rome to the Rise of Medieval Europe* (New York: Anchor, 1996), argues that Western civilization's learning was preserved in Irish monasteries.

salt, and, occasionally, vegetables. Then they sang a thanksgiving hymn and went to sleep on their straw beds.

From Augustine to Charlemagne

The Barbarians in Rome[130]

While monasticism was developing, the empire was changing. In 378, the Emperor Vallens lost his life and his army at the battle of Adrianople. He and his troops fell victim to an "uncivilized" group known as the Visigoths, and this inaugurated a new crisis between the Roman Empire and the Germanic tribes who had crossed the empire's borders. During the next two centuries, the Holy Roman Empire would be conquered and divided by these barbarians.

There was a lot of interaction between the barbarians and the Roman armies, with the barbarians serving in the army in greater and greater numbers. The Germanic tribes also provided outlets for Roman goods. There was a slow cultural assimilation between the two groups. It was also at about this time that the Germanic tribes came into contact with Christianity.

It is difficult to differentiate sharply between Romans and Goths. The Germanic tribes admired Roman civilization, and in many ways sought to assimilate Roman civilization into their own. However, at the beginning of the fifth century, the Visigoths attacked the weakened empire, beginning in the East, and conquered Greece, as far as Sparta, as well as Constantinople, which they captured in 410. Between 410 and 455, in many ways Roman power and authority were destroyed in Britain, France, Spain, and North Africa.[131] Because they wished to be associated with the great culture and "authority" of Rome, the barbarian kings technically were servants of the Roman state, but this was a Rome that had lost her former power.

Just as in times of war armies assume great significance, so now it was the military generals who controlled the Roman Empire. But, by the end of the fifth century (i.e., in 476), the barbarians completely controlled Italy, continuing to dominate the world until the Emperor Justinian I, who ruled from 527 to 565.

Justinian I attempted to reconquer the Western Empire. First, he took North Africa from the Vandals, and then he successfully wrested Italy from the Ostrogoths. Theologically speaking, the Vandals and Ostrogoths were Arian, and in many ways at this time "theological" Arianism was defeated.[132]

> *It is difficult to differentiate sharply between Romans and Goths. The Germanic tribes admired Roman civilization, and in many ways sought to assimilate Roman civilization into their own.*

---

130. Jacques Le Goff, tr. Julia Barrow, *Medieval Civilization 400–1500* (Oxford: Basil Blackwell, 1988), 3–36.

131. Le Goff, *Medieval Civilization*, 17: "The most spectacular episode was the siege, capture and sack of Rome by Alaric and the Visigoths in 410."

132. Heussi, *Kompendium*, 116.

After Justinian, no one was able to continue the fight against the Germanic people, and by 568 the Lombards reinvaded the Italian peninsula.[133]

The Growth of the Papacy[134]

Beginning in the fourth century, Bishop Damasus (366–84) began to describe the church in Rome, of which he was the bishop, as the "apostolic see." He attempted to strengthen the preeminence of the church of Rome among the churches of the West, even over those of the East. By the end of the fourth century, Rome possessed a special role and authority among the churches of both the Eastern and Western parts of the empire.

Leo I (440–61), also known as Leo the Great, further attempted to establish the power of the papacy, so that technically he may be referred to as the first pope. He insisted on Peter's primacy among the apostles and that Peter's heirs, the popes, inherited his role as the supreme ruler and teacher in the church. Leo even began to talk about Peter speaking in and through the pope. The Council of Chalcedon (451) solidified the power of the papacy by maintaining that Peter had spoken through the mouth of Leo. Finally, the emperor put the icing on the pope's cake, so to speak, by declaring that the pope held all power over the other provinces of the Western church, at least.

The rise of the power of the bishop of Rome was concomitant with the barbarians' invasion of the Roman Empire. As the power of the Roman Empire faded, the pope's power increased. As the empire lost control, the pope, the visible representation of Rome's power, grew increasingly important. The bishop of Rome became the symbol both of apostolic authority and Roman power.

This power shift contributed to a rift between the Eastern and the Western churches. During the time of Pope Felix III (483–92), the church of Rome excommunicated the patriarch of Constantinople. This was the first recorded "schism" in the institutional church. This schism was resolved in the year 519, and this resulted in strengthening papal power.

About a century later, Gregory I (590–604), also known as Gregory the Great, came to power.[135] By this time, the Visigoths and Lombards had abandoned Arianism. Pope Gregory undertook the conversion of the Anglo-Saxons, a task entrusted to the monk Augustine and his companions. Willibrord and Boniface began working to convert Frisia (modern Netherlands) and Germany during the first half of the eighth century.[136]

> The rise of the power of the bishop of Rome was concomitant with the barbarians' invasion of the Roman Empire. As the power of the Roman Empire faded, the pope's power increased.

133. Heussi, *Kompendium*, 116. Justinian I was also against Monophysitism.
134. Walker, *History*, 151.
135. Heussi, *Kompendium*, 119.
136. Le Goff, *Medieval Civilization*, 21.

Kings and the Pope

Generally, from the fall of Rome until Charlemagne, political rule was local and based on much smaller units than at the time of the Roman Empire's power. Until the late Middle Ages, no king had a well-established bureaucracy. The papacy continued to have the best administration and the largest rule of the relatively ineffective clergy.[137] Additionally, since literacy was basically confined to the clergy, the papacy's services to kings were extremely helpful. They were needed to write any type of laws or legal or political recommendations.

Besides literacy, the papacy had other powers. The pope could crown kings. For example, Pepin the Short, son of Charles, desired to be crowned king of France, and he requested coronation by the pope. The pope agreed and commissioned the missionary Saint Boniface to crown Pepin as king of the Franks. This was done in 752.[138] Shortly afterward, Pepin came to the pope's rescue. He crossed the Alps with an army and contained the Lombards, who had attacked in Italy. Pepin had to cross the Alps again the following year, in 756, and he severely defeated the Lombards. Because of the Lombards' defeat, Pepin took land they had seized and made a direct donation of that land to the pope. This substantial gift became known as the famous "Donation of Pepin." Given the legal theory of the time, a donation of lands won by military conquest was a legal gift.[139] It also is probable that Pepin forged what became known as the "Donation of Constantine." This "donation" gave the pope direct political sovereignty over the western half of the Roman Empire![140]

Pepin died in 768. He divided his kingdom between his two sons, Charles, known as "the Great" (and thus Charlemagne), and Carloman. It was with Charlemagne that the empire was reestablished in the West. Charlemagne's long reign (768–814) was notable for the fact that the ruler of the West had lands that were greater than those held by the emperor in Constantinople.[141]

Charlemagne was a brilliant leader. He appointed legions of nobles and clergy who were loyal to him. His empire was vast. He fought the Saxons for twenty-three years and made them accept Christianity. He defeated

> *Additionally, since literacy was basically confined to the clergy, the papacy's services to kings were extremely helpful. They were needed to write any type of laws or legal or political recommendations.*

137. Stewart Easton, *The Western Heritage* (Holt, Reinhart & Winston: New York, 1961), 184–90.

138. Le Goff, *Medieval Civilization*, 21: "The eighth century was indeed the century of the Franks."

139. Walker, *History*, 186: This "donation remained the legal instrument by which the popes maintained their lands in Italy until the 19th century."

140. Le Goff, *Medieval Civilization*, 23. Walker, 186, underlined the fact that the donation was known to be false as early as the 1430s. The "donation" legally lasted until the year 1870, when the State of Vatican City was established within the nation of Italy.

141. Stewart C. Easton, *The Western Heritage* (New York: Holt Rhinehart, 1961), 190–94.

Asiatic tribes and also compelled them to convert to Christianity. Notably, his only defeat was in Spain against the Basques.[142]

Charlemagne's administrative system was simple. Each free man swore an oath of allegiance, and each lord had certain duties that he needed to perform for the king. Although he was what is called an autocrat, he recognized his responsibility to God as a ruler.[143]

Charles the Great had an interesting relationship with the pope (named Leo III). Charles never considered the pope to be his political superior. At best, the pope was viewed as a useful collaborator. Charlemagne gave the pope honor as the representative of God and head of the church, but he also felt free to summon synods himself and to declare bishops heretical, as well as to pronounce ecclesiastical sentence. In fact, during the time of controversy with Pope Leo, who was accused of various sins, Charles required the pope to take an oath declaring his innocence. Thus, Charles actually sat in judgment over the pope.

On Christmas day 800, Pope Leo III crowned Charles emperor in Saint Peter's cathedral in Rome. Scholars have questioned whether this inauguration was planned on Charles's part or whether it happened spontaneously, as Charlemagne alleged. Depending on the textbook, one can take a position either way.

Emperor Charlemagne

Conclusion

Profound changes occurred in the Christian worldview over the eight-hundred-year span of this chapter. Christianity went from the catacombs to the cathedrals. Various forms of Christian literature proliferated, articulating core beliefs, liturgical practices, and high moral standards. As persecution steeled Christian resolve to persist in the midst of virulent opposition, apologists defended the new faith. Various schools and theologians developed Christian doctrines, which clearly differentiated belief and practices from heresies and other forms of unbelief. Although different emphases emerged among early thinkers, councils convened to articulate doctrine and to oppose false ideas. Christians observed the downfall of the mighty Roman Empire and the rise of "barbarian" Germanic powers. The church struggled with persecution from without to become a "persecutor" from within. The church took positions against contemporary philosophical influences and in favor of such influences. Believers struggled against the state, and in some senses they helped to rule over the state. Thus, the stage is set for further development in the chapters that follow.

> *Charlemagne's administrative system was simple. Each free man swore an oath of allegiance, and each lord had certain duties that he needed to perform for the king. Although he was what is called an autocrat, he recognized his responsibility to God as a ruler.*

---

142.   See the map from Walker, *History*, 178.

143.   Hans von Schubert, *Geschichte der Christlichen Kirche im Frühmittelalter* (Tübingen, Germany: Mohr, 1921), 346.

For Further Reading

Bruce, F. F. *The Growing Day: The Progress of Christianity from the Fall of Jerusalem to the Accession of Constantine.* Eerdmans: Grand Rapids, 1953.

Chadwick, H. *The Early Church.* Penguin History of the Church. Grand Rapids: Eerdmans, 1968.

Cochrane, Charles Norris. *Christianity and Classical Culture: A Study of Thought and Action.* New York: Oxford University Press, 1944.

Duchesne, Louis. *Early History of the Christian Church from Its Foundation to the End of the Fifth Century.* London: Murray, 1965.

Gamble, Richard C. "Medieval Monasticism," *Tabletalk* (January 1995).

Kelly, J. N. D. *Early Christian Doctrines.* 5th ed. London: Black, 1972.

Kidd, B. J. *A History of the Christian Church to AD 461.* Oxford: Oxford University Press, 1922.

Le Goff, Jacques. Translated by Julia Barrow. *Medieval Civilization 400–1500.* Oxford: Basil Blackwell, 1988.

Markus, R. A. "Victorinus and Augustine," *The Cambridge History of Later Greek and Early Medieval Philosophy.* Cambridge: Cambridge University Press, 1970.

Nash, Ronald H. "The Christian Rationalism of St. Augustine," in *The Word of God and the Mind of Man: The Crisis of Revealed Truth in Contemporary Theology.* Phillipsburg, NJ: Presbyterian and Reformed Publishing, 1982.

Nash, Ronald H. *The Light of the Mind: St. Augustine's Theory of Knowledge.* Lexington: The University of Kentucky Press, 1969.

Needham, N. R. *2000 Years of Christ's Power. Part One.* London: Grace Publications Trust, 1997, 2002.

Quasten, Johannes. *Patrology.* Westminster, MD: Newman Press, 1951.

Schaff, Philip. *History of the Christian Church.* 2 vols. Eerdmans: Grand Rapids, 1979.

Stark, Rodney. *The Rise of Christianity: A Sociologist Reconsiders History.* Princeton, NJ: Princeton University Press, 1996.

Stark, Rodney. *The Rise of Christianity: How the Obscure, Marginal Jesus Movement Became the Dominant Religious Force in the Western World in a Few Centuries.* San Francisco: Harper and Row, 1997.

Warfield, B. B. *Studies in Tertullian and Augustine.* Oxford: Oxford University Press, 1930.

Wiles, Maurice, and M. Santer. *Documents in Early Christian Thought.* Cambridge: Cambridge University Press, 1975.

For Further Discussion

1. What is the Nicene Creed, and why is it important for the church today?

2. What is the Chalcedon Creed, and why is it important for the church today?

3. What is the content and impact of the Pseudo-Dionysus, and who was Boethius of Rome?

4. Give five reasons why studying church history is helpful.

5. Name five apostolic fathers and/or apologists and provide a one-sentence biography for each?

6. Identify Irenaeus of Lyons, including his biography, writing, and theology?

7. Identify Arius, including biography and theology?

8. Who was Athanasius? Include biography, writing, and theology.

9. Who was Gregory of Nyssa? Include biography, writing, and theology.

10. Describe and evaluate the period of persecution.

11. Why did the Roman Empire fall?

12. Was the emperor Constantine really a Christian?

13. Why did monasticism develop?

14. What was the relationship between the pope and the emperor during this period?

5

Medieval Theology and the Roots of Modernity

Peter J. Leithart

Looking back from the perspective of a culturally and intellectually fractured modernity and postmodernity, the medieval world can look enticingly unified. Long, long ago in a place far, far away a culture was united by a single worldview. For Christians, the attraction is especially powerful, since the whole of medieval life and thought was infused with Christianity. Medieval revivals have been a regular feature of modern Christianity.

Nostalgic though it is, this portrait is true in many respects. Medieval thinkers and writers attempted to understand every feature of the world through the lenses provided by Christian faith. Political thought was thoroughly infused with theological principles.[1] The economic issues that dominated medieval discussion, the just price and usury, were hashed through using biblical texts and theological principles. Aesthetics was not a separate branch of thought but simply one part of theology.[2] When Henry of Langenstein set out to write on science, he modeled his work after the

> *Long, long ago in a place far, far away a culture was united by a single worldview. For Christians, the attraction is especially powerful, since the whole of medieval life and thought was infused with Christianity.*

1. See Walter Ullmann, *A History of Political Thought: The Middle Ages* (Baltimore: Penguin, 1965); id., *Principles of Government and Politics in the Middle Ages* (London: Methuen, 1961); Ernst Katorowicz, *The King's Two Bodies: A Study of Medieval Political Theology* (Princeton, NJ: Princeton University Press, 1957). For a wonderful collection of texts in medieval (as well as patristic and Renaissance) political theology, see Oliver and Joan Lockwood O'Donovan, eds., *From Irenaeus to Grotius: A Sourcebook in Christian Political Thought* (Grand Rapids: Eerdmans, 1999).

2. Umberto Eco, *The Aesthetics of Thomas Aquinas*, trans. Hugh Bredin (Cambridge, MA: Harvard, 1988); id., *Art and Beauty in the Middle Ages*, trans. Hugh Bredin (New Haven, CT: Yale, 1986).

days of creation in Genesis 1.[3] Philosophical concerns raised by Plato, Neoplatonists such as Plotinus and Porphyry, and Aristotle were evaluated according to their consistency with Scripture and Christian tradition. Fine arts were replete with Christian themes and principles, and theater consisted of biblical stories (mystery plays) or allegories (morality plays). The lives of ordinary people were ordered by Christian rituals and festivals.[4] Entry into a cathedral enabled worshipers to relive their incorporation into the church, as well as to walk imaginatively through the events of the history of redemption.

We can be even more specific, for medieval thought and culture orbit, almost obsessively, around the nature and interpretation of signs, including linguistic signs, literary imagery, artistic symbols, meaningful rituals and gestures, pictures in architecture, and stained glass. Drawing on Augustine's treatment of signs in his classic text *On Christian Teaching* and on the hierarchical symbolic philosophy of Pseudo-Dionysus the Areopagite, medievals approached life with a "symbolic worldview." Marcia Colish says that "People who read books on the medieval mind are familiar with the dictum usually found on page one of any book on this subject: 'Medieval man thought in terms of symbols.' "[5] Despite a hint of irritation in that sentence, Colish does not dispute the dictum. Instead, she sets out to explain how "four major medieval figures actually thought that signs functioned in the acquisition and transmission of knowledge."[6]

The unity of medieval life and thought can, however, be exaggerated, and scholars have recently paid much closer attention to the fractures and breaches within the medieval world.[7] One illustration will suggest the variety and complexity of medieval thought. A thirteenth-century French clergyman known to us as Guillaume le Clerc composed a rhyming bestiary that surveyed the habits and symbolic features of animals, both

Guillaume le Clerc

> *Medieval thought and culture orbit, almost obsessively, around the nature and interpretation of signs, including linguistic signs, literary imagery, artistic symbols, meaningful rituals and gestures, pictures in architecture, and stained glass.*

3. G. R. Evans, *The Language and Logic of the Bible: The Earlier Middle Ages* (Cambridge: Cambridge University Press, 1984), vii.

4. John Bossy, *Christianity in the West, 1400–1700* (Oxford: Oxford University Press, 1985).

5. *The Mirror of Language: A Study in the Medieval Theory of Knowledge* (rev. ed.; Lincoln, NE: University of Nebraska Press, 1983), vii. This, interestingly enough, appears on the first page of Colish's own book.

6. Ibid. For more on this theme in general, see, for example, M. D. Chenu, *Nature, Man, and Society in the Twelfth Century: Essays on the New Theological Perspectives in the Latin West*, trans. and ed. Jerome Taylor and Lester K. Little (Chicago: University of Chicago Press, 1968), chap. 3: "The Symbolist Mentality"; Bernard J. Cooke, *The Distancing of God: The Ambiguity of Symbol in History and Theology* (Minneapolis: Fortress, 1990), chaps. 5–7; Michal Kobialka, *This Is My Body: Representational Practices in the Early Middle Ages* (Ann Arbor: University of Michigan Press, 1999); Eugene Vance, *Mervelous Signals: Poetics and Sign Theory in the Middle Ages* (Lincoln: University of Nebraska, 1986); Stephen G. Nichols Jr., *Romanesque Signs: Early Medieval Narrative and Iconography* (New Haven, CT: Yale, 1983); Ross G. Arthur, *Medieval Sign Theory and Sir Gawain and the Green Knight* (Toronto: University of Toronto, 1987).

7. See the survey in John van Engen, "The Christian Middle Ages as an Historiographical Problem," *American Historical Review* 91 (1986), 519–52.

real and legendary. Of the unicorn, Guillaume wrote,

> Now I will tell you of the unicorn,
> A beast which has but one horn
> Set in the middle of its forehead.
> This beast is so daring
> So pugnacious and so bold,
> That it picks quarrels with the elephant. . . .
> That it fears no hunter
> They that would ensnare it
> Go there first to spy
> When it has gone to disport itself
> Either on mountain or in valley.
> When they have found its haunt
> And have well marked its footprints
> They go for a young girl
> Whom they know well to be virgin.
> Then they make her sit and wait
> At its lair, for to capture the beast
> When the Unicorn is come back
> And has seen the damsel
> Straight to her it comes at once
> In her lap it crouches down
> And the girl clasps it
> Like one submitting to her.
> With the girl it sports so much
> That in her lap it falls asleep
> Those who are spying at once rush out
> There they take it and bind it
> Then they drive it before the king
> By force and despite its struggles.[8]

> *How do we evaluate the "worldview" of people credulous enough to believe that unicorns can be tamed by virgins but so obsessively Christ-centered that they turn the unicorn's legendary habits into an allegory of the incarnation?*

From this, medieval writers concluded that the unicorn was a fitting symbol of the incarnation, since Christ, too, was an untamable being who submitted to being slaughtered by placing himself in the lap of a virgin.[9] That medievals apparently believed unicorns existed and behaved this way points to an important feature of medieval thought and culture. That they saw an allegory of Christ in the habits of the unicorn points to a feature even more fundamental.

The picture becomes even more charmingly complex when we recall that while Guillaume was composing his bestiary, scholastic theologians in Paris were studying Aristotelian philosophy and engaging in sophisticated debates about the nature of angels, the meaning of essence and existence, and whether or not there is a single "active intellect" shared by all human beings. How do we evaluate the "worldview" of people credulous enough to believe that unicorns can be tamed by virgins but so obsessively Christ-

---

8. Quoted in Rodney Denys, *The Heraldic Imagination* (New York: Clarkson N. Potter, 1975), 163–64.

9. Louis Charbonneau-Lassay, *The Bestiary of Christ* (New York: Arkana, 1991), 365–75.

centered that they turn the unicorn's legendary habits into an allegory of the incarnation? How do we evaluate the "worldview" of a civilization that can produce a playful portrait of unicorns alongside dense, deadly, and earnest treatises in metaphysics? If there is a unity behind this, it is not, to say the least, obvious on the surface of things.[10]

Viewing Worldview

Further questions arise about the category of worldview itself. Is this concept "worldview" adequate to deal with something as richly chaotic as medieval thought and culture. Whose worldview, after all, are we talking about? Thomas Aquinas used Aristotelian categories to attempt to penetrate the nature of things, but did a Parisian merchant selling English woolens down the street from Thomas's rooms at the university share his worldview? Would he have understood the first thing Thomas was saying? Where, moreover, is the medieval worldview to be sought? Does the "medieval worldview" refer to a set of categories or a map of the universe in the heads of medieval people (and, again, which people)? Or, is it found in texts, and if so, what kinds of texts—philosophical, poetic, epistolary? Or, is it located in the assumptions made by writers of texts, in things everyone takes so much for granted that they never need to say them out loud? Or, is it embodied in practices, institutions, and artifacts, in the traceries of Gothic rose windows, in the pageantry of a feudal ceremony of vassalage, or in the theatrical celebrations that accompanied the Corpus Christi festival? In the last case, is there any significant difference between the "worldview" and "culture." Furthermore, on what basis do we conclude that there is a single "worldview" shared by people in a particular historical epoch? Is this an assumption or a metaphysical or moral necessity? Or is there empirical evidence that this is the case?

To control some of these complexities, I have written mainly about developments in medieval "theology,"[11] as well as the social and cultural setting and ramifications of those developments. Though "worldview" usually has a broader scope than "theology," my focus on theology is defensible for several reasons. First, medieval thought, as noted above, was shot through with Christian language, symbols, and ideas, and many medieval figures studied today as philosophers (e.g., Scotus and Ockham) were in the first instance theologians. For medieval thinkers, "theology" was as broad a subject as "worldview" is for modern evangelicals. Second, tracing developments in theology gets at the very pretheoretical judgments and beliefs that "worldview" analysts are interested in. Finally, my training is in

> *Further questions arise about the category of worldview itself. Is this concept "worldview" adequate to deal with something as richly chaotic as medieval thought and culture. Whose worldview, after all, are we talking about?*

---

10. Of course, variety of outlook was not unique to the Middle Ages. Scratch just below the surface of any age, and you find bewildering, incomprehensible diversities.

11. As will be noted below, the word "theology" also is a loaded term. It also has a history, and a controversial one.

theology rather than literature, art history, or philosophy, and therefore I am more confident that I can offer helpful guidance here.

The Shape of the Story

The story of medieval theology has often been told, with great variety. For many evangelicals, Thomas Aquinas is the syncretistic villain of the story, the evil genius who smuggled Aristotle into the church under cover of orthodoxy, and who thereby assisted the development of the evils of the modern culture: the autonomy of reason and nature, secularism in politics and society, foundationalist epistemology, the primacy of scientific modes of knowledge, and knowledge understood as functional control over the world. More recently, John Duns Scotus has become the *bête noire*. His advocacy of the univocity of being, in contrast with the Thomist analogy of being (see below), provided the foundation for all the violent antinomies whose clashes are the story of modernity.[12]

One way to state this story is that it traces the development of what Heidegger called "onto-theology." Many have taken Heidegger as an opponent of any theology that makes metaphysical claims about what really is the case with the world. For Heidegger, however, "onto-theology" refers to a style of theology subordinated to and constrained by philosophical commitments from outside theology. For onto-theology, "God" comes to the world "only insofar as philosophy, of its own accord and by its own nature, requires and determines how the deity enters into it." Heidegger had nothing but scorn for a god who can be controlled by philosophy: we "can neither pray nor sacrifice to this god. Before the *causa sui*, man can neither fall to his knees in awe nor can he play music and dance before this god."[13] The Christian God, the Creator and Redeemer, the God of exodus and resurrection, is precisely the God who enters the scene wherever and whenever he pleases, the God who interrupts, the God who surprises, the God who is constrained by nothing, certainly nothing so feeble as human ideas.

I am adopting a version of this story line, for it seems incontestable that the medieval world contained some of the seeds that grew into modern thought and civilization. No medieval thinker went so far as to subordinate theology to philosophical conceptions. But before onto-theology could develop, philosophy and theology had to be separated from one another, so they could begin their struggle for domination. If philosophy is

> *No medieval thinker went so far as to subordinate theology to philosophical conceptions. But before onto-theology could develop, philosophy and theology had to be separated from one another, so they could begin their struggle for domination.*

12. Scotus and the voluntarist movements of the later Middle Ages are targeted especially by theologians in the Radical Orthodoxy movement. See John Milbank, *Theology and Social Theory: Beyond Secular Reason* (Oxford: Blackwell, 1990), 14; Catherine Pickstock, *After Writing: On the Liturgical Consummation of Philosophy*, Challenges in Contemporary Theology (Oxford: Blackwell, 1998), 121–66; Conor Cunningham, *Genealogy of Nihilism*, Radical Orthodoxy (London: Routledge, 2002), 16–58.

13. Both quotations from Merold Westphal, *Overcoming Onto-Theology: Toward a Postmodern Christian Faith* (New York: Fordham University Press, 2001), 2.

seen as internal to theology, onto-theology is impossible.[14] The process of separating philosophy and theology began during the High Middle Ages, in the two-and-a-half centuries following the reforms of Pope Gregory VII. I argue here that the main mechanism for this rupture was the separation of theological and philosophical "questions" from reading and interpreting of the text of Scripture.[15]

I depart from the common stories in two ways. First, there was no pristine Christian purity in patristic, or even the apostolic, Christianity. The New Testament is the infallible Word of God, but many heard the gospel through the filter of Hellenistic conceptualities that distorted the sound waves. One cannot read Justin Martyr without realizing that he is in a very different thought world from the apostle Paul. Hellenistic static distorts the gospel message in even the greatest of the fathers. Augustine very nearly struggled free of his Neoplatonic roots, but remained to the end ambivalent about the goodness of material creation, a fact especially evident in his ambivalence about sexual passion. The development of the Christian theology in the West is not a story of patristic rise and Thomistic (or Scotist) fall. It is a much more complex picture, with significant progress in the medieval era as well as significant wrong turns.

Abelard and Heloise

Second, I offer a third choice for the villain of the story, Peter Abelard, a choice that suggests that medieval thought took a wrong turn earlier than Thomas or Scotus. I offer this option not out of lust for innovation (which would place me alongside my villain) but for two reasons: first, because the issues that Abelard raises and the methods he employs are the issues and methods of medieval thinkers throughout the following centuries; and, second, because examining Abelard will help us to locate precisely where the shifts in theology took place and precisely how medieval theology moved toward onto-theology. Attention to detail is essential here, for in many respects the *substance* of medieval thought changed little between 1050 and 1400. At the beginning of that period, every thinker believed in an almighty Creator who made a good creation that was corrupted by sin but became flesh to redeem the world, to gather his church, and to bring history to a glorious consummation. At the end of the period, every thinker believed the same things. The shift is less in the *substance* of thought than in the *style* and *language* in which it was discussed and elaborated. Abelard marks an important moment in that shift, which, though a change in style,

The process of separating philosophy and theology began during the High Middle Ages .... I argue here that the main mechanism for this rupture was the separation of theological and philosophical "questions" from reading and interpreting of the text of Scripture.

14.   It seems that the opposite might also be true: If theology is simply ignored, as it is in much modern philosophy, it would seem that onto-theology is impossible. But, Heidegger claimed that philosophy had always had a hidden theological agenda, and thus was inherently onto-theological.

15.   One way to state the point is that the twelfth century marked the beginning of interest in theological method. I have critiqued method in an essay review in *Pro Ecclesia* 9:3 (2002): 356–62.

is simultaneously a subtle change in the substance of theology. Both shifts, moreover, are part of a broader revolution in medieval civilization.[16]

Abelard and the Adventure of Scholasticism

Rupert of Deutz smelled a rat and wanted to sniff it out, remove it from the church, and give it a decent burial. In 1117, he made a trip from his monastery at Saint-Laurent of Liege to Laon to take on two masters of theology, William of Champeaux and Anselm of Laon.[17] Rupert was a learned biblical commentator, an "enthusiast for the richness and vividness of the Bible's imagery, the myriad pictures countercharging and reflecting one another in its pages."[18] Everywhere, he displayed his love of "the details of the sacred text, tracing patterns and connections, passages in the Old Testament which have echoes in the New, prophecies fulfilled."[19] Rupert was not the least opposed to the liberal arts, but saw them as tools to be used for the study of Scripture, not as independent subjects for study in themselves. Without the discipline of Scripture, he said, the liberal arts are nothing but "silly giggling girls." Put into service of scriptural reading, interpretation, and preaching, they become *ancillae*, handmaidens of theology.

William and Anselm had already been involved in a war of treatises with Rupert on the problem of evil. William and Anselm had attempted to reconcile God's omnipotence with the existence of evil by positing a distinction between a permissive will and an approving will, a distinction based partly on observation of the workings of the human will.[20] Rupert protested that this distinction had no basis in Scripture, and he insisted that scriptural language be employed to explore the mystery of evil. In the book of Job, one reads not of a permissive will but "of the patience of God; a patience which is not a 'specific' way of willing evil, but merely goodness and forbearance and benevolence."[21] If this did not completely solve the intellectual problem, so be it. Rupert had no problem resting in mystery and standing before the dark glass of faith.

Rupert's struggle with William and Anselm of Laon was many-sided. Rupert recognized that the authority of Scripture was at stake: "Whatever can be thought up apart from sacred scripture or fabricated out of argumentation," he argued, "is unreasonable and therefore pertains in no way to the praise or acknowledgment of the omnipotence of God."[22] Rupert's insistence

> *William and Anselm had attempted to reconcile God's omnipotence with the existence of evil by positing a distinction between a permissive will and an approving will, a distinction based partly on observation of the workings of the human will.*

---

16. I should make explicit an assumption that is no doubt already apparent: I reject the separation of form and content as a modern innovation, an early form of which is found in Abelard. Like "worldview" and "theology," this conception has a history.

17. *PL* 170, 482–83, quoted in Chenu, *Nature, Man, and Society*, 270.

18. Evans, *Logic and Language of the Bible*, 13–14.

19. Ibid., 14.

20. Chenu, *Nature, Man, and Society*, 271.

21. Ibid., 271–72.

22. Quoted in ibid., 272.

on Scripture's centrality in all theology was characteristic of the monastic schools in which he was trained. William and Anselm, by contrast, had forged their habits of thought in cathedral schools, in which a master (not an abbot) taught students (not novice monks). The social differences between the monkish theologian and the school theologian could hardly be starker: Monks were rooted to a single place, while the masters of the schools were mobile, the original of the rootless Western intellectuals who later populated Russian novels. Monks were bound to obedience; masters made a living in a competitive environment, which encouraged innovation in order to win students. Monks were scholars of Scripture and used rhetoric and grammar as means for making Scripture plain; masters employed dialectic (logic) to resolve "questions." Monks sought union with God through meditation and a kind of unbounded free association on the text; masters pursued propositional truth through the application of logic and the concoction of disputations, and attempted to summarize Christian truth and organize it in systematic ways.[23] Rupert's protest against the masters was an early skirmish in the battle over a new kind of theology that no longer focused on study of sacred Scripture and no longer sought wisdom (*sapientia*). Instead, the masters' theology was increasingly understood as a "science" constructed through logical argumentation.[24] Although earlier scholarship had arisen from the text and from the practical needs of the monastic liturgy,[25] the new scholarship was a product of sheer human curiosity.

According to the early medieval conception, Christendom was a single **ecclesia**, *ruled jointly by priests and princes. Both ecclesiastical and civil rulers were seen as holding sacred offices.*

Eleventh-Century Foundations

In some important senses, the die had already been cast in the mid-eleventh century. Institutionally, Pope Gregory VII had, in his famous battle with Henry IV, asserted and achieved papal primacy over the emperor. More importantly, though, Gregory's reform movement had driven a wedge between the two leading poles of early medieval society. According to the early medieval conception, Christendom was a single *ecclesia*, ruled jointly by priests and princes. Both ecclesiastical and civil rulers were seen as holding sacred offices. For centuries, medievals thought of the royal anointing as a sacrament, analogous to ordination. In various ways, however, Gregory's program split this unified social and political reality. By insisting that priests remain celibate, Gregory detached the clergy from the networks of kingship that constituted society, so that the clergy became a

---

23. Anselm of Canterbury (different from Anselm of Laon) is *sui generis*, both exemplifying the monastic approach and departing significantly from it. Anselm's works all begin in meditation and prayer, but he rarely cites Scripture at all, much less offers free-ranging allegories on it. See Evans, *Language and Logic*, 17–23; more fully, R. W. Southern, *St. Anselm: A Portrait in a Landscape* (Cambridge: Cambridge University Press, 1990).

24. On the development of theology as a "science," see M.-D. Chenu, *La theologie comme science au XIIe Siecle*, 2nd ed. (Paris: Librairie J. Vrin, 1943).

25. R. W. Southern, *The Making of the Middle Ages* (New Haven, CT: Yale, 1953), 186–87.

"class" unto themselves. Gregory considered Henry IV "merely" a layman, and his heated rhetoric was an implicit "secularizing" of political power. A century later, the king's anointing was downgraded from a full sacrament to a "sacramental." Clergy became identified with the "church" and the "literal priesthood," while laymen were considered as only "metaphorically" priests. Though his intentions were quite different, Gregory's reform transformed a unified society with twin rulers into two societies, the church, on the one hand, and the "state" or society, on the other. Gregory thus laid institutional foundations for the later development of separated areas of study. After Gregory, it became reasonable to think of "politics" as an area of study distinct from "theology," which pertained specifically to the church. These developments were centuries in the making, but Gregory set them in motion.[26]

Gregory's papal reforms were inspired by reform movements within Benedictine monasticism. By the mid-eleventh century, many monks had become disenchanted with the Cluniac revival of monasticism of the previous century, regarding Cluniac monks as too comfortable and soft. They revived the more rigorous ascetic monasticism of the early church. When these reforming monks, such as Gregory VII himself, because leaders of the church, they sought to spread their ascetic ideal throughout the church, and indeed throughout the world. At least the clergy could be reformed into a holy and ascetic class.[27]

Other cultural shifts in the mid-eleventh century also helped prepare for the birth of scholasticism and the early development of onto-theology. Fresh devotion to the humanity of Jesus, Anselm's theory of the atonement that emphasized the importance of his human sufferings, and renewed attention to the literal sense of Scripture all indicated a new affirmation of the goodness of the material creation.[28] By the mid-eleventh century, Islam had become somewhat moribund and was less of a threat to Europe. Europeans began to move out into the Mediterranean world and the Middle East, and by the end of the century, Crusaders were fighting Muslims in the Holy Land. Wars with Islam were a common feature of the Early Middle Ages, particularly during the Carolingian age. In those wars, however, Franks had been fighting off a Muslim advance. By the eleventh century, Europeans were on the offensive. Technological changes also contributed to the formation of a new outlook: "The importation of the horse collar and stirrup gave them a much greater use of available horsepower," and "Euro-

> *Though his intentions were quite different, Gregory's reform transformed a unified society with twin rulers into two societies, the church, on the one hand, and the "state" or society, on the other. Gregory thus laid institutional foundations for the later development of separated areas of study.*

---

26. For more discussion and for evidence for these claims, see my "The Gospel, Gregory VII, and Modern Theology," *Modern Theology* 19:1 (2003): 5–28. Note that the formation of a new social entity—the "state"—was historically prior to the formulation of theories about that entity, i.e., political science.

27. Norman Cantor, *The Civilization of the Middle Ages* (New York: HarperCollins, 1993), 243–49. Cantor describes the Gregorian reform as the first "world revolution" in Western European history.

28. Southern, *Making of the Middle Ages*, chap. 5: "From Epic to Romance."

peans also began to make use of water power" to grind grain and cut lumber.[29] Rising population, increasing wealth, and the beginnings of urbanization also lent energy to the age. Christopher Dawson claimed: "there is no doubt that the eleventh century marks a decisive turning point in European history—the end of the Dark Ages and the emergence of Western culture. . . . with the eleventh century a movement of progress begins which was to continue almost without intermission down to modern times."[30]

In an illuminating study comparing developments in medieval architecture and scholarship, Charles M. Radding and William W. Clark point to the spirit of experimentation that gripped both builders and masters in the eleventh century:

> From being craftsmen who took the learning and styles of the past and adapted them to contemporary use, builders and masters [scholars] had by 1100 transformed themselves into self-aware and consciously innovating members of disciplines. But 1130s saw a quantum leap in the level of intellectual sophistication required of masters and builders as they shifted their attention from solving individual issues to constructing whole systems of solutions to intellectual and aesthetic problems. Masters moved from dealing with isolated texts that could be glossed or *quaestiones* for which definite answers could be proposed to constructing systems of thought in which the effects of an answer on one issue impinged upon the answer to other equally complex issues. . . . builders . . . not endeavoring to devise increasingly complex and integrated spaces, found themselves having to design small details with an eye to the effects each decision would have on the whole.[31]

Pope Gregory VII

In scholarship, the new approach showed itself in the debates over Berengar's Eucharistic theories, the theological *cause celebre* of the eleventh century.[32] Architecturally, the new spirit was evident in innovative uses of Romanesque style that prepared the way for Gothic style in the following centuries. Behind the diversity of Romanesque styles was a basic design plan, which Radding and Clark call the "modular conception." Architects treated the various component spaces of a church, for example, as discrete spaces set off from one another by columns, half-columns, and so on.[33] Details aside, there is an evident resemblance between the architectural practice of organizing smaller, semi-independent units into a larger whole

Rising population, increasing wealth, and the beginnings of urbanization also lent energy to the age.

---

29. Ibid., 228–29.

30. Christopher Dawson, *The Making of Europe: An Introduction to the History of European Unity* (New York: Times Mirror, 1952), 239.

31. Radding and Clark, *Medieval Architecture, Medieval Learning: Builders and Masters in the Age of Romanesque and Gothic* (New Haven, CT: Yale, 1992), 57.

32. Ibid., 22–27.

33. At Saint-Sernin of Toulouse, for example, the apse at the east end of the church was circumscribed by a walkway (ambulatory), which led out into five alcove-like chapels that radiated from the main building. Each of the chapels was considered a modular unit distinguished in some way (columns, half-columns, etc.) from the ambulatory. This had two practical benefits: later builders who continued the project would be able to work from the original design without altering the overall plan, and modules could be added without disrupting the whole (ibid., 37–44).

and the scholarly practices of scholasticism, which summarized theological issues in a series of "questions" as part of a larger systematic pattern.[34]

This new spirit of optimism or adventure creeping into the medieval mind manifested itself institutionally in the formation of universities. E. Harris Harbison writes:

> From the point of view of intellectual history, the first half of the twelfth century (1100s) was the most exciting fifty years since the fall of Rome. The long fight for sheer survival had finally been won and Europe was beginning to feel her energies flowing. The Crusades had begun, and Western European scholars were traveling in Spain, Sicily, and Asia Minor, ransacking Moslem libraries, and translating into Latin the scientific and philosophical works of the ancient Greeks, preserved and commented upon by the Arabs. The intellectual excitement was widespread, but Paris soon became its focus. In the twelfth century Paris became "a city of teachers," the first the medieval world had known.[35]

Yet, nowhere was the new attitude toward life more evident than in literature. Two related changes are evident. Beginning in the eleventh and twelfth centuries, traveling poets in southwestern France known as *troubadours* began composing what has come to be known as "courtly love" poetry. C. S. Lewis called courtly love a "real change in human sentiment," which was very rare: "there are perhaps three or four [such changes] on record." Troubadours "effected a change which has left no corner of our ethics, our imagination, or our daily life untouched, and they erected impossible barriers between us and the classical past or the Oriental present. Compared with this revolution, the Renaissance is a mere ripple on the surface of literature."[36]

According to the definition of Andreas Capellanus, one of the "theorists" of courtly love, love is suffering induced by seeing the beauty of a member of the opposite sex.[37] Love comes as a wound from an arrow shot by the god of love that enters the eye and pierces the heart. Classic treatments of this theme were found in the thirteenth-century French allegory, *The Romance of the Rose*, and in the intense longings of Troilus in Chaucer's *Troilus and Criseyde*. For many courtly lovers, love is pain because the beloved is inaccessible—either married or scornful of the lover. A courtly lover, however, is utterly devoted to his lady, so that she becomes almost a replacement for his feudal lord, and the lover's passion inspires him to undertake great deeds of daring. For the courtly love tradition, therefore,

> C. S. Lewis called courtly love a "real change in human sentiment," which was very rare: "there are perhaps three or four [such changes] on record." Troubadours "effected a change which has left no corner of our ethics, our imagination, or our daily life untouched . . . ."

34. The classic study of the connections between medieval theology and architecture is Erwin Panofsky, *Gothic Architecture and Scholasticism: An Inquiry into the Analogy of the Arts, Philosophy, and Religion in the Middle Ages* (New York: Meridian, 1951).

35. E. Harris Harbison, *The Christian Scholar in the Age of the Reformation* (Grand Rapids: Eerdmans, 1983).

36. Lewis, *The Allegory of Love: A Study in Medieval Tradition* (Oxford: Oxford University Press, 1936), 4.

37. Andreas Capellanus, *The Art of Courtly Love*, trans. John Jay Parry (New York: W. W. Norton, 1941), 28.

love made the lover in every way a better man. This last characteristic of courtly love is perhaps the most innovative of all the features of this perspective. Ancient writers often rhapsodized on the character-building potential of love, but they were talking about the love of one man for another. Only this kind of male love could inspire virtue. For courtly love poets, passion for a woman had a similar effect.[38]

Courtly love poetry quickly became intertwined with the adventure literature that was making its appearance in the same period. According to the Marxist historian Michael Nerlich, this marked a significant and permanent new development in Western history. Adventure stories existed from antiquity, but Nerlich argues there was a fundamental difference between ancient and medieval adventure: Ancient adventurers (such as Odysseus) were driven unwillingly into their adventures, but for medievals after the twelfth century, "adventures are undertaken on a *voluntary* basis, they are *sought out*, (*la quete de l'aventure*, the quest for adventure), and this quest and hence the adventurer himself are glorified." The very meaning of the term "adventure" underwent significant change: "*Adventure*, which in its literary occurrences before the courtly romance, means fate, chance, has become, in the knightly-courtly system of relations, an event that the knight must seek out and endure, although this event does continue to be unpredictable, a surprise of fate." Nerlich examines how these medieval motifs assisted in the development of capitalist economic practices, a connection still evident in phrases such as "venture capital" and "business ventures." He goes so far as to say that the first truly modern man was the twelfth-century poet Chretien de Troyes, the first and greatest writer of Arthurian romance.[39]

These eleventh-century developments in culture and literature provide the setting for a significant shift in theology, especially in theological method. Moreover, these shifts signaled one of the key revolutions in medieval worldview, a revolution associated in the first instance with the adventurous work of Peter Abelard and with the movement known as "scholasticism."

The Invention of "Theology"

For many moderns, "scholasticism" carries connotations of aridity and conservatism and exudes the noxious odor of dust and death. In the twelfth and thirteenth centuries, however, scholasticism was an innovative movement, riding the wave of adventure and experimentation that we have glanced at above. Scholasticism took its name from the fact that its practitioners taught in a "school" setting rather than a monastic setting, and their methods of theology reflected the contentious setting of the early universi-

> *Courtly love poetry quickly became intertwined with the adventure literature that was making its appearance in the same period. According to the Marxist historian Michael Nerlich, this marked a significant and permanent new development in Western history.*

---

38. C. Stephen Jaeger, *Ennobling Love: In Search of a Lost Sensibility* (Philadelphia: University of Pennsylvania Press, 1999).

39. Michael Nerlich, *Ideology of Adventure: Studies in Modern Consciousness, 1100–1250: Volume 1*, Theory and History of Literature, 42, trans. Ruth Croley (Minneapolis: University of Minnesota Press, 1987), 3–12.

ties.[40] On the surface, scholasticism was a systematic way of organizing theology and a method for resolving apparent contradictions in the tradition. Medieval theologians inherited a rich and varied tradition but one that was not always internally consistent. When Augustine says X, and Ambrose says Y, and the Bible says Z, what are we to do? Is this a contradiction, or are they speaking of different things or of the same thing in different ways? Add Aristotle into the mix, and you have most of the sources for scholastic theology. Scholasticism also was an attempt to harmonize faith and reason, an effort to demonstrate that the truths of Christian faith did not contradict logic and reason. This effort preceded Aristotle's renewed invasion of the West, for in the eleventh century Anselm already was offering rational defenses of the atonement, sophisticated linguistic treatments of the doctrine of the Trinity, and ontological "arguments" for the existence of God. But, again, adding Aristotle to the mix complicated things immeasurably.

On the other hand, from the beginning there was a more "conservative" impulse in scholasticism. Both intellectually and politically, scholastic theology strove to tame a rapidly changing and sometimes chaotic world. In an intriguing work on modernity, Stephen Toulmin argues that Descartes and his successors were reactionaries who wanted to bring the intellectual and political energies of the Renaissance under control.[41] Something similar was going on in the twelfth and thirteenth centuries. As Europe grew into a bumptious toddler, scholastics intervened to discipline it.[42] R. W. Southern explains the aims:

> From a scholarly point of view, it was the twelfth-century innovators who first introduced systematic order into the mass of intellectual material which they had inherited in a largely uncoordinated form from the ancient world. The general aim of their work was to produce a complete and systematic body of knowledge, clarified by the refinements of criticism, and presented as the consensus of competent judges. Doctrinally the method for achieving this consensus was a progression from commentary to questioning, and from questioning to systematization. And the practical aim of the whole procedure was to stabilize, make accessible, and defend an orthodox Christian view of the world against the attacks of heretics within, and unbelievers . . . outside the area of Christendom.

> *On the surface, scholasticism was a systematic way of organizing theology and a method for resolving apparent contradictions in the tradition. Medieval theologians inherited a rich and varied tradition but one that was not always internally consistent.*

This "conservative" motif was mingled with an astonishingly ambitious agenda. Underlying scholasticism was a desire to participate in the reversal of Adam's fall: "In principle, they aimed at restoring to fallen mankind, so far as possible, that perfect system of knowledge which had been in the possession or within the reach of mankind at the moment of Creation."[43]

40. For a brief summary of the rise of the universities, see Charles Homer Haskins, *The Renaissance of the Twelfth Century* (Cambridge, MA: Harvard, 1927), chap. 12.
41. Toulmin, *Cosmopolis: The Hidden Agenda of Modernity* (Chicago: University of Chicago Press, 1992).
42. Southern, *Making of the Middle Ages*, 179.
43. Southern, *Scholastic Humanism and the Unification of Europe: Volume 1: Foundations* (Oxford: Blackwell, 1995), 4–5. Note the similarities between the scholastic agenda

Of the early scholastic works, Peter the Lombard's *Four Books of the Sentences* had the greatest overt impact on later generations, but the origin of the scholastic drive for rational inquiry was the work of Peter Abelard (1079–1142).[44] Abelard is of interest in many respects. His colorful life, involving a love affair that ended with his castration, has often been recounted, first by himself. His Trinitarian speculations landed him in difficulties with Bernard of Clairvaux and other church leaders. He was among the earliest proponents of a form of the philosophical position called "nominalism," the view that every really existing thing is particular (see on Ockham below). As Norman Cantor points out, Abelard's autobiography, *The History of My Calamities*, was of a piece with his philosophical agenda. By emphasizing the uniqueness of his life, he was protesting against the "Platonic absorption of the individual into the universal."[45] For my purposes, Abelard is of interest for his contribution to the separation of theology and philosophy and the development of new ways of pursuing theology. Abelard was one of the early thinkers to treat "theology" as a "scientific" pursuit. He established the "summary" (*summa*) as the unit of theology, and he organized theology around topics, rather than following the contours of the biblical text.

Anselm, following Augustine, had said his theology was a matter of "faith seeking understanding." In his autobiography, Abelard says that his students demanded from him theology in precisely the opposite direction, for one cannot believe what he does not first understand.[46] Though Abelard coyly puts the demand for rational theology in the mouths of his students, it is clearly his own theological agenda. The seriousness with which he took the abilities of reason to penetrate and explain Christian faith is evident in his claim that he was able to penetrate the mysteries of the Trinity. When challenged, Abelard protested that he had no desire to subordinate Christ to philosophy. In a much-cited letter to his lover Heloise, he wrote, "I will

Page from Peter Lombard's **Sentences**

"Anselm, following Augustine, had said his theology was a matter of "faith seeking understanding." In his autobiography, Abelard says that his students demanded from him theology in precisely the opposite direction, for one cannot believe what he does not first understand.

---

and the aims of many worldview thinkers.

44. For introductions to Abelard, see John Marenbon, *The Philosophy of Peter Abelard* (Cambridge: University of Cambridge Press, 1997); M. T. Clanchy, *Abelard: A Life* (Oxford: Blackwell, 1997); more briefly, David Luscombe, *Medieval Thought,* History of Western Philosophy 2 (Oxford: Oxford University Press, 1997); Adriaan H. Bredero, *Christendom and Christianity in the Middle Ages,* ed. Reinder Bruinsma (Grand Rapids: Eerdmans, 1994), chap. 8. Haskins says that twelfth-century philosophy was not dependent on the infusion of Arabic and Greek texts into the West, pointing to Anselm, Abelard, and Roscillinus as examples of philosophical theologians prior to the main Aristotelian revival (*Renaissance of the Twelfth Century*, 349).

45. Cantor, *Civilization of the Middle Ages*, 332.

46. Abelard wrote that "[pupils] asked for the human and philosophical reasons and insisted that it was not enough for something just to be said—it had to be understood. Indeed, they said that it was vain to utter words if they were not then understood, nor could anything be believed in unless it was first understood, and that it was ridiculous for someone to preach to others what neither he nor those he taught could grasp with their intellects, for then (as Christ complained) the blind lead the blind" (quoted in Marenbon, *Philosophy of Peter Abelard*, 54).

never be a philosopher, if this is to speak against St. Paul; I would not be an Aristotle, if this were to separate me from Christ."[47] Yet, his use of logic pushed him in the direction of onto-theology.

With regard to "theology" as a science, Abelard's work was a crucial moment in the invention of "theology" as a discipline.[48] In earlier centuries, monastic writers had "done theology" by expounding the text of Scripture, applying it wherever it happened to lead. They did not describe themselves as "theologians" but as "masters of the sacred page." This interpretive scholarship was not seen as a separate "discipline" alongside other disciplines but merely an evangelical use of Scripture, which the liberal arts served. Because it centered on the study of texts, monastic interpretation made fuller use of grammar and rhetoric than of dialectic or logic. Abelard, however, was one of the first to use the word "theology" to describe a distinct kind of treatise and a separate course of study. The newness of the usage is evident in Bernard's reaction. In his controversy with Abelard, Bernard never used "theology" to describe his own work but only pejoratively to describe Abelard's, and Bernard frequently used the neologism "*stultilogia*" ("idiotology") as a synonym.[49]

Fittingly in an age of questing, Abelard's method in theology was a method of questioning. Questions about the text of Scripture were inevitable, and commentators during the earlier Middle Ages frequently digressed to explain particular words or grammatical forms or to address theological concerns that arose from the text. Abelard normally followed this technique as well, addressing the issues in sequence as they come up in Scripture. Yet, Abelard intended to move past this textually based method into one more fully guided by logic. According to Manchy's summary, for Abelard "the 'reading of the divine books' of the Scriptures was the way a conventional student of divinity proceeded. A theologian, on the other hand, proceeded by reasoning from first principles."[50] Dissatisfied with the method of "reading" with commentary and explanation (*lectio*), Abelard aimed to provide "reasons" that were satisfying to the human intellect.[51]

> "Because it centered on the study of texts, monastic interpretation made fuller use of grammar and rhetoric than of dialectic or logic. Abelard, however, was one of the first to use the word "theology" to describe a distinct kind of treatise and a separate course of study.

47. Quoted in Edward Grant, *God and Reason in the Middle Ages* (Cambridge: Cambridge University Press, 2001), 57.

48. According to J. Riviere, Abelard was the first to use "theology" to describe "une etude raisonnee, general ou partielle, de la doctrine chretienne, soit, par extension, un ouvrage consacre a ce genre de travail" (quoted in Chenu, *La theologie comme science*, 85, fn. 2).

49. G. R. Evans, *Bernard of Clairvaux*, Great Medieval Thinkers (Oxford: Oxford University Press, 2000), 48; Clanchy, *Abelard*, 264–65. For other evaluations of Abelard's method, see Roger French and Andrew Cunningham quoted in Grant, *God and Reason*, 59; Louis Bouyer, *Cosmos: The World and the Glory of God* (Peterham, MA: St. Bede's, 1982); Chenu, *Theologie comme la science*, 64.

50. Clanchy, *Abelard*, 264.

51. In this, Abelard was a transitional figure, who still valued the spiritual reading of the monks. Beryl Smalley points out that Abelard advised Heloise to attend to the *lectio divina*, the traditional monastic reading of Scripture, and to learn Hebrew to enhance her grasp of it (*The Study of the Bible in the Middle Ages* [Notre Dame: University of Notre Dame Press, 1964], 79).

Gradually, the method of "questioning" was pried away from the context of the "reading," so that theology became detached from exegesis, and eventually reason from faith, and philosophy from theology.

Abelard's separation of the substance of theology from its biblical form was deeply rooted and at least partly self-conscious. A form-content opposition appears repeatedly in different contexts in his work. He advised his son Astralabe not to accept a teacher or writer on the basis of eloquence or personal love. Rather, the best teachers speak plainly and organize their teaching logically and systematically. Style and personal character (ethos) are bracketed off; what counts is the disconnected, impersonal logic of a teacher or a book.[52] His ethics, moreover, focused on intentions to such an extent that he could write: "external things do not commend us to God," a statement that nearly everyone in the previous century would have rejected. As Stephen Jaeger summarizes it, Abelard introduced a wholly new system of education and a wholly new approach to scholarship: "An entire system of education was caught in a conflict between a traditional kind of teaching that tended toward the acquisition of human qualities and a new kind of teaching that tended toward knowledge and rational inquiry."[53]

Though Bernard won his battles with Abelard in his lifetime, Abelard had the final say, for Peter the Lombard (ca. 1095–1161) consolidated theology in an Abelardian key, and Lombard's text became the leading theology textbook of the medieval period until displaced by Thomas's *Summa theologiae* many years later. Lombard's *Sentences* was a rather modest compilation and harmonization of the Christian tradition, not yet a systematic work on the scale of the later scholastic *summas*. But, the continuity is evident. Chenu claims that a text like Peter Lombard's *Sentences* "made it possible to foresee already how the questions would become more important than the texts being commented upon,"[54] though he fails to note Abelard's centrality in this process. Abelard, after all, wrote his *Sic et non* prior to Lombard's text, and Lombard was an assiduous reader of Abelard's work, probably heard Abelard lecture, and patterned his *Sentences* after Abelard's earlier treatise.[55] Although apparently a dispute about a few isolated theological issues and abstruse questions of theological method, the conflict between Bernard and Abelard actually was a basic "worldview" conflict about the role of human reason, the relationship of God and man, and the purposes of study and education. It was a conflict fraught with the future.

> *Abelard's separation of the substance of theology from its biblical form was deeply rooted and at least partly self-conscious. A form-content opposition appears repeatedly in different contexts in his work.*

52. To put it into contemporary terms: earlier monastic teachers could not have imagined "distance" learning, learning detached from personal relationship. Abelard could. This is not to say, however, that Abelard invented the Internet, which, everyone knows, was the work of a former American vice president.

53. This entire paragraph is indebted to C. Stephen Jaeger, *The Envy of Angels: Cathedral Schools and Social Ideals in Medieval Europe, 950–1200* (Philadelphia: University of Pennsylvania Press, 1994), 229–34.

54. Chenu, *Nature, Man, and Society*, 295.

55. Evans, *Language and Logic*, 135. The separation of scriptural interpretation from speculative theology also is discussed in Smalley, *Study of the Bible*, esp. chap. 6.

Synthesis of Faith and Reason, Thomas Aquinas, 1224–74

Although Abelard planted the seeds of scholastic theology, it was only in the thirteenth century that they bore abundant fruit. One key new factor was the rediscovery of various works of Aristotle on logic, which contributed to the creation of the "new logic." Several of Aristotle's works on logic had long been known in the West through the mediation of Boethius. During the latter part of the twelfth century, however, other works were newly translated into Latin and began to be employed in theology.[56] In addition to the texts themselves, Arabic commentaries from Averroes and Avicenna were translated into Latin and widely used. In the fourteenth century, Dante still spoke of Averroes as the author of the "great commentary," though, admittedly, Averroes was confined in hell at the time.

Naturally enough, Western authorities were suspicious of Aristotle, first because he was a pagan and second because he was introduced to the West by Islamic scholars. Many believed that Aristotle (or his commentators) taught things that contradicted Scripture, such as the eternity of matter and the idea that there is a single "active intellect" in which all human intellects participate. Siger of Brabant (1240–84) and others toyed with the Averroist idea of "double truth," the notion that truths of philosophy are different from truths of faith, though equally valid. Various church authorities issued condemnations, the most important of which was the Condemnation of 1277, which denounced various Aristotelian beliefs as inconsistent with the Christian confession of the sovereign omnipotence of God.

Nature and Supernature in Thomas

According to some accounts, Thomas's reconciliation of faith and Aristotelian philosophy was achieved through a version of the "double

Thomas Aquinas

---

56.   Charles Homer Haskins gives a concise summary of the situation: "Of his works the early Middle Ages had access only to the six logical treatises of the *Organon* as translated by Boethius, and as a matter of fact all of these except the *Categories* and the *De interpretatione* dropped out of sight until the twelfth century. These two surviving treatises came to be known as the *Old Logic*, in contradistinction to the *New Logic*—the *Prior* and *Posterior Analytics*, *Topics*, and *Elenchi*—which reappeared in various forms soon after 1128. By 1159 the most advanced of these, the *Posterior Analytics*, was in the course of assimilation, and the whole of the Aristotelian logic was absorbed into European thought by the close of the century. The *Physics* and lesser works on natural science, such as the *Meteorology*, the *De generatione*, and *De anima* were translated not long before 1200, though . . . traces of their teachings can be found somewhat earlier, coming from both Greek and Arabic sources. About 1200 came the *Metaphysics*, first in a briefer and then in the complete form. In the course of the thirteenth century the rest of the Aristotelian *corpus* was added: the various books *On Animals*, the *Ethics* and *Politics*, and, imperfectly, the *Rhetoric* and *Poetics*, accompanied and followed by a considerable mass of pseudo-Aristotelian material, so that by ca. 1260 the surviving works of Aristotle were known and men were busy comparing the texts of the versions from the Arabic with those derived immediately from the Greek" (*Renaissance of the Twelfth Century*, 345–46).

truth" theory. Francis Schaeffer admitted that "the origin of modern man could be traced back to several periods," but he begins with Aquinas. According to Schaeffer, Thomas operated with a two-story view of reality. On the top level is grace (including the concepts God, heaven, unseen, soul, and unity), while nature is a lower sphere (the created, earth, visible, man's body). After Thomas, there was a constant struggle to unify nature and grace. Because of Thomas's work, "Man's intellect became autonomous." The sphere of autonomous nature takes the form of "natural theology," and by this method Thomas detached philosophy from theology and destroyed the unity of the Christian worldview.[57] Although Schaeffer does not use this phrase, Thomas opened the possibility of a "secular" sphere for scholarship, philosophy, politics, economics, and so on that could be pursued without any recourse to the Bible or revelation.[58]

This view of Thomas has been challenged on a number of fronts in recent years. Within Catholic theology, the main attack has come from Henri de Lubac and the "new theologians" influenced by him.[59] According

Although Abelard planted the seeds of scholastic theology, it was only in the thirteenth century that they bore abundant fruit. One key new factor was the rediscovery of various works of Aristotle on logic, which contributed to the creation of the "new logic."

57. *Escape from Reason* (Downers Grove, IL: InterVarsity, 1968), 9–11. A similar assessment may be found in Gordon H. Clark, *Thales to Dewey: A History of Philosophy* (Grand Rapids: Baker, 1957), 269–84. More sophisticated versions are found in Cornelius Van Til, *A Christian Theory of Knowledge* (Nutley, NJ: Presbyterian and Reformed, 1969), 169–75, and Herman Dooyeweerd, *A New Critique of Theoretical Thought*, trans. David H. Freeman and William S. Young, 2 vols. (Ontario, Canada: Paideia Press, 1984), 1.179–81. A more sympathetic evangelical treatment of Thomas is available in Colin Brown, *Christianity and Western Thought: A History of Philosophers, Ideas & Movements, Volume 1: From the Ancient World to the Age of Enlightenment* (Downers Grove, IL: InterVarsity, 1990), 117–34, and a thorough Protestant appreciation of Aquinas is found in Arvin Vos, *Aquinas, Calvin, and Contemporary Protestant Thought: A Critique of Protestant Views on the Thought of Thomas Aquinas* (Washington, DC: Christian College Consortium, 1985). Interestingly, Norman Geisler, an evangelical Thomist, appreciates Thomas only by adopting the view that Thomas separates philosophy and theology: "We may take Aquinas' theism without buying into his theology" ("A New Look at the Relevance of Thomism for Evangelical Apologetics," *Christian Scholar's Review* 4 [1974]: 200, quoted in Vos, *op. cit.*, xii, fn. 1).

58. This view is regularly repeated in textbooks on medieval theology and philosophy. Marcia Colish, in a highly sophisticated study of medieval intellectual life, describes Thomas's "natural philosophy" derived from Aristotle and adds "Thomas coordinates this natural philosophy with supernature, clarifying what we can know in each subdivision, how we can know it, and how these areas are related. Embracing the entire physical world under the heading of nature, Thomas thinks that Aristotle's explanation of it is basically correct.... The fact that a pagan philosopher could arrive at these conclusions, without revelation and faith, is Thomas' empirical rationale for rejecting Bonaventure's pan-illuminationism. In the realm of nature, reason alone is sufficient. In the realm of supernature, however, reason, while important, is subordinate to faith. Here, our starting point is faith, not metaphysical first principles" (*Medieval Foundations of the Western Intellectual Tradition, 400–1400,* Yale Intellectual History of the West [New Haven, CT: Yale, 1997], 298).

According to some accounts, Thomas's reconciliation of faith and Aristotelian philosophy was achieved through a version of the "double truth" theory.... According to Schaeffer, Thomas operated with a two-story view of reality.

59. See especially *The Mystery of the Supernatural*, trans. Rosemary Sheed (New York: Herder & Herder, 1967). On the revised Thomism of the twentieth century, see now Fergus Kerr, *After Aquinas: Versions of Thomism* (Oxford: Blackwell, 2002). According to de Lubac, the dualistic interpretation of Thomas, rather than originating with Thomas himself, originates with Cajetan, a cardinal of the sixteenth century and interpreter of Thomas. In de Lubac's opinion, Cajetan simply misconstrues Thomas, and nearly everyone after was simply presenting a Cajetanian misinterpretation of Thomas, rather than Thomas himself.

to de Lubac, Thomas did not operate with a two-story theory, and he did not give any autonomy to natural reason. There has, furthermore, been a resurgence of interest in the Neoplatonic structures and direction of Thomas's thought. Thomas quoted Pseudo-Dionysus frequently, though not as frequently as Aristotle, and Thomas's frequent citations of Augustine also point to a Neoplatonic influence.[60] Far from being a thoroughgoing Aristotelian, the Thomas of recent scholarship emerges as some kind of Platonist.

Given this scholarship, it may be that Dante was a more accurate reader of Thomas than many have realized. Nearly the first word of Dante's *Paradiso* is "glory," and this theme dominates much of the canticle.[61] Employing the image of light, Thomas Aquinas, the greatest of the medieval theologians, later explains more fully this view of created glory. Everything "which dies and all that cannot die/ reflect[s] the radiance of that Idea which God the Father through His love begets" (*Paradiso* 13.52–54). By "Idea" Aquinas means the eternal Son of God, the second person of the Trinity, who became flesh in Jesus. He is the "Idea" of the Father, as he is the Father's Word, because in him all the Father's mind is expressed. Aquinas also calls the Son the "Living Light," who "streams forth" from the Father. The Father is the "radiant Source" of the Light that is the Son, but the Light "never parts" from the "Source," which is the Father, nor from "the Love which tri-unites with them," that is, the Holy Spirit (*Paradiso* 13.55–57).

All created things reflect the "radiance" of the Son. This is so because the "Living Light" that is the Son "of Its own grace sends down its rays, as if / reflected, through the nine subsistencies / remaining sempiternally Itself" (*Paradiso* 13.58–60). The nine subsistencies may refer to the nine spheres of Paradise or to the nine orders of angels that Pseudo-Dionysus identified, but it does not really matter which. The Light of the Son is diffused as it moves from the higher reaches of the universe to the lower. Like a light penetrating water, it becomes dimmer at the lower end, so that different parts of creation reflect the Light of the Son in different degrees. Though its parts display different degrees of glory, all the diverse things of creation are ordered into a brilliant display of beauty and light. The glory of which Dante spoke in the first line of *Paradiso* is the glory of the "One Who moves all things." Just as each thing reflects its particular degree of the Light of the Son, so also everything moves toward the place that is appropriate to its degree of glory.

This theology of light, borrowed from Pseudo-Dionysus (whose works had begun to circulate widely in the twelfth century) as well as from Thomas, had a direct effect on the architectural theories and practices of

> *According to de Lubac, Thomas did not operate with a two-story theory, and he did not give any autonomy to natural reason. . . . Thomas's frequent citations of Augustine also point to a Neoplatonic influence. Far from being a thoroughgoing Aristotelian, the Thomas of recent scholarship emerges as some kind of Platonist.*

60. See Wayne Hankey, "Denys and Aquinas: Antimodern Cold and Postmodern Hot," in Lewis Ayres and Gareth Jones, eds., *Christian Origins: Theology, Rhetoric, and Community* (London: Routledge, 1998), 139–84, though Hankey's article is as much about contemporary theology as about Aquinas.

61. The following paragraphs are condensed from my *Ascent to Love: An Introduction to Dante's Divine Comedy* (Moscow, ID: Canon, 2001), 141–44.

Abbot Suger. He designed the monastic church at Saint-Denys in France to manifest the fact that all creation is illumined with divine light. As described by Georges Duby,

> It was in the choir of the new church . . . that the mutation in aesthetics took place. Suger naturally placed the glowing center, the point where the approach to God became most dazzling, at the other end of the basilica, at the culmination of the liturgical procession turned toward the rising sun. At this point he therefore decided to take away the walls and urged the master builders to make fullest use of the architectonic resources of what until then had been merely a mason's expedient, the ribbed vault. And so the years between 1140 and 1144 saw the construction of a "semicircular sequence of chapels, which caused the entire church to glow with marvelous uninterrupted light, shining through the most radiant of windows."[62]

If Dante's reading of Aquinas was correct, Thomas must have been delighted at Suger's achievement. Few medievals read Thomas, but those who worshiped at Saint-Denys were confronted with Thomism in stone and glass.

For my purposes, the differences between these interpretations of Aquinas are of less interest than the overall question of whether Thomas is guilty of syncretism: did Thomas mold Christian faith into an Aristotelian or Neoplatonic shape, or did he employ Aristotelian and Neoplatonic tools as handmaids that enabled him to expound the Christian faith?

Videtur Quod

It would seem that Thomas did separate nature and grace, giving considerable autonomy to nature and natural reason, and thus was the grandfather of secular modernity and modern onto-theology. Numerous passages in Thomas appear to support Schaeffer's reading. First, we have the massive evidence of his use of Aristotle. Though Thomas does not always agree with Aristotle, and in some fundamental ways modifies Aristotelian philosophy, he depends in many respects on Aristotelian categories. His treatment of the real presence in the Lord's Supper, for example, is entirely framed in terms of the Aristotelian ideas of "substance" and "accident." To that extent, he clearly considered Aristotle's account of the nature of things to be correct, and just as clearly Aristotle was not deriving his ideas from revelation.

Furthermore, Thomas frequently distinguished between faith and reason in a way that seems to imply a dualistic view of reality. At the beginning of the *Summa theologiae* he wrote: "Although those things which are beyond man's knowledge may not be sought for by man through his reason, nevertheless, once they are revealed by God they must be accepted by faith" (*ST* I, 1, 1). Later in the *Summa*, Thomas asked whether man can know apart from grace. Citing Augustine's comments on Psalm 50, he concluded in the affirmative. Using the metaphor of light, he explicated a distinction

It would seem that Thomas did separate nature and grace, giving considerable autonomy to nature and natural reason, and thus was the grandfather of secular modernity and modern onto-theology. Numerous passages in Thomas appear to support Schaeffer's reading.

---

62. Duby, *The Age of the Cathedrals: Art and Society, 980–1420*, trans. Eleanor Levieux and Barbara Thompson (Chicago: University of Chicago Press, 1981), 100–101.

between what man can know by natural light and what he can know by an added supernatural light (*ST* I–II, Q 109, a 1).[63]

Thomas also distinguished between the interests and objects of philosophy and theology. Philosophy pertains to that realm in which natural reason operates; theology pertains to the realm where grace operates.[64] Philosophy addresses theological questions, but the second form of theology is "higher than the other divine science taught by the philosophers, since it proceeds from higher principles," namely, the principles of revelation and faith. Theistic proofs offer further evidence that Thomas believed in a certain degree of autonomy for natural reason, since he explicitly defends the notion that man can know God from natural reason without the assistance of grace.[65] Evidence like this could be multiplied at great length, especially from the early portions of the *Summa theologiae*.

Sed Contra

As Thomas would say, "on the other hand" (*sed contra*) there are other passages in Thomas that point in a very different direction, passages in which faith and reason are not set up as antinomies or as sharply different ways of knowing and where theology and philosophy are integrated. In other words, there are passages where Aquinas was not a dualist of nature/supernature but offered a profoundly unified and profoundly Christian view of the world.[66]

---

63. Thomas used similar language and the same metaphor in his commentary on Boethius's "On the Trinity." See Ralph McInerny, ed., *Thomas Aquinas: Selected Writings* (New York: Penguin, 1998), 111, 113.

64. In his commentary on Boethius's treatise on the Trinity, he writes: "There are two kinds of science of the divine. One according to our mode, which uses the principles of sensible things to make the divine known, and so it was that philosophers developed a science of the divine, calling divine science first philosophy. Another following the mode of divine things themselves, which grasps divine things in themselves, which indeed is impossible in this life, but some share in and likeness to divine knowledge comes about in us in this life insofar as through infused faith we adhere to first truth for its own sake" (ibid., 131).

65. Defending the notion that the existence of God can be demonstrated, Thomas wrote that "the existence of God and other like truths about God, which can be known by natural reason, are not articles of faith, but are preambles to the articles; for faith presupposes natural knowledge, even as grace presupposes nature, and perfection supposes something that can be perfected. Nevertheless, there is nothing to prevent a man, who cannot grasp a proof accepting, as a matter of faith, something which in itself is capable of being scientifically known and demonstrated" (*ST* I, 1, 2).

66. John Milbank's comment on the deceptive simplicity of Aquinas is worth noting: "Only superficially is he clear, but on analysis one discovers that he does not at all offer us a decently confined 'Anglo-Saxon' lucidity, but rather the intense light of Naples and Paris which is ultimately invisible in its very radiance. . . . Of course it is true that Aquinas does indeed refute shaky positions with supreme economy, simplicity and clarity of argumentation, but the arcanum of his teaching lies not here. It resides rather in the positions he does affirm often briefly and like a kind of residue, akin to Sherlock Holmes's last remaining solution, which must be accepted in all its implausibility, when other solutions have been shown to be simply impossible" (Milbank and Catherine Pickstock, *Truth In Aquinas*, Radical Orthodoxy [London: Routledge, 2001], 20–21).

Summa Theologiae

For starters, an initial, obvious point about the *Summa*: It is "divine science" (*scientia Dei*) from beginning to end. In a brief prologue, Thomas said that a master of catholic truth should not only teach the proficient but also "instruct beginners" and he claimed to have composed the *Summa* for those beginners(!): "We purpose in this book to treat of whatever belongs to Christian Religion, in such a way as may tend to the instruction of beginners. . . . We shall try, by God's help, to set forth whatever is included in this Sacred Science as briefly and clearly as the matter may allow."

Thomas defined this "sacred science" in the opening question of the *Summa* by categorizing different sciences in terms of their origins. Some sciences proceed from the light of intelligence and some from principles of a higher science. Sacred doctrine is a science "because it proceeds from principles established by the light of a higher science, namely, the science of God and the blessed. Hence, just as the musician accepts on authority the principles taught him by the mathematician, so sacred science is established on principles revealed by God." Thus true theology—sacred science—is the knowledge of the blessed, the knowledge of those who have achieved the vision of God. Theological science does not rise to this level, but is derived from it. This is the context in which Thomas offered the proofs of God's existence, employed Aristotelian concepts and ideas, and discussed the virtues.

Structurally, the *Summa* is a treatise on theology. The whole is divided into three parts, the second part of which is divided into two parts (they are numbered I, I–II, II–II, and III). Aquinas explained the purpose of each part at the beginning of question 2: "Because the chief aim of sacred doctrine is to teach the knowledge of God, not only as He is in Himself, but also as He is the beginning of things and their last end, and especially of rational creatures, as is clear from what has been already said, therefore, in our endeavour to expound this science, we shall treat: (1) Of God; (2) Of the rational creature's advance toward God; (3) of Christ, who as man, is our way to God" (*ST* I, 2).[67]

In examining this passage, Fergus Kerr has noted the narrative and eschatological orientation of Thomas's whole enterprise: "Thomas's theology is entirely dominated by the promise of human participation in God's own blessedness," and "the plan is clear—to treat the moral life as a journey to beatitude (*secunda pars*) in the middle of the treatment of God as beginning and end of all things (*prima pars*) and the treatment of the God-man Christ as the beginning of the new creation (*tertia pars*). The exposition of sacred doctrine, then, has the narrative structure of a journey from

> *Thomas also distinguished between the interests and objects of philosophy and theology. Philosophy pertains to that realm in which natural reason operates; theology pertains to the realm where grace operates.*

> *Some sciences proceed from the light of intelligence and some from principles of a higher science. Sacred doctrine is a science "because it proceeds from principles established by the light of a higher science, namely, the science of God and the blessed."*

---

67. On this point, Dante, in my view, misread Thomas. Dante introduced a separation of pagan and sacred learning, symbolized by the fact that his initial guide, the pagan poet Virgil, yields to Beatrice and then to Bernard when Dante arrives in Paradise. Thomas would not have countenanced that separation. In a truly Thomistic *Inferno* and *Purgatorio*, Virgil would have been consistently losing his way.

God as created to God as beatifying in raising the dead—from creation to beatitude." As Kerr says elsewhere, what Thomas offered was an "eschatological foundationalism," rather than a rationalistic foundationalism like Descartes. The foundation of knowledge is not, as in Descartes, unquestionable truth available to every human being but the intuitive and direct knowledge available to the blessed in glory. This gives a striking eschatological shape to Thomas's entire theology.[68]

Within this context, we can make better sense of Thomas's use of Aristotle, which he frequently put into service to expound the Christian faith.[69] One example will illustrate the point. One of the key questions regarding the use of Aristotle in Thomas's time was the relation of Jesus' soul to his dead body in the tomb. The problem arose from the Christian application of Aristotelian hylomorphism in anthropology. "Hylomorphism" is a compound of two Greek words, *hyle* (matter) and *morphe* (form). According to Aristotle and Aquinas, every created substance or thing is hylomorphic, a combination of matter and form. Thomas applied this to human beings by insisting that the soul is the form of the man, the principle that "shapes" material stuff into a particular kind of thing, a man. But, this raises obvious difficulties for the Christian conception of life after death. At death, the soul and body are separated, and this implies both that forms can exist independently of matter (which Aristotle denies) and that the body in the grave reverts to prime, formless matter. In particular, what happened to the body of *Jesus* in the three days between his death and resurrection? Did Jesus' body cease to exist, and then come back into existence at the resurrection? To relieve this problem somewhat, some medieval thinkers multiplied the number of forms in a human being. In addition to the soul (or substantial form), each human being has a "corporeal form," which keeps the body in existence after death.

Thomas stuck with Aristotle and consistent hylomorphism. Thomas believed there was only one substantial form in a human being, a theory known as the "unicity of substantial form." Instead, he forced the question back to the hypostatic union of the divine and human natures of Jesus. What linked the dead body of Jesus with his risen body was the union of the second person of the Trinity with his human soul and body. Preservation of Jesus' body did not depend on his human soul at all, but on the Son's union with human nature. Strikingly, by dogged adherence to Aristotle, Thomas was also adhering more fully than his opponents to a specifically Christian belief, namely, the incarnation (*ST* III, 50, 5). For Thomas, philosophical theology was a tool for exploring and expounding sacred doctrine, not a separate study in itself.

> *The exposition of sacred doctrine, then, has the narrative structure of a journey from God as created to God as beatifying in raising the dead—from creation to beatitude.... what Thomas offered was an "eschatological foundationalism," rather than a rationalistic foundationalism like Descartes.*

---

68. Kerr, "Thomas Aquinas," in G. R. Evans, ed., *The Medieval Theologians: An Introduction to Theology in the Medieval Period* (Oxford: Blackwell, 2001), 211. Kerr's comment resonates with Yves Congar's view that Part II of the *Summa* is about ecclesiology.

69. The following example is drawn from ibid.

Indeed, this is evident also from his fundamental epistemological outlook. As Ralph McInerny says, the concept of "participation" is a key idea in Aquinas that runs through all of his thought.[70] Aristotelian though he was, at this point he Platonizes Aristotle, much as the Neoplatonists had Aristotelianized Plato. All reason is rational by virtue of participation in divine reason. This applies not only to reasoning about divine things or to a superadded realm of grace. *All* intellectual light is participation in the divine light. For Thomas, "the intellectual power of the creature is called an intelligible light, as it were, derived from the divine light, whether this be understood of the natural power, or of some perfection superadded of grace or glory" (*ST* I, 12). Moreover, "the intellectual light which is in us, is nothing else than a participated likeness of the uncreated light, in which are contained the eternal types. By the seal of the Divine light in us, all things are made known to us" (*ST* I, 84, 5).[71]

Reason and faith, therefore, are not different in kind but in degree of participation. Thus, in *Summa* I, 12, 13, Thomas described grace as an intensification of the divine light: "Human knowledge is assisted by the revelation of grace. For the intellect's natural light is strengthened by the infusion of gratuitous light; and sometimes also the images in the human imagination are divinely formed, so as to express divine things better. . . while sometimes, sensible things, or even voices, are divinely formed." Theology and philosophy are not distinct sciences, but are poles in a continuum of sciences. Theology is definitely in the master's position. Sacred doctrine "does not depend upon other sciences as upon the higher, but makes use of them as of the lesser, and of handmaidens" (*ST* I, 5, 2).[72] Natural reason is not autonomous but requires correction by revelation.[73] Later, in article 6 of the first question, he concluded, citing 2 Corinthians 10, "Whatsoever is to be found in other sciences contrary to any truth of this science must be

> *Reason and faith, therefore, are not different in kind but in degree of participation. Thus, in* **Summa** *I, 12, 13, Thomas described grace as an intensification of the divine light: "Human knowledge is assisted by the revelation of grace."*

---

70.   McInerny, "Introduction," in *Selected Works*, xxx.

71.   Knowledge by participation is rooted in an ontology of participation. See Thomas's notion of "truth in things" (*ST* I, 16, 1). Proportion or "correspondence" between the truth of a thing and the intellect participates in beauty, and thus there is an aesthetic dimension to knowing anything.

72.   He continues, "That [sacred science] thus uses [lesser sciences] is not due to its own defect or insufficiency, but to the defect of our intelligence, which is more easily led by that which is known through natural reason . . . to that which is above reason." For Thomas, this noetic defect has less to do with sin than with our position in redemptive history. So long as we are still "in the way" (*in via*), we see through a glass darkly and need the assistance of lesser sciences, but when we arrive at our homeland (*in patria*), we will have direct, intuitive knowledge of God. There is no room to explore this, but only to say that the conception of signs implied here is very faulty. See my *Priesthood of the Plebs: The Baptismal Transformation of Antique Order* (Eugene, OR: Wipf & Stock, 2003), chap. 1.

73.   "Even as regards those truths about God which human reason could have discovered, it was necessary that man should be taught by divine revelation; because the truth about God such as reason could discover, would only be known by a few, and that after a long time, and with the admixture of error" (*ST* I, 1, 1).

condemned as false." Thomas was willing to use Aristotle, but if Aristotle runs contrary to faith, Aristotle is the one to go.

Thomas's eschatological foundationalism in epistemology was grounded in an eschatological foundationalism in ontology. Everything is known by participation in divine intellect, and furthermore, everything *is* according to its participation in divine intellect. It is true that created things are images of things in God's mind in a static sense. Yet, since God is the end of all things, things are also images in the dynamic teleological sense that they are becoming more and more what they are, or, better, that their essence is not what they *now* are but what they *will be*. This is a synthesis of Christian eschatology and Aristotelian teleologism, but for Thomas, the teleological was theological: a thing fulfills its end when it is "copying God in its own manner, and tending to existence as knowledge in the divine Mind."[74]

Thomas's eschatological ontology is clear in his description of the "good,"[75] which he defined in a "teleological" or "eschatological" fashion. To say something is "good" is to say that it is actualized, however incompletely, and therefore to say something is "good" without qualification means that it is entirely perfected and completed. A thing becomes better as it becomes more and more actualized, and will not be completely good or completely be until the eschaton.[76] He expressed this by reference to the Aristotelian notion of causes. According to Thomas, the *first* cause of a being is its final purpose, its ultimate purpose. Before a carpenter begins to make a table, he intends to use the table for a particular purpose—say, for writing—and this purpose is, in Aristotelian terms, the "final cause" of the table, even though it occurs before other causes. Only when he has planned a particular end does the carpenter begin to gather wood (material cause) and use his tools (efficient cause) to make a table. So also God, as the agent for the whole universe, makes everything for the sake of an end, and this end is the ultimate reason for a thing's existence. A thing exists in order to be fully actualized, to become perfectly what it is. And this is what, in a complete sense, we mean by saying that a thing is "good."[77]

All this supports the conclusion of Mark Jordan, who claims that for Thomas, philosophy is related to theology as "part to whole" and that

> *Thomas's eschatological foundationalism in epistemology was grounded in an eschatological foundationalism in ontology. Everything is known by participation in divine intellect, and furthermore, everything **is** according to its participation in divine intellect.*

---

74. Pickstock, *Truth in Aquinas*, 9.

75. A similar structure pervades Thomas's understanding of "truth." See Milbank and Pickstock, *Truth in Aquinas*, chaps. 1–2.

76. According to Aquinas, all created things are substances, and all are good insofar as they have being. But, for Aquinas, "substance" implies the notion of life, self-sharing, and dynamic self-communication. Substance is not a substratum but the concrete thing in its constant movement toward self-transcendence. See Kerr, *After Aquinas*, 48–50.

77. This principle relates not only to individual items in the creation but also to the creation as a whole. See *Summa Contra Gentiles* 3, 24, 2052; more fully, Oliva Blanchette, *The Perfection of the Universe According to Aquinas: A Teleological Cosmology* (University Park: Pennsylvania State University Press, 1992).

Thomas's goal is "theology's transforming incorporation of philosophy."[78] To use Dooyeweerd's language, the "ground motif" of Thomas's thought was profoundly Christian and quite astonishingly biblical. Thomas did not posit a static world of immobile being but a dynamic, becoming world in constant motion, directed by God to its last end. Thus his epistemology and ontology are shaped by the already-not yet structure of the gospel. Had I space, I also would point to the centrality of the cross and resurrection in Thomas's structure, where they function as the means and path by which all things are directed, in the living head, Jesus, to their ultimate end in the kingdom of heaven. From this perspective, Thomas's first name for God was not "Being" (see below), but the biblical name, "Alpha and Omega."[79]

Responsio

And yet, at another level, Thomas undeniably accommodated Christian theology to the conceptuality and language of philosophy. The language and a good bit of the structure of the *Summa* are philosophical, even if the content usually is scriptural. Giving Christian theology a philosophical shape is a matter of indifference only because Aquinas already had assumed an Abelardian separation of form and substance. A single illustration of this point will have to suffice.

Thomas's metaphysics build on a series of related contrasts—form and matter, act and potency, existence and essence.[80] Although the terms are not interchangeable, they correspond as follows: form-act-existence on one side, matter-potency-essence on the other. Following Aristotle, Thomas believed substances are a combination of form and matter. Matter does not exist in itself, since without form it is mere potency and has no actual existence. ("Form" here does not mean "shape," though it is an analogous concept; it refers to the metaphysical principle by which featureless matter becomes a particular kind of matter.) Once prime matter is "informed" by a form, it becomes a particular substance. Bronze becomes a statue when informed by the form of a statue, though bronze itself is already informed matter, prime matter turned into bronze by combination with the form of bronze.

For medieval theologians, this Aristotelian account of substances raised a problem, namely, angels. They are immaterial, yet they are substances. How can they be substances without being a composite of form

> *Thomas's thought was profoundly Christian and quite astonishingly biblical. Thomas did not posit a static world of immobile being but a dynamic, becoming world in constant motion, directed by God to its last end. Thus his epistemology and ontology are shaped by the already-not yet structure of the gospel.*

---

78. Mark D. Jordan, "Theology and Philosophy," in Norman Kretzmann and Eleonore Stump, *The Cambridge Companion to Aquinas* (Cambridge: Cambridge University Press, 1993), 248.

79. Here again, Dante's image of Paradise as a *dance* in the presence of the eternally active Trinity is soundly Thomist.

80. Among the standard accounts of these distinctions, I have found the work of David Burrell particularly concise and helpful. See Burrell, *Knowing the Unknowable God: Ibn-Sina, Maimonides, Aquinas* (Notre Dame: University of Notre Dame Press, 1986), chap. 2; id., *Aquinas: God and Action* (Notre Dame: University of Notre Dame Press, 1979).

and matter? Perhaps angels are pure form, but then we have a problem in the opposite direction: how do angels differ from God himself?

Aquinas solved this by saying that angels are composite beings not because they are a compound of form and matter but because they are composed of "essence" and "existence." Essence specifies "what a thing is" while existence means "that a thing is." Essences are in themselves only potential. We can define angels without knowing whether they actually exist or not, just as we can describe an orc or a hobbit without committing ourselves to belief in their actuality. For an angel to *be*, existence (or "being") must be added to essence. God, by contrast, is entirely simple[81]—pure being, pure act, pure form, without any composite character at all. God's essence *is* existence, since he alone is a necessary being. As soon as we define God, we define an existing being, who is Being itself. This solution enabled Thomas to maintain orthodox positions on two fronts: angels are not material, and they are not equal to God, since they are composite and he is simple.

All this is quite subtle, and the conclusion is fundamentally orthodox, for it is true that God cannot not-be. One of Thomas's overriding purposes in pursuing these questions, moreover, was to protect the metaphysical difference between God and creation. Yet, it also seems evident that he has changed the context for a discussion of God's character and has left the biblical portrait of God far behind.[82] Thomas appealed to Exodus 3:14 ("I am that I am"),[83] but the philosophical elaboration of this passage only highlights the fact that Thomas was developing his doctrine of God through rational exploration in an Aristotelian mode, rather than through exegesis of Scripture. Clearly, Thomas's philosophical claim was not elaborated in terms of the narrative of the text but instead a single phrase is pulled from its narrative context in order to be made the foundation for philosophical speculation. In form, if not yet in content, this is onto-theology—a theology that works within the

One of Thomas's overriding purposes in pursuing these questions, moreover, was to protect the metaphysical difference between God and creation. Yet, it also seems evident that he has changed the context for a discussion of God's character and has left the biblical portrait of God far behind.

81. Given his premises, Thomas must maintain that God is simple in order to protect God's ultimacy. Compound beings, in Thomas's system, are compounded by an efficient cause that transcends the component parts. God cannot be compound without ceasing to be ultimate, without ceasing to be God.

82. One virtue of my argument is that it does not depend much on the intricacies of interpreting Thomas, whose theology is contested at many points. My argument turns on the blindingly obvious fact that he did theology in the mode of "science," concentrating on answering questions in the pursuit of systematic knowledge, rather than in the mode of exegesis, concentrating on explicating the text in order to form persons and communities.

83. Thomas was not the first to discover an ontology in Exodus 3. This was common currency in the patristic period. Etienne Gilson offered a spirited defense of Aquinas's use of Exodus 3:14: "No hint of metaphysics, but God speaks, *causa finita est*, and Exodus lays down the principle from which henceforth the whole of Christian philosophy will be suspended. From this moment it is understood once and for all that the proper name of God is Being and that, according to the word of St. Ephrem, taken up again later by St. Bonaventure, this name denotes His very essence" (*The Spirit of Mediaeval Philosophy,* Gifford Lectures, 1931–32, trans. A. H. C. Downes [New York: Charles Scribner's Sons, 1940], 51).

confines set by an alien philosophical system.[84] Contrary to Aquinas and his defenders, "Being" is not the first name of God in Scripture. Instead, God's "name" is unfolded in creation, event, act, narrative, and *torah*—in action and speech that come to a climax in Jesus, at which point God's name is revealed as Father, Son, and Spirit. Such a God cannot be encompassed by the name "Being," not least because that word has a "wild and woolly sort of sound" (Chesterton), not least because we sense that "being" names something vaguely "like breathing, only quieter" (J. L. Austin).[85]

Later Medieval Theology: Scotus and Ockham

Thomas is, by all accounts, the high point of scholasticism, bringing unprecedented rigor to the scholastic enterprise. In many accounts, later medieval theology was corrupt and decaying. Certainly, European civilization was marked by regular crises—natural, political, and ecclesiastical. The black death ravaged Europe in the mid-fourteenth century, leaving carnage and fear on an unprecedented scale and inspiring prophets announcing the second coming. For seventy years, the papacy was exiled in Avignon, and when the pope finally returned to Rome, the church broke into open schism. The response to the crisis of later medieval civilization was varied. Some groups determined that the church was incorrigibly corrupt, and broke off into sects, some of which the church condemned as heretical. On the far edges of the church, the "Brethren of the Common Life" organized houses of lay Christians, men and women living together according to an "apostolic" pattern of sharing everything in common. Beyond the far edges was an exotic array of Waldenses, Cathars, Bogomils, and other groups, which had begun to appear as early as the twelfth century. Scholasticism, once an exciting and innovative movement, hardened into schools, with Franciscans and Dominicans battling each other and full of party spirit. Arid scholastic systemization induced a reactionary mysticism, which

Black Plague, ***The Dance of Death****,* *Hans Holbein the Younger*

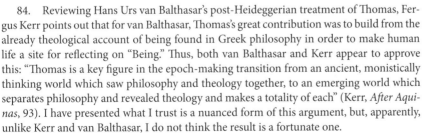

Contrary to Aquinas and his defenders, "Being" is not the first name of God in Scripture. Instead, God's "name" is unfolded in creation, event, act, narrative, and torah—in action and speech that come to a climax in Jesus, at which point God's name is revealed as Father, Son, and Spirit.

84.   Reviewing Hans Urs van Balthasar's post-Heideggerian treatment of Thomas, Fergus Kerr points out that for van Balthasar, Thomas's great contribution was to build from the already theological account of being found in Greek philosophy in order to make human life a site for reflecting on "Being." Thus, both van Balthasar and Kerr appear to approve this: "Thomas is a key figure in the epoch-making transition from an ancient, monistically thinking world which saw philosophy and theology together, to an emerging world which separates philosophy and revealed theology and makes a totality of each" (Kerr, *After Aquinas*, 93). I have presented what I trust is a nuanced form of this argument, but, apparently, unlike Kerr and van Balthasar, I do not think the result is a fortunate one.

85.   Robert Jenson makes the important point that the "philosophy" that Thomas and others of his time regarded as nothing more than the light of "natural reason" was in fact historically contingent, a specific tradition: "it comprised a part of the theology that Greek religious thinkers . . . had provided for the cults of Mediterranean antiquity." Jenson also sketches a genealogical descent from this high medieval acceptance of natural theology to modern theology, in which philosophical and especially epistemological prolegomena set the coordinates for theology (*Systematic Theology*, 2 vols. [Oxford: Oxford University Press, 1997], 1.7, 9).

eschewed doctrine and speculation in favor of personal devotion to God. The conciliarist movement, an effort to resolve rival claims to the papal see through a universal council, took root. Despite some success at the Councils of Constance, it soon lost strength and ultimately left the papacy more entrenched and the church more centralized than ever.

Anticlericalism and antipapalism usually are associated with Luther and other Reformers, but the Reformers' claim that the pope was the Antichrist had a strong medieval pedigree. A fourteenth-century allegorical work in English, William Langland's *Piers the Plowman*, provides a good example of medieval critiques of the clergy.[86] The poem opens with a description of a plain full of people, which represents Langland's world, dominated by money and self-interest. An alternative view of life is spelled out in the prologue: devotion to love and conformity to the cardinal virtues. Truly Christian living is at the margins from the beginning of the poem, however. The world is weighted against righteousness, not only because wicked people outnumber righteous people, but because laws are set up to promote self-interest rather than self-sacrifice. Langland's critique takes on a sharper focus in the second "Passus," or chapter, which focuses on Lady Meed, the personification of mammon, and a false church modeled on the whore of Babylon, from Revelation. Because of Meed's domination, everything is for sale—a consumerism sanctioned by law, which is itself for sale. Even the church has been invaded by the spirit of Meed, and the personified representative of theology defends this dominance by arguing that money keeps society together, serving as the bond between a lord and his servants.

As Langland saw things, the main flaw in the late medieval system was the lack of spiritual guidance. Instead of faithful pastoral "plowmen" who provide spiritual nourishment to their flocks, the church was dominated by friars who preyed on the people and who were wholly in the service of Meed. Langland's confused character, Haukyn, manifests the condition of the laity. Encouraged to sin by the easy confessions offered by friars, Haukyn has descended into debauchery and greed. Through the ministrations of Piers, the true Plowman, Haukyn is washed, given new clothes, and sets out on a life of repentance. For Langland, Christendom's social ills come down to one essential cause: the failure of the clergy to guide the laity.

A plowman in medieval times

Analogy versus Univocity

In this tumultuous cultural and political context, theological scholarship underwent dramatic changes. Both Duns Scotus and William of Ockham, the greatest of late medieval theologian-philosophers, departed in significant ways from the Thomistic synthesis of faith and reason. There is a family resemblance between movements such as the Brethren of the Common Life and the theological movements of the later medieval period. In

---

86.   One could also reference the clerical figures in Chaucer's more widely read *Canterbury Tales.*

both cases, we see a reaction to corrupting worldly influence and an effort to secure the bounds of faith. The Brethren of the Common Life retreated from a worldly church into enclaves of piety; Scotus and Ockham retreated from worldly philosophy in defense of their Franciscan conviction that God can be known only in revelation and not through reason.[87] Unfortunately, their effort to purify theology from the contamination of natural reason accepted the dualistic social and intellectual world that had been established since the time of Gregory VII and Abelard. Instead of rejecting the earlier sundering of theology from text, they accepted and even deepened the separation. Instead of protesting the autonomy of philosophy, they accepted that autonomy. They insisted only that theology be left in peace, but at the cost of allowing philosophy to retain its autonomy.[88]

A detailed illustration of this tendency will clarify this point. Thomas taught what was later called an "analogy of being," which grounds his account of how human language can be used in talking of God. Analogy is the alternative to "univocal" and "equivocal" language. A word is used "univocally" when it means exactly the same thing in several different contexts, and "equivocally" when it means different things in different contexts. "Leaf" is used equivocally in the sentences "Put the leaf in the table" and "Don't pull that leaf off the tree," and "man" is used univocally in the sentences "Socrates is a man" and "Duns is a man." When applied to theological language, each of these alternatives is an unhappy one. If theological language is equivocal, then we cannot say anything true about God, but if it is univocal, God is reduced to a creaturely level.

Thomas believed that the solution to this was to say that theological language is "analogical." When we say "God is wise" and "Socrates is wise," "wise" is used analogically. We are not using "wise" in exactly the same way, but we are not using "wise" in completely different senses, either. There is an "analogy" or "similarity" between the two uses. Thomas applied this to all the attributes of God, including the fundamental attribute of "existence" (Being). God's existence is his essence, but this is not true of other beings. Thus, in the sentences "God exists" and "My toenail exists," the word "exists" is being used in an analogical way.

By contrast, John Duns Scotus (1266–1308) defended the "univocity of being." Though it pertains to theological language, the dispute has much larger implications.[89] Scotus did not deny analogy *per se*. Terms are

> *As Langland saw things, the main flaw in the late medieval system was the lack of spiritual guidance. Instead of faithful pastoral "plowmen" who provide spiritual nourishment to their flocks, the church was dominated by friars who preyed on the people and who were wholly in the service of Meed.*

> *When applied to theological language, each of these alternatives is an unhappy one. If theological language is equivocal, then we cannot say anything true about God, but if it is univocal, God is reduced to a creaturely level.*

87. Cantor, *Civilization of the Middle Ages*, 533.

88. Frederick Artz put his finger on this commonality when he claimed that Scotus "opened a door . . . to philosophical agnosticism, on the one hand, and to a mystical conception of theology, on the other," and by his characterization of Ockham as insisting that "the great religious truths could never be proved by reason and could be really understood only as the result of a mystical religious experience." *The Mind of the Middle Ages: An Historical Survey, A.D. 200–1500*, 3rd ed. (Chicago: University of Chicago Press, 1980), 269b–c.

89. The following summary is taken from Alexander Broadie, "Duns Scotus and William Ockham," in Evans, ed., *The Medieval Theologians*, 250–65.

not predicated of God and creatures in exactly the same way, and Scotus believed that analogy is necessary because "creatures are only imperfect representations of the divine." Yet, he said that without some univocity within the analogy, there can be no analogy. In brief, "analogy presupposes univocity." More fully, "If of two things one is the measure of the other, then they must have something in common that permits the first to be measured of the second, and the second to be measured of the first. If of two things one exceeds the other by some quantity or degree, however great, then they must have something in common with respect of which the first exceeds the second."[90]

"Animality" is the shared characteristic that makes it possible to compare man and donkey. Without that shared characteristic, the comparison makes no sense.

Scotus argued that similar points must be true of our language about God and creation. God is more perfect than man, but that raises the question: a more perfect *what*? What is the common term? God is more perfect in "wisdom" and "justice." But if this is to make any sense at all, then "wise" and "just" must be used univocally. Unless we are able to form a concept "wisdom" that will encompass both God's and man's wisdom, the analogy is impossible.

Scotus also wanted to apply this to the concept "being." It is possible to form a concept of being, Scotus argued, that is "neutral between the being of God and the being of creatures, and is contained in both."[91] We can thus form a concept of being "simpliciter," and then qualify this concept when it is applied to a particular being, God or man. "Infinite" and "finite" are therefore qualifications of one being. Scotus does not believe that "being simply speaking" actually exists anywhere. All being exists only as finite or infinite, created or uncreated. Being *simpliciter* is a concept arrived at by abstraction, and in our minds exists only insofar as we form a concept of beings that exist in determinate ways and then by abstraction form an undetermined concept of being.

Interpreting Scotus is difficult, not only for his famed subtlety, but also because most of his works are fragmentary and incomplete. In some respects, his arguments in favor of univocity seem correct, yet his treatment has radical implications for the relationship of theology and philosophy. Richard Cross points out that God's ineffability, his transcendence of all our concepts of him, is weakened in Scotus's account, so that "we can

> *Interpreting Scotus is difficult, not only for his famed subtlety, but also because most of his works are fragmentary and incomplete. In some respects, his arguments in favor of univocity seem correct, yet his treatment has radical implications for the relationship of theology and philosophy.*

90. As Scotus put it, "Things are never related as the measured to the measure, or as the excess to the excedent unless they have something in common. . . . when it is said, 'This is more perfect than that' then if it be asked 'A more perfect what?' it is necessary to ascribe something common to both, so that in every comparison something determinable is common to each of the things compared. For if a human being is more perfect than a donkey, he is not more perfect *qua* human than a donkey is; he is more perfect *qua* animal" (quoted in ibid., 253).

91. Ibid., 255.

know quite a lot about God."[92] That seems to put the case too mildly. More deeply, Scotus's views have, paradoxically, both a monistic and a dualistic tendency. Although Scotus protested that "God and the creature share in no reality" that encompasses both of them, his univocal concept of being pushes in the other direction, implying that there is some common metaphysical principle—being—that includes both God and man. As a result, God is paled on a continuum with his creation, and the Creator-creature distinction is blurred. God is infinite being, but this can suggest only that he is an unbounded version of finite being—hence the monist tendency.

At the same time, Scotus led in a dualistic direction that set God over against his creation as pure, infinitely powerful will. This is evident in Scotus's denial that creatures, including man, have a created urge toward self-transcendence. For Thomas, as we have seen, every substance strives toward the realization of its good, which is ultimately found in God. For Scotus, since the creation already is participant in "being" and already in some sense "part of" the infinite being, there is no drive toward self-transcendence. Man sits at one end of the spectrum and God at the other, without a created impulse to unite. God and man are not inevitably joined in covenant or communion, but stare at one another through an infinite field of undifferentiated being.[93]

John Duns Scotus

As throughout this essay, the central concern is to examine how Scotus construed the relationship of philosophy and theology, and what contribution he made, if any, to the development of onto-theology. His contribution is vast. By distinguishing God and man as two "degrees" (finite and infinite) of a single concept ("being"), he flattens out the Creator-creature distinction. Since metaphysics is the science of Being, moreover, metaphysics seems to be the all-embracing science, with theology subordinated to it. Though this is a plausible inference from Scotus's thought, this is not the direction he takes. Instead, because of the dualistic tendency inherent in his monism of being, he separates theology and philosophy in a way that Aquinas would not have recognized.

Theology as Science

The difference between Thomas and Scotus can be seen in their different conceptions of the "scientific" status of theology. Aquinas believed that theology was a science, but in a peculiar way. In his Aristotelian conception, all sciences are axiomatic and deductive systems, along the lines of modern mathematics. But, some sciences have their axioms within themselves, as the Pythagorean theorem is internal to geometry. In these sciences, the first principles are self-evident, at least to those who understand the principles of the science. Other sciences, however, derive their first

> *At the same time, Scotus led in a dualistic direction that set God over against his creation as pure, infinitely powerful will. This is evident in Scotus's denial that creatures, including man, have a created urge toward self-transcendence.*

92.   Richard Cross, *Duns Scotus* (Oxford: Oxford University Press, 1999), 45.
93.   For this strange tension in Scotus, see especially Conor Cunningham, *Genealogy of Nihilism*, 28–32.

principles from another science. For both Aquinas and Bonaventure, theology was a science of this second kind, what they called a "subalternate" science. Bonaventure said that the first principles of theology derive from Scripture, while Aquinas, as we have seen, said that they derive from the intuitive knowledge that the blessed have of God.

There already were significant problems with these arrangements, for both schemes attempted to fit theology into an intellectual schematization borrowed from Aristotle. But, Duns Scotus made things worse. According to Scotus, it is theoretically possible for God to reveal himself directly to the theologian, in which case theology would not need to be a subalternate science. Failing that, however, the theologian is left with the Scriptures, which can be used to construct a theology that "falls far short of this possible science."[94] This indicates not only that biblical theology is an unfortunate "second best" kind of theology but more clearly than ever shows how far theology had become detached from concern with the specifics of the biblical text. An index of the distance that Scotus placed between philosophy and theology is the fact that he never appealed to a theological principle as a decisive argument in any of his philosophical treatises.[95] Scotus was both philosopher and theologian, but he was not a philosopher-theologian. Scotus the philosopher operated with different categories and lived in a different world from Scotus the theologian. In an effort to protect the uniqueness of theological study, Scotus conceded the entire world of philosophy, and implicitly the entire world of political, aesthetic, economic, and social thought, to the non-theologians.

What's Real?

The Condemnation of 1277 had at least two effects on the later development of medieval theology. First, it made it clear that theological claims had precedence over philosophical ones. Second, by emphasizing the omnipotence and sovereignty of God's will, it encouraged theologians to emphasize the will of God as his leading attribute (voluntarism). Both of these effects are evident in William of Ockham.

Ockham, like Scotus, was an opponent of the Thomistic synthesis and distrusted the use of Aristotle in theology or philosophy. He considered the Platonic and Aristotelian concept of "universals" to be the worst mistake in the history of philosophy. We use the word "horse," for instance, to refer to innumerable individual horses, yet each of these horses is quite different from all others, in color, size, age, shape, history, strength, speed, and so on. What, then, are we naming when we say "horse" without further specification? For both Plato and Aristotle, we are naming a "universal," an entity (some have called it "horseness") that actually exists outside our

> *Ockham, like Scotus, was an opponent of the Thomistic synthesis and distrusted the use of Aristotle in theology or philosophy. He considered the Platonic and Aristotelian concept of "universals" to be the worst mistake in the history of philosophy.*

---

94. John Marenbon, *Later Medieval Philosophy (1150–1350)* (London: Routledge & Kegan Paul, 1987), 80–82.

95. Cross, *Duns Scotus*, 13.

minds. For Plato, this universal existed in a transcendent world of Ideas, while for Aristotle the universal was embedded within specific individuals. For both, the universal was really real. For many centuries, most Christian thinkers followed this scheme, modifying it in a Christian direction. Some, of a more Neoplatonic disposition, placed the Ideas in the mind of God, while others, more Aristotelian, believed that the universals existed only within actual creatures. Anyone who believed in the real existence of universals was called a "realist."

Ockham rejected the whole scheme. Universals are no more than concepts or words ("names," or *nomina*), and have no reality outside the mind. We arrive at these concepts by a principle of abstraction. As we get to know many individual horses, we come to realize how much they resemble each other. We subtract all the variable factors and come up with a concept that can be applied to every horse we know and to any we might get to know in the future. Ockham's anti-realist metaphysics had immediate implications for epistemology. For realists, one knows an individual thing through the intermediation of the universal: We know Seabiscuit only through the universal "horse," and we never can be said to "know" the individual in a strong sense. Ockham, however, believed that the universal was just a name, a tool, useful for navigating our way through life. We can know individual things directly and immediately, without having to look at them through the screen of universals.

Ockham and Modernity

Ockham's "nominalist" epistemology often has been seen as an important development in the formation of modern science. His emphasis on empirical experience as a way of knowing is similar to the methods of the modern "scientific method." Yet, the science that developed from Ockham is of a peculiar kind, as can be seen from a comparison of Thomas's understanding of the order of things with Ockham's. Throughout his work, Ockham employed the "principle of annihilation." According to this principle, "Every absolute thing, distinct in subject and place from another absolute thing, can exist by divine power even while [any] other absolute thing is destroyed."[96] Whatever cannot remain in existence after all else is annihilated is not, strictly speaking, a thing. Things are only things if they are self-standing (though everything is immediately dependent on God). Ockham gave philosophical ground for knowing particular things, but they are fundamentally detached things. In Thomas's earlier conception, every thing not only is "ordered to" God but also is ordered to other things, so that no individual can be understood except as part of a web of things in the world. Modern science built on Ockham's conception, examining individual things

> *Ockham rejected the whole scheme. Universals are no more than concepts or words ("names," or nomina), and have no reality outside the mind. We arrive at these concepts by a principle of abstraction.*

---

96. Quoted in Amos Funkenstein, *Theology and the Scientific Imagination: From the Middle Ages to the Seventeenth Century* (Princeton, NJ: Princeton University Press, 1986), 135.

and breaking them into component parts, ignoring the wider networks and attachments in which every thing actually is embedded. Only in the last century has science begun to pull away from this Ockhamist inheritance to develop scientific theories in which relatedness is as basic as individuality.

Ockham's particularism also led to shifts in aesthetics. For Thomas, aesthetics was inherent in the nature of the world and the act of knowing. When we know, there is a proportion or harmony between God's intellect and ours that Thomas described as "partaking of beauty." All knowing is a kind of "art." Ontologically, Thomas saw everything interrelated in a beautiful harmony, like Dante's dance in Paradise. For Ockham, individual things are self-standing in relation to other created things, not organized into a harmonious dance. Any aesthetic order has to be constructed by the human mind. It is not, as in Thomas, "divined" from the actual nature of things. Not only did this diminish the role of aesthetics, but it also helped to form aesthetics as a distinct set of problems, rather than as a concern internal to theology.[97] In other ways, Ockham's influence on art was to emphasize the uniqueness of individual things and people. As Eco says, the particularism of Scotus and Ockham affected the development of Gothic architecture, which, in its later manifestation, was "more concerned with the particular than with ensembles," more interested in the multiplicity of things than to "discern the form shining in objects." Flemish miniaturists such as van Eyck operate in a world first imagined by Ockham.[98]

Ockham's radically individualistic view of reality was consistent with his understanding of God's nature and his relation to the world. Ockham, like other late medieval thinkers, followed the Condemnation by emphasizing the will of God, developing the distinction between God's "absolute" and "ordained" power. This distinction had a significant impact on the late medieval understanding of salvation, especially of justification.[99] In some respects, later medieval theology prepared the way for the Reformation. Alongside the semi-Pelagian system of Gabriel Biel, known as the *via moderna*, was a revival of Augustinianism, led by Thomas Bradwardine, among others. Eliminating "universals" also cleared the ground for new ways of thinking about grace.

Yet, there were some crucial flaws in the late medieval outlook, flaws that helped to produce radical changes in anthropology, politics, and society. As John Milbank has argued, late medieval theologians did not work through issues of the will of God in a Trinitarian framework and thus came to see God's relation to the world as a "bare divine unity starkly confront[ing] the other distinct unities which he had ordained." Furthermore, since God was seen as primarily will, man, as the image of God,

> *As John Milbank has argued, late medieval theologians did not work through issues of the will of God in a Trinitarian framework and thus came to see God's relation to the world as a "bare divine unity starkly confront[ing] the other distinct unities which he had ordained."*

---

97. Eco, *Art and Beauty*, 88–89.

98. Ibid., 87.

99. On this debate, see Heiko A. Oberman, *The Harvest of Medieval Theology* (Grand Rapids: Baker, [1983] 2000); Alister E. McGrath, *Iustitia Dei: A History of the Christian Doctrine of Justification*, 2 vols. (Cambridge: Cambridge University Press, 1986), vol. 1.

was most godlike when exercising unimpeded willpower: "men . . . when enjoying unrestricted, unimpeded property rights and even more when exercising the rights of a sovereignty that 'cannot bind itself' came closest to the *imago Dei*." Thus, theologians helped to construct a "secular" social space, an arena of social, economic, and political life where sovereignty and dominion ruled, unconstrained by any religious principle.[100] Such a conception of divine power fit easily into the absolutist politicians beginning to slouch across the landscape of the late medieval world. In his political treatises, Ockham attempted to maintain a balance of spiritual and secular authorities, but his tendency to spiritualize and privatize the church set a worrying precedent for the future, and his emphasis on divine power was attractive to the powerful.[101] It is not an accident that he spent his last years as an imperial apologist in the court of Emperor Louis IV.

More fundamentally, these developments were the outworking of processes set in motion in the eleventh and twelfth centuries. It was only possible for a secular space to be formed because Gregory had already, self-protectively, dug a chasm between the clergy and laity. It was possible to consider God as abstract absolute power because philosophical conceptions of "deity" had been separated from theological ones. All this was intellectually feasible only because theology already had been detached from the scriptural revelation of a triune God of love.

Page from an illuminated manuscript from the Middle Ages

Medieval Questions and the Development of Modern Thought

In a study of the medieval uses of reason and logic, Edward Grant has argued that the Middle Ages were simultaneously an "Age of Faith" and an "Age of Reason." He claims that medieval attention to "questions" developed into the questioning spirit of modern science, social science, and technology: "The question format remained in extensive use for some four centuries. By the time it was abandoned in the seventeenth century, to be replaced by treatises that were given topical treatment, the question approach to natural philosophy was engrained in Western thought."[102] As Grant playfully puts it, the High Middle Ages bequeathed to the West a "culture and spirit of 'poking around.' "

That is a fine summary of the developments we have surveyed, but it fails to reckon with the precise nature of the revolution of the High Middle Ages. Questions, after all, had been posed by Christian thinkers for some centuries, beginning with Augustine's *Confessions*, which, like *Hamlet*, is dominated by the interrogative mood. Scholasticism is new not only because questions arise from a source other than Scripture but also because the answers often are provided from sources other than Scripture. Philosophical

In his political treatises, Ockham attempted to maintain a balance of spiritual and secular authorities, but his tendency to spiritualize and privatize the church set a worrying precedent for the future, and his emphasis on divine power was attractive to the powerful.

---

100.   Milbank, *Theology and Social Theory*, 14–15.

101.   See the summary of Ockham's political views, along with selected texts, in O'Donovan and O'Donovan, *From Irenaeus to Grotius*, 453–75.

102.   Grant, *God and Reason*, 357.

speculation was detached from attention to the details of the biblical text, and, formally if not substantively, reason was treated as a relatively autonomous source of truth. This detachment of the *quaestio* from the *lectio* was the decisive revolution of high and late medieval thought. The Reformation raised a protest and initiated a counterrevolution, but later Protestantism in many ways remained mired in the dualism of post-Gregorian, post-Abelardian thought and culture. In many ways, this breach has yet to be healed.

For Further Reading

Chenu, M. D. *Nature, Man, and Society in the Twelfth Century: Essays on the New Theological Perspective in the Latin West.* Chicago: University of Chicago Press, 1968.

Colish, Marcia L. *Medieval Foundations of the Western Intellectual Tradition, 400–1400.* New Haven, CT: Yale, 1997.

Duby, Georges. *The Age of the Cathedrals: Art and Society, 980–1420.* Translated by Eleanor Levieux and Barbara Thompson. Chicago: University of Chicago Press, 1981.

Eco, Umberto. *Art and Beauty in the Middle Ages.* Translated by Hugh Bredin. New Haven, CT: Yale, 1986.

Evans, G. R., ed. *The Medieval Theologians: An Introduction to Theology in the Medieval Period.* Oxford: Blackwell, 2001.

Funkenstein, Amos. *Theology and the Scientific Imagination: From the Middle Ages to the Seventeenth Century.* Princeton, NJ: Princeton University Press, 1986.

Grant, Edward. *God and Reason in the Middle Ages.* Cambridge: Cambridge University Press, 2001.

Jaeger, C. Stephen. *Ennobling Love: In Search of a Lost Sensibility.* Philadelphia: University of Pennsylvania Press, 1999.

Jaeger, C. Stephen. *Envy of Angels: Cathedral Schools and Social Ideals in Medieval Europe, 950–1200.* Philadelphia: University of Pennsylvania Press, 1994.

Kantorowicz, Ernst. *The King's Two Bodies: A Study in Medieval Political Theology.* Princeton, NJ: Princeton University Press, 1957.

Kerr, Fergus. *After Aquinas: Versions of Thomism.* London: Routledge, 2002.

Lewis, C. S. *The Allegory of Love: A Study in Medieval Tradition.* Oxford: Oxford University Press, 1936.

Lewis, C. S. *The Discarded Image: An Introduction to Medieval and Renaissance Literature.* Cambridge: Cambridge University Press, 1964.

de Lubac, Henri. *Medieval Exegesis.* 2 vols. Grand Rapids: Eerdmans, 1998, 2000.

Macy, Gar. *Treasures from the Storeroom: Medieval Religion and the Eucharist.* Collegeville, MN: Liturgical Press, 1999.

McInerny, Ralph, ed. *Thomas Aquinas: Selected Works.* New York: Penguin, 1998.

Oberman, Heiko. *The Harvest of Medieval Theology.* Grand Rapids: Baker, [1983] 2000.

[In scholasticism] philosophical speculation was detached from attention to the details of the biblical text, and, formally if not substantively, reason was treated as a relatively autonomous source of truth.

Southern, R. W. *The Making of the Middle Ages*. New Haven, CT: Yale, 1969.

Southern, R. W. *Scholastic Humanism and the Unification of Europe, Volume I: Foundations*. Oxford: Blackwell, 1995.

Van Engen, John. "The Christian Middle Ages as an Historiographical Problem," *American Historical Review* 91 (1986): 519–52.

For Further Discussion

1. What is meant by a "symbolic worldview"? Should Christians try to develop this kind of worldview?

2. What is the proper relationship between theology and philosophy? What role should the Bible play in forming our worldviews and philosophies?

3. What is scholasticism? Is it a good method for trying to answer theological questions? Should theology be considered a "science"? In what sense?

4. Identify some contemporary examples of the "courtly love" view of human love. Hint: There are thousands.

5. During the Middle Ages, ideas found their way into cultural artifacts like Dante's poetry and Suger's architecture. How would you express your church's theology in poetry, painting, sculpture, or architecture?

6. Evaluate Thomas's "hylomorphic" view of human nature biblically.

7. Do you think that form and substance are separable? For example, can you summarize a poem in prose without changing the poem? Can you systematize the Bible without changing the meaning of the Bible?

8. What does it mean to say that God is "Being"? Is that true?

6

The Renaissance

Carl Trueman

W hen discussing the "worldview" of the Renaissance, immediately we face a number of problems that require careful consideration. Foremost among these is the definition of the Renaissance itself. Like all terms used by later historians with reference to earlier periods of historical development, it involves the ordering and reification[1] of something that may not have had such a self-conscious identity or unity at the time. If this is true of the Reformation, which contained numerous theological and ecclesiastical movements that can be subsumed under this singular noun, how much more is this true of the Renaissance—a movement with no obvious beginning or ending points, no single geographical center, no broadly unified intellectual program, and no self-conscious identity? This raises a second problem regarding worldview and the Renaissance: is it at all meaningful to speak of "*the* worldview" of such a diverse and diffuse phenomenon? I suspect not. Therefore, in this chapter I will trace the various threads that form the warp and woof of the movement we call the Renaissance, rather than present a single set of dogmas, as if such were sufficient to define "the Renaissance worldview."[2]

> *In this chapter I will trace the various threads that form the warp and woof of the movement we call the Renaissance, rather than present a single set of dogmas, as if such were sufficient to define "the Renaissance worldview."*

1. Regarding something abstract as a material thing.
2. Inevitably, there is a considerable body of literature surrounding the notion of what constitutes the "Renaissance." Petrarch probably was the first person to reject medieval historical periodization, dubbed the Middle Ages, as dark and obscurantist, arguing that this period in which he lived represented a "rebirth" of classical cultural values. The picture is further complicated by the scholarly recognition that the Renaissance in southern Europe took a different form from the Renaissance in northern Europe, though there is no consensus regarding how best to define this difference. For further discussion, see J. B. Bullen, *The Myth of the Renaissance in Nineteenth-Century Writing* (Oxford: Clarendon Press, 1994); Wallace K. Ferguson, *The Renaissance in Historical Thought: Five Centuries of Interpretation* (Cambridge, MA: Houghton and Mifflin, 1948); Denys Hays, ed., *The Renaissance Debate* (New York: European Problem Studies, 1965).

Humanism

Central to the intellectual reforms represented by the Renaissance was the movement, or movements, known as humanism. Humanism is notoriously difficult to define in terms of its doctrinal content because it embraced a wide variety of figures, from relativizing skeptics such as Pomponazzi, to conservative Catholics such as Sir Thomas More, to Lutheran Reformers such as Philipp Melanchthon.[3]

Contrary to some popular discussions, scholasticism and humanism are not mutually exclusive categories, with the former representing a rigid, logical, systematizing tendency and the latter a more literary, exegetical, poetic tendency. Scholasticism and humanism are entirely separate categories of discourse. Scholasticism is an academic approach to learning, whose home is the university; humanism, as we will see, is a cultural attitude based on the reappropriation of classical literature. Thus, it was entirely possible to be a scholastic and a humanist, just as today one can be a university academic and an author of epic poetry. The two forms of discourse are not mutually exclusive, and attempts to make them so actually commit a category mistake.[4]

Humanism emerged in Europe between 1200 and 1400 as a result of the spread of French culture and the influence of classical models of literature and learning, particularly those provided by Cicero. Although the term *humanism* arose later, the *studia humanitatis*, or "humanistic studies," came to represent an established intellectual and cultural curriculum focused on grammar, rhetoric, history, poetry, and moral philosophy. The

> *Scholasticism is an academic approach to learning, whose home is the university; humanism ... is a cultural attitude based on the reappropriation of classical literature. Thus, it was entirely possible to be a scholastic and a humanist, just as today one can be a university academic and an author of epic poetry.*

---

3. As with the term *renaissance*, the term *humanism* also has been subjected to heated debate over the years. The nineteenth-century writers Georg Voigt and Jakob Burckhardt both saw humanism as a decisive break with the values of the Middle Ages. Voigt focused on Petrarch, and Burckhardt, influenced by Hegel, believed the essence of the movement lay in a nebulous "spirit of the age." Since 1945, scholars have tended to acknowledge the complexity of the relationship between humanism and other elements of medieval culture, seeing no clean break but rather various areas of development, discontinuity, competition, and assimilation, with a particular focus on the appropriation of classical literature in the construction of cultural values. See, for example, Hans Baron, *The Crisis of the Early Italian Renaissance: Civic Humanism and Republican Liberty in an Age of Classicism and Tyranny*, 2nd ed. (Princeton, NJ: Princeton University Press, 1966); Eugenio Garin, *Italian Humanism: Philosophy and Civic Life in the Renaissance*, trans. Peter Munz (Westport, CT: Greenwood Press, 1975); Paul Oskar Kristeller, *Renaissance Thought: The Classic, Scholastic, and Humanist Strains* (New York: Harper and Row, 1961). Kristeller's approach, focusing as it does on the writings and activities of the humanists themselves, is perhaps the most influential in current studies. A useful collection of essays focusing on the nature of humanism in northern Europe is F. Akkerman, G. C. Huisman, and A. J. Vanderjagt, *Wessel Gansfort (1419–1489) and Northern Humanism* (Leiden: Brill, 1993).

4. See Kristeller, *Renaissance Thought*; Erika Rummel, *The Humanist-Scholastic Debate in the Renaissance and Reformation* (Cambridge: Cambridge University Press, 1995); Willem Van Asselt and Eef Dekker, eds., *Reformation and Scholasticism: An Ecumenical Enterprise* (Grand Rapids: Baker, 2001); also Carl R. Trueman and R. Scott Clark, eds., *Protestant Scholasticism: Essays in Reassessment* (Carlisle, PA: Paternoster, 1999).

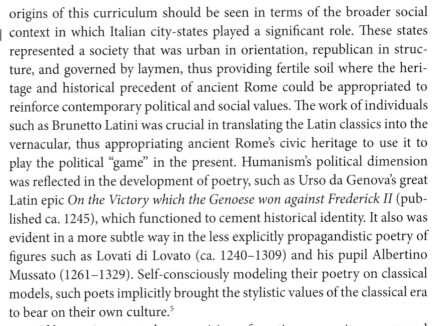

CARL TRUEMAN

OUTLINE

► Humanism ◄
Renaissance
Philosophy
Renaissance
Science
Renaissance Politics
Renaissance Litera-
ture and Art
Conclusion

origins of this curriculum should be seen in terms of the broader social context in which Italian city-states played a significant role. These states represented a society that was urban in orientation, republican in structure, and governed by laymen, thus providing fertile soil where the heritage and historical precedent of ancient Rome could be appropriated to reinforce contemporary political and social values. The work of individuals such as Brunetto Latini was crucial in translating the Latin classics into the vernacular, thus appropriating ancient Rome's civic heritage to use it to play the political "game" in the present. Humanism's political dimension was reflected in the development of poetry, such as Urso da Genova's great Latin epic *On the Victory which the Genoese won against Frederick II* (published ca. 1245), which functioned to cement historical identity. It also was evident in a more subtle way in the less explicitly propagandistic poetry of figures such as Lovati di Lovato (ca. 1240–1309) and his pupil Albertino Mussato (1261–1329). Self-consciously modeling their poetry on classical models, such poets implicitly brought the stylistic values of the classical era to bear on their own culture.[5]

If humanism started as a revision of poetic canons, it soon spread to include prose and rhetoric. Central to the poetic and prose revolutions was the figure of Francesco Petrarca, or Petrarch (1304–74), who stressed the centrality of the classics for any conception of literature, placing Virgil and Cicero at the center of the poetry and prose agendas.[6] As noted above, it is important to grasp the stylistic, political, and cultural significance of what was transpiring. Petrarch, a true intellectual pioneer, fashioned Italian humanism into a self-conscious movement, developed early text-critical methods through his rediscovery of Latin manuscripts, and played an important role in the development of the genre of autobiography (taking his cue in this from Augustine). Although he did not know classical Greek, the intellectual trajectories he established ultimately bore philological fruit in the works of Marsilio Ficino (1433–99) and Desiderius Erasmus (1466–1536). Regarding the revolution in rhetoric, Petrarch's six surviving orations are medieval in style. He also provided a great service by identifying and analyzing the Latin rhetorical tradition. One of humanism's most impor-

Francesco Petrarca

5. On humanism in general, see Kristeller, *Renaissance Thought*; also Jill Kraye, *The Cambridge Companion to Renaissance Humanism* (Cambridge: Cambridge University Press, 1996). On its origins, see Roberto Weiss, "The Dawn of Humanism," *Bulletin of the Institute of Historical Research* 42 (1969), 1–16; Ronald Witt, "Medieval Italian Culture and the Origins of Humanism as a Stylistic Ideal," in Albert Rabil, ed., *Renaissance Humanism: Foundations, Forms, and Legacy*, 3 vols. (Philadelphia: University of Pennsylvania Press, 1988), 1:29–70.

6. A selection of Petrarch's work in translation can be found in David Thompson, ed., *Petrarch: A Humanist among Princes* (New York: Harper and Row, 1971); also E. Cassirer, P. O. Kristeller, and J. H. Randall Jr., eds., *The Renaissance Philosophy of Man* (Chicago: University of Chicago Press, 1948). On Petrarch's thought and influence, see Charles Trinkaus, *The Poet as Philosopher: Petrarch and the Formation of Renaissance Consciousness* (New Haven, CT: Yale University Press, 1979).

180

tant contributions was its classically oriented revision of rhetoric, which transformed the medieval university curricula. For example, the rhetorical arts displaced logic in importance. Pier Paolo Vergerio (1370–1444) and Leonardo Bruni (1370–1444) figured prominently in the revision of rhetoric. Bruni's famous *Praise of the City of Florence* marked a watershed in the development of a full-blooded Ciceronian rhetorical style.[7]

The significance of all this is simple, yet far-reaching: the political climate of northern Italy led to the transformation of intellectual pursuits in a manner that facilitated respect for and appropriation of classical models for contemporary cultural pursuits. This was no static phenomenon. The general concern for classical culture that early humanism exhibited was bound to culminate in major pedagogical achievements, perhaps most significantly in the development of textual criticism and the rise of a new interest in languages—first Greek, then Hebrew, and so on. Thus, the subtle—and sometimes not so subtle—use of antiquity as a means of legitimizing civic values led to a basic restructuring of attitudes toward the past. Although such a change manifested itself primarily in grammatical and stylistic revolutions, it went much deeper. Thus, it is clear that the humanist cry of "*Ad fontes!*" ("Back to the sources!") heralded a far more politically and socially significant statement than at first we might imagine.

Although scholars have noted the different ways that humanism influenced various spheres of power in late medieval Europe—Italy, Spain, Germany and the Low Countries, and England—concern for style, rhetoric, and access to the original sources actually bound together the various humanist trajectories in these areas. Thus, what began as a movement concerned with poetry soon led to a massive industry throughout Europe involved in producing and studying classical texts and juxtaposing classical and medieval learning in a manner that generally proved most unfavorable to the latter. It also had a profound impact on the university curriculum. The medieval emphasis on logic, which had led to a flourishing of complex logical handbooks, was slowly but surely supplanted by an emphasis on rhetoric. Logic was pared down and simplified, as evidenced in the shorter, more concise handbooks of logic that became the vogue in the sixteenth and seventeenth centuries, and in the works of specific thinkers, for example Peter Ramus (1515–72).[8] The emphasis on rhetoric and on the past as

> *Petrarch, a true intellectual pioneer, fashioned Italian humanism into a self-conscious movement, developed early text-critical methods through his rediscovery of Latin manuscripts, and played an important role in the development of the genre of autobiography....*

> *The significance of all this is simple, yet far-reaching: the political climate of northern Italy led to the transformation of intellectual pursuits in a manner that facilitated respect for and appropriation of classical models for contemporary cultural pursuits.*

7. On these issues, see Rabil, *Renaissance Humanism*; also Jerrold E. Seigel, *Rhetoric and Philosophy in Renaissance Humanism: The Union of Eloquence and Wisdom, Petrarch to Valla* (Princeton, NJ: Princeton University Press, 1968). For discussion of the impact of rhetoric on intellectual life in England, see Quentin Skinner, *Reason and Rhetoric in the Philosophy of Hobbes* (Cambridge: Cambridge University Press, 1996).

8. Scholarship traditionally has downplayed the impact of Renaissance patterns on university education; see W. T. Costello, *The Scholastic Curriculum at Early Seventeenth Century Cambridge* (Cambridge, MA: Harvard University Press, 1958). More recently, the downgrading and simplification of logical training has been noted; see Mordechai Feingold, "The Humanities," in Nicholas Tyacke, ed., *The History of the University of Oxford IV: The Seventeenth Century* (Oxford: Clarendon Press, 1997), 211–357; cf. Jennifer E. Ashworth,

a source of style and learning constituted a powerful tool that could be appropriated for various ideological ends.[9]

From the Christian perspective, the most obvious and important result of this was the increasing prominence of biblical languages and the development of patristic studies. Prior to the rise of humanism, most theological work in Western Europe was conducted using the Latin text of the Vulgate Bible and various collections of authoritative quotations from earlier generations that functioned as aids to exegesis and theological synthesis. With the rise of textual and linguistic studies, humanists were able, so they thought, to bypass the interpretative accretions of the medieval period and directly access the original sources for themselves. For Christianity, this methodological and cultural shift was earthshaking. On one level, it allowed scholars to examine the validity of certain claims of the church that were based on allegedly historical documents. Long-held assertions regarding Roman primacy and the autonomy of church power had been grounded for centuries on the "Donation of Constantine," but careful textual study enabled Nicholas of Cusa and Lorenzo Valla to prove that this document was fraudulent and probably an eighth-century forgery. All other arguments built on its historicity also were undermined. At another level, it led directly to the production of critical editions of the early church fathers, providing, for almost the first time in history, a more general access to their thought that allowed their individual statements to be set in a wider textual context.

Undoubtedly, the availability of patristic texts proved a major factor in driving the development of Reformation theology. The Reformers tended to downplay the intellectual competence of the Middle Ages and to claim patristic precedent for their reforming activity, whether within the Catholic Church (e.g., Erasmus) or without it (e.g., Melanchthon). Indeed, with only a little exaggeration one could argue that the Reformation was essentially a debate about which party could lay claim to the most accurate interpretation of Augustine, and this debate could only take place, as it did, in a world whose attitude and access to the past had been so decisively shaped by the

> *Undoubtedly, the availability of patristic texts proved a major factor in driving the development of Reformation theology. The Reformers tended to downplay the intellectual competence of the Middle Ages and to claim patristic precedent for their reforming activity . . . .*

"The Eclipse of Medieval Logic," in N. Kretzmann, Anthony Kenny, and Jan Pinborg, eds., *The Cambridge History of Later Medieval Philosophy* (Cambridge: Cambridge University Press, 787–96); also idem, "Traditional Logic," in Charles B. Schmitt, ed., *The Cambridge History of Renaissance Philosophy* (Cambridge: Cambridge University Press, 1988), 143–72; idem with Lisa Jardine, ibid., 173–98. On Ramus, see Walter Ong, *Ramus: Method and the Decay of Dialogue* (Cambridge, MA: Harvard University Press, 1958); James Veazie Skalnik, *Ramus and Reform: University and Church at the End of the Renaissance*, Sixteenth Century Essays and Studies (Kirksville, MO: Truman State University Press, 2002).

9. A number of observations can be made regarding the relationship between Renaissance patterns of thought and later Protestantism. For example, Richard Muller has noted that the appropriation of Renaissance rhetoric led to a recasting of the classical proofs for God's existence in Reformed theology, whereby the metaphysical and logical thrust of the medieval arguments was set within the rhetorical context of the consent of the nations. See Richard A. Muller, *Ad fontes argumentorum: The Sources of Reformed Theology in the 17th Century*, Utrechtse Theologische Reeks 40 (1999), 18.

developments of humanism. This is why, with the notable exception of Martin Luther, almost all of the other major Reformers were deeply schooled in the kind of humanist program advocated by Erasmus.[10]

At the most important level, Erasmus's production of a critical edition of the Greek New Testament proved most decisive for theological changes in the sixteenth century. Erasmus's scholarship formed part of a wider linguistic and cultural enterprise that sought to bring the classics to bear on the present day.[11] His interest in Greek extended far beyond the biblical text. By 1506, he produced two verse translations of plays by Euripides; and in 1518, he translated the Greek grammar of Theodore Gaza into Latin. Additionally, he worked on translations of such writers as Isocrates, Plutarch, and Lucian, and he edited the complete works of Jerome and contributed to a similar project on the works of Augustine. Thus, his work on the New Testament text must be seen as part of this wider interest in ancient texts and as the result of the kind of philological and linguistic work that he developed with reference to this wider classical background. The result was a careful fusion of Christian thought and the classical tradition that found expression in works such as *The Praise of Folly* and *The Handbook of the Christian Soldier*. In the former, Erasmus used literary techniques in a devastating satire of the church of his day. *The Praise of Folly* exemplifies how the classical tradition that humanism appropriated could be used in a highly ideological fashion to contrast simple Christian purity with the corrupt accretions of the medieval era. For example, Erasmus's discussion of monasticism makes great play of the physical filth, ignorance, and general loud-mouthed arrogance of the monks whom he depicted not simply as objects of ridicule but as being positively harmful to society:

> Among them [the monks] are some who make a great thing out of their squalor and beggary, who stand at the door bawling out their demands for bread . . . depriving other beggars of no small share of their income. And in this manner, these most agreeable fellows, with their filth, ignorance, coarseness, impudence, recreate for us, as they say, an image of the apostles.[12]

> *At the most important level, Erasmus's production of a critical edition of the Greek New Testament proved most decisive for theological changes in the sixteenth century. Erasmus's scholarship formed part of a wider linguistic and cultural enterprise that sought to bring the classics to bear on the present day.*

---

10.   On the "Donation of Constantine," see Lorenzo Valla, *The Treatise on the Donation of Constantine*, trans. Christopher B. Coleman (Toronto: University of Toronto Press, 1993). On the fathers in the Renaissance and Reformation, see the relevant essays in Irena Backus, ed., *The Reception of the Church Fathers in the West*, 2 vols. (Leiden: E. J. Broll, 1997), vol. 2. The trajectory of linguistic scholarship established by the Renaissance continued into the seventeenth century; see Stephen G. Burnett, *From Christian Hebraism to Jewish Studies: Johannes Buxtorf (1564–1629) and Hebrew Learning in the Seventeenth Century* (Leiden: Brill, 1996); Peter T. van Rooden, *Theology, Biblical Scholarship and Rabbinical Studies in the Seventeenth Century: Constantijn L'Empereur (1591–1648), Professor of Hebrew and Theology at Leiden*, trans. J. C. Grayson (Leiden: Brill, 1989).

11.   On Erasmus, see Cornelius Augustijn, *Erasmus: His Life, Works, and Influence*, trans. J. C. Grayson (Toronto: University of Toronto Press, 1991); James McConica, *Erasmus* (Oxford: Oxford University Press, 1991); Marjorie O'Rourke Boyle, *Erasmus on Language and Method in Theology* (Toronto: University of Toronto Press, 1977).

12.   *The Praise of Folly*, trans. Clarence H. Miller (New Haven, CT: Yale University Press, 1979), 98–99.

Indeed, if monks were treated with such scorn, the pope fared little better. Given that popes are meant to be vicars of Christ and thus to imitate him with regard to poverty, service, and the cross, Erasmus argued that it was remarkable how they had filled up warehouses with riches and wealth and power beyond imagining.[13] The satire is biting; the outrage is tangible; and the criticism is typical of the content of many a Protestant tract or pamphlet during the sixteenth century. Yet it is vital that Erasmus's criticism be understood as operating essentially at the level of practical morality. Whereas Protestants eventually attributed the corruption of the church to theological deficiencies, Erasmus interpreted the church's corruption as the result of bad practices. Thus Erasmus's cultural humanism and criticism stood in serious continuity with that of Melanchthon and Calvin, and so reflected a broad-based intellectual disdain for the corruption of the church. However, we should not read too much theological common ground into such critiques,[14] as Erasmus made clear in his *The Handbook of the Christian Soldier*.[15]

In the *Handbook,* Erasmus developed the notion of a moderately undogmatic Christianity built around a practical philosophy of life that takes the example of Christ as its benchmark for behavior and practice. For Erasmus, one of the major problems of late medieval religion was the radical divorce he perceived to have developed between practical piety and the kind of arid, disputatious doctrinalism that afflicted the schools. In critiquing this situation, he targeted two kinds of problematic Christianity: the nitpicking intellectualism of the theologians and the superstitious, mindless piety of the masses, wedded as they were to pilgrimages, relics, and so forth. In *The Handbook of the Christian Soldier*, Erasmus sought to reunite a basic Christian doctrinal commitment with a fruitful personal piety by developing twenty-two rules. These rules covered remedies for ignorance; a commitment to move from lower, material things to higher, spiritual realities (revealing the Platonic tendency of Erasmus's own ontology); and an emphasis on the need for charity. Erasmus wove together doctrine and practice in a sophisticated manner that always pointed to Christ as the great example. Indeed, at one or two points where Erasmus discusses Christian beliefs, his analysis is informed by a strong moralistic tone.[16]

Therefore, it is not surprising that the relationship between Protestant theology and Erasmus's *Handbook* is ambivalent. Although the English Reformer William Tyndale translated Erasmus's work into English as

Erasmus

13. Ibid., 111–12.

14. For a useful study of Erasmus's religious satire in the context of his thought as a whole, see M. A. Screech, *Erasmus, Ecstasy, and the Praise of Folly* (London: Penguin, 1980). To locate Erasmus within the theological debates of his day, see Marjorie O'Rourke Boyle, *Erasmus' Civil Dispute with Luther* (Cambridge, MA: Harvard University Press, 1983).

15. The best translation is in *The Collected Works of Erasmus* 66, ed. J. W. O'Malley (Toronto: University of Toronto Press, 1988).

16. *Handbook*, 93–94.

a summary of the Christian faith, this happened early in Tyndale's career when the trajectories of his thought were more informed by the wider humanist movement than by specifically Lutheran concerns.[17] We need to remember as well that humanism promulgated a cultural attitude, not a set of dogmas. Thus, the kind of Christianity advocated by Erasmus was not part of the essence of humanism as such, although the concern for a cultured society built on classical virtues, broadly conceived, was something that was part and parcel of the program at various points. Other humanists, such as Philipp Melanchthon and John Calvin, would develop very different attitudes to dogma and religion, while retaining respect for classical learning and for a stable, virtuous society.[18] But, in its desire to return to a form of Christianity found in the early sources and to bypass medieval scholasticism, the *Handbook* represents a clear humanist agenda and thus bears a formal similarity to other works produced by more radical theological figures. Indeed, works such as this earned Erasmus his lasting reputation as the quintessential Christian humanist and, at least until his dispute with Luther, as an outspoken critic of the church.

To return to the issue of the New Testament text, Erasmus decisively influenced biblical studies in several ways. First, he produced a critical Greek edition of the New Testament. This was not without problems; the early omission of the Johannine "comma" stirred controversy over Erasmus's Trinitarian orthodoxy, and the comma was duly replaced in later editions.[19] Second, his text facilitated the production of vernacular Scriptures across Europe, most controversially by William Tyndale in England, a country where, since the late fourteenth century, Bible translation had been synonymous with heresy and political subversion.[20] Third, more than anyone Erasmus helped to place the study of Greek—and then Hebrew—firmly within the curricula of universities and colleges. Without this ped-

> *In the **Handbook**, Erasmus developed the notion of a moderately undogmatic Christianity built around a practical philosophy of life that takes the example of Christ as its benchmark for behavior and practice.*

> *Erasmus decisively influenced biblical studies in several ways. First, he produced a critical Greek edition of the New Testament. . . . Second, his text facilitated the production of vernacular Scriptures across Europe . . . .*

17. Cf. the discussion in Carl R. Trueman, *Luther's Legacy: Salvation and English Reformers, 1525–1556* (Oxford: Clarendon Press, 1994), 46.

18. The literature on the relationship between humanism and the Reformation is vast. A good place to begin is Heiko A. Oberman, *Masters of the Reformation: the Emergence of a New Intellectual Climate in Europe*, trans. Dennis Martin (Cambridge: Cambridge University Press, 1981). On Calvin, see Richard A. Muller, *The Unaccommodated Calvin* (New York: Oxford University Press, 2000), which represents an impressive critique of the earlier interpretation of Calvin vis-à-vis the Renaissance offered by William J. Bouwsma, *John Calvin: A Sixteenth Century Portrait* (New York: Oxford University Press, 1988). On Melanchthon, see Timothy J. Wengert, *Human Freedom, Christian Righteousness: Philip Melanchthon's Exegetical Dispute with Erasmus of Rotterdam* (New York: Oxford University Press, 1998); also the essays in Karin Maag, ed., *Melanchthon in Europe* (Grand Rapids: Baker, 1999).

19. The Johannine comma is found in 1 John 5:7–8 and consists of the bracketed words in this KJV translation: "For there are three that bear record [in heaven, the Father, the Word, and the Holy Ghost: and these three are one. And there are three that bear witness in earth], the Spirit, and the water, and the blood: and these three agree in one."

20. On Tyndale, see David Daniell, *William Tyndale: A Biography* (New Haven, CT: Yale University Press, 1994).

agogical development, there could have been no widespread scholarly access to the New Testament in the original languages and, quite simply, no Reformation. Only when they had access to the Greek New Testament could scholars discern the subtle semantic differences between Greek and Latin vocabulary, particularly in the families of words surrounding notions of justice and justification, which held massive theological significance. In the early years of the Reformation, linguistic factors lay at the root of much of the debate between Protestants and Catholics. Additionally, the boost that such textual work gave to the production of Bible translations, combined with comparatively cheap printing and distribution methods and the slowly but surely rising literacy rates, helped fuel the ecclesiastical crisis.

We should note at this point the so-called Reuchlin Affair. This was a fierce controversy between a converted Jew, Johannes Pfefferkorn (1469–ca. 1522), and Philipp Melanchthon's uncle, Johann Reuchlin (1455–1522), regarding whether Jewish literature should be systematically destroyed. Although some scholars portray this affair as a clash between anti- and pro-Jewish factions, such was not the case, since in the sixteenth century neither side had any love for practicing Jews. Instead, it was a clash over the value of non-canonical literature, with Reuchlin representing a humanism that valued textual, and (perhaps just as important) contextual study as integral to the humanist project. Although the debate had limited religious significance, it facilitated the rise of Semitic studies and resulted in one of the most clever, ruthless, and influential religious satires of the sixteenth century, the *Letters of Obscure Men* (2 vols., 1515–17), which helped to implant in popular imagination the image of the opponents of humanism as obscurantist fools.[21]

> *Humanism helped develop and reinforce other less obvious attitudes that bore huge ideological significance. The clear connection between humanism and the ideologies of the Italian city-states found its counterpart in other European countries.*

Humanism helped develop and reinforce other less obvious attitudes that bore huge ideological significance. The clear connection between humanism and the ideologies of the Italian city-states found its counterpart in other European countries. Issues of national identity are never far removed from the development of a culture that reinforces and maintains that identity. A movement like humanism, rooted in the desire to appropriate the distant past to legitimize the present against the recent past, proved ideally suited to such purposes in a Europe where nation-states were just starting to emerge as major players in the political and economic scene. Thus, for example, in Spain humanism quickly became allied with the imperial ambitions of the royal family, most significantly those of Charles V (Holy Roman emperor, 1519–56), without doubt the most powerful man in the Europe of his day and the person who marked the high point of Spanish international influence. Under his rule, many humanist poets lent their weight to the creation of an ideological hegemony that facilitated

---

21. On the controversy, see Heiko A. Oberman, *The Roots of Anti-Semitism in the Age of Renaissance and Reformation*, trans. James I. Porter (Philadelphia: Fortress Press, 1984), 24–37.

Spanish dominance in mainland Europe by lauding Spanish virtues and histories. Unsurprisingly, the death of the most influential Spanish humanist poet of his generation, Garcilaso de la Vega, while fighting on behalf of his king, became a powerful symbol of the alliance between cultural pursuits and military exploits in the Spanish world at this time. To write poetry for the empire and to fight on the battlefield for the empire were two parts of the same political project. One also might add that the Jesuits, with their deep roots in Spanish culture, were in part the beneficiaries of such developments; and indeed, key Jesuit thinkers, such as Francisco Suarez, emerged as clear products of the new learning pioneered by the humanists (1548–1617). Nor was this a specifically Catholic phenomenon. Humanism, as has been noted, was not a set of dogmas but an approach to culture, a way of using culture. On the Protestant side, humanism also was allied to nascent nationalism in Germany and the Low Countries. German humanists effectively used their literary tools to protest the financial exploitation of Germany by the Italians and to develop a notion of German identity that depicted its honest, hard-working values in stark contrast to the alleged laziness and effeminacy of the Italian world. Indeed, it is again perhaps not a surprise that one of Luther's early and most violent supporters, Ulrich von Hutten, combined the callings of poet and knight and used the skills of both professions to push the line of German nationalism and independence.[22]

One final point that needs to be made about Renaissance humanism relative to developments in the Reformation is the phenomenon of "common places" or, to use the Latin term, *loci communes*. The technique used by humanists when faced with analyzing a given text was to identify the common places, or major topical headings, and then arrange the analysis of the textual matter in terms of these common places. The technique itself was connected to patterns of book production in the Renaissance that facilitated the gathering of data under such topically arranged structures.[23] This approach presupposed a belief that coherent arguments and data in a text could be drawn out and rearranged in a systematic manner. The theological impact of this was enormous. For example, it lay directly behind the appropriately titled *Loci Communes* of Philipp Melanchthon, which from 1521 onward represented the first major attempt to draw up a systematic statement of Lutheran doctrine under a series of common place headings. It also shaped the way in which Melanchthon and others read the Bible. Faced with

> *The technique used by humanists when faced with analyzing a given text was to identify the common places, or major topical headings, and then arrange the analysis of the textual matter in terms of these common places.*

22. On Spain, see Ottavio Di Camillo, "Humanism in Spain," in Rabil, 2:55–108; Carlos G. Norena, *Studies in Spanish Renaissance Thought* (The Hague: Nijhoff, 1975). On Germany and the Low Countries, see Anthony Goodman and Angus MacKay, eds., *The Impact of Humanism on Western Europe* (London: Longman, 1990); Heiko A. Oberman and Thomas A. Brady, *Itinerarium Italicum: The Profile of the Italian Renaissance in the Mirror of Its European Transformations* (Leiden: Brill, 1975).

23. For an excellent discussion, see Ann Moss, *Printed Commonplace Books and the Structuring of Renaissance Thought* (Oxford: Clarendon Press, 1996).

the massive content of the book of Romans, for example, Melanchthon drew out the common place headings with which Paul implicitly operated and then structured his own commentary on the epistle in the same way. This method had a direct influence on the way in which John Calvin finalized the arrangement of topics in his own common place book, *The Institutes of the Christian Religion*. Again, we see here that the influence of humanism is a formal, technical one, rather than directly material. Yet a relationship clearly exists—albeit highly complex—between the way a text is read and what the text is thought to say.[24]

Since Catholic and Protestant nations and movements were able to use humanism for their own ends, it is clear that humanism is not a worldview, if such is construed in terms of specific and detailed dogmatic commitments or a unified way of looking at the world. Instead, humanism emerges as a cultural attitude that was peculiarly adaptable to the conditions of early modern Europe where it could be appropriated and deployed to great effect by different sides on the great religious and political issues of the time. Humanism played a central role in the Renaissance project, and so many issues that flow from the Renaissance were positively connected to it. Nevertheless, to reduce the Renaissance to humanism would be grossly inaccurate. Other factors, particularly those of philosophy and politics, also need to be taken into account.

Renaissance Philosophy

> *Humanism emerges as a cultural attitude that was peculiarly adaptable to the conditions of early modern Europe where it could be appropriated and deployed to great effect by different sides on the great religious and political issues of the time.*

In contrast to much modern philosophy, Renaissance thinkers, as we might expect from what we have seen above, pursued their philosophy in careful and conscious dialogue with the past. The rationalism and pragmatism of later ages that tended to depreciate the work of previous generations and to define itself over against what had gone before, rather than in developmental continuity with it, was, by and large, alien to Renaissance patterns of thought. Thus, major trajectories of reflection tended to be set by those from the classical tradition, whether Aristotelian, Platonic, or Stoic. Indeed, without much exaggeration we can say that Renaissance philosophy served in some sense as a running footnote to the streams of classical learning that it found in the original sources. We should not overplay the unity that such terminology implies. To say that Renaissance thinking was, for example, Aristotelian, is not to say that all Renaissance thinkers agreed about even the most basic of Aristotelian positions. Rather, it means that the Aristotelian corpus provided a textual canon or dialogue point in

---

24.   On Melanchthon's common place method, and its theological impact, see Robert Kolb, "Melanchthonian Method as a Guide to Reading Confessions of Faith: The Index of the Book of Concord and Late Reformation Learning," *Church History* 72 (2003), 504–24. On the impact of Melanchthon on Calvin, see Muller, "Establishing the *ordo docendi*: The Organization of Calvin's *Institutes*, 1536–1559," in *The Unaccommodated Calvin*, 118–39.

relation to which philosophers conducted their speculations. One might therefore say that widely accepted textbooks and a common language provided the unity to Renaissance philosophy; beyond this, the philosophical picture became much more diverse and complicated.[25]

The translation of Aristotle's works into Latin proved decisive to Renaissance philosophy. Although only two books, translated by Boethius, were available at the start of the twelfth century, soon these were joined by other Boethian translations of Aristotle's logical works to form what is now known as the *Organon*, which formed the backbone of medieval training in logic. Then, in the late twelfth and thirteenth centuries, more and more Aristotelian texts, including the important works on physics and metaphysics, accompanied by translations of his principal Arabic commentators, such as Ibn Rushd, became available in Western Europe. One obvious fruit of this was the transformation of Christian theology at the hands of Albert the Great and, even more so, Thomas Aquinas, who developed a full Christian theology that took into account the need to interact critically with the language and concepts of these newly accessible philosophical texts. The Latin translations of Aristotle played an additional critical role, since Latin was the universal language of learning in Europe up to the time of the early Kant. Thus, by providing a canon of texts in this universal language, the translators of Aristotle gave the whole of Western Europe a philosophical resource that could be used in Edinburgh as easily as in Rome and which therefore could bind together institutions from all over Europe in a common project.[26]

Boethius teaching his students

This Aristotelian corpus eventually formed the core of philosophical discussion in Western Europe, until the Enlightenment began to make significant inroads into university curricula in the late seventeenth century. Nevertheless, it would be highly inappropriate to talk about "the Aristotelian worldview" of the Renaissance. The appropriation and development of Aristotle's philosophy was eclectic and highly diverse. In fact, the only meaningful way in which Renaissance philosophy could be characterized as "Aristotelian" is if the term is taken strictly to mean that all Renaissance philosophy took the Aristotelian canon as one of its basic starting points for philosophical exploration and reflection. One might, perhaps, draw an analogy with Augustinianism and Western medieval theology: all Western medieval theology is "Augustinian" in that it takes Peter Lombard's *Four*

This Aristotelian corpus eventually formed the core of philosophical discussion in Western Europe, until the Enlightenment began to make significant inroads into university curricula in the late seventeenth century.

25. On Renaissance philosophy, see Brian P. Copenhaver and Charles B. Schmitt, *Renaissance Philosophy* (Oxford: Oxford University Press, 1992); Charles B. Schmitt, *Aristotle and The Renaissance* (Cambridge: Cambridge University Press, 1983); Charles B. Schmitt et al., *The Cambridge History of Renaissance Philosophy* (Cambridge: Cambridge University Press, 1991).

26. See Schmitt, *Aristotle and the Renaissance*. For Aquinas, see Brian Davies, *The Thought of Thomas Aquinas* (Oxford: Clarendon Press, 1992). On Aristotle's impact in the Middle Ages, see the various primary source readings in Arthur Hyman and James J. Walsh, eds., *Philosophy in the Middle Ages* (Indianapolis: Hackett, 1973).

Books of Sentences as its starting point—a book that draws heavily on the Augustinian corpus for many of its texts. Thus, that which binds, say, the philosophical approaches of Padua and Cambridge together is not a core of doctrinal agreement but a canon of texts that form the basis of philosophical reflection.[27]

Given the diverse nature of Renaissance Aristotelianism, no adequate treatment of the subject as a whole is possible here. Nevertheless, we can savor some of this diversity by glancing briefly at a few of the central figures. One such person, Leonardo Bruni (1370–1444), was a major figure in the Florentine Renaissance. A translator of Plato, he also wrote a history of Florence and translated Aristotle's *Nicomachean Ethics*. Significantly, he also provided an analytic introduction to the *Ethics* that depicted Aristotle as a wealthy man, engaged in public affairs, and highly skilled in the art of eloquence—precisely the kind of ideal citizen a place like Florence needed. Additionally, in typical humanist fashion, he took pains to contrast his own translation favorably with those of the past, and he extolled the virtues of Latin as a suitable vehicle for capturing the beauty of Aristotle's Greek. The move was brilliant, because it effectively appropriated Aristotle for the humanist project, reading him through the lens of Ciceronian priorities, and thus made him a legitimate source for Renaissance models of what a philosopher should be: not simply a logician or metaphysician but also a politician with a deep interest in eloquence and rhetoric. When Bruni became chancellor of Florence, he may well have interpreted this appointment as legitimized by the reading of Aristotle he advocated.[28]

Another significant contribution resulted from Bruni's controversy with the Spaniard, Alfonso of Cartagena, regarding translation. Alfonso contended that the only purpose in translation was to bring out the transcendent content, or *ratio*, of a text. Bruni, however, argued that it is necessary to preserve the original author's style as well. At one level the debate seems merely a matter of style, but it has philosophical significance because Bruni insists that the translator be cognizant of the historical particularity of a text, and this points toward an early kind of historicism, or historical sense, that had been signally absent from previous scholarly endeavors. Thus, a concern for style emerged as a factor in the rise of historicism in the context of Aristotelian philosophy in the Renaissance. To translate a text, one needed more than just a dictionary and a grammar; one also needed

> *All Western medieval theology is "Augustinian" in that it takes Peter Lombard's* **Four Books of Sentences** *as its starting point .... Thus, that which binds, say, the philosophical approaches of Padua and Cambridge together is not a core of doctrinal agreement but a canon of texts that form the basis of philosophical reflection.*

---

27. The diversity of Renaissance Aristotelianism is brought out clearly in the essays in Charles B. Schmitt, *Studies in Renaissance Philosophy and Science* (London: Variorum, 1981). For the significance of this to Reformed theology, see Richard A. Muller, "Reformation, Orthodoxy, 'Christian Aristotelianism,' and the Eclecticism of Early Modern Philosophy," *Nederlands Archief voor Kerkgeschiedenis* 81 (2001), 306–25.

28. For Bruni, see L. Bruni, *The Humanism of Leonardo Bruni: Selected Texts*, ed. and trans., G. Griffiths et al. (New York: Center for Medieval and Early Renaissance Studies, 1987).

to comprehend the wider cultural and linguistic context within which the text occurred and into which it was to be translated.[29]

Another major person in Renaissance Aristotelian philosophy was the controversial figure of Pietro Pomponazzi, or Pompanatus (1462–1525). Pompanatus exemplified a person steeped in the method of medieval scholasticism and receptive to many of humanism's insights. Trained by Thomists and Scotists to appreciate medieval philosophy, Pompanatus developed a philosophy that, in a sense, adumbrated some of the skepticism and naturalism that began to surface. Teaching at Padua, Ferrara, and Bologna, Pompanatus exerted a wide influence in Italian circles. Because of the international reputation and student body of Padua in particular, Pompanatus became a philosophical figure of European stature. He developed his philosophy as a philosophy of nature that, controversially, tended to exclude miracles by always seeking natural causes for any alleged miraculous event. Just as controversial, though hardly without precedent, even within the trajectories of orthodox Christian thought, he also argued that philosophy could not demonstrate the immortality of the soul. In this context, Pompanatus exploited obscurity in Aristotle's own teaching on the immortality of the soul. Thus, as stated above, Pompanatus proposed a philosophical position that was Aristotelian more in the sense that it took Aristotle as a point of departure than as an authoritative text that simply needed to be exegeted to arrive at the truth.[30]

Renaissance philosophy, however, was eclectic. If Aristotle provided the central canon of texts, philosophers also appropriated other elements—from Plato and Neoplatonism to hermetic and mystical philosophy. Indeed, even in a narrow philosophical realm like ethics, it is easy to discern streams of thought that are more strictly Aristotelian, Platonic, Stoic, and Epicurean. All developed in dialogue with the Aristotelian ethical corpus, but all appropriated and interpreted this corpus within frameworks developed from eclectic engagements with other philosophical texts and trajectories.[31] Indeed, there was a healthy market for the production and distribution of non-Aristotelian classical philosophical sources. For example, Plato's complete works went through more than thirty printings and three revisions in the sixteenth century, indicating a keen appetite for such philosophy. Figures such as Marsilio Ficino (1433–99) spent much of their working lives in Florence under the patronage of the Medici, working on, among other things, the careful appropriation of classical philosophy

"Renaissance philosophy, however, was eclectic. If Aristotle provided the central canon of texts, philosophers also appropriated other elements—from Plato and Neoplatonism to hermetic and mystical philosophy.

---

29. See Ibid., 201–12, 217–29.

30. On Pomponazzi, see Copenhaver and Schmitt, 103–12; on his views of the soul, see Paul Oskar Kristeller, "A New Manuscript Source for Pomponazzi's Theory of the Soul from his Paduan Period," *Revue internationale de philosophie* 5 (1951), 144–57.

31. In addition to the works by Schmitt, the collection of philosophical texts edited by Jill Kraye gives some idea of the diversity of philosophical approaches within the Renaissance: *Cambridge Translations of Renaissance Philosophical Texts*, 2 vols. (Cambridge: Cambridge University Press, 1997).

for contemporary intellectual construction. Thus, in addition to engaging in extensive translations of Plato, Ficino also elaborated a thoroughgoing system of thought based on Platonic notions of love and contemplation, something that underlined the fact that he despised the activity of civic humanists. Ficino promoted a vision of the good life as one of contemplation and ascetic disregard for the material world. Nevertheless, he managed to maintain the importance of the active life by stressing its role as a step on the hierarchical ladder of being, thus retaining an ideological justification for such a life. He also argued for the importance of religion as a means of infusing human life with dignity, thus raising it above that of the beasts. However, this, too, had a strong Neoplatonic dimension to it, because Ficino interpreted religion's obsession with the body as something that is, perhaps, not its strongest point.[32] Ficino also worked extensively on hermetic texts, the mysticism of which proved relatively congenial to anyone sympathetic with the mythological pose of much Neoplatonic thought. Indeed, for a while Ficino emphasized the role of Hermes Trismegistus as a contemporary of Moses and as a source of equally ancient, though pagan, wisdom. We see here the typical impact of humanist concerns as an influence that shaped philosophy: the appeal to antiquity and the classical texts as means of discerning wisdom and knowledge. In contrast to Pompanatus, Ficino also developed an elaborate defense of the soul built upon, among other authors, Plato, Plotinus, Augustine, and Aquinas, demonstrating once again the eclectic nature of Renaissance philosophy.[33] In this context, the Neoplatonic tendency of Ficino's thinking and piety is evident in the way that he regarded prayer as essentially an inner conversion of the soul toward God.[34]

In short, we can see that Renaissance philosophy, while predominantly Aristotelian because of its basic starting point in the Aristotelian corpus, was a diverse and eclectic phenomenon that is difficult to define in terms of specific dogmatic positions. One might also add that it is not always easy to distinguish what should be considered Renaissance philosophy from what we might regard as medieval philosophy. For example, although Thomas

> *Thus, in addition to engaging in extensive translations of Plato, Ficino also elaborated a thoroughgoing system of thought based on Platonic notions of love and contemplation, something that underlined the fact that he despised the activity of civic humanists.*

32. E.g., Letter 83: "I believe that the human race would be less happy than any beast if it were deprived of the worship of God. I leave out of account its involved and ceaseless obsession with the helpless, feeble, and continually ailing body. But if hope for the divine be removed, rational enquiry, the very activity which seems to make us superior to beasts, undoubtedly renders us more miserable than the beasts, through regret for the past, dread of the future, anxiety over the present, knowledge of evils and insatiable desire for innumerable possessions." *The Letters of Marsilio Ficino*, ed. Paul Oskar Kristeller, 4 vols. (London: Shepheard-Walwyn, 1975–88), 1:132.

33. For Ficino, see Paul Oskar Kristeller, *The Philosophy of Marsilio Ficino*, trans. V. Conant (New York: Columbia 1964); also Konrad Eisenblicher and Olga Zorzi Pugliese, eds., *Ficino and Renaissance Neoplatonism* (Ottawa: Dove House, 1986). One other figure who greatly utilized hermetic thought as part of his philosophical project is Tommaso Campanella; see John M. Headley, *Tommaso Campanella and the Transformation of the World* (Princeton, NJ: Princeton University Press, 1997).

34. Kristeller, *The Philosophy of Marsilio Ficino*, 315–16.

Bradwardine (1290–1349) and John Wycliffe (ca. 1329–84) lived when Renaissance philosophy was well under way, generally speaking, both are regarded as figures of the Middle Ages, not the Renaissance. To this there is no obvious answer other than to point to the problem of imposing too prescriptively the categories of later historians on epochs and movements that were not clearly defined or obviously discrete phenomena.

Renaissance Science

Copernicus

Given the importance of Aristotle's writings for all Renaissance intellectual endeavors, it is not surprising that the impact of his works was felt in the world of science as well. Since Pompanatus used Aristotle as a dialogue partner to develop a natural philosophy, Aristotle's works significantly influenced Renaissance scientific endeavors. Indeed, given the comprehensive nature of the topics covered by the Aristotelian corpus, its language, ideas, and agenda inevitably would continue to dominate scientific studies until some equally comprehensive, alternative paradigm was available, something that did not happen until the flourishing of the Enlightenment in the eighteenth century.

There were various scientific figures who were central to the Renaissance project. The most famous of these are Nicolaus Copernicus (1473–1543), the Polish astronomer, and Galileo Galilei (1564–1642), the Italian mathematician, physicist, and astronomer, whose suffering for his cause at the hands of the Catholic Church means that he now looms large as a martyr for enlightened scientific thinking over against religious obscurantism.

Copernicus's major contribution was his theory, based on astronomical observation, that the earth revolves around the sun, not vice versa, as the traditional Ptolemaic view would have it. Copernicus's theory challenged significant trajectories in biblical exegesis and raised questions about the centrality of human existence in the universe, not only physically but also metaphysically. Indeed, Copernicus himself sensed the revolutionary nature of his conclusions so acutely that he pondered them for twenty-six years before daring to go public.[35]

The Copernican system found its most able defender in Galileo, who made numerous scientific contributions in his early career, including an attempt to formulate laws of motion. His most famous work, however, was his experimental verification of a Copernican view of the universe. Galileo developed his argument in the context of a lifetime of critical interaction with Aristotelian texts and ideas, and his innovative conclusions do not

Copernicus's theory challenged significant trajectories in biblical exegesis and raised questions about the centrality of human existence in the universe, not only physically but also metaphysically.

35. On Copernicus, see I. Bernard Cohen, *The Birth of a New Physics* (New York: W. W. Norton and Co., 1985). Three of his works are available, with an annotated bibliography, in *Three Copernican Treatises*, trans. Edward Rosen (New York: Dove, 1959). For an interesting account by an influential philosopher of science, see Thomas Kuhn, *The Copernican Revolution: Planetary Astronomy in the Development of Western Thought* (Cambridge, MA: Harvard University Press, 1957).

represent a clean break with all the science that had gone before. Aristo-telian philosophy, in all its forms, was essentially empirical; it emphasized the importance of matter and sensory perception to knowledge. Thus, as regards the natural sciences, Aristotelian philosophy contained the seeds of its own destruction. Many of the philosophical claims it made about the universe ultimately would prove to be untenable when tested. Given the technical work of men such as Tycho Brahe (1546–1601), who developed and refined the tools necessary for increasingly precise astronomical measurements, Aristotle's claims, based on far inferior instruments, inevitably would prove vulnerable, as would the physics and metaphysics built on them. Galileo played the crucial role as these scientific developments unfolded. Between 1602 and 1609, Galileo engaged in a series of experiments. On the basis of these experiments, Galileo began to articulate a theory of motion that regarded Aristotle's approach to this subject as deeply flawed. In 1610, through observation and analysis, Galileo discovered that Venus revolves around the sun, thus demonstrating to his own satisfaction the validity of the Copernican theory.[36]

The significance of what happened subsequently—Galileo's trial and persecution at the hands of the church—represents a significant moment, not simply in the history of the church's relationship to science but of the increasingly problematic relationship of learning to religion. As its own empiricism led to a rejection of some of Aristotle's central ideas regarding motion and the order of the universe, the hold of the Aristotelian corpus began to slip. The rising science offered radically new paradigms for understanding reality, and these paradigms effectively excluded God from the picture. Although Neoplatonic and hermetic mysticism flourished in some intellectual circles, the need for an esoteric metaphysic to understand reality in a coherent fashion began to diminish. This could only pose problems for a church that had sought to offer a comprehensive view of reality that now had been revealed as severely flawed.

It is interesting that in his *Letter to the Grand Duchess of Tuscany*, one of Galileo's defenses of his own work and that of Copernicus, Galileo made extensive use of Augustine and Augustinian themes to justify his work. Arguing that his conclusions were not unscriptural, Galileo quoted Augustine to the effect that reason should guide Christian thinking in those areas regarding the physical universe that Scripture has left somewhat obscure. Additionally, Galileo astutely noted that scriptural language should not always be taken in a realistic or literal sense, because in biblical revelation God often condescends or accommodates himself to our limited capac-

> " As its own empiricism led to a rejection of some of Aristotle's central ideas regarding motion and the order of the universe, the hold of the Aristotelian corpus began to slip. The rising science offered radically new paradigms for understanding reality, and these paradigms effectively excluded God from the picture.

---

36. On Galileo, see I. Bernard Cohen, *The Birth of a New Physics* (London: Heinemann, 1970). For his defense of Copernicus, see Galileo Galilei, *Dialogue concerning the two chief world systems, Ptolemaic and Copernican*, trans. Stillman Drake (Berkeley, CA: University of California Press, 1975).

ity to grasp infinite, divine truths.[37] In fact, in this letter Galileo makes two significant points: God has endowed human beings with reason as a means to exploring the nature of reality, and there is ample precedent in the history of the church to justify the kind of method and conclusions that his scientific work represents. One could be cynical and argue that Galileo was doing little more in this letter than trying to legitimize his approach by using the authorities his opponents accepted. However, that would be speculative. It is more charitable and historically accurate to acknowledge that Galileo was demonstrating that his project was not motivated by a desire to undermine Christianity. As he closes the work with a hymn of Ambrose and a quotation from Proverbs, his knowledge of, and respect for, traditional Christianity scarcely can be doubted.

Significant advances in science emerged in fields other than astronomy. In the same year that Copernicus published *On the Revolution of the Heavenly Spheres*, Vesalius published a groundbreaking study of human anatomy, *On the Structure of the Human Body*. Again, we can discern in this kind of work the empirical orientation of a science that took seriously Aristotle's empirical epistemology. We also see the inevitable demise of Aristotle as an authority on anatomy, because his own anatomical claims would not withstand the scrutiny of empirical investigation. Growing concern for anatomical study is reflected in the artistic work of men such as Michelangelo and Leonardo da Vinci, in which proportion and body structure are prominent concerns. In short, empirical concerns of Renaissance science resulted in subjecting physical and metaphysical claims to close scrutiny and finding many of them wanting. In years to come, this science became a powerful tool in the hands of secularists who undermined the plausibility of church teaching.

> *The rise of city-states in Italy and nation-states within the wider Europe significantly affected Renaissance views of the political order. ... Parallel developments in political thinking facilitated the kind of activities in which these various cities and states wished to engage.*

Renaissance Politics

The rise of city-states in Italy and nation-states within the wider Europe significantly affected Renaissance views of the political order. We have already seen how literature and other disciplines helped form and reinforce national identities. Parallel developments in political thinking facilitated the kind of activities in which these various cities and states wished to engage. Inevitably, in the late medieval/early modern world, no genuine separation of religious and political issues into discrete entities existed, since public discourse embodied both. Thus, we find that some of the most interesting political figures also are fascinating religious leaders.[38]

---

37.   The text of the letter is available at http://www.fordham.edu/halsall/mod/galileo-tuscany.html.

38.   On Renaissance politics, see the selection of texts in Kraye, *Cambridge Translations*, vol. 2; also Quentin Skinner, *The Foundations of Modern Political Thought*, 2 vols. (Cambridge: Cambridge University Press, 1978), esp. vol. 1.

Girolamo Savonarola (1452–98), a Dominican preacher, exemplified the integration of religion and politics. He combined political reform with a powerful apocalyptic vision, thereby anticipating elements that eventually became part and parcel of the Reformation political order in the 1500s. The late fifteenth century witnessed some political chaos in northern Italy that culminated in the invasion and conquest of Naples in the late summer of 1494 by Charles VIII of France, followed by the proposed surrender of Florence to him by the Medici. Riots ensued in Florence, followed by the rapid departure of the Medici. Savonarola, already a popular visionary preacher in Florence, interpreted these events as fulfillment of biblical prophecy. He identified Charles with Cyrus and, in an orgy of apocalyptic preaching, was catapulted to prominence as head of an embassy sent to Charles to seek terms that, after some tensions, he obtained.[39]

In subsequent months and years, Savonarola played a key role in the combined religious and political reform of Florence, helping to develop a new form of government, based on Venetian models, of one large representative council. The council fulfilled a mandate for the moral and political reformation of the city, a reformation that involved burning books and artwork considered suggestive and imposing strict moral codes on the citizens. Savonarola's ambition, which he believed he achieved but which modern scholars seriously question, entailed bringing the members of the artisan class to political prominence, thus displacing the old-style nobility as the major political force. Eventually, Savonarola ran afoul of the papacy and was excommunicated. In a situation where simultaneous devotion to Savonarola and to the papacy was impossible, Savonarola fell from power and was executed, though the immediate cause was his humiliation in a bizarre trial by fire of the validity of his prophetic utterances.

Savonarola's significance lies in a number of points. First, he clearly perceived the rising importance of the artisan class in a society whose public values conflicted with society's changing economic structure. Although his attempts at reform apparently were not as successful as he thought, this should not blind us to the ideological implications of his program. But we need to be cautious. It would be anachronistic to construe his efforts at reforming the council structure as conscious precursors of modern liberal democracy. His reforms did not anticipate the modern principle of universal suffrage. However, they did represent the rise to prominence of the commercial classes over the old nobility. In this context, Savonarola's use of the Venetian model indicates a conscious response to social and economic changes that emerged across Europe. Additionally, it is interesting to note that Savonarola pointedly used religious rhetoric and theology to justify and implement his program of social reform. Although that is hardly exceptional, given the absence of a separate secular vocabulary for politics

Savonarola

39. On Savonarola, see D. Weinstein, *Savonarola and Florence* (Princeton, NJ: Princeton University Press, 1970).

at this time, it is interesting that Savonarola stressed the importance of personal and social piety, a point indicative of the times. Savonarola adapted Christianity, expressed in individual practice and behavior, in the secular sphere to undermine the old hierarchical approach to religious calling that typified medieval Christianity. The parallels with Luther's own emphasis on the sacredness of even the most secular tasks are obvious.[40]

These secularizing tendencies in Renaissance political thought figure most prominently in the work of Machiavelli and in the development of Erastianism. Niccolo Machiavelli (1469–1527) admired the way in which Savonarola nuanced the content of his religious message to suit the changing political times and to maintain his audience appeal. A true son of the Renaissance, Machiavelli developed his political theories in careful dialogue with classical sources. Thus, studying the different leadership strategies of Scipio and Hannibal provided him with a base for a pragmatic understanding of how armies should be controlled, depending on the temperaments of generals and soldiers. He also argued strongly for cities to develop their own military structures in order to free themselves from dependence on the services of mercenaries. This point touches on a central aspect of Machiavelli's thought—the concept of fortune or the state of being dependent on others for one's welfare, power, or even survival. It is obvious that this is a clear product of an age of rising local and national political units and identities.[41]

Machiavelli's great political treatise, *Discourses on the First Ten Books of Titus Livius*, is a classical piece of Renaissance composition. In its extended reflection on the work of the historian, Livy, it represents precisely the kind of mining of the classical past for present wisdom that we noted earlier. By taking the development of the early Roman city-state as his subject of study, Machiavelli moved toward analyzing precisely what facilitated the effective running of such an Italian state in his own time. Indeed, the opening words of the first chapter set the tone for the whole:

> Those who read what the beginning of Rome was, and what her lawgivers and her organization, will not be astonished that so much virtue should have maintained itself during so many centuries; and that so great an empire should have sprung from it afterwards.[42]

Here the typical humanist concern for the classical past as a source of knowledge united with a typical Machiavellian theme, that of virtue, which is more than just the common notion we might have of a quality or habit

> *Savonarola's ambition, which he believed he achieved but which modern scholars seriously question, entailed bringing the members of the artisan class to political prominence, thus displacing the old-style nobility as the major political force.*

> *A true son of the Renaissance, Machiavelli developed his political theories in careful dialogue with classical sources.... He also argued strongly for cities to develop their own military structures in order to free themselves from dependence on the services of mercenaries.*

40. A translation of Savonarola's major political work is available as *Liberty and Tyranny in the Government of Men*, trans. C. M. Flumiani (Albuquerque, NM: American Classical College Press, 1976).

41. On Machiavelli, see Quentin Skinner, *Machiavelli* (Oxford: Oxford University Press, 1981); J. G. A. Pocock, *The Machiavellian Moment: Florentine Political Thought and the Atlantic Republican Tradition* (Princeton, NJ: Princeton University Press, 1975).

42. Machiavelli, *The Prince and the Discourses*, ed. Max Lerner (New York: The Modern Library, 1940).

that is morally praiseworthy. For Machiavelli, it also connoted the ability to rule well and to maintain political control and stability. In short, virtue may not be something that always is morally praiseworthy in the typical manner; it may well involve the ability to operate within the conventions of Realpolitik. Thus, for example, Machiavelli regarded deceit in the context of warfare as a thoroughly laudable thing.[43] Furthermore, promises extracted by force are not binding;[44] and, in a classic anticipation of the hermeneutic of suspicion, mistakes made by an enemy should be assumed to be part of a deliberately deceptive strategy.[45]

Regarding the practice of political leadership, Machiavelli developed a theory that was built on the central, powerful figure of the prince, or ruler, who was the very embodiment of virtue understood along the distinctive Machiavellian lines mentioned above. Thus, the best prince is one capable of instilling the necessary civic spirit and discipline into his people by charisma, craftiness, and military skill—the very qualities that constitute virtue in the Machiavellian scheme—and by so doing maintain his people's dependence on him in whatever circumstances.[46] The prince also should be prepared, where necessary, to engage in whatever activity he finds necessary to maintain himself in power. In other words, with respect to the prince's power, normal rules of social morality and behavior simply do not apply to him.[47] Furthermore, Machiavelli praised the policy of keeping the people—and indeed all political underlings in the power structure—confused about political strategy by adopting unpredictable and apparently illogical courses of action. The prince also should give the appearance of being a man of good faith in public, whatever his hidden agenda and secret actions might be. By acting in such a way, the prince could better maintain and safeguard his power.[48] Again, as with the *Discourses*, much of the argument in *The Prince* rests upon ancient historical precedent.[49]

In *The Prince*, Machiavelli advocated a politics thoroughly secular in orientation, a form of pragmatic Realpolitik whereby ends frequently justify the means. In the *Discourses*, he made it clear that the basic unit of loyalty is the basic unit of politics, the city or the state, and that ties of

> *The best prince is one capable of instilling the necessary civic spirit and discipline into his people by charisma, craftiness, and military skill—the very qualities that constitute virtue in the Machiavellian scheme—and by so doing maintain his people's dependence on him in whatever circumstances.*

43. "Although deceit is detestable in all other things, yet in the conduct of war it is laudable and honorable; and a commander who vanquishes an enemy by stratagem is equally praised with one who gains victory by force." Ibid., 526. The particular exemplar of this for Machiavelli is Hannibal.

44. Ibid., 528.

45. Ibid., 537–38.

46. "Therefore, a wise prince will seek means by which his subjects will always and in every possible condition of things have need of his government, and then they will always be faithful to him." Ibid., 39.

47. Ibid., 56.

48. Ibid., 63–66.

49. E.g., the discussion of civil stability after the Alexandrine conquests in chapter 4 (Ibid., 15–18), which acts as a preface to a series of chapters devoted to contemporary discussion of pacifying and ruling subject nations.

friendship and family—in other words, private commitments—should not be allowed to interfere with this wider public commitment to the political success of the city or nation.[50] As noted above, within the Machiavellian context virtue has little to do with traditional Christian notions, and religious faith would appear to be only one of a number of tools that the prince has at his disposal for social control. The work also can be read as a response to a particular moment of time, as a plea for the rise of a strong, powerful leadership, identified by Machiavelli as the Medici, to rise up, unite the people, expel the foreign powers on the Italian peninsula, and make Italy glorious. Thus, in one sense it is a bleak and pessimistic book, very much the product of a Europe where old boundaries and old values were in flux and where representatives of the old, ruling noble elites lived in danger of being displaced by the rise to power of new social and economic groups. Against this, Machiavelli looked to his prince as a redeemer figure and to the Medici as those charged with the redemption of Italy.[51]

Machiavelli

Erastianism is another significant stream of Renaissance political thought that finds expression in the works of medieval thinkers such as John Wycliffe, Marsilio of Padua (1275/80–1342/3), and then in later philosophers including Thomas Hobbes (1588–1679). This stream of thinking viewed the church as essentially a branch of the state and therefore subject to the control of the established secular authorities. On this level, it represents a trajectory of thinking that is continuous with aspects of Machiavelli's program whereby another potential social tie that could cause a division of loyalty, that is, to the church, is effectively neutralized through its identification with the state. This kind of thinking provided the foundation for the English Reformation, particularly in the policies pursued by Thomas Cromwell in the 1530s—Cromwell being greatly influenced by his reading of Marsilio of Padua's *Defensor Pacis* (1324), which developed a secular notion of the state by means of a careful appropriation of Aristotle's *Politics*. Cromwell used Erastianism to justify the dissolution of the monasteries and the seizure of church revenues for the crown. In his theoretical work, Hobbes adapted Erastianism to make religion effectively a means of social control—one tool among many to use to impose coherence and order on society. As a thoroughgoing materialist, Hobbes retained little place for religion as a metaphysical system; it was simply a political tool. Thus, like Machiavelli, Hobbes placed pragmatic considerations, rather than doctrinal content, at the center of his thinking about religion.[52]

> In the **Discourses**, *[Machiavelli] made it clear that the basic unit of loyalty is the basic unit of politics, the city or the state, and that ties of friendship and family—in other words, private commitments—should not be allowed to interfere with this wider public commitment to the political success of the city or nation.*

50.   Ibid., 536–37.

51.   See his last chapter, "Exhortation to liberate Italy from the barbarians," which is an extended plea for a man to arise to liberate Italy, closing, appropriately enough, with a quotation from Petrarch which looks to the achievements of the past for inspired leadership in the present: "Valour against fell wrath / Will take up arms; and be the combat quickly sped! / For, sure, the ancient worth, / That in Italians stirs the heart, is not yet dead." Ibid., 98.

52.   See Skinner, *Reason and Rhetoric in the Philosophy of Hobbes* (Cambridge: Cambridge University Press, 1996).

Renaissance Literature and Art

It should be clear from what we have seen that the Renaissance offered no single, unifying worldview. Instead *Renaissance* is a term that embraces a variety of views and perspectives on a whole range of issues. Therefore, when we examine the Renaissance's influence on art and literature, we confront the obvious problem that we cannot simply trace out the effect of a single idea or system of ideas on literary form and material representation. Nevertheless, some obvious points are worth noting. A significant factor in both literature and art, however, is the wider social and economic context in which artists and writers pursued their crafts. In discussing humanism, we noted the close connection between literature and the political concerns of those the humanists sought to serve. Then, in looking at the political theories of the time, we noted the importance of localized politics, of the rising city-state or nation, for the role of religion and other ideological tools in the development of political theory and practice. These same factors apply to literature and art.

First, one of the hallmarks of Renaissance literature from the earliest period was the desire to write in the vernacular and to do so in a manner that was self-conscious about literary style. In this, we see a confluence of the concern for the particularity of the local context intersecting with the typical concern for rhetoric and style that arises from the political appropriation of the classical past. Thus, the great Italian poet Dante Alighieri (1265–1321) composed a major work on use of the vernacular, *De vulgari eloquentia*, in which he wrestled with how to classicize vernacular Italian. The concern is implicit, perhaps surprisingly, in the work of Petrarch who publicly dismissed his vernacular verse as youthful folly and yet devoted significant time and energy editing his own Italian poetry, the *Canzoniere*.

Concern with vernacular prose style continued and intensified when underlying ideological issues received a powerful religious dynamic in the rise of Protestantism, which emphasized the necessity of providing ordinary people with a comprehensible translation of God's Word. The work of later humanists, such as John Calvin, showed a clear desire to wed vernacular writing with the religious concerns and demands of the Protestant church.

Dante's work, particularly the *Divine Comedy*, exemplified the appropriation of a classical genre, "epic," and a classical figure, Virgil (as guide). Dante's works also united classical culture with contemporary Catholic beliefs and church concerns. In its critique of the papacy, the *Divine Comedy* anticipated many of the polemical concerns of later Renaissance figures. Indeed, criticism of the church was not an uncommon feature of other Renaissance writing, as witnessed by the works of Boccaccio (1313–75) and Erasmus. Additionally, we can see the impact on Dante of Thomistic thinking, reminding us once again that the medieval period and the

> *One of the hallmarks of Renaissance literature from the earliest period was the desire to write in the vernacular and to do so in a manner that was self-conscious about literary style.*

Renaissance were not chronologically discrete eras but are terms that can be applied to different aspects of the same period.

The works of Dante, Boccaccio, and Petrarch also came to form something of a canon within the Renaissance itself. By the fifteenth and sixteenth century, the works of these men occupied a central place in the literary canon, although Dante was the least significant of the three, with more than 160 editions of the works of Petrarch and even more of Boccaccio produced. Thus, the authority of the classical period was supplemented by the elevation to classical status of more-recent works that then served as models for those who wished to follow. This canonical status for particular figures and works made them a unifying factor in the Renaissance, as epitomized by the appropriation of Dante's *Divine Comedy* by a variety of figures of cultural significance. Intellectuals lectured on it; politicians quoted it to give their speeches an air of sophistication; Galileo spent time calculating the precise dimensions of the Inferno; and artists such as Domenico da Michelino, Giorgio Vasari, Michelangelo, and others depicted scenes from the work—a tradition that continued beyond the Renaissance, as the work of the English mystic and poet William Blake indicates. [53]

The classical heritage, so crucial to the ideological validation of Renaissance Italy's political and social ambitions, was an absolute gold mine for the visual artists of the era. Sponsored in many instances by precisely the people who prospered financially and socially from the rising commerce of the Italian states, the artists inevitably reflected something of the cultural values that legitimized their sponsors in their work. Thus, classical scenes abound in Renaissance painting, and, more subtly, we find a classical aesthetic system that placed a premium on proportion and measurement as characteristics of painting and sculpture. Many biblical scenes depicted by great Renaissance figures such as Donatello and Michelangelo reflect the humanist desire to bring classical values to bear on contemporary work. Indeed, when we look at statues such as Michelangelo's *David* and those of Donatello, we see a definite shift from medieval aesthetics to something self-consciously akin to the aesthetics that governed classical pagan sculpture. Additionally, the rise of individual portraiture as a major genre of artistic production resulted in no small measure from the system of financing artistic production, whereby wealthy individuals and families provided money for many of the commissions.[54]

Again, as with humanism and Renaissance literary culture, these aesthetic values originated in the particular context of the Italian Renaissance

> *The classical heritage, so crucial to the ideological validation of Renaissance Italy's political and social ambitions, was an absolute gold mine for the visual artists of the era.*

---

53. On the reception of Dante in the Renaissance, see Deborah Parker, *Commentary and Ideology: Dante in the Renaissance* (Durham, NC: Duke University Press, 1993). A good translation of *The Divine Comedy* is that by C. H. Sisson (Oxford: Oxford University Press, 1998).

54. On Renaissance artists, see the contemporary account in Giorgio Vasari, *Lives of the Artists*, ed. and trans. Julia Conway Bondanella and Peter E. Bondanella (Oxford: Oxford University Press, 1998); also Frederick Hartt, *History of Italian Renaissance Art*, 4th ed., rev. David G. Wilkins (London: Thames and Hudson, 1994).

but soon spread north of the Alps. Thus, by the early sixteenth century, Albrecht Dürer produced artwork that reflected the aesthetic values of the Italians and wrote handbooks on proportion and measurement in which he introduced his audience to what was happening in Rome and similar places.[55]

Conclusion

The underlying assumption of this chapter is that the Renaissance did not represent a unified set of universal values that one might characterize as a worldview in the singular. Instead, the term *Renaissance* embraces various cultural responses offered by the European cultural elite to the social and economic disruption initiated at the dawn of the modern era by the rising power of the commercial classes and the consequent realignment of political power in its wake. This means that the relationship of Renaissance thought to medieval antecedents and to Reformation, Protestant and Catholic, is complex and cannot be dealt with as if it were a discrete force in simple antithesis to these others. In literature, the emphasis on classical languages and textual criticism fed directly into the production of editions of the early fathers and, more importantly, of Scripture itself, paving the way for the kind of theological critique we find in the Reformers. Furthermore, the emphasis on the vernacular and on the development of linguistically localized literature finds its parallels in the rise of Bible translations and, perhaps just as importantly, in the use of German, English, and French to disseminate new religious ideas. Additionally, as humanism initially was driven to find historical precedent for the political situations developing in Italy in the thirteenth century and beyond, so this use of history spread throughout Europe. This caused scholars to return to the original sources, and in religious circles—whether Protestant or Catholic—it intensified the need to lay claim to the Christian past as a way of legitimating one's stand in the present.

Perhaps the connections between Protestant Reformation and Renaissance philosophy, science, and politics are not as obvious as those with humanism, but again we might note that each of these spheres challenged old patterns of authority. Philosophy and science, while continuing to use the Aristotelian corpus as the basic point of departure, used that corpus to undermine old Aristotelian certainties, particularly in the scientific realm, where the peripatetic empirical epistemology ultimately proved lethal to the old peripatetic cosmology and physics. In politics, the rise of commerce, city-states, and nations demanded a theoretical framework for

> *In literature, the emphasis on classical languages and textual criticism fed directly into the production of editions of the early fathers and, more importantly, of Scripture itself, paving the way for the kind of theological critique we find in the Reformers.*

55. For examples of Dürer's work, see T. D. Barlow, *Woodcuts of Albrecht Dürer* (London: Penguin, 1948); on his life see Erwin Panofsky, *The Life and Art of Albrecht Dürer* (Princeton, NJ: Princeton University Press, 1971); also Jane Campbell Hutchinson, *Albrecht Dürer: A Biography* (Princeton, NJ: Princeton University Press, 1990).

local action. Savonarola, Machiavelli, and Marsilio of Padua, along with the streams of thought that followed in their wake, provided ideological models for this new situation—models that undermined old notions of how European Christendom should be governed. If the Reformers did not pick up all of their thinking, it still served a useful purpose in breaking up the established patterns.

As for art, the classical aesthetics of the Renaissance transformed painting and sculpture. More significantly, the related erosion in the minds of certain Renaissance thinkers between the sacred and the secular realism, fuelled by the satires of men such as Boccaccio and the religious attitude of Savonarola, ultimately bore fruit in the development of an aesthetic of the everyday life. We see this adumbrated in the rapid development of individual portraiture, which resulted from the rise of wealthy families and patrons in the Renaissance world.

Dante

In short, the Renaissance did not offer a single worldview as an alternative to the Middle Ages or the Reformation. Indeed, the very nature of the Renaissance calls into question the usefulness of using *worldview* when addressing the complex ways in which human beings interact with their environment. The various strands that make up the movement indicate the complexity of the relationship between the Renaissance and the Middle Ages, on the one hand, and the Reformation, on the other. This reminds us, once again, to avoid reducing any cultural movement to the level of a simplistic sound bite. It also serves as a warning against attempting to understand a worldview simply as the product of a disembodied thought process, rather than as the result of a cultural moment that combines intellectual and material factors in a complicated ideological web of intellectual, economic, and political factors.

For Further Reading

Copenhaver, Brian P., and Charles B. Schmitt. *Renaissance Philosophy.* Oxford: Oxford University Press, 1992.

Kraye, Jill. *The Cambridge Companion to Renaissance Humanism.* Cambridge: Cambridge University Press, 1996.

Kristeller, Paul Oskar. *Renaissance Thought: The Classic, Scholastic, and Humanist Strains.* New York: Harper and Row, 1961.

Oberman, Heiko A. *The Roots of Anti-Semitism in the Age of Renaissance and Reformation*, trans. James I. Porter. Philadelphia: Fortress, 1984.

Oberman, Heiko A., and Thomas A. Brady. *Itinerarium Italicum: The Profile of the Italian Renaissance in the Mirror of Its European Transformations.* Leiden: Brill, 1975.

Rummel, Erika. *The Humanist-Scholastic Debate in the Renaissance and Reformation.* Cambridge: Cambridge University Press, 1995.

Schmitt, Charles B. *Aristotle and The Renaissance.* Cambridge: Cambridge University Press, 1983.

> "*The various strands that make up the movement indicate the complexity of the relationship between the Renaissance and the Middle Ages, on the one hand, and the Reformation, on the other. This reminds us, once again, to avoid reducing any cultural movement to the level of a simplistic sound bite.*

Schmitt, Charles B., Quentin Skinner, Eckhard Kessler, and Jill Kraye, eds., *The Cambridge History of Renaissance Philosophy*. Cambridge: Cambridge University Press, 1991.

Seigel, Jerrold E., *Rhetoric and Philosophy in Renaissance Humanism: The Union of Eloquence and Wisdom, Petrarch to Valla*. Princeton, NJ: Princeton University Press, 1968.

Skinner, Quentin. *The Foundations of Modern Political Thought*, 2 vols. Cambridge: Cambridge University Press, 1978. (Esp. vol. 1.)

For Further Discussion

1. What are some difficulties entailed in articulating a Renaissance worldview?

2. Why does Trueman call Petrarch "a true intellectual pioneer"?

3. How does the phrase *ad fontes* capture the spirit of humanism and illustrate the importance of classical studies to Renaissance thinkers?

4. How did Christianity benefit from the rise of humanist studies?

5. How does Erasmus epitomize the popular phrase "Renaissance man"? Evaluate his contributions in *The Praise of Folly* and *Handbook of the Christian Soldier*.

6. Several times I have argued that humanism was more of a cultural attitude than a set of dogma. Evaluate that claim.

7. Why was the humanist technique of *loci communes* of such revolutionary significance?

8. How would you compare/contrast the medieval and Renaissance usages of Aristotelianism?

9. How does continuity and discontinuity with the past figure prominently in Renaissance thought? Are such perspectives still apparent today?

10. I have argued that Renaissance philosophy was eclectic. What do you consider the advantages and disadvantages of eclecticism in a person's worldview?

11. Read Galileo's *Letter to the Grand Duchess of Tuscany* at the link cited. Which of my interpretations of Galileo seems more likely?

12. How do the passages cited from Machiavelli's *The Prince* reflect a

secularization of the traditional understanding of virtue?

13. How are the major themes of the Renaissance manifest in Renaissance literature and art?

14. Though the Renaissance may not have manifested a singular worldview, how did its various figures adapt the classical past and portend the rise of modernity?

7

The Reformation as a Revolution in Worldview

Scott Amos

The Reformation[1] in the sixteenth century was many faceted.[2] Social convulsions produced popular uprisings including the Peasant Revolt in Germany and the Pilgrimage of Grace in England. Western powers established colonies that spanned the globe, taking the first auspicious steps toward European world domination that endured some 450 years. New industries and the influx of precious metals from the Spanish Empire's New World colonies resulted in an economic boom that ensured the increasing influence and wealth of the middle class. Discoveries and inventions in science and technology initiated the "Age of Science" that would come fully into its own in the succeeding century. Politically, the titanic struggles between the Hapsburgs of Spain and the Holy Roman Empire, on the one hand, and the Valois of France, on the other, signaled the rise of the nation-states. Moreover, with the coming of the Turks to the very walls of Vienna, Europe was threatened with invasion in a manner it had not faced since the early Middle Ages.

For the purposes of this essay, the Reformation represented a religious upheaval and, therefore, a revolution in worldview.[3] If one turns to

> *The Reformation represented a religious upheaval and, therefore, a revolution in worldview. If one turns to contemporary historiography regarding this signally important period, it would be easy to lose sight of this fact, since the period is more commonly referred to as Early Modern Europe.*

---

1. I would like to express my gratitude to W. Andrew Hoffecker for inviting me to contribute to the present volume and my indebtedness to his earlier work, *Building a Christian Worldview*, 2 vols. (Phillipsburg, NJ: Presbyterian and Reformed, 1986, 1988), especially his essay and that by Gary Scott Smith, which have informed much that I have written below in terms of content and structure.

2. The complexity of the period is well presented in Thomas A. Brady Jr., Heiko A. Oberman, and James D. Tracy, eds., *Handbook of European History, 1400–1600*, 2 vols. (Grand Rapids: William B. Eerdmans, 1994).

3. Two excellent studies of the theological character of the period are Steven Ozment, *The Age of Reform, 1250–1550: An Intellectual and Religious History of Late Medieval and*

contemporary historiography regarding this signally important period, it would be easy to lose sight of this fact, since the period is more commonly referred to as Early Modern Europe.[4] Without denying the value of contemporary scholarship and the obvious fact that the Reformation brought social, economic, and political developments of the first magnitude, what struck many at the time was its character as a religious revolution. In significant parts of Europe, the religious teachings of Protestant Reformers brought irrevocable change; and for many who accepted these teachings, the transformation involved a shift in worldview as well. If for no other reason than the density and rapidity of change, sixteenth-century Europe experienced a transformation in worldview that was more nearly a revolution in the conventional sense of the term than perhaps almost any other comparable period in history.

With respect to worldview issues, the Reformation was a religious revolution whose leading figures expressed an intensely theocentric perspective in their writings. The Reformers juxtaposed the power, majesty, and holiness of God with human weakness and sinfulness. Thus, they emphatically opposed the more decidedly anthropocentric orientation of the Renaissance, with its highly optimistic view of human ability—"Man is the measure of all things." Though the contrast with the medieval outlook was less stark, the Reformers nevertheless rejected the medieval synthesis[5] of the human and the divine in its balance of reason and revelation. Although the medieval synthesis was still formally theocentric, it was (as the Reformers perceived) a compromised theocentricity that tended, in some respects, towards a more anthropocentric understanding of the world.[6]

The theocentric orientation of the Reformers inclined them to look first to God's revelation for direction in all of life. For all but a radical fringe, this meant looking to the Bible. The Reformers' common focus on the Bible enables us to speak of a "Reformation worldview," for apart from this emphasis no other significant commonality existed among the myriad of parties

> *The Reformation was a religious revolution whose leading figures expressed an intensely theocentric perspective in their writings. The Reformers juxtaposed the power, majesty, and holiness of God with human weakness and sinfulness.*

Reformation Europe (New Haven, CT: Yale University Press, 1980), and Jaroslav Pelikan, *The Christian Tradition: A History of the Development of Doctrine*, Volume 4: *Reformation of Church and Dogma (1300–1700)* (Chicago: University of Chicago Press, 1984), 126–385. A good, balanced history of the period to 1559 is Lewis W. Spitz, *The Protestant Reformation, 1517–1559* (New York: Harper & Row, 1985).

4.   A survey of history courses offered at many colleges and universities confirms this is a common designation. On the one hand, it permits the inclusion of the Renaissance and Reformation under a common name, and on the other hand, it tends to minimize, if not elide, the religious character of the age. Cf. Hans J. Hillerbrand, "Was There a Reformation in the Sixteenth Century?" *Church History* 72:3 (September 2003), 525–52.

5.   The medieval synthesis is the synthesis of faith and reason, or more pointedly, biblical revelation and Greek philosophy, supremely expressed in the work of Thomas Aquinas.

6.   Examples of a "compromised" theocentricity (at least as the Reformers would see it) would be the recourse medieval theologians made to the philosophy of Aristotle as a starting point for theology, and a greater reliance on natural theology and confidence in human reason. Consider, for instance, the sharp comments of Luther in the course of his disputation on scholastic theology.

Reformation Wall, Geneva: Guillaume Farel, Jean Calvin, Theodore Beza, and John Knox

and individuals who made up the Reformation. The centrality of the Bible pervaded the spectrum of Reformation opinion and decisively shaped the Reformers' conviction that all aspects of life have a religious dimension. Whether one looks to the Lutherans, the Reformed, the Anabaptists, or even (to a lesser degree) the Catholics, the Reformation, regarded collectively, bore witness to a concerted effort to make the Bible authoritative for all of life in a manner not seen since the early church. A broad spectrum of Christians became self-conscious in applying Scripture's teaching to all of life in a way that resulted in a "worldview." In this regard, pride of place belongs to the Reformed "wing" of the Reformation. Certainly, the Lutherans, especially in the person of Martin Luther, developed a worldview based on the Bible. Indeed, especially in matters of faith, Luther clearly recognized the antithesis between the Bible and the heritage of the classical world. The Anabaptists also developed a distinctive understanding of the world that involved a decisive break with the recent past and the world around them and a concerted effort to apply the Bible to all areas of life. Yet in terms of developing a fully elaborated Christian view of culture, the political order, and the relationship between church and state, the work of John Calvin and other Reformed Protestants demonstrated the broadest application of a biblical worldview.

This chapter will selectively discuss and explore key elements of the revolution in worldview that took place during the Reformation. Lutherans are best represented by Martin Luther, whose Reformational role is so significant that it will receive the majority of our attention. Anabaptists, who are too diverse to be represented by one person, will be examined in terms of an early confessional statement—the Schleitheim Confession—that presents their distinctive beliefs. Reformed Christians are best represented by John Calvin. In each case, the principal issues we will address are epistemology, theology, and anthropology—all key worldview components. Additionally, we will consider how the Reformation worldviews influenced culture, especially in the areas of church and society. Then, we will consider the result of Reformation worldviews collectively in the arts and literature. Finally, we will address the extent to which a shift in worldview occurred in the Catholic Reformation.

The Background of the Reformation

The intellectual factors that led to the Reformation form the substance of heated historiographical debate, one that we will not join here.[7] However, the starting point for discussing the Reformation as a revolution

---

7. For instance, see: Heiko A. Oberman, *Forerunners of the Reformation: The Shape of Late Medieval Thought* (Philadelphia: Fortress Press, 1966); Steven E. Ozment, *Age of Reform* and *The Reformation in the Cities: The Appeal of Protestantism to Sixteenth-Century Germany and Switzerland* (New Haven, CT: Yale University Press, 1975); and Alister McGrath, *The Intellectual Origins of the European Reformation* (Oxford: Blackwell, 1987).

in worldview must be its leaders' intensive focus on the Bible. This focus was a dramatic departure from the church's practice in the immediately preceding centuries. It stemmed from a growing dissatisfaction among the elites and the wider populace (especially in the cities) with the current Christian doctrine and practice. This dissatisfaction stemmed from two key developments of the High Middle Ages: the attempt to synthesize Greek philosophy and biblical teaching and the attempt to supplement the authority of the Bible with philosophical teaching—a supplementing that in some ways became a supplanting.

The recovery of a substantial part of Greek philosophy, particularly the works of Aristotle, and the synthesis of these works with biblical thought constituted a supreme intellectual achievement of the Middle Ages.[8] No one figures more prominently in this effort than Thomas Aquinas (1225–74), whose magnum opus, *Summa Theologiae,* epitomized medieval scholasticism.[9] Aquinas attempted to reconcile the tensions that were perceived to exist between Greek and biblical worldviews. Because of his fundamental conviction that all truth was God's truth, Aquinas believed such a synthesis was possible and that even pagans such as Aristotle understood truth to a significant degree. Aquinas believed that where Aristotle erred, he could be corrected from Scripture, and where rational speculation alone could not penetrate divine things, Scripture could supply the lack.

By the later Middle Ages, it was clear that efforts to synthesize disparate elements in Greek and biblical perspectives created severe tensions in scholastic thought. New philosophical movements, such as the nominalism of William of Ockham (following paths marked out by John Duns Scotus), challenged Thomas's synthesis of reason and revelation. The seeds of the intellectual conflict of the later Middle Ages were sown in the synthesis that Aquinas attempted.[10]

Additionally, a growing number of scholars in the later fifteenth and early sixteenth centuries realized the Bible had lost its unique authoritative position in theology and in thinking about the Christian life and worldview issues. Medieval theologians believed the Bible was central to everything they did[11]; each of them would have thought he was doing nothing more than interpreting and applying the Bible's teaching. But, from the twelfth century on, there was a division between studying the Bible and

> *A broad spectrum of Christians became self-conscious in applying Scripture's teaching to all of life in a way that resulted in a "worldview." In this regard, pride of place belongs to the Reformed "wing" of the Reformation.*

> *By the later Middle Ages, it was clear that efforts to synthesize disparate elements in Greek and biblical perspectives created severe tensions in scholastic thought. ... The seeds of the intellectual conflict of the later Middle Ages were sown in the synthesis that Aquinas attempted.*

8.   See: David Knowles, *The Evolution of Medieval Thought* (New York: Vintage, 1962), 185–92; and Marcia L. Colish, *Medieval Foundations of the Western Intellectual Tradition, 400–1400* (New Haven, CT: Yale University Press, 1997), 265–301.

9.   See Peter Leithart's chapter above in the present volume.

10.   See Ozment, *The Age of Reform*, 22–72.

11.   The two volumes of G. R. Evans make this clear: *The Language and Logic of the Bible: The Earlier Middle Ages* (Cambridge: Cambridge University Press, 1984); *The Language and Logic of the Bible: The Road to Reformation* (Cambridge: Cambridge University Press, 1985).

the study of theology as an academic discipline.[12] Initially, the latter developed on the basis of biblical exposition and involved grappling with difficult hermeneutical questions. Gradually, however, analyzing and resolving these questions became an end in itself. Theology's focus shifted from the Bible to the disputed questions, leading to a literary genre called "question literature."[13]

The most significant works in this genre were Peter Lombard's *Sentences* and Thomas Aquinas's *Summa Theologiae*. Along with the Bible, Lombard's *Sentences* became the central text for teaching theology in the Middle Ages.[14] As scholars developed this approach to sacred studies, they made greater recourse to writings other than the Bible to answer questions that originally arose from biblical study. Theology became more speculative as the questions led to more subtle issues generated not by the Bible but by Greek philosophy. Theology became significantly more "profound" at the expense of becoming increasingly speculative and removed from the biblical text, from the church's life, and from the lives of Christians. A quick survey of the works of leading theologians of the later Middle Ages, such as John Duns Scotus, William Ockham, and Gabriel Biel, reveals that none of these men wrote commentaries nor was their theological teaching based directly on the text of Scripture. Therefore, despite their intent to use the Bible to develop theology, systematic speculation based on reason replaced close attention to the biblical text.

Immediately prior to the Reformation, Renaissance biblical humanists in northern Europe issued a strong critique of the medieval synthesis and resulting diminution of the Bible in theology and the Christian life.[15] Like their secular counterparts, who were predominant in Italy, the biblical humanists called for a return to the sources of antiquity (summed up in the slogan: "*Ad fontes*"—"*Back to the sources!*"). For biblical humanists, this meant the sources of *Christian* antiquity—the Bible in its original languages (Hebrew and Greek) and the writings of the church fathers (Latin and Greek), especially Augustine, but also Jerome, Ambrose, and Chrysostom.

> *Immediately prior to the Reformation, Renaissance biblical humanists in northern Europe issued a strong critique of the medieval synthesis and resulting diminution of the Bible in theology and the Christian life. [They] called for a return to the sources of antiquity.*

12.   In addition to the two volumes of Evans, see also M.-D. Chenu, *Nature, Man, and Society in the Twelfth Century: Essays on New Theological Perspectives in the Latin West*, ed. and trans. Jerome Taylor and Lester K. Little (Chicago: University of Chicago Press, 1968; repr. Toronto: University of Toronto Press, 1997), 146.

13.   Ibid., 295–96.

14.   Marcia L. Colish, *Peter Lombard*, 2 vols. (Leiden: Brill, 1994); for the broader intellectual context of the twelfth century, Marcia L. Colish, *Medieval Foundations of the Western Intellectual Tradition* (New Haven, CT: Yale University Press), 274–88.

15.   A very good survey of the Renaissance, with attention to the Northern Renaissance as well, is Charles G. Nauert, *Humanism and the Culture of Renaissance Europe* (Cambridge: Cambridge University Press, 1995). Excellent on the tensions between humanists and scholastics is Erika Rummel, *The Humanist-Scholastic Debate in the Renaissance and Reformation* (Cambridge, MA: Harvard University Press, 1994), on which I have drawn for the present essay with respect to both Reformers.

The greatest and most influential of the biblical humanists was Erasmus of Rotterdam.[16] Erasmus differed substantially with the Reformers—especially Luther—on many fundamental issues. For instance, he had a much more positive view of human nature. Additionally, Erasmus came to regret being considered an intellectual patron by many Reformers. Nevertheless, Erasmus's famous *Novum Instrumentum* (1516), a critical edition of the Greek New Testament accompanied by a fresh Latin translation and critical annotations, was a material contribution to the Reformation. Erasmus also strongly advocated returning to a biblically centered and practically oriented theology. He expressly criticized scholastic tendencies to construct intellectual systems that appealed only to rational speculation. In both respects, he inspired first-generation Reformers (particularly those who would become important in the Reformed tradition) to devote themselves to intensive Bible study and to develop a biblically grounded and rooted theology.

Martin Luther

Of the Reformation's many causes, Martin Luther (1483–1546)[17] and his answer to the question "What must I do to be saved?" are the greatest of all. Ironically, Luther, who was more responsible for the dissolution of the medieval synthesis than anyone else, was a product of the very system he repudiated[18]; and throughout his career, he continued to exhibit characteristics of his scholastic training. For a time, Luther's positions appeared to resonate with the concerns of biblical humanists including Erasmus, but there were fundamental differences between them; agreements were more accidental and apparent than intentional and real.

Luther's radical departure from medieval thought resulted from his work in exegeting Scripture, not in "doing theology." Luther never created a theological system. Instead, as a university professor of the Bible, he developed a way of thinking theologically that made the interpretation and appli-

> *Luther's radical departure from medieval thought resulted from his work in exegeting Scripture, not in "doing theology." Luther never created a theological system. . . . He developed a way of thinking theologically that made the interpretation and application of biblical truth the foundation of his life's work.*

16. Two excellent works on Erasmus are Cornelis Augustijn, *Erasmus: His Life, Works, and Influence*, trans. J. C. Grayson (Toronto: Toronto University Press, 1991); and James McConica, *Erasmus* (Oxford: Oxford University Press, 1991). Augustijn also provides the context of biblical humanism that was so important for Erasmus.

17. The literature on Luther is enormous. An exhaustive biographical study is found in the three-volume biography by Martin Brecht, translated by James L. Schaaf: *Martin Luther: His Road to Reformation, 1483–1521*; *Martin Luther: Shaping and Defining the Reformation, 1521–1532*; and *Martin Luther: The Preservation of the Church, 1532–1546* (Philadelphia: Fortress Press, 1985, 1990, 1993, respectively). The classic one-volume study is Roland H. Bainton, *Here I Stand: A Life of Martin Luther* (Nashville: Abingdon Press, 1950). Of more recent vintage is James Kittleson, *Luther the Reformer: The Story of the Man and His Career* (Minneapolis: Augsburg, 1986). Finally, a helpful sketch of Luther, and of Calvin as well, can be found in Timothy George, *Theology of the Reformers* (Nashville: Broadman Press, 1988).

18. See the first volume of Brecht's biography, cited above, for exhaustive detail.

cation of biblical truth the foundation of his life's work.[19] Lecturing as well as preaching on Scripture were the substance of his daily life throughout his career. In the course of lecturing on the Bible between 1512 and 1521, Luther hammered out the fundamentals of his critique of the medieval synthesis and articulated his "Reformation discoveries." The "progress" he made towards the Diet of Worms[20] and his dramatic confrontation with the secular and ecclesiastical powers of his day should be understood in terms of his lectures on Scripture: Genesis (1512), Psalms (1513–15), Romans (1515–16), Galatians (1516–17), Hebrews (1517–18), and Psalms again (1518–21). Among other writings, Luther's intensive study of the Bible resulted in works written for a wide audience, especially his three "Reformation Treatises" of 1520: *An Appeal to the Ruling Class*, *The Babylonian Captivity of the Church* (or *The Pagan Servitude of the Church*), and *The Freedom of a Christian*.[21] Although strictly speaking these works were not expositional, they were firmly grounded in biblical interpretation; they were the practical fruit of Luther's years of studying and expounding the Bible.

Luther's insistence on the authority of Scripture did not mean he rejected all teaching from the Christian past. Although fully conscious of having made a sharp break with scholastic practice in teaching of theology, Luther deeply valued the teachings of the fathers, especially Augustine. Yet, Luther called upon the fathers, including Augustine, only insofar as they grounded their teaching in the Bible.

> Now if anyone of the saintly fathers can show that his interpretation is based on Scripture, and if Scripture proves that this is the way it should be interpreted, then the interpretation is right. If this is not the case, I must not believe him.[22]

Thus, Luther allowed a place for the role of tradition alongside Scripture, but clearly he stressed the priority of the latter.[23]

Hence, the fundamental point for understanding Luther and the Reformation as a whole with respect to worldview is the first of three Latin slogans frequently used to characterize Luther's "Reformation" teaching: *sola Scriptura* ("Scripture alone"), the so-called "Scripture principle." Luther's conviction regarding the centrality of Scripture for Christians'

Martin Luther

19. The best recent survey of Luther's theology is Bernhard Lohse, *Martin Luther's Theology: Its Historical and Systematic Development*, trans. and ed. Roy A. Harrisville (Minneapolis: Fortress Press, 1999).

20. The phrasing of this sentence echoes the title of Gordon Rupp's book, *Luther's Progress to the Diet of Worms* (New York: Harper Torchbooks, 1964).

21. All three can be found in John Dillenberger, ed., *Martin Luther: Selections from His Writings* (New York: Anchor Books, 1961).

22. Luther, "Sermons on the Second Epistle of St. Peter," trans. Martin H. Bertram in *Luther's Works*, vol. 30, ed. Jaroslav Pelikan (St. Louis: Concordia, 1967), 166, quoted in George, *Theology of the Reformers*, 82.

23. Luther's rejection of medieval practice did not entail jettisoning tradition—his view was not *nuda Scriptura*, Scripture without any reference to historical exposition and interpretation of biblical truth in the past.

lives came to concrete expression in his translation of the Bible into German. Although Luther did not write a treatise on the doctrine of Scripture, his radical return to Scripture as the source of and fundamental authority for life and doctrine informed everything he wrote. As such, *sola Scriptura* lies at the root of Luther's epistemology, theology, and anthropology—the key elements of a worldview—and it forms the foundation for the wider implications of this worldview for the church and society.

Epistemology

To the central epistemological question "How do we know?" the Middle Ages answered "through reason and revelation." Aristotle's philosophy provided the authority for reason, and Scripture supplied the basis for revelation. Luther became a theologian within this framework, but as he became immersed in biblical studies in the 1510s, he repudiated the primary recourse to reason.

Indeed, Luther's study of *theology* provided the context for his most radical statements about epistemology. Luther vehemently rejected the centrality of the Aristotelian corpus—specifically Aristotelian dialectic and its categories—as preeminent in the realm of knowledge. Luther rejected Aristotle primarily because of the exalted place he and human reason had been accorded in scholastic theology, but this does not obscure the fact that Luther took a dim view of the Stagirite.[24]

> It is a wrong thing to say that a man cannot become a theologian without Aristotle (against the generally accepted opinion). The truth is that a man cannot become a theologian unless he becomes one without Aristotle. In short, compared with the study of theology, the whole of Aristotle is as darkness is to the light (against the scholastic theologians).[25]

Luther directed these remarks at contemporaries who esteemed Aristotle and his method as the means of doing systematic theology.

Rather than beginning theological studies with Aristotle's writings, Luther argued vigorously for the primacy of Scripture in our effort to understand God, since God has revealed himself in Scripture. All theological knowledge should derive from God's revelation, not from unaided human reasoning. Nevertheless, Luther retained a place for reason in theology, as shown most clearly in his famous declaration at the Diet of Worms on April 18, 1521.

> Unless I am convinced by the testimony of the Scriptures or by clear reason, for I do not trust either in the pope or councils alone, since it is well known that they have often erred and contradicted themselves, I am bound by the Scriptures I

> *Luther's insistence on the authority of Scripture did not mean he rejected all teaching from the Christian past. . . . Luther deeply valued the teachings of the fathers, especially Augustine. Yet, Luther called upon the fathers . . . only insofar as they grounded their teaching in the Bible.*

> *Sola Scriptura lies at the root of Luther's epistemology, theology, and anthropology—the key elements of a worldview—and it forms the foundation for the wider implications of this worldview for the church and society.*

24. Aristotle is sometimes referred to by this term because he was born in Stagira.
25. Luther, *Disputation Against Scholastic Theology*, theses 43, 44, and 50, in *Luther: Early Theological Works*, ed. and trans. James Atkinson (Philadelphia: Westminster Press, 1962), 269–70.

have quoted and my conscience is captive to the Word of God. I cannot and I will not retract anything, since it is neither safe nor right to go against conscience. I cannot do otherwise, here I stand, may God help me. Amen.[26]

Notice, however, that Luther's conscience ultimately was bound by Scripture, not reason. According to Luther, reason's place is ministerial, serving Scripture, not magisterial, lording it over Scripture. Although Luther's Catholic opponents maintained the same position in theory, Luther's vigorous insistence on Scripture's primacy struck at the root of their *practice* of the medieval synthesis.

Luther's advocacy of Scripture's primacy as the basis for knowledge had profound consequences for his epistemology and, especially, for his theology.

> In temporal affairs and those which have to do with men, the rational man is self-sufficient . . . : here he needs no other light than reason's. Therefore, God does not teach us in the Scriptures how to build houses, make clothing, marry, wage war, navigate, and the like. For here the light of nature is sufficient.[27]

Regarding day-to-day matters, Luther was conventional and complacent about reason's role in the development of knowledge.

Theology and Anthropology

Luther's epistemological elevation of Scripture to a place of primacy constituted a revolution in the practice of theology. Instead of relying on Aristotelian philosophy to develop theology, Luther relied on the teaching of Scripture. Luther repudiated the speculative way scholastic theology treated God as a concept—the First Mover or the Necessary Being, two categories taken from Aristotelian philosophy. Luther believed speaking of God in this fashion made him impersonal and utterly remote, resulting in a view of God radically opposed to the way Scripture presents the God and Father of Jesus Christ, the God who sent his Son to die on the cross.[28]

Similarly, Luther developed his revolutionary view of salvation from an intensive study of Scripture. His study of Paul's letters, especially Romans, resulted in the doctrines encapsulated in two other Reformation slogans: *sola fide* and *sola gratia* ("by faith alone" and "by grace alone"). Together, these phrases answered how one can be justified before God—"what must I do to be saved?" Luther's answer overturned the medieval understanding of salvation, which emphasized the role of works in salvation. The crucial text for Luther was Romans 1:17. Toward the end of his life, Luther described

> *Luther developed his revolutionary view of salvation from an intensive study of Scripture. His study of Paul's letters, especially Romans, resulted in the doctrines encapsulated in two other Reformation slogans: **sola fide** and **sola gratia** ("by faith alone" and "by grace alone").*

---

26. As quoted in Ozment, *Age of Reform*, 245.
27. From the Postil for Epiphany, on Isaiah 60:1–6, quoted in B. A. Gerrish, "Luther's Belief in Reason," excerpted in *Luther: A Profile*, ed. H. G. Koenigsberger (New York: Hill and Wang, 1973), 198.
28. George, *Theology of the Reformers*, 59.

the moment he understood this text (the date of which is much debated by historians) and reflected on the events that led to his break with Rome.

> At last, by the mercy of God, meditating day and night, I gave heed to the context of the words, namely, "In it the righteousness of God is revealed, as it is written, 'He who through faith is righteous shall live.'" There I began to understand that the righteousness of God is that by which the righteous lives by a gift of God, namely by faith. And this is the meaning: the righteousness of God is revealed by the gospel, namely, the passive righteousness with which merciful God justifies us by faith, as it is written, "He who through faith is righteous shall live." Here I felt that I was altogether born again and had entered paradise itself through open gates.[29]

As adumbrated here and fully developed in later writings (most winningly and concisely in *The Freedom of a Christian*[30]), Christians are saved not on the basis of any meritorious works (a teaching prevalent in one form or another in the medieval church) but solely through faith in Christ, who gave his life on the cross as an atoning sacrifice for the sins of those who believe (the gospel to which Luther refers). Through faith, believers receive the righteousness of Christ, imputed to them by the Father, and on this basis their sins are forgiven. Finally, the act of faith is through grace alone; it is a gift from God.

Closely connected with this renewed biblical view of salvation, Luther recovered a biblical (and Augustinian) understanding of anthropology. As is well known, Augustine had a low view of human ability in the aftermath of the fall. He maintained that the power of sin pervaded human nature so thoroughly that individuals are unable to secure God's favor, a view articulated most clearly in his controversy with Pelagius.[31] Although medieval theologians held Augustine in high esteem and formally repudiated Pelagius's teaching, a form of semi-Pelagianism flourished in the later Middle Ages, obscuring the biblical and Augustinian understanding of the power of sin. The starting point of this development appeared in Thomas Aquinas (though it had begun to develop before him), who believed that through good works performed while in a state of grace a person could cooperate in securing salvation. Thus this teaching implied a more optimistic understanding of human nature than Augustine's. Without denying the necessity of God's grace for salvation, late scholastic theologians believed an individual could earn "semi-merit," which God was obligated to reward with meritorious, efficacious grace. This notion developed around the phrase: *facientibus quod in se est Deus non denegat gratiam*, "God will not deny grace to those who do what lies within them."[32]

Christians are saved not on the basis of any meritorious works . . . but solely through faith in Christ. . . . Through faith, believers receive the righteousness of Christ, imputed to them by the Father, and on this basis their sins are forgiven. Finally, the act of faith is through grace alone; it is a gift from God.

---

29. Quoted from Luther's preface to his Latin writings, as printed in Dillenberger, ed., *Martin Luther: Selections*, ed. Dillenberger, 11.

30. Printed in Ibid., 42–85.

31. In this, I have drawn upon Ozment, *Age of Reform*, 22–41, and 233–34; see also Oberman, *Forerunners of the Reformation*, 123–41.

32. Oberman, *Forerunners of the Reformation*, 129. The concept could be expressed in our day by the slogan, "Do your best, and God will do the rest," a phrase that is more col-

In thesis sixteen of the Heidelberg disputation in April 1518, Luther categorically rejected such a position: "If a man thinks he will come to a state of grace by doing 'what in him lies,' he merely piles one sin upon another and is doubly sinful."[33] Luther contended that late medieval teaching on this point denied the biblical teaching of the power of sin, assumed far too optimistic a view of human nature, and distorted the proper understanding regarding salvation. Again, the shift in Luther's thinking resulted from his close attention to the teaching of Scripture, particularly Paul's letter to the Romans. In an excursus on Romans 5:4 in the course of his 1515–16 lectures, Luther identified original sin as the fundamental problem of human nature.

> Due to original sin, our nature is so curved in upon itself at the deepest levels that it not only bends the best gifts of God toward itself in order to enjoy them (as the moralists and hypocrites make evident), nay, rather, "uses" God in order to obtain them, but it does not even know that, in this wicked, twisted, crooked way, it seeks everything, including God, only for itself.[34]

Luther displayed an overwhelming sense of sin's power in his writings and an understanding of how it enslaved those whom it holds captive. His understanding of sin as intensive and extensive contributed in no small way to the vibrancy of his recovery of Paul's teaching on justification, grace, and faith through which believers are liberated from the power of sin. It also provided the premises for his magisterial repudiation of Erasmus's challenge to Pauline anthropology.

From the time of Luther's emergence as an opponent of the Catholic Church, conservatives pressured Erasmus to enjoin the German reformer in debate (in part because there was a suspicion that he had sympathies for Luther). After several years of temporizing, Erasmus finally entered the lists against Luther in September 1524 with the publication of *A Diatribe on the Freedom of the Will*.[35] In essence, Erasmus argued that since Scripture was not clear on the subject (a point that infuriated Luther, who maintained the perspicuity of Scripture), reason and experience must decide the issue. Erasmus argued that it is self-evident that humans make choices, and because they are commanded in Scripture to *choose* between good and evil, it follows that they *must* be able to do so. Thus, the will, though damaged by the fall, remains free to choose or reject the grace necessary for salva-

> *Luther displayed an overwhelming sense of sin's power in his writings and an understanding of how it enslaved those whom it holds captive. His understanding of sin as intensive and extensive contributed in no small way to the vibrancy of his recovery of Paul's teaching.*

---

loquial than one would find in scholastic discourse, but that is reminiscent of what Johann Tetzel, the indulgence-seller whose actions drove Luther to post his ninety-five theses and "start" the Reformation, might have used.

33.   Luther, *Disputation Held at Heidelberg, April 26, 1518*, in *Luther: Early Theological Works*, 276–307, here 277.

34.   Luther, *Lectures on Romans*, ed. and trans. Wilhelm Pauck (Philadelphia: Westminster Press, 1961), 159.

35.   Erasmus, *On the Freedom of the Will, a Diatribe or Discourse*, in *Luther and Erasmus: Free Will and Salvation*, trans. and ed. E. Gordon Rupp and Philip S. Watson (Philadelphia: Westminster Press, 1969), 35–97.

tion. In short, Erasmus argued that obligation entails ability, that "ought" implies "can."

Luther responded in December 1525 with his treatise *The Bondage of the Will*,[36] a thorough and scathing critique of Erasmus that provides further evidence of the revolution in worldview Luther wrought—in this instance the difference between the Reformation and the Renaissance, as much as between the former and the medieval synthesis. To a degree, Luther's view of the human will parallels what he said of reason: regarding mundane affairs unrelated to moral and religious issues, Luther agreed the human will is operative and free to choose, just as reason suffices for knowledge in mundane matters.

> Free choice is allowed to man only with respect to what is beneath him and not what is above him. That is to say, a man should know that with regard to his faculties and possessions, he has the right to use, to do, or to leave undone, according to his own free choice, though even this is controlled by the free choice of God alone, who acts in whatever way he pleases.[37]

Erasmus

However, regarding religion, the human will left to itself is not free but is in bondage—caught in a cosmic struggle between God and Satan, between good and evil.

> On the other hand, in relation to God, or in matters pertaining to salvation or damnation, a man has no free choice, but is a captive, subject and slave to either the will of God or the will of Satan.[38]

Luther cited Scripture to respond to the many texts that Erasmus had urged in support of his position. He also clearly reflected the influence of Augustine in describing the will as caught between God and Satan. In fact, Luther used a simile employed by Augustine to clarify this point.

> Thus the human will is placed between the two [God and Satan] like a beast of burden. If God rides it, it wills and goes where God wills . . . . If Satan rides it, it wills and goes where Satan wills; nor can it choose to run to either of the two riders or to seek him out, but the riders themselves contend for the possession and control of it.[39]

Above all, Luther was concerned in *The Bondage of the Will* to establish the absolute necessity of the grace of God in salvation, including the necessity of grace to enable the individual to have faith. Therefore, Luther emphasized the sinfulness of humans apart from the grace of God.

> "*Above all, Luther was concerned in The Bondage of the Will to establish the absolute necessity of the grace of God in salvation, including the necessity of grace to enable the individual to have faith. Therefore, Luther emphasized the sinfulness of humans apart from the grace of God.*

36. Luther, *On the Bondage of the Will*, in Rupp and Watson, *Luther and Erasmus*, 101–334.

37. Ibid., 143.

38. Ibid.

39. Ibid., 140.

217

When a man is without the Spirit of God, he does not do evil against his will, as if he were taken by the scruff of the neck and forced to it . . . but he does it of his own accord and with a ready will. . . . Free choice without the grace of God is not free at all, but immutably the captive and slave of evil, since it cannot of itself turn to the good.[40]

The human will by nature was utterly incapable of choosing between good and evil, to accept the grace necessary for salvation or to reject it. In short, Luther argued that obligation does not entail ability, that "ought" does not imply "can."

Because humans by nature are evil, and because of original sin, they willingly choose the evil they do; only through the grace of God are humans able to choose the good in matters of faith. Luther's teaching reprised Augustinian and, above all, biblical anthropology, and firmly rejected the trajectory of late medieval thought, as well as the thought of the Renaissance.

The Church and Society

One practical and immediate consequence of Luther's biblical worldview involved the church. Luther had no intention of "founding" a new church. Instead, he sought to reform the existing church into which he had been born and of which he believed himself to be a continuing member. Two of his "Reformation Treatises" reveal important aspects of his thinking on the church. Luther's understanding of the church was radical because he insisted that Scripture serves as the foundation of the church and is the guarantor of its authority, instead of affirming that the church guaranteed Scripture's authority, as the Roman Church maintained. Once again, the primacy of the Bible undergirded Luther's doctrine.

In *An Appeal to the Ruling Class*,[41] Luther directly assaulted the institutional church's claims that it was a realm unto itself. In this work, Luther called on the German nobles to reform the church, since it so clearly refused to reform itself. Luther identified and assaulted the three "walls" the church had erected to defend itself against any attempts by outsiders to intrude into its affairs. He denied any distinction between clergy and laity (the first "wall")—a distinction that had developed in the Middle Ages to make the clergy supreme within the church.[42] Luther countered with his doctrine of the "priesthood of all believers," asserting on the basis of Scripture (1 Peter 2:9) that *all* believers are priests, having only one supreme high priest, Jesus Christ. All Christians have direct access to Christ; they do not need an intermediary class to intercede for them. Priesthood involves

> *The human will by nature was utterly incapable of choosing between good and evil, to accept the grace necessary for salvation or to reject it. In short, Luther argued that obligation does not entail ability, that "ought" does not imply "can."*

---

40. Ibid., 139, 141.

41. Luther, *An Appeal to the Ruling Class of German Nationality as to the Amelioration of the State of Christendom*, as printed in *Martin Luther: Selections*, 403–85.

42. Ibid., 407–12.

service to others, and each believer in this sense serves as priest to other believers. No one is a Christian alone. Luther combined the legitimacy of the individual believer with the fact that the church also is a communion, indeed a community, of saints, that is, the body of all believers whether lay or ordained to a specific office. With Augustine, Luther maintained that the visible church is a mixed body, including believers and unbelievers, a point on which Luther and Calvin agreed against the Anabaptists.

Second, Luther assaulted the claim that the church (especially the pope) possessed the sole, authoritative responsibility for interpreting the Bible.[43] Instead, Luther asserted the right of believers to read and interpret Scripture for themselves and not *blindly* accept the teachings of the church, thus granting to the laity (specifically the rulers) the wherewithal and authority to carry out necessary reforms. Rome's third "wall" asserted that only the pope, as head of the church, could call a council to reform the church, a claim buttressed by the first two "walls" and a claim that was the immediate object of repudiation in Luther's treatise.[44] Luther urged the nobility of Germany to call such a council. In sum, Luther challenged the church's claim to be an institutional structure set apart from and independent of the rest of society, as represented by the church's understanding of the pope and the clergy. Instead, Luther argued that the church is a body that embraces all believers, each of whom has a part to play in its work in this world.

Luther also developed his revolutionary teaching on the church in *The Pagan Servitude* (or, *Babylonian Captivity*) *of the Church*,[45] in which he conducted a devastating, Scripture-based critique of the sacraments, by reducing them from seven to three (and later two, baptism and the Lord's Supper), thus eliminating confirmation, marriage, holy orders, and extreme unction (and later, penance). This was revolutionary because the sacramental theology of the medieval church had buttressed the standing of the clergy; they alone could dispense grace through the sacraments. Luther's critique further removed the props that supported the unique status the clergy embraced to distinguish themselves from the laity.

The implications of Luther's Scripture-based shift in worldview extended into the wider cultural milieu. Luther's thinking about society rested on his distinction between two kingdoms, a kind of dualism already present in his teachings on epistemology and anthropology, in which the world is divided into a spiritual realm and a temporal realm. In both areas, Luther applied a biblical worldview more strenuously to the first kingdom than to the second. This dualism also is apparent in Luther's thinking about the state, where we see a profound and fundamental antithesis between the kingdom of God and the kingdom of the world (of the devil). Ultimately,

> *Luther assaulted the claim that the church (especially the pope) possessed the sole, authoritative responsibility for interpreting the Bible. Instead, Luther asserted the right of believers to read and interpret Scripture for themselves and not **blindly** accept the teachings of the church.*

---

43. Ibid., 412–15.
44. Ibid., 415–17.
45. Luther, *The Pagan Servitude of the Church*, printed in *Martin Luther: Selections*, 249–59.

Luther's dualism hindered applying a thoroughly biblical worldview to *all* of life.

Luther, like Calvin, was a "magisterial" Reformer; he effected his reforms in cooperation with and under the auspices of the secular authority (the magistrate), as we have seen in his *An Appeal to the Ruling Class*. In this respect, he broke with the Catholic Church, which claimed to be independent of any external authority. The "magisterial" character of Luther's Reformation reflected his understanding of the state and its relationship to the church.[46]

Luther's "two kingdoms" view of the state was based on his interpretation of Romans 13 and 1 Peter 2:13–14 and drew on Augustine's distinction between the city of God and the city of man.

> We must divide all the children of Adam into two classes; the first belong to the kingdom of God, the second to the kingdom of the world. Those belonging to the kingdom of God are all true believers in Christ and are subject to Christ. . . . All who are not Christians belong to the kingdom of the world and are under the law. . . . For this reason God has ordained two governments; the spiritual, which by the Holy Spirit under Christ makes Christians and pious people, and the secular, which restrains the unchristian wicked so that they must needs keep the peace outwardly, even against their will.[47]

Thus the state has a negative, though important, function. Luther maintained that God ordained the state for the purpose of restraining evil and maintaining order and peace. Through it, God works his will, though in a hidden way, whereas in the kingdom of God, he works in an open way. Therefore, Luther repudiated any attempt to rebel against it, even if the ruler was a tyrant, though he did maintain that a Christian should not obey a tyrant if the latter commanded something sinful. For this reason, Luther vehemently condemned the Peasant Revolt, even though he sympathized with the plight of the peasants and understood why many would wish to rise in arms against their rulers.[48]

Luther believed that Christians did not *need* the government of this world, which would in fact be unnecessary if all people were Christians, but he insisted, nevertheless, that they should submit to their rulers.[49] Furthermore, he maintained that although the state was not a Christian institution, Christians should not seek to withdraw from it, as the Anabaptists

Wartburg Castle in Eisenach where Luther translated the New Testament into German

---

46. Luther and Calvin differed on the relation between church and state, as we shall see, and the magisterial Reformers were opposed in these matters by the Anabaptists—an opposition that was reciprocated.

47. Luther, *Secular Authority: To What Extent It Should Be Obeyed*, printed in *Martin Luther: Selections*, 363–402, here 368 and 370.

48. On this dark chapter in Luther's life, see Kittleson, *Luther the Reformer*, 191–92, for a brief discussion.

49. Luther, *Secular Authority*, 373.

did, for God ordained it, and Christians can and should participate in it.[50] However, Luther did not develop a concept of the Christian magistrate.

Luther's understanding of the two kingdoms and two governments naturally leads us to consider the relationship between church and state. Luther developed his position in opposition to the Anabaptists, on the one hand, and the Roman Catholics, on the other. We already have touched on the Anabaptists with respect to their withdrawal from the world and from any association with government, and we will return to them later in this chapter. In the case of the Catholics, Luther repudiated what he held to be the pretensions of the medieval church, which had maintained—in theory at least—that the pope (and thus the church) possessed the superior authority in society, could rightly intervene in affairs of government, and had jurisdiction in secular affairs, generally. According to Luther, there must be no confusion between the two, nor should one seek superiority over the other.

> These two kingdoms must be sharply distinguished, and both be permitted to remain; the one to produce piety, and the other to bring about external peace and prevent evil deeds; neither is sufficient in the world without the other.[51]

Luther argued that God uses both institutions to achieve his ends in the world. The church guides the inner man; the state governs the outer man. Luther adamantly insisted that the two forms of government should not be confused and that the authority of the church and that of the state should remain separate. However, the two forms of government should not exist in tension but in cooperation. The church preached obedience to the state, and the state protected the church and enabled it to conduct its work.

But, in practice, Luther's language sharply distinguished between the two governments and thereby obscured their fundamental unity under God. This had the practical effect of encouraging a passivity on the part of Christians to reform the institutions of government and was a consequence of Luther's disparagement of the idea that the government of the world can be made to conform more perfectly to the government of the kingdom of Christ.[52]

In conclusion, Luther effected a substantial and radical break with the medieval synthesis of reason and revelation, on the one hand, and Scripture and philosophy, on the other. More than any single individual of the Reformation, Luther contributed to a return to Scripture as the supreme authority in theology and thus the supreme authority for our view of God and the world. And yet, as we have seen, Luther did not develop a comprehensive biblical worldview. The dualism that characterized his thought—the division of the world into spiritual and temporal, the kingdom of God

*Luther believed that Christians did not **need** the government of this world, which would in fact be unnecessary if all people were Christians, but he insisted, nevertheless, that they should submit to their rulers. . . . he maintained that although the state was not a Christian institution, Christians should not seek to withdraw from it.*

Luther's language sharply distinguished between the two governments and thereby obscured their fundamental unity under God. This had the practical effect of encouraging a passivity on the part of Christians to reform the institutions of government.

---

50. Ibid., 371.
51. Ibid.
52. Ibid.

and the kingdom of this world—precluded that. Luther tended to limit the activity and sovereignty of God to the former of these two spheres, and so, in effect if not in theory, Luther minimized the influence a comprehensive biblical worldview could have had for all of life.

The Anabaptist Tradition

Another significant Reformational era protest directed against the early sixteenth-century status quo was Anabaptism. The use of the term "Anabaptism" is purely a matter of convenience; the movement it denotes was so multifarious that it defies convenient categorization. Frequently, "Anabaptism" is used as an alternative to "the Radical Reformation," though the latter is a more accurate way to describe the phenomenon of the multiple sects that developed on the fringes of the magisterial Reformation of Luther and Calvin.[53] Among Anabaptists, Menno Simons's (1496–1561)[54] importance and influence were comparable to those of Luther and Calvin in their circles, though he lacked the authority among Anabaptists that Luther had among Lutherans and that Calvin had among the Reformed. As mentioned earlier in the chapter, we will examine the Schleitheim Confession as a benchmark of Anabaptist belief, rather than Menno Simons or any other Anabaptist individual.[55]

Anabaptists shared some of the primary concerns of all Protestants:[56] they used the language of faith in Christ and his work; they rejected the conception of the church held by the Catholics, including the concept of a separate priesthood that acted as mediators between believers and God; and, above all, they held to the concept of *sola Scriptura*. But, whereas Luther and Calvin did not believe that *sola Scriptura* excluded use of the interpretive tradition of the church, on the whole, the Anabaptists did. In other words, Anabaptists read Scripture without reference to how Christians in previous centuries had read it. Their commitment to Scripture

> "Whereas Luther and Calvin did not believe that **sola Scriptura** excluded use of the interpretive tradition of the church, on the whole, the Anabaptists did. In other words, Anabaptists read Scripture without reference to how Christians in previous centuries had read it.

53. In this essay, "Anabaptist" refers to those early Protestants whose descendants are best represented by the Mennonites and Amish but who to a certain degree also influenced Baptists and various independent churches. The authoritative work in this area is George Huntston Williams, *The Radical Reformation*, 3rd ed. (Kirksville, MO: Sixteenth Century Journal Publishers, 1992). Also important: William R. Estep, *The Anabaptist Story* (Grand Rapids: Eerdmans, 1963). A fine, brief discussion of the Anabaptists can be found in Roland H. Bainton, *The Reformation of the Sixteenth Century* (Boston: Beacon Press, 1958), to which I am indebted for the general outline below.

54. For a short life of Menno Simons, see George, *Theology of the Reformers*, 252–307.

55. *The Schleitheim Confession: Brotherly Union of a Number of Children of God Concerning Seven Articles*, in *Creeds of the Churches: A Reader in Christian Doctrine from the Bible to the Present*, rev. ed., ed. John H. Leith (Atlanta: John Knox Press, 1973), 282–92.

56. As a group the Anabaptists were less interested in theological questions than in the practical application of biblical teaching, specifically the ethics of the New Testament as found in the Sermon on the Mount. For that reason, in this section we will not address issues such as epistemology or even theology *per se*, certainly not to the extent that these are considered in other sections.

was biblicist—quite literally, the Bible alone (*nuda Scriptura*). Frequently, though not always, this raised serious doctrinal problems. For example, some groups among the Anabaptists avoided speaking of the Trinity, since the word itself is not found in the Bible. Less controversially, Anabaptist biblicism caused them to reject infant baptism, since no explicit instance of the practice appears in Scripture.[57]

The Anabaptist worldview focused primarily on their distinctive understanding of the church. The magisterial Reformers conducted a *reformation* of the *existing* church; they corrected doctrinal and practical errors and so assumed continuity between the church into which they were born and the earliest church—a continuity of the church through the centuries. The Anabaptists, however, sought a *restitution* or *restoration* of primitive, biblical Christianity; they did not see continuity in the history of the church over the ages. Therefore, their rejection of the Catholic Church as an institution was all the more radical.[58] Anabaptists sought to restore what had been lost and to do so according to a strict reading and application of the Bible. They attributed the downfall of the church to its recognition by Constantine, its eventual establishment as a state church, and, especially, the identification of church and society as one and the same.[59]

By enumerating the genuine signs of the true church, the Schleitheim Confession of 1527 established the parameters of what the Anabaptists wished to restore. Their teaching on the church includes several elements. First, the church consists only of heartfelt believers who have experienced conversion, or the new birth. The Anabaptists restricted church membership to adult believers who had undergone "believer's baptism."

> Baptism shall be given to all those who have learned repentance and amendment of life, and who *believe* truly that their sins are taken away by Christ, and to all those who walk in the resurrection of Jesus Christ.[60]

Thus membership in an Anabaptist congregation was voluntary, and the movement affirmed the autonomy of each congregation.

Second, the church is completely separate from the world around it, constituting what is termed a "gathered" society.

> A separation shall be made from the evil and from the wickedness which the devil planted in the world; in this manner, simply that we shall not have fellowship with them [the wicked] and not run with them in the multitude of their abominations.[61]

The Anabaptists, however, sought a restitution or restoration of primitive, biblical Christianity; they did not see continuity in the history of the church over the ages. . . . Anabaptists sought to restore what had been lost and to do so according to a strict reading and application of the Bible.

57. See the *Schleitheim Confession*, Article One, 284.
58. Ibid., Article Four, 285–87.
59. Ibid., Introduction and Article Four in particular, 282–84, 285–87.
60. Ibid., Article One, 284. Emphasis mine. Cf. also Article 3: "All who wish to break one bread in remembrance of the broken body of Christ, and all who wish to drink of one drink as a remembrance of the shed blood of Christ, shall be united beforehand by baptism in one body of Christ which is the church of God whose Head is Christ."
61. Ibid., Article Four, 285.

Everything which is not united with our God and Christ cannot be other than an abomination which we should shun and flee from. By this is meant all popish and antipopish works and church services, meetings and church attendance, drinking houses, civic affairs, the commitments [made in] unbelief and other things of that kind, which are . . . carried on in flat contradiction to the command of God.[62]

Thus the church is a community of saints who together strive for perfection in this life, following the ethic of the Sermon on the Mount. According to the Anabaptists, the sermon taught an ethic that was to be taken literally and was not restricted to monks, as the Catholic Church taught.

Anabaptists espoused a negative view of the larger culture—"the world," which they saw as hopelessly corrupt. Therefore they rejected the belief that church and society can be coterminous, unless society was to consist of the converted and no other.

For truly all creatures are in but two classes, good and bad, believing and unbelieving, darkness and light, the world and those who [have come] out of the world, God's temple and idols, Christ and Belial; and none can have part with the other.[63]

He [the Lord] further admonishes us to withdraw from Babylon and the earthly Egypt that we may not be partakers of the pain and suffering which the Lord will bring upon them.[64]

Although pessimistic that the larger culture could in any way experience redemption, Anabaptists expressed optimism about the gathered church,[65] as seen in their assumption that members of the true church could achieve moral perfection in this life.

Anabaptists recognized that some among their number would fall into serious sin. Church discipline, including the ban—that is, excommunication from the fellowship of the gathered society—was the means by which congregations as a whole were to be kept pure.

The ban shall be employed with all those who have given themselves to the Lord, to walk in His commandments, and with all those who are baptized into the one body of Christ and who are called brethren or sisters, and yet who slip sometimes and fall into error and sin, being inadvertently overtaken.[66]

Thomas Muentzer, one of the founders of the Anabaptist movement

However, the consequences of the ban went no further than exclusion. Unlike medieval Catholicism, the ban did not include capital punishment or any other form of civil penalty, as did the magisterial Reformation. The Anabaptists did not identify church and society, as did the Catholics and, to an extent, the magisterial Reformers. For opponents of Anabaptism, excom-

62. Ibid., Article Four, 286.
63. Ibid., Article Four, 286.
64. Ibid., Article Four, 286.
65. Bainton, *Reformation of the Sixteenth Century*, 96.
66. *Schleitheim Confession*, Article Two, 284–85.

munication not only meant being placed outside the pale of church but also of society, since the two were different expressions of the same reality.

Third, Anabaptists maintained a complete separation of church and state, as well as church and society, because they believed God established the church for the saved and the state for sinners.

> The sword is ordained of God outside the perfection of Christ. It punishes and puts to death the wicked, and guards and protects the good.[67]

Anabaptists believed government is necessary for the world but that it plays no positive part for the church.[68] Anabaptists denied any overlap of the two. This worked in both directions. On the one hand, Anabaptists believed that magistrates should not take part in the affairs of the true church. Anabaptists had no conception of a Christian magistrate;[69] they viewed involvement of secular officials in the church as one of the evil consequences of Constantine's conversion. Because the Anabaptists believed in the complete separation of church and state, the state could not coerce belief; the Anabaptists strongly favored religious liberty and freedom of conscience.[70]

On the other hand, according to Anabaptist belief, just as believers were to be separate from the world, so they should not take part in affairs of state.[71] Because the state existed for sinners, it was to be administered by sinners alone. Anabaptists also were strict pacifists; they refused to take up the sword for self-defense or in service of the state.[72] They willingly accepted persecution for all these beliefs and believed their persecution confirmed their claim to be the restored New Testament church.

The differences between the worldviews of the Anabaptists and the magisterial Reformers should be evident. In the light of Luther's teaching about the distinction between the kingdom of God and the kingdom of this world, one might think his position and that of the Anabaptists on this topic are linked. However, it is more accurate to speak of similarities, rather than any sort of linkage. As magisterial Reformers, Luther and Calvin adamantly opposed the Anabaptists on these points.[73] By the same token, Anabaptists were equally opposed to the magisterial Reformation. Because of their strong emphasis on ethics, Anabaptists criticized the major Reformers for leading a Reformation that did not result in changed lives among their followers. In the opinion of Anabaptists, believers in Wittenberg, Geneva, and Zurich did not live lives that were noticeably different from how they lived prior to the Reformation. The magisterial Reformers responded that Anabaptists were guilty of

> *According to Anabaptist belief, just as believers were to be separate from the world, so they should not take part in affairs of state. Because the state existed for sinners, it was to be administered by sinners alone.*

> *Because of their strong emphasis on ethics, Anabaptists criticized the major Reformers for leading a Reformation that did not result in changed lives among their followers.*

---

67. Ibid., Article Six, 287.
68. We can see a resonance on this point between the Anabaptists and Luther.
69. Ibid., Article Six, 289.
70. Bainton, *Reformation of the Sixteenth Century*, 99.
71. *Schleitheim Confession*, Article Six, 288–89.
72. Ibid., Article Six, 288.
73. See Bainton, *Reformation of the Sixteenth Century*, 96–97, for a brief discussion of the relationship between magisterial Reformers and the Anabaptists.

resorting to monastic notions of perfection and of winning salvation by works and not faith. The Anabaptists replied that they understood works to be an exhibition of the fruits of salvation, not the cause or ground of it.

The Anabaptist understanding of the church and its relationship to society and, more specifically, to the state troubled the magisterial Reformers more than any other Anabaptist distinctive. Here the difference between Anabaptist and Reformed worldviews is most pronounced. Although the magisterial Reformers maintained the separation of church and state in their functions, they believed church and society should remain united, even if society consisted of many unbelievers. Following Augustine, Calvin and Luther recognized that the visible church is a mixed body, consisting of believers and unbelievers, and that to maintain the church should consist only of saints was to aspire to something that is impossible and not taught in Scripture. Although the magisterial Reformers maintained a distinction of church and state, they rejected the *absolute* separation of the two that the Anabaptists maintained. As the generic term "magisterial" suggests, Calvin and Luther believed church and state should cooperate, because God instituted both for the benefit of people in this life. Cooperation between the two institutions contributes stability and peace to the world and demonstrates that both are instruments of the same God and Lord. Therefore, Anabaptist teachings were seen as a major threat to the basic structures of society. This was confirmed when extreme Anabaptists took over the city of Münster in 1535, with chaotic and anarchic consequences.[74]

Anabaptists were as committed as Luther to the authority of the Bible for the Christian life. They contributed to the broader movement of the Reformation, helping to foster its decisive break with the medieval outlook. Because the Anabaptist movement primarily was led by lay people, not scholars and theologians like Luther and Calvin, and focused on local congregations, it helped diffuse a biblical outlook more widely still. Nevertheless, profound differences separated Luther and the Anabaptists, even in areas of apparent similarity—for example, the division of the world into two realms, where sharp distinctions were drawn between church and state. The sectarian practices of the Anabaptists exacerbated these distinctions, and their withdrawal from the world restricted the power of a biblical worldview to their own gathered societies.

*Although the magisterial Reformers maintained a distinction of church and state, they rejected the **absolute** separation of the two that the Anabaptists maintained. ... Calvin and Luther believed church and state should cooperate, because God instituted both for the benefit of people in this life.*

John Calvin and the Reformed Tradition

John Calvin (1509–64) was a second-generation Reformer who built on the achievements of his predecessors.[75] In that sense, Calvin was less

74. On the debacle and its background, see Williams, *Radical Reformation*, 553–88.

75. The best one-volume study of Calvin's thought remains François Wendel, *Calvin: Origins and Development of His Religious Thought*, trans. Philip Mairet (New York: Harper and Row, 1963). Also useful is Ronald S. Wallace, *Calvin, Geneva and the Reformation: A Study of*

revolutionary in his break with the medieval synthesis than first-generation Reformers like Luther; he was more of a consolidator and refiner of what already had been achieved. Nevertheless, Calvin made momentous contributions in his own right, most significantly by formulating a comprehensive, all-pervasive worldview.

Although Calvin owed a theological debt to Luther, Calvin's doctrinal formulations followed a different trajectory from Luther's, because Calvin applied the fundamental Reformation principle *sola Scriptura* more consistently. Although Calvin did not initiate the Reformed tradition, which had many significant contributors—Ulrich Zwingli (1484–1531), Martin Bucer (1491–1551), Heinrich Bullinger (1504–75), and Theodore Beza (1519–1605), to name a few—he so thoroughly put his stamp on the movement that scholars refer to it as the Calvinist tradition. Calvin's teaching decisively shaped the doctrine and worldview of the Reformed tradition. Despite tensions that arose between the Lutheran and Reformed traditions, especially early on, and although Calvin entered into disputes with a number of Luther's later followers, Calvin expressed deep respect for Luther.[76]

Although Calvin's early education prepared him for a career in the church, by training he was a lawyer, and by inclination he was an aspiring humanist scholar, as evidenced by his first literary production, a scholarly commentary on Seneca's *De Clementia* (1532). Thus, Calvin brought to the Reformation refined argumentative skills and advanced abilities in literary and textual analysis. Consequently, Calvin emerged as one of the greatest expositors of and commentators on the Bible. He focused intensely on studying the Bible, not primarily as history or literature but as the true Word of God that instructs its readers how to think about God and how to live. Calvin's reputation rests primarily on his *Institutes of the Christian Religion*,[77] a handbook of Christian doctrine noted for its clarity and organization. When Calvin produced his first edition in 1536, he intended it to be a manual for students who wished to study the Bible. Hence, it was ancillary to the main task for all aspiring theologians—the study and application of the Bible. Although he expanded the work over the years until it reached final form in Latin in 1559, Calvin retained in the preface the declaration found in the first edition that the work was to aid in the study of Scripture.[78] Calvin did not intend the *Institutes* to be studied for their own sake or independently from Scripture.[79]

> *Calvin's doctrinal formulations followed a different trajectory from Luther's, because Calvin applied the fundamental Reformation principle **sola Scriptura** more consistently.... Calvin's teaching decisively shaped the doctrine and worldview of the Reformed tradition.*

Calvin as Social Worker, Churchman, Pastor and Theologian (Grand Rapids: Baker, 1988). For Calvin's life, see T. H. L. Parker, *John Calvin: A Biography* (Philadelphia: The Westminster Press, 1975), and the sketch by George, *Theology of the Reformers*, 163–251, both of which I follow.

76. Parker, *John Calvin*, 137, where Parker quotes from a letter by Calvin to Bullinger regarding Luther.

77. John Calvin, *Institutes of the Christian Religion*, 2 vols., ed. John T. McNeill, trans. Ford Lewis Battles (Philadelphia: The Westminster Press, 1960).

78. Ibid., "John Calvin to the Reader," 4–5.

79. When one looks at the literature on Calvin, his commentaries on virtually every book of the Bible, combined with his published sermons, far outweigh all other works that

Epistemology

At the beginning of the *Institutes*, Calvin asks what constitutes true wisdom. This is a question about epistemology and theology. Thus, at the outset Calvin sets the theocentric tone that permeates the rest of his work and his worldview. This demonstrates the difference between his approach to these questions and that of the medieval synthesis. Calvin's treatment of these questions lacked Luther's polemical cast: Calvin did not single out Aristotle, and he was not particularly concerned to repudiate reason as a source of authority for theology.

From the outset of his work, Calvin saw God's self-revelation as central to knowing God. Calvin did not begin his discussion with the question of God's being or with arguments for God's existence—unlike Aquinas's inductive, empirical method—but instead began by investigating how we know God and ourselves (and by extension, the world around us), which together constitute true wisdom.

> Nearly all the wisdom we possess, that is to say, true and sound wisdom, consists of two parts: the knowledge of God and of ourselves. But, while joined by many bonds, which one precedes and brings forth the other is not easy to discern. In the first place, no one can look upon himself without immediately turning his thoughts to the contemplation of God, in whom he "lives and moves" . . . indeed, our very being is nothing but subsistence in the one God. . . . Again, it is certain that man never achieves a clear knowledge of himself unless he has first looked upon God's face, and then descends from contemplating him to scrutinize himself.[80]

Calvin does not demonstrate God's existence; he presupposes it on the basis of God's revelation. Knowledge of God is intuitive: we all have a *sensus divinitatis*, "an awareness of divinity,"[81] and within each of us is implanted a *semen religionis*, "a seed of religion" that serves as the subjective aspect of our knowledge.[82] Indeed, all creation proclaims the knowledge of God, because what God has made reveals him, thus making this an objective knowledge.[83] Therefore, we are surrounded and pervaded by God's testimony to himself; it is inescapable. Nevertheless, as Calvin points out, we suppress the truth that we intuitively and objectively know; we distort it and refuse to acknowledge God and give him the worship he is due as our Creator. Suppressing the truth about God is a consequence of original and actual sin, and because of sin, we cannot know God by unaided natural reason.

John Calvin

---

came from his pen. Here the volumes of T. H. L. Parker are invaluable: *Calvin's Old Testament Commentaries* (Edinburgh: T. & T. Clark, 1986); *Calvin's New Testament Commentaries*, 2nd ed. (Louisville, KY: Westminster/John Knox Press, 1993); *Calvin's Preaching* (Louisville, KY: Westminster/John Knox Press, 1992).

80. *Institutes*, I.1.1, I.1.2.

81. Ibid., I.3.1.

82. Ibid., I.4.1.

83. The question of what Calvin taught about natural revelation (and whether this meant he allowed for a natural theology) has been a hotly disputed topic that we shall not address.

At this point, Scripture's role in knowing God and ourselves is crucially important, because only on the basis of Scripture are we able truly to know God and ourselves, especially as we are led by the work of the Holy Spirit to trust Scripture's testimony. Thus, in practical terms, the foundation for the fullness of our knowledge is the Bible.

In likening the effect of sin to an impairment of vision, Calvin argues that the Bible serves as spectacles to overcome the lack of clarity in our perception of the world around us.

> Just as old or bleary-eyed men and those with weak vision, if you thrust before them a most beautiful volume, even if they recognize it to be some sort of writing, yet can scarcely construe two words, but with the aid of spectacles will begin to read distinctly; so Scripture, gathering up the otherwise confused knowledge of God in our minds, having dispersed our dullness, clearly shows us the true God.[84]

Calvin addressed objections to such a reliance on Scripture as the source of our knowledge of God by saying:

> The testimony of the Spirit is more excellent than all reason. For as God alone is a fit witness of himself in his Word, so also the Word will not find acceptance in men's hearts before it is sealed by the inward testimony of the Spirit. The same Spirit, therefore, who has spoken through the mouths of the prophets must penetrate into our hearts to persuade us that they faithfully proclaimed what had been divinely commanded.[85]

Thus, Calvin underscored God's sovereignty, and his words echo Luther's regarding reason's role in matters of faith. Neither Calvin nor Luther rejected reason out of hand, but clearly they subordinated it to God's testimony to himself. Reason's limits in matters of faith become more evident in Calvin's chiding of those who relied on external proofs of the veracity of the Bible: "those who wish to prove to unbelievers that Scripture is the Word of God are acting foolishly, for only by faith can this be known."[86]

To sum up, we do not achieve true knowledge of God through autonomous human reason, because sin renders reason incapable of attaining such knowledge. Only by virtue of the Spirit's work and Scripture's testimony can we acquire such knowledge, and only the faithful believers do so.

Furthermore, our knowledge about God is both objective and subjective. We come to know God objectively through Scripture and creation. Because of the *sensus divinitatis,* our knowledge of God also is subjective and personal; we come to know him as our Creator, Savior, and Lord. Our knowledge of God consists of a dynamic interrelationship of the objective and subjective, which in turn requires a response from us: worship and a

Calvin saw God's self-revelation as central to knowing God. Calvin did not begin his discussion with the question of God's being or with arguments for God's existence . . . but instead began by investigating how we know God and ourselves.

Only on the basis of Scripture are we able truly to know God and ourselves, especially as we are led by the work of the Holy Spirit to trust Scripture's testimony. Thus, in practical terms, the foundation for the fullness of our knowledge is the Bible.

84. *Institutes*, I.6.1.
85. Ibid., I.7.4.
86. Ibid., I.8.13.

life of piety, which Calvin defines as a combination of reverence for and love of God—the prerequisite for a true knowledge of God.[87]

Theology and Anthropology

If one phrase encapsulates Calvin's worldview, it is "the sovereignty of God."[88] We saw this in our discussion of Calvin's epistemology; it is characteristic of all his thinking and teaching. Because of this emphasis, Calvin's teaching and the Reformed tradition have the most consistently biblical worldview.

Calvin's emphasis on God's sovereignty led him to insist that our concern should not be with what God is in and of himself but with what kind of God he is and what our business with God is.

> What is God? Men who pose this question are merely toying with idle speculations. It is more important for us to know of what sort he is and what is consistent with his nature.[89]

Therefore, Calvin's break with the medieval synthesis was as decisive as Luther's and is best characterized as a return to biblical, as opposed to Greek, epistemological categories for understanding God. God is personal, and he is known as a person, not as a Prime Mover or First Cause.

As a personal God, he is active in his creation as the Creator and the Sustainer of all that he has made.[90] God's personal, continual, and active involvement in his creation to sustain, govern, and guide it is part of Calvin's doctrine of providence. God's sovereignty comes to concrete expression as he works providentially in his world. Therefore, with respect to God's sovereignty, creation cannot be divided into temporal and spiritual realms—the kingdom of God and the kingdom of this world; God is Lord of all. His care permeates all that he has made. Although God is not removed from his creation, in no way does Calvin confuse God with his creation. God is distinct from it, though involved in it.

Therefore, for Calvin, God's sovereignty is not an abstract concept; it is vividly concrete, and it undergirds Calvin's understanding and perception of the world and our place in it. Because of this, God's sovereignty has immense practical value for Christians and for our worldview. Because of God's providential control of all creation, Christians can live confidently and engage in their everyday activities to God's glory.

> "As a personal God, he is active in his creation as the Creator and the Sustainer of all that he has made. God's personal, continual, and active involvement in his creation to sustain, govern, and guide it is part of Calvin's doctrine of providence.

87. Ibid., I.2.1 and 2.

88. There has been much debate about whether there is a so-called central dogma in Calvin's teaching, a debate that need not concern us here. In any case, our concern is with the matter of worldviews, and thus the assertion of the crucial importance of God's sovereignty should not be taken to indicate that it is *the* central dogma of Calvin's theology.

89. *Institutes*, I.2.2.

90. Calvin identifies a twofold knowledge of God: God as Creator, and God as Redeemer; see *Institutes*, I.2.1. It is with the former that we are now concerned. We will return to the latter momentarily.

Therefore the Christian heart, since it has been thoroughly persuaded that all things happen by God's plan, and that nothing takes place by chance, will ever look to him as the principal cause of things. . . . Then the heart will not doubt that God's singular providence keeps watch to preserve it, and will not suffer anything to happen but what may turn out to its good and salvation. But since God's dealings are first with man, then with the remaining creatures, the heart will have assurance that God's providence rules over both.[91]

Calvin's use of providence precludes understanding God as an abstract, remote being, removed from creation. He is the God we come to know in the Old and New Testaments, not the one we learn about in Greek philosophy. Calvin's understanding reflects the character of the Reformation in general as a *biblical* revolution in theology and worldview.

Calvin's application of biblical and Augustinian categories also dominated his understanding of anthropology, which sets the stage for his teaching about the sovereignty of God in salvation. Calvin's emphasis on the corruption wrought by original sin reiterated the teaching of Luther, Augustine, and ultimately the apostle Paul.

> We are so vitiated and perverted in every part of our nature that by this great corruption we stand justly condemned and convicted before God, to whom nothing is acceptable but righteousness, innocence, and purity.[92]

The consequences of original sin pervade the whole of our existence from one day to the next.

> This perversity never ceases in us, but continually bears new fruits—the works of the flesh that we have already described—just as a burning furnace gives forth flame and sparks, or water ceaselessly bubbles up from a spring. . . . for our nature is not only destitute of good, but so fertile and fruitful of every evil that it cannot be idle. . . . Whatever is in man, from the understanding to the will, from the soul even to the flesh, has been defiled.[93]

We already have observed the consequence of this regarding the knowledge of God. Here Calvin asserted that the corruption is so complete that we can neither will nor do anything pleasing to him apart from his grace. Indeed, the only remedy is a new nature, produced by the sovereign regeneration of the Holy Spirit.

Calvin's particular contribution to understanding salvation was his pronounced emphasis on human inability and the fact that redemption is entirely the work of God's sovereign, electing grace.[94] Calvin made the doctrine of election central to his teaching on salvation, because it emphasizes

> *Calvin's use of providence precludes understanding God as an abstract, remote being, removed from creation. He is the God we come to know in the Old and New Testaments, not the one we learn about in Greek philosophy.*

---

91. *Institutes*, I.17.6.
92. Ibid., II.1.8.
93. Ibid., II.1.8.
94. For reasons of space, we cannot take time to discuss Calvin's doctrine of salvation. Additionally, this essay is not an analysis of doctrine *per se*. For a discussion of this subject, see Wendel, *Calvin*, 185–284.

the gracious choice of God to save those whom he would call to be his own, to be united to his Son, Jesus Christ, and to receive the Holy Spirit. In its outworking, election is therefore Trinitarian. Calvin's emphasis on election (and predestination) was not simply a logical consequence of his emphasis on God's sovereignty. Instead, above all else, it was his application of what he understood Scripture to teach. Consistently, Calvin grounded all he taught in what he understood Scripture to teach. Like Luther, Calvin maintained that we are justified by faith, not works, and that saving faith is a gift of God. If anything, however, Calvin was more intent on stressing God's electing grace and sovereignty, while at the same time emphasizing the complete inability of humans to effect or contribute to their salvation in any way.

Church and Society

As in our consideration of Luther, we turn to two particular applications of Calvin's biblical worldview: his thinking regarding the church and the relationship of church and state. In some important respects, Calvin's understanding of the church was broadly similar to Luther's. Calvin maintained that the invisible church was the true church and that the visible church was a mixed body, consisting of wheat and tares, believers and unbelievers.[95] Like Luther, Calvin maintained that all believers shared in the priesthood, in opposition to the Catholic understanding of the priesthood as a separate class unto itself, though he grounded this doctrine more firmly in the priesthood of Christ and did not frequently use the term.[96]

Calvin had a more developed doctrine of the visible church than Luther, especially its character and structure, relation to the invisible church, and how it was to be distinguished from that which was false. According to Calvin, Scripture teaches that the marks of the true church are the preaching of the Word of God and the proper celebration of the sacraments—the Lord's Supper and baptism.[97] Calvin came close to making discipline a third mark of the church, though he never did so, instead characterizing it as forming the sinews of the body, which is the church.[98]

Calvin also studied church government, seeking to discover its correct *biblical* form. Although he was not dogmatic about the matter, he believed that what we know as Presbyterian government was the proper biblical form; and, based on Scripture, he identified four offices: teacher, pastor, elder, and deacon.[99] Calvin taught that members of the church itself, not the magistrate, should control church affairs, including electing ministers, elders, and deacons,[100] who then should determine the form of worship,

Martin Bucer

95. *Institutes*, IV.1.7–8.
96. Ibid., II.15.6.
97. Ibid., IV.1.9–12.
98. Ibid., IV.12.1.
99. Ibid., IV.3.4–9.
100. Ibid., IV.3.13–15.

exercise discipline, and oversee the work of the church.[101] Calvin believed the basic unit of the church is the local congregation. This, combined with an emphasis on the importance of discipline, reflects the influence of Martin Bucer and, through him, the Anabaptists on Calvin's thinking.[102]

Nevertheless, Calvin and Bucer repudiated Anabaptist separatism and their rejection of participation in society. Calvin's understanding of the relationship of church and society are best seen in his understanding of the relationship of church and state. Like all magisterial Reformers, Calvin worked within the framework of the *corpus Christianorum*, the assumption of a close and necessary relationship of church and society—an inheritance from the Middle Ages that influenced the thinking of many Reformers. Unlike Luther, Calvin did not work within a set of dualisms—the spiritual and the temporal, the kingdom of God and the kingdom of this world. Since Calvin affirmed that God is Lord of all, no part of life or of society should be excluded from his dominion.

Unlike Luther and the Anabaptists, who affirmed a basic discontinuity between church and state, Calvin sought to bring the two institutions into congruence with each other under the principle of order. Calvin used the concept "covenant" to explain God's relationship to man, as well as the basic relationship between men. Calvin believed that politics and the willingness to establish a civil order result from man's essential nature: "there is in all men some seed of political order, which is a strong argument that no one is destitute of the light of reason concerning the government of the present life."[103] Calvin taught that God's appointed end or goal for civil government is "to cherish and protect the outward worship of God, to defend sound doctrine of piety and the position of the church, to adjust our life to the society of men, to form our social behavior to civil righteousness, to reconcile us with one another, and to promote general peace and tranquility."[104] Thus civil government existed to enforce both "tables" of God's law—those dealing with our vertical relationship with God and those dealing with our horizontal relationship with our fellow human beings.

Although the state in Calvin's teaching remains an instrument for social control, as Luther emphasized, Calvin's description has none of the pessimism that characterized other contemporary views of the state; Calvin brought secular government into conjunction with religious society. Calvin believed the state is as much the creation of God as is the church. Although they are independent, they possess a concurrent and common activity: the maintenance of order. The state exists to enforce order and punish wrongdoers, as Luther taught, but for Calvin the state has an addi-

> *Calvin also studied church government, seeking to discover its correct **biblical** form. Although he was not dogmatic about the matter, he believed that what we know as Presbyterian government was the proper biblical form.*

> *Calvin believed the basic unit of the church is the local congregation. This, combined with an emphasis on the importance of discipline, reflects the influence of Martin Bucer and, through him, the Anabaptists on Calvin's thinking.*

---

101.   Luther posited something like this as well, but only in a theory; he never advocated its application in practice.

102.   For Bucer's influence on Calvin, see Wendel's sketch in *Calvin*, 137–44.

103.   *Institutes*, II.2.13.

104.   Ibid., IV.20.2.

tional positive function: to provide the means "whereby man is educated for the duties of humanity and citizenship that must be maintained among men."[105] Unquestionably, Calvin had a high view of civil government's place in God's created order. He saw the state as the instrument by which God educated man and as the agency for man's improvement and advancement in this world.

Calvin's thinking about the relation of church and state included an additional distinctive not found in Luther or the Anabaptists: the concept of a Christian magistrate. In Book IV of his *Institutes*, Calvin included civil government, along with the church, as a "means of grace," and he discussed the role of the magistrate in this context. Calvin expressed the highest regard for the magistrate, and he viewed all leaders, kings included, as ministers (servants) of God. The calling of the magistrate, "the most sacred and honorable," derives from God himself, and the magistrate should perform as befits so noble an office.[106]

Thus, in effect, Calvin created a political or governmental counterpart to the pastorate. Magistrates were to "apply themselves with the highest diligence to prevent the freedom (whose guardians they have been appointed) from being in any respect diminished, far less be violated."[107] Calvin went so far as to say that any dereliction in this duty, either from negligence or design, would make them "traitors to their country."[108] The function of magistrates was to "execute judgment and justice," to "receive into safekeeping, to embrace, to protect, vindicate, and free the innocent." Consequently, magistrates were to "withstand the boldness of the impious, to repress their violence, to punish their misdeeds."[109] In exercising justice, a magistrate should utilize both severity and clemency with prudence, "lest by excessive severity he either harm more than heal," or alternatively "by superstitious affectation of clemency, fall into the cruelest gentleness, if he should (with a soft and dissolute kindness) abandon many to their destruction."[110] In the end, magistrates are responsible to both God and men, a point developed by Calvin in his commentary on Romans 13:4.

> Since they [magistrates] have been chosen by God and do His business, they are answerable to Him. But the ministry which God has committed to them has reference to their subjects. They have also therefore an obligation to them.[111]

> *Calvin had a high view of civil government's place in God's created order. He saw the state as the instrument by which God educated man and as the agency for man's improvement and advancement in this world.*

105. Ibid., III.19.15.

106. Ibid., IV.20.4.

107. Ibid., IV.20.8.

108. Ibid., IV.20.8. This points us to the potentially revolutionary character of Calvin's teaching regarding the right to resist tyrants. A good introduction to this subject can be found in Quentin Skinner, *The Foundations of Modern Political Thought*, vol. 2, *The Age of the Reformation* (Cambridge: Cambridge University Press, 1978), 189–348.

109. Ibid., IV.20.9.

110. Ibid., IV.20.10.

111. *The Epistles of Paul the Apostle to the Romans and to the Thessalonians*, trans. Ross Mackenzie, ed. David W. Torrance and Thomas F. Torrance (Grand Rapids: Wm. B. Eerdmans Publishing Company, 1980), 282.

Just as the arrangement between God and men, and between men themselves, is characterized by a covenantal (and, in that respect a biblical) structure, so, too, is the relationship between God and the magistrate, and between the magistrate and his people.

Calvin's contribution to a "Reformation" worldview was the most comprehensive in scope and substantial in content of any of the Reformers. As a biblical worldview, it was firmly rooted in Scripture, to which Calvin devoted his life in study and exposition; and on the basis of the witness of Scripture, Calvin consistently maintained the sovereignty of God in all areas of life, not only in matters relating to theology and the church. More than either of the other traditions we have touched upon, the Reformed tradition, following its most lucid teacher, Calvin, has maintained a profound sense of God's authority and rule over all aspects of our existence. Thus Reformed theology offers the most consistent alternative to the medieval synthesis and the modern secular worldview.

The Reformation and Culture[112]

The Reformers often are charged with having led a movement whose zeal to apply biblical principles helped destroy much surrounding culture.[113] On one level, this charge has substance: the Reformation resulted in the physical destruction of much that was aesthetically beautiful, for example, statues, stained glass, painting in the form of altar pieces, and many other objects of religious art, which was the major form of art in the preceding centuries. The rationale for much of this destruction was an application of the second commandment, the prohibition against idolatry, and thus was often consistent with an application of a biblical worldview—at least as the adherents of the Reformed tradition in the sixteenth and seventeenth centuries understood it. Indeed, iconoclastic outbreaks emerged in regions where the Reformed tradition predominated; such demonstrations occurred less frequently in Lutheran areas.

Apart from Lutheran areas that produced artists such as Lucas Cranach and Albrecht Dürer, for example, the visual arts were not a medium for expressing the Reformation worldview.[114] One might argue that since the con-

> *More than either of the other traditions we have touched upon, the Reformed tradition ... has maintained a profound sense of God's authority and rule over all aspects of our existence. Thus Reformed theology offers the most consistent alternative to the medieval synthesis and the modern secular worldview.*

---

112. Because of their brevity, remarks in this section are intended only to be suggestive. The subject requires fuller treatment than I have given it here. I have found Francis A. Schaeffer, *How Should We Then Live? The Rise and Decline of Western Thought and Culture* (Old Tappan, NJ: Fleming H. Revell, 1976), 79–100, to be helpful. Spitz's book, *The Protestant Reformation*, contains a concise discussion of the Reformation and culture, 365–83. For a detailed discussion of visual art and the Reformation with reference to Germany, see: Carl C. Christensen, *Art and the Reformation in Germany* (Athens: Ohio University Press, 1979). For the Reformed tradition and the arts, see, e.g., Charles Garside, *Zwingli and the Arts* (New Haven, CT: Yale University Press, 1966).

113. A representative judgment of the Reformation in this light can be found in Kenneth Clark, *Civilisation: A Personal View* (New York: Harper and Row, 1969), 159.

114. Spitz, *The Protestant Reformation*, 367–70.

tent of the visual arts continued to be largely religious, and since Reformed people applied the biblical worldview more consistently than did Lutherans, including a strong concern to apply the second commandment, we find visual arts continuing among Lutherans but not among the Reformed. However, this point should not be pressed beyond the level of suggestion.

On the other hand, in the areas of music and literature, there is a more substantial and broadly based artistic application of the Reformational worldview, one to which Lutherans and Reformed contributed alike. Regarding music,[115] the Reformation witnessed the genesis of two important forms of congregational singing: Lutheran hymnody and the psalmody of the Reformed tradition. Both were concrete reactions against the clerical domination of the church, where singing in worship was a clerical function. More positively put, hymnody and psalmody can be understood as attempts to involve the laity in worship as active participants, and not merely as observers. Examples of Lutherans include Martin Luther, Johann Walther, and (later) Hans Leo Hassler and Michael Praetorius. These men, and others like them, established a musical and choral tradition that would culminate in the supreme genius of Johann Sebastian Bach. Among the Reformed, Louis Bourgeois, Claude Goudimel, Clement Marot, and Theodore Beza versified and set to music the Psalms. In England, while the influence of the Reformation resulted in a minimization of visual arts, it led to a heightened emphasis on the Word and its exposition. Thus it contributed to a flowering of the literary arts (even among those who would not otherwise be described as Protestant). Two names from opposite ends of the religious spectrum are sufficient to make the point: William Shakespeare, and John Milton.[116]

The Catholic Response

What was the Catholic Church's response to the challenge of the Reformation?[117] Initially, after condemning the Protestant Reformers, some Catholics sought reconciliation, which entailed acknowledging, to some degree, the failings of the late medieval church. The Catholics who spearheaded efforts at reconciliation were Cardinal Gasparo Contarini and Georg Witzel, both of whom worked largely within the context of the Holy Roman Empire. The supreme expression of efforts at reconciliation was

> *The Reformation witnessed the genesis of two important forms of congregational singing: Lutheran hymnody and the psalmody of the Reformed tradition. Both were concrete reactions against the clerical domination of the church.*

115. Ibid., 371–72.

116. This is not to suggest that neither would have emerged without the Reformation. It is merely to observe that both wrote within a cultural context dominated by the Reformation and its emphasis on the Word.

117. In what follows, I am guided by Ozment's brief discussion in *Age of Reform*, 398–409, and Spitz, *The Protestant Reformation*, 283–316. For a recent survey of the subject, see Michael A. Mullet, *The Catholic Reformation* (London: Routledge, 1999). A still useful discussion of the Catholic Reformation is H. O. Evennett, *The Spirit of the Counter Reformation* (Cambridge: Cambridge University Press, 1968).

the Colloquy at Regensburg in 1541, where leaders of Catholicism in the empire met with mediating Reformers including Melanchthon and Bucer. An agreement of sorts was achieved on the matter of justification, but the process broke down entirely on the question of the eucharist. In any case, Luther rejected the compromise statement on justification.

After the failure of Regensburg, conservatives in the Catholic Church gathered their strength, and from 1545 to 1563, the church held the Council of Trent, a prolonged deliberation on the state of the church and how to respond to the challenge of the Reformation. The decrees that came forth from Trent were, in effect, a direct repudiation of the Reformation. They affirmed what the Reformers collectively had decried, and they strengthened much of the medieval synthesis.[118] This repudiation is clearest regarding Scripture: where the Reformers maintained the sole authority of the Bible for faith and life, Trent affirmed the equality of the Bible and tradition, as both were interpreted by "Holy Mother Church."[119] Furthermore, where the Reformers promoted the reading of the Bible by the laity and, consequently, the translation of the Bible into the common languages of Europe, Trent reaffirmed the authority of the Latin Vulgate.[120]

Albrecht Dürer

Trent also explicitly rejected the Protestant understanding of justification by faith, maintaining that faith is but the beginning of one's salvation and that salvation is not wholly the work of God—it requires human cooperation, in the form of works.[121] Furthermore, the council affirmed that believers receive grace through the sacraments as administered by the church[122] and that the Mass is a sacrifice.[123] Trent also confirmed many practices that had been subjected to criticism by the Reformers, for example, indulgences and the veneration of the saints. Finally, the council also reasserted the supreme authority of the pope,[124] and there was a resurgence of Aquinas's thought as the authoritative expression of the faith,[125] thus restoring the medieval synthesis to its former position in the church.

Conclusion

Much more could be said about the Reformation as a shift in worldview. Space has not allowed us to discuss, for example, the implications of Reformation thinking for the cultural mandate (Gen. 1:28) and how the biblical worldview was applied to the family and to economics, to name

> *The decrees that came forth from Trent were, in effect, a direct repudiation of the Reformation. They affirmed what the Reformers collectively had decried, and they strengthened much of the medieval synthesis.*

118. A text of portions of the decrees can be found in *Creeds of the Churches*, 400–439, and the Creed of the Council of Trent is found on 440–42.
119. "Decrees of the Council of Trent," in Ibid., 401–4.
120. "Decrees of the Council of Trent," in Ibid., 403.
121. "Decrees of the Council of Trent," in Ibid., 408–24.
122. "Decrees of the Council of Trent," in Ibid., 425–27.
123. "Decrees of the Council of Trent," in Ibid., 437–39.
124. *Creed of the Council of Trent*, in Ibid., 441.
125. Spitz, *The Protestant Reformation*, 285.

but a few interesting topics. In the present chapter we have focused on epistemology, theology, and anthropology, the building blocks of a biblical worldview. In these areas we best see the radical nature of the Reformation, vis à vis the medieval synthesis, and as a worldview that continues to challenge our contemporary approaches to life's issues.

The common denominator for all the Reformers was the return to the Bible as the primary, if not the only, authority for faith and practice. Consistently, we see the Reformers continually referring to the Bible, and not only in matters of theology, narrowly understood. As we have seen, there were other sources for Reformational thought; the Reformers did not discard the inheritance of the past, as some Anabaptists had done. Because various Reformers interpreted the Bible differently, it is difficult to speak of a single "Reformation" worldview. But to the extent that the Reformers shared a common focus on the Bible as their ultimate authority for faith and practice, they shared a common approach to life's questions.

What of those who listened to the preaching and teaching of the Reformers? What did they take away from it all? The realization, in a way not fully grasped by the wider populace prior to this period, of the centrality of the Bible for *their* lives—a Bible that, on account of the Reformation, was now in their hands and in their language, and that would for centuries after the Reformation be the fundamental guide for earnest believers of all confessions. In the end, perhaps this was the most revolutionary application and result of the revolution in worldview that was effected in the Reformation—that there was now a much broader segment of the body of Christ that could develop a more authentic biblical worldview, mediated by the teaching of the church, yes, but built as well upon the book they now had in their homes.

The common denominator for all the Reformers was the return to the Bible as the primary, if not the only, authority for faith and practice. Consistently, we see the Reformers continually referring to the Bible, and not only in matters of theology, narrowly understood.

For Further Reading

Calvin, John. *Institutes of the Christian Religion*. 2 vols. Edited by John T. McNeill. Translated by Ford Lewis Battles. Philadelphia: The Westminster Press, 1960.

George, Timothy. *Theology of the Reformers*. Nashville: Broadman Press, 1988.

Kittleson, James. *Luther the Reformer: The Story of the Man and His Career*. Minneapolis: Augsburg, 1986.

Lohse, Bernhard. *Martin Luther's Theology: Its Historical and Systematic Development*. Translated and edited by Roy A. Harrisville. Minneapolis: Fortress Press, 1999.

Luther, Martin. *Martin Luther: Selections from His Writings*. Edited and with an introduction by John Dillenberger. New York: Anchor Books, 1961.

McGrath, Alister. *The Intellectual Origins of the European Reformation*. Oxford: Blackwell, 1987.

McGrath, Alister E. *Reformation Thought: An Introduction.* 4th ed. Oxford: Blackwell, 1999.

Ozment, Steven. *The Age of Reform, 1250–1550: An Intellectual and Religious History of Late Medieval and Reformation Europe.* New Haven, CT: Yale University Press, 1980.

Parker, T. H. L. *John Calvin: A Biography.* Philadelphia: The Westminster Press, 1975.

Pelikan, Jaroslav. *The Christian Tradition: A History of the Development of Doctrine,* Volume 4: *Reformation of Church and Dogma (1300–1700).* Chicago: University of Chicago Press, 1984.

Spitz, Lewis W. *The Protestant Reformation, 1517–1559.* New York: Harper & Row, 1985.

Wallace, Ronald S. *Calvin, Geneva and the Reformation: A Study of Calvin as Social Worker, Churchman, Pastor and Theologian.* Grand Rapids: Baker, 1988.

Wendel, François. *Calvin: Origins and Development of His Religious Thought.* Translated by Philip Mairet. New York: Harper and Row, 1963.

Williams, George Huntston. *The Radical Reformation.* 3rd ed. Kirksville, MO: Sixteenth Century Journal Publishers, 1992.

In the end, perhaps this was the most revolutionary application and result of the revolution in worldview that was effected in the Reformation—that there was now a much broader segment of the body of Christ that could develop a more authentic biblical worldview, mediated by the teaching of the church, yes, but built as well upon the book they now had in their homes.

For Further Discussion

1. Why might one argue that the leaders of the Reformation were more theocentric in their worldview than were the leaders of medieval Christendom?

2. To what extent was Luther's thought a revolutionary break with his scholastic training, and to what extent can one discern an underlying conservatism and continuity?

3. To what extent can it be argued that, among all the Protestant movements in the sixteenth century, the Reformed tradition was the most comprehensive, consistently theocentric, and biblical revolution in worldview?

4. In what respect could the Anabaptists have argued that they were the most consistently biblical in their worldview? How would the magisterial Protestants respond to this?

5. In what way could the Reformation be understood as the most "revolutionary" of the various revolutions in worldview, at least for Christians?

8

Enlightenments and Awakenings:
The Beginning of Modern Culture Wars

W. Andrew Hoffecker

T raditional treatments of the seventeenth and eighteenth centuries used the singular "Enlightenment" as an inclusive term to describe philosophical and cultural developments in Europe and America. Summaries of this age emphasize the following: new epistemological methods in philosophy produced an "age of reason" in which autonomous methods of rationalism or empiricism replaced traditional alliances between philosophy and theology in the search for truth; rising confidence in Newtonian science provided powerful new perspectives on nature and the laws by which it operates; a new intellectually elite class, the *philosophes*, believed that reason mated with science could inaugurate an era of progress politically, economically, and socially; and new religions such as deism and Unitarianism challenged outmoded faiths of Protestantism and Catholicism.[1]

> *A new intellectually elite class, the **philosophes**, believed that reason mated with science could inaugurate an era of progress politically, economically, and socially.*

This chapter will present a different perspective in two ways.[2] First, rather than depicting a homogenous period, marked by virulent hostility to religion, we will show that the plural "Enlightenments" more appropriately

---

1. Peter Gay's two-volume work *The Enlightenment: An Interpretation* (New York: W. W. Norton & Company, 1966) remains the classic interpretation; the subtitles of the two volumes indicate his particular interpretation: "The Rise of Modern Paganism" and "The Science of Freedom." Gay's work responded to Carl Becker's claim in *The Heavenly City of the Eighteenth Century Philosophers* (1932) that the *philosophes* possessed a naïve faith in reason's autonomy and capacity to produce an earthly utopia.

2. Recent studies of the Enlightenment have spawned fresh appraisals of this era. Some venture to contend that little unanimity exists concerning the Enlightenment—its intellectual program, as well as its chronological, geographical, and social boundaries. See Dorinda Outram, *The Enlightenment* (Cambridge: Cambridge University Press, 1995).

portrays the diversity of perspectives in this period.[3] We will examine the plurality of views that developed in Britain, France, Germany, and America. What emerges are a series of Enlightenments—some radical, which attempted a total recasting of thought, and others more moderate, which sought to accommodate new ideas with traditional religion that radicals sought to replace.

Second, this chapter will juxtapose another trajectory of movements, which paralleled the Enlightenments—a series of "Awakenings": the Evangelical Awakening in Britain, Jansenism in France, Pietism in Germany, and the Great Awakening in America. Each exerted significant influence not only on prevailing religious milieus but also on the broader cultural context in which they appeared.[4] Surveys of Western civilization often consign Awakenings to sections separate from the Enlightenment. Isolating Enlightenment and religious movements into the public or "real world" of secular life and the private, inner world of "religious" life, however, ignores what should be obvious—that *both* Enlightenments and Awakenings competed for the public mind. Seeing both as worldviews, instead of qualitatively different phenomena, that is, "religious" and "secular," provides a more appropriate way of appraising them. Our procedure corrects a misconception that Enlightenments were more culturally significant. In the era we are studying, religious phenomena still carried cultural weight. Only as secular views took hold in the nineteenth and twentieth centuries did the sharp differentiation between public and private become commonplace.

Both Enlightenments and Awakenings of the early modern period manifest what has been called a "subjective turn," a decisive shift in worldview from theocentric thinking to various degrees of anthropocentrism. Differences will become evident as we examine various figures and movements in Europe and America. The movement toward human self-sufficiency is most pronounced in radical enlighteners in their espousal of autonomy as the dominant theme of modern thought. More complex is the extent to which a turn toward the subjective manifests itself in evangelical and traditional Christianity. Clearly a spectrum exists on which we may differentiate pietist Jacob Spener, Methodist John Wesley, Jansenist Blaise Pascal, and latter-day Puritan Jonathan Edwards.

> **Both** Enlightenments and Awakenings competed for the public mind. Seeing both as worldviews, instead of qualitatively different phenomena, that is, "religious" and "secular," provides a more appropriate way of appraising them.

---

3.   Henry May modified "Enlightenment" by the terms "moderate," "skeptical," "revolutionary," and "didactic." Henry May, *The Enlightenment in America* (New York: Oxford University Press, 1976).

4.   Ironically, the metaphors that both groups used to define themselves—"Enlightenment" and "Awakening"—are closely related in the imagination and proved effective in gaining adherents. Enlighteners described the past as intellectual and moral darkness from which society would be delivered, if people embraced the modern worldview offered by philosophy and science. Awakeners, on the other hand, portrayed the West as stifled by spiritual lethargy. Only dramatic religious experience, grounded in traditional Christianity, could wrench individuals and the culture from the clutches of moral and spiritual decay and infuse them with new life.

Our treatment also will validate "revolutions" as the larger theme of this book. In fact, the onset of modernity initiated the "culture wars." Although the term usually describes late twentieth-century struggles in public life, we will argue that initial skirmishes emerged far earlier as various thinkers and movements vied for intellectual and moral leadership in public life.

Enlightenment and Awakening in Britain

The Rise of Science and Rational Religion: The Transition to Deism

Francis Bacon (1561–1626) epitomized the Renaissance from the past and foreshadowed the modern age ahead.[5] Although he distinguished himself in politics, law, literature, and philosophy, his contributions in science instigated a revolution in the method and motivation for scientific work. The aphorisms in *Novum Organum* (1620) posited a new "interpretation of Nature and the Kingdom of Man." First, he proposed that modern man, "the servant and interpreter of nature," needed a method that is "altogether better and more certain" than traditional deduction, which "flies from the senses and particulars to the most general axioms." An inductive method, by contrast, "derives axioms from the senses and particulars rising by a gradual and unbroken ascent, so that it arrives at the most general axioms last of all." Bacon foresaw a new science, patient and diligent in method, steady in approach, and ready to rethink in light of new discoveries. Issuing the clarion call of Enlightenment thinkers, Bacon argued: "we must begin anew from the very foundations."[6]

Sounding like an Old Testament prophet, Bacon called for the overthrow of idols and false ideas that afflict peoples' thinking. He enumerated four idols fit for destruction: those of the Tribe, which are rooted in human nature; Idols of the Cave, which are errors due to each person's individuality, living in his own "cave" or "den" in the world; Idols of the Market-place, which arise from peoples' association with others, "the apprehension of the vulgar"; and Idols of the Theatre, which infiltrate peoples' thinking from the systems of philosophies that are nothing more than "so many stageplays, representing worlds of their own creation."

Bacon's insistence that the elimination of idols will produce a new, impartial science heralds the modern preoccupation—even obsession—

Francis Bacon

---

5. Cf. Catherine Drinker Bowen, *Francis Bacon: The Temper of a Man* (Boston: Little, Brown and Co., 1963); Anthony Quinton, *Francis Bacon* (New York: Hill and Wang, 1980); Jerry Weinberg, *Science, Faith, and Politics: Francis Bacon and the Utopian Roots of the Modern Age, A Commentary on Bacon's Advancement of Learning* (Ithaca, NY: Cornell University Press, 1985).

6. Bacon's *Novum Organum* was only a part of his *Instauratio Magna*, a great restoration of thinking that had been centuries in decay. Although historians traditionally credit Descartes with initiating "foundationalism" in philosophy, clearly Bacon harbored similar thoughts for science.

with finding the one true method by which thinkers can settle all disputes about matters of fact or truth. Just as religious idolatry requires a change of mind for genuine faith to succeed, so modern people must repent of false worldviews.[7]

Within a few years of Bacon's use of religious terminology to propagate a new science, the seminal proposal for natural, or rational, religion—deism—appeared.[8] In *De Veritate* (1624), Lord Herbert of Cherbury (1582/3–1648) proposed a radical change in religious a priori from revealed doctrine and piety to rational truth.[9] Herbert contended that principles of natural religion derive not from Scripture, confirmed by the inner testimony of the Holy Spirit, but from reason itself. An advocate of innate ideas, he enumerated five "Common Notions of Religion" as the basis for all religions: belief in the existence of a Supreme Being; this deity ought to be worshiped; virtue and piety are the proper forms of worship; sins ought to be expiated by repentance; rewards and punishments exist both in this life and the next. Because these principles are derived from reason a priori, they are universal and form the basis for a purely natural religion.

What immediately impresses the reader of *De Veritate* is the absence of prominent Christian beliefs—the incarnation, atonement, and Jesus' resurrection, as well as traditional Christian piety. Herbert did not explicitly deny doctrines that go beyond common notions, and his view of miracles is unclear.[10] However, the tone of the treatise and skepticism regarding the Trinity prefigured future unbelief. In a subsequent writing, Herbert intensified his opposition to traditional notions by directly attacking revelation and challenging biblical authority. Although some argue that Lord Herbert posed his work as an alternative to skepticism, as well as to Protestant and Catholic dogmatism, he clearly established the modus operandi for

> *Bacon's insistence that the elimination of idols will produce a new, impartial science heralds the modern preoccupation—even obsession—with finding the one true method by which thinkers can settle all disputes about matters of fact or truth.*

> *Lord Herbert of Cherbury (1582/3–1648) proposed a radical change in religious a priori from revealed doctrine and piety to rational truth. Herbert contended that principles of natural religion derive not from Scripture, confirmed by the inner testimony of the Holy Spirit, but from reason itself.*

7.   Bacon portended a new age in which inductive science opened up mastery of nature. Some interpreted Bacon as advocating the Christian worldview, by following the cultural mandate in Genesis 1:26–28 to exercise dominion over God's creation, subject to God's laws. Others saw in Bacon a much bolder anticipation of rational man becoming the great controller of nature. According to this view, Bacon synthesized the Christian view of providence with the Promethean myth that gave humans power to control nature and by experimentation to shape it according to their whims.

8.   The earliest use of "deist," dating from 1564, is by Pierre Viret, a disciple of Calvin who claimed it was used by intellectuals who believed in God but denied Jesus and Christian doctrines. They used "deist" to distinguish themselves from "atheists." Viret, like many others in the sixteenth to eighteenth centuries, rejected such contentions, blatantly calling them "atheists." Ernest Campbell Mossner, "Deism," *The Encyclopedia of Philosophy*, vol. 1, Paul Edwards, ed. (New York: Macmillan, 1966). Cf. Michael Hunter and David Wooton, eds., *Atheism from the Reformation to the Enlightenment* (Oxford: Clarendon Press, 1992), and Alan Charles Kors, *Atheism in France, 1650–1729*, vol. 1, *The Orthodox Sources of Disbelief* (Princeton, NJ: Princeton University Press, 1990). For a selection of deist writings, see Peter Gay, *Deism: An Anthology* (Princeton: Van Nostrand, 1968).

9.   Cf. John A. Butler, *Lord Herbert of Cherbury 1582–1648: An Intellectual Biography* (Lewiston, NY: Edwin Mellon Press, 1990).

10.   Ironically, Herbert claimed a sign from heaven in answer to his prayer whether to publish his treatise!

> Locke's greatest accomplishment was his summation of the English mind in the late seventeenth century. He presented religious ideas in "plain and intelligible" terms so that anyone could understand them.

deism—affirm only what common notions of reason allow, and attack elements of any religion that do not meet rational criteria.

John Locke (1632–1704), England's foremost Enlightenment thinker, added to the growing intellectual ferment. His works covered a multitude of fields: epistemology (*An Essay Concerning Human Understanding*, 1690), toleration (*Letter on Toleration*, 1689), government (*Two Treatises of Government*, 1688), and several works on religion (*The Reasonableness of Christianity*, 1695; *Paraphrase and Notes on the Epistles of St. Paul*, 1705–7; and *A Discourse on Miracles*, 1706). His synthesis reexamined the foundations in each field of thought and attempted to unite the emerging fields of science and rationalism with prevailing Christian thinking.

Philosophers emphasize that Locke founded modern empiricism. His representational epistemology, or direct realism, challenged the theory of innate ideas, including Herbert's earlier deism. Prior to experience of the world through the senses, the human mind is a mere *tabula rasa* ("blank slate").[11] Therefore, ideas are not a priori but a posteriori; they enter the mind only through experience, which consists of sensation and reflection. A person has no direct knowledge of the world; such knowledge is mediated through the senses. Locke's empiricism, which at first blush promised knowledge based on simple and complex ideas, proved problematic. Instead of producing certainty, his probing of primary and secondary qualities resulted in skepticism.[12] Locke's epistemology could not assure the knower that ideas correspond with the objects they represent. Nevertheless, Lockean empiricism seemed fully compatible with the rising tide of science.

Likewise, in political thought, Locke's treatises broke new ground. Not only did he join others in denying the divine right of kings, Locke justified England's Glorious Revolution by appealing to natural law and the teaching of the Bible. He also proposed a new contractual basis for the state. Rather than the state resulting from a covenant between ruler and subjects, as Reformed thinkers argued, the new contractual theory viewed the state as democratic, based on the consent of the governed. Consistent with these changes, Locke also espoused a theory of toleration that permitted religious liberty for all dissenting religious groups, with the exception of Catholics.

Locke's greatest accomplishment was his summation of the English mind in the late seventeenth century. He presented religious ideas in "plain and intelligible" terms so that anyone could understand them. Locke criti-

---

11.   By positing the mind as *tabula rasa*, Locke not only rejected Descartes' rational apriorism but also Calvin's view that all people are imbued with a sense of divinity imprinted in their hearts.

12.   Although primary qualities ("bulk, figure, and motion of parts") are "real" qualities of objects, secondary qualities ("heat, whiteness, or coldness") are not: "[They] are no more really in them than sickness or pain is in manna. Take away the sensation of them; let not the eyes see light of colours, nor the ears hear sounds; let the palate not taste, nor the nose smell, and all colours, tastes, odours, and sounds, as they are such particular ideas, vanish and cease . . ."

cized Herbert's deism, but he had little to say about the Trinity, the atonement, and the deity of Christ. He defined a Christian as one who believes in Jesus as the Messiah, repents of sins, and tries to live according to the teaching of Jesus. He also espoused traditional apologetic strategies that affirmed fulfilled prophecy and miracles as primary means for defending the truths of Christian faith.

Locke gave reason a different role from the ones it previously enjoyed. For Locke, reason was not just a tool to prepare for faith (Aquinas) or to explain the faith (Augustine); it was the standard for judging revelation and the judge of truth claims. Locke distinguished three types of propositions: those that are according to reason (e.g., the existence of God), whose truth we can verify by examining ideas arising from sensation and reflection; those that are above reason (e.g., the resurrection), whose truth we accept but are beyond reason's grasp; and those that are contrary to reason (e.g., the existence of more than one God), because they are inconsistent with our ideas. Using these distinctions, Locke treated religion almost entirely as a matter of individual intellectual belief. Assent to what passed the test of reason captivated his attention. What claimed to be revelation must submit to reason's judgment.[13]

> *Locke gave reason a different role from the ones it previously enjoyed. For Locke, reason was not just a tool to prepare for faith (Aquinas) or to explain the faith (Augustine); it was the standard for judging revelation and the judge of truth claims.*

An example of Locke's rationalist revision of Christianity is his acquiescence to Socinianism's rejection of original sin. Not only is the human mind a *tabula rasa*, but people are born with a moral nature untrammeled by sin. Although mortal, humans are morally neutral; the child is "denuded of all beliefs, opinion, and inclinations," with the exception of seeking pleasure and avoiding pain. Whether people are good or evil depends on their education, which consists of habit formation: "Of all the men we meet with nine parts of ten are what they are, good or evil, useful or not, by their education. It is that which makes the great difference in mankind." Original sin in its Augustinian form, therefore, is a fiction. Continued belief in inherited corruption from our first parents undermines morality.[14]

Although Locke never judged any Christian doctrine to have failed the test of reason, his rationalistic approach made religion primarily a private matter. Christianity consists in believing certain tenets that pass the test

---

13. Colin Brown contends that Locke's attempt to combine traditional apologetics with his rationalism established still another form of foundationalism, which demanded that belief rest on reasonable grounds. Colin Brown, *Christianity and Western Thought: A History of Philosophers, Ideas and Movements*, Vol. 1 (Downers Grove, IL: InterVarsity Press, 1990), 225.

14. By advocating education as the means by which mankind can become morally better, Locke put forth a secular method of redemption that was contrary to the traditional Christian view that God's grace alone can save. Thus, Locke paved the way for various modern forms of the belief that human beings are perfectible. Because of Locke's influence, many viewed education as the secular equivalent of Arminian and Wesleyan prevenient grace. Whether one attributed confidence in human perfectibility to a secular basis or to a revised view of grace, the result was the same—a revolution in how people viewed human nature and the means of human redemption.

of reason. However, Christianity so conceived is marginalized from public life because it focuses on individual belief and moral behavior. Regardless of how one tries to categorize Locke's views—as consistent with or as a departure from traditional Christianity—his minimalist view of Christian doctrine illustrates a transition that culminated in the deistic controversy.[15]

Herbert's natural religion and Locke's theorizing opened the door for additional challenges to traditional worldviews. The seismographic impact of Newtonian science transformed this possibility into a reality. Sir Isaac Newton's (1642–1727) *Principia* (1687) is the culmination of a line of scientific inquiry that began with Nicholaus Copernicus and continued in Galileo Galilei, Tycho Brahe, and Johannes Kepler. Copernican cosmology had replaced the Ptolemaic model, thus producing a radical change in the West's worldview.

Newton's calculations produced a powerful new synthesis for understanding the physical universe. Newton's three laws[16] explained the motion of heavenly bodies and of motion *anywhere* in the universe. His formulas enabled scientists to calculate the masses of the earth, its planets, and the sun. Using Newton's laws, scientists could calculate paths of the planets and determine the times of future eclipses.

In *Optics* (1730), Newton enunciated principles that testified to his theistic beliefs. He reiterated the traditional view of creation: ". . . God in the beginning formed matter . . . of such sizes and figures, and with such other properties, and in such proportion to space, as most conduced to the end for which he formed them . . . " Newton repudiated the existence of occult properties as bases for understanding objects. Because creation displays clear signs of intelligence, "it's unphilosophical to seek for any other origin of the world, or to pretend that it might arise out of a chaos by the mere laws of nature." He further denied the power of "blind fate" to move the planets. The uniformity and intricacies of design in creatures confirm that "nothing else than the wisdom and will of a powerful everliving agent" could have created them. Newton opposed pantheism and panentheism[17]

Isaac Newton

15.   For a sympathetic account of Locke's religious beliefs, see Victor Nuovo, "Locke's Theology 1694–1704" in M. A. Stewart, ed., *English Philosophy in the Age of Locke* (Oxford: Oxford University Press, 2000). Nuovo argues that Locke's *The Reasonableness of Christianity* constituted an apologetic against deism and rendered his views compatible with traditional views of biblical interpretation. Also see S. G. Hefelbower, *The Relation of John Locke to English Deism* (Chicago: University of Chicago Press, 1918).

16.   First Law: *Inertia*. Every object persists in its state of rest or uniform motion in a straight line unless it is compelled to change that state by forces impressed on it. Second Law: *Acceleration*. Force is equal to the change in momentum (mV) per change in time. For a constant mass, force equals mass times acceleration—F=ma. Third Law: *Reciprocal Actions*. For every action, there is an equal and opposite reaction.

17.   Pantheism and panentheism differ from traditional theism, which clearly distinguishes God as creator of and separate from the world he created. Pantheism stresses the immanence of God by identifying God with the universe. Panentheism on the other hand holds that while God is immanent, God also transcends the world.

by defining God's distinction from creation and by affirming that the universe is "open" so that God may "vary the laws of nature."[18]

As scientific knowledge became available, profound questions followed. Is the universe a self-sufficient system? If events can be explained as part of the larger system, why posit a personal God who providentially orders history; why posit the existence of spirits and demons? If the cosmos is simply the most intricate watch or machine, should our conception of God change from the biblical image of a personal Father? How does one reconcile belief in fixed laws of nature with the personal God of the Bible? These and similar queries led people to view the heavens as autonomously ordered and structured. Newton himself maintained a deep sense of wonder, believing that creation is the work of God's hands. He viewed the universe as a marvelously coordinated system, a masterpiece produced by a grand designer. For him, God's existence was absolutely necessary for the operations of nature. As a master lawgiver or mechanic, God could and did intervene to perform miracles and correct irregularities in the universe.[19]

Newton's successors did not follow his lead.[20] They were convinced that the new science, allied with the new rationalism, resulted in a radically different worldview that required eliminating the old Christian perspective. Newton's disciples outstripped themselves as they invented metaphors to redefine the character of the universe: a vast machine or a watch designed so wisely by a watchmaker that it runs on its own without outside intervention. Nature no longer was an organism; now it had a mechanical nature and operated according to Newton's laws. Newton's accomplishments led to numerous accolades, but none more effusive than Alexander Pope's famous epitaph for Newton:

> Nature and Nature's Laws lay hid in night:
> God said, Let Newton be! And all was Light.

*Newton's calculations produced a powerful new synthesis for understanding the physical universe. Newton's three laws explained the motion of heavenly bodies and of motion **anywhere** in the universe.*

Newton's successors did not follow his lead. They were convinced that the new science, allied with the new rationalism, resulted in a radically different worldview that required eliminating the old Christian perspective.

18.   Newton's greatness is revealed in this statement made toward the end of his life: "I know not what the world will think of my labors, but to myself it seems that I have been but as a child playing on the seashore; now finding some pebble rather more polished, and now some shell rather more agreeably variegated than another, while the immense ocean of truth extended itself unexplored before me," in John L. Beatty and Oliver Johnson, eds., *Heritage of Western Civilization*, vol. 2 (Englewood Cliffs, NJ: Prentice Hall, 1991), 53. This humble assessment of his remarkable discoveries, especially in the context of his Christian faith, stands in sharp contrast to the later hubris that sometimes characterized popularizers of science.

19.   Newton outwardly maintained his faith as a professing Christian. In fact, in addition to his remarkable accomplishments in science, he cultivated an intense interest in minute theological matters. He published works on the Old Testament prophet Daniel and John's Apocalypse. Although his theological views displayed heterodox tendencies—he rejected the central dogma of the Trinity—he nevertheless believed that science and Christian faith were totally compatible.

20.   See Richard Olson, *Science Deified and Science Defied: The Historical Significance of Science in Western Culture*, Vol 2: 1620–1820 (Berkeley: University of California Press, 1990) and Simon Schaffer, "Newtonianism" in *Companion to the History of Modern Science*, ed. Robert Olby (New York: Routledge, 1990).

> *Tindal's **Christianity as Old as Creation** was the highest expression of English deism and so was nicknamed "the Deists' Bible." Tindal argued that natural religion, which is eternal and unchangeable, always has existed as a perfect religion.*

The inroads of rationalism and science culminated in the deist controversy of the early eighteenth century. As laws restricting freedom of expression softened, hundreds of books and pamphlets on religion appeared. John Toland's *Christianity not Mysterious, Showing that there is nothing in the Gospel Contrary to Reason, nor above it; And that no Christian Doctrine can properly be Call'd a Mystery* (1696) and Matthew Tindal's *Christianity as Old as the Creation: or, the Gospel a Republication of the Religion of Nature* (1730) indicate by their titles that the seminal ideas in Herbert developed into a full-blown deism, yet ironically retained the name "Christian."

Toland's treatise[21] reveals his desire to move well beyond Lockean rationalism.[22] Denying Locke's tripartite distinction of reason, Toland insisted that any religious claim be fully intelligible. Those that fall outside, that is, above reason, belong in the category of the mysterious, which he ascribed to pagan influences. He introduced the phrase "deceit of priests" as the motivation behind Christianity's sacraments. In contrast to Jesus who taught simple moral truths, priests copied pagan practices of adding mysterious ceremonies to baptism and the Lord's Supper and thus deceived worshipers into believing that salvation consisted of participation in celebrations controlled exclusively by priests. Medieval "worship" became the very antithesis to "religion," which consists in moral behavior. The standard of every religion, including Christianity, must be the eternal, intelligible truths of reason. Toland denounced doctrines at the heart of the gospel, and he expressed special repugnance for the doctrine of Christ's propitiatory atonement.

Tindal's *Christianity as Old as Creation* was the highest expression of English deism and so was nicknamed "the Deists' Bible." Tindal argued that natural religion, which is eternal and unchangeable, always has existed as a perfect religion.[23] Not only are additions, whether doctrinal or ceremonial, unnecessary, but they result in evil by detracting from the essential elements of natural religion. He changed the nature of the religious a priori from glorifying God to doing good: "to do all the good we can, and thereby render ourselves acceptable to God in answering the end of our creation."[24] Because God's natural laws always and exclusively determine the events in nature, neither mystery nor miracles exist. Tindal argued "the more that the mind of man is taken up with the observation of things which are not of a moral nature, the less it will be able to attend to those that are."

21. Cf. Margaret Jacob, *The Radical Enlightenment: Pantheists, Freemasons and Republicans* (London: Allen and Unwin, 1981), and Robert E. Sullivan, *John Toland and the Deist Controversy: A Study in Adaptations* (Cambridge, MA: Harvard University Press, 1982).

22. Locke repudiated his admirers' efforts to move beyond his tripartite distinction of reason.

23. Cf. John Leland, *A View of the Principal Deistical Writers: British Philosophers and Theologians of the 17th and 18th Centuries*, 3 vols. (London: B. Dod, 1756–57; reprint New York: Garland Publishing, 1977).

24. Tindal's religious views directly counter the Puritans' classic expression in the Westminster Shorter Catechism's first question and answer: "What is the chief end of man?" "To glorify God and enjoy him forever."

As radical as the Herbert-to-Tindal deistic trajectory sounds, English deism remained relatively conservative in nature. Despite opposition to doctrines including the Trinity, original sin, and the atoning work of Christ, they portrayed their ideas as consistent with Christianity, instead of as a replacement for it. Although "Christian deist" may appear a contradiction in terms, English deists believed they were merely developing Christianity to its next, rational stage, not distorting it. Later, more radical deists aggressively denounced Christianity by repudiating miracles and supernatural revelation and by engaging in radical criticism of the Bible.

The British Enlightenment reached its most radical expression in the writings of David Hume (1711–76), specifically his *Enquiry Concerning Human Understanding* (1758) and his *Dialogues Concerning Natural Religion* (published posthumously in 1779). Hume's writings are every bit as controversial as John Locke's. Whereas Locke's works summarized the English mind leading up to the deist controversy, Hume captured his era's philosophic mind in its most skeptical form.[25]

Hume insisted that the human mind is severely limited in what it knows. By taking Locke's representational assumptions to their logical conclusion, Hume affirmed that what people ordinarily claimed to know about the world, themselves, and God resulted from habits of association. Upon careful analysis, human knowledge consists of a series of constructs based on sense data. Regarding substance, for example, Hume stated, "The idea of substance as well as that of a mode is nothing but a collection of simple ideas, that are united by the imagination, and have a particular name assigned to them, by which we are able to recall, either to ourselves or others, that collection." We clearly perceive sense data, but we cannot know whether anything lies behind them. From this he concluded that while we think we know cause and effect, the idea of any connection between the two arises from our recalling similar events in past experience, rather than any direct knowledge of cause between two events.

In a similar vein, Hume reduced our supposed knowledge of the self to a series of perceptions, which is very different from knowledge of the soul.[26] Gaps of self-perception and the cessation of self-perception associated with sleep and one's death only reinforced Hume's skepticism about the soul. Although another person might believe in the self, Hume concluded: "All I can allow him is, that he may be in the right as well as I, and that we are essentially different in this particular. He may, perhaps, perceive something simple and continued, which he calls himself; though I am certain there is no such principle in me."[27]

> "Hume captured his era's philosophic mind in its most skeptical form.... Hume affirmed that what people ordinarily claimed to know about the world, themselves, and God resulted from habits of association. Upon careful analysis, human knowledge consists of a series of constructs based on sense data.

---

25. An excellent account of Hume's skeptical empiricism is found in Brown, *Christianity and Western Thought*, 235–58.

26. Hume's treatment of the self reflects the emergence of the modern autonomous self, as distinguished from traditional language about the soul and its relation with God (as made in the image of God) that was rooted in biblical revelation.

27. Cited by Brown, *Christianity and Western Thought*, 241.

Hume also achieved notoriety for developing the conclusive argument against miracles. Miracles had long been used as a primary apologetic in defense of supernaturalism, but deists mounted the initial attacks on miracles, claiming they were inconsistent with belief in the laws of nature.[28]

Since Hume claimed that genuine knowledge could be found only in mathematics and experimental disciplines, he summarized his view of theology and metaphysics this way: "If we take in our hand any volume; of divinity or school metaphysics, for instance; let us ask, Does it contain any abstract reasoning concerning quantity or number? No. Does it contain any experimental reasoning concerning matter of fact and existence? No. Commit it then to the flames: for it can contain nothing but sophistry and illusion."

Hume's ideas have elicited vigorous debate. Did his empiricism simply take Locke's representationalism to its logical conclusion? Were his views reducible to atheism, agnosticism, skepticism, a modern Epicureanism, or even a radically new fideism? None of these reductionisms can fully capture the complexity of his ideas. To the philosophical mind, he posed such profound questions that they prompted Immanuel Kant to rethink human reason. Hume achieved the reputation for demolishing several conventions: knowledge of the ego or self, knowledge of God or metaphysical reality, knowledge of cause and effect that serves as the basis for modern science, and knowledge of miracles that proves the truth of revealed religion.

The English Evangelical Awakening

The Enlightenment occupied only part of seventeenth- and eighteenth-century English worldviews. In addition to dramatic shifts associated with the rise of reason, modern science, and deism, England also experienced remarkable religious phenomena based on traditional theism—the evangelical awakening.

Evangelicalism in the early decades of the eighteenth century offered a decisive, alternative worldview that profoundly affected the Church of England and helped counter the rising tides of secularism and the threat of cultural decay. Because of the comprehensive nature of the evangelical vision and its ability to galvanize English social life in new directions, many historians believe it was a benchmark worldview event, equal in stature and cultural influence to the French and the Industrial Revolutions.

David Hume

28. See Colin Brown, *Miracles and the Critical Mind* (Grand Rapids: Eerdmans, 1984), 79–100, which probes Hume's decisive role in countering miracles as part of the Christian apologia. Of special interest in light of our treatment of Jansenism below is Brown's discussion of Hume's refusal to accept reports of miracles that met his own tests, because of his conviction of the inviolability of the laws of nature.

The term "evangelical"[29] is associated primarily with John Wesley (1703–91),[30] whose indefatigable organizing, preaching, and advocacy of social measures epitomized the movement.[31] Wesley insisted that Christianity differed radically from natural religion, with its minimalist theology and moralism. Wesley also stressed worship and holiness, which deists found so distasteful because, in their opinion, they distracted from moral behavior as the essence of religion. Wesley's evangelicalism also differed from Anglican formalism in worship. Wesley prized evangelistic preaching and activism that led to conversion and social reform.

Theologically, Wesley maintained the themes of the Protestant Reformation. However, German Pietism and Enlightenment thinking clearly influenced his worldview, as seen in his moving away from Christianity's view of authority, human nature, and sanctification. In his famous "quadrilateral," Wesley based his theology on four principles of religious authority: Scripture (the Reformers' *sola scriptura*), reason, tradition (influenced by Richard Hooker's views of natural law in *Laws of Ecclesiastical Polity*), and experience (reflecting the influence of pietism and Moravianism).[32] Wesley developed a careful revision of Dutch Arminianism.[33] His description of salvation deviated from the monergistic views of Augustine, Luther, and Calvin.[34] Although retaining some emphasis on the sovereignty of God, at the same time Wesley attempted to preserve a place for autonomous human choice, understanding salvation to be an act of synergistic cooperation between God and humans.

> "Evangelicalism in the early decades of the eighteenth century offered a decisive, alternative worldview that profoundly affected the Church of England and helped counter the rising tides of secularism and the threat of cultural decay.

29. David Bebbington's *Evangelicalism in Modern Britain: A History from the 1730s to the 1980s* (London: Unwin Hyman, 1989) enumerates evangelicalism's four defining characteristics: conversionism based on justification by faith; activism, a tidal wave of participation in ministries including missions, prison reform, and the abolition of slavery; ardent biblicism, where the Bible stood as the final authority for belief and practice; and crucicentrism, which held to Christ's atoning death as the preeminent core of Christian truth. For the emergence of evangelicalism, see Mark A. Noll, *The Rise of Evangelicalism: The Age of Edwards, Whitefield and the Wesleys* (Downers Grove, IL: InterVarsity, 2004).

30. See A. C. Outler, ed., *John Wesley* (New York: Oxford University Press, 1964); Robert G. Tuttle, *John Wesley: His Life and Theology* (Grand Rapids: Zondervan, 1978); Henry D. Rack, *Reasonable Enthusiast: John Wesley and the Rise of Methodism* (Nashville: Abingdon, 1992).

31. In addition to the awakening in England, evangelical movements broke out in other parts of Great Britain such as the Cambuslang revival in Scotland.

32. Cf. Donald A. Thorsen, *The Wesley Quadrilateral: Scripture, Tradition, Reason and Experience as a Model of Evangelical Theology* (Grand Rapids: Zondervan, 1990), and Thomas C. Oden, *John Wesley's Scriptural Christianity: A Plain Exposition of His Teaching on Christian Doctrine* (Grand Rapids: Zondervan, 1994).

33. Named for Dutch theologian Jacob Arminius (1560–1609), who spearheaded the Remonstrance movement against scholastic Calvinism. Arminians attempted to de-emphasize Reformed theological distinctives, going so far as to urge significant changes in the Belgic Confession and the Heidelberg Catechism on doctrines associated with original sin, predestination, the atonement, the work of the Holy Spirit, and perseverance.

34. Monergism is the belief, rooted in Pauline and Augustinian theology, that due to the pervasiveness of human sin, the sovereign grace of God is the only cause of a person's salvation. Monergism stands in opposition to synergism, which posits some cooperation or reciprocation between God's will and the will of the individual.

> "Theologically, Wesley maintained the themes of the Protestant Reformation. However, German Pietism and Enlightenment thinking clearly influenced his worldview, as seen in his moving away from Christianity's view of authority, human nature, and sanctification.

In describing salvation, Wesley distinguished between prevenient, justifying, and sanctifying grace. Prevenient grace[35] was a universal process by which the Holy Spirit works in people's hearts between conception and conversion. Wesley did not deny original sin, but he redefined its effects. Because of original sin, God must initiate the relationship with the sinner. The Holy Spirit prevents persons from falling so far away from God that they cannot respond to the preaching of the gospel. Justifying grace consists of Christ's righteousness being imputed to the believer and is manifested by an instantaneous conversion effected by the Holy Spirit. For Wesley, faith is the free human choice to accept God's grace. Finally, according to Wesley, sanctifying grace is the work of the Holy Spirit from conversion to death. Paradoxically, it is both an instantaneous event (sometimes called "entire sanctification") and a process that culminates in an experience of pure love devoid of self-interest.

Wesley also called sanctification "scriptural holiness."[36] Sanctification begins at the new birth, by means of the Holy Spirit, and progresses gradually until the instant of "entire sanctification," which results in love of God and neighbor. Because of conceptual similarities between Wesley's view of holiness and the modern belief in human perfectibility, controversy raged over Wesley's "perfectionism." At times, Wesley stated that believers come to a place in Christian experience that enables them to rule their lives without sin. More often, Wesley described perfection more as a goal than as a completed act. Wesley also emphasized perfection of motive and avoidance of conscious sin. Scholars debate whether Christian perfectionism, such as Wesley's, resulted more from his quadrilateral or from the moderating influences of enlighteners, who argued for perfection based not on grace but on human ability.[37]

Wesleyan Arminianism became the driving force of British evangelicalism. Evangelicals affirmed justification by faith and pressed for conversion in their preaching, but they did so on the basis that God's grace is unlimited and free. Although some evangelicals maintained a Calvinist perspective—George Whitefield is an obvious example[38]—evangelicalism as a whole proceeded from a different set of assumptions about God's sovereignty in salvation and human freedom in appropriating that salvation. Evangelicals preached a gospel of salvation that assumed universal human sinfulness. But sin had not so corrupted the human will that it could not

> "Although some evangelicals maintained a Calvinist perspective—George Whitefield is an obvious example—evangelicalism as a whole proceeded from a different set of assumptions about God's sovereignty in salvation and human freedom in appropriating that salvation.

---

35. According to Hodge, prevenient grace is a divine influence that precedes any good effort, which if acted upon receives "the merit of congruity." As Wesley redefined it, prevenient grace becomes a universal process that keeps people from being so enveloped by sin that they cannot choose to respond to the gospel.

36. Cf. John Wesley, *A Plain Account of Christian Perfection* (London: Epworth, 1952), and Kenneth J. Collins, *The Scripture Way of Salvation: The Heart of John Wesley's Theology* (Nashville: Abingdon, 1997).

37. Cf. the discussion of perfectibility espoused by French *philosophes* below.

38. Wesley and Whitefield had a sharp falling out over the issue of predestination. Whitefield, who held a Calvinist worldview, preached throughout Great Britain and America.

respond to the offer of salvation. God's sovereignty was limited to his making salvation available to everyone in Christ's death on the cross. Individuals could freely respond to the good news by choosing to accept Christ as savior from sin. Thus, a person's salvation resulted from a synergy of the divine and human wills.

Enlightenment and Awakening in France

From Cartesian Foundationalism to the *Philosophes*

Just as Bacon's *Instauratio* launched the English Enlightenment by calling for a methodological revolution in science (inductivism), René Descartes (1596–1650) initiated a radically new approach to knowledge in his *Discourse on the Method* (1637). He wrote his *Discourse* to refute Pyrrhonism, a flourishing skepticism that threatened to banish all certainty in thinking. Descartes proposed a method premised on the superiority of the mind as distinguishing humans from the lower animals. He acknowledged the force of the Pyrrhonist contention that past philosophies led only to uncertainty. Ancient moralists lauded the virtues, but their intellectual edifices lacked sound foundations. Although he revered the teaching of the Roman Catholic Church, he could not understand it because it rested on divine authority. Despite philosophers' attempts to explain the nature of reality, their speculations lay shrouded in doubt and subject to dispute. The sciences fared no better, as evidenced by the spurious practices of alchemy and astrology.

Descartes believed only a fresh start in thinking would save philosophy from the grips of skepticism. Although an individual lacked the ability to reform a state or the sciences as a whole, he could rebuild his own thinking. And although he did not use the term worldview, clearly Descartes had in mind a radical reformulation of his mind. He laid out a clear, rational plan. Although he relinquished the goal of infallibilism, the belief that absolute truth or certainty in knowledge is attainable, he retained his belief that the lack of certainty and the root of disagreement in philosophy resulted from not appropriating the proper method in thinking. If carefully followed (cf. Bacon's elimination of idols), rational principles would comprise the true method that led to knowledge: accept only what is so clear and distinct as to exclude all ground of doubt; divide each difficulty into as many parts as possible; begin thinking about those parts from the simplest to the most complex; and engage these in thought so comprehensive that nothing is omitted.

Descartes' new foundation for thinking rested in systematic doubt. Only by systematically doubting everything could he hope to arrive at certainty. Everything—the opinions of others, what he received through the senses, indeed what had ever passed through his mind—fell under the grand principle of *dubito* ("I doubt"). His mind thus cleared, Descartes reflected on his very act of thinking. Even if he were deceived in every

> *Descartes' new foundation for thinking rested in systematic doubt. Only by systematically doubting everything could he hope to arrive at certainty. Everything—the opinions of others, what he received through the senses, indeed what had ever passed through his mind—fell under the grand principle of* **dubito** *("I doubt").*

idea, the fact that he thought demonstrated that he, the thinker, existed. Although he might doubt all else, the very act of doubting established one indisputable truth—that he existed. He summarized this conclusion in the famous phrase *cogito, ergo sum* ("I think, therefore I am.") and made it the unshakeable basis of certainty and the starting point of all philosophy.

Archbishop William Temple identified the day that Descartes sequestered himself to gain certainty as the most disastrous day in European history. Descartes' methodical doubt and belief that individual existence is the indisputable starting point for philosophy resulted in an entirely new perspective—a shift from God-centered thinking to human-centered philosophizing. Temple stated: "There was an urgent need to find some new foundation on which the habitation of the spirit of man could be securely built. If the individual could not find it in the whole scheme of things in which he was placed, he must find it in his own integrity."[39] Cartesian rationalism effectively inaugurated the "modern self" or the "subjective turn," a shift from knowledge as objectively rooted in biblical revelation to knowledge as authenticated and demonstrated by human reason.[40]

The disparity between the Enlightenment and philosophy that preceded it is illustrated by the irony that Augustine actually used a *cogito* argument centuries earlier in *Contra Academicos* to dispute skepticism. However, Augustine's and Descartes' use of the argument reveals a fundamental disparity in their worldviews. Augustine formulated the *cogito* in the *context* of objective Christian belief, in which knowing God took preeminence. Certainty of his own existence served the higher end of knowing God. His *cogito* formed but a small part of thought that would center on God, who alone is self-existent and self-sufficient.

Descartes' use of the *cogito*, on the other hand, launched the whole project of modernity. Self-authenticating, rational self-sufficiency was the basis of Cartesian foundationalism.[41] No matter what form epistemology took in the ensuing seventeenth- and eighteenth-century discussions, its formulators used assumptions that furthered Descartes' break with the past. Descartes' radically new method—*dubito, cogito ergo sum*—provided a subjective, rational starting point—the intellectual fulcrum of human autonomy—that set the agenda for all future philosophical discussion. Although Cartesianism was but the first of many systems that occupied European thought, it placed the debate on new ground—a human-centered, secular perspective.

René Descartes

39. *Nature, Man and God*, Gifford Lectures 1932–34 (London: Macmillan, 1934), 57.

40. Cf. Charles Taylor's thorough treatment of the rise of the modern autonomous self in *Sources of the Self: The Making of the Modern Identity* (Cambridge, MA: Harvard University Press, 1989) and Jeffrey Stout, *The Flight from Authority: Religion, Morality and the Quest for Autonomy* (Notre Dame: Notre Dame Press, 1981).

41. "Foundationalism" refers to any epistemological theory that maintains beliefs are justified (known) on the basis of "basic beliefs," i.e., "foundational beliefs." According to foundationalism, basic beliefs are self-justifying or self-evident and serve as the basis for other beliefs.

However, Descartes did not neglect God, nor did most of the Enlightenment philosophers. Having established rational autonomy as the basis for his knowledge, Descartes moved to the question of God. Descartes formed his own version of the ontological argument: his idea of God differed from other ideas because of its metaphysical nature, and since a less-perfect nature cannot produce the idea of a perfect nature, then the idea of a perfect nature must originate from a being that is more perfect, that is, from God. At first glance, God appears to play a crucial role as the second idea in Descartes' system. But this is not the case; God is reduced to a functional role within the Cartesian system as a whole. As James Collins comments:

> [Descartes' use of the idea of God] does not mean that the rationalist systems were religious or theocentric in structure. Quite the contrary, God was made to serve the purposes of the system itself. He became a major cog, but still a cog, in the over-all program of answering skepticism, incorporating the scientific spirit, and building a rational explanation of the real.[42]

Thus, Descartes used the idea of God as the bridge between the *cogito* and knowledge of the real world. Descartes' subordination of God to the aims of his system contributed to the modern marginalization of religion. Privately, Descartes remained a faithful Catholic—he lit a candle to the Virgin when he formulated the *cogito*, but Catholicism remained a matter of his personal faith, not a governing element in his public philosophy. Descartes' philosophical treatment of God illustrates the modernist shift from seeing God as a transcendent, personal sovereign, who is worthy of worship, pious devotion, and personal obedience, to seeing him as a "deity" who serves the philosopher's ends by tying together his system as a whole.

By the conclusion of the Enlightenment, compartmentalization of religious faith as a matter of private belief separate from philosophical speculation epitomized the modern worldview. What previously captivated thinkers in the Reformation—seeing public life as the arena where Christian faith in a personal, transcendent God would manifest itself in a diversity of vocations that would transform every aspect of cultural life—now became the prerogative of the secular use of reason and science.

Philosophers in the age of reason in the seventeenth century prepared the way for the more dramatic shift in worldview that appeared in the eighteenth-century *philosophes*: Voltaire, Rousseau, Diderot, Helvetius, d'Holbach, and Condorcet.[43] These men were not professional philoso-

Cartesian rationalism effectively inaugurated the "modern self" or the "subjective turn," a shift from knowledge as objectively rooted in biblical revelation to knowledge as authenticated and demonstrated by human reason.

By the conclusion of the Enlightenment, compartmentalization of religious faith as a matter of private belief separate from philosophical speculation epitomized the modern worldview.

42. James Collins, *God in Modern Philosophy* (Chicago: Henry Regnery Co., 1959), 56. Temple makes essentially the same point. Even though God was the "pivot" of his philosophy, "yet it is still not a religious philosophy, for it sets no value on God in Himself, but only as the lynch-pin of its own mechanism. It does not interpret the world in the light of knowledge of God, but makes use of God to vindicate its own interpretation of the world. . . . He is to be used for our purpose, not we for his," *Nature, Man and God*, 84.

43. "Philosophes" is French for "philosophers," including this French group of eighteenth-century Enlightenment intellectuals. Although the primary figures were French, and

> *Voltaire . . . epitomized the French Enlightenment with his demand "Ecrasez l'infame"—"Wipe out the infamy [of organized Christianity]." . . . he categorically upbraided Catholicism as an oppressive and scurrilous superstition.*

phers but champions of the epistemological revolution that began with the age of reason.

Whereas Toland and Tindal conceived themselves as "Christian deists," taking Christianity to its next level of development, French deists severed all ties with Christianity. The perception of the Enlightenment as a rabidly anti-Christian reprise of ancient paganism stems from the attacks by these thinkers against throne and altar—dominance of French life by the monarchy and the Catholic Church. Philosophes sought to break the *anciene regime's* stranglehold on French culture. They contended that Christianity's insistence on revelation, asceticism, and mysticism and the inadequacy of humans to save themselves without divine grace resulted in a tragic "failure of nerve" among Greek and Roman leaders. Ancient thinkers failed in their aspiration to achieve a life of reason because the church fathers appropriated Greek philosophy and subordinated it to revelation and Christian theology. Although Christianity captured the Western mind early, the modern period represented the philosophes' frontal attack to reverse the process. Seizing what rightfully belonged to the philosophers and propounding a new spirit of the age, their goal was nothing less than "the recovery of nerve."

Voltaire (1694–1778) epitomized the French Enlightenment with his demand *"Ecrasez l'infame"*—"Wipe out the infamy [of organized Christianity]." Unleashing a barrage of pamphlets, plays, poems, manuscripts, and treatises, he categorically upbraided Catholicism as an oppressive and scurrilous superstition. Twice he fled in exile when public opinion turned against the violence of his critique of Christianity and Judaism.[44] He pilloried every major theological belief—the Trinity, original sin, the atonement, Mary's virginity, the Eucharist—as antithetical to rational, natural religion. He issued a diatribe characterized by wit, verve, and indignation. Echoing Lord Herbert's rationalistic reductionism, Voltaire defined natural religion in a single phrase "the principles of morality common to the human race." Any act that went beyond the worship of a Supreme Being by these means was a distortion: "The only gospel one ought to read is the great book of nature, written by the hand of God and sealed with his seal. It is as impossible that this pure and eternal religion should produce evil, as it is that the Christian fanaticism should not produce it." Voltaire did not seek to purify Christianity but to rid France of Christianity altogether.

Despite his virulent hostility to Christianity, Voltaire was not an atheist.[45] He claimed to be a theist. In his *Treatise on Metaphysics*, Voltaire

---

although Paris became the capital of modern discourse, the *philosophes* were an international group whose goal was to take the achievements of the seventeenth-century worldview to their logical conclusion.

44. See the citation at the beginning of our chapter on the Old Testament in this volume. Voltaire also attacked Pascal's *Pensées*.

45. Scholars frequently mention that the eighteenth century witnessed all degrees of deism but relatively few atheists. Several figures, however, qualify for this term, among

propounded Thomist arguments for the existence of God. However, his refusal to accept all evidence from revelation, his denial of providence, and his questioning even the goodness of God because of the problem of evil identify him as a radical deist. He once uttered the statement that if God did not exist, it would be necessary for man to invent him. In his most famous play, *Candide*, Voltaire rejected the facile optimism that sometimes characterized rationalism. When the tragic earthquake and tidal wave devastated Lisbon on All Saints' Day in 1755, killing thousands who worshiped in churches while sparing others in brothels, Voltaire questioned how the presence of such evil could characterize Pope's dictum "whatever is, is right" and Leibniz' belief in this as the best of all possible worlds. But in *Lettres philosophique*, he disagreed just as vociferously with Pascal's acceptance of miracles and the Augustinian beliefs of the fall (original sin), predestination, and the necessity of divine grace.

The philosophes' redefinition of religion and confidence in the powers of reason and science resulted in rising confidence in human progress.[46] As science became separated from theological ends, the medieval idea of theology as the "queen of the sciences" gave way to science as a series of autonomous disciplines that not only provide information independent of revelation but furnish humanity with the tools by which to transform the political order. Newton's discovery of the laws of motion led people to believe we could discover similar laws that determine human behavior. Modern scientism[47] grew out of the belief that an exact parallel existed between nature and human affairs. Just as universal laws govern events in nature, so universal laws of human nature lay ready to be discovered. The science of human affairs needs only its "Newton" to pave the way for continued human progress.[48]

> *As science became separated from theological ends, the medieval idea of theology as the "queen of the sciences" gave way to science as a series of autonomous disciplines that not only provide information independent of revelation but furnish humanity with the tools by which to transform the political order.*

---

them Paul-Henry D'Holbach (1723–89), author of *Systeme de la Nature*; and Denis Diderot (1713–84), editor of the definitive *Encyclopedie*.

46.　See Carl Becker, *The Heavenly City of the Eighteenth-Century Philosophers* (New Haven, CT: Yale University Press, 1974) and John Passmore, *The Perfectibility of Man* (New York: Scribners, 1970).

47.　Scientism is the belief that the quantitative methods of science are the only means by which knowledge may be attained, coupled with the denial of all qualitative disciplines, e.g., ethics and religion. The most concise definition of scientism is that of Albert H. Hobbs: "Scientism as a belief that science can furnish answers to all human problems, makes science a substitute for philosophy, religion, manners and morals," *Social Problems and Scientism* (Harrisburg, PA: The Stackpole Company, 1953).

48.　Condorcet represents Enlightenment hope in human progress based on the proper use of reason and science. His *Sketch for a Historical Picture of the Progress of the Human Mind* (1795) divided history into ten epochs, each distinguished by remarkable cultural events. Throughout, he maintained that Christianity is responsible for the oppression, barbarity, and superstition that marked declines. The appearance of Enlightenment forces in his last era demonstrated the greatest opportunity in history for overcoming evil and establishing a just society. Condorcet believed that reason, joined with science, could prophetically map the future destiny of man and successfully eradicate individual and social evils.

Religious Movements in France

Jansenism and Blaise Pascal

Two religious movements, each espousing a distinctive worldview, opposed the French Enlightenment—Jansenism in the seventeenth century and the anti-philosophes in the eighteenth century. Blaise Pascal (1623–62), a Jansenist, countered Cartesian rationalism with its inherent confidence in autonomous reason.[49] Noted for his mathematical genius, experiments on the effects of the vacuum, and inventing the calculator, Pascal collected ideas, published as the *Pensées*, for a new Catholic apologetic. He defended Jansenism, a Catholic reform movement that reprised Augustine's monergistic emphasis on the absolute necessity of divine grace over against the synergism and moral casuistry of the Jesuits.[50]

The *Pensées* provided a profoundly different worldview from Pyrrhonic skepticism, Cartesian rationalism, and the theological and moral teachings of the Jesuits. Some of Pascal's defense mimics traditional apologetics—use of miracles and fulfilled prophecy. But he also proffered a striking psychological analysis of the human soul. He called man a monster who paradoxically manifests greatness and misery. Although Pyrrhonism, rationalism, and dogmatism can explain part of the human paradox, only the Christian doctrines of the fall and the incarnation explain both. The solution to the human dilemma consists neither in analyzing the Cartesian mind and its doubts nor in moral casuistry but in exploring the human heart.

Pascal combined a radical subjective probing of the human heart with an appeal to the objective authority of the Bible that was reminiscent of Augustine. The Bible poses the *Deus absconditus* (the God of Isa. 45:15), hidden from the speculations of discursive reason but also inaccessible to speculation, due to the willfulness of human sin. Despite human greatness, philosophers who pursue God through Cartesian reason cannot find him. Pascal especially decried the way Descartes used God merely to put the world in motion and then had no further use for him. By confining God to a deductive model, Pascal argued, Descartes misused reason and its method, which were designed for geometry and science, not for Christian faith.

Pascal's most suggestive method posits the heart as the intuitive and synoptic center of human experience: "The heart has its reasons of which

Blaise Pascal

49. Cf. A. J. Krailsheimer, *Pascal* (Oxford: Oxford University Press, 1980); D. Wetsel, *Pascal and Disbelief: Catechesis and Conversion in the Pensées* (Washington, DC: Catholic University of America Press, 1994); Marvin R. O'Connell, *Blaise Pascal: Reasons of the Heart* (Grand Rapids: Eerdmans, 1997).

50. Cf. Alexander Sedgwick, *Jansenism in Seventeenth Century France* (Charlottesville, VA: University Press of Virginia, 1977), and Dale Van Kley, *The Jansenists and the Expulsion of the Jesuits from France 1757–1765* (New Haven, CT: Yale University Press, 1975).

reason knows nothing."[51] Hereby, Pascal affirmed the heart as the central experiential human faculty, and the heart's purpose is to apprehend first principles, from which the rest of human thought is derived. Pascal did not disparage genuine reason, but only its Cartesian misuse. Although Descartes argued rationally, Pascal contended that the heart sees intuitively through immediate awareness. What the heart apprehends comes not by ideas mediated through syllogisms. Instead, the heart knows first principles by instinct or sentiment, which is not mere emotional feeling but the assurance of faith. The heart intuits first principles as a matter of direct experience. One knows oneself and God not by the logic of the *cogito* and an argument from ontology but from the intuitive awareness in the heart. Thus, Pascal concluded it is the heart that perceives God, not the reason.

But Pascal does not thereby espouse an irrational fideism. Although the number of intuited first principles[52] is relatively small, reason's task is to form a coherent perspective within the confines provided by biblical revelation. Since the heart, not reason, experiences God, Pascal did not define faith primarily in cognitive terms; Pascal used affective terms (God felt by the heart), and he affirmed that faith is God's gift. Faith differs from proof; one is human, the other is a gift of God. God himself instills faith into the heart resulting not in *scio* ("I know") but in *credo* ("I believe").

Pascal did not eliminate objective truth from his worldview. He appealed to the authoritative teaching of the Bible as the basis for comprehensive knowledge. Without Scripture, which has Jesus Christ as its object, we cannot know anything but darkness. Genuine wisdom, therefore, consists in avoiding two extremes: excluding reason altogether and appealing only to reason. On the one hand, if we appeal only to reason, faith has no mysterious or supernatural dimension; on the other hand, if we reject reason, religion is absurd.

The cure for human complacency in the seventeenth-century mind lay in existential shock, and Pascal wielded this quite effectively. He issued his most provocative challenge to the modern worldview in a wager directed to the cool, detached French gambler, who faces life's greatest risk; the ultimate wager is either God exists or he does not. If one wagers for God and God exists, the result is ultimate gain, eternal life. On the other hand, if a person bets on God who does not exist, or another bets against God who does not exist, neither loses anything of ultimate value. However, at the opposite extreme, gambling against God if God exists produces infinite loss. How could anyone who knows the stakes of life possibly wager for the latter![53]

> *Pascal combined a radical subjective probing of the human heart with an appeal to the objective authority of the Bible that was reminiscent of Augustine. . . . Pascal's most suggestive method posits the heart as the intuitive and synoptic center of human experience: "The heart has its reasons of which reason knows nothing."*

> *Pascal did not eliminate objective truth from his worldview. He appealed to the authoritative teaching of the Bible as the basis for comprehensive knowledge. Without Scripture, which has Jesus Christ as its object, we cannot know anything but darkness.*

51. See Bernard Ramm, *Varieties of Christian Apologetics* (Grand Rapids: Baker, 1976), 39.

52. "For the knowledge of first principles, as space, time, motion, number, is as sure as any of those which we get from reasoning. And reason must trust these intuitions of the heart, must base them on every argument . . . Principles are intuited, propositions are inferred, all with certainty, though in different ways."

53. Cf. Nicholas Rescher, *Pascal's Wager: A Study of Practical Reasoning in Philosophical Theology* (Notre Dame: University of Notre Dame Press, 1985).

Pascal never finished his comprehensive apologetic for Christianity. He intended to defend Christianity as the only worldview capable of providing certainty for the doubtful, and he intended to expose the folly of a bald rationalism. Only the heart divested of pride and denuded of pretense can begin to know God. Pascal's critique of prevailing worldviews challenged the human-centered perspectives that characterized the Enlightenment. He countered autonomous subjectivism on its own terms. He posited the heart's response to God's grace and authoritative revelation as the ground for truth, as opposed to autonomous reason. The dispute between the Pyrrhonists and Descartes illustrates reason's inability to attain certainty in knowledge. By itself, reason lacks the foundation that Descartes believed he established in the *cogito*. Pascal enjoined the heart, with its reasons, to take up the task of using revelation to subdue the arrogant claims of reason. Enlightenment figures disparaged such demands as the latest version of heteronomy, or "failure of nerve." Thus, Pascal's intention in the *Pensées* was unmistakable—to refute the early success of rationalism and to induce a conversion in worldview among cultured French intellectuals.[54]

The Anti-philosophes

Just as Cartesian philosophy evoked a sharp response from Pascal in the seventeenth century, so a vigorous anti-Enlightenment movement emerged in eighteenth-century France. The foes of the Enlightenment identified their enemy as *philosophie*.[55] The anti-philosophes claimed unaided human reason subverted faith, multiplied error, and showed itself anything but autonomous. Philosophes placed great confidence in the mind, eliminated traditional piety, removed restraints necessary for righteous living, and opened the way for human passion to control behavior. Utilitarian tendencies to substitute pleasure and pain as the primary motivators of behavior succeeded only in producing immoral and criminal activity. Loosening traditional morality and undercutting family values could result only in further pollution of the political order.

Just as Cartesian philosophy evoked a sharp response from Pascal in the seventeenth century, so a vigorous anti-Enlightenment movement emerged in eighteenth-century France. The foes of the Enlightenment identified their enemy as philosophie.

54.   Pascal's other worldview battle opposed the moral casuistry of the Jesuits, the Company of Jesus, founded in 1534 by the Spaniard Ignatius Loyola. The Jesuits were known for their missionary and educational successes and for their tenacious devotion to the papacy. Pascal wrote the anonymous *Provincial letters* to criticize their probabilism in ethical matters. Jesuit ethical guidelines allowed moral leeway to pursue questionable behavior when probable arguments supported it, even if counterarguments actually weighed more heavily. To Pascal, this approach went beyond subtlety and introduced moral uncertainty into areas demanding straightforward answers. While recognizing the difficulty of ethical decisions, Pascal argued that probabilistic casuistry introduced unnecessary ambiguity into public thinking, making flexibility into the highest virtue. Pascal criticized the church for abandoning the teaching of its greatest teacher (Augustine) in favor of contemporary Jesuit morality.

55.   The lack of scholarly attention to those who opposed the philosophes and supported the old regime has recently been filled by Darrin M. McMahon, *Enemies of the Enlightenment* (Oxford: Oxford University Press, 2001). The analysis that follows draws upon ch. 1, pp. 18–53.

Anti-Enlightenment writers accused their foes of spreading republican and democratic ideas by speaking eloquently of the sovereignty of the people, equality between all classes, and the merit of social contracts. Charges of "Anglomania" permeated their writings. They linked together church and king: "Whoever does not fear God, will not respect his king," wrote one journalist. Tolerance in religion resulted from Protestant influences that would dilute belief into a vapid relativism.

To support their allegations, anti-Enlightenment advocates needed only to cite from the philosophes. One journalist made a blanket charge: "I defy you to cite me an error, however absurd . . . that the *philosophes* have not adopted [guided solely] by the torch of reason."[56] McMahon quotes the following broadside made in 1787 by anti-philosophe author Rigoley de Juvigny:

> The destructive spirit that dominates today no longer has anything to stop it. *Philosophisme* has penetrated everywhere, has corrupted everything. . . . And indeed how could morals remain pure when an all-consuming *luxe* corrupts them? when everything gives off a spirit of independence and liberty that leads us to sever the ties that attach to State and Society, making of us egotists who are as indifferent to evil as to good, to virtue as to vice? when an ungrateful and false *philosophie* seeks to snuff out filial piety in our hearts, the love that we possess, from birth, for our kings, the attachment we owe to our country . . . ? when, in a word, we have lost all idea of duty, of principle, every rule of conduct, and every sentiment of religion?[57]

The antidote to Enlightenment errors lay in recovering tradition. Long before Edmund Burke's scathing analysis of the French Revolution, anti-philosophes argued that if people cut themselves off from traditional religious beliefs, virtues, and customs, then chaos would result. France should resist the world's tendency toward Enlightenment secularism. Only traditional Catholicism could hold families together, restrain people from committing hideous crimes, and inspire self-denial and respect for legitimate authority.

Thus, France also witnessed the earliest skirmishes of the modern culture wars. Both sides held adamantly to positions totally at odds with the other. Philosophes were convinced that only the Enlightenment could save France from further decline at the hands of outmoded religion and government. Anti-philosophes equally believed in the utter necessity of retaining traditional religion. Each side appealed to principles they deemed self-evidently true, as they engaged in a fierce polemic for the French mind. Enlightenment forces rejoiced in the victory of their principles in 1789, and when the revolution went awry with Robespierre, the anti-Enlightenment forces claimed vindication for their principles.

The antidote to Enlightenment errors lay in recovering tradition. Long before Edmund Burke's scathing analysis of the French Revolution, anti-philosophes argued that if people cut themselves off from traditional religious beliefs, virtues, and customs, then chaos would result.

56. Ibid., 33.
57. Ibid., 41.

German Enlightenment and Awakening

German Pietism

Pietism,[58] the evangelical awakening on the continent in the seventeenth century, bears a genuine similarity to the Anabaptists of the sixteenth-century Reformation. Both considered Luther's forensic view of justification—*sola gratia* and *sola fide*—an objective revolution in theology that needed to be completed with a corresponding subjective revolution in the individual—a personal conversion experience. Philipp Jakob Spener (1635–1705), a pastor in Frankfurt, became disillusioned with the dead orthodoxy of Lutheran scholasticism. Spener was profoundly impressed with the experiential reflections of English Puritans.

Spener believed the church's loss of ardor required major changes in the understanding of Christianity. Drawing on Christianity's broad mystical tradition, Spener said Christianity is not so much an intellectual belief as it is a practical faith. In 1675, Spener outlined his views in *Pia Desideria*—"Heartfelt Desires for a God-Pleasing Reform of the True Evangelical Churches"—in six propositions.

1. Christians ought to study the Bible, not with an academic goal in mind but with the aim of increasing personal devotion.
2. Christians should return to Luther's priesthood of believers to foster greater lay participation. Lay ministry should awaken people from spiritual passivity by mutual instruction and correction.
3. Christianity is not so much a doctrine to be believed as a way of life. Here is the heart of Pietism—its emphasis on experiential faith and its tendency to dichotomize what others believed should remain united.
4. Christian apologetics should be concerned with winning the whole person more than winning theological arguments. A moderate, charitable spirit in theological discussion should replace polemical debate.
5. Because pastors ought to model piety to their people, ministerial education should stress experiential, in addition to intellectual, preparation for ministry. Moral and spiritual qualifications should rank above intellectual prowess when selecting pastors.
6. Evangelical preaching on practical experience should replace didactic sermons on theology. Preaching should be simple, designed to build up the piety of the people: "Since our entire Christianity consists in the inner or new man, and its soul is faith, and the effects of faith are the fruits of life, I regard it as of the greatest importance that sermons should be wholly directed to this end."

Philipp Jakob Spener

---

58. Cf. F. Earnest Stoeffler, *German Pietism During the Eighteenth Century* (Leiden: Brill, 1973) and *The Rise of Evangelical Pietism* (Leiden: Brill, 1965).

These principles gave rise to practices that distinguished the Pietist worldview in everyday life. Pietists articulated Christianity primarily in individual, subjective terms by demanding that everyone experience a conscious, datable conversion experience—a new birth. Although Pietists never rejected the objective nature of salvation (forensic justification), they placed a greater emphasis on subjective experience (regeneration, conversion, and sanctification). In turn, Pietists de-emphasized the intellectual aspects of piety in favor of practical Christian living. Genuine faith manifests itself not primarily in an orthodox confession but in a strenuous ethic characterized by ascetic practices, such as moderation in food, drink, and dress, and by abstaining from attending the theater and participating in dances and card playing.

Pietists mollified legalistic tendencies, however, by their avid participation in philanthropic and missionary enterprises. Under the leadership of Spener's successor August Hermann Francke (1663–1727), the University of Halle flourished as Pietism's intellectual center. Francke established three special programs: a school, the Paedagogium (1696), which carefully monitored children's piety through regular prayer and devotions; the Orphan House (1696), which soon housed 130 children; and the Danish Halle Mission, which pioneered the sending of missionaries (sixty went to South India).

The influence of Pietism as a worldview goes beyond its appearance and gradual decline in the eighteenth century. Although it began within German Lutheranism, Pietism exerted a powerful effect on Moravianism, Methodism, and other denominations in Europe and America. Pietism's most lasting legacy is its leavening effect on modern evangelicalism as a whole with its individualism, conversionism, moralism, and activist tendencies.

Immanuel Kant

In the figure of Immanuel Kant (1724–1804), the German Enlightenment reached its peak of influence.[59] Kant recast epistemology, ethics, and theology, and he epitomized the spirit of the Enlightenment in all of its diverse manifestations.

Ironically, Kant's life illustrated the tension that developed between theocentric and anthropocentric thinking. Because Kant grew up in a Pietist home, his early life was worlds removed from the severities of philosophical reasoning. Kant's mother summarized their religious environment by the following entry in the family Bible: "In the year 1724, on Saturday the 22nd of April at 5:00 in the morning, my son Immanuel [NB, "God with

> *Pietists articulated Christianity primarily in individual, subjective terms by demanding that everyone experience a conscious, datable conversion experience—a new birth.*

> *The influence of Pietism as a worldview goes beyond its appearance and gradual decline in the eighteenth century. … Pietism's most lasting legacy is its leavening effect on modern evangelicalism as a whole with its individualism, conversionism, moralism, and activist tendencies.*

59. See Ernst Cassirer, Stephan Korner, and James Haden, *Kant's Life and Thought* (New Haven, CT: Yale University Press, 1986); Paul Guyer, ed., *The Cambridge Companion to Kant* (Cambridge: Cambridge University Press, 1992); Norman Kemp Smith, *Commentary to Kant's Critique of Pure Reason* (Chicago: University of Chicago Press, 1960); Stephan Korner, *Kant* (New Haven, CT: Yale University Press, 1982); Allen W. Wood, *Kant's Rational Theology* (Ithaca, NY: Cornell University Press, 1978); Bernard Reardon, *Kant as Philosophical Theologian* (Totowa, NJ: Barnes and Noble, 1988).

us"!] was born into the world and on the 23rd received holy baptism . . . . May God preserve him in His covenant of grace unto his blessed end, for Jesus Christ's sake, Amen." But the young Kant recoiled at the strict religious regimen at the Collegium Fridericianum, which he attended for eight years. Because each child was coached to exhibit deep religious feelings, Kant is reported to have said fear and trembling overtook him whenever he recalled those days of youthful slavery and that he could never engage in prayer or hymn singing for the remainder of his life.

For years, Kant labored in virtual obscurity at the University of Königsberg. But with the publication of his revolutionary writings on epistemology, Kant became the central philosophical figure of the new Enlightenment era. We will focus on four writings, each of which articulated the leitmotif (dominant, recurring theme) of all Kant's thinking—the necessity of human autonomy in all phases of human life.

What do we know and how do we know it? Kant answered this epistemological question in his *Critique of Pure Reason* (1781), which revolutionized Western thought. Claiming Hume's skepticism woke him from his "dogmatic slumbers"—a complacent acceptance of rationalist metaphysics—Kant undertook a reappraisal of human reason in which he cemented several developments that had been initiated by his predecessors. Kant's thesis that all knowledge begins with sensory experience, but all knowledge does not arise from sense experience brought together rationalist and empiricist threads. By synthesizing rationalism and empiricism, Kant addressed Hume's skepticism[60] and eliminated any possibility of revelation as a factor in knowledge. Kant claimed that his distinction between the phenomenal world of things and the noumenal realm of ideas saved science and religion, but at the expense of a twofold dichotomy—an ontological dualism in the realm of being and an epistemological dualism between knowledge and faith.[61] Scientists can labor unhindered in their quest to pursue nature and the laws by which it operates, resulting in "knowledge," and theologians can continue their speculations about God and the nature of the soul, resulting in "faith." Not only did Kant give epistemic superiority to science; he left science and theology with nothing to say to each other. Kant introduced a conflict between facts and values that continues to this day.

By analyzing judgments that reason makes, Kant contended that the mind does not contain innate ideas; it contains twelve categories, or "pure concepts of understanding" (e.g., causality, substance), that organize what it receives through the senses. Kant called this operation of the mind a "Copernican revolution," because objects conform to the operation of the

> *Not only did Kant give epistemic superiority to science; he left science and theology with nothing to say to each other. Kant introduced a conflict between facts and values that continues to this day.*

---

60. Some have flippantly argued that in *The Critique of Pure Reason*, Kant merely handed back to Hume his original problem as the solution!

61. While scholars debate whether previous philosophies such as Plato's and Aquinas's qualify as ontological and epistemological dualisms, Kant's "wall" between phenomenal reality and noumenal reality clearly qualifies.

mind and not the mind to objects. Strictly speaking, according to Kant, the mind does not create knowledge, but what it knows is shaped by the knower's categories of understanding. What the mind can know is limited by sensory perception. The mind cannot penetrate beyond physical appearance to apprehend the "thing-in-itself" ("*Ding an sich*"), such as Plato's forms. They remain unknowable. Furthermore, reason certainly cannot know what transcends the world of phenomenal things. Kant said when reason attempts to probe such matters as the existence of God, the soul, or freedom, it becomes hopelessly entangled in irresolvable antinomies. Although such ideas possess a regulative function in ordering our thoughts about the world and our place in it, they do not constitute genuine knowledge.

Kant's transcendental deduction of the categories by which the mind thinks and the control they exercise in shaping knowledge laid the groundwork for his coining the term weltanschauung, which is the subject of this book. At stake for Kant was the autonomy of human reason. Kant maintained that the categories with which we think have their own legitimate integrity and function and do not refer to anything external to the mind, such as revelation. If they did, this would be heteronomy—reason governed by a law "other" than its own inherent authority. Heteronomy would undermine the mind's self-sufficiency to think for itself. According to Kant, heteronomy simply perpetuates the condition of previous eras, which rendered people incapable of thinking for themselves.

Kant further developed his argument for the necessity of human autonomy when he addressed a growing uncertainty about the Enlightenment enterprise. Because of the many different answers to modern questions, many people questioned whether there was an inner coherence to the Enlightenment, and if so, what was it? To explore the issue, a Berlin newspaper posed the question "What is Enlightenment?" and solicited answers from its most prominent representatives. Kant submitted his answer in 1784:

> Enlightenment is man's emergence from his self-imposed immaturity. Immaturity is the inability to use one's understanding without the guidance of another. This immaturity is self-imposed when its cause lies not in lack of understanding but in lack of resolve and courage to use it without guidance from another. *Sapere Aude!* [dare to know] "Have courage to use your own understanding!"—that is the motto of enlightenment.

Although he wrote this after his first *Critique*, Kant hereby revealed the leitmotif of all his works—human reason must function autonomously, if it is to be enlightened. The human mind is *autonomous* (self-sufficient) and must not be subservient either willingly or under coercion to any authority outside itself. Such servitude would constitute *heteronomy* (submitting to law or principle other than its own inherent categories).

Kant illustrated his motto, "Dare to know," by singling out freedom to speak publicly in criticism of religion as essential to an age of enlighten-

At stake for Kant was the autonomy of human reason. Kant maintained that the categories with which we think have their own legitimate integrity and function and do not refer to anything external to the mind, such as revelation.

ment.[62] Privately, a church or denomination may require a pastor or scholar to adhere to its confessional standards. A pastor is obligated to adhere to the church's creed in catechizing, teaching, and preaching. But publicly, a scholar or pastor must have "complete freedom, indeed even the calling, to impart to the public all of his carefully considered and well-intentioned thoughts concerning mistaken aspects of that symbol, as well as his suggestions for the better arrangement of religious and church matters." Kant drew a clear line between public life and private religion that is based on the dualism affirmed in his *Critique*. Kant argued that as moderns progress in their rational inquiry, and as their religion becomes increasingly rational—ceases in the "perpetuation of absurdities"—this double standard of truth will become increasingly unnecessary.

In *Critique of Practical Reason* (1788), Kant answered a third major question: "What is the good and how do we do it?" Just as humans possess a priori categories of pure reason that determine what is, they also possess an a priori category of practical reason—a sense of duty that commands without exception. Kant called this the "categorical imperative": "Act only by that maxim by which you can at the same time will that it should become a universal law." Although Kant's wording bears outward resemblance to Jesus' statement "Do to others as you would have them do unto you" (Luke 6:31 NIV), Kant insisted that morality rests not upon divine authority—that would be heteronomy—but upon the autonomy of reason. The human mind contains the moral principle that determines the good; it is not dependent upon external authority, interior motive, or perceived consequences.[63]

Kant affirmed freedom of the will, immortality of the soul, and the existence of God, but these are not matters that we know. They are nothing more than *necessary postulates* that satisfy the demands of human moral experience. In the same way that Descartes made God the means by which he could bridge between the *cogito* and the real world, Kant made freedom, the soul, and God serve the purposes of the *summum bonum*, the highest good, where virtue and happiness are harmonized. Kant assumed that being commanded implies our ability to fulfill the command; therefore, in order to fulfill the categorical imperative, we must hypothesize that the will is morally free. But the ideal is never fulfilled in this life. Good does not always result in happiness, nor is evil always punished. Therefore, we must assume unending time when people (immortal souls) can improve their behavior and when those who never received just recompense for their actions in this life will be rewarded. In order to guarantee this ideal,

Immanuel Kant

---

62. In the same essay, Kant posed the question whether he lived in an enlightened age and answered: "No, but we do live in an age of enlightenment."

63. In another major work, *Foundations of the Metaphysics of Morals* (1785), Kant stated: "Autonomy of the will is that property of it by which it is a law to itself independently of any property of objects of volition."

we also must postulate the existence of a being who is altogether fitted to judge, order, and effect perfect happiness and virtue, that is, God. In this manner, Kant gave God a place in his philosophy, but he clearly made God subservient to his system, not its determining basis. By separating ethics from divine authority, Kant prepared the way for the fourth and concluding issue—the nature of religion.

In *Religion within the Limits of Reason Alone* (1793), Kant addressed the question: "What is religion, and how do we become right with God?" in terms that were consistent with the notion of human autonomy he had developed in his preceding writings. Although many scholars neglect this work, its title, content, method, and conclusion form a capstone to Kant's entire enterprise; summarize Enlightenment revolutions in worldview; and bring Kant's Copernican revolution to its conclusion by recasting Christianity as a moralistic deism.[64]

Although Kant upheld Christianity as the ultimate ethical religion, he divested it of all its distinctive doctrines. His denial of key elements of the Christian worldview and his reinterpretation of others lead many to call him "the philosopher of [nineteenth-century, liberal] Protestantism." Kant began by asserting the presence of "radical evil" in human nature. For Kant, radical evil means choosing sensual over moral incentives (Kant's interpretation of Adam and Eve in Genesis 3). Subordinating the categorical imperative to other faculties such as the sensual appetites corrupts the moral disposition, which for Kant was the ultimate maxim that influences all other moral choices resulting in perversity of heart. But "perversity of heart" is far from the wickedness of a "rebel" who repudiates the moral law: "Man (even the most wicked) does not under any maxim whatever, repudiate the moral law in the manner of a rebel (renouncing obedience to it)."

Thus, Kant proposed what has become the modern view of human nature: although evil exists in human nature, it can be overcome. According to Kant, there is bad news: "There is in man a natural propensity to evil. . . . This evil is radical because it corrupts the ground of all maxims; it is moreover, as a natural propensity, inextirpable by human powers, since extirpation could occur only through good maxims, and cannot take place when the ultimate subjective ground of all maxims is postulated as corrupt. . . ." Many interpreted Kant's "radical evil" as nothing less than a reinstatement of original sin,[65] and a contemporary derided Kant as "slobbering on his philosopher's robe" for suggesting such a "natural propensity" as something "inextirpable." Nevertheless, Kant continued by saying "at the same time it must be possible to overcome it since it is found in man, a

> *Kant insisted that morality rests not upon divine authority—that would be heteronomy—but upon the autonomy of reason. The human mind contains the moral principle that determines the good; it is not dependent upon external authority, interior motive, or perceived consequences.*

> *[Kant] divested [Christianity] of all its distinctive doctrines. His denial of key elements of the Christian worldview and his reinterpretation of others lead many to call him "the philosopher of [nineteenth-century, liberal] Protestantism."*

---

64.   See Allen W. Wood, *Kant's Rational Theology* (Ithaca, NY: Cornell University Press, 1978). So important is this work that Nicholas Wolterstorff in his critique of foundationalism inverts Kant's title in his *Reason within the Bounds of Religion* (Grand Rapids: Eerdmans [1976], rev. ed. 1984).

65.   Kant cited Paul's classical text for human sin, Romans 3:9–10: they are "all under sin . . . 'there is none righteous [in the spirit of the law], no, not one.' " "Extirpate" means "eradicate."

being whose actions are free." Thus, Kant's analysis of the presence of evil and his belief in the possibility of moral improvement derive from autonomous human reason and presuppose moral freedom. This understanding of evil, moral improvement, human reason, and moral freedom has come to be the primary characterization of the modern worldview.

Kant's view of human nature diverges far from traditional views of an inherited corruption or the federal imputation of Adam's sin. For Kant, the fall was not a historical event that plunged the human race into sin. Kant argued that in "rational religion," the least acceptable ("most inept") explanation for the origin of evil is a historical one. Therefore, one must look for a rational origin where "Adam" is not the first man but stands for everyman, where he is a rational depiction of what every human does to corrupt his disposition. After summarizing Genesis 2 and 3, Kant stated: "From all this it is clear that we daily act in the same way, and therefore 'in Adam all have sinned' [Rom. 5:12] and still sin. . . ."

According to Kant, since the Bible teaches that human will was not inherently corrupt but fell prey to temptation by "a spirit of an originally loftier destiny," then human nature must "still [be] capable of improvement" because a seed of goodness remains. Therefore, according to Kant, the human will retains the content of the moral law (the categorical imperative) and possesses the moral freedom needed to choose to reinstate the moral incentive to its position of dispositional dominance. In other words, according to Kant, all humans know the categorical imperative and have the moral freedom necessary to choose to live by its dictates. Kant categorically depicted the modern view of human nature: "Man *himself* must make or have made himself into whatever, in a moral sense, whether good or evil, he is or is to become." He cited John 3:5, the classical Pietist text for "the new birth," to affirm that a moral revolution, not gradualism, is required: "He can become a new man only by a kind of rebirth as it were a new creation."[66] Kant realized this contradicted what he said earlier regarding the corruption of maxims being inextirpable (incapable of being completely destroyed). But the contradiction only highlights the incompatibility between moral and theological dogmatics.

This led Kant to distinguish between religions that are genuine, that is, moral, and those that are inauthentic, that is, religions of worship. The latter flatter people by teaching that they can become happy by the remission of sins (i.e., by performing acts that win favor from God, such as prayer and ritual performances) "without . . . having to become . . . better" by performing acts of *good life conduct.* In Kant's system, morality and worship differ so radically from one another that the religious goal of "salvation" or becoming "right with God" changes from total dependence on God's grace to performing works that merit God's blessing. Kant stated categorically,

> *Kant's analysis of the presence of evil and his belief in the possibility of moral improvement derive from autonomous human reason and presuppose moral freedom. This understanding of evil, moral improvement, human reason, and moral freedom has come to be the primary characterization of the modern worldview.*

---

66. Kant conflated John 3:5 and 2 Cor. 5:17. He also borrowed Paul's wording that a person "puts on the new man."

"It is not essential, and hence not necessary, for every one to know what God does or has done for his salvation; but it is essential to know *what man himself must do* in order to become worthy of this assistance." That statement changes Christianity from a religion of grace, where God does for humans what they are not able to do for themselves—that is, God forgives their sins—to a bootstrap religion, where people lift themselves up by their own internal moral revolution.

Kant further delineated the modern view of Jesus Christ, whom he never mentions by name but only by such titles as "Teacher" and "Master." Kant interpreted Jesus as "the Personified Idea of the Good Principle" as the meaning of John 1:1–13 and John 3:16." Jesus is not the eternal, onto-logical Son of God, sent by the Father to atone for human sin, but a rational archetype, a personification of moral goodness that lies resident in reason. Kant taught that although humans need no empirical example of what they already possess in reason, the Bible accommodates itself with the anthro-pomorphism of God sending his Son as a sacrifice for others' sins—an idea, however, carrying "the most injurious consequences." That is, some might actually "transform it into a *schematism of objective determination.*" For Kant, such an idea was morally reprehensible. Kant set the moral tone for modern religion by denying that "radical evil" is a "*transmissible* liability which can be made over to another like a financial indebtedness where it is all one to the creditor whether the debtor himself pays the debt or whether some one else pays it for him" (cf. Anselm's *Cur Deus Homo*). Instead, said Kant, "[the debt of sins] is the most personal of all debts . . . which only the culprit can bear and which no innocent person can assume even though he be magnanimous enough to wish to take it upon himself for the sake of another."[67] Belief in a substitutionary atonement, therefore, rather than forming the foundation for redemption, actually constitutes the ultimate ethical irresponsibility.

Kant also applied the principle of autonomy to the process of salva-tion by emphasizing the subjective nature of conversion. The internal con-version of the disposition becomes the locus of salvation, as the individual experiences the "death of the old" man and carries out "the crucifying of the flesh." "These the new man undertakes in the disposition of the Son of God, that is merely for the sake of the good, though really they are due as *punishments* to another, namely to the old man (for the old man is indeed morally another)." Thus Kant substituted the subjective work in the heart of the believer for the objective work of Christ on the cross, while retaining aspects of the biblical language.

> *Kant also applied the principle of auton-omy to the process of salvation by empha-sizing the subjective nature of conversion. . . . [He] substituted the subjective work in the heart of the believer for the objec-tive work of Christ on the cross, while retaining aspects of the biblical language.*

67. Kant directly attacked the legitimacy of atonement with remarks such as "how could a reasonable person . . . in all seriousness believe" in such an idea, and "no thought-ful person can bring himself to believe" the idea of substitution. Kant thus denies both the Pauline and Johannine views of Jesus' death as a propitiation and expiation for sin.

> Immanuel Kant's
> reformulation of
> Christianity was a
> towering accom-
> plishment in reshap-
> ing the modern
> mind, and it trans-
> formed Christianity
> into the ultimate
> deist religion that
> needs no confirming
> miracles or external
> verification.

Finally, Kant's comments on founding the kingdom of God and on acts of devotion round out his modern interpretation of religion. Kant taught that the goal of rational religion is to unite individuals into a community, a social commonwealth that displays the genuine signs of the "kingdom of God on earth." Kant applied four categories he adopted in his first *Critique* to depict the "true visible church": Quantity (universality)—numerical oneness: there must be no sectarian divisions; Nature (quality)—purity: it must not consist of superstitious or fanatical elements that pollute its essential moral character; Relation (freedom): true moral communities will not allow any hierarchicalism or "illuminatism" that differentiates some individuals from others; and Modality (unchangeableness): it must consist of settled principles, primordial laws that are not arbitrary and subject to contradiction.[68]

According to Kant, pure religious faith must focus on moral teaching that is consistent with the religion of reason, especially where claims of historical revelation appear. Citing 2 Timothy 3:16–17, a classical text for biblical authority and inspiration, Kant stated that the main purpose of revelation is to teach moral truth, "the highest principle of all Scriptural exegesis." All interpretations of the Bible must pass the test of reason and not rest on feeling. Kant bridled at a proposal that involved acquiescing to the morality of the imprecatory Psalms. Kant retorted, "I should try as a first alternative, to bring the New Testament passage into conformity with my own self-subsistent moral principles. . . ." Kant disparaged Judaism as a qualitatively inferior religion because its ceremonial laws lacked moral content, and the notion of a chosen people based on ethnicity excluded the vast majority of people from its membership.

Immanuel Kant's reformulation of Christianity was a towering accomplishment in reshaping the modern mind, and it transformed Christianity into the ultimate deist religion that needs no confirming miracles or external verification. His a priori contrasted religions of morality with those of pseudo-worship. False religion consists of any practice that goes beyond good-life conduct. Thus, Kant opposed any acts of religious devotion as manipulative magic conceived to win God's favor. These Kantian principles laid the intellectual foundations for nineteenth-century liberalism in Christian theology. Although Schleiermacher and Hegel drastically reworked Christianity again, they did so on the same basis that Descartes and Kant did in the eighteenth century; they adapted Christianity to the thought forms of their day. If enlighteners before him had stressed human autonomy, Kant made it the focal point of his writings.

---

68. Cf. the followers of magisterial Reformers' designation of the signs of a true visible church: preaching of the gospel, celebration of the sacraments (baptism and the Lord's Supper), and discipline of its members, as well as the seven signs of the church in the Anabaptist *Schleitheim Confession*: Believer's Baptism, the Ban (discipline), Breaking Bread (the Lord's Supper), Separation from the World, Pastors called by Congregations, Prohibition of the Sword, and Prohibition of Oaths.

American Enlightenment and Awakening

The American Enlightenment

America experienced the various phases of the Enlightenment manifested in Europe—the moderate Enlightenment of England, the skeptical Enlightenment of France, and the didactic Enlightenment from Scotland.[69] Enlightenment thought made its most significant impact in the American political realm. The secularism that led to denials of traditional theological beliefs also led to dramatic changes regarding how to conceive of the political order—the nature of government, how to legitimate its power, and the most pressing issue of modern times, under what conditions people have the right to revolt against unjust powers.

Thomas Paine (1737–1809) championed new views of freedom and independence in England, France, and America. Born a Quaker, Paine associated with radical dissent in England before writing three influential treatises: *Common Sense* (1776), a defense of the American War of Independence; *The Rights of Man* (1791), an answer to Edmund Burke's *Reflections on the French Revolution*; and *The Age of Reason* (1794–95), which mounted such a savage attack on revealed religion that people renamed the era "The Age of Pain." Although Paine appealed to Samuel's arguments against Israel's desire for a king in order to repudiate monarchy as a legitimate form of government (see 1 Sam. 8:6–22), the preponderance of his writings lack any reference to revealed authority. Instead, Paine cites the "natural rights of mankind," "the concern of every man to whom nature hath given the power of being," "the influence of reason and principle," and "the universal order of things," as the basis for "common sense." He affirmed his rational autonomy by fiat: "My principle is universal. My attachment is to all the world, and not to any particular part, and what I advance is right, no matter where or who it comes from."

Having established his epistemic base, Paine proposed in *The Rights of Man* a totally secular basis for government. Paine adopted Locke's view of the "consent of the governed," eliminating any theistic grounds as the basis for the state. Locke may be interpreted as applying the Protestant principle of the priesthood of believers to the political realm as the philosophical underpinning for a commonwealth like the old Latin *civitas*.

However, more radical ideas were afoot than merely affirming a new basis for government, for the question arose regarding how to justify a break from England. Although Christians had debated the legitimacy of revolution for centuries, now the issue arose afresh in the colonies. Burke had contended that French philosophes grounded their case for revolution in atheism and denial of the organic traditions from the past. Paine, how-

Thomas Paine

The secularism that led to denials of traditional theological beliefs also led to dramatic changes regarding how to conceive of the political order—the nature of government, how to legitimate its power, and . . . under what conditions people have the right to revolt against unjust powers.

---

69. The latter was manifested more in the nineteenth century in the proliferation of Scottish Common Sense Realism in intellectual life. Cf. May, *Enlightenment in America*.

ever, challenged British hierarchical thought by affirming that government rested purely on the equal rights of all people. Locke based human government on God's granting to husband and wife the liberty to form a conjugal society. But Paine foresaw a republic founded on the common belief of the natural rights of people: "Every age and generation must be as free to act for itself, *in all cases*, as the ages and generations which preceded it. . . . Every generation is, and must be competent to all the purposes which its occasions require." Whereas past governments rested on priests imposing their will through superstitions and conquerors ruling through coercion, the modern era, the age of freedom, must base its government on "the *individuals themselves*." Paine summed up his case: ". . . each in his own personal and sovereign right, *entered into a compact with each other* to produce a government: and this is the only mode in which governments have a right to arise, and the only principle on which they have a right to exist."

Paine's arguments fueled the American drive for independence. He exalted liberty as the most important cause of mankind: "We have it in our power to begin the world over again. A situation similar to the present has not happened since the days of Noah until now." But it fell to Thomas Jefferson to spell out in the Declaration of Independence, in more reserved terms, the rights of revolution on which both theists and deists could agree. The declaration served as a revolutionary worldview document because it affirmed that government rested on certain self-evident truths about God, man, and government that broke from English hierarchical precedence. The document primarily summarizes grievances that violate assumptions about rights of individuals and the social contract. Although much debate still surrounds the basic ideas of Jefferson's political document, the most significant fact about it is that it established a precedent for revolution drawn from both Reformation and Enlightenment principles. The Reformation provided the belief that all liberties rest on freedom from sin and that revolution should proceed under the leadership of under-magistrates, not by mob action. Locke's and Paine's writings lent more secular appraisals of human rights and liberties.

> *The declaration served as a revolutionary worldview document because it affirmed that government rested on certain self-evident truths about God, man, and government that broke from English hierarchical precedence.*

America's Great Awakening

The religious scene in the New World manifested characteristics we traced in Europe. America exhibited both a great diversity of denominations and a remarkable revivalism that swept the colonies and the new nation into the nineteenth century. The Enlightenment took its toll on traditional religion, as evidenced by the spread of Unitarianism, principally in New England, and the brief impact that deism had, especially among the political leadership until the War of 1812. But the underlying beliefs during the colonial period testify to the continuing influence of traditional theism as the prevailing worldview.

While New Light awakeners Gilbert Tennent, Theodore Frelinghuysen, and George Whitefield labored might and main to revive the colonial churches, the dominant figure of eighteenth-century America was Puritan Jonathan Edwards (1703–58), pastor, evangelist, theologian, philosopher, and apologist. He shaped the American mind by defending the Great Awakening, articulating a view of religion as consisting of religious affections, and detailing a credible defense of traditional Calvinism against the secular worldviews of Enlightenment thinkers.[70]

Edwards participated in and defended the Great Awakening. In *A Faithful Narrative*, the first of several works supporting the legitimacy of evangelical revivalism, he chronicled the 1734–35 revival in his Northampton congregation in great detail. Against detractors who repudiated the awakening as mere "enthusiasm," because of emotional outbursts that accompanied dramatic conversions, Edwards portrayed the revival as "the surprising work of God." While denouncing abuses of some co-revivalists, Edwards's classic *Faithful Narrative* describes the genuine marks of the Holy Spirit, distinguishing them from those that do not prove the genuineness of revivals, one way or the other. Edwards systematically dismissed anti-revivalist objections to emotional manifestations (which he called "negative signs"), because such phenomena are of no value in judging whether revivals are God's work or a counterfeit of Satan.

Instead, Edwards pointed to "positive signs," characteristics that satisfied biblical criteria in 1 John as "distinguishing marks" of the work of God's Spirit. Genuine revivals enhance worship of Christ, reject sin and the works of Satan, and promote love for the Scriptures and true Christian love. Anyone opposing the awakenings, therefore, faced the danger of opposing God. Additionally, by placing the awakenings in a broad historical context, Edwards denied the revivals were merely provincial phenomena. American awakenings were the most recent of God's periodic acts of renewing the church, and they happily coincided with Pietist renewals in Germany under Hermann Francke. Thus, in several works, Edwards articulated the classic defense of revivalism, based on a Calvinist worldview, that served as evangelicalism's foundational interpretation until revivalism's worldview changed radically in the next century.

In *Treatise on Religious Affections* (1747), Edwards defended the religious a priori of the awakeners. He repudiated two extremes: radical New Lights, who by their manipulative practices deluded their hearers, and Old Lights, who made religion simply a matter of cognitive belief. Neither affec-

> *Genuine revivals enhance worship of Christ, reject sin and the works of Satan, and promote love for the Scriptures and true Christian love. Anyone opposing the awakenings, therefore, faced the danger of opposing God.*

---

70. See Robert Jenson, *America's Theologian: A Recommendation of Jonathan Edwards* (New York: Oxford University Press, 1988); Norman Fiering, *Jonathan Edwards's Moral Thought and Its British Context* (Chapel Hill, NC: University of North Carolina Press, 1981); Sang Hyun Lee, *The Philosophical Theology of Jonathan Edwards* (Princeton, NJ: Princeton University Press, 1988); Gerald McDermott, *Jonathan Edwards Confronts the Gods: Christian Theology, Enlightenment Religion, and Non-Christian Faiths* (New York: Oxford University Press, 2000); Robert E. Brown, *Jonathan Edwards and the Bible* (Bloomington, IN: Indiana University Press, 2002).

tions nor intellect alone constitute the seat of religion. By insisting that genuine religion consists of "holy love," Edwards joined the affective and the cognitive faculties: "True religion in great part, consists in holy affections."

Edwards delineated twelve signs of "truly gracious and holy affections."[71] Signs four and five, "spiritual understanding" and "conviction," show the subtlety of Edwards's synthesis of intellect and affections. By the former, Edwards disposed of anti-revivalists who reduced religion to reasonable belief: "Holy affections are not heat without light; but evermore arise from some information of the understanding, some spiritual instruction that the mind receives, some light or actual knowledge." But mere notional understanding, while grasping information, does not engage the will. Therefore he used the biblical terminology of the heart, the unifying center of the person, as the seat of religion: "The Holy Scriptures do everywhere place religion very much in the affections; such as fear, hope, love, hatred, desire, joy, sorrow, gratitude, compassion and zeal." The believer does not merely assent to a truth but manifests a sense or taste that transcends perception and inclines the heart. Edwards likened philosophical reasoning, by which "persons are guided in their judgment of the natural beauty, gracefulness, propriety, nobleness and sublimity of speeches and actions," to a "divine taste given and maintained by the Spirit of God, in the hearts of the saints, whereby they are in like manner led and guided in discerning and distinguishing the true spiritual and holy beauty of actions. . . . " Edwards refused to contrast the head and the heart.

The fifth sign adds to cognitive apprehension a conviction that grasped and moved the total self. Conviction follows understanding and is impossible without its preceding function. Conviction also manifests an immediacy of experience: "the Spirit of God's enlightening the mind, to have right apprehensions of the nature of those things, and so as it were unveiling things, or revealing them, and enabling the mind to view them and see them as they are." With these remarks, Edwards summarized not only his religious a priori but also his epistemology. Religion and knowledge possess an objective cognitive element, as well as an equally important subjective component. The biblical category of the heart joins these elements to characterize the unity of human experience. Although Edwards's language may sometimes reflect a faulty psychology, he succeeded better than many in holding together human understanding, emotions, imagination, and will. The remaining six signs confirm this. Revealing his Puritan heritage, Edwards claimed that only God knows those who are genuinely redeemed; no definitive method exists by which to judge the human heart. However, he added, "gracious and holy affections have their exercise and fruit in Christian practice."

> *Holy affections are not heat without light; but evermore arise from some information of the understanding, some spiritual instruction that the mind receives, some light or actual knowledge.*

71. Here I follow George Marsden's excellent analysis in *Jonathan Edwards: A Life* (New Haven, CT: Yale University Press, 2003), 284–90. Cf. William J. Wainwright's treatment of Edwards's view of emotions guiding reason in *Reason and the Heart: A Prolegomenon to a Critique of Passional Reason* (Ithaca, NY: Cornell University Press, 1995).

Edwards's final contribution may well have been his most significant—a lifelong pursuit to articulate a credible Christian worldview in the face of secular alternatives.[72] Edwards believed Reformed Christianity alone provided a satisfying, coherent worldview, in contrast with the heralded advances of the Enlightenment, which were only "dimly reflected light." Throughout his life, Edwards remained thoroughly engaged with the intellectual milieu in America and abroad, and he read widely across the disciplines of the arts, sciences, philosophy, and theology. In addition to his explicitly theological defenses of Calvinism in *Freedom of the Will* and *Original Sin,* in which he responded to modern views of human autonomy and perfectibility, he also planned a massive, comprehensive work to demonstrate how all of the arts and sciences, as they are developed, will add to the glory of God and show themselves as evidences of God's providence.

Jonathan Edwards

Later, Edwards completed two dissertations, which partially fulfilled this goal: *The End for which God Created the World* and *The Nature of True Virtue* (published posthumously in 1765). In the former, Edwards enunciated a fundamental perspective, and in turn countered the premises of modern freethinkers. Enlightenment philosophers erred, Edwards argued, because they viewed everything from the viewpoint of human happiness, not from the perspective of God's purpose in creating the universe. Whereas thinkers from Descartes comprehended and interpreted everything based on human autonomy, Edwards insisted that all things, not just theology proper, could be understood fully only as they relate to God. Drawing on his Augustinian heritage, Edwards made the Trinity and God's communication of love for the well-being of his creatures his point of departure.

Edwards's interpretation takes on even greater significance when viewed against his unique view of creation. Edwards believed that human speculation functions properly only when it does so within a theological and teleological context. The end for which God created the world was the glory of God.[73] Edwards concluded that providence means that God did not create out of nothing just at the beginning of time; God creates out of nothing at every moment in time. Adapting the Pauline benediction in Romans 11:36 as the leitmotif for this prolegomena to all that he wrote, Edwards consistently interpreted everything, including human happiness, in the larger context of God's glory: "The beams of glory come from God, and are something of God, and are refunded back again to their original. So that the whole is *of* God, and *in* God, and *to* God; and God is the beginning, middle and end in this affair." Marsden comments, "[this sentence]

> *Edwards's final contribution may well have been his most significant—a lifelong pursuit to articulate a credible Christian worldview in the face of secular alternatives. Edwards believed Reformed Christianity alone provided a satisfying, coherent worldview.*

72. Marsden's development of Edwards's worldview contribution is excellent. Marsden, *Jonathan Edwards*, 459–89.

73. In an earlier writing, Edwards had expanded on what he considered Newton's excellent work on the laws of nature: "if gravity should be withdrawn, the whole universe would in a moment vanish into nothing." The laws of nature are not just explanations of mechanical causality but a description of God's direct action in maintaining the cosmos, as Paul stated in Col. 1:17: "And he is before all things, and by him all things consist" (KJV).

encapsulated the central premise of his entire thought." Instead of the god who fills the gap between the *cogito* and rest of reality, or reveals things subject to the dictates of human reason, or the wise moral governor of a kingdom of ends, Edwards posits the sovereign God of redemption, infinitely involved in sustaining the world, whose glory elicits praise from creatures united with him. God's self-revelation opens up a cosmic perspective in which creation, fall, and redemption fill the chronicles of human history and in which believers enjoy union with God. Herein lies genuine human happiness: "The more happiness the greater union; when the happiness is perfect, the union is perfect." Whereas moral behavior formed an important element of Edwards's religious devotion (few could match his Puritan zeal for moral discipline), worship, prayer, and other acts of piety formed the appropriate means by which people expressed their worship of the glory of God.

The second dissertation, *The Nature of True Virtue*, addressed prevailing assumptions that philosophy awaited its own Newton to establish an autonomous morality that would garner the same recognition and respect as modern science. Such a grand scheme would possess both a rational and empirical base in keeping with the belief that "self-evident" principles are built into the very structure of reality.

Edwards exploited this confidence with the all-important caveat derived from his first dissertation regarding the glory of God: "Nothing is of the nature of true virtue in which God is not the *first* and the *last*." Rather than quoting Scripture passages, as he did in abundance in *The End for which God Created the World*, Edwards mounted a transcendental argument based on the proposition that true virtue essentially consists in benevolence to Being in general. Seeing everything within the context of God and his will means that benevolence is possible only from a converted heart and is radically inferior unless it takes into consideration the widest possible horizon for the expression of love, that is, God himself.

Edwards's argument resembles Augustine's hierarchical conception of various loves and forms of peace in *The City of God*, wherein anything less than love of and peace with God is but a splendid vice. "For he that is influenced by private affection, not subordinate to regard to Being in general, sets up its particular or limited object *above* Being in general; and this most naturally tends to enmity against the latter." Edwards concludes: ". . . these *schemes* of religion or moral philosophy, which, however well in some respects they may treat of benevolence to *mankind*, and other virtues depending on it, yet have not a supreme regard to God, and love to him, laid in the *foundation* and all other virtues handled in a *connection* with this, and in a *subordination* to this, are no true schemes of philosophy, but are fundamentally and essentially defective."

Edwards's religious and ethical schemes form a coherent whole. Only as humans are united to God and order their lives so that they love what

> "For he that is influenced by private affection, not subordinate to regard to Being in general, sets up its particular or limited object **above** Being in general; and this most naturally tends to enmity against the latter."

God loves will God's happiness be their happiness and benevolence and justice with others come to fruition. Edwards proposed a theistic worldview that contextualized the biblical perspective in opposition to modernity's philosophical project, which is based on human autonomy.

Conclusion: The Beginning of the Culture Wars

The era of Enlightenments and Awakenings witnessed enormous changes in worldview in Western thought. At the opening of the modern era, theistic orthodoxy prevailed in Europe and America in various forms of established religions, the dominant churches being Lutheran, Calvinist, Anglican, and Roman Catholic. Although religious worldviews differed in doctrinal tenets, as well as in acts of piety or devotion, traditional religions maintained their heritage as traced in previous chapters.

Throughout the seventeenth and eighteenth centuries, however, new philosophical and religious trajectories confronted traditional views. A radical diversity of worldviews resulted, ranging from militantly anti-Christian deism and explicitly secular perspectives to various modifications of traditional theism. Challenges to traditional cosmology from the scientific revolution and competing philosophical perspectives of modern philosophers quickly gained momentum. The term "Enlightenment," regardless of the form it took, came to signify a new way of seeing things, primarily not through the category of revelation but through rational demonstration and empirical investigation. As human autonomy replaced divine autonomy, the heavens looked different, miracles seemed inconsistent with natural law, authorities based on revelation no longer compelled belief, and traditional schemes of redemption rather than offering hope and comfort appeared repugnant to the modern sensitivities. The religious a priori among Enlightenment thinkers became decidedly moralistic, achievable by human effort with some assistance from God.

Over against Enlightenment ideas, various forms of evangelical religion in England, France, Germany, and America stood as alternatives to secularism. Although in some instances subjective tendencies emerged, evangelicals championed biblical authority, heartfelt conversion experiences, and involvement in public good works based on Christ's redemptive work on the cross. The radical differences in worldviews clearly set the stage for the struggle for the Western mind—a veritable culture war.

Many analyses of the contemporary culture war trace its beginnings to the nineteenth century, as early forms of postmodernism emerged in Romantic, Marxist, Darwinian, and Nietzschean philosophies that repudiated traditional ideas. But the roots for the culture war lay in an earlier era, as evidenced by the radical disparity of worldviews we have examined. None of the protagonists believed their worldviews were merely a matter of private belief. None wanted their views to be relegated to the pri-

The roots for the culture war lay in an earlier era, as evidenced by the radical disparity of worldviews we have examined. None of the protagonists believed their worldviews were merely a matter of private belief. None wanted their views to be relegated to the private dimension of human life.

vate dimension of human life. Enlighteners and awakeners alike believed their worldviews competent to guide both private and public life, and they fought aggressively to attain that end. Their agendas also looked similar. They defended their perspectives and launched polemics against competitors. They articulated both individual and social moralities to achieve their ends, since they believed their ideas had political, economic, and social implications. In short, all participants viewed their worldviews as holistic commitments that transcended their own particularity and thus applied to the universal human condition.

For Further Reading

Baumer, Franklin. *Modern European Thought: Continuity and Change in Ideas*. New York: Macmillan, 1977.

Becker, Carl L. *The Heavenly City of the Eighteenth-Century Philosophers*. New Haven, CT: Yale University Press, 1932.

Bebbington, David W. *Evangelicalism in Modern Britain: A History from the 1730s to the 1980s*. London: Unwin Hyman, 1989.

Brown, Colin. *Christianity and Western Thought: A History of Philosophers, Ideas and Movements*. Vol. 1, *From the Ancient World to the Age of Enlightenment*. Downers Grove, IL: InterVarsity Press, 1990.

Brown, Dale W. *Understanding Pietism*. Grand Rapids: Wm. B. Eerdmans, 1978.

Campbell, Ted. *The Religion of the Heart: A Study of European Religious Life in the Seventeenth and Eighteenth Centuries*. Columbia, SC: University of South Carolina Press, 1991.

Collins, James. *God in Modern Philosophy*. Chicago: Henry Regnery Company, 1959.

Copleston, Frederick C. *A History of Philosophy*, 9 vols. Garden City, NY: Image Books, 1962–65.

Gay, Peter. *The Enlightenment*. Vol. 1, *The Rise of Modern Paganism*. New York: W. W. Norton, 1966.

———. *The Enlightenment*. Vol. 2, *The Science of Freedom*. New York: W. W. Norton, 1969.

Marsden, George M. *Jonathan Edwards: A Life*. New Haven, CT: Yale University Press, 2003.

May, Henry. *The Enlightenment in America*. New York: Oxford University Press, 1976.

McMahon, Darrin M. *Enemies of the Enlightenment: The French Counter-Enlightenment and the Making of Modernity*. Oxford: Oxford University Press, 2001.

Outram, Dorinda. *The Enlightenment*. Cambridge: Cambridge University Press, 1995.

Passmore, John. *The Perfectibility of Man*. New York: Scribners, 1970.

Schneewind, Jerome B. *Invention of Autonomy: A History of Modern Moral Philosophy*. Cambridge: Cambridge University Press, 1997.

Enlighteners and awakeners alike believed their worldviews competent to guide both private and public life, and they fought aggressively to attain that end.... In short, all participants viewed their worldviews as holistic commitments that ... applied to the universal human condition.

Stoeffler, F. Ernest. *The Rise of Evangelical Pietism*. Leiden: Brill, 1965.

Toulmin, Stephen. *Cosmopolis: The Agenda of Modernity*. Chicago: University of Chicago Press, 1990.

Turner, James. *Without God, Without Creed: The Origins of Unbelief in America*. Baltimore: Johns Hopkins University Press, 1985.

For Further Discussion

1. What commonality exists between Enlightenment and Awakening thinkers?

2. What contemporary views of religious Awakenings/revivals are argued in support of the privatization and marginalization of religion?

3. How did Francis Bacon's inductive method and Newtonian physics establish a new paradigm of thinking for the modern period?

4. Although "theism" and "deism" are etymologically cognate, how have they come to exemplify diametrically different worldviews? What comes immediately to mind when you hear these two words?

5. How do previous Christian thinkers and the thinkers in this chapter differ in their explanation of the structure and reliability of reason?

6. How does Kant's view of what constitutes a genuine "religious act" differ from those of previous eras from the Old Testament to the Reformers?

7. How does Kant's term "radical evil" sound similar to but actually differ from Christianity's "original sin"?

8. Nicholas Wolterstorff has rephrased Kant's major work on religion and written a book titled *Reason within the Limits of Religion*. What are the implications of that change?

9. How does Wesley's quadrilateral differ from Reformation thinkers' views of authority?

10. How do the various formulations of Wesley's perfectionism compare with the optimistic views of human nature espoused by the philosophes?

11. Speculate how Descartes would respond to Pascal's critique of Cartesian reason.

12. Of the various uses of faith and reason in this chapter, which do you find most satisfying? Which do you find least satisfying? Explain your selections.

13. Do you think the demands of the Pietists represent a legitimate expression of Christianity? Why or why not?

14. Summarize the differences between the philosophes and anti-philosophes. How did the anti-philosophes differ from Pascal?

15. Evaluate Kant's claim that his epistemology represented nothing less than a "Copernican revolution" in philosophy.

16. Explore the various nuances of meaning in Kant's definition of Enlightenment: "Dare to reason." How does his challenge to his contemporaries compare with the use of reason in the Middle Ages, Renaissance, and Reformation?

17. Explain how Kant differentiated between autonomy and heteronomy.

18. Why did Kant believe religions of worship are "inauthentic"?

19. What are some implications of the double standard of truth (confessional and academic) introduced by Immanuel Kant? What evidences do we have that such a standard still exists today?

20. How does human autonomy exercise a controlling influence in Thomas Paine's various works?

21. Contrast the various ideas of conversion represented in the following figures: Martin Luther, John Calvin, Philipp Spener, John Wesley, Immanuel Kant, and Jonathan Edwards.

22. How does Jonathan Edwards fit the stereotype of the term "Puritan"? How does he break the mold of that stereotype?

23. Compare Kant and Edwards on the definition of "religion." How would each critique the other's work?

The Age of Intellectual Iconoclasm: The Nineteenth Century Revolt against Theism

Richard Lints

I f ever the description "revolution" was appropriately applied to a century, surely it describes the nineteenth. Whatever else, this was an era of intellectual upheaval. At the beginning of the period, faith and reason generally were thought to be mutually compatible. Scholars routinely interpreted the rise of early modern science as grounded in Christian claims about the orderliness of the created order.[1] By the end of the century, faith and reason were more generally perceived as enemies, forever locked in violent conflict. A. D. White could write representatively of the "warfare between science and religion."[2] In Europe and America, belief in God was much more fragile at the end of the nineteenth century than at its beginning.

At the heart of the revolution was a conflict over the foundational claims of biblical theism—belief in the existence of a God who created the world, who orders history, who will bring all things to their proper consummation, and in whose image human beings are created. Idolatry was the attempt to

> *At the heart of the revolution was a conflict over the foundational claims of biblical theism— belief in the existence of a God who created the world, who orders history, who will bring all things to their proper consummation, and in whose image human beings are created.*

---

1.   A vast body of literature addresses the controversy whether modern science is influenced, at least in part, by Christian origins. A fair and balanced set of essays can be found in Gary B. Ferngren, ed., *Science and Religion: A Historical Introduction* (Baltimore: Johns Hopkins University Press, 2002). On the question of how evangelicals have related to the rise of modern science, see David N. Livingstone, D. G. Hart, and Mark A. Noll, eds., *Evangelicals and Science in Historical Perspective* (New York: Oxford University Press, 1999). A dated but still helpful overview of the central issues is R. Hooykaas, *Religion and the Rise of Modern Science* (Grand Rapids: Eerdmans, 1972). For the purposes of this chapter, it simply needs to be said that early modern science was not originally thought to be antagonistic to Christian belief.

2.   Andrew Dickson White, *A History of the Warfare of Science with Theology in Christendom: Two Volumes in One* (Buffalo, NY: Prometheus Books, 1993).

Abraham Kuyper

fashion a god in our own image. Ironically, intellectuals of the nineteenth century concurred that idolatry was abhorrent. However, they turned the problem upside down, for the secular prophets concluded that Christianity manifested the clearest instance of intellectual idolatry—fashioning a god in human form, or at least according to deep-seated human needs. Radical thinkers supposed the God of Christianity looked too much like an ideal human being—kind, merciful, courageous, and forgiving—to be taken seriously. Therefore, they expended great intellectual energy destroying the idols of religion. These thinkers unmistakably borrowed the language of religion as the chief means of denuding it, if not also destroying it.

Although unbelief remained a remote option for most laypersons, biblical theism increasingly came under attack by intellectuals.[3] The burden of proof had shifted during the century. As the century wore on, atheism, earlier considered intellectually indefensible, became a much more reasonable alternative. By the end of the century, many of the significant voices we will hear in this chapter would have thought atheism on a relative par, intellectually speaking, with biblical theism. As atheism became less repugnant, theism became much more precarious in Europe and America.

If belief in God were to be retained even in part, the deity could remain simply as a God of the gaps—a being who merely fills the empty spaces in mankind's ever-expanding scientific knowledge. Where mystery remained, God might continue to exist. When science eliminated mystery, God no longer would be needed. Because of these critical intuitions, as God was pushed out, he also was pushed inside as a projection of human needs and desires. The counterpart of this intellectual revolution was the emergence of a new breed of religious belief, designed to withstand the critical assaults launched in the academy. In many religious traditions, faith had become separated from its intellectual moorings and had begun to float free in the sea of human experience. Many no longer labored to demonstrate the reasonableness of religious conviction, since reason and religion inhabited two separate spheres, and neither had much to do with the other. Reason reigned supreme in matters of science and history, but in religious matters, reason did not matter. To the newly emerging traditions of idealism and romanticism, free and full expression of one's creative and free experiences mattered most. Thus, the nineteenth century became an age not of religious unbelief so much as an age of transformed religious belief. The vast majority of ordinary people would

---

3. The Enlightenment was largely an intellectually inspired movement, and thus for most of its life it remained isolated among a university-related people. The implications of rising secularism did not influence popular culture for well over a century. As James Turner remarks, "Despite the perils supposed to beset belief [in God], unbelief in fact remained unthinkable to all but a tiny handful [in the 18th century]," in *Without God, Without Creed: The Origins of Unbelief in America* (Baltimore: The Johns Hopkins University Press, 1985), 35. Turner's work and May's *The Enlightenment in America* (New York: Oxford University Press, 1976) are both helpful treatments of the diffusion of Enlightenment thinking into the American mainstream.

still have voiced a resolute belief in God, though that belief had become more generic, increasingly ambiguous, and sharply severed from the mind.

From one important perspective, the nineteenth century represented a critical assault on the historical claims of Christianity. Religious scholars became more confident in objecting to biblical theism's traditional claims about past events.[4] A significant consequence of this growing historical criticism was the attempt to refashion Christian beliefs in such a manner that they would be immune to the historical criticism being leveled against them. Remove the historical claims of Christianity, for example, the incarnation and resurrection, and the problems would dissolve—or so many thought. Hoping to protect a remnant of Christian belief, leading intellectuals abandoned core Christian beliefs so that nothing but a generic civil religion remained—a Christianity refashioned into everyone's own image. Before long, in the academic marketplace, the gospel was relegated to the backwaters of apologetic and theological discussions.[5]

Biblical theism had some able defenders in this period, but they were voices crying in the wilderness, all but overlooked by their opponents. Critics branded confessional Protestant scholarship as naïve and highly partisan. Not until the late twentieth century did Christian scholarship again receive a modicum of respect by non-evangelical scholars.[6] Rather than relegating historical claims to the periphery of Christianity, B. B. Warfield, Abraham Kuyper, and Herman Bavinck stressed the absolute centrality of the historical events recorded in Scripture.[7] Although employing widely divergent apologetic strategies in defense of these claims, they argued that the historicity of the gospel claims was the greatest apologetic concern in the nineteenth century.[8]

This chapter will chart the revolutionary changes in the intellectual climate from the beginning of the nineteenth century to its conclusion. Two

> *The counterpart of this intellectual revolution was the emergence of a new breed of religious belief, designed to withstand the critical assaults launched in the academy.*

> *Hoping to protect a remnant of Christian belief, leading intellectuals abandoned core Christian beliefs so that nothing but a generic civil religion remained—a Christianity refashioned into everyone's own image.*

4. See Jeffrey Stout, *Flight from Authority: Religion, Morality, and the Quest for Autonomy* (Notre Dame, IN: University of Notre Dame Press, 1981).

5. In this regard, see George Marsden's work on the secularization of the American universities: *The Soul of the American University: From Protestant Establishment to Established Nonbelief* (New York: Oxford University Press, 1994).

6. This so-called "evangelical renaissance" in the disciplines of history, philosophy, and sociology emerged in the 1980s. As a sign of the times, Harvey Cox included evangelical scholarship in his book *The Secular City: Toward a Postmodern Theology* (New York: Simon and Schuster, 1984), seeing it as one of the two major forces moving culture beyond modernism. Also, see Robert Wuthnow, *The Restructuring of American Religion: Society and Faith Since World War II* (Princeton, NJ: Princeton University Press, 1988), and George Marsden, *The Outrageous Idea of Christian Scholarship* (New York: Oxford University Press, 1997).

7. Representatively, see B. B. Warfield, "Faith in Its Psychological Aspects," in his *Studies in Theology* (Carlisle, PA: Banner of Truth Trust, 1988); Abraham Kuyper, *Principles of Sacred Theology*, trans. J. Hendrik de Vries (Grand Rapids: Wm. B. Eerdmans Pub. Co., 1954); and Herman Bavinck, *Our Reasonable Faith*, trans. Henry Zylstra (Grand Rapids: Wm. B. Eerdmans Pub. Co., 1956).

8. Warfield defended a traditional variety of natural theology as a prologue to the dogmatic claims of the Christian faith, but Kuyper and Bavinck stressed the fallenness of human reason and therefore viewed natural theology as bankrupt.

of the greatest minds of the modern era demarcate the century: Immanuel Kant (1724–1804) at the beginning and Friedrich Nietzsche (1844–1900) at the end. Since Kant's work has been investigated in the previous chapter, only the rough contours of his thought need concern us here. Kant's intellectual shadow dominated the agenda of the nineteenth century unlike any thinker dominated an age before or since. At the other end of the century, Nietzsche brought the Kantian enterprise to a close. Traces of Kant lingered for another fifty years, but in a severely weakened form. As the next chapter shows, Nietzsche's work foreshadowed much of what now passes as the postmodern revolution. For this reason, the "Age of Intellectual Iconoclasm" stands between the two great intellectual projects of modernism and postmodernism. Within these two frameworks, religious belief underwent significant changes, most especially in its relationship to the life of the mind.[9]

Immanuel Kant: The Bridge from the Enlightenment to the Nineteenth Century

Alfred North Whitehead wrote famously that the history of philosophy was but a footnote to Plato. How much more can we say that the nineteenth century was but a footnote to Immanuel Kant? No figure of any age so dominated philosophical discourse in the succeeding age as Kant. Whatever one thinks of his conclusions, nearly every thinker of consequence in the nineteenth century believed Kant had set the agenda to which serious intellectuals must respond.[10]

Kant's central project entailed grounding natural sciences in a critical philosophical framework influenced by empirical and rationalist traditions. In contrast with the empirical traditions of Locke and Hume, however, Kantians argued there is a "natural ordering" of the impressions according to certain mental categories, the filters through which the mind apprehends and interprets the phenomenal world. Categories of reason provide the glue that holds the impressions of the world together. These categories do not exist "out there"; they are the epistemological means by which we make sense of the world "out there."

In the Kantian tradition, one, and only one history existed, and Kantian-inspired thinkers contended that this history was not and could not be glued together providentially. If there is providential glue, it is invisible to

> *Whatever one thinks of his conclusions, nearly every thinker of consequence in the nineteenth century believed Kant had set the agenda to which serious intellectuals must respond.*

---

9. This chapter primarily follows thematic lines, rather than strictly chronological ones. There is an argument in the chapter about the "flow of ideas" that matters to students of worldviews and that is abundantly clear in the nineteenth century. The chronology of the century's thinkers restrains us from putting "ideas" into the flow of the argument wherever one arbitrarily chooses. Paying attention to the time line is important. However, it is more important for our concerns to understand the thematic patterns that run through the century and thereby hold it together. May we be concerned not to miss the forest for the trees.

10. Since Kant properly belongs to the previous chapter ("Enlightenments and Awakenings"), only the briefest of summaries is included here.

the eye of human reason and therefore must be discarded as intellectually insignificant. Purpose does not reside in history, only in one's interpretation of it. History gives us facts, nothing more.

By the opening of the nineteenth century, the Enlightenment's challenge to older forms of institutional authority was well entrenched.[11] Kant effectively formalized what often has been called the "subjective turn."[12] The individual subject (at least among those individuals teaching in prestigious universities of Europe) was seen as the preeminent authority in matters pertaining to the constituents of the real world and how that world was known. The working assumption was that a disinterested scholar occupies a far superior vantage point from which to know the world as it really is than any religious cleric. This precipitated a crisis regarding the proper grounds for believing in God. One compelling option located the origin of religion within our own psychological needs. This alternative believed scholars should pay attention to the natural origins of religion, that is, those elements of human nature that give rise to religious belief. The search for these naturalized origins took thinkers in many different directions, though they commonly assumed that the source of religion is not to be found in the historical and verifiable past, or in a transcendental and absolute future. Religion belongs to the inner emotional (and nonrational) nature of persons.

Kant's legacy effectively divided intellectual inquiry into two separate domains: the secular world of science—the realm of facts and data—and the sacred world of religion—the world of faith and trust. The secular world prized objectivity and hardheaded skepticism. In the religious world, blind belief and obedience to authority ruled. Virtually no interaction transpired between these two domains nor, according to Kant, should that be worrisome. To hardened skeptics after Kant, the task was less to defend the secular domains of knowledge than to wonder aloud why the sacred world was still needed. Although it may not have appeared so at the time, the nineteenth century witnessed the swallowing up of the sacred by the secular.

> *Kant's legacy effectively divided intellectual inquiry into two separate domains: the secular world of science—the realm of facts and data—and the sacred world of religion—the world of faith and trust.*

11. David Ray Griffin suggests that the heart of the Enlightenment lay in its claim that the supernatural God, i.e., the God of traditional Western (Augustinian) Christian theology, has died. Rejecting the fundamental authority of God entails repudiating other institutional forms of authority, such as the church and the king. See his "Introduction: Varieties of Postmodern Theology" and "Postmodern Theology and A/Theology: A Response to Mark C. Taylor" in David Ray Griffin, William A. Beardslee, and Joe Holland, eds., *Varieties of Postmodern Theology* (Albany, NY: State University of New York Press, 1989), 1–8, 29–62.

12. See the generally critical account of this "subjective turn" in Jeffrey Stout, *The Flight from Authority: Religion, Morality, and the Quest for Autonomy* (Notre Dame, IN: Notre Dame Press, 1981). For an interpretive essay with a concern for the larger social implications, see May, *The Enlightenment in America*. Standard histories of philosophy normally see this "subjective turn" as the explanatory key for understanding modern philosophy, starting with René Descartes in the seventeenth century. See e.g., Frederick Copleston, *A History of Philosophy*, vols. 4–6. See also the highly influential essays in the collection titled *The Linguistic Turn*, ed. Richard Rorty (Chicago: University of Chicago Press, 1967), which charts the extension of the "subjective turn" in the twentieth century in the form of a "linguistic turn."

The Secular Prophets: Idolatry and Intellectual Iconoclasm

The intellectual momentum headed in the direction of religious unbe-lief, though much of that did not appear in the English-speaking world until the early 1900s.[13] Prominent intellectual voices mostly spoke German in the nineteenth century and tended to accept Kant's sacred/secular divide, but they pressed the dichotomy in a fashion unforeseen by Kant. Starting with Ludwig Feuerbach and culminating in Friedrich Nietzsche, the secular all but gobbled up the sacred. Traditional religious belief was on trial, and a guilty verdict echoed in the writings of the German secular prophets.

At the end of his first major work, *Critique of Pure Reason*, Kant argued that the objects of the noumenal world (God and self) were not objects of knowledge but objects of faith. The secular prophets accepted this prem-ise, but instead of viewing objects of faith as protected from the inroads of empirical inquiry (as Kant had hoped), they rejected these objects as irrelevant and frequently damaging to human progress. After Kant (and Hegel), these radical thinkers wondered aloud why people believed in God, given the total lack of empirical evidence for him. Moreover, exploiting the Christian tradition in which many of them were reared, they borrowed the most powerful conceptual tool of criticism from that tradition—idolatry—and used it against the tradition. Instead of searching for an explanation for unbelief, they sought an explanatory framework for religious belief. If God does not exist, why do people still believe in him?

Georg Wilhelm Friedrich Hegel (1770–1831)

Kant's primary interlocutor was G. W. F. Hegel. Although Hegel accepted some of Kant's critical realism, he found it profoundly insensitive to larger metaphysical realities. Hegel thought he might be able to turn the clock back—reversing trends unleashed by Kant and the shift toward empirical investigations. As one of the last grand metaphysicians of the era, Hegel provided a perfect foil for the later radical secular prophets to use to appropriate Kant for their own purposes. As it turned out, most German intellectuals saw Hegel as the last gasp of an outmoded religion—the reli-gion that believed in things that could not be seen or heard. Therefore, to understand the nineteenth century, we must make a quick detour through Hegel, before arriving at the main critique of the radical secular prophets.

Hegel contended that history has a purpose that is displayed in the outworking of the "Absolute Mind."[14] History unfolds inexorably as the self-

> *The intellectual momentum headed in the direction of religious unbelief, though much of that did not appear in the English-speaking world until the early 1900s. . . . Traditional religious belief was on trial, and a guilty verdict echoed in the writings of the German secular prophets.*

13. The rise of logical positivism in the 1920s was a major turning point in the Eng-lish-speaking world in switching the burden of proof from atheism to theism. Two recent sympathetic histories are Friedrich Stadler, *The Vienna Circle: Studies in the Origins, Devel-opment, and Influence of Logical Empiricism*, trans. Camilla Nielsen et al. (Vienna: Springer, 2001), and Michael Friedman, *Reconsidering Logical Positivism* (Cambridge: Cambridge University Press, 1999).

14. Earlier generations might have referred to the Absolute Mind as God, but Hegel believed that granting Absolute Mind a name reduced the metaphysical ground of all being

actualization of this Absolute Mind. In other words, ideas move history—a movement that is neither linear nor circular but dialectical. Human history progresses by means of tension between great ideas. Simply put, historical movement consists of thesis, antithesis, and synthesis.[15] Most momentous ideologies of history are one-sided. They capture a great truth but only part of it. Inevitably, an opposing ideology appears that captures other aspects of truth. The clash between these antithetical ideologies results in a synthesis of the two, which in time is opposed by another ideology. In religion, for example, Hegel supposed that animism was the earliest worldview, opposed at some later point by pantheism. A resulting synthesis of sorts arises in polytheism, which in turn was later opposed by theism. Theism persisted until it clashed with deism, and the resulting synthesis was Hegel's own brand of religious idealism. Hegel believed this synthesis brought the dialectical movement of religious history to its climax. This cycle of conflicting religious worldviews is neither haphazard nor accidental but manifests the rational outworking of Absolute Mind. Thus, history makes determined progress toward a goal. In this case, the goal was Hegel's own religious views.

G. W. F. Hegel

Hegel's religious views enigmatically blended Platonism and Christianity. Plato contended that the purpose and meaning of objects in the world lay in a world beyond history. Christianity assumed that the purpose and meaning of objects in the world lay in the meaning granted them by a transcendent deity. Hegel combined the two by collapsing the transcendent world and the historical realm into one. For Hegel, history never should be reduced merely to temporal and empirical events. The unfolding of Absolute Mind frames the central relational institutions of Western culture (husband/wife, employer/employee, and master/slave) as relationships of power to achieve an end or purpose. All relationships either contribute to or detract from this end or purpose. The exercise of power, the power of one side over the other, constitutes the only means to achieve those means. There are no "neutral" relationships contributing to the well-being of others. This was the consequence of viewing history primarily as the result of ideological conflict.

Hegel's followers divided into two camps: those who believed his system compatible with Christianity (Right Wing Hegelians) and those who did not (Left Wing Hegelians). The vastly more influential Left Wing Hegelians sought to press the radical demands of history (as they perceived them) on all ideologies, especially religious ones. In part, they reversed the priority of ideas over history that Hegel believed so critical. Rather than ideas moving history, the radicals believed concrete, empirical history provides the

This cycle of conflicting religious worldviews is neither haphazard nor accidental but manifests the rational outworking of Absolute Mind. Thus, history makes determined progress toward a goal. In this case, the goal was Hegel's own religious views.

---

into a merely humanized deity. See G. W. F. Hegel, *The Phenomenology of Spirit*, trans. A. V. Miller (Oxford: Clarendon Press 1977).

15.   See G. W. F. Hegel, *Science of Logic*, trans. A. V. Miller (New York: Humanities Press, 1976).

only source for ideas. The Left Wing Hegelians included biblical scholars such as D. F. Strauss and F. C. Baur, who sought to undermine the ancient conviction about the Bible being a word from outside history. They argued that the Bible was merely a product of its own historical contexts. Other Left Wing Hegelians, such as Ludwig Feuerbach and Karl Marx, claimed that all convictions about God were, in fact, merely disguised assertions about humanity. In their hands, theology became anthropology.

Among the radicals, the central remaining element of Hegel's thought was the place of dialectical conflict in history. In contrast to Enlightenment views of historical progress, radicals posited that history always entails struggle. Religious, political, and social conflicts operate at the center of human history. Far from trying to achieve a state of perfection, real social science should study and validate these historical tensions. History shows that civilizations spread by conquest. In earlier times, military conquest moved history forward, but in later eras, conflict between worldviews generated cultural change. The clash of worldviews often legitimates the conquest by armies. According to Left Wing Hegelians, in cultural change the physically stronger and mightier prevail, not the morally superior.

In retrospect, Hegel's focus on the dialectical movement of history gave rise to a strained interpretation of historical conflict. Historians wrote of the church and philosophy, for example, as if at most two prominent and opposed views existed at any given time, resulting in a synthesis. Hegelian historiography tended to polarize ideas (and to downplay any similarities between worldviews) and to marginalize ideas, movements, or people that did not fit into the two dominant views. This oversimplification of historical movement prevailed throughout the nineteenth century because it provided a "clean" alternative to Christian views of God's providence over history. It appeared to provide a safely secular way to explain history.

Ludwig Feuerbach (1804–72)

Feuerbach emerged as one of the best-known Left Wing Hegelians—and surely one of the most radical. He published his first work in 1830 as a searing criticism of Christianity, claiming it to be inhuman and egotistic. Feuerbach gained a reputation as an ardent atheist. His zeal cost him a permanent appointment as a university professor in Germany, but for his twentieth-century followers, it earned him the status of a prophet of secularism.

Feuerbach sought to undermine confidence in Christianity's supernatural claims.[16] He did not argue that the Christian church was particularly detrimental to civilization; it simply misplaced a trust it should have had in itself with a loyalty to a non-existent deity. At times, Feuerbach portrayed the church as the last remnant of superstition left in the West, which left it holding an unfortunate grip on Western culture. Feuerbach

> *Other Left Wing Hegelians, such as Ludwig Feuerbach and Karl Marx, claimed that all convictions about God were, in fact, merely disguised assertions about humanity. In their hands, theology became anthropology.*

16.   See, most especially, Ludwig Feuerbach, *The Essence of Christianity*, trans. George Eliot (New York: Harper, 1957).

did not seek to destroy the church but to cleanse it of superstitions. Later, an important commentator would write of Feuerbach:

> His principal aim was to change the friends of God into the friends of man, believers into thinkers, worshippers into workers, candidates for the other world into students of this world, Christians, who on their own confession are half-animal and half-angel, into men—whole men.[17]

Feuerbach believed Christian religion confessed loyalty to a being who did not exist. In the study of religion, therefore, we learn about the religious yearnings of human beings, not about some transcendent reality. Although such religious impulses may be perfectly natural and normal, they are misplaced when viewed as fulfilled by a distant, sky-dwelling deity. Feuerbach did not propose to eliminate religion but to naturalize it, to tame it, and to refocus its energies for the betterment of humankind.

Feuerbach believed human beings were prone to create God in their own image as a projection of their ideals. The problem was not as much believing that the abstract ideal was real, but in trusting the abstraction to solve the enduring problems of human experience. Inevitably, despair would result when the abstraction proved incapable of solving real world crises. Hope in an abstraction should be replaced by a hope in the possibility of humanity's own progress. The ideal may have been useful as a goal toward which humankind was to strive, but when the abstraction replaced the concrete realities of human nature, it had become dangerous. Feuerbach contended that the invention of God alienated human beings from their true nature.[18]

Behind this prophetic warning lay Feuerbach's conviction that self-consciousness is a great glory and a great danger. Self-consciousness separates humans from the beasts and permits civilization to emerge. It also prompts the creation of idols. The ability to name oneself as a species (in contrast to the animals) leads to the illusion that abstract objects like "human species" exist over and above individual human beings. Belief that abstract concepts do not actually exist but are merely names given to mental categories of understanding often is called "nominalism." Feuerbach was both a nominalist and a materialist, believing that the only kind of reality that existed was physical matter. Concepts such as God or beauty or truth exist only as concepts in the mind.

For Feuerbach, therefore, no actual, concrete, ideal human by any name—much less a deity—exists in human image. Only concrete particular human beings exist. In Feuerbach's wonderfully ugly phrase, "Man is what he eats"—nothing more, nothing less. Combining all the desirable human character traits results in believing in a perfect human character

Feuerbach believed human beings were prone to create God in their own image as a projection of their ideals. The problem was not as much believing that the abstract ideal was real, but in trusting the abstraction to solve the enduring problems of human experience.

17. Karl Barth, "Introductory Preface" to Feuerbach, *The Essence of Christianity*.

18. See Ludwig Feuerbach, The *Essence of Religion: God the Image of Man*, trans. Alexander Loos (New York, A. K. Butts, 1873).

and calling this "God." Feuerbach believed that to understand this illusion was to be cured of it. The difficult task, however, consists in seeing it. What better way for Christians finally to see this than to refashion the language of idolatry? The Old Testament prophets charged Israel with believing in false gods, created in their own image. They well understood the powerful human drive to construct a deity who serves selfish interests by protecting and providing for them. What these prophets failed to recognize, according to Feuerbach, was that Yahweh was Israel's original idol, created in the image of a powerful overlord who would protect them against the rulers of the ancient world and provide them with a promised land. Railing against the idols of pagans, they failed to see their own idolatry.

An idol symbolized a god who did not exist. Nevertheless, the power of an idol was profound and often enduring. Although the gods of ancient Greece were viewed as fictional figures in mythical stories, once they demanded absolute loyalty from their human subjects. Some gods demanded that children be sacrificed to them. Others demanded ritual prostitution. City-states became powerful precisely because their local gods were powerful—or so the ancients believed. So it is with Christianity, Feuerbach argued.

The Roman Empire replaced ancient polytheistic civilizations and united much of the known world. No longer content with local deities, Roman gods must be universal and absolute. Their culture demanded monotheism and what better place to look than to ancient Israel, not in its original Semitic context but in its reshaped Hellenized form—Christianity.[19] The Romans borrowed Christianity as the ideological means to justify their place in the world. However, the world has changed, and it must now be freed from Roman idols. Feuerbach did not seek a new set of idols to replace the old; he sought the removal of all idols. He desired a culture that simply believed in itself.

Overcoming the idols of religion would be a long and arduous task. People were comfortable with idols and could not easily give them up. The way out of idolatry was to look inside the human heart and discern those needs that give rise to creating idols. Exposing the needs that give rise to religious belief will hasten the end of the edifice built on those foundations, Feuerbach believed. Feuerbach called this process the psychogenetic method. By identifying the psychological origins of a belief, one undermines its validity.

According to Feuerbach, God was only the objectification of human aspirations. "What humans are not, but what they will to be, just that and

Ludwig Feuerbach

---

19. Apart from the fact that Feuerbach's historical argument had no actual evidence in its favor, his contention possessed a simple elegance in its explanatory power. This "alternative explanatory framework" justified greater freedom for secularists from ecclesiastical control. This note of liberation originally sounded in the Enlightenment continued unabated in the nineteenth century. See Van A. Harvey, *Feuerbach and the Interpretation of Religion* (New York: Cambridge University Press, 1995).

only that is God."[20] Hoping for peace, people create a God who will bring peace. Humans hope for love, and so create a God of love. They hope for victory, and create a God who will bring them victory. Humans create a God as the mirror of their hopes. "If God were a being of the birds, he would have been a winged creature."[21]

According to Feuerbach, God must be humanized. The proper object of worship is humankind. It is important to locate the essence of perfection within human beings, not outside of human experience. Doing this will change the worship of God into the worship of humankind. It also will place squarely on the shoulders of humankind the responsibility to work for peace and to show love—to exhibit the very characteristics humans have misplaced on God. Humans need to exert their own wills, not believe someone or something else will solve their problems.

To this end, Feuerbach attempted to translate Christianity into a language without any transcendent entities—without any gods. In a calculating fashion, Feuerbach believed he could rid the world of idolatry by translating the historic Christian confession into a language without any theological overtones. This was the central aim of his most influential work, *The Essence of Christianity*. Feuerbach tried to use the same terms Christians had, but he gave them an entirely different meaning. He wrote of performing "pneumatic hydrotherapy"—throwing out the baptismal water and replacing it with real water.[22] Humans needed to eliminate magic water and get about the business of cleaning themselves with real water. Feuerbach hoped the sacred would be swallowed by the secular.

A brief critical note now should be sounded regarding Feuerbach's setting the agenda for the secular prophets. Like many of his contemporaries, Feuerbach failed to wrestle with radical evil, particularly radical social evil. He expressed naïve optimism about unbridled human progress, freed from the religious constraints of the past. Later, thinkers in the Left Wing Hegelian tradition attempted to address evil more responsibly, although they still located all good inside of human nature, and this was their blind spot. Anytime God is humanized, humankind is deified. When God is excluded from the picture, human nature must assume the roles of creator and creature, and normally this is too much weight for humanity to bear.

Ironically, Feuerbach and the secular prophets had no way to account for their own naïvely optimistic views of humankind. They could not secure human dignity without a transcendent source. If humans are merely cosmic accidents, they have no eternal significance. Feuerbach was convinced that in contrast to animals, humans possess a lofty dignity; but in hindsight, it appears he borrowed this idea from the Judeo-Christian

> *According to Feuerbach . . . Yahweh was Israel's original idol, created in the image of a powerful overlord who would protect them against the rulers of the ancient world and provide them with a promised land.*

> *According to Feuerbach, God must be humanized. The proper object of worship is humankind. It is important to locate the essence of perfection within human beings, not outside of human experience. Doing this will change the worship of God into the worship of humankind.*

20. Feuerbach, *The Essence of Christianity*, 24.
21. Ibid., 28.
22. Ibid., 236.

> *Although humans
> are intrinsically
> valuable by virtue
> of being human,
> we also possess an
> "exchange value"—
> the value we have in
> the economic system
> in which we labor.
> A farmer has sig-
> nificant value in an
> agrarian society and
> a banker in an early
> capitalist society.*

tradition, although without any borrowing rights! After Feuerbach, think-ers attempted to ground human dignity in something intrinsic in human culture, though it remained always fragile, given the temporal character of human life. They trumpeted human freedom as an important element of that dignity, but freedom loosed from moral constraints often resulted in moral anarchy. In a richly ironic turn of events, a natural explanation for unbelief appeared—to escape the moral demands of the Creator. With-out recognizing it, secular prophets had unleashed a counterargument to their own claims. Feuerbach did not notice it at the time, but if irreligion could be located within a psychological need, then its claims could likewise be undermined. That counterargument would await the beginning of the twentieth century before it would be launched effectively.

Karl Marx (1818–83)

Marx was appalled by the extreme conditions of the early stages of the Industrial Revolution in England. Factory laborers were exploited with menial labor, low wages, and painfully long hours. Young children suf-fered under similar conditions, as they worked to support their families. Often, they received just enough food to sustain their existence. Workers were treated as commodities, useful only insofar as they could contribute to factory production. Ruled by laws of supply and demand, the workplace crushed many of the laborers in its grip. Jobs were scarce and pay was min-imal, which meant that demand (for jobs) exceeded supply (opportunities for work). This permitted owners to abuse workers as they saw fit. Essen-tially, Marx believed, workers had become slaves of owners.

Following Feuerbach, Marx believed abstract, transcendental meta-physical terms did not describe human nature. Humans are merely the matter from which they have come. Nothing exists over and above the material world. Unlike Feuerbach, however, Marx was pessimistic about human nature. Apart from social pressures asserted by the community for its good, humans are intrinsically selfish. Social ties exist before individual moral standards and are the only ground for those standards. The collec-tive good of the society precedes any moral principles that elevate the dig-nity of the individual.

Following the Hegelian tradition, Marx believed conflict lay at the center of human history and was the force that pushed it forward. Marx believed progress was inevitable but could be accomplished only through struggle—a struggle best described in terms of social and economic class conflict, rather than as a clash of ideas. Class struggle can best be under-stood by understanding human nature. Marx believed working is the essence of human nature. Although humans are intrinsically valuable by virtue of being human, we also possess an "exchange value"—the value we have in the economic system in which we labor. A farmer has signifi-cant value in an agrarian society and a banker in an early capitalist society.

Updating the illustration, rock stars are valuable only in an entertainment culture.

Workers can be exploited when their exchange value is controlled by individuals who seek their own good, rather than the community's good. Given the opportunity, deviant social organizations, as well as individuals, will exploit workers, as happened throughout England during the early days of the Industrial Revolution. As a result, workers were alienated from their own labor, controlling neither its value nor its conditions. Assembly line workers were alienated from the products of their labors because they did not produce the final product, only a part of a larger whole. Workers became cogs in a machine they did not own. Drudgery and tedium further alienated industrial workers from themselves, and this convinced many that work no longer was meaningful. Behind this dehumanizing and degrading system were the owners of the factories and capitalist intuitions that legitimized their oppression. Marx concluded that capitalism was the root cause of the problem.[23]

Karl Marx

Usually, capitalism was justified by appealing to religious grounds in general and to Christianity in particular. Religion was not the cause of the problem; it was the worldview that legitimized it. Capitalism came first and latched onto a religion that could support it. Religion in the West, Marx famously stated, was the "opium of the people," a drug that kept people addicted to capitalism. Religion was the sentiment of a heartless world and the soul of a soulless condition.[24]

According to Marx, the origin of religion reveals it to be a determined oppressor. People sought meaning beyond themselves and created a god in their own image. Dominant economic forces manipulated this fantasy figure to justify their system. In capitalist contexts, this god required obedience to masters and humility and meekness in the face of hardship. Above all, this god promised rewards in another life. Each of these religious "virtues" helped make workers servile to their masters by convincing them this was religiously faithful behavior.

For Marx, the criticism of religion was the presupposition of economic criticism.[25] He disparaged religion, believing it justified oppressive economic conditions. Religion was idolatrous; it created a god who served the economic interests of masters. Workers held onto religion to protect themselves against the inhumanity of the industrial workplace. Religion gave them hope in a hopeless world. Owners used religion to cement their power. Religion helped workers cope with their oppressive existence. In

> "Capitalism came first and latched onto a religion that could support it. Religion in the West, Marx famously stated, was the "opium of the people," a drug that kept people addicted to capitalism. Religion was the sentiment of a heartless world and the soul of a soulless condition.

23. See Karl Marx, *The German Ideology*, with Friedrich Engels (Amherst, NY: Prometheus Books, 1998).

24. This phrase is borrowed from Merold Westphal in one of the very best treatments of Marx's critique of religion, *Suspicion and Faith: The Religious Uses of Modern Atheism* (Grand Rapids: Eerdmans, 1994).

25. See the representative collection of essays, *Marx on Religion*, ed. John Raines (Philadelphia: Temple University Press, 2002).

both cases, religion conserved the status quo. According to Marx, progress required unmasking these idols. This unmasking could be accomplished only as workers mounted a determined revolt against capitalism and exploitation, broke the shackles of religion, and embraced atheistic humanism. Until humans believed in themselves, they would not throw off the burdens of their oppressors.[26]

In his most influential work, *Capital*, Marx outlined his antidote to capitalism.[27] In *Capital*, Marx presented a program to abolish private property, jettison religion, and allow the human community to flourish. Marx assumed that in the absence of a capitalist economy, cooperation would emerge among communities and nations. Collectives would produce goods according to the ability of the workers and distribute them according to human need.

With the hindsight of the twentieth century, Marx's vision appears utopian and incredibly naïve. Marx did not take individual evil seriously; he hoped systemic economic and political changes would eradicate it. Contrary to Marx's assumptions, communities can be just as oppressive as individuals can. However, lest we dismiss Marx too easily, we should note—as with Feuerbach—that idolatry appears as easily in Christian communities as it does in non-Christian ones. Justification of greed and oppression often wear a religious face. Above all people, Christians should take their liability to evil seriously, realizing that even their own religious convictions may be used to legitimate actions that are repugnant to the gospel.

Marx did not see that religious confession could function as a prophetic voice against human injustice precisely because it offers a word from "outside." The transcendent voice of God's Word judges all people; it is precisely the tool Marx yearned for with which to criticize culture. One only need read the Old Testament prophets to see this. Without a transcendent word, the only judge of human actions can be human words, which are always corruptible, individually and corporately.

Charles Darwin (1809–92)

Darwin is not normally included in the list of Left Wing Hegelians, and rightfully so. He was not a member of this tradition in any formal way! However, in a book describing worldviews, Darwin provides a key philosophical component in the overall development of the criticism of religion by the secular prophets. Without Darwin, intellectuals would not have taken these voices so seriously toward the end of the nineteenth cen-

Charles Darwin

26. The outlines of this argument are found in summary form in Karl Marx, "Theses on Feuerbach," in *The German Ideology: Including Theses on Feuerbach*, with Friedrich Engels (Amherst, NY: Prometheus Books, 1998). These can be accessed online at: http://www.marxists.org/archive/marx/works/1845/theses/theses.htm.

27. Karl Marx, *Capital: A Critique of Political Economy*, trans. Ben Fowkes (New York: Penguin Books, 1992).

tury and beginning of the twentieth. For this reason, we include him in the section on the secular prophets. A brief word of context is needed first.

The natural world under Copernicus, Galileo, and Bacon became a "machine" by the seventeenth century. The famous "clockwork" image of the universe dominated Europe in the eighteenth century. The world moved with mathematical precision because it operated under the quantifiable laws of mathematics. Galileo put the matter this way:

> Philosophy is written in the grand book, the universe, which stands continually open to our gaze. However, the book cannot be understood unless one first learns to comprehend the language and read the letters in which it is composed. It is written in the language of mathematics, and its characters are triangles, circles, and other geometric figures without which it is humanly impossible to understand a single word of it; without these one wanders about in a dark labyrinth.[28]

People understood the world more as a machine than as a living, breathing spirit. Machines invariably followed laws that could be studied and adequately delineated by science. Kant may have believed these laws of nature were divinely ordered, but no religious beliefs were required to interpret them or discover them. In the century before Kant, the old dualism of heaven and earth had been slowly dismantled; the earth became simply another planet, included under the same scientific rubric as the rest of the heavens, and all became subject to the universal laws of terrestrial mechanics. Man no longer needed to appeal to a "plan of God" to explain the movements of the heavenly bodies, even if most people still believed God created these laws. The appeal to internal natural forces at work in the world meant that efficient causes replaced discussion of final cause.[29] Transcendent purpose gave way to empirical facts.

Given this picture of the universe, it no longer seemed reasonable to believe God was constantly tinkering with his machine or that he was moving the world in any direct sense. God may have been in charge, but essentially, he became an absentee landlord for those committed to a mechanistic explanation of the world. In the eighteenth century, people viewed natural law as the divine mechanism that directed the world on its proper course. By the middle of the nineteenth century, natural law was the glue that held the world together, without any need to suppose that there was a glue maker (God).

If God dropped out of the picture, as some of the more radical Enlightenment thinkers had hoped, the puzzling question of the origin and structure of the world still persisted. If there was no watchmaker, how and why did the "watch" work? To religious skeptics, this question

> *Idolatry appears as easily in Christian communities as it does in non-Christian ones.... Above all people, Christians should take their liability to evil seriously, realizing that even their own religious convictions may be used to legitimate actions that are repugnant to the gospel.*

> *God may have been in charge, but essentially, he became an absentee landlord for those committed to a mechanistic explanation of the world.*

---

28. Galileo, *The Assayer* (1623), as quoted in Franklin Baumer, *The History of Modern European Thought* (New York: Macmillan, 1977), 50.

29. The distinction between efficient and final causes is an important one in the history of philosophy. Efficient cause refers to the thing or person that brings something to pass. Final cause refers to the goal or purpose for which something comes to pass.

> *More revolutionary still was his explanation of natural selection as the internal natural mechanism that could explain change without appeal to supernatural forces. Natural selection entails that in a natural environment where food is scarce, those species best able to adapt to the struggle for food would most likely survive.*

remained unanswered. Christians of this era supposed that the "design" of the world/machine proved the existence of a "Great Designer" (God).[30] As the story of the nineteenth century unfolded, this argument was turned on its head, becoming a powerful force that undermined belief in a benevolent God. Darwin supplied the conceptual mechanism by which the "Great Designer" was reckoned superfluous.

Born in England and raised in a nominally Christian home, Darwin studied medicine at the University of Edinburgh and then divinity at Cambridge University. In both cases, he did not distinguish himself. Consequently, he accepted an invitation to join a surveying expedition on the British ship *The Beagle*, which sailed around the tip of South America from 1831 to 1836. More than any other experience in his life, this trip helped to frame the questions that were most important to Darwin: How does change occur in nature? Is there an explanation intrinsic to nature that can account for natural change?

After returning from *The Beagle* expedition, Darwin read Malthus's *Essay on the Principles of Population* (1836), in which Malthus argued that population increases geometrically while food increases arithmetically. This suggested that severe natural struggles for food, and therefore for survival, occurred in nature. In these struggles, favorable variations among populations tend to be preserved, and unfavorable variations tend to be destroyed. Darwin concluded that new species emerged from the natural struggle for survival, and he advanced this thesis to explain the amazing diversity among species he observed during his almost five years of research work with *The Beagle* expedition.

Initially, Darwin's systematic summary of his conclusions in *On the Origin of the Species* (1859) attracted support from few natural scientists. Two central elements in the proposal created the most controversy—the natural evolution of life and the mechanism of natural selection, which best accounted for that natural evolution. Evolutionary frameworks did not originate with Darwin, but his systematic presentation of life as gradually developing over millions of years from a common ancestry was novel. More revolutionary still was his explanation of natural selection as the internal natural mechanism that could explain change without appeal to supernatural forces. Natural selection entails that in a natural environment where food is scarce, those species best able to adapt to the struggle for food would most likely survive. Nature selects its own survivors, so to speak.

A significant aspect of the controversy that ensued after the publication of *On the Origin of the Species* was that social scientists adopted its general theory of evolution more quickly than did natural scientists. Within a decade of its publication, Darwin's explanation of natural change

---

30. The most notable example is William Paley's *Lectures on Natural Theology* (Houston, TX: St. Thomas Press, 1972), which depended heavily on this analogy in the teleological argument for the existence of God.

formed a virtual orthodoxy among anthropologists, sociologists, and, to a lesser extent, philosophers. Change had become the primary ontological category, and understanding nature's ability to change without invoking external entities removed the need for any appeal to religious factors, most especially when human beings also are seen as products of nature. Adoption of Darwinian categories by social scientists to explain human beings constitutes yet another of the various "Copernican revolutions" in the history of worldviews.

Although Darwin may have been religiously ambivalent, his explanations were not. Darwin's observations impelled him to rescind earlier arguments that invoked the need for God to explain the order of nature. Nature no longer needed a Creator. According to Darwin, the hinge of a bivalve shell may be beautiful in the eyes of a human observer, but obviously, it was not made by an intelligent being, as is the hinge of a door by a craftsman. Darwin wrote: "There seems to be no more design in the variability of organic beings and in the action of natural selection than in the course of which the wind blows."[31] Consequently, God was no longer necessary to explain the natural order. Science could get along quite well without God—or so Darwinian social scientists thought.

By all accounts, Darwin unwittingly confirmed Hegel's intuition that history changes through struggle. Hegel located the source of change in the struggle of ideas. Darwin naturalized Hegel's framework by locating the source of struggle within nature itself. Therefore, Darwin's scheme filled one of the last important conceptual gaps for the radical secular prophets. We no longer need religion to explain nature; after Darwin, nature can explain itself. The enormity of this philosophical consequence cannot be underestimated. After reading *On the Origin of the Species* in the early 1860s, both Marx and Engels stated it confirmed their suspicions that the dialectic of history needed nothing over and above the natural order. Above all, thinkers now pronounced religion irrelevant to the system. Evolution removed the need for God or any notion of providence. The evolutionary point of view could now explain every part of the natural order. Darwin's theory metastasized, as it were, into every intellectual domain. No questions remained that could not be answered by appealing to evolution. Or so the post-Darwinian secular prophets claimed.

Because of Darwin's work, the Western view of humankind underwent a profound change. Prior to this point, under Enlightenment pressures, Western thinkers held largely optimistic views of human nature. The myth of progress pervaded America in particular, and utopian social visions sprang up everywhere. But Darwin pictured humankind as caught in a brutal struggle for survival, and indeed the human race survived because of barbaric tendencies over the rest of nature. Humans thrived because they

> *Darwin's scheme filled one of the last important conceptual gaps for the radical secular prophets. We no longer need religion to explain nature; after Darwin, nature can explain itself. The enormity of this philosophical consequence cannot be underestimated.*

31. Charles Darwin, *On the Origin of the Species* (New York: New York University Press, 1988), 103.

were stronger, smarter, and more cunning than the rest of the animal world. Humankind's brutality, not moral superiority, explained our survival. Henceforth, a sea change that focused on humankind's darker side and irrational nature engulfed social scientific studies. The links to the animal kingdom became more prominent and philosophically more significant. Evolutionary biology may have been half a century away, but social Darwinism became all the rage before the final decade of the nineteenth century.

Christian responses to Darwin in the nineteenth century varied. Darwin never sought to make a direct connection between evolution and religious belief. Others were more than happy to fill in those gaps, but the gap itself resulted in differing responses to Darwin's work by Christians. Those who understood evolution as fundamentally opposed to religious belief—by virtue of being a pseudo-religion itself—harshly criticized the theory. Those who interpreted evolution as having only a narrow application within plant and animal life sought to preserve space for it within a larger theistic worldview. These thinkers proposed that God created an evolutionary mechanism within the natural order while also being fully able to contravene the system when he so desired. Debates within the Christian community over a suitable response to Darwin reinforced the notion that evolutionary science could not be ignored.

Sigmund Freud (1856–1939)

Placing Freud in the chronological sequence of the nineteenth century secular prophets stretches the temporal construct almost to the breaking point. Freud belongs most fully to the twentieth century, and the fact that he was not a philosopher or a theologian renders dubious our inclusion of him in our narrative. However, there is no clearer representative of the final flowering of the secular prophets than Freudian psychology. Freud distilled the larger claims of the secular prophets into a working framework that influenced worldviews well beyond the midpoint of the twentieth century. And although Freud's primary frame of reference was psychology, his ideas infiltrated the entire religious spectrum. Freud's treatment of the neurotic character of religion brought the tradition of the secular prophets to its most aggressive criticism of Christian belief. Leaving aside Freud's developed thought on psychological structures, his central contribution to naturalism's rising dominance was his psychological depiction of the rise of religion. Freud depicted religion as a psychological disorder that is common to humankind. Religion has developed because of an inner conflict within each person,[32] a conflict of dependence on others and the yearning for independence from others. Natural forces war within each person's soul. The "normal" state of this conflict depends on one's own life journey. At birth, each person is naturally more predisposed toward dependency

Sigmund Freud

---

32. Sigmund Freud, *Totem and Taboo: Some Points of Agreement Between the Mental Lives of Savages and Neurotics*, trans. and ed. James Strachey (New York: W. W. Norton, 1989).

on others for survival. As natural development takes place, maturing individuals eventually reach a stage where they become self-reliant. Failure to work through this transition from dependence to independence results in various neuroses. Taken collectively, these neuroses express themselves most prominently in religious ways.

Freud assumed religion had no actual insight into the "way things are."[33] He dismissed religious claims about the existence of God because they had no basis in fact. The more pressing question could be stated: if there is no God, why is there religion in the first place? This question provided the context for Freud's psychological explanation of religious belief.

Freud depicted a hypothetical ancient tribal context as the clearest way to explain the emergence of religion in society. The chief of the tribe was viewed as the primal father in the tribe. By virtue of his office as chief, he held complete authority. This was largely justified by the need to establish order in the surrounding chaotic world. Because of their natural desire for independence, those outside the power structure eventually revolted against the chief and killed him. However, far from gaining freedom from the tyranny of authority, the younger warriors suffered great loss and guilt. Loss of leadership led to chaos and disruption. To repair the moral fabric that appeared to hold the tribe together, the young murderers created a totemic religion where memories of the dead chief restored order and meaning. The young warriors worshiped the chief as if he were still alive, creating representations of him out of wood and stone. Soon someone claimed that the chief actually was still alive and existed spiritually in some distant heaven. The projection of the chief's image was identified as a "Supreme Being" and eventually referred to as "God." The will of the chief again became absolute, and this helped the warriors find forgiveness.

Freud intended his mythical depiction to describe the collective "Oedipal complex," on the basis of which religion may be explained. Given the metaphors of "family" within Christianity (e.g., Father and Son), Freud discredited religious belief by claiming it evoked a neurotic psychological dependence that social scientists had otherwise seen only in human families. Religion was nothing other than an immature child, refusing to shed its dependence on a parent-figure. The social structures built to support the myth of religion proved strong enough to sustain this totemic worldview for several thousand years. With the coming of modernity, however, Freud envisioned a time when people would break the shackles of religion and gain their (psychological) independence.

Thus the root of religion is fear—fear that one cannot stand alone. It is fear of the unknown—especially of nature. Nature presents many imposing dangers. Storms of immense power and natural forces beyond human control threaten our survival. The first step in dealing with fears of the unknown is to

> *Freud depicted religion as a psychological disorder that is common to humankind. Religion has developed because of an inner conflict within each person, a conflict of dependence on others and the yearning for independence from others. Natural forces war within each person's soul.*

> *Freud assumed religion had no actual insight into the "way things are." He dismissed religious claims about the existence of God because they had no basis in fact.*

---

33. Sigmund Freud, *The Future of an Illusion,* trans. and ed. James Strachey (New York: Norton, 1989).

> *Those who desire
> freedom from the
> constraints of reli-
> gious authority
> simply need to cast
> away their shackles.
> Recognizing the
> neurosis is the larger
> part of curing it. After
> a correct diagnosis, a
> determined exercise
> of the will is the lone
> missing ingredient.*

attempt to tame nature itself. Freud supposed that early animists humanized nature by projecting spiritual qualities onto it. However, when nature continued to treat humankind arbitrarily, tossing destructive storms at them, a stronger solution had to be found. If nature could not be tamed, a supernatural force was needed. This supernatural force had to be powerful enough to control nature's threats and compassionate enough to care for those threatened by nature. It would be better still if this supernatural force were personal and had much in common with humankind. This would assure us that the supernatural force would be loyal to those whom nature threatened. Thus, according to Freud, people created an idol in the image of those in need, but stronger and smarter, as a mechanism to overcome their fears. However, far from granting them solace from their fears, this idol kept them in a perpetual state of dependence, because it always demanded obedience.

The failure to mature beyond the stage of dependence created the opportunity for religion. And religion all but guaranteed humans would never achieve the independence for which they yearned. Up to a point, Freud's diagnosis seemed irrefutable. It offered no evidence that could contravene it; it depended solely on the explanatory power of its suggestions. Those who desire freedom from the constraints of religious authority simply need to cast away their shackles. Recognizing the neurosis is the larger part of curing it. After a correct diagnosis, a determined exercise of the will is the lone missing ingredient.

Freudian explanations of religion were fairly neat and tidy. And like its predecessors, the explanations were conceptually dependent on biblical notions of idolatry. Biblical religion had offered resources that in turn could (and were) used against it. The blind spot for Freud's use of idolatry was the problem of "self-referential incoherence." Any criticism of religion that ultimately depends on a psychological depiction of it is vulnerable to the same exact charge. If corrupting motives lay behind religion, could not a similar tale be told with respect to the motives behind the critique? If there is a psychology of belief, clearly there may also be a psychology of unbelief.[34] The presence (or absence) of psychological motives behind (ir)religious beliefs entails neither the truth nor falsity of the beliefs in question. Freud, as the secular prophets had before him, assumed a naturalistic worldview, and on this basis went looking for the only possible cause of religion—a natural one.

However, as with Marx, so with Freud—one should not dismiss these criticisms too easily. Scripture is replete with examples of idolatrous beliefs and actions within the visible covenant community of God. If secular prophets are required to identify modern forms of idolatry within Christendom, then woe to the modern church. The church should be better equipped to think about itself critically in an age of great temptation. In part, we owe a

---

34. In a thoughtful but far too brief account, R. C. Sproul turned the tables on the cultured despisers of religion of the nineteenth century in just this manner. See R. C. Sproul, *The Psychology of Atheism* (Minneapolis: Bethany Publishers, 1974).

debt to Freud for exposing tendencies of psychological dependence that often influence how we see God. In the present environment, too frequently these dependencies mean that God's primary responsibility is to look out for our wealth and well-being—the "gospel" of health and wealth. Is not the church responsible to reflect the living and true God's desire for truth, beauty, and justice? Religion can be psychologically manipulated, and the dangers in an individualist culture like ours are precisely the abuses Freud identified.

However, secularists from Feuerbach to Freud hardly understood the scriptural presentation of God's holiness. The tame god of civil religion was an easy target for them, but far less so the overwhelming and terrifying God confronted in the pages of Job, Isaiah, Hebrews, and Revelation. When we see Job overwhelmed by God's presence, we cannot imagine that this Yahweh is the sort of God Job would have created.[35] The same thing is true regarding Isaiah's terrifying vision of God's holiness. Is this terrifying portrayal of God merely a figment of Isaiah's imagination, created to meet his private needs? The author of Hebrews well understood the costliness of salvation in Christ; one cannot reasonably argue he would have created this gospel if given the opportunity to make things easy for himself. Likewise, the suffering and martyrdom portrayed throughout the book of Revelation makes it highly unlikely that any person looking for comfort and convenience would have created a God that brought so much suffering into the lives of his people. In these and other ways, the biblical message resounds with a message too overwhelming to be simply a product of an idolatrous imagination. Nevertheless, in the face of the withering critiques from secular prophets, today's church should seek to recover the full-orbed holiness of God.

> *In part, we owe a debt to Freud for exposing tendencies of psychological dependence that often influence how we see God. In the present environment, too frequently these dependencies mean that God's primary responsibility is to look out for our wealth and well-being—the "gospel" of health and wealth.*

Friedrich Nietzsche (1844–1900)

No one comprehended the stark contrast between belief and unbelief like Nietzsche, and therefore none of the secular prophets depicted the implications of atheism as clearly as he did. Nietzsche brought the tradition of the secular prophets to its conceptual end by proclaiming that atheism was extremely costly. After Nietzsche, easy belief and easy unbelief proved impossible. As the culminating voice of the nineteenth century, Nietzsche foreshadowed the postmodern tradition that effectively eradicated the easy confidence in human nature and in rationality that was trumpeted by his Enlightenment predecessors.

Nietzsche's classical education developed in him an early love for Greek poetry and mythology. His love of ancient pagan authors convinced him of the repressive nature of Christian morality. The Christian worldview undermines the full moral autonomy of the individual. To Nietzsche, nothing surpassed the importance of human freedom—not simply the

---

35. See especially Job 38–40.

> *To Nietzsche, nothing surpassed the importance of human freedom—not simply the ability to choose between alternative actions but the larger sense of being free from any moral constraints whatsoever. Throughout his life, Nietzsche developed this fundamental intuition with a vengeance.*

ability to choose between alternative actions but the larger sense of being free from any moral constraints whatsoever. Throughout his life, Nietzsche developed this fundamental intuition with a vengeance.

After reading the radical Left Wing Hegelians while at university, Nietzsche abandoned his Christian upbringing. By all accounts, Nietzsche possessed one of the greatest minds of Western intellectual history, and he became one of Christianity's sharpest critics. The University of Leipzig granted Nietzsche a full academic doctorate, although he had not fulfilled any of the core requirements nor written a doctoral dissertation. More amazing still, Nietzsche attained the rank of full professor in philology the year after receiving his doctorate, having never taught a class nor written a book. In this light, we see why Nietzsche prized intellectual genius and saw it as a flowering of the ancient virtue of creativity. This also helps us see why Nietzsche understood Christianity as repressing such creativity and as civilization's worst enemy.

Unlike the cool and dispassionate analyses of earlier post-Enlightenment thinkers, Nietzsche made no pretense of objectively sifting the evidence for and against the gospel. "Disinterestedness has no value either in heaven or on earth."[36] As a tool in the service of desire, a tool that can only clarify the stark choices facing all humans, reason cannot be objective. The first and most important choice concerns God. Nietzsche passionately believed that if there is a God, human beings cannot be free. If human beings are free, there cannot be a God. It was that simple—and yet that terrifying. If this was the beginning of the story, it was also the end.

In his most notable work, *Thus Spake Zarathustra*, Nietzsche painted a picture of two competing worldviews. He referred to one as the "logic of life" and the other as the "logic of reason." In the former, human existence was the most primal datum. All else came from this. It accepted life simply as it was: to be celebrated and enjoyed. The logic of reason, on the other hand, imposed a framework of meaning around life in such a manner that human existence is interpreted through a moral and religious framework. Nietzsche represented these conflicting worldviews by using the mythological figures of Dionysius and Apollos. Dionysius, the god of wine and song, celebrated life in all its pleasures and all its dangers. By contrast, for Apollos, the god of order and balance, life was not so much to be celebrated as to be organized and interpreted. For Apollos, beauty was the celebration of harmony and symmetry. For Dionysius, beauty had no existence except in that which flowered from creative genius. For Dionysius, beauty was what is enjoyed when life is lived to the fullest. By contrast, Apollos preached, "Know thyself, and do nothing in excess." Dionysius proclaimed: "Celebrate the excess of life always."

---

36. Frederich Nietzsche, *The Gay Science*, trans. Walter Kaufmann (New York: Viking, 1974), 128.

Whom shall we choose: Dionysius or Apollos? According to Nietzsche, the fundamental choice between the logic of life and the logic of reason cannot be settled by appeal to reasons—for that would already assume the conclusion, which the evidence was intended to support. The choice was absolute, but also absolutely arbitrary. Life cannot be chosen *because* it is "right," for this would be to choose the logic of reason. There can be no reasons in favor of reason or in favor of life.

In effect, Nietzsche claimed that in the end all morality and all truth are arbitrary, since every argument must begin with premises that cannot be supported. The original foundation of every argument is merely "suspended in air." First principles are simply and only arbitrary choices, if they are indeed the principles upon which all other principles stand. In this regard, first principles cannot be reasonable or rational, if they are genuine *first principles*, for there would be no principles prior to first principles by which to judge whether the first principles satisfied them as reasonable.

Friedrich Nietzsche

If we think of foundationalism as that system of logic committed to rational first principles, then Nietzsche heralded the end of foundationalism. At the time, most thought of foundationalism as the logical framework of Christian belief. Christians believed in first principles as laid out in Holy Scripture. Few realized that the Enlightenment critiques of Christian belief were every bit as foundational in structure. "Trust only empirical evidence" may seem like a reasonable first principle—but on what basis is it reasonable? None, unless one also assumes that only empirical evidence is reasonable.

The upshot was that Nietzsche saw rationality as a function of human choice. It is located in human subjectivity, rather than any objective rational order. This entails that humans create their own meaning—the logic that makes sense of our lives. Humans can cede this responsibility to others, but to do this makes them slaves of those to whom they cede this responsibility. In this regard, religious people are the worst culprits. They consign themselves to be defined absolutely by another, thus losing altogether what makes them truly human: the awful responsibility to choose for oneself.

Nietzsche referred to this "awful responsibility" as "the will to power." It is the assertion of the self as the source of meaning. It is the intuition that man creates the world, rather than discovers a world in which meaning is fixed. Humans do not find truth so much as they make truth. In contrast to Christianity and the history of the Western philosophical tradition, Nietzsche believed humans did not have a fixed nature. They bore the burden of having to create meaning out of nothing. The Christian tradition gave the illusion that God bore the burden, but in so doing, Christians had abandoned their true humanity. "We should not place perfection above in the heavens or in a place of time nor should we set ourselves a perfection which is unattainable. Man is what man can make of himself."[37]

> *Nietzsche claimed that in the end all morality and all truth are arbitrary, since every argument must begin with premises that cannot be supported. The original foundation of every argument is merely "suspended in air."*

37. Frederich Nietzsche, *On the Genealogy of Morals*, trans. Walter Kaufmann (New York: Vintage, 1967), 32.

If the will to power is the essence of what it means to be human, there cannot be a being who exercises the will to power over another.[38] Most especially, Nietzsche argued, if humans exercise their will to power, then God cannot be. God must die if man is to live. For this reason, Nietzsche declared that God was dead. And if God is dead, then humankind must face up to their plight: there is no ultimate meaning to life, only the meaning that individuals create for themselves. There is no absolute good and evil, either. The only good left is that which enhances the feeling of power in individuals to determine their destiny.

Nietzsche believed that in the absence of God and meaning, individuals must assert a dialectical courage. This is courage to face up to the consequences of meaninglessness, no longer holding on to the illusion that real, absolute meaning could be found or created. This is a call to courage when one knows ultimately that courage will not save. This is the courage to live meaninglessly. Nietzsche understood that few could ever fully face this reality. Those who could overcome the hopelessness of the human plight by the sheer force of their will to power, Nietzsche called "Übermensch" (superman). In this, Nietzsche was profoundly influenced by the tragic heroes of ancient Greek mythology, who fought the gods rather than merely accepting their fate.

With the foundation of theism destroyed and nothing but the will to power left, Nietzsche believed Judeo-Christian morality eventually would crumble. If God were dead, the moral constructs of good and evil would vanish. There would be no room for guilt if there were no longer right and wrong. The only good left would be those actions that are life-affirming. All traditional morality was turned upside down; Nietzsche called this the "transvaluation of all values." Whereas traditional morality valued love of God and love of neighbor and abhorred love of self, Nietzsche believed the only value left is love of self. Christianity celebrated humility and meekness, obedience and loyalty. These were moral values for slaves, the weak, and the feeble. The courage to face up to the meaninglessness of life on one's own terms demanded a morality for masters.

Nietzsche believed the rejection of traditional morality in part is accomplished by locating the genesis of moral development, what he called a "genealogy of morals." By locating morality within the story of the past, the pretense to an eternal and transcendent beginning could be abolished. The story of the two moralities (slave and master) arose in cultures that denied desire and endorsed the weaknesses of the masses. The slave morality developed out of fear and hatred of the master class. The impotent, unable to conquer their worthier and physically more powerful foes, sought "spiritual revenge." They made everything that was opposed to the master class "good." Aligning God with their cause, they endorsed the eter-

> *All traditional morality was turned upside down; Nietzsche called this the "transvaluation of all values." Whereas traditional morality valued love of God and love of neighbor and abhorred love of self, Nietzsche believed the only value left is love of self.*

---

38. See Frederich Nietzsche, *The Will to Power*, trans. Walter Kaufmann and R. J. Hollingdale, ed. Walter Kaufmann (New York: Random House, 1967).

nal damnation of everyone who violated their moral standards. According to Nietzsche, eternal damnation, the ultimate revenge, shows that Judeo-Christian morality is rooted in hatred and vengefulness, not in love.

Nietzsche believed this genealogy of morals was sufficient to undermine the slave morality of Christianity by showing the stark differences between the two moralities.[39] Christianity is for weak people. Atheism demands a passionate embrace of strength. Christianity seeks to sublimate the core instincts and desires of humanity. Atheism declares that primal instincts and desires should be affirmed. Christianity imposes order by introducing absolutes. Atheism celebrates the chaos of life. Christianity defends the slave morality. Atheism rejects the slave morality and rejoices that everyone is his or her own master.

The choice between these alternative moralities and worldviews is clear and unavoidable. For making that choice clear and unavoidable, Christians should thank Nietzsche. More than anyone else, Nietzsche was willing to face the consequences of atheism. Liberal Christianity had tried to naturalize religion, making it appear more "civilized," but had denuded it in the process, while trying to avoid the spiritual and moral consequences of their naturalism. The earlier secular prophets had eliminated God, but because of their optimistic assumptions about human goodness, they believed there was ample room for a meaningful existence without him. Nietzsche saw more starkly than his predecessors that without God, there is no goodness left in humankind or anywhere else. Just as the earlier secular prophets put to death "easy believism," Nietzsche did the same for "easy atheism." Believing in God left no room for making God in one's own image. By mirror reasoning, Nietzsche believed atheism leaves no room for naïve hope and optimism. Without God, life is meaningless.

Nietzsche lived the courage of his convictions. He left academic life, believing it survived by creating an artificial cocoon of ideas. For a time, he served in the ambulance corps in the Franco-Prussian War of 1870–71, in some measure because of his own ill health. During the decade of the 1880s, while suffering from deep depression and wandering around Europe, he wrote his most penetrating and cryptic works. At the end of the decade, severe mental illness set in, probably caused by a venereal disease acquired during many earlier promiscuous sexual encounters. During his last decade, Nietzsche lived in the care of his mother and sister. It is a strange irony that Nietzsche died while hallucinating that he was Jesus Christ, his greatest enemy.

"Nietzsche saw more starkly than his predecessors that without God, there is no goodness left in humankind or anywhere else. . . . Nietzsche believed atheism leaves no room for naïve hope and optimism. Without God, life is meaningless.

Eclectic Movements: From Romanticism to Pragmatism

Leaving aside the core thematic argument of the nineteenth century's ideological revolution, it is important to turn our attention to the vast array of

---

39. Frederich Nietzsche, *The Antichrist*, trans. Walter Kaufmann, in *The Portable Nietzsche* (New York: Viking, 1954).

intellectual movements that swirled throughout the century. The nineteenth century saw a vast proliferation of worldviews. Underneath the surface, these worldviews appeared to emerge from a common intuition: the past should be radically reinterpreted. Earlier in this chapter, we explored the main contours of that intuition as it came to prominence in the secular prophets. Now we will examine the diverse nineteenth-century intellectual movements that arose from this intuition. The following descriptions survey the movements as distinct but overlapping worldviews. Most of them are interesting primarily as historically peripheral movements that left few successors. The historical details are less important than the movements' major convictions.

Romanticism and Transcendentalism

Although romanticism and transcendentalism technically are different movements, their central intuitions are virtually identical. Both were reactions against the strongly rationalistic tone of the Enlightenment. They also were sympathetic with the Enlightenment's critique of traditional religious belief. Both movements valued the liberating spirit of the Enlightenment and were disparaging in their view of Christianity. Religious belief was important only as an expression of a genuinely human emotion. It was much less important as a set of doctrines that sought to express timeless truths.

Romanticism betrays a simple, easy description as a unified worldview. As a movement, Romanticism dates to the last two decades of the eighteenth century and the first three decades of the nineteenth century. Romanticism came to expression primarily in the arts and literature and only derivatively in the academy. Its lasting impact was in music, and to a lesser extent in poetry. The chief figures of the Romantic Movement were Friedrich von Schlegel (1772–1829), Percy Bysshe Shelley (1792–1822), Johann Wolfgang von Goethe (1749–1832), Samuel Coleridge (1772–1834), William Wordsworth (1770–1850), and Thomas Carlyle (1795–1881). Most of these were literary authors and poets, rather than formal philosophers. They shared a deep appreciation for the beauty of nature. Each in his own way sought to exalt the emotions over reason, speaking of human experience, rather than of objective truths. They shared a preoccupation with the heroic individual who was separated from the masses by a robust set of passions and creativity. They all devalued the classical style of harmony and balance, believing the center of human meaning is found in each person's creative spirit. The mystical and mysterious played unusually large roles in their writings.

Johann Wolfgang von Goethe

As a worldview, romanticism was hostile to traditional religious belief, but its authors made much of the figures of God and the devil in their writings. Romanticism did not have a clear view of the meaning of history or of death. It was entirely sympathetic with the Enlightenment's attack on formal religion and the church in particular, but it never espoused anything approaching a structured set of beliefs. It drew on religious imagery without any pretense of believing in anything religious. Its writers felt free to draw on biblical themes in the same way that earlier writers drew on Greek mythology, with as little conviction and as much irreverence.

Transcendentalism was a more coherent movement than romanticism, but it was narrower in its influence. Transcendentalism came to expression in the first half of the nineteenth century among a group of New England authors and artists centered in Boston. Its most prominent members included Ralph Waldo Emerson (1803–82), Henry David Thoreau (1817–62), and Margaret Fuller (1810–50). Each believed the individual is the center of the spiritual universe and that an individual's inner light provides the best clue to the meaning of life. Like romanticism, the transcendentalists greatly admired nature for its beauty, rather than its law-like behavior. Thus, for transcendentalists, the empirical sciences were less significant than they were for the figures of the Enlightenment. The transcendentalists believed genuine happiness was not the result of studying nature analytically but of uniting oneself to nature in a mystical and transcendent way. They also believed human virtue primarily consists in restraining animal passions and embracing the spiritual forces of nature.

Transcendentalists resisted the mechanization of modern life that resulted from the Industrial Revolution. They saw the danger of imposing mechanistic categories, based on factory operations, on human life. Humans are not cogs in a machine, and human significance cannot be equated with what we produce, transcendentalists argued. Contemplation of mystery and beauty are far more important for enriching human experience. Transcendentalists saw contemplation as a form of intuition, not rational analysis.

The transcendentalists sound overtly religious, but their convictions cannot be identified with any recognizable religious group or creed. At times, their use of "God" sounded more like a place marker for some nebulous life force than as reference to a God who has spoken and acted decisively in history. The transcendentalist "God" could be found everywhere and in everything. Thus, transcendentalism was a form of pantheism. And as is true for most forms of pantheism, in some sense evil is illusory; there is no ultimate distinction between good and evil. On the surface, the transcendentalists also were pacifists, although their defense of this conviction rested more on instinct than argument.

Although transcendentalism faded as a coherent movement by the 1850s, its legacy continued to be felt in the literature and reform movements of the latter part of the nineteenth century. Most of the transcendentalists were writers: they wrote voluminous personal journals, sermons, letters, manifestoes, poems, translations, and essays. Emerson's *Essays* and Thoreau's *Walden* were outstanding literary works that influenced a generation of authors and poets and offered a distinct alternative to traditional European forms of literature.[40] Thoreau's writings on civil disobedience helped shape the articulate

> *[Romantics] devalued the classical style of harmony and balance, believing the center of human meaning is found in each person's creative spirit. The mystical and mysterious played unusually large roles in their writings.*

> *Transcendentalists resisted the mechanization of modern life that resulted from the Industrial Revolution.... Human significance cannot be equated with what we produce, transcendentalists argued.*

40.   See Ralph Waldo Emerson, *The Collected Works of Ralph Waldo Emerson* (Cambridge, MA: Harvard University Press, 1971), and Henry David Thoreau, *Walden, and Civil*

and nonreligious branches of the abolitionist movement. Finally, Margaret Fuller was seen as a prominent role model for feminist intellectuals in the progressive era at the beginning of the twentieth century.

Idealism

Like romanticism, idealism was not so much a well-defined movement as a set of common intuitions. Unlike romanticism, idealism was confined largely to the philosophical academy. Its only sizeable religious influence was among some liberal theologians in the middle part of the nineteenth century. Idealism flourished in Britain and Germany. Although the more prominent idealists were German, at the beginning of the twentieth century two Englishmen, G. E. Moore and Bertrand Russell, hard-core empiricists in the tradition of David Hume, dealt idealism its death blow. The most prominent and most complex idealist of the nineteenth century was G. W. F. Hegel, whom we mentioned earlier in this chapter. Two later idealists, Arthur Schopenhauer (1788–1860) and Friedrich Wilhelm Joseph Schelling (1775–1854), came to embody most clearly what is now referred to as German idealism. F. H. Bradley (1846–1924) was the most famous and philosophically influential of the British idealists.

As a general theory, idealism stood in contrast to materialism's teaching that ultimate reality is material in nature. Idealists, on the other hand, believed ultimate reality consists of mentally related phenomena (ideas).[41] There were many different versions of idealism, as well as many hybrid theories, some of which even combined elements of materialism. Plato's contribution to ancient Greek thought often was seen as a kind of idealism, since he defined ultimate reality in terms of non-material Forms. However, Plato also affirmed the full reality of the physical world, thus making it questionable to identify his philosophy as a type of idealism. Enlightenment philosophy commonly assumed that ideas represent material objects. Using this assumption, nineteenth-century idealists argued that the only evidence of the material world was our perception of it. However, perceptions are not material objects; they are mental pictures. And since these "pictures" are the only entities to which the mind had immediate and certain access, idealists concluded the only things we really know are ideas, not the objects they supposedly represent. Ideas, not material objects, are the ultimate reality.

With the rise of logical positivism and the critical scientific spirit that accompanied it, the grand metanarrative of idealism came crashing down in the first half of the twentieth century. However, there are some recent signs that the positivists prematurely announced idealism's death.

> *With the rise of logical positivism and the critical scientific spirit that accompanied it, the grand metanarrative of idealism came crashing down in the first half of the twentieth century.*

Disobedience: Complete Texts with Introduction, Historical Contexts, and Critical Essays, ed. Paul Lauter (Boston: Houghton Mifflin, 2000).

41. See F. H. Bradley, *Appearance and Reality* (Oxford: Clarendon Press, 1893), who gave classic expression to this conviction.

Anti-realism and linguistic idealism, both recent theories, deny materialism's fundamental postulate that ultimate reality is material. Moreover, we should note that contemporary Christian philosophical thought has battled the related errors of absolute idealism and absolute materialism—though for very different reasons than the anti-realists.

Theological Liberalism

In the aftermath of the Enlightenment, deism revived, accompanied by literature sharply critical of the Christian Scriptures. This gave rise to what we now call "theological liberalism"—a loose coalition of biblical scholars, theologians, and historians of religion. The movement centered mostly in Germany, though its tentacles spread far and wide. The central theological figures associated with the movement were Friedrich Schleiermacher (1768–1834), Albrecht Ritschl (1822–89), and Adolf von Harnack (1851–1930), along with the biblical scholars C. J. Wellhausen (1844–1918), F. C. Baur (1792–1860), and David F. Strauss (1808–74). In retrospect, Schleiermacher's work cast the longest shadow and still is theologically significant.

Schleiermacher was a fervent advocate of reunion between the diverse branches of the Protestant church in Germany. Interestingly, he was best known in his own day for providing the critical edition and translation of Plato's dialogues. He was important in the founding of the classic modern University of Berlin, in which the diverse disciplines revolved around a philosophical center. At Berlin, Schleiermacher also gave expression to the now-common, fourfold division of the theological disciplines: biblical, dogmatic, historical, and pastoral. Schleiermacher believed religious disciplines should be governed by the universal principle intrinsic to all academic disciplines, namely, critical historical inquiry. As a result, theology became religious studies.

According to Schleiermacher, religion is not a form of knowing but a form of doing.[42] It is primarily ethical in orientation. In this regard, religion has to do with a feeling or consciousness of absolute dependence, as opposed to believing in an absolute being. God is not an object; he is the essence of all that is. General religious experience confirms there is ultimate meaning. The raw experience of feeling dependent on reality could be conceptualized by different cultures in many different ways, each of which mistakenly supposed that its conceptualization was true. However, religious experience points to the ambiguity of ultimate truth. For Schleiermacher, this suggested Christian faith should be construed less in terms of specific doctrinal claims and more in terms of doing good to one's neighbor. This is the heart of what we can glean from Jesus' example, as recorded in the biblical texts that still can be trusted.

> *According to Schleiermacher, religion is not a form of knowing but a form of doing. It is primarily ethical in orientation. In this regard, religion has to do with a feeling or consciousness of absolute dependence, as opposed to believing in an absolute being.*

---

42. Friedrich Schleiermacher, *The Christian Faith*, ed. H. R. Mackintosh and J. S. Stewart (Edinburgh: T. & T. Clark, 1989).

Underlying theological liberalism's reinterpretations was a critical attack on the veracity of Scripture.[43] Although by the nineteenth century that attack was more than a century old, it received a renewed vigor in this period's climate of historicism. Historicism is the claim that truth is a function of historical contexts. In this vein, religion is best understood not by examining its ultimate claims but by studying its historical origins. Thus, for example, the gospel accounts of Jesus' life can be read much more fruitfully if the mythic and supernatural elements are removed and the real, earthly history uncovered. There may be much to learn about ancient cultures by understanding their motives for creating the miracle stories, but no self-respecting nineteenth-century religious scholar would have believed that miracle stories were literally true. Thus, liberal Protestants began to discuss how the mythic elements in the scriptural tradition began, not the importance of this religious tradition itself. Tradition became something that told the nineteenth century liberal scholars more about the prejudices of the earlier age. They believed that early Christians were motivated by political and economic factors to create a tradition that ostracized those who disagreed with them. The Scriptures informed them who was more powerful, not what was true. Under the influence of historicism, many in the nineteenth century came to believe that victors wrote the history books (the Bible) and thereby defined orthodoxy.[44]

The critical assumptions of theological liberalism came under increasing scrutiny, especially in the first three decades of the twentieth century. The "real earthly history" that was the goal of liberal enquiry often resulted in finding a history that merely agreed with the assumptions of the liberal historians. When searching for the historical Jesus, liberals often found a figure who merely mirrored their own convictions. When historicism became absolute, all claims to truth (even of a liberal persuasion) were reduced to mere opinion. And this left liberalism with no place to stand.

Existentialism

Properly speaking, existentialism primarily was an ideological movement of the twentieth century that was associated most notably with the French critics Jean-Paul Sartre and Albert Camus. However, the forerunners of this movement, and original thinkers in their own right, can be found in the nineteenth century: Søren Kierkegaard (1813–55) and Friedrich Nietzsche. Having examined Nietzsche in some detail, we now turn our attention to Kierkegaard. Although Nietzsche and Kierkegaard share some common themes, their differences are more important. Kierkegaard's

Søren Kierkegaard

43. A good, brief account of biblical criticism in the nineteenth century can be found in John Rogerson, Christopher Rowland, and Barnabas Lindars, The *History of Christian Theology*, vol. 2, *The Study and Use of the Bible* (London: Marshall Pickering, 1988), 318–80.

44. See Adolf von Harnack, *History of Dogma*, trans. Neil Buchanan (Gloucester, MA: Peter Smith, 1976).

goal was a revitalized religion of the heart; Nietzsche's goal was God's death. Kierkegaard saw "dead faith" as a Christian's worst enemy; Nietzsche saw faith of any sort as our worst enemy. These differences should not be overlooked when considering existentialism's roots in Kierkegaard and Nietzsche's works.

In nineteenth-century Denmark's state-sponsored church, Christianity had been reduced to conformity to external formalities; its inward transformation was being ignored. Hypocritical religious leaders to whom public recognition meant more than a sincere faith incensed Kierkegaard. These men preached high and lofty sermons, but their lives were testimonies to greed and jealousy. They had an intellectual faith, but their hearts were dead. Therefore, Kierkegaard called for an experiential choice that was rooted in a religious passion to know God with the fullness of one's heart.[45] This could not be a choice rooted in reason, for then it would forever waver under the weight of further inquiry. Kierkegaard believed the most significant choices were not dictated by reason but were the result of passionate, individual commitments. Reason's constraints drained life of its vitality and energy.

A common thread throughout Kierkegaard's writings is the "stages on life's way."[46] The first stage is the aesthetic stage, where we are driven by pleasure and committed to satisfying our desires. Pain and boredom, enemies of this life, may lead us to the edge of despair where we recognize that our hedonistic drive is superficial. Despair may call us to the next stage, the ethical, where we adopt moral principles to guide our lives. However, moral principles can prove difficult. Because they place moral constraints on life, we are tempted to retreat to the aesthetic stage, or we may take a leap of faith into the religious stage.

In *Fear and Trembling*, Kierkegaard uses the figure of Abraham to describe the transition from the ethical to the religious stage.[47] In demanding that Abraham sacrifice Isaac, God required something contrary to moral law. Children should not be sacrificed! However, God's demands are greater than any ethical principle. From an aesthetic or ethical perspective on life, the demands God placed on Abraham appear ludicrous. However, the religious stage of life calls us to suspend ordinary morality and make a genuinely religious choice, which Abraham passionately embraced and which we should emulate. It is a choice for God and against reason. It is only in making a religious choice of this sort that one can truly find one's self.

> The "real earthly history" that was the goal of liberal enquiry often resulted in finding a history that merely agreed with the assumptions of the liberal historians. When searching for the historical Jesus, liberals often found a figure who merely mirrored their own convictions.

> Kierkegaard called for an experiential choice that was rooted in a religious passion to know God with the fullness of one's heart. This could not be a choice rooted in reason, for then it would forever waver under the weight of further inquiry.

45. Søren Kierkegaard, *Either/Or*, trans. David F. Swenson, Lillian M. Swenson, and Walter Lowrie (Garden City, NY: Anchor Books, 1959).

46. Søren Kierkegaard, *Stages on Life's Way*, trans. Walter Lowrie (Princeton, NJ: Princeton University Press, 1945).

47. Søren Kierkegaard, *Fear and Trembling*, trans. Howard V. Hong and Edna H. Hong (Princeton, NJ: Princeton University Press, 1983).

Pragmatism

America's most distinct contribution to philosophy lay in the movement we now call pragmatism. Pragmatism, which originated in the latter half of the nineteenth century, found its intellectual home at Harvard University. The chief architects of the movement were Harvard philosopher William James (1842–1910), the founder of pragmatism, C. S. Peirce (1839–1914), the intellectual force behind the movement, and John Dewey (1859–1952), the propagator of the movement. The pragmatists' core conviction was that beliefs are to be valued according to their practical consequences. Philosophy is not primarily a rational enterprise; it should be more concerned with beliefs that help us get along in life. The meaning and truth of any idea are functions of its practical outcomes. A secondary conviction of the pragmatists was that all ideas should be regarded as working hypotheses, not absolutely true axioms. Human knowledge is always evolving, and further enquiry should not be excluded.

According to pragmatists, no theory is ever determined by the data. There are always conflicting theories that could be "proven" by the data, though two conflicting theories could not be true. Because differing theories could equally well account for the evidence, no appeal to the data can finally determine which hypothesis is true. How could one reasonably decide which to believe? According to pragmatists, the determinative truth test is the proven usefulness of a belief.

Originally, pragmatism was less a theory of truth than a theory of meaning. The meaning of any term was ultimately the actions that it elicited. The sensible effects of a term or theory were the only way humans could discover what the term meant. In contemporary language, the meaning of a term was its "cash value." This suggested to later pragmatists such as John Dewey that education be reframed as a project oriented toward action, rather than abstract ideas. It should help students solve actual practical problems. A truly modern education should challenge students to test rival hypotheses against their own experiences in order to lead them toward reasonable conclusions and ever more coherent and concrete actions. Dewey granted that the results of this process always would be open to criticism and revision, so that nothing was ever finally absolutely true.

Pragmatism was less a system of ideas than a method by which ideas were to be tested. At times, it appeared openly hostile to religion, at other times it was an ardent defender of belief in God, or at least it was critical of critiques of God. The contemporary revival of pragmatism at the end of the twentieth century is decidedly agnostic.[48] Its commitment to an evolutionary epistemology made it strongly suspicious of any notion of religious truth "delivered once and for all."

> *The pragmatists' core conviction was that beliefs are to be valued according to their practical consequences. . . . The meaning and truth of any idea are functions of its practical outcomes.*

---

48. See Richard Rorty, *The Consequences of Pragmatism* (Minneapolis: University of Minnesota, 1982).

Concluding Comments on the Revolution

It would be a mistake to conclude from the preceding narrative that religious belief was either absent or sickly at the end of the nineteenth century. Popular religious belief was pervasive in the English-speaking world as the century ended. Many, in fact, trumpeted the claim that the twentieth century would prove to be the "Christian Century."[49] However, religious belief was all but unthinkable to most social movers and shakers in turn-of-the-century America.[50] The nineteenth century had witnessed one of the largest revivals in the history of Christendom—the Second Great Awakening.[51] However, the strength of religious belief in culture largely lay outside the world of ideas at the end of the century. Intellectual momentum had turned, though popular movements may not yet have testified to this.

From the perspective of Protestant orthodoxy, the nineteenth century produced a wide array of highly influential theologians, among them Charles Hodge, Benjamin B. Warfield, and Augustus Strong. They spoke a common philosophical language and carried a common commitment to defending the historic confession of the Christian tradition. This common philosophical language was "common sense realism." One could justifiably suggest that the *lingua franca* of intellectual discourse in the nineteenth century was not German idealism or its successors but the common sense realism of Hodge, Warfield, and Strong—a philosophical movement not discussed here.[52] The common sense tradition was an entirely different trajectory from the earlier British empiricists. Immanuel Kant believed one must accept the central assumptions of David Hume's critical assault on religious belief, and so he worked out a system to salvage knowledge. The earliest of the common sense realists, Thomas Reid and his successors, refused to accept Hume's central assumptions.[53] They believed there was a direct and immediate apprehension of common truths, most notably those of perception and memory. In other words, they believed there was a "foundation" that was stable and secure, upon which the traditional claims of religious belief could be built. It would be wrong to suppose that the common sense realist project was not influential in the nineteenth century. However, it also would be an exaggeration to

> *[Common sense realists] believed there was a direct and immediate apprehension of common truths, most notably those of perception and memory. In other words, they believed there was a "foundation" that was stable and secure, upon which the traditional claims of religious belief could be built.*

---

49. This is the origin of the name given to the widely influential journal "Christian Century."

50. See Turner, *Without God, Without Creed*, esp. chap. 1.

51. See William G. McLoughlin, *Revivals, Awakenings, and Reform* (Chicago: University of Chicago Press, 1978).

52. The central figure of common sense realism, Thomas Reid, belongs to the eighteenth century, which is why he is not included in this chapter. Reid is better known for providing an alternative response to David Hume's skepticism than is Kant. See Thomas Reid, *Inquiry into the Human Mind on the Principle of Common Sense*, ed. Timothy Duggan (Chicago: University of Chicago Press, 1970). The best treatment of Reid's significance for the history of philosophy is Nicholas Wolterstorff, *Thomas Reid and the Story of Epistemology* (New York: Cambridge University Press, 2001).

53. See Wolterstorff, *Thomas Reid*, for an extended treatment of Reid's relationship to Hume.

say that it exerted a significant intellectual counterweight to the post-Kantian criticisms of religion. By the beginning of the twentieth century, there was nary a common sense realist to be found of any intellectual note.[54] Whatever else may be said of the intellectual vitality of this movement, its irrelevance to the rest of the academy at the start of the twentieth century is striking.

Looking back on the nineteenth century, it is important to understand it ideologically on its own terms and to treat it with the respect it deserves. As this chapter frequently has argued, thoughtful Christians should take seriously the project of naturalizing religion. Wherever there is sin, the danger of religious belief being crafted to serve human need is always present. The idolatry of the church is a temptation as old as the golden calf and as threatening as Nietzsche supposed. The church must take its own corruption seriously, and for that, we can thank the secular prophets.

However, as we have emphasized, the secular prophets were dependent on a set of assumptions that now appear dubious, at best. The naïve optimism in human progress, whether of a religious or atheistic variety, now has been largely discredited. In addition, the central plank in the naturalist argument—that religion is historically conditioned and thereby not true—may as easily be turned against the naturalists, namely, that unbelief is historically conditioned and thereby not true. As the twentieth century will bear witness, historical conditions should not be dismissed superficially or viewed as absolutely determinative.

The nineteenth century was a time when great ideas mattered and intellectual discourse took seriously the notion of worldview. Life was to be lived in the parameters of a worldview. The nineteenth century also was a period when too much confidence may have been placed in intellectual discourse, in turn giving rise to the notion that religious belief could be intellectually dismissed. Although many supposed religion would never be the same again, there were others who hoped the church might wake up, take its critics seriously, and take its responsibilities before the living God more seriously. Ideas do matter, especially those that echo into eternity.

For Further Reading

Thomas Reid

Kant, Immanuel

Critique of Judgement. Translated by W. S. Pluhar. Indianapolis: Hackett Publishing Co., 1987.
Critique of Practical Reason. Translated by L. W. Beck. New York: Macmillan Publishing Co., 1993.

---

54. One of the great ironies of this story is that the revival of common sense realism in the middle part of the twentieth century also was a precursor, of sorts, to the renaissance of evangelical scholarship. See especially the work of Alvin Plantinga and Nicholas Wolterstorff, *Faith and Rationality* (Notre Dame: University of Notre Dame, 1983).

Critique of Pure Reason. Translated by N. K. Smith. London: MacMillan and Co., 1963.

Religion within the Limits of Reason Alone. Translated by T. M. Greene and H. H. Hudson. New York: Harper and Row, 1960.

Hegel, G. W. F.

The Phenomenology of Spirit. Translated by A. V. Miller. Oxford: Clarendon Press, 1977.

Science of Logic. Translated by A. V. Miller. New York: Humanities Press, 1976.

Feuerbach, Ludwig

The Essence of Christianity. Translated by George Eliot. New York: Harper, 1957.

The Essence of Religion: God the Image of Man. Translated by Alexander Loos. New York: A. K. Butts, 1873.

Marx, Karl

Capital: A Critique of Political Economy. Translated by Ben Fowkes. New York: Penguin Books, 1992.

The Communist Manifesto, with Friedrich Engels. New York: Penguin, 2002.

The German Ideology: Including Theses on Feuerbach, with Friedrich Engels. Amherst, NY: Prometheus Books, 1998.

Marx on Religion: Selections. Edited by John Raines. Philadelphia: Temple University Press, 2002.

Charles Darwin

On the Origin of the Species. New York: New York University Press, 1988.

The Descent of Man. Chicago: Encyclopedia Britannica, Inc., 1990.

Sigmund Freud

Civilization and its Discontents. Translated and edited by James Strachey. New York: W. W. Norton, 1989.

The Future of an Illusion. Translated and edited by James Strachey. New York: Norton, 1989.

Moses and Monotheism: Three Essays. Translated and edited by James Strachey. London: The Hogarth Press and the Institute of Psycho-analysis, 1974.

Totem and Taboo: Some Points of Agreement Between the Mental Lives of Savages and Neurotics. Translated and edited by James Strachey. New York: W. W. Norton, 1989.

Friedrich Nietzsche

The Antichrist. Translated by Walter Kaufmann. In *The Portable Nietzsche*. New York: Viking, 1954.

The Complete Works of Friedrich Nietzsche. Edited by Oscar Levy. New York: Russell and Russell, 1964.

> *The central plank in the naturalist argument—that religion is historically conditioned and thereby not true—may as easily be turned against the naturalists, namely, that unbelief is historically conditioned and thereby not true.*

> *The nineteenth century was a time when great ideas mattered and intellectual discourse took seriously the notion of worldview. Life was to be lived in the parameters of a worldview.*

Romanticism

Coleridge, Samuel Taylor. *Lectures on the History of Philosophy.* Edited by J. R. de J. Jackson. Princeton, NJ: Princeton University Press, 2000.

———. *On Humanity.* Edited by Anya Taylor. New York: St. Martin's Press, 1994).

von Goethe, Johann Wolfgang. *Collected Works.* Princeton, NJ: Princeton University Press, 1994.

von Schlegel, Friedrich. *The Philosophy of History.* Translated by James Burton Robertson. New York: AMS Press, 1976.

Transcendentalism

Emerson, Ralph Waldo. *The Collected Works of Ralph Waldo Emerson.* Cambridge, MA: Harvard University Press, 1971.

Thoreau, Henry David. *Walden, and Civil Disobedience: Complete Texts with Introduction, Historical Contexts, Critical Essays.* Edited by Paul Lauter. Boston: Houghton Mifflin, 2000.

Idealism

Bradley, F. H. *Appearance and Reality.* Oxford, Clarendon Press, 1893.

Schelling, Friedrich Wilhelm Joseph. *System of Transcendental Idealism.* Translated by P. Heath. Charlottesville, VA: University Press of Virginia, 1981.

Schopenhauer, Arthur. *On the Freedom of the Will.* Translated by K. Kolenda. New York: Bobbs Merrill, 1960.

———. *The World as Will and Representation.* Translated by E. F. J. Payne. New York: Dover, 1969.

Theological Liberalism

Harnack, Adolf von. *History of Dogma.* Translated by Neil Buchanan. Gloucester, MA: Peter Smith, 1976.

———. *Liberal Theology at Its Height: Selections.* Edited by Martin Rumscheidt. San Francisco: Collins, 1989.

Schleiermacher, Friedrich. *The Christian Faith.* Edited by H. R. Mackintosh and J. S. Stewart. Edinburgh: T. & T. Clark, 1989.

———. *On Religion: Speeches to Its Cultured Despisers.* Translated and edited by Richard Crouter. New York: Cambridge University Press, 1996.

Søren Kierkegaard

Concluding Unscientific Postscript. Translated by David F. Swenson. Princeton, NJ: Princeton University Press, 1941.

Either/Or. Translated by David F. Swenson, Lillian M. Swenson, and Walter Lowrie. Garden City, NY: Anchor Books, 1959.

Fear and Trembling. Translated by Howard V. Hong and Edna H. Hong. Princeton, NJ: Princeton University Press, 1983.

Stages on Life's Way. Translated by Walter Lowrie. Princeton, NJ: Princeton University Press, 1945.

Pragmatism

Dewey, John. *The Early Works 1882–1898, The Middle Works 1899–1924,* and *The Later Works 1925–1953.* Edited by Jo Ann Boydston. 36 vols. Carbondale, IL: Southern Illinois University Press, 1961–90.

James, William. *The Works of William James.* Edited by Frederick H. Burkhardt, Fredson Bowers, and Ignas Skrupskelis. 19 vols. Cambridge, MA: Harvard University Press, 1981–88.

Peirce, C. S. *The Collected Papers of Charles S. Peirce.* Edited by Charles Hartshorne, Paul Weiss, and Arthur Burks. 8 vols. Cambridge, MA: Harvard University Press, 1931–35, 1958.

Secondary Sources

Copleston, Frederick. *A History of Philosophy.* Vol. 7, Parts I–II. New York: Image Books, 1965.

Wilkens, Steve, and Alan G. Padgett. *Christianity and Western Thought.* Vol. 2. Downers Grove, IL: InterVarsity Press, 1990.

For Further Discussion

1. Give reasons why intellectuals in the nineteenth century claimed that religious belief arose from natural sources.

2. What are the similarities and differences in the critiques of Christianity offered by Feuerbach, Marx, Darwin, and Freud?

3. Is there an enduring significance to Marx's criticism of capitalism?

4. Why are arguments about Darwin's evolutionary theory still going on today?

5. How does Nietzsche both affirm and criticize the secular prophets of the nineteenth century?

6. How might you compare the criticism of idolatry by the Old Testament prophets and the criticism of idolatry by the secular prophets of the nineteenth century?

7. How revolutionary was the nineteenth century?

⎡ 10 ⎤

Philosophy Among the Ruins: The Twentieth Century and Beyond

Michael W. Payne

The culture of any society at any moment is more like the debris, or "fall-out," of past ideological systems than it is itself a system, a coherent whole.
Victor Turner

Suddenly, there is a curve in the road, a turning point. Somewhere, the real scene has been lost, the scene where you had rules for the game and some solid stakes that everybody could rely on.
Jean Baudrillard

> *In many ways, the twentieth century was simply a continuation of the principal debates and themes discussed earlier in this book. In another sense, it represents the final resting place of what once were thought—wrongly, it appears—to be matters worth considering again.*

Both Turner's and Baudrillard's descriptions offer vivid philosophical metaphors for illuminating our century and the one that immediately preceded it. In many ways, the twentieth century was simply a continuation of the principal debates and themes discussed earlier in this book. In another sense, it represents the final resting place of what once were thought—wrongly, it appears—to be matters worth considering again. For some issues, multiple streams converge and in various ways are refreshed and re-directed (e.g., the recent renaissance in Aristotelian studies relative to virtue ethics).[1] For others, the streams dry up, since they were fed by sources that have themselves self-imploded (e.g., foundationalism, Cartesian rationalism, etc.).[2]

1. For example, see the work of Alasdair MacIntyre in his *After Virtue* 2nd ed. (Notre Dame: University of Notre Dame Press, 1984) and Martha Nussbaum's *Love's Knowledge* (Oxford: Oxford University Press, 1990).

2. Nicholas Wolterstorff, *Reason Within the Bounds of Religion* (Grand Rapids: Eerdmans, 1976, rev. ed. 1984); Nancey Murphy, *Beyond Liberalism and Fundamentalism* (Valley Forge, PA: Trinity Press International, 1996) and *Anglo-American Postmodernity: Philosophical Perspectives on Science, Religion, and Ethics* (Boulder, CO: Westview Press, 1997).

In fact, Phillip Blond refers to the twentieth century as one of *failed conditions*. By this, he means that we late moderns seem bound to the horns of a dilemma. Either we celebrate some projected transcendental a priori that is supposed to validate our practical and pragmatic choices, or we opt for a more celebratory, self-legislating sense of purpose, acknowledging that whatever we say or do, it is always bound up with language and power, as Nietzsche and Foucault taught.[3] Both are human constructions and projections.[4] As Blond writes,

> Always and everyday those trapped in such worlds practice the violence of denial. They deny that any world or order might precede them; through turning away from the transcendent they violate that which is present alongside and before them, and with the intoxicating compulsion of *ressentiment* they complete it all with the refusal of a future, taking being-towards-death (*Sein zum Tode*) as the definitive mark of the only subjectivity to come. Death, they say, is the only future that both you and I can authentically have as individuals.[5]

Before we succumb to the Nietzschean "agony of the 'in vain,' " which for Nietzsche meant surrendering to the ultimate nothingness that our lives eventuate in, once we recognize there is no inherent purpose or beauty in the world, a world that "aims at nothing and achieves nothing,"[6] we need to engage in a little philosophical archaeology of our own. One thing seems certain: a synchronic analysis is insufficient; we need a diachronic approach, since ideas do not appear *de novo* or exist in hermetically sealed containers, unaffected by surrounding forces.[7]

How best can we explore the most salient turning points in twentieth-century intellectual history[8] that have propelled us into the twenty-first century? In keeping with the overall thrust of this book, we will analyze three interconnecting, primary revolutions that have created the current philosophical environment of postmodernism.[9] These include revolutions

> One thing seems certain: a synchronic analysis is insufficient; we need a diachronic approach, since ideas do not appear de novo or exist in hermetically sealed containers, unaffected by surrounding forces.

---

3. See Michel Foucault, *The Order of Things: An Archaeology of the Human Sciences*, trans. unnamed (New York: Vintage Books, 1973).

4. Phillip Blond, "Introduction: Theology before Philosophy" in *Post-Secular Philosophy: Between Philosophy and Theology*, ed. Phillip Blond (London: Routledge, 1998), 1–66.

5. Ibid., 3.

6. Friedrich Nietzsche, *The Will to Power*, trans. Walter Kaufmann and R. J. Hollingdale, ed. Walter Kaufmann (New York: Vintage Books, 1968), §12.

7. This echoes MacIntyre's understanding of "tradition" as something historically extended and socially embodied.

8. This is a work dedicated to examining "ideas" and not social or political movements as such. There are implications deriving from these ideas and these are worth examining in detail, but that is another work altogether.

9. The subject of postmodernity, postmodernism, the postmodern, etc., has been analyzed to death. Later in this essay, we will revisit the subject out of necessity. A good general (although somewhat superficial) survey of the issues, and one limited in terms of its own analytical choices, is Steven Best and Douglas Kellner, *Postmodern Theory: Critical Interrogations* (New York: The Guilford Press, 1991). See also the sequel by Best and Kellner, *The Postmodern Turn* (New York: The Guilford Press, 1997). John Milbank has offered a tantalizing twist on "postmodern" as really the second phase of modern critical thought.

in (1) language and epistemology, (2) science, and (3) ethics. All three revolutions have had a major impact on our understanding of truth, which has undergone a major revision since the latter part of the twentieth century. These various revolutions should not be understood as "sequential" or "chronological" developments.[10] Instead, they all occurred simultaneously and form what Richard Bernstein describes as a "new constellation"—appropriating Walter Benjamin and Theodor Adorno—of "changing elements that are irreducible to a common denominator"—something like a "force field" of interactions between old and new ideas.[11] Multiple forces converge to create new organisms, each of which has some of its forbears' traits. The remainder of this essay will explore these topics more fully, beginning with the linguistic turn and its parallels in epistemology and science.[12]

Ludwig Wittgenstein

According to Milbank, "The Sublime in Kierkegaard" in *Heythrop Journal* 37 (1996): 288, "In the first phase, inaugurated by Kant, the sublime or the indeterminable was safely off-limits for the proper exercise of theoretical reason, which is confined to notions that can be 'schematized' within finite space and time. In the second phase, by contrast, sublimity is perceived to contaminate even what is deceptively taken for finitude, so that it is precisely our 'here' and 'now' which cannot be finally characterized, but are only seized in their passing evanescence." There were, according to Milbank, premodern "postmodern" anticipations! Milbank elaborates further on this theme in "Problematizing the Secular: The post-Postmodern Agenda" in Philippa Berry and Andrew Wernick, eds. *The Shadow of Spirit* (London: Routledge, 1992). Toulmin seems to suggest something similar in his *Cosmopolis* (see note below), as does Louis Dupre in his *Passage to Modernity* (New Haven, CT: Yale University Press, 1993). Recent assessment of the "postmodern" include the incisive analysis provided by Pierre Manent, *The City of Man*, trans. Marc le Pain (Princeton, NJ: Princeton University Press, 1998); Nicholas Boyle, *Who Are We Now?: Christian Humanism and the Global Market from Hegel to Heaney* (Notre Dame: University of Notre Dame Press, 1998); David Toole, *Waiting for Godot in Sarajevo: Theological Reflections on Nihilism, Tragedy, and Apocalypse* (Boulder, CO: Westview Press, 1998); Terry Eagleton, *The Illusions of Postmodernism* (Oxford: Basil Blackwell, 1996); Catherine Pickstock, *After Writing: On the Liturgical Consummation of Philosophy* (Oxford: Basil Blackwell, 1998); Philip Blond, ed., *Post-Secular Philosophy: Between Philosophy and Theology* (London: Routledge, 1998); John Milbank, *Theology and Social Theory* (Oxford: Blackwell, 1993).

10. By making this somewhat "non-chronological" assertion, I am not succumbing to the "postmodernist" temptation to deny historical sequence or development (as a falling back on Enlightenment principles and appeals to "metanarratives"). Instead, I am suggesting that the historical process is not *reducible* to a mechanistic or deterministic notion of history and development, i.e., not just "any" history will do. See Nicholas Boyle's excellent analysis of this issue in his *Who Are We Now? Christian Humanism and the Global Market from Hegel to Heaney* (Notre Dame: University of Notre Dame Press, 1998), 290.

11. Richard Bernstein, *New Constellation* (Cambridge, MA: Polity Press, 1991).

12. The following exploration and analysis is unapologetically tendentious by design. I have chosen "language" as the device whereby I connect what might appear otherwise as "disconnected" discourses, i.e., epistemology, science, and ethics. The revolution in linguistics and language philosophy directly bears on each of these discourses. This should become apparent as we continue.

Introduction: The Revolution in Language and Epistemology

Perhaps no other issue has had a more singular impact on twenty-first century thought than the "linguistic turn"[13] that occurred in the twentieth century, primarily through the influence of Ludwig Wittgenstein, whose writings and reflection on language parallel the great shifts of momentum in other areas of philosophy and science.[14] What follows is a brief intellectual history—the roots of the revolution—leading up to Wittgenstein, followed by a sketch of where the paths diverge, namely, the developments in ordinary language philosophy that followed on the heels of his work. Wittgenstein is uniquely qualified to serve as the principal actor in this historical and philosophical drama. His life and thought epitomized an unquenchable thirst for resolution of some of the most important questions confronting philosophy in the twentieth century. His answers are not always satisfying, but they elicit responses that trigger further reflection and new ways of considering possible alternatives.[15]

All three revolutions [language and epistemology, science, and ethics] have had a major impact on our understanding of truth, which has undergone a major revision since the latter part of the twentieth century.

13. For an excellent introduction to this revolution in philosophy, see the compilation of essays edited by Richard Rorty, *The Linguistic Turn: Essays in Philosophical Method* (Chicago: The University of Chicago Press, 1992). Also see A. J. Ayer et al., *The Revolution in Philosophy* (London: Macmillan, 1956); A. N. Flew ed., *Logic and Language* (Oxford: Oxford University Press, 1953). An insightful contribution to this discussion also can be found in Ian Hacking's *Why Does Language Matter to Philosophy?* (Cambridge: Cambridge University Press, 1978).

14. Ludwig Wittgenstein, *Tractatus Logico-Philosophicus*, trans. D. F. Pears and B. F. McGuiness (London: Routledge and Kegan Paul, 1961). Hereafter cited as *T*. See also the later and posthumously published work by Wittgenstein, *Philosophical Investigations*, trans. G. E. M. Anscombe (New York: Macmillan, 1958). Hereafter cited as *PI*. In addition, see *The Blue and the Brown Books*, ed. Rush Rhees (Oxford: Blackwell Publishers, 1958; 2nd ed, 1960), 4. Hereafter cited as *BL/BRBK*. An excellent study of the intellectual environment in which Wittgenstein's early thought developed is found in Allan Janik and Stephen Toulmin, *Wittgenstein's Vienna* (New York: Simon & Schuster, 1973). An absorbing account of Wittgenstein's life can be found in Ray Monk, *Ludwig Wittgenstein: The Duty of Genius* (New York: Free Press, 1990). Additional resources include: Fergus Kerr, *Theology After Wittgenstein* (Oxford: Blackwell, 1986); J. Koethe, *The Continuity of Wittgenstein's Thought* (Ithaca, NY: Cornell University Press, 1996); J. Coffa, *The Semantic Tradition from Kant to Carnap* (Cambridge: Cambridge University Press, 1993); Judith Genova, *Wittgenstein, A Way of Seeing* (New York: Routledge, 1995); J. Cook, *Wittgenstein's Metaphysics* (Cambridge: Cambridge University Press, 1994); Norman Malcolm, *"Nothing is Hidden": Wittgenstein's Criticism of His Early Work* (Oxford: Blackwell, 1986); David Stern, *Wittgenstein on Mind and Language* (Oxford: Oxford University Press, 1995); G. E. M. Anscombe, *From Parmenides to Wittgenstein: Collected Philosophical Papers* (Oxford: Blackwell, 1981); Hans Sluga and David G. Stern eds., *The Cambridge Companion to Wittgenstein* (Cambridge: Cambridge University Press, 1996); Cora Diamond, *The Realistic Spirit: Wittgenstein, Philosophy and the Mind* (Cambridge, MA: MIT Press, 1991).

15. For a fascinating, though overly optimistic, reading of Wittgenstein "the man" with particular emphasis on his relationship to the Christian faith, see James Wm. McClendon Jr.'s "Wittgenstein: A Christian in Philosophy" in his *Systematic Theology Vol. 3: Witness* (Nashville: Abingdon Press, 2000), 227–70.

Perhaps no other issue has had a more singular impact on twenty-first century thought than the "linguistic turn" that occurred in the twentieth century, primarily through the influence of Ludwig Wittgenstein, whose writings and reflection on language parallel the great shifts of momentum in other areas of philosophy and science.

The Designative (Representationalist) and the Expressive

Attempts to explain the history of the "linguistic turn" in philosophy frequently appeal to the basic distinction between "designative" and "expressive" views of language and meaning.[16] After examining this distinction and its two components, we will use it to look at the history of the linguistic turn, with an eye toward epistemological and linguistic considerations.

The Distinction Itself

Designative theories of language begin with the correlations that exist between words, terms, expressions, and so forth on the one hand, and things, objects, and states of affairs in the world on the other. Words "designate" things—objects in the world—and the meaning of sentences is found in their correspondence or lack thereof to states of affairs in the world (i.e., the role of truth conditions). Such theories "make meaning something relatively unpuzzling, unmysterious."[17] Designative theories of meaning are compatible with the nature of modern scientific thought, where there is the intention of avoiding subjectivity at all costs. On the other hand, expressive theories of meaning are inherently mysterious. According to such theories, there is no way to extract the subject from the expression. Taylor writes,

> The meaning of an expression cannot be explained by its being related to something else, but only by another expression. Consequently, the method of isolating terms and tracing correlations cannot work for expressive meaning. Moreover, our paradigm-expressive objects function as wholes.[18]

Expressive accounts cannot and do not attempt to avoid the "subject-relatedness" of meaning, because expression is the very power of a subject. Expressions "manifest things, and hence refer us to subjects for whom these things can be manifest."[19] Their meaning cannot be paraphrased or translated into an objective language, that is, they simply cannot be explained in terms of something else.[20] Expressive accounts of language and meaning give no purchase to scientific theories of language or to the possibility of creat-

Designative theories of meaning are compatible with the nature of modern scientific thought, where there is the intention of avoiding subjectivity at all costs. On the other hand, expressive theories of meaning are inherently mysterious.

16. I am following closely the work of Charles Taylor, "Language and Human Nature," in his *Philosophical Papers Vol. I: Philosophy and Human Agency* (Cambridge: Cambridge University Press, 1985). Also see Taylor's *Philosophical Arguments* (Cambridge, MA: Harvard University Press, 1997), 61–99. Another singularly important work in this regard is George Steiner, *After Babel: Aspects of Language and Translation* (Oxford: Oxford University Press, 1976). For further explorations, see John Milbank, "The Linguistic Turn as a Theological Turn," in *The Word Made Strange: Theology, Language, Culture* (Oxford: Blackwell, 1998), 84–122.

17. Charles Taylor, "Language and Human Nature," 220.

18. Ibid., 221.

19. Ibid.

20. This is the later Wittgenstein's criticism of "philosophy" as the failed attempt to "explain" or service "explanations." In the end, all philosophy can do and is allowed to do is to offer "descriptions."

ing objective accounts of meaning. Designative theories, on the other hand, which build on a more or less atomic notion of reality as constituted by "bits" of facts, and so forth, can produce or be identified objectively and so provide a model that fits with natural science. In the end, designative theories demythologize or demystify language and meaning, thus finding a home in the positivist environment of language and science in the early twentieth century.

Historical Roots

The unnecessary dualism between designative and expressive theories of meaning has driven philosophy, science, and ethics from past to present. Understanding the history of this dualism will help us better understand the present philosophical situation.

The Greeks are the starting point for all things philosophical. Not surprisingly, therefore, we find some discussion of descriptive and expressive theories of meaning in Plato's *Cratylus*.[21] The *Cratylus* is concerned with the correctness of names (383a4–b2), especially whether their correctness is by nature or by convention. For Plato, contrary to the Protagorean (conventionalist) view, there is something about external reality that makes it right to classify things in one way rather than another. For example, consider the word *ousia* (being). According to the conventionalists, the *ousia* of things is private to each person (385e5), and this means the word *ousia* is "unstable"—an unhappy state of affairs.

There was an inextricable link in the Greek way of thinking between "saying, language and reason."[22] This is reflected in the use of *logos*, whose root means "to say" (*legein*). For the Greeks, thought was characterized along the lines of discourse and expressed the same things language generally does. Thus, the Greeks used *logos* to refer to "reason" and "reasoned account." By extension, the Greeks viewed reality as a kind of discourse. According to Plato, "Ideas" ground the world of sensible things, and the ways we use words—to discourse, to speak, to describe, and so forth—should accord with the nature of reality. Therefore, there is an emphasis on nature (*phusei*), as opposed to convention, in Plato's understanding of the relationship between words and reality.[23]

Plato's theory contains a view that later was articulated in more detail by the Neo-Platonist, the early fathers, Augustine, and others.[24] This view

> In the end, designative theories demythologize or demystify language and meaning, thus finding a home in the positivist environment of language and science in the early twentieth century.

---

21. J. Burnet, ed. *Platonis Opera*, 5 vols. (Oxford: Oxford University Press, 1968). All citations are from this edition.

22. Taylor refers to this as a "discourse-modeled notion of thought"—see "Language and Human Nature," 222.

23. John Milbank, "The Linguistic Turn as a Theological Turn," 88.

24. Here, see especially the work of John Milbank, "The Linguistic Turn as a Theological Turn," 84–122. The point that needs to be made is how one's theories of God, the world, and language are interrelated. For illustrations in Augustine on this subject, see his *On Christian Doctrine*, 1.8, 1.2.2; 2.10.15; 3.59; 3.10.14.

is embedded in Plato's belief that the sensible world is a copy of an ideal world, the world of "Forms" or "Ideas." The sensible world is patterned after the logos; it is the concrete expression of these Ideas. Although Plato has no doctrine of God in a Christian sense, his language echoes a familiar biblical theme, that is, the world is the "speech of God." Thus, for Augustine the divine *Verbum* (Word/Logos) is expressed in creation itself. Therefore, everything is a sign (signifier) of something else, namely, God's thoughts. Likewise, men also employ signs—words and language—as the clothing for our thoughts.

What emerges from Plato is a theory of language and meaning directly linked to an ontology—an understanding of the nature of reality. Since God is an "expressivist," so to speak, our approach to language and meaning will follow an expressivist line. Our expectations that this will be the case are fulfilled in the medieval and Renaissance periods of history, where "semiological ontologies" that depicted the world as inscribed with order by the Creator (like a giant text!) prevailed. This view of the world, as a meaningful order designed in its various domains to reveal or embody the very thoughts of the Creator, held sway until the seventeenth century (with precursors in late medieval nominalism) and the scientific revolution.[25]

Nominalists rebelled against this ontologizing (realism). This rebellion promoted a designative view of language that elevated the importance of words to new heights. Medieval nominalism thoroughly rejected Platonic and Augustinian views of reality, since the latter believed God's thoughts—universals, essences—were embedded in everyday language and the particulars of the world. Nominalists do not believe in universals or essences. They believe that although we use universals in our thinking, this is simply the result of practice and habit. In other words, "universals" are nothing more that the results of linguistic habits. Thus, for nomalists, generalities and universals do not reveal the real world; they reveal how we use language. Consequently, language is purely designative. Words simply name things. And in the absence of things, there is no meaning. For nominalists, the world is not a "meaningful order"; it is not ordered by the very speech of God.

A new view of the world emerged that corresponded with this understanding of language and meaning—a view of the world as "objective" and "machinelike."[26] Medieval theologians such as William of Ockham sought to protect God's freedom—a freedom easily extended to humans as well—by promoting an anti-Aristotelian view of the world that was non-teleological and non-realist and by arguing that God is absolutely free to act

> *What emerges from Plato is a theory of language and meaning directly linked to an ontology—an understanding of the nature of reality. Since God is an "expressivist," so to speak, our approach to language and meaning will follow an expressivist line.*

25. See the work of Louis Dupre, *Passage to Modernity* (New Haven, CT: Yale University Press, 1993). Also see the fascinating analysis provided by R. K. French and Andrew Cunningham, *Before Science: The Invention of the Friars' Natural Philosophy* (London: Solar Press, 1996).

26. For a fuller explication of the implications and genesis of these ideas, see Francis Oakley, "Christian Theology and the Newtonian Science," *Church History* 30 (1961): 433–57.

by fiat whenever and wherever he chooses. However, this view resulted in understanding the world as operating autonomously, according to observable rules and processes, independent of God's power or presence.

That view of the world is reflected in Descartes' philosophy (and the revolution he inspired in epistemology), which was built on a nominalist foundation. In Cartesian methodology, the thinking subject is primary, not a correspondence between mind and the order present in the world. Certainty in knowledge results from the mind (not God) forming representations of the world in accordance with established canons of rational thought. The mind is a mirror; its primary function is representational.[27] To understand the world, first we must disassemble the phenomena and then reassemble them in our thoughts. As Thomas Hobbes later would put it in *De Cive* (11.14):

John Locke

> For everything is best understood by its constitutive causes. For as in a watch, or some such small engine, the matter, figure and motion of the wheels cannot be well known, except it be taken asunder and viewed in its parts; so as to make a more curious search into the rights of states and duties of subjects, it is necessary, I say, not to take them asunder, but yet that they be so considered as if they were dissolved.

How does this view come to expression in a theory of language? Words help us perform the tasks described above. To avoid ambiguity and confusion, we need transparent language and terms. Language must fit its subject. Since the world increasingly is seen as process and machinelike, our terms and language must follow suit. Language should not contain mystery; the terms we use should enable us to describe the true course and nature of the world accurately. Therefore, we must designate the connections between words and what they describe. This "designated connection" gives words their meaning.

Descartes' rationalist slant is paralleled by Locke's empiricist orientation in the seventeenth century and by Condillac in the eighteenth century. As discussed earlier in this volume, Locke's theory of understanding reveals how language is to be understood.[28] Believing they were philosophically redundant, Locke rejected the notion of "innate ideas." Why, Locke asked, would God create us so that we acquire basic ideas through the use of our senses and also endow us with a set of innate ideas? Locke believed we collect individual particulars of experience and form them into coherent wholes, creating a lexicon of meaningful terms in the process. The unanswered question is "what is each sensation 'about'?" This fundamental dilemma of "reflection" eventually led Kant (1724–1804) to critique empir-

Since the world increasingly is seen as process and machinelike, our terms and language must follow suit. Language should not contain mystery; the terms we use should enable us to describe the true course and nature of the world accurately.

27. Richard Rorty, *Philosophy and the Mirror of Nature* (Princeton: Princeton University Press, 1979).

28. John Locke, *An Essay Concerning Human Understanding* (Amherst, NY: Prometheus Books, 1994), 2.2.2.

icism altogether.[29] Each individual impression—sensation—we have of the world is a piece of information. What enables us to discriminate among these various sensations? Sensations are about something, what Kant eventually called "intentionality." The subject (knower) must be able to "place" the sensation (particular) somewhere, that is, give it a location in a world already familiar to the knower. Otherwise, Kant argued, "it would be possible for appearances to crowd in upon the soul, and yet to be such as would never allow of experience." One's perceptions "would not then belong to any experience, consequently would be without an object, merely a blind play of representations, less even than a dream."[30]

If empiricists are correct, language is a collection of independent words or "sounds" (atomism), without the necessary framework (the linguistic dimension itself) being elaborated. Thus, the presuppositions of language and meaning are implicit; they are "beyond" the empirical. Such a designative, or representational, view of language formed the foundation the logical atomists and positivists built on when they initiated the twentieth-century's linguistic turn.

The Twentieth Century: The Heyday of "Words"

In the twentieth century, the turn toward language emerged with greater force and significance. "Logical atomism" and the work of Ludwig Wittgenstein (1889–1951) had as their backdrop the substance of our earlier discussion about designative and expressive views of language. In the early part of the twentieth century, the scientific mind was gripped by the designative theory of language and meaning—known in its modern form as the representationalist, or *depictive*, theory. Although expressivism was rekindled by Herder, Hamman, and others in the eighteenth and nineteenth centuries in the guise of Romanticism, in the twentieth century it was eclipsed by a resurgence of Enlightenment scientism—what came to be known as "positivism." Interestingly, however, expressivism returned in the writings of the "later" Wittgenstein—something we will discuss below.

Why did language acquire a greater importance for philosophy in the early twentieth century, especially the representational, or depictive, view of meaning? Considering Nietzsche's views and the pragmatism of James and Dewey, this is a perplexing question. It is best to see the positivist period (early Wittgenstein) as a parenthesis, bracketed by Nietzsche (1844–1900) on one side and the "later" Wittgenstein on the other. Nietzsche portended the collapse of the Kantian resolution to the Cartesian and empiricist conundrum. Kant, as discussed earlier in this book, wanted it both ways: a vigorous "ego-subject," whose innate categories of understanding constitute

> *In the early part of the twentieth century, the scientific mind was gripped by the designative theory of language and meaning—known in its modern form as the representationalist, or depictive, theory.*

---

29. Immanuel Kant, *Critique: Kritik der reinen Vernunft*, Prussian Academy ed., in Kant's *Werke*, vol. 4 (Berlin, 1968), A104, 112.

30. Ibid., A111, 112.

knowledge, and an ineffable *Ding-an-sich*, the "thing-in-itself," that anchors our representations (a policing function). Nietzsche observed that however functionally important this *Ding-an-sich* was for Kant, it was only a postulation—a wheel that when turned, turned nothing else, because it was not actually a part of the mechanism itself. Because the *Ding-an-sich* performs no "real" function, it can be eliminated without effect, leaving us with nothing more than one representation after another. This destroys the meaning of "*Ding-an-sich*," for the metaphor of representation is premised on the possibility of there being something to represent. Wittgenstein described this futile enterprise as comparable to buying several copies of the same newspaper to verify the accuracy of its front-page headline. Without the anchor, which was only a fabrication anyway, one needs a new metaphor. Nietzsche suggested that the metaphor for the new age is *interpretation* and that man is the willful imposer of meaning. As Nietzsche put it, " 'Interpretation,' the introduction of meaning—not 'explanation.' . . . There are no facts, everything is in flux, incomprehensible, elusive; what is relatively most enduring is—our opinions."[31] Nietzsche's ideas would not carry the day, however. His insights were eclipsed by a renewed emphasis in philosophy and logic on empiricist methodologies and on representationalism. Nietzsche's criticisms of metaphysics did not apply to the Vienna Circle—philosophers committed to satisfying an unquenchable thirst to "explain." In the vacuum created by the anti-metaphysical bias of Nietzsche and his successors, the scientism of logical positivism arose—a kind of "joyous, nihilistic positivism." It was an attempt to secure finiteness, which is grounded in an awareness of the infinite, with a joyful positivity that only an absolute historicism could provide. This move toward positivity propelled the linguistic turn. Under this regime, "truth" became nothing more than a property of logical form and language, where the emphasis on formalization through mathematical representation was thought to reproduce the mechanics of the world and the mind.[32]

In our earlier discussion about the emergent nominalism associated with the rise of representationalist (designative) theories of language and meaning, we saw that one of the motivations was to find an adequate language for science. One of Locke's primary concerns, for example, was to ground our picture of the world on the foundation of clear and unequivocal definitions of basic terms. But how was one to do this? By correct representations that would enable one to affirm a true knowledge of the object. A key epistemological issue regarded the need to eliminate any contributions the knowing subject might make to the actual representation of things. This became the overriding twentieth-century concern regarding language, namely, how language can be a vehicle for knowledge, as modern epistemology understands it.

> *In the vacuum created by the anti-metaphysical bias of Nietzsche and his successors, the scientism of logical positivism arose—a kind of "joyous, nihilistic positivism." . . . Under this regime, "truth" became nothing more than a property of logical form and language.*

---

31. F. Nietzsche, *The Will to Power*, ed. Walter Kaufmann, trans. W. Kaufmann and R. J. Hollingdale (New York: Random House, 1967), section 604.

32. George Steiner, *After Babel*, 206.

The Ideal Language Approach

According to Richard Rorty (1931–2007), in the early twentieth century two approaches emerged regarding the issue of language: the Ideal Language School and Ordinary Language Analysis.[33] The Ideal Language School is closest, in form, structure, and interest, to the early Wittgenstein.[34]

In his "Notes on Logic" (1913), Wittgenstein stated: "Philosophy consists of logic and metaphysics: logic is its basis."[35] In the *Tractatus*, he developed the idea that language mirrors reality and that logic is the essence of language. According to Wittgenstein, reality has the same form, or structure, as logic; that is, it has a logical form. Wittgenstein wrote, "how can logic—all embracing logic, which mirrors the world—use such peculiar crotchets and contrivances? Only because they are all connected with one another in an infinitely fine network, the great mirror" (*Tractatus*, 5.511). In many ways, this is a reflection of what is known as "logical atomism," a view codified by Russell and Whitehead in their *Principia Mathematica*. According to logical atomism, reality ultimately is composed of atomic facts, each distinct from all others. Essentially, these atomic facts are empirical data. When combined, they form molecular facts that are then "truth-functional." By this he meant that atomic facts are represented by atomic propositions and molecular facts by truth-functional compounds of atomic propositions. Philosophy's task is to "explain" and "clarify" these facts and their corresponding propositions. Thus, genuine philosophical problems are confusions that result from a disjunction between the way we speak—what Rudolf Carnap referred to as the "grammatical syntax"—and the "logical syntax" that reflects the true nature of things.[36] This logical syntax is at the heart of language as it is meant to be understood—at least in terms of its bearing any relation to truth or falsity.[37] As Wittgenstein described the matter, the world is made up of simple

Rudolf Carnap

33. Richard Rorty, "Introduction," *The Linguistic Turn*, 15–24.

34. I am not interested in pursuing the issue(s) surrounding the notion of "development" or "change" relative to the "early" and "later" Wittgenstein. There is sufficient "continuity," as well as "discontinuity," to validate a variety of positions on the matter. For further considerations on this topic, see J. Koethe, *The Continuity of Wittgenstein's Thought*; Norman Malcolm, *"Nothing is Hidden": Wittgenstein's Criticism of His Early Work*; J. Cook, *Wittgenstein's Metaphysics*.

35. Ludwig Wittgenstein, *Notebooks, 1914–1916*, eds. G. H. von Wright and G. E. M. Anscombe, trans. G. E. M. Anscombe (Oxford: Blackwell, 1961; 2nd ed., 1979), 106.

36. Rudolf Carnap, *Logical Structure of the World* (Berkeley: University of California Press, 1967), 327–28. A brilliant (if misguided) analysis of similar considerations is found in Gilbert Ryle, "Systematically Misleading Expressions," reprinted in *The Linguistic Turn*, 85–100.

37. Carnap developed what is referred to as a "semantic theory of truth" that differentiates between those sentences capable of being "true," e.g., "object sentences" or "token sentences," and those that are not, namely "pseudo-sentences." The latter include "metaphysical" utterances, e.g., religious, ethical, etc. For more information, see Rudolf Carnap, *Introduction to Semantics* (Cambridge, MA: Harvard University Press, 1942), and his *Meaning and Necessity: A Study in Semantics and Modal Logic* (Chicago: University of Chicago Press, 1947).

objects (atoms) that are the basis of all analysis, and this is what prevents indeterminacy, that is, the rule of absolute contingency. Thus, without these objects (and the worldview implied in such a theory), "it would be impossible to frame any picture of the world (true or false)" (*T* 2.0212). This is what prevents an infinite regression in propositional knowledge. Otherwise, there could be no definite meaning (*T* 3.23). Without "reference," there is no "meaning." Why? Because there would only be convention, which is fundamentally arbitrary. The "simples" (i.e., simple objects) thus supply what Russell referred to as the "furniture of the world."

Building from this point, Wittgenstein developed his tractarian views in the *Tractatus*. "Simple objects" create "states of affairs" (*Sachverhalt*) that are either "possible" or "actual." As Wittgenstein described it, "Each thing is, as it were, in a space of possible 'states of affairs' " (*T* 2.013). The possibilities are fixed for each thing. This is the "form" of the object. The *Tractatus* maintains that the world as a whole has a form, that is, a fixed number of possible states of affairs: "The existence and non-existence of states of affairs is reality" (*T* 2.06); "the sum total of reality is the world" (*T* 2.063). Granting this "picture" of reality, philosophy now could give a complete analysis of the world in terms of propositions: "A proposition is a picture of reality" (*T* 4.01). A proposition has "sense" if it pictures a possible state of affairs. Its truth or falsity is determined by empirical verification. Wittgenstein's views on the nature of language and the role of philosophy can be summarized as follows. (1) Ordinary language is inherently vague and ambiguous (T 4.014–015, 4.002). (2) Clarity and accuracy are appropriate to sentences that "picture" or "record" facts (or states of affairs). This form is "logical," not grammatical, and where there is a correspondence between the content of the sentence and that which it represents. (3) Philosophy's role is to remove misunderstandings that directly result from linguistic confusions.[38]

> In the **Tractatus**, [Wittgenstein] developed the idea that language mirrors reality and that logic is the essence of language. According to Wittgenstein, reality has the same form, or structure, as logic; that is, it has a logical form.

The Logical Positivists

Implicit in (2) above is a common understanding regarding what the "facts" are as we scrutinize them. Number (1) also begs the question regarding what are the criteria for determining clarity and ambiguity. The logical positivists pursued both of these issues in an attempt to establish with finality the basis of science, as opposed to metaphysics. They believed their method could free science from human sentiment and subjectivity (value) and establish it solidly on observation and verification.

The logical positivists argued for a sharp distinction between fact and value. They said value statements (judgments) are "unverifiable" (and hence *neither* "true" nor "false"), but scientific statements (statements of fact) are "verifiable" (and are *either* "true" or "false"). As we saw above, Wittgenstein proposed that language "pictures" the real state of affairs, that is, the real

> The logical positivists argued for a sharp distinction between fact and value. They said value statements (judgments) are "unverifiable" (and hence neither "true" nor "false"), but scientific statements (statements of fact) are "verifiable" (and are either "true" or "false").

38. Dudley Shapere, "Philosophy and the Analysis of Language," in *The Linguistic Turn*, 279–80.

atomic facts of the objective world. As far as language does this successfully, it can be said to be "true." What really was at stake for the logical positivists was the "test of rationality," that is, what counts as rationally justifiable. We need criteria of rationality, or rational justification, that consist of a list, or canon, of acceptable rules that would then determine "in advance" what would or would not be allowed to stand as "cognitively meaningful." Hilary Putnam describes the goals of logical positivism as follows:

> Not only was the list or canon that the positivists hoped "logicians of science" (their term for philosophers) would one day succeed in writing down supposed to exhaustively describe the "scientific method;" but, since, according to the logical positivists, the "scientific method" exhausts rationality itself, and testability by that method exhausts meaningfulness ("The meaning of a sentence is its method of verification"), the list or canon would determine what is and what is not a cognitively meaningful statement.[39]

Granting the analytic-synthetic distinction that classifies statements in terms of their potential for truthfulness, which is judged on the basis of their being "true by definition" (analytic) or "true by testing" (synthetic), moral and ethical language was exiled to the land of pseudo-sentences or emotionally grounded language. Vivian Walsh writes,

> Consider the "putative" proposition "murder is wrong." What empirical findings, the positivists would ask, tend to confirm or disconfirm this? If saying that murder is wrong is merely a misleading way of reporting what a given society believes, this is a perfectly good sociological fact, and the proposition is a respectable empirical one. But the person making a moral judgment will not accept this analysis. Positivists then wielded their absolute analytic/synthetic distinction: if "murder is wrong" is not a synthetic (empirically testable) proposition it must be an analytic proposition, like (they believed) those of logic and mathematics—in effect, a tautology. The person who wished to make the moral judgment would not accept this, and was told that the disputed utterance was a "pseudo-proposition" like those of poets, theologians, and metaphysicians.[40]

It was not long, however, before philosophers influenced by Wittgenstein's own reasoning began to criticize the canons of logical positivism. As Walsh points out, by the end of the 1950s most of these ideas had been abandoned. As she describes the situation, "Their theory of 'cognitive significance,' needed to deny meaning to moral uses of language, had fallen."[41]

Dichotomies like those are based on the presumption that such hard and fast distinctions may exist in reality—a distinction that W. V. O. Quine noted, with some irony, was simply unreal: "the lore of our fathers is black with fact and white with convention, but there are no *completely* white

> As Walsh points out, by the end of the 1950s most of these ideas had been abandoned. As she describes the situation, "Their theory of 'cognitive significance,' needed to deny meaning to moral uses of language, had fallen."

39. Hilary Putnam, *Reason, Truth and History* (Cambridge: Cambridge University Press, 1981), 105.

40. Vivian Walsh, "Philosophy and Economics," in *The New Palgrave: A Dictionary of Economics*, eds. Peter Newman, John Eatwell, and Murray Milgate (New York: The Stockton Press, 1987), 862.

41. Ibid.

threads and no quite black ones."[42] Once the theory was applied to science, further weaknesses began to emerge. As Walsh observes,

> Another retreat, forced upon logical empiricism by the needs of pure science, opened the way for a further rehabilitation of moral philosophy. The old positivist attack on the status of moral judgments had required the claim that each single proposition must, at least in principle, be open to test. It became evident that many of the propositions of which the higher theory of pure science are composed could not survive this demand.[43]

In other words, it is simply naïve to assume that one could apply the method of verifiability to each "fact," one fact at a time, which is essential to the credibility of the final, overall statement of "fact," according to logical positivism. Quine pointed out that such a position is reductionistic in the extreme and leads to sheer folly. He noted that "our statements about the external world face the tribunal of sense experience not individually but only as a corporate body."[44] And this body of knowledge is composed of theoretical propositions that are far from "verifiable," in any empirical sense of the word. Walsh noted that in a vain attempt to emend the theory, logical empiricists decided that "theoretical propositions became 'indirectly' meaningful if part of a theory which possessed (supposed) observation statements which had empirical confirmation to some degree (never mind that the theoretical statement/observation statement dichotomy itself broke down!); but the clear fact/value distinction of the early positivists depended upon being able to see if each single proposition passed muster."[45] In the end, logical positivism and the verification principle were recognized by most philosophers[46] as self-refuting for at least two reasons: (1) the criterion is not analytic, and (2) the theory is not testable by its own standards (i.e., it is not empirical).

In the end, logical positivism and the verification principle were recognized by most philosophers as self-refuting for at least two reasons: (1) the criterion is not analytic, and (2) the theory is not testable by its own standards (i.e., it is not empirical).

The Later Wittgenstein, Ordinary Language Analysis, and Overcoming Epistemology: The Heyday of "Sentences"

The second movement, ordinary language analysis, emerged in the latter half of the twentieth century. In many ways, it was a repudiation of

42. Willard Van Orman Quine, "Carnap on Logical Truth," in P. A. Schlipp, ed., *The Philosophy of Rudolf Carnap* (LaSalle, IL: Open Court, 1963).

43. Vivian Walsh, "Philosophy and Economics," 862.

44. Willard Van Orman Quine, "Two Dogmas of Empiricism," in *From a Logical Point of View* (Cambridge, MA: Harvard University Press, 1996), 41. Quine notes that he is building on the insights of Pierre Duhem, *La Theorie physique: son objet et sa structure* (Paris, 1906), 303–28.

45. Walsh, "Philosophy and Economics," 862.

46. It is one of the ironies of philosophy that even though logical positivism was abandoned as a formal approach because of these weaknesses, it has nonetheless been institutionalized by modern culture. On this point, see Hilary Putnam's analysis in *Reason, History and Truth*, 106, 127–28.

some of the central insights of the Ideal Language approach. However, it was far more than simply a repudiation of what preceded; it was the continuation of a revolution that began with the criticism of "science" as free from subjectivity and context, and it extended to a complete revision of ethics and epistemology. We now turn our attention to examining the epistemological roots of ordinary language analysis and to an examination of its primary attributes.

As we have seen, the developments in language philosophy—the linguistic turn—were closely paralleled by developments in epistemology and science. Specifically, this epistemological tradition's emphasis on representation—the mirroring function of the mind—drove early positivists and the Ideal Language School forward. Additionally, this early version of the linguistic turn was a continuation of an ongoing dispute between natural sciences—with their claim that objectivity is achieved through methodological clarity and certainty—and human sciences, which focused on studying the human subject—sociology and history—individually and collectively.[47]

A Brief Introduction to a Mid-Century Crisis

To use Phillip Blond's evocative image, the mid-century crisis was one of *failed conditions*. What caused this failure? Primarily, the quest for a clear and precise logic of the world lost steam and failed because of its inherent inner contradictions, as we saw earlier. The dream of a universal logic and an Ideal Language to reflect the true picture of the world lies at the heart of the Enlightenment and the modern age. At the core of this vision, however, is a contradiction. No one has expressed more eloquently the paradox at the heart of this vision than Baudelaire, who in 1863 noted, "Modernity is the transient, the fleeting, the contingent; it is the one half of art, the other being the eternal and the immutable."[48] It was the "project of modernity," to borrow an expression from Habermas, to find the immutable, unchanging core of things, that is, to avoid the rule of contingency that lay at the heart of Hume's skepticism and empiricism. Accordingly, there was only one possible correct answer to any question, a belief taken as axiomatic by Enlightenment and modernist thinkers. Therefore, if we construct the picture correctly, we can rationally order and control the world. This aspiration was based on the belief that there is "one correct mode of representation" that if discovered will enable us to achieve the Enlightenment's goals. Nietzsche and others profoundly criticized this.

> It was the "project of modernity," to borrow an expression from Habermas, to find the immutable, unchanging core of things, that is, to avoid the rule of contingency that lay at the heart of Hume's skepticism and empiricism.

---

47. The discussion and elaboration of this distinction is most eloquently expressed in the work of Wilhelm Dilthey, especially in his *Gesammelte Schriften,* 18 vols. (Stuttgart: Teubner, 1968). For a simple introduction to Dilthey and his interaction with ideas found in Schleiermacher, see his "The Rise of Hemeneutics," trans. Fredric Jameson, *New Literary History* 3 (1972), 229–44. Also see Hans-Georg Gadamer, *Truth and Method*, trans. and ed. Garrett Barden and John Cumming (New York: Seabury Press, 1975).

48. Quotation found in David Harvey, *The Condition of Postmodernity* (Oxford: Blackwell, 1990), 10.

Nietzsche observed that the idea of a "true world" belonged to an ongoing illusion philosophers had perpetrated as far back as Plato (and his world of Forms) and that continued through Kant. As Nietzsche put it, "*becoming* has no goal and underneath all becoming there is no grand unity." Any postulation of "unity" is simply that, a postulation, a vain attempt to escape from contingency by passing "sentence on this whole world of becoming as a deception and to invent a world beyond it, a true world."[49] Nietzsche argued that parallel to this "true world" are the "higher values" created to sustain it. In fact, these "higher values," which most often are religiously based—eternal peace, the afterlife, justice, and so on—eventually lose their power to sustain themselves. As Nietzsche expressed it,

> The feeling of valuelessness was reached with the realization that the overall character of existence may not be interpreted by means of the concept of "aim," the concept of "unity," or the concept of "truth." Existence has no goal or end; any comprehensive unity in the plurality of events is lacking: the character of existence is not "true," it is false. One simply lacks any reason for convincing oneself that there is a true world.[50]

Charles Baudelaire

Søren Kierkegaard (1813–55) echoed an earlier and similar disenchantment with "totalizing" notions—"true world" pictures. The misleading narrative, or "system," as Kierkegaard called it, was Hegel's idealism (1770–1831). Hegel took the goal of explaining everything to an end Kierkegaard found threatening to the general philosophical enterprise and to "faith." Hegel attempted to transcend the particular "local" nature of human explanations in order to offer an explanation that ultimately appealed to one singular concept or set of concepts. In Hegel, the rational and the real perfectly coincided, and the result was a totalitarian epistemological regime. Differences that appear on a human and empirical level—for example, dualities such as mind/body, subject/object, finite/infinite, faith/reason, etc.—can be made to disappear into the higher conceptual synthesis of the "Absolute Idea." Because all differences will be absorbed into a higher identity, in the end everything will reveal itself as having been the same! Nothing will remain unexplained. Nothing will be left that disrupts our understanding. All that makes man restless and dissatisfied will have been overcome and fulfilled. As Kierkegaard put the matter, "the philosopher will be able to then transpose the whole content of faith into conceptual form."[51] "Faith" will then be rid of any residual mythical or mystical dimensions and reduced to more or less identifiable concepts and actions, just like any other phenomenon.[52]

" Nietzsche observed that the idea of a "true world" belonged to an ongoing illusion philosophers had perpetrated as far back as Plato (and his world of Forms) and that continued through Kant.

---

49. Friedrich Nietzsche, *The Will to Power*, trans. Walter Kaufmann and R. J. Hollingdale, ed. Walter Kaufmann (New York: Vintage Books, 1968), § 12.

50. Ibid.

51. Søren Kierkegaard, *Fear and Trembling*, ed. and trans. H. V. Hong and E. H. Hong (Princeton, NJ: Princeton University Press, 1983), 7.

52. Kierkegaard's concerns are echoed in the theological works of Barth and Bultmann.

The advent of World War I and the corresponding loss of optimism regarding mankind's upward march toward perfectibility helped precipitate an increasing commitment to diversity and a corresponding disregard for universality.

Therefore, according to Nietzsche and Kierkegaard, modernity's dream was based on fundamental philosophical mistakes. The dream also failed at the practical level. The "iron cage" of rationality (Max Weber, 1864–1920) implicit in this dream offered far more than it could ever hope to deliver. Although initially hospitable to the dream, the twentieth century soon resisted it. As Richard Bernstein observes,

> Weber argued that the hope and expectation of the Enlightenment thinkers was a bitter and ironic illusion. They maintained a strong necessary linkage between the growth of science, rationality, and universal human freedom. But when unmasked and understood, the legacy of the Enlightenment was the triumph of . . . purposive-instrumental rationality. This form of rationality affects and infects the entire range of social and cultural life encompassing economic structures, law, bureaucratic administration, and even the arts. The growth of [purposive-instrumental rationality] does not lead to the concrete realization of universal freedom but to the creation of an "iron cage" of bureaucratic rationality from which there is no escape.[53]

As early as the late nineteenth century, artists, writers, and others reflected a growing dissatisfaction with this picture. It was replaced by an awareness of diversity and multiplicity in the arts, particularly among writers and painters, for example, Flaubert, Baudelaire, and Manet. A similar awareness of diversity and multiplicity accompanied the intellectual crisis precipitated by non-Euclidean geometries (e.g., Lobachevesky and Bolyai—1820s–50s) and by Einstein's theory of relativity.[54] This challenge to Enlightenment and modernist uniformity and symmetry reached its zenith in literary and artistic terms between 1910 and 1915.[55] During this period works such as Proust's *Swann's Way* (1913), James Joyce's *Dubliners* (1914), Thomas Mann's *Death in Venice* (1914), and Stravinsky's *Rite of Spring* (1913) burst onto the scene. Woven throughout this period and its works is the uneasy marriage of universals and particulars—in Baudelaire's terms, the relationship between the "immutable" and the "contingent." These writers operated with an essentialist understanding of human beings, who, limited by the constraints of time and place, constantly strive to break free into some form of pure creativity. The advent of World War I and the corresponding loss of optimism regarding mankind's upward march toward perfectibility helped precipitate an increasing commitment to diversity and a corresponding disregard for universality. There was no one, unifying picture of the world, only a vast array of images that often conflicted violently with one another.

---

53. Richard Bernstein, ed., *Habermas and Modernity* (Cambridge, MA: MIT Press, 1985), 5.

54. See the fine article by Stephen F. Barker, "Geometry" in *The Encyclopedia of Philosophy*, 3:285–90.

55. Malcolm Bradbury and James McFarlane, *Modernism, 1890–1930: A Guide to European Literature* (New York: Viking Press, 1991). Also see Stephen Kern, *The Culture of Time and Space: 1880–1918* (Cambridge, MA: Harvard University Press, 1983).

Nevertheless, the inter-war period saw the growth of positivism and the development of positivist philosophy in the early Wittgenstein and the Vienna School of the 1920s and 1930s. In America especially, this extended into the post–World War II period, particularly in the development of architectural styles—suburbia, uniform space, and so forth—and the growing emphasis on science and technology as means whereby man could control his environment and destiny.[56] Houses, for example, became "machines for living in,"[57] and industry perfected the assembly line ("Fordism") as a model for economic—as well as human—development. This was particularly true in the United States and other industrialized countries.

Along with advances in technology and science, World War II triggered similar awakenings. Most of these awakenings were out of step with the optimism with which the century began (a sort of manifest destiny idea of Western society and civilization). No other philosophical movement better illustrates this crisis than existentialism. William Barrett notes that this philosophical movement was inextricably linked to the technology of World War II, in particular the atomic bomb: "The bomb reveals the dreadful and total contingency of human existence. Existentialism is the philosophy of the atomic age."[58]

Existentialism's roots are buried deep in the soil of late nineteenth-century Europe. They illustrate the crisis of modernity in European clothing. Just as in the 1880s Nietzsche noted that nihilism stood at Europe's door, and Kierkegaard had published his archeology of the spirit of the age using the categories of "sickness unto death" and "dread and anxiety" ("fear and trembling"), so in the early years of the twentieth century Martin Heidegger explored the implications of *Dasein*, the rule of finitude and contingency as the "place" of existence.[59] World War I began Europe's long process of realizing that all is not well with the human race.[60] Barrett notes, "August 1914 shattered the foundations of that world. It revealed that the apparent stability, security, and material progress of society had rested, like everything else, upon the void. European man came face to face with himself as a stranger."[61] For the most part, however, this sentiment was not shared by Americans who, as Barrett points out, were still experiencing economic progress and growth. Only later in the America of the 1960s would the effects begin to be felt. The shadow surrounding the Enlightenment project would fall on

Barrett notes, "August 1914 shattered the foundations of that world. It revealed that the apparent stability, security, and material progress of society had rested, like everything else, upon the void. European man came face to face with himself as a stranger."

---

56. David Harvey, *The Condition of Postmodernity* (Oxford: Blackwell, 1990). Also see David Harvey, *Spaces of Hope* (Berkeley: University of California Press, 2000).

57. A precursor to what Albert Borgman calls the "device paradigm." See his *Technology and the Character of Contemporary Life* (Chicago: University of Chicago Press, 1984).

58. William Barrett, *Irrational Man: A Study in Existential Philosophy* (New York: Anchor Books, 1958), 65.

59. Martin Heidegger, *Being and Time* (New York: Harper and Row, 1962).

60. The novels of Jean-Paul Sartre illustrate this trend. His novel *Nausea*, along with the novels of Albert Camus, e.g., *The Stranger* and *The Plague*, is paradigmatic of this sense of diagnostic pursuit.

61. Barrett, *Irrational Man*, 34.

America in the form known as postmodernism. The themes of contingency, limitations on reason, the threat to progress, a denial of certainty, and so forth, all would come under careful scrutiny over the following decades.

We are now in a position to explore in greater detail some particular manifestations of this crisis as they come to expression in language and epistemology. At the heart of this discussion is the shift from a naïve, disengaged approach to and understanding of reason and rationality to a more hermeneutical or engaged understanding of human knowledge and rationality. This discussion will prepare us for a final look at the revolutions in science and ethics and for an examination of postmodernity and the twenty-first century.

Language: The "Heyday of Sentences"

Wittgenstein's later works on language philosophy reflect a shift that began as far back as Immanuel Kant and that continued through philosophy's romantic period (Herder, Hamann, etc.). This shift was a reaction to the empiricism and rationalism of the seventeenth and eighteenth centuries, specifically the ideas of Descartes, Hume, and Locke.[62] The two primary features that characterize the modern rationalism of such philosophers are disengaged reason and proceduralism.[63] *Disengaged reason* refers to the thinking subject as occupying a "proto-variant" of Thomas Nagel's "view from nowhere."[64] By being "from nowhere," such a subject occupies no known space and has no history, culture, or "world," so to speak. This individual is an information-processing being, taking in bits of information and ordering them to construct a manageable, usable, livable world in which to live. The result—proceduralism—is an "atomism of input with a computational picture of mental function."[65] This picture is completed by the distinction between "fact and value" and its correlate of neutrality. Although Descartes and Locke had different methods and strategies, "both views call for reflexive self-policing in the name of a canonical procedure."[66] These views also redefined what post-Cartesian "science" and "scientific thought" consisted in: the pursuit of objectivity. However, objectivity itself was redefined. "Objectivity" is achieved only as we eliminate all possible distortions and see the world as it "really" is. Thomas Nagel puts it aptly as follows:

> The attempt is made to view the world not from a place within it, or from the vantage point of a special kind of life or awareness, but from nowhere in particular and no form of life in particular at all. The object is to discount for the features

*Illustration of a "duck-rabbit," as discussed by Ludwig Wittgenstein in his **Philosophical Investigations***

---

62. The reader should consult previous chapters in this book for greater elucidation of the contours of each of these philosophers' ideas and projects.

63. Charles Taylor, *Philosophical Arguments*, 61–78. Also see Taylor's *Sources of the Self*, 143–76.

64. Thomas Nagel, *The View From Nowhere* (Oxford: Oxford University Press, 1989).

65. Taylor, *Philosophical Arguments*, 65.

66. Ibid.

of our pre-reflective outlook that make things appear as they do, and thereby to reach an understanding of things as they really are.[67]

Although it would be advantageous to scrutinize our observations and calculations and eliminate distorting factors, this is not what modern rationalists do. The rationalists' fatal error was to define mind as functioning in a disengaged manner that lacks context or situation.[68] Rationalists believed that to provide useful results, thinking must transpire apart from any form of engagement and that it must follow a trustworthy procedure, although there was no agreement on exactly what that procedure should be.

What is missing is any explanation of the essential role "background" plays in this entire enterprise. What must be the case for any one perception to be counted as a perception? As we saw earlier, Kant's transcendental deduction, and various other arguments found in the *Critique of Pure Reason*, constituted a turning point in this regard. Kant noted there must be a conferring of intelligibility to make any single perception intelligible. In their various attempts to describe the process of understanding, Descartes, Hume, and Locke had masked the context of intelligibility. For something to be intelligible and to count as intelligible requires meeting certain conditions.

Wittgenstein built on a similar notion in his later reflections on language.[69] The transition in Wittgenstein's philosophy moved from an emphasis on lines of projection to an emphasis on methods of projection.[70] The earlier Wittgenstein was preoccupied with the implications of his own logical atomism and the ontology it seemed to imply—either words referred to substances that existed independently of language, or truth and falsity were simply constructions of an endlessly regressive process of signification. The referential emphasis in the early Wittgenstein was based on what seemed the only alternative to giving meaning absolute free play. Once Wittgenstein succumbed to the ontology of atomism ("logical simples"), truth functions then depended on demonstrating that the logical form operated pictorially—that language mirrored states of affairs in the world of objects. For the later Wittgenstein, logical form captures lines of projection between propositions and the world they represent. In the *Philosophical Investigations*, Wittgenstein said his earlier direction ("logical atomism") represented a gross misunderstanding of the way language actually works. A desire for "simples" led Wittgenstein to a "label view" of language that

> *Rationalists believed that to provide useful results, thinking must transpire apart from any form of engagement and that it must follow a trustworthy procedure, although there was no agreement on exactly what that procedure should be.*

> *In the **Philosophical Investigations**, Wittgenstein said his earlier direction ("logical atomism") represented a gross misunderstanding of the way language actually works.*

67. Thomas Nagel, *Mortal Questions* (Cambridge: Cambridge University Press, [1979] 1991), 208.

68. Taylor, *Philosophical Arguments*, 66. Such an "ontologizing" of reason and the rationalist methodology is canonized in the work of the *Port Royal Logic* in seventeenth-century France.

69. Ludwig Wittgenstein, *Philosophical Investigations*, trans. G. E. M. Anscombe (New York: Macmillan, 1958). Hereafter cited as *PI*.

70. Peter Winch, "Introduction: The Unity of Wittgenstein's Philosophy," in Winch, ed., *Studies in the Philosophy of Wittgenstein* (New York: Humanities Press, 1969), 1–19.

assumed its principal function is to correctly identify, or name, objects. We can refer to this phase as the early Wittgenstein's "explanation fixation." In the *Tractatus*, Wittgenstein emphasized the need to have "determinate" sense, that is, a fixed notion that corresponds to the simple, "objective" view of reality it is based on. In the *Investigations*, Wittgenstein discovered that "sense" is determined by use. It is not a result of correspondence between language and objects but of how we use language; it is a result of "language games." Meaning and sense result from practices and life forms.

The former reductionistic approach, based on projected lines between logical simples and states of affairs, failed to appreciate the mediated character of naming and defining. Naming presupposes a number of categories and procedures that make identification possible. As Wittgenstein put it, "Only someone who already knows how to do something with it can significantly ask a name."[71] Wittgenstein realized that basic facts cannot be discovered independently of methods of projection that guarantee their status as facts. Wittgenstein realized there are many ways of dealing with the facts in the world, many ways for language to project a relationship to the world. Therefore, philosophers should be concerned with the way utterances fit specific contexts and are used appropriately, not with whether a statement "pictures" the world. Wittgenstein introduced the notion of "language game" to explain the relation of language to world. He wrote, "I shall call the whole, consisting of language and the actions into which it is woven, the language game. . . . To imagine a language means to imagine a form of life."[72] Gone now was any pristine notion of a pure, ideal relation between mind and nature. Philosophical problems arise "when language goes on holiday" (*PI*, 116), when there is a "false and idealized picture of the use of language" (*PG*, 211).[73] Gone is the addiction to "explanation," which is the attempt to speak from a position that resides outside language. Philosophy can only "describe" what is going on, or as Wittgenstein puts it: "philosophy may in no way interfere with the actual use of language; it can in the end only describe it" (*PI*, 124). What is possible (and needed) is "description." Philosophical problems are really "direction problems," that is, not knowing our way about (*PI*, 123). Thus, description makes a way of escape from the philosophical problem by showing "the fly the way out of the fly-bottle" (*PI*, 309). An emphasis on "explanation" leads to a set of false problematics, the result of more or less ungrammatical applications of language that seek resolution outside language itself. As Wittgenstein stated, "Our illness is to want to explain."[74] Our "addiction to generality" is the result of attempting to

> In the **Investigations**, Wittgenstein discovered that "sense" is determined by use. It is not a result of correspondence between language and objects but of how we use language; it is a result of "language games." Meaning and sense result from practices and life forms.

71. Wittgenstein, *PI*, 31.

72. *PI*, 7, 19.

73. Ludwig Wittgenstein, *Philosophical Grammar*, ed. R. Rhees, trans. A. J. P. Kenny (Oxford: Blackwell, 1974), hereafter cited as *PG*.

74. Ludwig Wittgenstein, *Remarks on the Foundations of Mathematics*, eds. G. H. von Wright, R. Rhees, and G. E. M. Anscombe, trans. G. E. M. Anscombe (Oxford: Blackwell, 1956; 2nd ed., 1967; 3rd ed., 1978), 333.

move beyond the particular toward the general, which is characteristic of the explanatory approach. A type of therapeutic description will help us overcome this addiction. Wittgenstein insisted, "we may not advance any kind of theory. There must not be anything hypothetical in our considerations. We must do away with all explanation and description alone must take its place" (*PI*, 109). "Description" is about what "is" and decries metaphysical justification as a "pre-linguistic" notion altogether. In its place is the far more complex game of life. Among the multiple games (contexts, grammars) in which we participate, are multiple methods of projection (*Lebensform*) that affect every possible line of projection. As attractive as the world of the *Tractatus* may have appeared, it was not possible to live and communicate in that world. As Wittgenstein described it, "We have got on to slippery ice where there is no friction (the world of the *Tractatus*) and so in a certain sense the conditions are ideal, but also just because of that, we are unable to walk. We want to walk so we need *friction*. Back to the rough ground."[75]

Thus, the understanding of knowledge described in the *Tractatus* differs dramatically from the one outlined in the *Philosophical Investigations*. The earlier book emphasized "that" language and knowledge; the later emphasized "how" language as logically prior. Before we can point or identify something, we must be enmeshed in a world of language relations and meanings that make sense of the action of identification.[76] Altieri comments on the implications this has for philosophy:

> Analytic logic cannot be treated, even implicitly, as a means for specifying ultimate terms or determining the authority of philosophical arguments. Such logic is a tool, a line of projection that cannot interpret its own relevance as a method. Analytic logic assumes an ideal relationship between mind and world not influenced by methods of projection, and thus posits ideals which ultimately oversimplify the complexity of experience.[77]

Thus, the rough ground of the *Philosophical Investigations* is characterized by at least two features: (1) an emphasis on action and description, rather than on propositions, and (2) certainty derived from human conventions that are complex and nuanced, rather than a simple correspondence between terms/utterances and facts.

The Oxbridge parallel to the Canterbury Wittgenstein (who died in 1951) was J. L. Austin, professor of philosophy at Oxford from 1952 to 1960.[78] Austin is most often associated with what is now called "ordinary language philosophy." He illustrates the shift, initiated by Wittgenstein,

> *The Oxbridge parallel to the Canterbury Wittgenstein (who died in 1951) was J. L. Austin, professor of philosophy at Oxford from 1952 to 1960. Austin is most often associated with what is now called "ordinary language philosophy."*

---

75. *PI*, 107.

76. This line of argument is extended by Wittgenstein to include a critique of such erroneous notions as "private languages"; cf. *PI*, 243–44, 246, 261.

77. Altieri, *Act and Quality*, 45.

78. J. L. Austin, *Philosophical Papers*, ed. J. O. Urmson and G. J. Warnock (London: Oxford University Press, 1961); *Sense and Sensibilia*, ed. G. J. Warnock (Oxford: Clarendon Press, 1962); *How To do Things With Words* (Cambridge, MA: Harvard University Press, 1962).

from explanation-oriented approaches (positivism) toward more "descriptive" (i.e., non-designative) approaches.[79] Austin's central inspiration was that there are a great many uses of language other than designating, naming, labeling, and so forth (lines of projection)—those roles seized on by the positivists and constituted as "cognitive." Austin identified the positivist criteria that disqualified all other forms of speech, that is, those not verifiable empirically, as illustrative of what he called the "descriptive fallacy." Wittgenstein posited "description" as the therapeutic alternative to explanation, and his notion of description was quite distinct from that of the positivists. Wittgenstein identified the positivist craving for naming and explaining as a craving for generality that constantly drove the philosopher away from the actual way we use language to something more hypothetical and, in the end, illusory. Whatever therapy exists, it cannot be found "outside language" but rather inside it. There is no positing of "objective" reality; there is only the speaking of language, the "use" of language. The development of "language game" and *Lebensform* ("life form") was an attempt to overcome the monological character of positivist construals of language. It was those "illusions" that trapped philosophers like "flies in a bottle," from which first Wittgenstein and now Austin sought relief.[80]

Austin noted that speaking really is an action, so that speech acts, whether oral or written, are in a class with other purposeful acts (e.g., cooking, building, marrying, etc.). Speech acts are activities undertaken by a person who is using recognized means to achieve some end or goal. In the case of speech, the goal always is "saying something to someone." This constitutes the primary force or "illocutionary force" of language, whereby I perform an action by speech (the "performatives"). This becomes the conventional use and understanding of language that forms the core of how language generally functions.

When applied to utterances or terms like *truth*, for example, philosophers normally ask: is truth or *true* definable? The ordinary language analyst urges us simply to see how, in fact, the word *true* is used in ordinary language—and the result for many, once this is done, is to reconsider "P is true" as expressing agreement with someone who simply said "P." "P is true" has the force, more or less, of saying, "P: How true!" P. F. Strawson called this the *concessive use*.[81] The guiding principle was "use." The question appropriate to ask was "what are the conditions under which the

J. L. Austin's ***How to Do Things with Words***

79. Wittgenstein uses "description" as a contrastive term, in order to distinguish Enlightenment-driven methodologies, i.e., explanatory, positivistic approaches, from what might be called more instrumental approaches to language, i.e., denying the existence of anything beyond the sentence itself. Whether he is consistent or not (successful or not) in his endeavors is beyond the scope of this chapter. See the interesting analysis provided by Conor Cunningham, "Language: Wittgenstein after Theology," in *Radical Orthodoxy*, ed. John Milbank, C. Pickstock, and G. Ward (London: Routledge, 1999), 64–90.

80. Ludwig Wittgenstein, *PI*, 309, 109.

81. P. F. Strawson, "On Referring" in *Mind* 59 (1950): 320–44.

term or expression would be correctly used?" Philosophical problems only arise when one departs from the directives of the languages that define our forms of life. In other words, "don't ask for meaning . . . ask for use!"[82]

The Twentieth-Century Revolution in Science: Whose "Rationality" Is It Anyway?

"The World-Order Is Based on a Lie" (Kafka)

In our quest to compose a suitable picture of philosophical developments in the twentieth century, we have seen various themes merging and diverging. The most prominent theme, the one employed as a heuristic device for uniting the diversity that would otherwise overwhelm us, is language. We have seen that various views of language (designative vs. expressive) express fundamental disagreement about human knowledge of the world and how we are to understand and interpret our place in it. Growing out of the differences between depictive and descriptive theories of language are theories about the knowing subject's involvement in the interpretative process. Is this primarily an engaged or disengaged process? The Cartesian view, which is echoed in post-Cartesian theories of science and epistemology, advocated a disengaged way of reasoning (the pure *cogito*). Why? Because this guards against the pollution of perspective and more clearly reflects the way the mind operates and thus how the world should be understood. The early Wittgenstein, logical atomism, logical positivism, and related theories operated using this "scientific" and "objectifying" assumption; truth must be based on logic, and language must have similar precision and clarity. At this stage, we are operating in the world of "ideas"—what Hacking refers to as the "heyday of ideas," or the age of "mental discourse." This is the world of Descartes, Locke, Berkeley, Hobbes, and Hume.[83] It was Frege's attempt to ground analyticity in the general laws of logic—an attempt to overcome the potential for private languages that

> *Austin's central inspiration was that there are a great many uses of language other than designating, naming, labeling, and so forth (lines of projection)—those roles seized on by the positivists and constituted as "cognitive."*

> *Growing out of the differences between depictive and descriptive theories of language are theories about the knowing subject's involvement in the interpretative process. Is this primarily an engaged or disengaged process?*

---

82. There are innumerable difficulties arising from supposedly pure "use" or "instrumentalist" theories of language, e.g., take the sentence, "If I know that P, then Jones knows that P as well"—a simple conditional sentence. The expression "I know that P" clearly does not occur as a simple performative at all but as a straightforward declarative sentence that is capable of admitting truth-values similar to the way "Smith knows that P" occurs. This also is the case with "P is true" in a conditional such as, "If P is true then Q is false," where "P is true" states a condition for the falsity of Q: it does not express simple concurrence, i.e., as in a conversation, with what someone else may have said. The appeal of "use theories" derives from a "one at a time" gathering of sentences taken outside the larger discourse frameworks in which they would occur naturally. It was this insight that led to Wittgenstein's notion of *Lebensform*, "form of life," as essential to understanding both "use" and "formation" of language—an understanding that moves beyond simple word and meaning correspondences and even beyond sentence and meaning correspondences to larger "cultural" or "extra-linguistic" concerns of language. Hence, to understand a language is to understand a "form of life."

83. Ian Hacking, *Why Does Language Matter to Philosophy?* (Cambridge: Cambridge University Press, 1975).

MICHAEL W. PAYNE

*With the advent of
Wittgenstein's idea
of "language game,"
where a variety of
discourses operate
according to self-
determined rules
and grammars, the
important issues are
purely descriptive.
"How" becomes the
preeminent ques-
tion, not "what."*

seemed implicit in Locke and Hume—that helped point the early Wittgenstein toward focusing on notation as fundamental. The Vienna Circle's obsession with language played out the implications of both of these approaches.

With the shift that occurred in the later Wittgenstein's thoughts, the *cogito* as a disembodied, disengaged knower no longer is at center stage. The *cogito* has been replaced by the "human subject" engaged in public discourse that consists of sentences—hence, the emergence of the "heyday of sentences." There is nothing beyond sentences except the interconnecting web of sentences in discourses. With the advent of Wittgenstein's idea of "language game," where a variety of discourses operate according to self-determined rules and grammars, the important issues are purely descriptive. "How" becomes the preeminent question, not "what." In many ways, twentieth-century developments in science parallel these same paths. The insights gained by understanding the transition from "ideas" to "sentences" illustrate the crisis of truth and objectivity in science. To this, we now turn our attention.

The "new science" of Enlightenment modernity was validated, to an extent, by impressive achievements such as Copernicus' celestial mechanics, where the reigning theory of geocentrism was replaced with heliocentricism. This was followed by Newton's discoveries of the laws of gravity, and the advances go on and on from there. The major architects of this new worldview—Galileo, Bacon, Descartes, Newton—saw the cosmos as a machine governed by immutable laws that function in a predictable and orderly way, all of which can be understood and manipulated by the rational mind of man. Gone were the days when science was based on "first principles" (Aristotle); the shift from "qualitative" to "quantitative" had occurred. Teleological explanations and models of the world were rejected in favor of mechanistic ones, for example, cause and effect. The older, more expressivistic conceptions became the modern world's debris field. An early seventeenth-century attempt by Paduan skeptics to refute Galileo's discovery of Jupiter's moons illustrates the degree the crisis finally reached:

There are seven windows given to animals in the domicile of the head, through which the air is admitted to the tabernacle of the body, to enlighten, to warm and to nourish it. What are these parts of the microcosmos: Two nostrils, two eyes, two ears and a mouth. So in the heavens, as in a macrocosmos, there are two favourable [sp] stars, two unpropritious, two luminaries, and Mercury undecided and indifferent. From this and from many other similarities in nature, such as the seven metals, etc., which it were tedious to enumerate, we gather that the number of planets is necessarily seven.[84]

In Berthold Brecht's play, *Galileo*, the Paduan philosophers refuse to look through the telescope, preferring Aristotle's arguments over direct observation! After all, they remark, "Has it occurred to you that an eyeglass through

84. Steven Warhaft, ed., *Francis Bacon: A Selection of His Works* (Toronto: Macmillan of Canada, 1965), 17.

342

which one sees such phenomena might not be a too reliable eyeglass?" [85] The power of worldview is clearly displayed in this instance. The Paduan philosophers were certain they were correct to disparage the telescope and direct observation because the world embodied the same set of principles in different and varied domains (e.g., Aristotle). This is what the "language of correspondences" was all about; elements in different domains correspond to one another because they embody the same principle.

The rise of the modern paradigm put an end to such thinking. In many ways, Bacon's *Novum Organum* was a manifesto for a largely Western, anthropocentric worldview. Descartes approached the study of the world from a disengaged, rationalistic perspective that was grounded in a dualism between mind (*res cogitans*) and body (*res extensa*). Although not an empiricist, like Bacon he understood nature in mechanistic terms. Thus, to know reality is to have a correct representation of the world. This is attainable by correctly ordering ideas "in the mind." This order is not one I find or discover but one I build. This is not a construction without constraints. The primary constraint is certainty, and so the structure must generate certainty. How is this certainty to be achieved? It is achieved by developing a chain of clear and distinct ideas based on similarly clear and certain evidence. Thus, the rules developed by Descartes in his *Regulae* and later in the *Discours* are meant to guide us in this pursuit.

Hobbes and Spinoza extended Descartes' disengaged and proceduralist vision further. They rejected the Cartesian method's dualism in favor of a more consistent and mechanistic monism. Descartes had exempted human consciousness from mechanistic laws, but Hobbes claimed the human mind was a machine: "If this be so, reasoning will depend on names, names on the imagination, and imagination . . . on the motion of corporeal organs. Thus mind will be nothing but the motions in certain parts of an organic body."[86]

This reductionistic method of reasoning influenced Locke and Hume and spread throughout Europe through Newton's work. Eventually it attracted scholars in France—d'Holbach, d'Alembert, La Mettrie. It was La Mettrie who famously noted: "Let us conclude boldly then, that man is a machine and that there is only one substance, differently modified, in the whole world."[87] The modern mind conceived of nature as something man can master, understand, and subject to his or her own ends. Newton's *Mathematical Principles of Natural Philosophy* (1687) vindicated Bacon and Descartes by discovering universal laws of gravity and motion, along with the mathematical methods to describe them. The world was not mysterious nor was the process of

> " *La Mettrie . . . famously noted: "Let us conclude boldly then, that man is a machine and that there is only one substance, differently modified, in the whole world." The modern mind conceived of nature as something man can master, understand, and subject to his or her own ends.*

---

85.   Berthold Brecht, *Galileo*, in Berthold Brecht, *Seven Plays*, ed. Eric Bentley (New York: Grove Press, 1961), 353.

86.   Thomas Hobbes, *Leviathan* (Oxford: Oxford University Press, 1947), 5.

87.   Quoted in Floyd D. Matson, *The Broken Image: Man, Science and Society* (New York: Anchor Books, 1966), 13.

knowing it. The universe was like a well-regulated clock that abided by the rules of timekeeping. It was fully predictable, since everything past, present, and future was governed by the same universal laws of determinacy.

These laws were thought to govern human, or social, science, as well as natural science. *Scientism,* or positivism, was the application of these methods to secure the same kind of predictability one could achieve in the hard sciences. Thus, there was a sharp distinction between "fact" and "value," "objective" and "subjective." As with natural science, the goal was the "value free" research of various systems. "Social mathematics" and "social physics" would be based on "laws" of human behavior. This mechanistic vision was illustrated by the works of Saint Simon and his student Auguste Compte. As Compte wrote: "True liberty is nothing else than a rational submission to the preponderance of the laws of nature, in release from all arbitrary personal dictation."[88]

Thus, from the seventeenth to the twentieth centuries, the modern paradigm emerged and developed—a paradigm organized around the logic of determinism and rooted in the objectifying, mechanistic, abstract, and atemporal mode of thought that developed from the natural sciences. Science became the new God and scientism the new religion. Science and the scientific method formed the royal road to truth and certainty. In the world of modern science, the perceiving subject is a neutral observer, and the object is a pure datum of perception, unpolluted by the observer's participation. As Rorty notes, the mind was thought capable of representing the world through objective knowledge that was stable, certain, and accurate. After all, the mind was *the mirror of nature.*[89] Even language itself was thought to be impervious to pollution (e.g., logical positivism, the early Wittgenstein), since it, too, was distinct from the world of objects and able to represent them in objective terms. By the middle of the twentieth century, however, all this began to change.[90]

"We No Longer Live in the 'Modern' World" (Stephen Toulmin)

Several underlying presuppositions that made the modern scientific paradigm intelligible came in for criticism. These included the paradigm's purported objectivity, neutrality, linearity, incremental development, over-

Auguste Compte

88. Auguste Compte, *Social Physics: From the Positive Philosophy of Auguste Compte* (New York: Blanchard, 1850), 432.

89. Richard Rorty, *Philosophy and the Mirror of Nature* (Princeton, NJ: Princeton University Press, 1979).

90. The goal in this chapter is not to delineate in detail the forces that propel a "new" science in the twentieth century. However, they would include reflection on theories of dissipative structures that are based on principles of complexity, self-organization, and "chaos" theory, along with the rise of quantum mechanics, etc. For more on this, see Stephen Toulmin, *The Return to Cosmology: Postmodern Science and the Theology of Nature* (Berkeley, CA: University of California Press, 1982). Also see Frederick Ferre, "Religious World Modeling and Postmodern Science," in *The Reenchantment of Science: Postmodern Proposals*, ed. David Ray Griffin (Albany, NY: SUNY Press, 1988).

all consistency with what is "rational," and the rule of invariability. Once any one of these is challenged, the edifice that purportedly provides "clear, distinct, and certain" conclusions goes into a tailspin. A new kind of *anxiety* sets in, and the building begins to collapse. One term often used to identify the set of presuppositions outlined above is *foundationalism*. All knowledge claims must be grounded in unassailable foundations—beliefs that need no justification. We saw this in Descartes' elevation of "certain" ideas that form the foundation for everything else. Such ideas should be self-evident or obviously evident to the senses, which makes them certain, indubitable, and incorrigible.[91]

We also have observed a shift in science and rationality. Reflection began with the isolated atom, moved to the sentence, and now encompasses the larger framework or "web" of expression that makes knowledge possible. All these developments correspond to new ways of understanding reason and rationality. The notion of a disengaged reason, once the *sine qua non* of science, now is seen as an illusion. Each disciplinary matrix—whether physics, history, ethics, or religion—constitutes its own "language game," or paradigm, thus raising the stakes in any quest for certainty or truth.

Once the fully embodied, knowing subject overtakes the disembodied *cogito*, the full force of subjectivity and engaged reason results in the "curse of subjectivity" and loss of "absolute truth." Contributing to the demythologization of Descartes' myth of scientific objectivity was Thomas Kuhn's *The Structure of Scientific Revolutions* (1962), which was preceded by Michael Polanyi's *Personal Knowledge* (1958) and Peter Winch's *The Idea of a Social Science* (1958).[92] These three works challenged the older, representationalist views of rationality. They threatened the idea of a universal methodology, and this raised problems for being able to translate from one paradigm, or language game, to another—a problem known as incommensurability. Once the Kantian notion of universal categories is thrown into doubt, the specter of relativism raises its ugly head. In other words, once we stop believing that everyone sees and understands the same reality because they use the same a priori categories, then no one logic rules at all times and in all places. The following quote from Kuhn cast down the gauntlet:

> Nothing about that relatively familiar thesis [that theory-choice is not simply a matter of deductive proof] implies either that there are no good reasons for being persuaded or that those reasons are not ultimately decisive for the group. Nor does it even imply that the reasons for choice are different from those usually listed by philosophers of science: accuracy, simplicity, fruitfulness, and the like. What it

Thus, from the seventeenth to the twentieth centuries, the modern paradigm emerged and developed—a paradigm organized around the logic of determinism and rooted in the objectifying, mechanistic, abstract, and atemporal mode of thought that developed from the natural sciences.

*The notion of a disengaged reason, once the **sine qua non** of science, now is seen as an illusion. Each disciplinary matrix—whether physics, history, ethics, or religion—constitutes its own "language game," or paradigm, thus raising the stakes in any quest for certainty or truth.*

91. I am describing "classic foundationalism," as opposed to a "chastened or weakened" foundationalism. For the latter, see Alvin Plantinga, *Warrant and Proper Function* (New York: Oxford University Press, 1993).

92. Thomas Kuhn, *The Structure of Scientific Revolutions* (Chicago: University of Chicago Press, [1962] 3rd ed., 1996); Michael Polanyi, *Personal Knowledge* (Chicago: University of Chicago Press, 1958); Peter Winch, *The Idea of a Social Science and Its Relation to Philosophy* (London: Routledge & Kegan Paul, 1958).

should suggest, however, is that such reasons function as values and that they can thus be differently applied, individually and collectively, by men who concur in honoring them. If two men disagree, for example, about the relative fruitfulness of their theories, or if they agree about that but disagree about the relative importance of fruitfulness and, say, scope in reaching a choice, neither can be convicted of a mistake. Nor is either being unscientific. *There is no neutral algorithm for theory-choice, no systematic decision procedure which, properly applied, must lead each individual in the group to the same decision.* [Italics added]

Kuhn argued that "reasons" are really "values," not "rules for choice"—so much for the "fact-value" distinction! Everyone uses criteria for choosing that make sense only in the context of the prevailing paradigm within which they are working. These criteria really are "values" that reflect choices we have previously made—value-laden, informed choices. Thus, the "theory-ladenness" of all observation and calculation makes the post-Cartesian pursuit of "objectivity" absurd.

Peter Winch draws various conclusions from similar premises in his classic essay "Understanding a Primitive Society" (1970).[93] In this essay, Winch accuses Evans-Pritchard of imposing a monopolistic, Western conception of reason in his determination that the Azande tribe had no "science." This was because their practices did not fit the prevailing paradigm of Western science. Remember Wittgenstein's notions of "language game" and the importance of "use" in ordinary language analysis? When we hear the crowd at a baseball game shout "Kill the bum!" we don't for a minute assume they mean it literally.[94] But the dictionary meaning of "kill" is "kill." We "know" what we mean by "Kill the bum" at the ball game because of the experiences we have had in this same context, where this sentence is not a call to murder but to something else. This is what we earlier called "context conferring intelligibility." And this was precisely the point Wittgenstein was making with his analysis of "language games." One should not attempt to impose rules from one game on actions in another, different game. To do so would be to judge an activity according to the wrong rules. Thus, Winch writes:

> Criteria of logic are not a direct gift of God, but arise out of, and are only intelligible in the context of, ways of living or modes of social life. It follows that one cannot apply criteria of logic to modes of social life as such. For instance, science is one such mode and religion is another; and each has a criterion of intelligibility peculiar to itself. So within a science or religion actions can be logical or illogical. . . . But we cannot sensibly say that either the practice of science itself or that of religion is either illogical or logical.[95]

> *Kuhn argued that "reasons" are really "values," not "rules for choice"—so much for the "fact-value" distinction! Everyone uses criteria for choosing that make sense only in the context of the prevailing paradigm within which they are working.*

Thus, *incommensurability* is the problematic associated with the now-impossible task of translating across language games or paradigms; there is

---

93. Peter Winch, "Understanding a Primitive Society" in Brian R. Wilson, ed., *Rationality* (Oxford: Basil Blackwell, 1970), 78–111.

94. I owe this illustration to William Placher, *Unapologetic Theology* (Louisville: Westminster/John Knox, 1989), 58.

95. Peter Winch, *The Idea of a Social Science*, 100–101.

no word-to-word or term-to-term or concept-to-concept correspondence available among games. Under the older modern paradigm, the distinction between "natural science(s)" and "human science(s)" was an attempt to protect the former from the ever-present corruption of the thinking subject. As we have seen, the attempt to formalize scientific language illustrates the desire to avoid the equivocal and adaptable nature of ordinary human language. The fact-value distinction was intended to keep the agent out of the document or the data—to ensure as much as possible that the data were isolated from those intentions and meanings the subject might impose on them. The emphasis on discovering "law-like" relations external to the observer was to be a guarantee of their universal validity and significance. Objectivity was of premium value, and the more one could isolate the subject's input from the data, the better.

The scientific community has abandoned those beliefs or holds them with great suspicion. Mary Hesse summarizes the new post-empiricist account of natural science as it parallels the qualities of the older, post-Cartesian view of natural science that we have previously described:

1. In natural science, data [are] not detachable from theory, for what counts as data are determined in the light of some theoretical interpretation, and the facts themselves have to be reconstructed in the light of interpretation.
2. In natural science, theories are not models externally compared to nature in a hypothetico-deductive schema. Rather, they are the way the facts themselves are seen.
3. In natural science, the law-like relations asserted of experience are internal, because what count as facts are constituted by what the theory says about their interrelations with one another.
4. The language of natural science is irreducibly metaphorical and inexact. It is formalizable only at the cost of distortion of the historical dynamics of scientific development and of the imaginative constructions in terms of which nature is interpreted by science.
5. Meanings in natural science are determined by theory; they are understood by theoretical coherence rather than by correspondence with facts.[96]

The Twentieth Century: Ethics and the New Dark Ages (Nietzsche, Rorty and Pragmatism)

"Truth" is an army of mobile metaphors, metonyms, and anthropomorphisms— in short a sum of human relations, which have been enhanced, transposed, and

The fact-value distinction was intended to keep the agent out of the document or the data—to ensure as much as possible that the data were isolated from those intentions and meanings the subject might impose on them.

---

96. Mary Hesse, "In Defense of Objectivity" in her *Revolutions and Reconstructions in the Philosophy of Science* (Brighton, England: Harvester Press, 1980), 170–71.

embellished poetically and rhetorically and which after long use seem firm, canonical, and obligatory to a people. (Friedrich Nietzsche)[97]

If one considers chance to be unworthy of determining our fate, it is simply a relapse into the pious view of the Universe which Leonardo himself was on the way to overcoming when he wrote that the sun does not move. . . . we are all too ready to forget that in fact everything to do with our life is chance, from our origin out of the meeting of spermatozoon and ovum onwards. . . . We all still show too little respect for Nature which (in the obscure words of Leonardo which recall Hamlet's lines) "is full of countless causes ('ragioni') that never enter experience."

Everyone of us human beings corresponds to one of the countless experiments in which these "ragioni" of nature force their way into experience. (Sigmund Freud)[98]

The question of language is entrusted to that form of speech which has no doubt never ceased to pose it, but which is now, for the first time, posing it to itself. That literature in our day is fascinated by the being of language is neither the sign of an imminent end nor proof of a radicalization: it is a phenomenon whose necessity has its roots in a vast configuration in which the whole structure of our thought and our knowledge is traced. (Michel Foucault)[99]

Recall our earlier discussion of the designative and the expressivist views of language, with their corresponding views of the nature of the world and the role of the mind describing it. The former celebrates the "objectivity" of the world and the disengaged subject's role in mapping that world in a way that corresponds accurately to what is "really there." This emphasis on "universality" and "absoluteness" finds a home in the Enlightenment and rationalist traditions, with the rise of the "scientific revolution" and the epistemological tradition itself (e.g., Descartes, Locke, Hume). The episte-mological tradition illustrates what Michel Foucault calls a "history of the *Same*, a history of the order imposed on things."[100] This was paralleled in language by the emphasis on representation, where the hope was to devise "the great utopia of a perfectly transparent language in which things themselves could be named without any penumbra of confusion." This would be a world where words are no longer enigmatic (the expressivist world) but "sovereign" and where they capture "without residium and without opacity" the things of the world.[101] As we saw above, the positivist dream was only a dream. The "later" Wittgenstein illustrated and persuasively argued for a rethinking of language and its representational function.

Richard Rorty

97.   Friedrich Nietzsche, "On Truth and Lie in an Extra-Moral Sense," in *The Viking Portable Nietzsche*, trans. and ed. Walter Kaufmann (New York: Penguin, 1968), 46–47.

98.   Richard Rorty, *Contingency, Irony, and Solidarity* (Cambridge University Press, 1989), 31.

99.   Michel Foucault, *The Order of Things: An Archaeology of the Human Sciences*, trans. unnamed (New York: Vintage Books, 1973), 383.

100.   Michael Foucault, *The Order of Things*, 70.

101.   Ibid., 64, 117, 311.

Nietzsche, Rorty, and Pragmatism

As previously described, paralleling the development of the "later" Wittgenstein, philosophers of science recognized it was impossible to disentangle fact from value; there are no "pristine" or "immaculate" facts. Values and facts are interconnected and interlaced so that finding an "absolute" perspective,[102] or as Nagel refers to it, a "view from nowhere,"[103] became the never-ending quest of only a few. With the later Wittgenstein and ordinary language analysis,[104] the attention to genre and speech-act theory in Austin and Searle,[105] and the move from semiotics to semantics in Ricoeur,[106] language was released from the philosophical captivity that understood religious and ethical discourse as languages of projection. Now it was acknowledged that all language, whether scientific or moral, is value-laden.

All of this bode well for understanding ethical language as cognitively meaningful, but there is a downside as well.[107] In the new paradigm, all language is understood in terms of pure immanence. Because there is no "extra-linguistic" reality to which language refers, the result is what Kai Nielsen calls a "Wittgensteinian fideism."[108] The tribunal for determining what is "good," "true," or "meaningful" is found entirely within communal or inter-subjective experience. There is no court of appeal outside language, because language is a purely human convention.[109] Thus, there is no "essential"

> *In the new paradigm, all language is understood in terms of pure immanence. Because there is no "extra-linguistic" reality to which language refers, the result is what Kai Nielsen calls a "Wittgensteinian fideism."*

> *The tribunal for determining what is "good," "true," or "meaningful" is found entirely within communal or inter-subjective experience. There is no court of appeal outside language, because language is a purely human convention.*

102. See Bernard Williams's *Ethics and the Limits of Philosophy*, 132–55, for his distinction between "absoluteness" and "truth," a distinction that is meant to prize off a realm of "objective" fact that is somehow non-perspectivally true, from that which is "true" in the sense that it is "rightly assertable" within a specific language-game.

103. Thomas Nagel, *The View From Nowhere* (Oxford: Oxford University Press, 1986).

104. Ludwig Wittgenstein, *Philosophical Investigations*, 3rd ed., trans. G. E. M. Anscombe (Oxford: Blackwell, 1958).

105. J. L. Austin, *How to Do Things with Words*, 2nd ed. (Oxford: Oxford University Press, 1975), and John Searle, *Speech Acts: An Essay in the Philosophy of Language* (Cambridge: Cambridge University Press, 1969).

106. Paul Ricoeur, *Interpretation Theory: Discourse and the Surplus of Meaning* (Fort Worth, TX: Texas Christian University Press, 1976); also Paul Ricoeur, *Hermeneutics and the Human Sciences: Essays on Language, Action and Interpretation*, ed. John B. Thompson (Cambridge: Cambridge University Press, 1985), and Paul Ricoeur, *A Ricoeur Reader: Reflection and Imagination*. Ed. Mario J. Valdes (New York and London: Harvester Wheatsheaf, 1991).

107. The use of "cognitive" here is fraught with complications. Traditionally, the application of "cognitive" would suggest there are real moral propositions, i.e., propositions that are true or false, and potentially even verifiable against experience, thus making it possible to have "moral knowledge." Epistemologically speaking, however, the most to which contemporary philosophers will agree is some form of "reliabilism" or "coherentism," in terms of which "function" is the primary criterion. That is, does a term function in a "coherent" way; and is it "revisable," that is, open to adjustment in terms of the claims that are being made.

108. Kai Nielsen, "Wittgensteinian Fideism" *Philosophy* 62 (1967): 191–93. This consequence is most profoundly reflected in the works of Richard Rorty, e.g., *Contingency, Irony and Solidarity* (Cambridge: Cambridge University Press, 1989). Not all agree with Nielsen's analysis and his charge of fideism.

109. Rorty refers to this ancient preoccupation with "truth" and the "invisible" as "the disposition to use the language of our ancestors, to worship the corpses of their metaphors," *Contingency, Irony and Solidarity*, 21.

reality;[110] only "contingent" reality.[111] Therefore, there is only perspective, or "perspective seeing," as Nietzsche described it in *On the Genealogy of Morals*. Any attempt to ignore this would be to "castrate the intellect."[112] Expounding on this Nietzschean theme, Jacques Derrida describes the desire for "essence" as a misguided metaphysical quest that seeks a "cen- tered structure." He argues that whatever contingency or "play" there is "is based on a fundamental ground, a play constituted on the basis of a funda- mental immobility and a reassuring certitude, which is itself beyond play."[113] According to Derrida and other deconstructionists, such quests are at best illusory. In the end, Nietzsche's "strong poet" prevails over the scientist.[114]

What is the result of this renewed attention to contingency? In the words of Hilary Putnam, "the greatest pretensions of philosophy have collapsed."[115] A great "leveling" has occurred. There is no privileged status to which phi- losophy can appeal to adjudicate truth claims. Now "truth" and "value" are nothing more than the function of sentences strung together by people who create language.[116] Like science, ethics is one more area of discourse—one more language game—that deals with a different area of inquiry. Language is severed from any connection with external reality. Thus, we are freed from the impossible quest for certainty, whether in ethics or science.[117]

The shifts toward the ethical and the literary converge in the prag- matist line.[118] Ethics is no longer a second-class discourse because of its

> " *What is the result of this renewed attention to contin- gency? In the words of Hilary Putnam, "the greatest preten- sions of philosophy have collapsed." A great "leveling" has occurred.*

110. The problematic associated with positing a "reality" to which our value terms link or do not link is one pursued by Charles Taylor in his *Sources of the Self* (New York: Cam- bridge University Press, 1994). His analysis of this is directed toward his notion of "strong evaluations," where "the fact that these ends or goods stand independent of our own desires, inclinations, or choices, [indicates] that they represent standards by which these desires and choices are judged," 20.

111. The use of "essence" is burdened with all kinds of metaphysical freight that ulti- mately blurs our ability to see language doing more than function self-referentially. This is developed more fully by Ricoeur in *Interpretation Theory*.

112. Friedrich Nietzsche, *On the Genealogy of Morals*, ed. Keith Ansell-Pearson (Cam- bridge: Cambridge University Press, 1994), 92.

113. Jacques Derrida, *Writing and Difference* (Chicago: University of Chicago Press, 1978), 279.

114. More on this can be found in Alexander Nehamas, *Nietzsche: Life as Literature* (Cambridge, MA: Harvard University Press, 1985).

115. Hilary Putnam, "Taking Rules Seriously—A Response to Martha Nussbaum," in *New Literary History* 15 (1983), 199.

116. As Nietzsche poetically frames it in "On Truth and Lie in an Extra-Moral Sense," in *The Portable Nietzsche* (New York: Penguin Books, 1968), 46–47: "Truth is a mobile army of metaphors, metonyms, and anthromorphisms—in short a sum of human relations, which have been enhanced, transposed, and embellished poetically and rhetorically and which after long use seem firm, canonical, and obligatory to a people."

117. This misguided quest produced "Cartesian Anxiety," as Richard Bernstein labels it in his *Beyond Objectivism and Relativism: Science, Hermeneutics and Praxis* (Philadelphia, PA: University of Pennsylvania Press, 1983).

118. The increasing importance given to poetry and the novel as they relate to under- standing and explicating the "moral life" is directly linked to an awareness of the contin- gency of the world, most especially to our language. Postmodernists exaggerate this because they misconstrue the nature of language and because of their notions of contingency. For

subject matter but rather one of many discourses, each equally relevant to its own semantic domain. The emphasis in ethics is on description not prescription, since to be prescriptive is to assume a universality that is unjustifiable, given the purely immanent character of all reflection and knowledge.[119] Thus, according to Richard Rorty, identifying pragmatism as the heir apparent to the now-deceased representationalist paradigm is a major paradigm shift.[120] He writes:

> Pragmatism, by contrast, does not erect Science as an idol to fill the place once held by God. It views science as one genre of literature—or, put the other way around, literature and the arts as inquiries, on the same footing as scientific inquiries. Thus, it sees ethics as neither more "relative" nor "subjective" than scientific theory, nor as needing to be made "scientific." Physics is a way of trying to cope with various bits of the universe; ethics is a matter of trying to cope with other bits. Mathematics helps physics do its job; literature and the arts help ethics do its.[121]

Gone, according to Rorty and the modern pragmatists, is any quest for "objectivity" or interest in epistemology or metaphysics. The Platonic distinction between knowledge and opinion that resulted in the positivist split between empirical and transcendental harbored ill will toward the non-empirical and languished in the field of "correspondence." Where positivists failed to extract themselves from the dualisms of epistemology, the Kantian transcendentalist made the reverse error of hypostasizing "thought," and was left with a quasi-Platonic worldview. Allegedly, pragmatism frees us from both errors. Contrary to positivism, the pragmatist "drops the notion of truth as correspondence with reality altogether, and says that modern science does not enable us to cope because it corresponds, it just plain enables us to cope."[122] We are left with our language. There is no way to assume a position from the outside from which we can judge the adequacy of our language. As Rorty states, "it lets us see language not as a *tertium quid* between Subject and Object, nor as a medium in which we try to form pictures of

> *The Platonic distinction between knowledge and opinion that resulted in the positivist split between empirical and transcendental harbored ill will toward the non-empirical and languished in the field of "correspondence."*

---

illuminating analyses of the novel-ethics relationship see, e.g., S. L. Goldberg, *Agents and Lives: Moral Thinking in Literature* (Cambridge: Cambridge University Press, 1993); Geoffrey Galt Harpham, *Getting it Right: Language, Literature and Ethics* (Chicago: University of Chicago Press, 1992); J. Hillis Miller, *The Ethics of Reading: Kant, de Man, Eliot, Trollope, James and Benjamin* (New York: Columbia University Press, 1987); David Parker, *Ethics, Theory and the Novel* (Cambridge: Cambridge University Press, 1994); Leona Toker, ed., *Commitment in Reflection: Essays in Literature and Moral Philosophy* (New York: Garland, 1993).

119.   Arthur Allen Leff, "Unspeakable Ethics, Unnatural Law," *Duke Law Journal* 6 (1979), 1233–34.

120.   Thomas Kuhn, *The Structure of Scientific Revolutions*, 2nd ed. (Chicago: University of Chicago Press, 1970). Also see Mary Hesse, *Revolutions and Reconstructions in the Philosophy of Science* (Brighton, England: Harvester Press, 1980).

121.   Richard Rorty, *Consequences of Pragmatism* (Hempel Hempstead. England: Harvester Wheatsheaf, 1991), xliii.

122.   Richard Rorty, "Pragmatism and Philosophy" in *Consequences of Pragmatism*, (Minneapolis: University of Minnesota Press, 1982) as found in *After Philosophy*, eds. Kenneth Baynes, James Bohman, and Thomas McCarthy (Cambridge, MA: MIT Press, 1996), 30–31.

reality, but as part of the behavior of human beings."[123] Labels like "truth" and "goodness" are metaphysics under the carpet, and this only leads back to the Plato-Kant continuum, which has been made vacuous by critiques such as Nietzsche's. Ironists, like Rorty, celebrate nominalism and histori-cism. The ironist searches for new vocabularies not as a way of getting right something distinct from his vocabulary. After all, he doesn't take the point of discursive thought to be knowing, in any sense that can be explicated by notions like "reality," "real essence," "objective point of view," and "the corre-spondence of language and reality." For the *ironist*, the final vocabulary does not settle things finally, as if there were some criteria of adequacy. "Criteria, on their view, are never more than the platitudes which contextually define the terms of a final vocabulary currently in use."[124]

Much of this thinking finds its immediate historical roots in the philos-ophy of William James (1842–1910), "the" American pragmatist.[125] Accord-ing to James, philosophy's function should be to determine what difference it will make to you and me, at specific points in our lives, if this world-formula or that world-formula is true. This implies there is no way to tell if this or that world formula is correct or true. Only when two world formulas are incompatible with one another but compatible with everything known and knowable does the question "what definite difference will this make" arise. James sought to determine what it makes me feel happiest to believe, what it matters most to me to believe, what is good for me to believe, and so forth. Basically, that is what "pragmatic truth" means. Its only test is "what works best in the way of leading us, what fits every part of life best." Regardless of the answer, it is meaningless to treat it as "not true." After all, it would be a notion that was pragmatically successful. "Knowledge" is all about "positive science," according to James. To go beyond this is to exceed the limits of its possible competence. "Philosophy" is what we do when "knowledge goes on a holiday." Whatever issues there are in philosophy, they must be settled on a basis other than an appeal to cognition. Philosophical truth? Philosophical knowledge? With James and pragmatism, they became more like "moods"—the application of colors, depending on the mood we are in. There is no distinction between reality and appearance in James's pragmatism. There are simply multiple descriptions, alongside all the other descriptions—one more vocabulary alongside others. The goal of philosophy is to clarify, not to ground. As John Dewey, the other great pragmatist, noted (1859–1952):

William James

> When it is acknowledged that under disguise of dealing with ultimate reality phi-losophy has been occupied with the precious values embedded in social tradi-tions, that it has sprung from a clash of social ends and from a conflict of inher-ited institutions with incompatible contemporary tendencies, it will be seen that

123.   Ibid., 32.
124.   Ibid., 74–75.
125.   William James, *Pragmatism and the Meaning of Truth* (Cambridge, MA: Harvard University Press, 1978).

the task of future philosophy is to clarify men's ideas as to the social and moral strifes of their own day.[126]

There is no "universal validity" toward which to aim or on which to ground our ideas—an insight profoundly echoed in Wittgenstein. With pragmatism, "imagination is the chief instrument of the good . . . art is more moral than moralities. For the latter either are, or tend to become, consecrations of the status quo. . . . The moral prophets of humanity have always been poets even though they spoke in free verse or by parable."[127] This helps explain the convergence of literature and ethics in modern pragmatist writings.

For Rorty's ironist, literature serves an entirely different purpose than it does for the person who operates from the common-sense perspective—someone who still labors under the "objective truth" criteria. In the quest for a better final vocabulary, the ironist is not hoping to discover but to create; the goal is "diversification and novelty rather than convergence to the antecedently present."[128] These vocabularies are "poetic achievements." Orwell, Proust, D. H. Lawrence, along with others, should not be treated "as anonymous channels for truth but as abbreviations for a certain kind of vocabulary and for the sorts of beliefs and desires typical of its users."[129] One must play with the images each of these authors creates. Words like *should*, *ought*, *good*, and *bad* "name properties of sentences, or of actions and situations."[130] They are not extra-mental realities to which our words or actions conform. In Darwinian manner, language and meaning are seen as fundamentally adaptive strategies, so that "what is rational for us now to believe may not be true, [this] is simply to say that somebody may come up with a better idea. . . . a whole new vocabulary may come along"[131] and change things.

The pragmatist emphasis on the radical contingency of self and community emphasizes, or rather de-divinizes, the world. As Rorty somewhat poetically puts the matter:

> Once upon a time we felt a need to worship something which lay beyond the visible world. Beginning in the seventeenth century we tried to substitute a love of truth for a love of God, treating the world described by science as a quasi divinity. Beginning at the end of the eighteenth century we tried to substitute a love of ourselves for a love of scientific truth, a worship of our own deep spiritual or poetic nature, treated as one more quasi divinity.[132]

> *James sought to determine what it makes me feel happiest to believe, what it matters most to me to believe, what is good for me to believe, and so forth. Basically, that is what "pragmatic truth" means.*

> *In the quest for a better final vocabulary, the ironist is not hoping to discover but to create; the goal is "diversification and novelty rather than convergence to the antecedently present." These vocabularies are "poetic achievements."*

126.   John Dewey, *Reconstruction in Philosophy* (Boston: Beacon Press, 1948), 26.
127.   John Dewey, *Art as Experience* (New York: Capricorn Books, 1958), 348.
128.   Rorty, *Contingency, Irony, and Solidarity* (Cambridge: Cambridge University Press, 1989), 77.
129.   Ibid., 79.
130.   Dewey, *Art as Experience*, 327.
131.   Richard Rorty, *Objectivity, Relativism, and Truth* (Cambridge: Cambridge University Press, 1994), 23.
132.   Richard Rorty, *Contingency, Irony and Solidarity*, 22.

According to Rorty, philosophers such as Wittgenstein, Nietzsche, James, Dewey, and others have freed us from such delusions to the point "where we no longer worship *anything*, where we treat *nothing* as a quasi divinity, where we treat *everything*—our language, our conscience, our community—as a product of time and chance [emphasis in the original]."[133] Rorty and the pragmatists are opposed to possessing "final vocabularies" (the history of philosophy serves to illustrate the futility of such a quest); their concern is to develop new and ever-changing vocabularies. Human beings are all about "self creation." Coming to understand this constitutes self-knowledge. "The process of coming to know oneself, confronting one's contingency . . . is identical with the process of inventing a new language— that is, of thinking up some new metaphors."[134] We should not accept some-one else's description of ourselves—accept the prevailing language game— since that would be to discover oneself only as a "copy or replica."[135]

Irony vs. Common Sense

According to Rorty, each of us embodies a "final vocabulary"—a stock of words we use to justify our actions, beliefs, and lives. These are the words humans employ to tell "the story of their lives." It is a "final" vocabulary because "if doubt is cast on the worth of these words, their user has no non-circular argumentative recourse." There is nowhere else to go, except, perhaps, to force. A final vocabulary is made up of "thin" and "thick" terms. The former are represented by words such as "good," "truth," "beauty," and so forth. The latter consists of words such as "decency," "cruelty," "kindness," and so on.[136]

Regarding final vocabulary, people fall into one of two classes: either they are ironists, or they are committed to some form of common-sense strategy. Ironists accept the contingency of a final vocabulary; they have "radical and continuing doubts about the final vocabulary."[137] Usually, this is caused by ongoing encounters with other vocabularies, either in actual persons or in books. Ironists also realize that appeals to vocabulary cannot settle the incommensurability present in encounters with others. Lastly, ironists understand that one person's vocabulary is no closer to objective reality than is any other's. For ironists, there is no "metavocabulary" by which to measure one proposal against another.[138]

"Common sense" is the label Rorty attaches to those who "unself-consciously describe everything important in terms of the final vocabulary to which they and those around them are habituated."[139] When challenged by alternative vocabularies, such a person responds by appealing to crite-

> *According to Rorty, each of us embodies a "final vocabu- lary"—a stock of words we use to justify our actions, beliefs, and lives. . . . It is a "final" vocabulary because "if doubt is cast on the worth of these words, their user has no noncircular argu- mentative recourse."*

133. Ibid., 22.
134. Ibid., 27.
135. Harold Bloom, *The Anxiety of Influence* (Oxford: Oxford University Press, 1973).
136. Richard Rorty, *Contingency, Irony and Solidarity*, 73.
137. Ibid., *73*.
138. Ibid.
139. Ibid., 74.

ria, to standards of evaluation, as if there is a permanent, essential quality behind our evaluative terms. For the ironist, this is simply re-describing ourselves by using our vocabularies in the hope that "by this continual re-description, [we might] make the best selves for ourselves that we can."[140] Thus we are continually "revising" ourselves and in the process "doubts about our own characters or our own culture can be resolved or assuaged only by enlarging our acquaintance. *The easiest way to do that is to read books*"[emphasis mine].[141]

Conclusions: Life in a Hall of Mirrors

In this chapter, we have surveyed the growing awareness on the part of "moderns" and "late moderns"—postmodernists—about our contingency as creatures. We have seen that contingency extends to the nature of knowledge and the way we conceive, formulate, and communicate it. The Enlightenment reluctantly acknowledged contingency; postmoderns celebrate it. The twentieth century's fascination with language is not a passing fad. It is part of a larger revolution in the history of ideas. It lies at the heart of what has evolved in the human and natural sciences—our capacity to express and be limited by our expressions. We have given up on finding a "rock-bottom reality" that will enable us to validate our supposed certainties; we have given up on objectivity.[142] We have turned to another source that was anticipated by the romantics, Nietzsche, and the late nineteenth- and twentieth-century pragmatists (Dewey and James)—our *solidarity* as speakers and "doers." There is no "ugly ditch" that separates language from the world, because there is no "world" of objects. There are only our interpretations of the various relations within which discourse occurs. There is no "substance-property" distinction, no distinction between "appearance" and "reality," and no "language-fact" dualism. Late moderns argue that distinctions like those would secretly privilege one context over another—all the while denying there is any context, since all knowing, speaking, and describing already are bound to a context that cannot be objectified.[143] The choice is never between an "image" and "the real thing." It is simply a recognition and rejoicing in an ever enlarging and expanding set of images—a *hall of mirrors*.[144]

> The Enlightenment reluctantly acknowledged contingency; postmoderns celebrate it. The twentieth century's fascination with language is not a passing fad. It is part of a larger revolution in the history of ideas.

---

140.   Ibid., 78.

141.   Ibid., 79–80.

142.   Having moved beyond the fallacies of Cartesian and post-Cartesian "self-founding" strategies, Blumenberg argues that we should recover what lies at the heart of the Enlightenment—a "self-assertive" notion of humanity. See Hans Blumenberg, *The Legitimacy of the Modern Age* (Cambridge, MA: MIT Press, 1982).

143.   Hilary Putnam, *Representation and Reality* (Cambridge, MA: MIT Press, 1988), 89: "To ask a human being in a time-bound culture to survey all modes of human linguistic existence—including those that will transcend his own—is to ask for an impossible Archimedean point."

144.   This is the image employed by Richard Rorty in *Objectivity, Relativism, and Truth* (Cambridge: Cambridge University Press, 1991), 100. For a thoughtful and incisive rejoin-

The answer to the contingency and relativism of twentieth-century philosophy lies buried in the distinction between the "designative" and the "expressive." Philosophy would have taken a more productive course had it recognized these categories posed different kinds of questions and were not capable of subsuming all data and experience.[145] A more holistic account would have required a controlling figure, a "view from somewhere," a more integrative approach. The Christian worldview provides such a philosophy of "fact" and "interpretation"—a place where subject and object can dwell without falling prey to the idolatry that results from pursuing one extreme or the other. We live in a world created by God, and he knows his world exhaustively. Within God's creation, we can know truthfully without knowing exhaustively. We can pursue meaning, truth, and value, with humility, in a way that honors the Creator of all meaning, truth, and value.

A Christian worldview will celebrate the tearing down of the wall Enlightenment rationalism erected, a wall that circumscribed what could be accepted as true "knowledge." However, the celebration of *perspective* that atomizes all approaches to knowledge in the absence of an all-knowing God, who himself is the source of all knowledge, only creates the minimization of "content" (based on the need to achieve consensus) and the maximization of individual perspective (based on the need to celebrate human autonomy). In other words, the more *we* know the less we *know*.

The so-called "postmodern" world in which we live desperately needs more and not less content. Richard Rorty's celebration of "liberty" or "free inquiry" as the most we can hope for and the happiest of all epistemological and ethical settlements will not do. The balkanization of knowledge and ethics promoted by these late-moderns intensifies the scandal of rebellion that has defined human behavior since Genesis 3. Furthermore, the twenty-first century's association of "identity-based-on-truth" with *religion* does not bode well for any Christian attempt to make truth claims central to Christian identity; it makes Christians look like Islamists in disguise.

The story Christians need to tell is the one that makes all others intelligible. The gospel is not one story among many. The Christian worldview is not one option among a plethora of options, each of which will satisfy the human need for clarity and truth. The Christian worldview is true. As such, it makes the world intelligible and reveals the many half-truths in the aberrant worldviews with which it competes.

John Dewey

---

der to Rorty, see Cora Diamond, "Truth: Defenders, Debunkers, Despisers," *Commitment in Reflection*, ed. Leona Toker (New York: Garland Publishing, Ind., 1994), 195–221.

145.   Charles Taylor explores this question with great insight in "Language and Human Nature," 219. He notes how sentences do both; they designate and express: "to the objects it is about, in one; and to the thought it expresses, in the other."

For Further Reading

Allen, Barry. *Truth in Philosophy*. Cambridge, MA: Harvard University Press, 1993.

Bauman, Zygmunt. *Life in Fragments*. Oxford: Blackwell, 1995.

Baynes, Kenneth, James Bohman, and Thomas McCarthy, eds. *After Philosophy: End or Transformation?* Cambridge, MA: MIT Press, 1996.

Best, Steven, and Douglas Kellner. *The Postmodern Turn*. New York: The Guilford Press, 1997.

Blond, Phillip, ed. *Post-Secular Philosophy: Between Philosophy and Theology*. London: Routledge, 1998.

Heelas, Paul, David Martin, and Paul Morris, eds. *Religion, Modernity and Postmodernity*, Oxford: Blackwell, 1998.

Kern, Stephen. *The Culture of Time and Space: 1880–1919*. Cambridge, MA: Harvard University Press, 1983.

Lyotard, Jean-Francois. *The Postmodern Condition: A Report on Knowledge*. Translated by Geoff Bennington and Brian Massumi. Minneapolis: University of Minnesota Press, 1989.

MacIntyre, Alasdair. *After Virtue*. 2nd ed. Notre Dame, IN: University of Notre Dame Press, 1984.

Milbank, John. *Theology and Social Theory*. Oxford: Blackwell, 1990.

Schneewind, J. B. *The Invention of Autonomy: A History of Modern Moral Philosophy*. Cambridge: Cambridge University Press, 1998.

Stout, Jeffrey. *Ethics After Babel*. Boston: Beacon Press, 1988.

Taylor, Charles. *Sources of the Self*. Cambridge: Cambridge University Press, 1989.

Toole, David. *Waiting for Godot at Sarajevo*. Boulder, CO: Westview Press 1998.

Vanhoozer, Kevin J. *First Theology: God, Scripture and Hermeneutics*. Downers Grove, IL: InterVarsity Press, 2002

For Further Discussion

1. In what ways might the developments in linguistic philosophy help, rather than hinder, our understanding of biblical revelation?

2. How have Christians traditionally misconstrued the nature of "truth"? What are some consequences of this misconstrual?

3. How have Christians traditionally rightly understood the nature of "truth"? Search for examples to illustrate how even the church needs to be corrected at times in its handling of "truth."

4. Does the creation narrative of Genesis assist us in developing a proper view of language and truth? If so, how?

5. What does "getting it right" mean from a Christian perspective?

> *The Christian worldview provides such a philosophy of "fact" and "interpretation"—a place where subject and object can dwell without falling prey to the idolatry that results from pursuing one extreme or the other.*

> *The story Christians need to tell is the one that makes all others intelligible. The gospel is not one story among many. The Christian worldview is not one option among a plethora of options, each of which will satisfy the human need for clarity and truth.*

357

6. What are some of the dangers in making "perspective" everything? How can we protect ourselves from relativism?

7. How can we protect ourselves from the "hall of mirrors" effect discussed at the end of the chapter?

Glossary

absolute dependence. Friedrich Schleiermacher's term for the religious feelings of dependence people experience upon realizing their finitude—how small they are in an infinite universe.

absolute mind. G. W. F. Hegel's term for an abstract but real blueprint of ideas that determine how history progresses towards its inevitable goal.

Academy. Gymnasium in Athens where Plato taught; the Platonic school of philosophy.

active intellect. Aristotle's term for the aspect of intellect that abstracts concepts from sense experience. Aristotle distinguished the active from the passive intellect, which merely receives the data of the senses.

ad fontes. Latin meaning "to the sources" or "Back to the sources!" This term characterized the basic literary program of the humanists whereby they returned to the study of classical sources and texts. In the context of theology, this meant producing critical editions of complete works by the early church fathers that allowed a proper, overall assessment of patristic theology, rather than one filtered through the books of short extracts (called "florilegia" and "sentences"), which were typical of the Middle Ages.

already not yet. Designates the contrast between the present fulfillment of God's promises of salvation, and their future final and full realization in the new heaven and the new earth (Rev. 21:1–22:5). The "already" side includes what Christians already have been given as spiritual blessings in union with Christ (Eph. 1:3–14). The "not-yet" side includes all the blessings that have not yet been given but will be when Christ returns (Rom. 8:18–25). The two sides are related, because Christians now have the Holy Spirit as the "down payment" of future blessings (Eph. 1:14 ESV note). See also **inaugurated eschatology**; **union with Christ**.

Anabaptism. Literally "re-baptism." Practiced in the early stages of the Reformation by a broad spectrum of Protestants—Anabaptists—who rejected infant baptism. Anabaptists maintained baptism was to be received only on profession of faith, hence "believer's baptism." When, following this belief, they proceeded to baptize one another for the first time (as they saw it), their opponents dubbed them "re-baptizers," or Anabaptists.

analogy of being. Many theologians have concluded that language about God always is analogical. We say God is "creative" and an artist is "creative," but God's creativity is of a different order from the artist's. "Analogy of being" means that the word "being" has a similar but not identical meaning when applied to God and to man. We can say "God exists" and "man exists," but God's existence is the existence of a sovereign Creator, and thus is of a different order from human existence. See also **equivocation; univocity of being**.

anthropomorphic days. An understanding of the "days" of Genesis 1 as God's days, rather than natural, 24-hour days.

anti-philosophes. Opponents of the eighteenth-century French Enlightenment. They believed that philosophes' emphasis on autonomous reason corrupted morality and subverted French society. The anti-philosophes countered by stressing traditional Catholic piety and morality. See also **philosophes**.

Apollo. Greek mythological figure who came to represent harmony, order, and reason. Also known as the god of music and later, in Roman mythology, as the god of the sun.

apologists. Christians in the second and third centuries who wrote apologies, or defenses, of the faith to defend Christianity against pagan philosophy and state-sponsored persecution.

apostolic fathers. The earliest group of Christian writers after the New Testament, some of whom may have known or even studied with the apostles.

Arianism. Theological heresy denying the deity of Christ that threatened to engulf the church in the fourth century. Arius taught there was a time when Jesus was not the Son of God but was created like other beings. See also **Council of Nicaea**.

Arminianism. Theological movement named for seventeenth-century Dutch pastor/theologian Jacob Arminius, who revised traditional Calvinist doctrines on original sin, predestination, the atonement, and the work of the Holy Spirit.

atomic facts. Facts as experienced independent of criteria or framework.

atomism. Naturalistic view that reality is completely composed of tiny, indestructible bits of matter. Associated with Epicurus.

biblical minimalists. A group of modern scholars who deny there is much history in the biblical narratives.

categorical imperative. Kant's absolute moral law. Unlike conditional imperatives [if X do Y], it admits no exceptions. Basically, it is a restatement of the Golden Rule: "Act only on that maxim through which you can at the same time will that it should become a universal law."

categories of understanding. Kant's twelve forms of understanding that structure knowledge. Human reason is not a *tabula rasa*, as the empiricists claimed; the mind organizes sensory experience by means of this a priori categorical structure. See also *tabula rasa*; **Copernican revolution**.

class conflict, class struggle. Marx's contention that socio-economic differences between classes inevitably will result in inter-class conflict. Those in poverty are resentful of the affluent; the wealthy fear those below them. Marx believed the only solution was to abolish private property and thereby place everyone on the same economic plane.

cogito ergo sum. Latin meaning "I think, therefore I am." Used by Descartes to affirm his own existence as the starting point for epistemological certainty. This established the "subjective turn" as the foundation for modern thought. See also **subjective turn**.

common sense realism. Philosophical school rooted in the eighteenth-century work of Scottish thinker Thomas Reid. Resisted Hume's skepticism by teaching that ordinary common sense is generally a trustworthy source of knowledge.

common sense strategy. An approach to knowledge that pragmatists like Richard Rorty associate with metaphysics. The assumption that there is an order to things and some ultimate purpose. Contrasts with "ironist." See also **ironist**.

compatibilism. The view that human freedom is our ability to do what we want to do. Does not exclude causation of our actions by our desires, character, environment, heredity, or God. Therefore, is compatible with determinism. See also **incompatibilism**.

conciliarist movement. A fourteenth- and fifteenth-century movement that claimed the highest ecclesiastical authority resides in the assembled church council, not the pope.

concordist/day age view. An understanding of the "days" of Genesis 1 as sequential but of an indeterminable length of time.

contractual theory of the state. John Locke's view that society and government rest on a rational foundation of consent. Political society arises when people freely unite into a community for mutual benefit. The opposite of the medieval view that kings rule by divine right.

Copernican revolution. Kant's teaching that objects of knowledge conform to the operation of the mind, not the mind to the objects. Just as Copernicus' heliocentric cosmos replaced the geocentric cosmos, so Kant's formulation of reason meant that human reason is autonomous. See also **categories of understanding**.

cosmogony. From Greek *cosmos* ("world") and *ginomai* ("to be born"). Any theory of the origin of the universe or creation. Cosmology studies the cosmos in its existence; cosmogony speculates about its origin.

Council of Constance. A general council of the Roman Catholic Church (1414–18). Convened to end the schism in the Western church that had resulted in rival papacies. The high point of conciliarism. See also **conciliarism**.

Council of Nicaea. Called by emperor Constantine, theologians from the East and West met in 325 to debate Arianism and to discuss other practical questions. The council affirmed Athanasius's view of Jesus' deity (the Son was of the same substance as the Father) and denounced Arius's views. The council resolved practical matters (their decisions were called canons). In conjunction with the Council of Constantinople (381), the council developed what is now called the Nicene Creed. See also **Arianism**.

courtly love. A view of love that developed in European courts during the eleventh and twelfth centuries. Suffering induced by seeing the beauty of a member of the opposite sex. Influenced lyric love poetry, allegories, and chivalric romances. Made the lover strong, morally upright, and good looking. Courtly love poets often described tragic romances in which the lady is inaccessible to the lover, who suffers horribly as a result.

Dasein. Martin Heidegger's existentialist term for "Being," often translated "being there" to emphasize that we truly understand ourselves only as being-in-the-world. Involvement in the world is intrinsic to existential self-understanding.

deconstruction, deconstructionism. Associated most commonly with Jacques Derrida, French philosopher and thinker. Denies any metaphysical notion that might delimit or predetermine what words or sentences mean.

deism. Enlightenment rational religion. God created the world and ordered it by immutable, natural laws but thereafter does not interfere in its workings. Denies God's immanence. God is an "absentee landlord." Deism became aggressively opposed to traditional theism (Christianity) and substituted moral behavior for Christian worship and belief in revealed doctrine.

descriptive fallacy. J. L. Austin defined this as the fallacy of supposing that the meaning of an utterance is descriptive when it is not.

designative. The theory that words are arbitrarily chosen to identify or "designate" an object of experience or things in the world. The meaning of a sentence is its correspondence, or lack thereof, to states of affairs in the world. Meaning is not mysterious.

determinism. The view that every event is caused by another event. Every event has a cause; there are no uncaused events.

dialectic, dialectical. The Hegelian doctrine that reason and history develop progressively by means of fundamental conflicts. The dialectical tension between opposites results in a resolution—synthesis—where the opposites are neither fully extinguished nor fully embraced.

dialectical courage. Nietzsche's term for the courage to live meaninglessly that results in heroic acts performed without meaning and not motivated by rational argument.

Diet of Worms. A pivotal moment in Luther's career. In April 1521 at a meeting or "diet" of all the estates of the Holy Roman Empire in the city of Worms, Luther had a hearing before the emperor and the ecclesiastical German authorities. At this meeting, Luther uttered his famous "Here I stand" speech.

Ding an sich. German for "thing in itself." Immanuel Kant's expression for the "noumenal" realm as opposed to the "phenomenal" realm.

Dionysus. Figure of Greek mythology who came to represent ecstasy and disorder. The god of wine and orgy.

disengaged reason. The idea that reason functions in its purest and most effective way when it operates independently of any environmental influences.

Donation of Constantine and Donation of Pepin. Two eighth-century forgeries that supposedly gave earthly power to the bishop of Rome.

double truth theory. The Muslim scholar Averroes taught that truth can be arrived at along two paths—one philosophical, the other theological. Revelation is not needed to arrive at genuine truth about the world. Siger of Brabant, a Christian thinker, went further, claiming there were two truths, one scientific, the other religious. Condemned by the church in 1270 and 1277.

dubito. Latin meaning "I doubt." Descartes' systematic doubt (of the senses, religious belief, etc.) that precedes genuine knowledge. The mind accepts as true only what is indisputably clear to reason.

efficient cause. One of Aristotle's four philosophical causes. Efficient cause is the agent or event that brings something to pass, e.g., the sculptor causes the statue by chiseling the marble.

El Elyon. A Hebrew name for God that means "God Most High."

El Shaddai. A Hebrew name for God of uncertain derivation that is commonly translated as "God Almighty."

Elohim. A Hebrew name for God that emphasizes his power and might.

empiricism. An epistemological Enlightenment theory that knowledge is based primarily on experience, which consists of sensation and reflection. Empiricists such as John Locke denied the rationalists' belief in innate ideas and said the mind is empty until it receives sensory data. See also **rationalism**; **representationalism**; ***tabula rasa***.

Enlightenment. Seventeenth- and eighteenth-century movements in Europe and America that assumed various forms from moderate (Britain and America) to radical (France and Germany). Enlightenment thinkers debated new epistemologies (rationalism and empiricism), proposed the age of reason to replace traditional religion, advocated science as a new basis for certainty, and offered modern theories of government to replace traditional monarchies.

Epicureanism. The views of Epicurus, including materialism, atomism, indeterminism, and hedonism. Today, the term is mainly used only to indicate hedonism, especially a love of gourmet dining.

epistemology. The branch of philosophy that probes knowledge—its origin, structure, method, and validity. Epistemology plays a powerful role in one's worldview.

equivocation. A word's meaning is "equivocal" when it means several unrelated things in different contexts. The word "rose" refers to a fragrant flower but also functions as the past tense of "rise." When applied to theology, equivocation implies that terms mean something entirely different when they refer to God than they do when they refer to creation. Pure equivocation leads to skepticism about the possibility of knowing or talking about God. See also **analogy of being**; **univocity of being**.

Erastianism. The view that the church is subservient to the state. Named for sixteenth-century theologian Thomas Erastus who held that sin should be punished by the state, not disciplined by the church.

eschatological foundationalism. Catholic theologian Fergus Kerr's description of Thomas's epistemology, or view of knowledge. "Foundationalism" distinguishes between beliefs that are "basic" and beliefs derived from those basic beliefs. Knowledge is built on certain basic, unquestioned beliefs. For Thomas, the foundation of knowledge was not beliefs arrived at by rational deduction or empirical observation. The foundation of knowledge is the knowledge we will have when we see God face to face. This eschatological knowledge, which we look for in faith and hope, is what makes us confident we can know things now.

eschatological ontology. Aristotle's belief that everything has a nature that propels it to move and change in a certain direction. An end point, or "teleology," is hard-wired into things, and that trajectory is what makes the thing what it is. A seed is a seed because it has potential to grow into a flower; a seed finds its telos, or end, in becoming a flower. Aquinas borrowed this notion from Aristotle and gave it a Christian interpretation. Everything is created for God, and is moving toward the consummation in which God is all in all. Things are what they are because of their eschatological destiny.

eschatology. The doctrine of last things. Traditionally, "last things" designated the events involved in the second coming of Christ and the future transformation of the world, including the resurrection of dead, the final judgment, and the coming of the new heaven and the new earth. Discussions of various views of the millennium also fall under "eschatology." In the twentieth century, another, broader use of "eschatology" arose that included everything related to the fulfillment of Old Testament promises of climactic salvation and judgment. The coming of the kingdom of God during Jesus' earthly life, especially in his suffering, death, resurrection, ascension, and reign, were all then seen as "eschatological" events in this broad sense. See also **inaugurated eschatology**.

evangelical. Theological term from Greek *euangelion* ("good news," "gospel") that emphasizes doctrinal tenets such as the inspiration and authority of Scripture; the sinful condition of all humanity due to the fall in Adam; the person and work of Christ as the basis for salvation; and the necessity of missions and evangelism for people to be saved. Also a historical term for people (Augustine and the Reformers) and movements (awakenings in Britain and America) who have articulated these views.

exchange value. Marx's term referring to a person's worth based on the economic value he or she produces in a capitalist system.

existentialism. A movement in early twentieth-century philosophy most often associated with French thinkers Jean-Paul Sartre and Albert Camus. They claimed dignity and meaning were created by each person and have no eternal reference point. A person's choices determine their essence, in contrast to the notion that God created a person's character, from which choices arise. Stresses the independence and freedom of the individual in matters of ethics and self-definition.

ex nihilo. A Latin cosmogonic term meaning "out of nothing." Describes the creative activity of God in Genesis 1 and stands in opposition to Greek philosophies, which held to some type of eternal matter.

expressive, expressivism. "Subject-centered" theory of language. Contracts with "object-centered" (designative). Meaning cannot be separated from the individual who confers meaning. Thus meaning is more mysterious and puzzling.

fact/value distinction. The idea that there are "facts" that exist independently of a subject's description of them. The greater the distance between subjects and the facts, the more likely we are to arrive at truth.

fate. In Greek philosophy, an impersonal force that makes everything happen just as it does.

fideism. Epistemological theory of knowledge that asserts knowledge rests on premises accepted by faith. Fideism frequently is associated with Augustine's *credo ut intelligam*: "I believe in order that I might understand."

final cause. One of Aristotle's four philosophical causes. The final cause is the goal or purpose of an event or object. In Christianity, the final cause of all reality is to glorify God.

final vocabularies. An expression used pejoratively by Richard Rorty and other modern pragmatists to describe those who believe they can arrive at ultimate meaning that is contained in the words or descriptions employed. Contrasts with "ironists." See also **ironist**.

form/matter distinction. Matter is what something is made from; form is what it is made into. The form of something is its essential nature, what it really is. The matter is usually its physical composition. But since most physical components (e.g., wood, plastic, brick) are in turn made of other things, a search of the components of components eventually leads to what Aristotle called "prime matter," the ultimate constituent of everything, a matter that is not itself made of anything and which in itself has no form. Prime matter in this sense is indistinguishable from nothing.

formal cause. One of Aristotle's four philosophical causes. Adapted from Plato's use of forms or ideas, formal cause makes something to be what it is. An acorn, for example, becomes a tree, because it has within it the form of a tree.

forms. A form is what something essentially is. For Plato, however, a being must be perfect to realize its own essential nature. Although Bill is a man, he is not perfectly a man; his perfect manhood has not been achieved in this world. Similarly, for Plato, no form (e.g., triangularity, treeness, courage, virtue) exists perfectly in this world. But forms do exist in another world, "the world of forms." Forms in that world serve as perfect exemplars, criteria, standards for things in this world. Aristotle abandoned the world of forms and taught that forms exist in this world together with matter, the matter generally inhibiting the perfect development of the form. See also **form/matter distinction**; **formal cause**; **phenomenal/noumenal distinction**.

foundationalism. Any epistemological theory that asserts that knowledge rests on basic beliefs (foundations) that in turn justify other beliefs. Basic beliefs are self-evidencing; they need no justification. Certain truths are foundational for other truths. The debate among Enlightenment thinkers over rationalism and empiricism is a classical example over which foundation—rational ideas versus sense experience—serves as the foundation of knowledge. See also **rationalist foundationalism**; **self-authenticating**.

framework interpretation. An understanding of the "days" of Genesis 1 as a figurative description of actual events.

genealogy of morals. Nietzsche's term for the historical development of an ethical system. Discovering such a history undermines the claim that ethics are eternal and permanent.

Gnosticism. A philosophical-religious movement that reached its maximum influence in the second century AD. Gnostics claimed a "secret knowledge" of ultimate reality and held that everything in the world is an emanation of God and so is essentially divine. Many gnostics claimed to be Christian on the basis of supposed secret teachings of Christ. The orthodox churches rejected their claims. Gnosticism was never eradicated from the ancient church and various forms continue to this day.

Great Awakening. American revival movement that permeated the colonies in the 1730s and 1740s. Primary leaders were Puritan Jonathan Edwards, who preached an experiential Calvinism, and Anglican George Whitefield, who itinerated all the colonies preaching powerful sermons that called for conversion.

hedonism. The view that achieving pleasure (either individual or corporate) is the chief goal of human life.

henotheism. The worship of one god without denying the existence of other gods.

heteronomy. Literally "other law." Kant used heteronomy to describe belief that appealed to something other than the Enlightenment ideal of autonomous (self-sufficient) reason. Thus, appeal to revelation, the Bible, or the church was submitting to heteronymous authority. See also **self-authenticating**.

heyday of sentences. The period in the twentieth century when interest in language moved from words to sentences. Most often associated with Ludwig Wittgenstein and those influenced by him.

historicism. The claim that there are no forces in culture outside of its own historical development. There can be no eternal or transcendent influences on culture or its people. Results in a suspicion of any truth that appears to transcend time and place.

humanism. A movement that originated in Italy and spread to the whole of Western Europe. It should not be confused with modern uses of the term, which usually imply atheism. Humanism had a literary focus and was aimed at the renewal of culture through the rediscovery of the literature of classical Greece and Rome.

hylomorphism. From two Greek words *hyle*, which means "matter," and *morphe*, which means "form." Aristotle taught that everything in creation is a composite thing, composed of matter and a form. Matter is the stuff of things, but by itself, it is a shapeless and featureless blob. Form gives "blobby" matter specific features and attributes. When you join the form of a cow to un-bovine stuff, it becomes a cow.

idealism. Eighteenth- and nineteenth-century philosophy that claimed the material order was less real than ideas. Reason plays a central role in the developments of history. The central building blocks of reality consist of ideas, rather than material objects.

ideal language. A language purified from any subjective influences, e.g., mathematics.

ideas. In Plato, a synonym for "forms." See also **forms**.

illocutionary force. J. L. Austin described an "illocutionary *act*" as an act performed "*in* saying something," e.g., naming something, promising, commanding, etc. Contrasts with "locutionary act," the act *of* saying something, and "perlocutionary act," an act performed *by* saying something. Illocutionary *force* is the successful performance of an illocutionary act.

imago Dei. Latin meaning "in the image of God." Most often used to refer to the character of mankind's creation in Genesis 1.

Immanuel principle. The Hebrew word "Immanuel" means "God with us." The central aspect of the covenant relationship between God and Israel.

inaugurated eschatology. Many Old Testament predictions concern future acts of God in which he will bring about climactic salvation and judgment. Inaugurated eschatology is the view that these predictions have been partially fulfilled, or have begun to be fulfilled, in the work of Jesus Christ on earth—especially in his suffering, death, resurrection, ascension, and present reign (Eph. 1:20–21)—and that the completion of fulfillment awaits the second coming of Christ. The word "eschatology" is here used broadly to include everything belonging to climactic salvation and judgment—not simply the future bodily resurrection of believers but their present new life in Christ (Col. 3:1–4). The word "inaugurated" indicates that God's purposes announced in the Old Testament have begun to be fulfilled but that they are not yet complete. See also **already not yet**; **eschatology**; **inaugurated eschatology**.

incommensurability. Thomas Kuhn's notion that scientific paradigms are exclusive and hence "incommensurable," i.e., antithetical to one another.

incompatibilism. The view that no human act can be free if it is caused by anything outside the human will; contrasts with "compatibilism." Human free actions cannot be caused by God, heredity, environment, character, or even our own desires. Thus, freedom is incompatible with determinism. See also **compatibilism**.

indeterminacy. An event not caused by another is an indeterminate event. A libertarian or incompatibilist view of the human will is sometimes called "indeterminacy." A broader form of indeterminacy is the denial of determinism. See also **determinism**; **incompatibilism**; **libertarianism**.

invisible/visible church. The invisible church is composed of all whom God has elected to salvation. Thus, only God knows with certainty who is a member. The visible church is the institutional church in this life, consisting of elect and non-elect—those who are only outwardly members and who will fall away. Augustine and many of the Reformers articulated this distinction to guard against equating membership in the visible church with salvation.

iron cage of rationality. Max Weber's idea that the Enlightenment's understanding of reason locked us into certain explanations that by definition disallow the possibility of other explanations, e.g., reason over tradition.

ironist. Richard Rorty's term that describes pragmatism's approach to ethical or moral living. See also **common sense strategy**; **final vocabularies**.

irrational fate. Insofar as fate is considered impersonal, its causality is irrational. It does not cause events by virtue of reasoning. It is irrational. See also **fate**.

irrationalism, irrationalist. The view that human reason (or any kind of reason) is incapable of understanding the world.

Johannine "comma." Also known as "the Three Witnesses." This is an interpolation in the text of 1 John 5:7–8, as in the KJV (with the comma in italics): "For there are three that bear record *in heaven, the Father, the Word, and the Holy Ghost, and these three are one. And there are three that bear witness in earth*, the Spirit, the Water, and the Blood, and these three agree in one." The Johannine Comma only occurs in Latin manuscripts from ca. 800. It is found in no Greek manuscripts prior to 1200.

ladder of being. Many Greek philosophers taught there are degrees of being, some higher, some lower. A higher degree is in some sense more real than a lower degree. Thus, in Plato forms are higher than matter; and among the forms, the form of the good is highest. In Aristotle, the Prime Mover is the highest. In Gnosticism and Neoplatonism, the supreme being sends forth lower forms of being in different degrees—emanations of itself. The material world is the lowest form of being. The remedy to the sufferings of human life is for souls to climb beyond the material world through various higher levels of being, until they are absorbed into the supreme being. "Ladder of being" metaphorically describes this structure.

language game(s). Ludwig Wittgenstein's notion that language games are language practices governed by certain rules and practices unique to each language game, e.g., science, literature, religion, etc.

Lebensform. German for "life form" or "form of life." Wittgenstein came to view language and meaning as arising from life circumstances and experiences that include more than mathematical or scientific judgments.

Left Wing Hegelians. Nineteenth-century radical intellectual descendents of Hegel who argued that Prussian society was still in need of revolutionary reforms. Believed Hegelianism was not compatible with Christianity. See also **Right Wing Hegelians**.

libertarianism. The view that human free acts are not caused by anything other than the human will: neither by God, nor heredity, nor environment, nor character, nor one's own desires. See also **compatibilism**; **determinism**; **incompatibilism**; **indeterminacy**.

lines of projection. Expression indicative of the "early" Wittgenstein's approach to language as governed by an overly scientific approach to meaning.

linguistic turn. Expression used to identify the twentieth century's fascination with language as an attempt to overcome the perceived failures of traditional philosophy.

loci communes. Latin meaning "common places." Common place books were a standard way of organizing knowledge in the Renaissance. Texts were analyzed to find the "common places" or topics they contained, and this material could then be organized under these topical headings. Such an approach was soon adapted to theological use, as a way of extracting theology from the biblical text. The most famous example, the various editions of Melanchthon's *Loci Communes* from 1521 onwards, became a standard expression of Lutheran theology and paved the way for later theological treatises such as Calvin's *Institutes*.

logical atomists. Refers to the "early" Wittgenstein, Bertrand Russell, and Rudolf Carnap. A "mathematical" approach to solving the riddles of philosophy based on a materialistic understanding of reality.

logical positivists. Also known as the "Vienna Circle." Philosophers and linguists who saw the earlier views of the logical atomists as unsatisfactory and in need of revision. They believed that for any sentence to be meaningful it had to be analytic (its truth is determined solely by analyzing its meaning) or empirically verifiable.

logic of life. Nietzsche's term referring to the celebration of life apart from a rational interpretation of human existence.

logic of reason. Nietzsche's term referring to the rational explanation of human life and history.

logos. In Heraclitus and other Greek philosophers, a principle of rationality in the world, corresponding to the rationality of the human mind and enabling the mind to understand the world. In the Bible, the speaking of God, preeminently in Jesus Christ (John 1:1–14).

logos doctrine. The belief that a deity created the universe by mere verbal fiat.

magisterial Reformers. Reformers such as Luther, Zwingli, Calvin, and Cranmer, who worked in cooperation with the magistrate (the secular, governing authority) in conducting the Reformation, were known as magisterial Reformers, in contrast with Protestant groups such as the Mennonites, who sought reformation without entanglement with secular authorities.

marks of the church. Protestant Reformers such as Luther and Calvin identified a number of characteristics or marks that defined what was a true church (as opposed to the claim of apostolic continuity or succession made by the Roman Church). The marks were the true preaching of the Word of God and the valid celebration of the sacraments of baptism and the Lord's supper. Later Reformed thought maintained that the practice of church discipline constitutes a third mark.

material cause. One of Aristotle's four philosophical causes. What something is made of. The material cause of a statue is the marble or granite from which it was carved. See also **form/matter distinction**.

materialism/naturalism. The view that everything is material, that matter is all there is. The universe is a closed system that operates entirely according to natural laws. Among the Greeks, the Epicureans and Stoics were materialists.

meaning as use. The "later" Wittgenstein's teaching that meaning is a function of how language is used. Words are defined by use, not by what they refer to in the external world or to mental states we associate with them.

medieval synthesis. One of the supreme intellectual achievements of the High Middle Ages was the reconciliation of classical philosophy (especially Greek thought, i.e., Plato and Aristotle) with biblical thought in a supreme synthesis. Best represented in the work of Thomas Aquinas. Subjected to searching criticism in the fourteenth and fifteenth centuries by William of Ockham and others.

messianism. The belief that God will send a heavenly redeemer to crush his enemies and deliver his people.

metaphysics. The branch of philosophy concerned with the ultimate nature of reality. Traditionally, metaphysics (from Greek *meta*, "after," and *physika* "things of nature") followed the study of nature because it probed beyond the physical order and was more difficult to understand.

methods of projection. The "later" Wittgenstein saw meaning as part of the process of experience that is shared by communities of language users who then describe experience in different ways.

mind mirrors nature. Richard Rorty's metaphor to describe the failure of representationalist epistemology, which understands the purpose of knowledge to be "getting things right," i.e., reflecting the true nature of the world. There is no "true nature of the world," according to Rorty.

miracle. An extraordinary visible act of God. Miracle often is distinguished from "providence," when the latter term is used to describe the more ordinary events brought about under God's governance. See also **providence**.

monergism. Theological view rooted in Pauline and Augustinian theology. Due to the pervasiveness of human sin, God's sovereign grace is the only cause of a person's salvation. Contrasts with "synergism," which posits some cooperation or reciprocation in salvation between God's will and ours. See also **synergism**.

monism, monist. The view that there is only one reality, not many. Parmenides and Plotinus were monists.

monotheism. The belief that only one God exists.

natural rights. Universal rights viewed as inherent in the nature of people and not dependent on legal or divine precedent.

Neoplatonism. A school of thought following the writings of Plotinus. Neoplatonists believed in one supreme being, "The One," from which everything else emanated. (Therefore, all are divine.) Among those emanations, some are higher or better than others. Matter is the lowest form, the source of evil. The human task is to rise beyond the realm of matter, through reason and mysticism, and seek union with the One. See also **ladder of being**.

New Lights. Congregationalists and Presbyterians who supported America's Great Awakening in the seventeenth century. Stressing Puritan piety as indispensable to Calvinist theology, they believed true faith required a vital conversion experience and personal holiness as signs of regeneration. New Lights charged that Old Lights, who stressed only orthodox belief as evidence of salvation, often were unconverted. See also **Old Lights**.

nominalism, nominalist. Throughout the later Middle Ages, there was a running debate between realists and nominalists about "universals." Universals are general categories of things: We see many specific trees, and they are all very different. What makes them all trees? For "realists," the answer is that they all participate in a metaphysical reality, the "universal" or "form" of tree. We never have actual contact with universals, but they are real nonetheless. Nominalists denied the reality of universals. We call oaks and maples and cedars "trees" because they share certain similarities. The only universal that unites them is the name (Latin, *nomina*) we give them all. Abstract names or universal terms exist only as ideas in the mind. Only particular things exist; only individuals are real. There are no universal predicates. Only as words refer to "real" individual things can they be said to have meaning.

nuda Scriptura. Latin meaning "bare Scripture." Contrasts with "*sola Scriptura*." Did not exclude the value of the Christian tradition as a source for theological reflection but only emphasized the primacy of Scripture for doctrine. *Nuda Scriptura* refers to seeing Scripture without any reference to historical exposition and interpretation of biblical truth in the past.

occult properties. Aristotelian term for qualities that lay hidden in objects that explain their movement. Newton refuted this notion by his three laws of motion.

Old Lights. Congregationalists and Presbyterians who opposed revivalist phenomena associated with America's Great Awakening in the seventeenth century. Claiming that genuine faith is evidenced exclusively by theological orthodoxy, they opposed New Lights for their "enthusiasm" (emotional conversions) and intruding into Old Light pulpits. See also **New Lights**.

onto-theology. The subordination of theology to the categories of philosophy. It is a theology that gives more respect to the God of the philosophers than to the God of Abraham, Isaac, and Jacob. Onto-theology speaks of God in abstract, static ways, in contrast to the Bible, which teaches that God is an active, dynamic, living God.

ontology. The branch of metaphysics that studies being—existence itself. Moderns like Kant distinguished between noumenal reality, "real existence," and phenomenal reality, "appearance." See also **phenomenal/noumenal distinction**.

ordinary language analysis. View associated with the "later" Wittgenstein where meaning is to be found in "use."

ordinary language philosophy. Wittgenstein's students (e.g., J. L. Austin and John Searle) applied Wittgenstein's "later" views in an expansive way as an attempt to finally demythologize the work of philosophy.

Orphism. A religious movement among the disciples of Pythagoras that influenced Plato. Taught that the human soul was a divine being imprisoned in the body. The soul undergoes reincarnation until it is sufficiently purified to return to the divine realm. Our souls are divine because they are rational. Thus, salvation comes through knowledge.

pantheism. The view that all reality is God, and God is all reality. Pantheism denies the creator-creature distinction. Hegel and Schleiermacher espouse forms of pantheism.

Peasant Revolt. An uprising of peasants that began in south Germany and Austria in 1524 in protest against the increasingly desperate economic and social circumstances they faced. By 1525, it spread to all of Germany. It was the most serious social revolt of the early modern period and was linked by some to Luther's doctrines. Because of this, he responded with some of his harshest writing in opposition to the peasants.

perfectionism. Belief that human nature is improvable or perfectible. Perfectionists fall into several groups, according to the means that they propose to achieve perfection. Enlightenment thinkers believed perfection attainable by reason or the application of the scientific method. Thinkers such as Wesley contended perfection resulted only by God's grace.

performatives. J. L. Austin's view of a form of speaking that "does" what it says it does. A justice of the peace who says "I declare you man and wife" not only is saying it but in saying it is "doing" it. *See also* speech acts.

personal absolute being. A being who is both absolute (the ultimate reality, the cause of all, the all-powerful) and personal (thinks, plans, speaks, loves, etc.) Among all the religions and philosophies, only the biblical God is both absolute and personal.

perspective seeing. Nietzsche's view that there are no "facts," only perspectives.

phenomenal/noumenal distinction. Kantian distinction that we can only know phenomena—appearances (objects apprehended by the senses). The noumenal realm, which consists of objects independent of the mind (e.g., Platonic forms), is not knowable. Kant postulated the existence of the noumenal realm to explain the existence of freedom. See also **forms**.

philosophes. French philosophers in the eighteenth century who advocated reason and education as means by which ignorance and superstition could be overcome.

philosophy, philosophers. Literally, philosophy is "love of wisdom." In Greece and elsewhere, philosophy was understood as the attempt to understand the fundamental principles of reality by reason alone, without help from religion or cultural tradition. Of course, this restriction is not necessary, and Christians, under the guidance of Scripture, have long investigated the questions asked by philosophers.

pneumatic hydrotherapy. Feuerbach's term that refers to the abandonment of the sacrament of baptism in favor of ordinary and rational uses of water in human societies.

polytheism. The belief in many gods.

positivism. Sometimes referred to as "The Vienna Circle," it was an attempt on the part of numerous analytical philosophers in 1920s Vienna to find a unified theory of science, expressed in a common language, through logical analysis.

postmodern, postmodernism. A term used to identify a mid-to-late twentieth-century approach to philosophy and culture that celebrates the failure of Modernity (Enlightenment) to achieve universally valid conclusions on truth, beauty, etc.

pragmatism. Philosophical conviction that knowledge arises primarily in the performance of tasks. Practical consequences are prized as the primary evaluation of a belief. A sentence can be understood as true only if one understands how its terms work in ordinary life.

prevenient grace. In medieval thought, prevenient grace is a divine influence that precedes any good effort that if acted upon receives the merit of congruity. As Wesley redefined it, prevenient grace becomes a universal process that keeps people from being so enveloped by sin that they cannot choose to respond to the gospel.

Prime Mover. Aristotle's term for the original cause of motion. Aristotle considered the Prime Mover a divine being and spoke of him as a person, although he offered no argument to justify this personal language.

principle of annihilation. William of Ockham's term for a philosophical test of the reality of things. According to this principle, "Every absolute thing, distinct in subject and place from another absolute thing, can exist by divine power even while [any] other absolute thing is destroyed." Whatever cannot remain in existence after all else is annihilated is not, strictly speaking, a thing. Things are things only if they are self-standing (though everything is immediately dependent on God). Ockham gave philosophical ground for knowing particular things, but they are fundamentally detached things rather than coinvolved with other things. In this way, Ockham gave philosophical support for modern individualism and scientific dissection.

proceduralism. Rationalism's teaching that achieving "certainty" is possible only if one employs the right procedures.

providence. God's continual sustaining, governing, and directing the world, including his bringing about specific events. Providence sometimes is used more narrowly to describe God's ordinary governance, in contrast to his extraordinary acts—"miracles." See also **miracle**.

psychogenetic method. Explaining an idea's meaning by tracing its origins in the psychological needs of those who believe it.

Pythagoreanism. The views of Pythagoras and his disciples, including Orphic religion, that objects in the world are the product of mathematical formulas.

quadrilateral. John Wesley's fourfold method for theological formulation that posits Scripture, tradition, reason, and experience as sources of authority.

qualitative atomists. Atomists who believe that the ultimate constituents of matter have different qualities, corresponding to the things of which they are parts, e.g., shapes, colors, tastes. See also **atomism**; **quantitative atomists**.

quantitative atomists. Atomists who believe that the ultimate constituents of matter are all the same, that atoms themselves do not have the qualities (e.g., shapes, colors, tastes, etc.) that exist in the larger objects made up of atoms. See also **atomism**; **qualitative atomists**.

radical evil. Kantian term for universal human sinfulness. Choosing sensual over moral incentives. Rather than traditional Christianity's belief in original sin, Kant posited a radical evil in each person that results from his or her corrupting the moral disposition, the human faculty that is the ultimate source of moral maxims.

ratio. This is a notoriously difficult word to translate. It can mean "reason," as in human rationality; it also can mean "rationale" and "account." In this context, it means the underlying meaning, or content, of a work, as distinguished from its form.

rational religion. Enlightenment term for religion considered from the perspective of reason alone. Eliminates revelation and subsequent Christian doctrines. Synonymous with "deism."

rationalism, rationalist. The belief that human reason is the final standard of truth and is more reliable than sense experience as a way to truth. See also **epistemology**.

rationalistic foundationalism. The teaching that basic beliefs must be rationally defensible. Various criteria are offered for establishing the rationality of basic beliefs. According to Descartes, basic beliefs had to be truths that everyone would acknowledge as true, and truths that were self-evident. In Cartesian foundationalism, Christian beliefs cannot be basic beliefs because they are not universally acknowledged and are not self-evident. Only beliefs like "I exist" qualify as basic beliefs. See also **foundationalism**.

recollection. Plato's teaching that all knowledge is recollection. In his view, knowledge is a knowledge of forms or ideas, not of the material world. Human souls once had direct access to the world of the forms, but they "fell" into the material world and now are trapped in material bodies. Yet they gain knowledge by their recollections of the forms. See also **forms**.

Reformation. Sixteenth-century evangelical movement in which European Protestants reacted against doctrines, practices, and abuses in Roman Catholicism by recovering elements of the biblical gospel.

Reformed. A party of the evangelical Reformation led by John Calvin, who stressed that "reform," based on biblical teaching, pertains to all areas of life: doctrine, piety, worship, sacraments, polity, and even culture itself.

reincarnation. The doctrine that after we die we return to earth in another physical form. This doctrine was taught by the Orphic religion and influenced Plato. See also **Orphism**; **recollection**.

relativism. The view that there is no absolute or objective truth but only truth for the individual. This view of the Sophists was attacked by Socrates and Plato.

Renaissance. From French for "rebirth." A scholarly term applied to the cultural movement that swept Europe from the thirteenth century and which witnessed dramatic cultural changes—particularly in literature, art, and politics—linked to a rediscovery of classical literature.

Representational, **representationalism**. The belief that the goal of epistemology is to represent the real world of things as accurately as possible in our minds and language. Representationalists believe we do not experience the external world directly. Our knowledge of it is mediated by ideas or our own interpretation.

Reuchlin Affair. Johannes Reuchlin (1454/5–1522) was an outstanding humanist and Hebraist. From 1509, he was embroiled in an affair in which he opposed the demands of the converted Jew, Johannes Pfefferkorn of Cologne, for an imperial ruling to have Jewish religious books destroyed. Reuchlin's opposition eventually earned him a heresy trial and a hefty fine. See also ***ad fontes***.

Right Wing Hegelians. Nineteenth-century moderate intellectual descendents of Hegel who argued that Prussian society was the zenith of Western cultural development. Believed Hegelianism was compatible with Christianity. See also **Left Wing Hegelians**.

romanticism. Eighteenth- and nineteenth-century movement in art and literature that reacted strongly against the rationalism of the Enlightenment and modern industrialization of Western culture. It stressed the importance of imagination and emotion in human identity and the significance of nature in its pure state. Celebrated subjectivity, passion, and emotion.

Schleitheim Confession. Early confessional document of the Anabaptist tradition stating seven genuine marks of church in contrast to those of the magisterial Reformers. The confession was drafted by Michael Sattler in 1527 for believers in the southwest German town of Schleitheim, shortly before his martyrdom in the same year.

scholasticism. A term used to describe university (i.e., school) discourse from the twelfth century onwards. Scholasticism was a pedagogical method, built upon the dialectical question and answer structure of medieval classroom discussion. It should not be misunderstood as implying a particular intellectual content (e.g., confusing it with rationalism).

scientism. Pejorative term for the belief that science and the scientific method constitute the exclusive means by which we can know the world. Natural and social sciences take precedence over other disciplines in their description of reality. Belief that the scientific method and its scrupulous application in all areas of life will achieve the greatest benefits for humanity.

self-authenticating. A proposition or set of ideas is self-authenticating when it contains within itself sufficient reasons for one to believe it.

self-referential incoherence. The charge by which an argument or term does not make sense according to its own self-defining conditions.

semen religionis. Latin meaning "seed of religion." Calvin used this term to affirm that all people possess a religious nature that moves them to engage in acts of worship. Because of the fall, all humans create false gods and engage in various forms of idolatry. The seed of religion is only directed towards the true God by his revelation in Scripture.

sensus divinitatis. Latin meaning "sense of the divine." Refers to a basic innate perception that God exists, a perception with which all humans are born, and which is the basis of all religion whether true or idolatrous.

Socinianism. A form of anti-Trinitarianism (Unitarianism) named for Lelio and Faustus Sozzini. The Polish Racovian Catechism (1605) summarizes Socinian beliefs; it rejected the deity of Christ. Its insistence that reason interpret the Bible led to a denial of original sin.

sola Christo. Latin meaning "Christ alone." Reformation phrase that means people can only be saved through the atoning work of Christ and not by any other means.

sola fide. Latin meaning "by faith alone." Refers specifically to justification by faith alone, one of the foundational doctrines advanced by Luther and taken up by the Protestant Reformation to indicate how believers come to salvation. The object of that faith is Jesus Christ.

sola gratia. Latin meaning "by grace alone." Refers to one of the foundational doctrines of the Protestant Reformation that declares that it is by God's grace or favor alone that believers come to have faith in Christ, which leads to their justification. This doctrine maintains that neither human works nor human will play any part in coming to faith. See also **monergism; synergism**.

sola Scriptura. Latin meaning "Scripture alone." Refers to the Reformation doctrine that maintains that the Bible should be the sole authoritative foundation for all theology. This doctrine does not exclude the value of the broader Christian tradition, including that of the interpretive tradition of the Bible, as a source for theological reflection and formulation, but it does insist on the absolute primacy of the Bible.

soli Deo gloria. Latin meaning "Glory to God alone." Protestant Reformers believed that since salvation was wholly the work of God, worship and glory should be ascribed only to him.

speech acts. J. L. Austin's term that emphasizes that by saying something we actually do something, e.g., an official ends a meeting by saying "I now declare this session closed." *See also* performatives.

stoicism. The views of Zeno of Cyprus and his followers. Stoicism is materialistic, deterministic, and monistic.

subjective turn. Term associated with Enlightenment emphasis on the individual subject (e.g., Descartes' *cogito ergo sum*) as the preeminent authority on matters relating to the real world and how it is known. The subjective turn was further formalized by Kant, whose Copernican revolution in epistemology posited human reason and experience instead of previous authorities (i.e., revelation and church teaching), as the basis for knowledge.

sui generis. Latin meaning "of its own kind." Refers to entities that cannot be included in a wider category or concept. Something is *sui generis* when it is unique.

summum bonum. Latin meaning "the highest good." Used to describe the ultimate end of human conduct, which is substantively good. In ethics, all people ought to pursue all other goods as subordinate to the highest good.

synergism. Theological view that salvation results from cooperation between human will and divine grace. See also **monergism**.

systematic doubt. See **dubito**.

tabula rasa. Latin meaning "blank tablet." Used by John Locke to refute the existence of innate ideas. Because the mind is empty at birth, ideas result only from experience and sense perception.

theory-laden. Thomas Kuhn's view that all language and methodology are bound up with a theory regarding the nature of the world and what we should be looking for in the world. There is no "objectivism."

theogonic, theogony. Refers to the origin of the gods. Primitive religions myths relate the origin of the gods to the origin of the cosmos. Elaborate rituals, usually yearly, reenact the myths to ensure the cosmic and societal order. Gods exist through the creative activity of other gods.

theological liberalism. Nineteenth-century movement in Germany that emphasized the need for radical change in the church's understanding of the Christian faith if the church was to adapt to modern culture. In particular, traditional understanding of the authority and inspiration of the Bible, the person and work of Christ, and God's supernatural interventions in history were abandoned.

Thomistic. Thomists are theologians who work within the framework of the theology of Thomas Aquinas. "Thomistic" theology is theology done within this framework. Methodologically, Thomists often employ the scholastic methods of Thomas himself. Substantively, Thomists are committed to the Christianized Aristotelian worldview that Thomas elaborated.

threefold state of man. Augustinian view of human nature in its pre-fall, post-fall, and redeemed states. Human nature as originally created by God before Adam's fall possessed freedom to sin or not sin (*posse peccare, posse non peccare*—able to sin, able not to sin). Human nature after the fall is characterized by original sin; apart from grace, people do not possess moral freedom (*non posse non peccare*—not able not to sin). Redeemed individuals in this life may sin or not sin (*posse non peccare*—able not to sin); in eternal life they cannot sin (*non posse peccare*—not able to sin).

tragic heroes. Protagonists of Greek dramas who typically challenge fate and suffer the consequences.

transcendentalism. Nineteenth-century movement in American intellectual circles that protested the over-rationalizing tendencies of organized religion. Sought to replace these tendencies with an emphasis on a natural spirituality that arises from human intuition. The transcendentalist movement included such luminaries as Henry David Thoreau, Ralph Waldo Emerson, and Bronson Alcott.

transvaluation of values. Nietzsche's term that refers to the revolutionary transformation of ethical values needed in Western culture. In particular, Nietzsche believed Christian morality was hostile to life and ought to be replaced with a morality of freedom and natural instincts.

tripartite soul. Plato's distinction between three aspects of the soul. The appetitive seeks physical necessities and pleasures; the spirited includes anger, ambition, desire for social honor; and the rational seeks knowledge for its own sake. Plato's distinction corresponds somewhat to the later common distinction between emotion, will, and intellect.

troubadour. The troubadours were traveling singers and lyrical poets of the eleventh and twelfth centuries. They were the original courtly love poets.

truth-functional. Truth-functional language is language capable of being either true or false.

two-story view of reality. According to a two-story view of reality, the world is divided into two virtually detached realms of being. On the weekends, human beings engage in worship, prayer, sacraments, and so forth as "religious" activities. During the week, they engage in work, play, family life, cooking and eating, and so on as "secular" activities. The religious activities have virtually no effect on the secular, and vice versa. Though few if any Christians hold to this view in such stark terms, modern Christians have very commonly set up less rigid barriers between religious and secular life.

unbounded. Anaximander's concept of the "infinite" or "indefinite" material of which everything is made. This material is neither earth, nor air, nor fire, nor water.

union with Christ. The saving fellowship of human beings with Christ. Through this fellowship, the benefits of Christ's work, such as forgiveness, adoption, justification, and resurrection life, are given to believers (Eph. 1:3–14). In the New Testament, the expressions "in Christ," "with Christ," and "through him" often designate some aspect of this fellowship.

univocity of being. Means that the word "exist" has exactly the same meaning in the sentence "God exists" as it does in the sentence "I exist." For most theologians, this is dangerous because it damages the Creator-creature distinction. God's existence is the existence of the eternal Lord and triune God, which is not true of any creature's existence. See also **analogy of being**; **equivocation**.

unmoved mover. Aristotle's Prime Mover. The Prime Mover causes movement but is not moved by anything else. See also **Prime Mover**.

via moderna. Latin meaning "modern way." Refers to a late medieval movement in theology. Gabriel Biel was its most famous exponent. The adherents of the *via moderna* were nominalists in philosophy and tended to be semi-Pelagian in their views of salvation.

weltanschauung. German meaning "worldview." Coined by Immanuel Kant. See also **worldview**.

will to power. Nietzsche's term referring to the power of the will to create one's own meaning and identity. Central to Nietzsche's repudiation of the traditional Christian worldview and his clarion call for new values without reference to God.

Wittgensteinian fideism. Belief that there are no universal criteria of rationality, and any and all religious beliefs can only be judged in the **Lebensform**, or contexts of life, associated with them.

world soul. Stoic belief that the world is a single reality governed by a pantheistic "god" who rules all by natural law. See also **Neoplatonism**.

worldview. From the German *weltanschauung*. Although Kant coined the term to refer one's sensible apprehension of reality, it has come to refer to the ultimate framework of ideas and beliefs by which a person understands and interacts with the world.

Yahweh. The Hebrew covenantal name for God that reflects his immutability and self-sufficiency.

Index of Scripture

Index of Personal Names

Index of Subjects

Recommended Resources for Exploring Worldviews

Allen, Diogenes. *Philosophy for Understanding Theology*. Atlanta: John Knox Press, 1985.

Baumer, Franklin. *Modern European Thought: Continuity and Change in Ideas*. New York: Macmillan, 1977.

Brown, Colin. *Christianity and Western Thought: A History of Philosophers, Ideas and Movements*. Vol 1, *From the Ancient World to the Age of Enlightenment*. Downers Grove, IL: InterVarsity Press, 1990.

Cahill, Thomas. *The Gifts of the Jews: How a Tribe of Desert Nomads Changed the Way Everyone Thinks and Feels*. New York: Random House, 1998.

Chenu, M. D. *Nature, Man, and Society in the Twelfth Century: Essays on the New Theological Perspective in the Latin West*. Chicago: University of Chicago Press, 1968.

Colish, Marcia L. *Medieval Foundations of the Western Intellectual Tradition, 400–1400*. New Haven, CT: Yale University Press, 1997.

Colson, Charles and Nancy Pearcy. *How Now Shall We Live?* Wheaton, IL: Tyndale House, 1999.

Copenhaver, Brian and Charles B. Schmitt. *Renaissance Philosophy*. Oxford: Oxford University Press, 1992.

Copleston, Frederick C. *A History of Philosophy*. 9 vols. Garden City, NY: Image Books, 1962–65.

Dooyeweerd, Herman. *In the Twilight of Western Thought*. Nutley, NJ: Craig Press, 1968.

Evans, G. R., ed. *The Medieval Theologians: An Introduction to Theology in the Medieval Period*. Oxford: Blackwell, 2001.

Frame, John M. *Apologetics to the Glory of God*. Phillipsburg, NJ: P&R Publishing, 1994.

———. *The Doctrine of God*. Phillipsburg, NJ: P&R Publishing, 2002.

———. *The Doctrine of the Knowledge of God*. Phillipsburg, NJ: P&R Publishing, 1987.

Gay, Peter. *The Enlightenment*. Vol. 1, *The Rise of Modern Paganism*. New York: W. W. Norton, 1966.

———. *The Enlightenment*. Vol. 2, *The Science of Freedom*. New York: W. W. Norton, 1969.

George, Timothy. *Theology of the Reformers.* Nashville: Broadman Press, 1988.

Grant, Edward. *God and Reason in the Middle Ages.* Cambridge: Cambridge University Press, 2001.

Guthrie, Donald. *New Testament Theology.* Downers Grove, IL: InterVarsity Press, 1981.

Heslam, Peter S. *Creating a Christian Worldview: Abraham Kuyper's Lectures on Calvinism.* Grand Rapids: Eerdmans, 1998.

Hoitenga, Dewey J. *Faith and Reason From Plato to Plantinga.* Albany, NY: State University of New York Press, 1991.

Holmes, Arthur F. *All Truth Is God's Truth.* Grand Rapids: Eerdmans, 1977.

———. *Contours of a World View.* Grand Rapids: Eerdmans, 1983.

———. *The Idea of a Christian College.* Grand Rapids: Eerdmans, 1975.

———. *Philosophy: A Christian Perspective.* Downers Grove, IL: InterVarsity Press, 1975.

Jones, Peter R. *The Gnostic Empire Strikes Back.* Phillipsburg, NJ: P&R Publishing, 1992.

Kaiser, W. C. *A History of Israel: From the Bronze Age Through the Jewish Wars.* Nashville: Broadman and Holman, 1998.

Kuyper, Abraham. *Lectures on Calvinism.* Grand Rapids: Eerdmans, 1943.

Lewis, C. S. *The Discarded Image: An Introduction to Medieval and Renaissance Literature.* Cambridge: Cambridge University Press, 1964.

Long, V. P., D. W. Baker, and G. J. Wenham, eds. *Windows into Old Testament History: Evidence, Argument, and the Crisis of Biblical Israel.* Grand Rapids: Eerdmans, 2002.

Marsden, George M. *The Outrageous Idea of Christian Scholarship.* New York: Oxford University Press, 1997.

Marshall, Paul A., Sander Griffioen, and Richard Mouw, eds. *Stained Glass: Worldviews and Social Science.* Lanham, MD: University Press of America, 1989.

McGrath, Alister E. *Reformation Thought: An Introduction.* 3rd ed. Oxford: Blackwell, 1999.

Nash, Ronald H. *Life's Ultimate Questions: an Introduction to Philosophy.* Grand Rapids: Zondervan, 1999.

———. *World Views in Conflict: Choosing Christianity in a World of Ideas.* Grand Rapids: Zondervan, 1992.

Naugle, David. *Worldview: The History of a Concept.* Grand Rapids: Eerdmans, 2002.

Oberman, Heiko. *The Harvest of Medieval Theology.* Grand Rapids: Baker, [1983] 2000.

Orr, James. *The Christian View of God and the World.* Grand Rapids: Kregel, 1989.

Ozment, Steven. *The Age of Reform, 1250–1550: An Intellectual and Religious History of Late Medieval and Reformation Europe.* New Haven, CT: Yale University Press, 1980.

Passmore, John. *The Perfectibility of Man.* New York: Scribners, 1970.

Pearcey, Nancy, R. *Total Truth: Liberating Christianity from Its Cultural Captivity*. Wheaton, IL: Crossway, 2004.

Plantinga, Alvin and Nicholas Wolterstorff, eds. *Faith and Rationality*. Notre Dame, IN: University of Notre Dame, 1984.

Ridderbos, Herman. *The Coming of the Kingdom*. Philadelphia: Presbyterian and Reformed, 1969.

Rummel, Erika. *The Humanist-Scholastic Debate in the Renaissance and Reformation*. Cambridge: Cambridge University Press, 1995.

Schmidt, Alvin, J. *Under the Influence*. Grand Rapids: Zondervan, 2001.

Schneewind, J. B. *The Invention of Autonomy: A History of Modern Moral Philosophy*. Cambridge: Cambridge University Press, 1998.

Sire, James W. *Habits of the Mind*. Downers Grove, IL: Inter Varsity Press, 2000.

———. *The Universe Next Door: A Basic World View Catalogue*. Downers Grove, IL: InterVarsity Press, 1975.

Southern, R. W. *Scholastic Humanism and the Unification of Europe*. Vol. 1: *Foundations*. Oxford: Blackwell, 1995.

Tarnas, Richard. *The Passion of the Western Mind: Understanding the Ideas That Have Shaped Our World View*. New York: Ballantine Books, 1991.

Taylor, Charles. *Sources of the Self: The Making of the Modern Identity*. Cambridge, MA: Harvard University Press, 1989.

Vanhoozer, Kevin J. *First Theology: God, Scripture and Hermeneutics*. Downers Grove, IL: InterVarsity Press, 2002.

Van Til, Cornelius. *A Christian Theory of Knowledge*. Nutley, NJ: Presbyterian and Reformed, 1969.

Walsh, Brian J., and J. Richard Middleton. *The Transforming Vision: Shaping a Christian World View*. Downers Grove, IL: InterVarsity Press, 1984.

Wolters, Albert M. *Creation Regained*. Grand Rapids: Eerdmans, 1985.

Wolterstorff, Nicholas. *Reason Within the Bounds of Religion*. 2nd ed. Grand Rapids: Eerdmans, 1984.

Turning Points in Worldview

Revolutions in Worldview has surveyed the prominent thinkers and movements whose ideas have driven Western history. The following timeline identifies those figures and events that stand out as the most significant because they mark major turning points or transitions in worldview.

1400 BC   Israelite Exodus from Egypt. The Mosaic revelation establishes a theocentric worldview: God, human nature, knowledge, creation, society, and ethics are developed within a framework of God as sovereign creator, providential ruler, and redeemer.

Eighth century BC   The Homeric poems *Iliad* and *Odyssey* provide the background from which Greek philosophy emerged. Zeus and the personal Olympian deities replace the earlier primitive Greek religion, which focused on magical forces at work in nature.

Sixth century BC   Thales, Anaximander, and Anaximenes found the Milesian pre-Socratic school in Miletus, Greece. They speculated that the source of order in the cosmos lay not in Homeric deities but in some ultimate natural phenomena.

Fifth century BC   Plato's *Republic* proposes philosophy as the new ideal. Transcendent world of ideas replaces Homeric deities as objects of religious devotion. Aristotle subsequently revised Platonic thought by emphasizing sensory experience.

AD 31   Jesus is crucified and resurrected. The incarnation of God in Jesus Christ establish the historical and ontological basis for the Christian worldview, in which redemption from sin and death form the core of the Christian gospel.

AD 36   Conversion of the apostle Paul. His letters and the gospels of the New Testament articulate the Christian view of redemption in continuity with Old Testament revelation.

313   Roman Emperor Constantine issues the Edict of Milan, which ends empire-wide persecution of Christianity. In 325 he convened the first ecumenical council of the church at Nicaea, which affirmed the deity of Jesus Christ.

419   Augustine's *On the Trinity* establishes the Christian alternative to classical Greek thought. The tripersonal God alone provides a transcendent basis for understanding all reality. His *City of God* articulates a teleological philosophy of history to replace the Greek cyclical view.

1120   Abelard's *Sic et non* initiates a new method of doing theology. His use of logic in the form of questions controlled the interpretation of biblical content that separated theology from biblical exegesis.

1274   Thomas Aquinas's *Summa Theologiae* combines Aristotelian philosophy and Christian teaching to form the classical medieval synthesis of faith and reason.

ca. 1285–1347   William of Ockham's nominalism denies the existence of universals, challenges Aquinas's synthesis of faith and reason, and provides the basis for modern science.

1304–74   Petrarch develops Renaissance humanism. His pioneering use of Latin manuscripts prompted the revival of classical writings, whose appeal superseded scholastic authorities as the way to legitimate civic values.

1503   Desiderius Erasmus publishes *Handbook of the Christian Soldier*, a nondogmatic Christian humanism. His *Praise of Folly* (1509), a stinging satire, attacked corrupt medieval practices and religious superstition.

1515   The publication of Niccolo Machiavelli's *The Prince* launches the modern view of politics, which espouses power as opposed to virtue as the goal of political action.

1522 Martin Luther refuses to recant his writings at the Diet of Worms in Germany. His recovery of Paul's teaching on justification by faith and his other writings launch the magisterial Protestant Reformation.

1527 The Schleitheim Confession inaugurates Protestant sectarianism's separation of church and state over against the magisterial Reformers' cooperation with the secular authorities.

1536 John Calvin publishes *Institutes of the Christian Religion*, which became a classic statement of Reformed theology. Calvin's theological and biblical writings, combined with his correspondence, articulated a worldview that called for the reform of all of life, based on the Bible's teaching.

1543 Nicholaus Copernicus's *On the Revolutions of the Celestial Spheres* proposes the heliocentric theory of the universe to replace the geocentric theory of Ptolemy. Galileo's telescopic investigations confirmed Copernicus' theory.

1624 Lord Edward Herbert of Cherbury enumerates five points of natural religion in *De Veritate*, which marks the beginning of English deism.

1637 René Descartes' *cogito ergo sum* in *Discourse on Method* initiates the "subjective turn" of the Enlightenment, which elevated individual reason as the means for determining truth and thus displaced previously accepted authorities, such as revelation and church teaching.

1675 Philipp Jakob Spener's *Pia Desideria* outlines the basic principles of pietism—Bible study, evangelical preaching, and vital religious experience over doctrinal belief as the primary elements of Christian faith.

1781 Immanuel Kant's *Critique of Pure Reason* creates a "Copernican revolution" in epistemology and provides a philosophical basis for his *Religion within the Limits of Reason Alone*, a moralistic reinterpretation of Christianity.

1841 Ludwig Feuerbach's *Essence of Christianity* attacks Christian teaching as merely a projection of the human spirit. By reinterpreting Christianity in human terms, he thought that man would take responsibility for attributes like love and peace that were misplaced on God.

1845 Søren Kierkegaard's *Fear and Trembling* introduces existentialism, which emphasizes freedom and individual choice as the determinants of the self and ethics.

1848 Karl Marx issues his *Communist Manifesto*, which called for the proletarian working class to unite in a revolution to overthrow the capitalist bourgeoisie in order to establish a classless society.

1859 Charles Darwin's *On the Origin of the Species* challenges the idea of fixity of species with his theory of evolution, according to which species change by a struggle for survival due to a process of natural selection.

1885 Friedrich Nietzsche's *Thus Spake Zarathustra* mocks traditional Christian thought and its morality and proposed in its stead that those who have the will to power should create their own meaning.

1907 William James's *Pragmatism: A New Name for Some Old Ways of Thinking* proposes an epistemology that focuses not on the act of cognition but on the practical consequences of an idea.

1922 Ludwig Wittgenstein's *Tractatus Logico-Philosophicus* initiates the "linguistic turn" in contemporary philosophy where analysis of language was used to solve traditional philosophical problems.

1962 Thomas Kuhn's *The Structure of Scientific Revolutions* rejects the idea that science develops by a linear accumulation of knowledge. Instead, he argued that science proceeds by paradigm shifts in which the nature of investigation changes abruptly.

1967 Jacques Derrida publishes three works that form the basis for deconstructionism, a major force in postmodernism. Deconstructionists deny the traditional notion of ultimate truth. All texts must be analyzed to ascertain their ideological biases.

Contributors

W. Andrew Hoffecker (MDiv, Gordon-Conwell Theological Seminary; PhD, Brown University) is professor of church history at Reformed Theological Seminary (Jackson), where he has taught church history, biblical worldview, and C. S. Lewis for ten years. He is ordained in the PCUSA.

Before joining Reformed Theological Seminary's faculty in 1997, he was professor of religion at Grove City College. His enthusiasm for worldview courses grew over twenty-five years of teaching undergraduates.

Dr. Hoffecker has also taught at the various RTS sites in Orlando, Charlotte, Washington, DC, Memphis, and Detroit, as well as in the Ukraine. He and his wife, Pam, enjoy tennis; and when they visit their three sons, who live in Washington, DC, Phoenix, and Atlanta, a pick-up game always follows.

John M. Frame (MDiv, Westminster Theological Seminary; MPhil, Yale University; DD, Belhaven College) is professor of systematic theology and philosophy at Reformed Theological Seminary (Orlando). He is an ordained minister of the Presbyterian Church in America.

Previously, he taught at Westminster Theological Seminary in Philadelphia (1968–80) and Westminster Theological Seminary in California (1980–2000).

He and his wife, Mary, have five children, three married and living in California and Oregon, and two single and attending college.

John D. Currid (MA, Gordon-Conwell Theological Seminary; PhD, University of Chicago) is Carl W. McMurray professor of Old Testament at Reformed Theological Seminary (Charlotte). He previously taught at Grove City College (1980–93) and at Reformed Theological Seminary (Jackson; 1993–2007). He is an ordained minister in the Presbyterian Church in America.

Before his move to RTS-Charlotte, Dr. Currid was the pastor of teaching at Providence Presbyterian Church in Clinton, Mississippi. He currently supplies the pulpit at Ballantyne Presbyterian Church (ARP) in Charlotte, North Carolina.

Dr. Currid has ten books in print. These include commentaries on Genesis (2 vols.), Exodus (2 vols.), Leviticus, and Deuteronomy in the Evangelical Press Study Commentary series, of which he is the editor. He and his wife, Nancy, have two grown children, one of whom resides in Indiana and the other in Texas.

Dr. Vern S. Poythress (BS, California Institute of Technology; PhD, Harvard University; ThM and MDiv, Westminster Theological Seminary; MLitt, University of Cambridge; ThD, University of Stellenbosch) is professor of New Testament interpretation at Westminster Theological Seminary, where he has taught for thirty years. He teaches Paul's letters, the gospels, the book of Revelation, topics of systematic theology, and hermeneutics. Dr. Poythress has a particular interest in interpretive principles, based on his background in linguistics and apologetics.

He also has taught linguistics at the University of Oklahoma. He has published books on Christian philosophy of science, theological method, dispensationalism, biblical law, hermeneutics, Bible translation, and the book of Revelation.

Dr. Poythress is a minister in the Presbyterian Church in America. He is married to Diane, and they have two children, Ransom and Justin. Dr. Poythress's side interests in science fiction, string figures, volleyball, and computers.

Richard C. Gamble (MA, Pittsburgh Theological Seminary; PhD, University of Basel) is professor of systematic theology at the Reformed Presbyterian Theological Seminary in Pittsburgh, Pennsylvania. He served as professor of systematic theology at Reformed Theological Seminary (Orlando), professor of historical theology at Calvin Seminary, director of the Meeter Center for Calvin Studies in Grand Rapids, Michigan, and as associate professor of church history at Westminster Seminary.

Peter J. Leithart (AB, Hillsdale College; MAR and ThM, Westminster Theological Seminary; PhD, University of Cambridge) is an ordained minister in the Presbyterian Church in America. He currently serves as senior fellow of theology and literature at New St. Andrews College, Moscow, Idaho, and as pastor of Trinity Reformed Church, also in Moscow. He is a contributing editor to *Touchstone* and *Credenda/Agenda*, and has written a number of books, including *1 & 2 Kings* (Brazos Theological Commentary) and *Solomon Among the Postmoderns* (Brazos, forthcoming). He and his wife, Noel, have ten children and one grandson.

Carl R. Trueman (MA, University of Cambridge; PhD, University of Aberdeen) is academic dean and professor of historical theology and church history at Westminster Theological Seminary, where he has taught for six years. Prior to that, he was a member of faculty at the University of Aberdeen and at the University of Nottingham.

His scholarly interests include the English Reformation, the life and thought of John Owen, and the connections between late medieval theology and the rise of Reformed orthodoxy.

He is a member of the Orthodox Presbyterian Church. He and his wife, Catriona, have two sons, John and Peter. His passions include marathon running, classic Westerns, and cheering on his boys in soccer and athletics.

N. Scott Amos (MA, The College of William and Mary; MDiv and ThM, Westminster Theological Seminary; PhD, University of St. Andrews; further study, University of Cambridge, University of Geneva) is assistant professor of history at Lynchburg College in Lynchburg, Virginia, where he has taught since 2002. He also teaches a two-semester course in church history at the Center for Christian Study in Charlottesville, Virginia, where he resides.

Dr. Amos's particular fields of interest include the work of the Strasbourg Reformer Martin Bucer; the early Reformed Tradition; the English Reformation through the Westminster Assembly; the Reformation as a whole; and the history of biblical interpretation (including the relationship of biblical exegesis and theological method). More broadly, he is keenly interested in the history of the church through the ages, and aims in his teaching of the subject to emphasize that a knowledge of the church's history gives substance to our belief in the communion of saints that we affirm in the Apostles' Creed.

Dr. Amos is married to Liesl, and they have two daughters, Miriam and Rachel.

Richard Lints (AM, University of Chicago; MA and PhD, University of Notre Dame) is professor of theology at Gordon-Conwell Theological Seminary in South Hamilton, Massachusetts. He is an ordained minister in the Presbyterian Church in America, having previously planted and pastored Redeemer Presbyterian Church in Concord, Massachusetts.

Dr. Lints has taught at Gordon-Conwell for twenty years. Prior to that, he was on the theological faculty at Trinity College, Bristol, England. He also has taught as a visiting professor of theology at Yale Divinity School, Reformed Theological Seminary, and Westminster Seminary California.

Dr. Lints is the author of *The Fabric of Theology*, the forthcoming *Radical Ironies: Religion*, and *The 1960s and the Rise of Postmodernity*. He is coauthor of *The Westminster Dictionary of Key Terms in Philosophy and*

Their Importance in Theology and editor and contributor to *Personal Identity and Theological Perspective*. He and his wife, Ann, have three grown children, all of whom reside in or around Boston.

Michael Payne (PhD, Westminster Theological Seminary) is currently interim pastor of Memorial Presbyterian Church, Montgomery, Alabama. Before coming to Memorial, Dr. Payne served as professor of theology at Reformed Theological Seminary (Jackson) from 1997–2006. From 2002–04 he served as professor of military ethics and leadership at the Air War College, Maxwell Air Force Base. He has lectured on ethics at the Army War College, Carlisle, Pennsylvania, and the Naval War College, Newport, Rhode Island.

From 1986–97, Dr. Payne served as a theological educator in Kenya at the Nairobi Evangelical Graduate School of Theology and at Daystar University. He has lectured in Germany, France, The Netherlands, South Korea, Hungary, and the Czech Republic.

Dr. Payne is married to Karen, and they have two daughters, Chalon and Kaley.